PROTECTING INTELLECTUAL PROPERTY IN THE ARABIAN PENINSULA

حماية حقوق الملكية الفكرية في شبه الجزيرة العربية:

This work examines the endeavours of the Arabian Peninsula States – namely the Gulf Cooperation Council member States of Bahrain, Kuwait, Oman, Qatar, Saudi Arabia and the UAE, as well as Jordan and Yemen as prospective GCC members – in establishing national intellectual property protection regimes which both meet their international treaty obligations and are also congruent with their domestic policy objectives. It uses the WTO's TRIPS Agreement of 1995 as the universal benchmark against which the region's laws are assessed. The challenges faced by the States in enforcing their intellectual property laws receive particular attention.

Protecting Intellectual Property in the Arabian Peninsula considers the changing nature of the States' intellectual property laws since 1995. It argues that the decade immediately following the TRIPS Agreement was marked by a period of foreign forces shaping or influencing the character of the States' intellectual property legislative regimes, primarily through multilateral or bilateral trade-based agreements. The second and current decade, however, see a significant shift away from foreign influences and a move towards domestic and regional imperatives and initiatives taking over.

The work also examines regional initiatives for the protection of traditional knowledge and cultural heritage, as areas of intellectual property which fall outside the parameters of the TRIPS Agreement, but which are of significant concern to the States and other developing countries, and to which they are giving increasing attention in terms of providing proper protection.

David Price is Associate Professor in Intellectual Property Law and Public International Law at Charles Darwin University, Australia.

Alhanoof AlDebasi is an Intellectual Property Law lecturer at Princess Nourah Bint Abdulrahman University (PNU), College of Business and Administration in Riyadh, Saudi Arabia.

Routledge Research in Intellectual Property

Copyright Industries and the Impact of Creative Destruction
Copyright Expansion and the Publishing Industry
Jiabo Liu

Health Technologies and International Intellectual Property
A Precautionary Principle
Phoebe Li

Intellectual Property, Traditional Knowledge and Cultural Property Protection
Cultural Signifiers in the Caribbean and the Americas
Sharon Le Gall

Intellectual Property and Traditional Knowledge in the Global Economy
Translating Geographical Indications for Development
Teshager W. Dagne

The Object of Copyright
A Conceptual History of Originals and Copies in Literature, Art and Design
Stina Teilmann-Lock

Well-Known Trade Marks
A Comparative Study of Japan and the EU
Hiroko Onishi

Contemporary Issues in Pharmaceutical Patent Law
Setting the Framework and Exploring Policy Options
Bryan Mercurio and Daria Kim

PROTECTING INTELLECTUAL PROPERTY IN THE ARABIAN PENINSULA

The GCC States, Jordan and Yemen

حماية حقوق الملكية الفكرية في شبه الجزيرة العربية:
دول مجلس التعاون الخليجي، الأردن واليمن

David Price and Alhanoof AlDebasi

Routledge
Taylor & Francis Group
LONDON AND NEW YORK

First published 2018
by Routledge
2 Park Square, Milton Park, Abingdon, Oxon OX14 4RN

and by Routledge
711 Third Avenue, New York, NY 10017

Routledge is an imprint of the Taylor & Francis Group, an informa business

British Library Cataloguing in Publication Data
A catalogue record for this book is available from the British Library

Library of Congress Cataloging in Publication Data
Names: Price, David, 1948-, author. | AlDebasi, Alhanoof, author.
Title: Protecting intellectual property in the Arabian Peninsula : the GCC states, Jordan and Yemen / David Price, Alhanoof AlDebasi.
Description: New York, NY : Routledge, 2017. | Series: Routledge research in intellectual property | Includes bibliographical references and index.
Identifiers: LCCN 2017023095 | ISBN 9781138211452 (hardback) | ISBN 9781138211476 (pbk.)
Subjects: LCSH: Intellectual property—Arabian Peninsula. | Intellectual property—Persian Gulf States. | Gulf Cooperation Council.
Classification: LCC KMC370. P755 2017 | DDC 346.5304/8—dc23
LC record available at https://lccn.loc.gov/2017023095

ISBN: 978-1-138-21145-2 (hbk)
ISBN: 978-1-138-21147-6 (pbk)
ISBN: 978-1-315-45297-5 (ebk)

Typeset in Galliard
by Keystroke, Neville Lodge, Tettenhall, Wolverhampton

CONTENTS

TABLES

PREFACE

This work examines the endeavours of the Arabian Peninsula States – namely the Gulf Cooperation Council member States of Bahrain, Kuwait, Oman, Qatar Saudi Arabia and the UAE, as well as Jordan and Yemen as prospective GCC members – in establishing national intellectual property protection regimes which both meet their international treaty obligations and are also congruent with their domestic policy objectives. It uses the WTO's TRIPS Agreement of 1995 as the universal benchmark against which the region's laws are assessed. The challenges faced by the States in enforcing their intellectual property laws receive particular attention.

This work examines the extent to which these statutory frameworks and their enforcement both meet the States' international treaty obligations and are congruent with their domestic policy objectives and needs. Particular attention is given to the foreign forces which have shaped or influenced the character of the Arabian Peninsula States' intellectual property legislative regimes. The work does not attempt to offer a detailed legal commentary on the text of each intellectual property law in each State law, but instead focuses on the salient features of each area of intellectual property protection.

The two decades since the creation of the WTO and the TRIPS Agreement see rounds of legislative activity by the States as they strive to meet their statutory obligations to introduce new laws or to make their current laws TRIPS-compliant and their enforcement effective. During the first decade, a major factor shaping the character of their laws is the bilateral strategy pursued by the United States as part of its strategy to create a Middle East Free Trade Area under US sponsorship. This round commences with a series of bilateral trade and investment agreements and continues with free trade agreements between the United States and Jordan (2000), Bahrain (2004) and Oman (2005), all three agreements incorporating extensive provisions on intellectual property.

However, the second decade of this phase is accompanied by an emerging diametric shift in the regional geopolitical dynamics, with a consequent change in the nature and pace of the development of national intellectual property protection regimes. The second decade is also marked by the GCC itself taking a more prominent role in regional intellectual property leadership. GCC-promoted regional patents and trademark registration schemes from the late 1990s gain increasing acceptance. The Unified Trademarks Law, for example, has already been formally adopted by four of the GCC member States, and there is speculation that the others may follow in the foreseeable future.

The work also examines regional initiatives for the protection of traditional knowledge and cultural heritage, being areas of intellectual property which fall outside the parameters of TRIPS, but which are of significant concern to the States and other developing countries and to which they are giving increasing attention in terms of providing proper protection.

ACKNOWLEDGEMENTS

The production of this work has been the result of a very fruitful and enjoyable collaboration across two rather different cultures and societies, and across two different generations – and which has demonstrated that differences can be, and have been, both beneficial and productive. Each collaborator has brought their own unique skills sets and expertise to this project to produce a work which we are confident will be both illuminating and instructive.

Particular thanks are extended to Olivia Manley and Katie Carpenter at Taylor & Francis for their expert and astute advice and guidance in the preparation and editing of the manuscript for publication.

I, David Price, owe an immeasurable debt of gratitude to my wife, Jane, to whom this book is dedicated. Without her undying encouragement, support and forbearance, this project would not have been possible.

I, Alhanoof AlDebasi, dedicate this book to my family who have always been supportive of dreams, and to my wonderful students for their valuable inputs and comments. Also, this journey would not have been completed without my co-author, David Price, who has been an amazing mentor and a great friend.

And most importantly, this book is for my mother '*Norah*' who taught me that the sky is the limit. Because she does not read English, the following lines are written in Arabic, as I owe her everything.

أهدى هذا الكتاب لوالدتي" نوره اباالخيل" لولا الله ثم هي لما كنت هنا اليوم. قصيدة معروف الرصافي اختصرت ما يجول في خاطري:

"أوجبُ الواجباتِ إكرامُ أمِّي إنّ أمِّي أحقُّ بالإكرام
حملتني ثقلاً ومن بعد حملي أرضَعَتني إلى أوانِ فِطامي
ورَعَتني في ظُلمةِ الليلِ حتّى تركت نومَها لأجلِ مَنامي
إنّ أمِّي هيَ التي خَلَقَتني بعدَ ربِّي فصرتُ بعضَ الأنام
فلها الحمدُ بعد حمدي إلهي ولها الشكرُ في مَدى الأيّام"

David Price
Charles Darwin University, Darwin, Australia
Alhanoof AlDebasi
Princess Nourah bint Abdulrahman University, Saudi Arabia

ABBREVIATIONS

AAA	Arabian Anti-Piracy Alliance
ACTPN	Advisory Committee for Trade and Policy Negotiations
AED	Emirati dirham
BD	Bahraini dirham
BIT	Bilateral Investment Treaty
BSA	Business Software Alliance
FTA	Free Trade Agreement
FTAA	Free Trade Agreement of the Americas
GATT	General Agreement on Tariffs and Trade
GCC	Gulf Cooperation Council
GI	Geographical Indication
ICSID	International Centre for Settlement of Investment Disputes
IDCAS	Industrial Development Centre for Arab States
IIPA	International Intellectual Property Alliance
ITAC-15	Industry Trade Advisory Committee on Intellectual Property Rights
KACST	King Abdul Aziz City of Science and Technology
KD	Kuwaiti dinar
KUNA	Kuwait News Agency
MEFTA	Middle East Free Trade Area
MFN	Most-Favoured Nation
NAFTA	North America Free Trade Area
OR	Omani rial
PCT	Patent Cooperation Treaty
PLT	Patent Law Treaty
PhRMA	Pharmaceutical Researchers and Manufacturers of America
QR	Qatari riyal

SR	Saudi riyal
TIFA	Trade and Investment Framework Agreement
TLT	Trademark Law Treaty
TRIPS	Trade-Related Aspects of Intellectual Property Rights
UAE	United Arab Emirates
UCC	Universal Copyright Convention
UNCITRAL	United Nations Commission on International Trade Law
UNCTAD	United Nations Commission for Trade and Development
UPOV	International Union for the Protection of New Plant Varieties
URAA	Uruguay Round Amendment Act, 1994 (US)
USTR	United States Trade Representative
WCT	WIPO Copyright Treaty
WIPO	World Intellectual Property Organisation
WPPT	WIPO Performances and Phonograms Treaty
WTO	World Trade Organisation
YER	Yemeni rial

1

PROTECTING INTELLECTUAL PROPERTY IN THE ARABIAN PENINSULA – INTRODUCTION AND CONTEXT

1.1 Introduction

This work builds upon the 2008 ground-breaking book by David Price entitled *The Development of Intellectual Protection Regimes in the Arabian Gulf States: Infidels at the Gates.* The primary objective of that earlier book was to examine the development of national legislative regimes for the protection of intellectual property rights in the six States of the Arabian Peninsula that constitute the Cooperation Council for the Arab States of the Gulf (the GCC),[1] namely, the Kingdom of Bahrain, the State of Kuwait, the Sultanate of Oman, the State of Qatar, the Kingdom of Saudi Arabia and the United Arab Emirates (UAE). That earlier work also included commentary on the development of intellectual property protection in the Republic of Yemen, as a prospective member of the GCC.[2]

This latest work continues along a similar but much expanded path, again concentrating its attention primarily on the GCC member States. However, it is much more than just a second edition of that earlier work, for a number of reasons.

1 The Gulf Cooperation Council (GCC) came into existence on 26 May 1981, in part as a response to perceived threats from an Islamic fundamentalist Iran, an imperialistic Ba'athist Iraq, the state of civil war in Yemen and the recent Soviet intervention in Afghanistan – all of which threatened to destabilise the ruling dynasties in the Gulf region and to involve their states in wider conflicts.

2 Yemen has been seeking membership of the GCC since 1996. Its application for membership has been sponsored by Oman and Qatar, but has been vetoed by Saudi Arabia, the main obstacle being the difference between Yemen's and the GCC members' political and economic systems. In January 2002, Yemen was granted observer status at GCC-affiliated non-political bodies and agencies, and in October 2002 Yemen and the GCC signed a protocol defining the relationship between the two sides – considered to be the first step towards Yemen's full membership of the GCC. As at the end of August 2017, Yemen was still seeking full membership of the GCC.

First, its scope has been extended to include the Kingdom of Jordan – the other Arabian Peninsula State that is a prospective member of the GCC.[3] Membership of the GCC will positively impact on Jordan's and Yemen's respective intellectual property protection regimes by providing the opportunity to adopt the GCC-sponsored regional harmonisation initiatives, currently in trademarks and patents.

Second, the work embraces a period of change and development in regional intellectual property covering almost a decade since the publication of the original book.

Third, this work acknowledges a noticeable shift in domestic intellectual property regimes away from foreign influences towards more regional-based influences.

And fourth, this work is the result of a team effort, with Alhanoof AlDebasi, of the Faculty of Law, Princess Noura University, Saudi Arabia, bringing her own expertise and unique local knowledge to the project.

As with its predecessor, this latest work examines the extent to which these legislative regimes and their enforcement both meet the States' international treaty obligations and are congruent with their domestic policy objectives and needs. Particular attention is given to the foreign forces which have shaped or influenced the character of the Arabian Peninsula States' intellectual property legislative regimes. Hence, the work examines the performance of the States in protecting intellectual property rights in the context of their accessions to World Trade Organisation (WTO) membership, the consequent compliance with the requirements of the WTO's Agreement on the Trade-Related Aspects of Intellectual Property Rights (1995) (TRIPS) and the international conventions for the protection of intellectual property rights upon which the Agreement draws and builds, notably the Paris, Berne and Rome Conventions.[4] The work does not attempt to offer a detailed legal commentary on the text of each intellectual property law in each State law, but instead focuses on the salient features of each area of intellectual property protection and its particular idiosyncratic features.

Accordingly, and appropriately, TRIPS serves as the benchmark for this work.

A secondary objective is to establish a substantive record of the nature of the States' intellectual property laws and the history of their recent development. Previous studies on intellectual property rights protection that have concerned the Middle East region have tended to concentrate either on one type of law,

3 Jordan has been seeking membership of the GCC since 1996. In May 2011, the GCC Supreme Council finally issued an invitation to Jordan to join the Council at a future (but unspecified) date. In 2015, Jordan and the GCC agreed on a five-year development plan for Jordan as a key element of its accession. At the same time, the GCC issued a (surprising) invitation to Morocco to also join the GCC.

4 The Paris Convention for the Protection of Industrial Property, the Berne Convention for the Protection of Literary and Artistic Works, the International Convention for the Protection of Performers, Producers of Phonograms, adopted at Rome on 26 October 1961, and the Treaty on Intellectual Property in Respect of Integrated Circuits, adopted at Washington on 26 May 1989. Although the Washington Treaty never entered into force, its provisions nevertheless became enforceable through TRIPS arts 35–8.

notably copyright, trademarks or patents, or on a few Arabian Peninsula States only. Selective studies on intellectual property protection in developing countries further afield have tended to pass over the countries in the region, with the occasional exception of Saudi Arabia or the UAE, in favour of a selection from a more active and industrially advanced group of developing countries. This work attempts to redress that imbalance. Although it focuses primarily upon patent, trademark and copyright protection, since these are the major areas of intellectual property concern, interest and activity within the States and the international community, it also encompasses the other significant areas of intellectual property as enshrined in TRIPS, such as industrial designs, geographical indications, integrated circuits, undisclosed information (trade secrets) and new plant varieties.

The work also examines regional initiatives for the protection of traditional knowledge and cultural heritage, being areas of intellectual property which fall outside the parameters of TRIPS, but which are of significant concern to the States and other developing countries and to which they are giving increasing attention in terms of providing proper protection.

An appreciation of the enforcement and recognition of intellectual property rights in the Arabian Peninsula would be incomplete without an understanding of the religious, political and cultural forces deeply rooted in Middle East history that shape the protection of intellectual property rights in the Middle East today.[5] Accordingly, the position of the *Shariah* as a major influence upon the intellectual property rights protection and the constitutional and judicial framework in which it resides is reviewed, as background and context for the examination of the region's intellectual property laws. The precedence of Islamic law, or the *Shariah*, as a legal imperative is unequivocal; its status has been described by one eminent commentator thus:

> Behind all secular law stands the *Shariah* law of Islam . . . the *Shariah* runs like a golden thread through the legal systems of the Arab Middle East.[6]

1.2 The Arabian Peninsula States and the development of intellectual property laws

What makes a study of these six GCC member States and Jordan and Yemen of current-day relevance and interest is that the emergence of each as a modern State is a fairly recent and ongoing occurrence and yet they have assumed a not insignificant regional and global influence in international affairs and trade. With

5 John Carroll (2000/2001), 'Intellectual Property Rights in the Middle East: A Cultural Perspective', 11, *Fordham Intellectual Property Media and Entertainment Law Journal*, p. 555.

6 W M Ballantyne (1986), *Commercial Law in the Arab Middle East: The Gulf States*, p. 2. See also W M Ballantyne (2011), *Essays and Addresses on Arab Laws*, pp. 58–78.

the arguable exception of Jordan and Saudi Arabia, the other six States have taken quantum leaps in their national development, to emerge from being quasi-feudal or disputative tribal regions under actual or effective foreign domination into stable and sophisticated independent sovereign States, in just two generations or less. Bahrain, Kuwait, Qatar and the seven sheikhdoms of the Trucial States (that later formed the UAE) were still part of the UK Persian Gulf interests until they gained independence in 1961 (Kuwait) and 1971 (Bahrain, Qatar and the seven sheikhdoms). Oman, although long an independent sovereign State, was still under British influence prior to 1970 and deemed the most feudal and withdrawn of all the Arab Peninsula countries; it did not start to emerge from this pseudo-feudal condition until the present Sultan succeeded his father in a British-backed palace coup in 1970.[7] Prior to 1990, Yemen existed as two separate States, the Yemen Arab Republic (North Yemen) and the pro-Marxist People's Democratic Republic of Yemen, until they formally united to create the Republic of Yemen on 22 May 1990. However, armed insurgency, separatist movements and civil war have continued to plague the country. Not surprisingly, therefore, Yemen has lagged behind the other States in terms of its emergence as a modern State generally, and in respect of the development of its intellectual property protection regimes.

As part of their ongoing respective political, economic and social metamorphoses, the legal systems of the States have undergone dramatic, radical and progressive change and development over the last 40 years or so and that change is continuing. The major trend has been a shift towards greatly increased codification of law and administered regulation which has entailed increasing substitution of institutionalised procedures for the former informal, discretionary exercise of personal authority sometimes based on local interpretation of *Shariah* legal principles.[8] With this movement towards codification of the law and the institutionalisation of the judiciary and government, there has emerged a growing tension between the protection of local and national interests and traditions and the governmental recognition of the need to embrace western-based legal and economic principles, practices and infrastructures.

The work argues that there has existed a disjunct between the formal expression of intellectual property protection through the States' laws and their practical application through the States' respective enforcement strategies and efforts. This

7 Oman has enjoyed independent status since it expelled the Portuguese in 1650. During the eighteenth century it established an empire encompassing Zanzibar, parts of East Africa and the southern Arabian Peninsula, and established effective trading control over parts of the Persian and Pakistan coasts. In 1800 Great Britain entered into a Friendship Treaty which recognised Oman's independence but which developed into Great Britain gaining effective control over Oman's foreign relations and over the affairs of non-Muslims in the Sultanate. Oman's regional influence and empire declined during the late nineteenth century as it retreated into a period of sustained isolationism until the 1970s.

8 Nicholas Angell (2006), 'An Overview of Legal Structures in the GCC Countries', World Service Group (December), available at www.worldservicesgroup.com/publications.asp?action=article&artid=1649, last accessed 26 May 2017.

disjunct arose as a consequence of the external pressures upon the States to adopt laws for which they had neither the resources nor the expertise nor the infrastructures to effectively execute to the level of satisfaction sought by the more demanding developed countries. The work speculates on the extent to which the legislative and operational responses of the States satisfy WTO/developed countries' expectations and what further changes might be sought in the future.

Since the 1960s and early 1970s, when most of the Arabian Peninsula States either gained their independence or emerged from sustained periods of international isolationism, they have undertaken a transformation of their intellectual property legislative regimes at an extremely rapid rate – virtually in the time frame of one or two generations. The period of this transformation has been marked by three major, but very different, phases in the development of the regimes. Each phase has been characterised by different degrees of foreign intervention which have directed or at least strongly influenced the construction of the States' intellectual property laws. But this foreign intervention has not necessarily caused the creation of laws which have been congruent with the States' needs or which have enabled the achievement of national objectives and international requirements in terms of their enforcement effectiveness.

The first of these phases, namely the pre-TRIPS period that existed until the mid-1990s and prior to the establishment of the WTO, was notable for the dearth of *sui generis* intellectual property laws in place in the States; the exceptions were few in number and existed in the fields of trademarks, patents and industrial designs, but even these laws were subject to foreign influence. However, this dearth of *sui generis* laws did not mean that protection for certain types of intellectual property rights was not available; it existed in an overarching perspective in the divine laws of social and moral conduct laid down in the *Qur'an* and the *Sunnah* of the Prophet. In a more corporeal and secular sense, and in the absence of any mainstream intellectual property framework, it also existed in the form of laws governing commercial activity and conduct. Protection in pre-TRIPS times was available for the benefit of the foreign merchant or the merchant's local agent, the trader and the consumer, instead of for the holder of an intellectual property right of foreign origin, but on occasion it coincided for the benefit of both groups. However, even these commercial laws were generally subject to foreign influence. In addition, the national frameworks for the control of publishing and public dissemination of printed material, which all States actively enforced, provided some limited protection for certain types of copyrightable material.

The second developmental phase is marked by the establishment of the WTO, the consequent entry into force of TRIPS and a post-TRIPS flurry of legislative activity by the Arabian Peninsula States as they endeavour to meet their statutory obligations to introduce intellectual property laws or to make their current laws TRIPS-compliant and their enforcement effective. TRIPS heralded a major shift in intellectual property by establishing unprecedented levels of protection to be enforced globally. However, the shift took shape by reference largely to the needs of the leading industrialised nations who were the major creators and exporters of intellectual property and sought the highest possible standards of protection for the accompanying rights. The World Intellectual Property Organisation (WIPO), which had already been a significance influence in shaping the States' pre-TRIPS intellectual property laws, continued to play a crucial role in guiding the States in their compilation of TRIPS-compliant laws and in their enforcement, structural and administrative capacity-building efforts. With fluctuating degrees of commitment, the States embarked on reshaping their intellectual property protection regimes during this period.

Hardly had the States come to terms with the enormity of the dimension of the transformation to their respective intellectual property protection regimes required by the TRIPS and post-TRIPS phase than they were faced with a new round of imposed changes as they entered the third phase – the TRIPS-plus phase. In the first half of this phase, generally the first post-TRIPS decade, a dominant driving factor shaping the character of their laws is the bilateral trade agreement strategy pursued by the United States. This new round commenced with a series of bilateral trade and investment agreements from the late 1990s, followed by free trade agreements (FTAs) by the United States with Jordan, Bahrain and Oman. All three agreements incorporate extensive provisions on intellectual property. The provisions constitute much higher standards of protection than those set by TRIPS and also remove and restrict the limited degree of manoeuvrability that TRIPS permitted developing and least-developed countries. The agreements are reinforced by demands that the signatory States not only adopt higher standards enshrined in the FTAs themselves but also adopt and adhere to a range of multilateral treaties which represents TRIPS-plus standards. Both the FTAs and the multilateral treaties reduce and restrict the flexibilities and exceptions provisions that TRIPS allows signatory States to craft their laws to take account of their respective national needs and objectives.

However, the second half of this phase – namely the second post-TRIPS decade or thereabouts – sees the GCC itself taking a more prominent role in regional intellectual property leadership. This developing role is evidenced by the GCC's willingness to expand its membership, and to launch a number of initiatives in regional intellectual property protection, namely a regional patents registration scheme, followed by a unified trademarks regulation and subsequent law, and more recently establishing a GCC intellectual property training centre. The trademarks law has already been formally adopted by four of the GCC member States, and there is speculation that the others may follow in the foreseeable future.

1.3 The WTO, TRIPS and the globalisation of intellectual property rights

1.3.1 The global pressures

A fundamental element of the emergence of the modern Arabian Peninsula is the move to gain membership of the WTO and the consequent perceived benefits of being a member of the global trade community (or the negative impact of not attaining membership). One consequence of such membership, however, is that legislation relating to trade and services, and to intellectual property in particular, must conform to the provisions of the international treaties in this area, notably TRIPS and the Paris, Berne and Rome Conventions. TRIPS set new international minimum standards of protection for each of the main categories of intellectual property by building on these major conventions and adding a requirement for effective enforcement regimes.

Since coming into effect in January 1995, TRIPS has generated considerable ongoing debate concerning the benefits and disadvantages that its standards of intellectual property protection bring to developed, developing and least-developed countries. According to some commentators, there exists a powerful lobby representing developed countries which believes that all intellectual property rights are good for business, benefit the public at large and act as catalysts for technical progress.[9] The rights are necessary to stimulate economic growth which, in turn, contributes to poverty reduction; by stimulating invention and new technologies, they increase agricultural or industrial production, promote domestic and foreign investment, facilitate technology transfer and improve the availability of medicines necessary to protect public health. The developed country lobby considers TRIPS to be a useful tool with which to achieve its objectives and holds that there is no reason why a system that works for developed countries could not work in similar fashion in developing countries.[10]

On the other side, there are those who believe that the protection of intellectual property rights according to the formula of the major industrialised countries is likely to cripple the progress of local industry and technology in developing countries, will harm their local populations and benefit none but the developed world.[11] Intellectual property rights do little to stimulate invention in developing countries, where the necessary human and technical capacity is absent, and they are ineffective in stimulating research to benefit the poor because they will not be able to afford the products, even if developed. They limit the option of technological learning through imitation and they allow foreign firms to drive out domestic competition by enabling these firms to obtain protection to service the market through imports rather than domestic manufacture. Very high standards of protection may be in the public interest in developed countries with highly sophisticated scientific and technological infrastructures, but this does not mean the same standards are appropriate in all developing countries.[12]

Harmonisation of intellectual property rights, whether as a regional or global initiative, is a contentious issue which still has much distance to travel. To its critics,

9 UK Department for International Development (DfID) (2002), *Report of the UK Commission on Intellectual Property Rights*, pp. 1–2.

10 Ibid.

11 Ibid.

12 Ibid.

harmonisation is the strategy devised by the leading developed nations to achieve and maintain global domination through control of international trade and to protect their commercial interests in the developing and least-developed countries. By that view, intellectual property rights are imposed by developed countries on the developing and least-developed countries as a non-negotiable total package, compliance with which is a prerequisite for membership of the international trade community of which WTO is the global representative. International intellectual property standard-setting has been dominated by western nations and intellectual property owners, and the dominant mechanism of standard-setting has been economic coercion, of which TRIPS has been the most potent multilateral expression.[13] Some commentators argue that TRIPS principally benefits the developed countries and the credibility of the WTO as an instrument to promote free trade in the interests of all countries is weakened:

> TRIPS does not involve mutual gain; rather, it positions the WTO primarily as a collector of intellectual property-related rents on behalf of multinational corporations (MNCs). This is a bad image for the WTO and in the view of many . . . reflects the 'capture' of the WTO by the MNCs.[14]

The States saw that WTO membership would give them the potential ability to exert some influence on international trade, whereas outside the WTO they would have no such ability. Yet the States really had little choice but to join the international community which the WTO represents. The perceived significance to the States of membership of the WTO and the requisite intellectual property legislative framework was a key national political and economic strategy. In both the legal and commercial contexts, global harmonisation can be an intrusive process that demands an active re-examination by the State of its laws and regulations. Arab countries were driven by pressures from a variety of sources, such as the WTO and individual developed countries, to review and upgrade their laws governing a wide range of economic activity and to introduce a widely embracing set of laws where none previously existed.[15]

1.3.2 The Arabian Peninsula States' response to the pressures

The question arises as to the extent to which the Arabian Peninsula States have succumbed to this pressure or whether they have managed to maintain their

13 Peter Drahos (2002), 'Developing Countries and International Intellectual Property Standard-Setting', 5, *Journal of World Intellectual Property*, p. 788.

14 See John Braithwaite and Peter Drahos (2002), *Information Feudalism: Who Owns the Knowledge Economy?*, pp. 9–13; see also Jagdish Bhagwati, quoted in 'Integrating Intellectual Property Rights and Development Policy', *Report of the UK Commission on Intellectual Property Rights*, op. cit. p. 160.

15 Howard Stovall (2000), 'Arab Commercial Laws – Into the Future', 34, *The International Lawyer*, p. 842.

integrity and to some extent outmanoeuvre the developed countries in some instances. Some intellectual property issues that have become of increasing importance to the States, such as the protection of indigenous rights, traditional knowledge and cultural heritage, have not yet been pursued with the same degree of aggression by the industrialised nations as they have moved to protect their rights and interest on copyright, patents and trademarks.

Critics of the performance of developing countries in displaying their commitment to the protection of intellectual property rights according to the standards set by TRIPS would argue that the States, as developing countries, are paying lip service to the rightful demands of the developed countries for the effective protection of intellectual property rights.[16] The States may be establishing the legislative regimes by adopting the intellectual property laws as required by the consortia of the developed countries, but they appear unwilling, uncommitted or unable to act as expeditiously and as fully as required with an effective implementation strategy and execution. To substantiate their complaints, the critics point to the perceived delays in introducing the necessary implementing regulations to give practical effect to the laws, the lack of structural reforms in the States' judicial, infrastructural and administrative areas, and enforcement actions which appear infrequent and do not conclude in successful judicial prosecutions and outcomes.[17]

The most challenging element of the TRIPS and TRIPS-plus phases, as perceived by both the States themselves and the industrialised nations, is the regional enforcement of the States' intellectual property protection obligations consistent with the standards enshrined in TRIPS, the TRIPS-plus treaties and the bilateral agreements to which the States have made commitments. Notwithstanding the presence of comprehensive sets of laws and treaty commitments, there nevertheless exists a disjunct between the principle of enforcement as enshrined in the various legislative regimes and the practice as exemplified by the degree of effective action. In all States, the practical application of compliance obligations through effective enforcement has been, and continues to be, the most difficult area with which to contend.

This disjunct is also experienced by many other developing and least-developed countries. Why and how this dichotomy emerges and what are, and might continue to be, the consequences for each State can be demonstrated by the comprehensive nature of the legislative regimes in light of the TRIPS minimum benchmark and the dimension of institutional and structural reforms being progressively initiated when contrasted with:

- implementation actions, as evidenced by policing actions against illegal activities, piracy and counterfeit goods; and

16 Carroll, op. cit., p. 594.
17 These criticisms would appear with regular frequency in the USTR's Annual Special 301 Reports. The Reports as they relate to the Arabian Peninsula States are discussed in greater detail in Chapter 8.

- the nature and frequency of judicial actions and the severity of penalties available and imposed.

One measure of the extent of this disjunct can be seen in the responses of the developed countries, as evidenced by the United States through the application of its USTR Annual Special 301 Reports, and the influence thereon of the powerful multinational industry lobby groups. For most States, the principal barriers to the elimination of intellectual property infringements, which lie at the heart of this disjunct, do not subsist so much in the substantive law as in their practical application. The reasons for these barriers, which this work explores, are many and do not rest solely with the enforcement authorities or the judiciary; entrenched local societal, cultural and commercial attitudes are also major contributing factors.

In the cause of securing membership of the international community, the States have had little option but to adhere to agendas set by the developed countries through the WTO and the major international treaties which they sponsor. Although the agendas may not necessarily have yet hampered the development of nationally appropriate intellectual property protection regimes, they are cementing in place conditions that will restrict the future freedom or discretion of the States to develop in directions which best deal with national imperatives or opportunities. Since becoming part of the international community, the States face, and will continue to face, direct pressure from some developed countries to accept the imposition of further enhanced levels of intellectual property protection, again with the objective of protecting the particular interests of the developed countries.

1.4 Multilateralism by the backdoor – the strategy of bilateralism

While TRIPS has set the minimum international standards for intellectual property protection, the nature of these standards and universal adherence to them has still created difficulties and challenges for the States, other developing countries and least-developed countries. It has also generated a significant degree of frustration and dissatisfaction for the major industrialised nations. In some respects, TRIPS has become somewhat superseded by the emergence of the new round of intellectual property law-making at the bilateral and regional levels in the post-TRIPS world. The WTO has stumbled at its recent ministerial meetings on efforts to liberalise global trade and to also inject a greater degree of equity and access into TRIPS. Failure to conclude the Doha Rounds after many years of largely fruitless negotiations calls into question the WTO's continuing prominence as the lead forum for the global trade and intellectual property agendas. At the same time, WIPO has been confronted with its own self-examination debate over proposals and counter-proposals which have the potential to significantly change its position and role in the global intellectual property arena.

The new 'international standard' of intellectual property protection in practical terms is becoming that which is defined by the terms enshrined in the latest bilateral or regional agreement in which the United States and the EU in particular may have participated and concluded. The 'highest international standards' have become very much a dynamic formula in a bilateral context rather than the multilateral forums.

While negotiations on intellectual property rights in the WTO are virtually paralysed and the launching of negotiations on investment finds strong opposition, developed countries have turned to bilateral dealings to advance their industries' economic interests and obtain higher levels of commitment from developing countries.[18] Powerful and influential multinational business interests actively push for progressively escalating standards and carefully monitor the progress and performance of the US government in imposing TRIPS-plus standards on weaker countries. Hence bilateral trade and investment agreements, particularly FTAs, typically contain extensive intellectual property protection provisions which are used to establish TRIPS-plus standards, to remove or reduce the flexibilities provided for in TRIPS and to establish protection in new areas of intellectual property rights which go beyond the parameters of TRIPS.[19]

Bilateral trade and investment agreements are promoted by their advocates as being stepping stones towards full integration of the participants into a global free market economy by ensuring governments implement the liberalisation, privatisation and deregulation measures of the globalisation agenda.[20] However, they have also been described as part of an insidious, fast-expanding and bewildering coercive web, popping up like Hydra's heads throughout the world and constructing in patchwork fashion what the developed nations have not been able to impose through such international forums as the WTO, or through multilateral negotiations.[21] They are seen as insidious because they are invariably conducted in unequal contest in closed session between unequal partners. With the stronger partner having an established objective to protect its own economic and trade interests, and having little or no interest in making allowance for the divergent or conflicting national and developmental interests of the weaker partner, the resultant agreement is both inevitable and predictable.

On intellectual property issues that really matter to it, the United States has utilised webs of coercion, and one of those webs is its strategy of establishing bilateral agreements which include the establishment of standards of intellectual

18 Carlos Correa (2000), *Intellectual Property Rights, The WTO and Developing Countries: The TRIPS Agreement and Policy Options*, p. 4.

19 See the Report of the Asian Regional Workshop on Bilateral Free Trade Agreements (2005), *Third World Network,* Kuala Lumpur, August, p. 8, available at www.twn.my/title2/twninfo253.htm, last accessed 26 May 2017.

20 Aziz Choudry (2004), 'Bombarded by Bilateral Trade and Investment Agreements', *Bilaterals.org*, March, p. 3, available at www.bilaterals.org/IMG/pdf/Bombarded_by_Bilatera_92909-2.pdf, last accessed 26 May 2017.

21 Aziz Choudry (2003), 'Bilateral Trade and Investment Deals a Serious Challenge to Global Justice Movements', *GRAIN,* December, p. 1, available at www.grain.org/article/entries/3620-bilateral-trade-and-investment-deals-a-serious-challenge-to-global-justice-movements, last accessed 26 May 2017.

property protection which may far exceed TRIPS standards and extend beyond the scope of TRIPS.[22] Developing countries operate within an intellectual property paradigm dominated by the United States, the European Union and international business; given the track record of the United States and the EU, developing countries can expect very few concessions on intellectual property issues in either a bilateral or a multilateral context.[23] However, developing countries are prepared to enter into bilateral agreements containing provisions on intellectual property rights in order to gain access to US and EU markets or to avoid losing access to them.

Having introduced intellectual property laws of largely foreign origin to satisfy the requirements to comply with TRIPS, the States are faced with the issues and challenges of their domestic implementation and enforcement. Even though the States have demonstrated a general willingness to address the complex and contentious issue of regional piracy – albeit with mixed success – they now face additional pressures from the United States to adopt TRIPS-plus standards of intellectual property protection. A crucial tool in the application of this pressure is the use of the USTR's Special 301 Annual Reporting provisions, which identify countries which fail to provide adequate protection of US intellectual property rights or deny market access to US companies and which threaten possible US retaliatory trade actions. Furthermore, the TRIPS-plus treaties are being used to apply the higher standards on the grounds that these treaties represent the new consensus on higher international standards for intellectual property protection. The intellectual property areas which receive the greatest attention under these bilateral actions are those of economic concern to the United States, particularly protection in the broadest sense of patents, pharmaceutical patents, copyright and neighbouring rights in the digital environment. In contrast, little or no effort is being made within these bilateral agreements to introduce protection of the States' traditional knowledge and cultural heritages, geographical indications of non-European origin, plant varieties and traditional agricultural practice.

This work includes an examination of the application of the US strategy of using bilateral trade agreements to achieve standards of intellectual property protection exceeding those enshrined in TRIPS. It also considers the impact of this strategy upon the States' intellectual property protection regimes and their degree of success in effectively enforcing them. It discusses the intellectual property provisions of the bilateral trade and investment agreements, and particularly the FTAs which the United States concluded with Bahrain, Jordan and Oman between 2000 and 2005. The role of the Office of the United States Trade Representative (USTR) and the Special 301 provisions as a coercive tool in the US bilateral strategy, receive particular attention.

During the Presidency of George W Bush, the United States declared its intention to establish a Middle East Free Trade Area (MEFTA) by 2013 as a crucial tool in

22 Drahos, op. cit., pp. 781–2.
23 Ibid., p. 788.

giving effect to its Middle East Peace Initiative and its global war against terrorism. This was to be achieved by the United States entering into an FTA with each GCC member State, creating a regional Gulf bloc and then promoting the benefits of this bloc as an incentive to other Middle East countries to participate. The FTAs with Jordan, Bahrain and Oman were to be the catalyst for further developmental change of this regional strategy. These FTAs required each State to make a number of significant concessions and commitments in the area of intellectual property protection which well exceeded TRIPS standards and which countered TRIPS flexibility provisions. The Bahrain FTA was based on the US model developed for Jordan, but set a new TRIPS-plus benchmark in terms of intellectual property protection in the Arabian Peninsula, while the Oman FTA raised it slightly higher.

However, with a change of US Presidents and Administrations came a change in global strategic geopolicy, with the MEFTA strategy being overtaken by the 'Asia Pivot' strategy, and a strengthened focus concentrating geopolitical and trade attention on East Asia and the Pacific Rim. Hence, the FTA negotiations commenced with Kuwait, Qatar and the UAE, which no doubt would have built on the Oman FTA and driven those intellectual property standards even higher, did not come to a successful conclusion, and FTAs did not eventuate.

1.5 Structure of the work

This chapter has introduced some background to the Arabian Peninsula States and briefly explored the paradigm in which the States have operated in the establishment of their legislative regimes for intellectual property protection.

Chapter 2 examines the regional and domestic moral fabric for intellectual property protection in the States under scrutiny in the book. It explores the idea of the *Shariah* as a 'golden thread' that runs through the constitutional, legal and judicial structures of the States, and the changing nature of its influence as the secular laws of the States have become increasingly codified. The work examines the extent to which the *Shariah* still drives or influences the regional protection of intellectual property rights.

Chapter 3 addresses the pre-TRIPS period of this study. It examines the recent history of intellectual property rights protection within the Arabian Peninsula and in each State. In so doing, it refers to examples of other laws which were outside a fledgling intellectual property framework, but which offered varying degrees of protection to some intellectual property rights by virtue of their common or overlapping objectives. The chapter also examines some of the foreign influences that have been brought to bear, directly and indirectly, on the development of the region's intellectual property laws. It also questions the impetus behind the States' decisions to join the international trade community and discusses the external inputs into the preparation of their legislative regimes as a precursor to their acceding to the WTO and to TRIPS.

Chapters 4 and 5 analyse the standards for intellectual property protection enshrined in TRIPS with the provisions of the States' current laws in the major intellectual property areas prescribed by TRIPS. They examine the extent to which the States comply with their obligations under TRIPS requirements and standards. They focus on the salient features of each area of intellectual property protection and its particular idiosyncratic features, rather than offering a detailed commentary on the text of each law. Chapter 4 addresses the status of the States' regimes for copyright and neighbouring rights protection. It includes a new section on the States' initiatives in respect of protection in the digital environment. Chapter 5 addresses the regimes in respect of the areas of industrial property as enshrined in TRIPS, namely trademarks and geographical indications, patents, industrial designs, integrated circuits, plant breeder's rights and trade secrets.

Chapter 6 continues the review process from Chapters 4 and 5 and examines the performance of the States against the enforcement standards and obligations required by TRIPS. It argues that, in the post-TRIPS environment, there exists a disjunct between the principle of intellectual property protection (as enshrined in the legislation) and the practice (as measured by its enforcement). It examines the enforcement provisions and sanctions within the States' major IP laws, and critically analyses the major discrepancies that exist between laws and between States. It briefly introduces criticisms on enforcement from foreign sources, notably the United States through its annual Special 301 Report on those sanctions and discrepancies.

Chapter 7 questions whether that enforcement challenge is a reflection of the political and societal commitment to enforcement, of a political and commercial attitude to intellectual property rights that differs from that of the major developed countries, or of the imposition by the major developed countries of inappropriate requirements and standards that are beyond the capacity of the States to implement effectively. It offers some possible reasons for the problems confronting the States in respect of achieving a strong compliance environment. In so doing, the work examines regional societal and cultural attitudes and obstacles, and the institutional and judicial capacity and limitations to enforcement within the respective States.

Chapter 8 explores the shift in the international intellectual property protection environment away from the multilateral context and towards the bilateral context. It considers the changing nature of foreign influence upon the States' intellectual property environment. It examines the TRIPS-plus elements of the FTAs concluded by the United States with Jordan, Bahrain and Oman. It examines the role of the USTR and its use of the Special 301 provisions as a tool to pressure States to adopt standards of protection much higher than those required by TRIPS.

Chapter 9 examines a 'TRIPS-minus' area of intellectual property rights protection – that is, areas of intellectual and creative activity that are not covered or protected by TRIPS. It discusses activities by the States in areas in which there has been little or no foreign interest in establishing standards of protection on behalf of the States or in the States themselves – notably traditional knowledge, expressions of cultural heritage and the offshoots of traditional medicines and indigenous plant species. The States for some years have taken a particular interest in these areas and have taken the initiative in introducing some protection standards in these areas.

In conclusion, Chapter 10 reviews the development of the States' intellectual property protection regimes and reports on the current status of the national laws and accessions to the major international forums and international conventions on intellectual property protection. It suggests that the development of the intellectual property rights protection regime in the Arabian Peninsula region has been impressive when the relatively short developmental timeframe is taken into account, and that the regime is therefore still 'work in progress'.

Finally, the Appendix lists the intellectual property laws and corresponding implementing regulations and ministerial orders that the States have issued during the timeframe encompassed by this study. The list also includes laws which are associated in one form or another with intellectual property protection, such as laws controlling the press and publications. The list of laws is not complete, but is still impressive and strikingly illustrates just how active the States have been over the last generation or so, and particularly during the current post-TRIPS period, with their law-making endeavours in the field of intellectual property protection.

1.6 Concluding remarks

The intellectual property laws of the GCC member States reflect a common heritage. They contain many similarities with each other, indicating an ongoing process of mutual collaboration and borrowings. They have also drawn much from countries in the region which progressed through an earlier modernisation/ westernisation process, notably Egypt, and other Arab States through their influence in regional groups such as the League of Arab States, and the GCC itself. But they have also drawn much from historical western sources, particularly French influences in the north and west and British influence, at least in the east and south of the Arabian Peninsula. A system of English law and justice prevailed throughout the eastern region until 1971 (except for Muslim nationals on matters within the province of the *Shariah*) and this influence, modified and added to by other western influences, continued well after independence.

However, the major influences in the construction of their legislative regimes and the character of the intellectual property laws have undoubtedly been threefold:

- the creation of the WTO, and the mandatory compliance with the TRIPs Agreement provisions as just one requirement of WTO membership;
- the World Intellectual Property Organisation (WIPO) as the administrator of the TRIPs Agreement, and the influence of the statutory models it provides through its various draft laws and technical assistance;
- and more recently the GCC as its members develop their own strategies and legal and organisational initiatives within the intellectual property framework as well as in the broader commercial and social contexts –

as the following chapters examine and discuss.

Finally, this work uses the terms 'Arabian Peninsula' and 'States' to refer to the eight States covered by the work, namely Bahrain, Jordan, Kuwait, Oman, Qatar, Saudi Arabia, the United Arab Emirates (UAE) and Yemen. It also uses the term 'GCC member States' when referring specifically and collectively to Bahrain, Kuwait, Oman, Qatar, Saudi Arabia and the UAE.

2

'THE GOLDEN THREAD THAT BINDS' – THE *SHARIAH* AND INTELLECTUAL PROPERTY PROTECTION

2.1 Introduction – 'the golden thread'

In its simplest definition, Islamic law, or the *Shariah*, is the corpus of rules and principles derived from the Holy *Qur'an* and *Sunnah* (Traditions) of the Holy Prophet which is aimed at regulating the spiritual as well as the temporal conduct of the Muslim in his relationship with God, with other Muslims and with non-Muslims. The precedence of Islamic law, or the *Shariah*, as a legal imperative is unequivocal; its status has been described thus:

> Behind all secular law stands the *Shariah* law of Islam . . . the *Shariah* runs like a golden thread through the legal systems of the Arab Middle East.[1]

Islam has been described as the cultural epicentre of identity in Arab Muslim life.[2] There exists an interrelational and reciprocal influence between its legal, religious and ethical aspects. As a divine-sourced religion, Islam, like many other religions, is characterised by:

- divine sources which are the highest primary sources and therefore possess supreme character and authority;
- other sources based on human reasoning which are therefore secondary and must defer to the primary sources, taking account of the settled rules and principles of Islamic methodology;
- divine sources which are free from errors whereas human sources are fallible;

1 William M Ballantyne (1986), *Commercial Law in the Arab Middle East: The Gulf States*, pp. 1–2.
2 Susan Rayner (1991), *The Theory of Contracts in Islamic Law*, p. 372.

- divine sources which form the framework outlining the general doctrines and principles, according to which the corpus of the detailed Islamic rules can be formulated.[3]

As the *Shariah* is a whole, comprehensive and interrelated corpus of rules, its application is subject to a single set of standards. Hence one does not find a separate discipline of Islamic law called, for example, intellectual property law. Instead, Islam has the *Shariah*, which deals with every aspect of human conduct regardless of its description as a personal, civil or international code of conduct.[4] Islamic jurisprudence (*fiqh*), as the body of rules and principles that is developed by the reasoning of Muslim jurists, then aims to approach as close as possible to the highest ideals of Islamic doctrinal aspiration.[5] The role of the Muslim jurist is to identify the detailed rules of Islamic law to meet the particular needs of time and place. The different views that emerge are seen not so much as an inconsistency or deficiency in the *Shariah* but rather a flexibility in its application which does not lose sight of the *Shariah* but still takes account of the unique time frame and facts of a particular circumstance or instance. Since Islamic law is set within these formulated rules, the doctrine of legal precedence of the common law system does not occupy an important place in the Islamic judicial system. The value of legal precedent in the Islamic context, which is therefore limited, lies in merely aiding consistency.

Over 35 years ago, William Ballantyne (1980) described what he perceived to be the impasse between *Shariah* law and western law as the classical situation of an 'irresistible force meeting an irremovable object':

> The problem is that the Arabs have, to a greater or less degree, in wishing to adopt the existing international world of commerce, come face to face with the classic situation: an irresistible force against an irremovable object. As is not uncommon in these circumstances (not by any means only in the Arab world) the question has been begged on all sides. It will be, to say the least, interesting to see for how long and to what extent this apparent anomaly can continue.[6]

3 Mahda Zahraa (2000), 'Characteristic Features of Islamic Law: Perceptions and Misconceptions', 15(2), *Arab Law Quarterly*, p. 169.

4 The *Shariah* or sacred law of Islam was developed and assembled during the first three centuries following the death of the Prophet Muhammad in 632 AD. While *Shariah* (literally, the way) is translated as 'Islamic law', it is neither canonical nor secular law because no such concept exists in Islam; it is rather a whole system of social and personal morality, prescribing the way a man should live if he is to act according to God's will. See Peter Mansfield, 'A History of the Middle East', 5, quoted by John Carroll, 'Intellectual Property Rights in the Middle East', (2000/2001), 11, *Fordham Intellectual Property, Media and Entertainment Journal*, p. 588.

5 Zahraa, op. cit., p. 174.

6 William Ballantyne (1980), *Legal Development in Arabia*, p. 121.

Ballantyne's 'irresistible force' is the ongoing codification of laws in the Arab States, particularly in the area of commercial activity, while the 'irremovable object' is the Islamic *Shariah*. The conundrum, at least at the time of Ballantyne's writing, was whether the anomaly could be sustained or whether there would be, legislatively at least, a clear domination by western-derived secular law, with Islamic law becoming an irrelevancy in all but personal matters. In the present age, Ballantyne's anomalous situation is being resolved insofar as a domination of western-derived secular laws over the *Shariah* in the commercial context has already arrived. The conundrum has now shifted to being one of whether the position of the *Shariah* in the civil, criminal and other legal contexts may be further eroded, maintained or even reasserted and enhanced.

Amin argues that, although Islamic law is complete in the sense that it supplies answers to all questions in all times and places, its very content and style leave it to jurists to answer the many questions unanswered in the original textual sources.[7] General and non-specific prescriptions existing in the classic textbooks in Islamic law are inadequate in the contemporary context. At the same time, the general principles and basic structure of Islamic *fiqh* leave ample room to manoeuvre, and jurists are thus given broad and general guidelines to regulate new issues in the contemporary context. New rules of law may also be developed through modern legislation and administrative regulations, incorporating concepts of secular thought and custom as appropriate. Unlike western legal theory, Islamic law and principles of morality in government, business and personal conduct are indivisibly linked.

Stovall suggests that the argument that Islamic law is irrelevant is a myth, as is its sister myth that Islamic law is also inherently unsuitable for modern commercial transactions. Practical minds have developed expedients to overcome these difficulties in most cases and hence Islamic law has continued to be revitalised in the Arabic world.[8] The application of the prohibition upon *riba* (usury, or interest charged upon money lent) is the classic example. Despite the universal prohibition in the *Shariah* upon *riba*, most Arab legal systems draw a distinction that permits interest charges on commercial transactions, at least under specified ceilings, but not on civil transactions. However, such expediency might be viewed as a practical solution or an unprincipled shortcut, depending on one's opinion of the underlying impasse, and such expediency might not offer permanent solutions. Stovall further suggests that this type of fine-tuning is likely to become more common in future throughout the Arab world, both in civil codes and in other laws.

Malkawi argues that, although intellectual property does not enjoy explicit legal protection in the *Shariah*, it has been protected through norms and concepts

7 S H Amin (1993), *Law of Intellectual and Industrial Property in Developing Countries: Muslim World*, pp. 36–7.

8 Howard Stovall (2000), 'Arab Commercial Laws – Into the Future', 34, *The International Lawyer*, pp. 841–2.

equivalent to today's laws and rights. However, there are problems regarding intellectual property protection in Arab countries due to religious beliefs, traditional societal culture, a lower degree of economic development and higher poverty levels. Moreover, the expansion of intellectual property rights and the challenges associated with new innovations render their justification under the *Shariah* more complicated.[9]

It is thus impossible to talk about a secular legal system in the Arabian Peninsula States in the real sense, suggests Rayner: legislation may appear to be secular, but the sources of reference and the consciences of its interpreters are innately religious.[10]

2.2 The *Shariah* and the Arabian Peninsula State constitutions

Throughout the States' constitutions, or constitution equivalents in the case of Oman and Saudi Arabia, the *Shariah* weaves its influence – as that common golden thread portrayed earlier by Ballantyne. But that weave varies in its paramountcy from state to state. Although the *Shariah* is still primary in all States, it is not always paramount.

Based upon their constitutional and political development, the States can be categorised into three groups:

- a largely western style, which is characteristic of the Bahraini, Jordanian, Kuwaiti and Emirati constitutions;
- a combination of quasi-western and traditional styles, as epitomised by Qatar's constitution; and
- the more fundamentalist style of the Omani and Saudi Basic Laws, and the Yemeni constitution.[11]

9 Bashar Malkawi (2013), 'Intellectual Property Protection from a Shariah Perspective', 16, *Southern Cross University Law Review*, p. 92.

10 Rayner, op. cit., p. 372.

11 Ahmad Saif (2004), 'Constitutionalism in the Arab Gulf States', *GCC Research Program – GCC Constitutions*, Gulf Research Centre, p. 17.

Bahrain first adopted a constitution on 26 May 1973, which came into effect on 6 December 1973. It adopted a new constitution on 14 February 2001, which came into effect one year later.

Jordan first adopted a constitution on 11 January 1952, but which has been subject to amendment on a number of occasions since. The most recent amendments were made in May 2016.

Kuwait achieved its independence from the United Kingdom on 19 June 1961 and gained its original constitution on 16 November 1962. This constitution remains in place.

Oman did not establish a form of constitution until 6 November 1996. By Royal Decree No. 101/1996, it established the Basic Law of the State, as the Sultanate's constitutional equivalent.

Qatar was granted a provisional constitution by the United Kingdom on 2 April 1970 and gained its independence on 3 September 1971. A new and permanent constitution was approved by national referendum on 29 April 2003.

The Kuwaiti, Bahraini, Qatari, Emirati and Jordanian constitutions are based on a common model drawing much from the French, United States and Egyptian constitutions, and the *Universal Declaration of Human Rights (1948)* (on which the Egyptian constitution was also partially based).[12] Since Kuwait received its constitution a decade before the other above-mentioned three GCC member States, its model formed a useful precedent. Kuwait's constitution has remained unaltered since it was first introduced more than 50 years ago, while the other States have since introduced new constitutions or significant changes in recent times. Oman and Saudi Arabia have each enacted a 'Basic Law', as distinct from constitutions, as a formal recognition of the higher status of the *Shariah* within those statutes, but they essentially serve the same purpose.

The constitutions have very strong common elements, each stipulating that the state is a sovereign independent and Islamic state with a hereditary constitutional monarchy (that is, except for Yemen, since it is a republic), that Islam is the religion of the state and that Arabic is its official language. However, although the position of the *Shariah* is primary, it is not by any means paramount in every case. The States each place the following degree of primacy on the *Shariah* within their constitutions:

- Bahrain, Jordan, Kuwait and the UAE provide that the *Shariah* is *a main source* of law;[13]
- Qatar declares that the *Shariah* is *the main source* of laws;[14]
- Oman mandates that the *Shariah* is *the basis* of legislation;[15]
- Yemen declares that the *Shariah* is *the source of all* legislation;[16]
- Saudi Arabia declares that the *Qur'an* and the *Sunnah* of the Prophet are not only *the sole source* of law but are also the constitution of the state.[17]

Saudi Arabia, like Oman, does not possess a formal constitution *per se*. It enacted, in March 1992, a Basic Statute of the Kingdom, which declares that the Holy *Qur'an* is the constitution of Saudi Arabia.

The UAE adopted a provisional constitution on 18 July 1971, which, with some minor amendments, was eventually confirmed on 2 December 1996 by the Constitutional Amendment Law No. 1 of 1996.

Yemen was established as a Republic in May 1990 on the unification of the Yemen Arab Republic (North Yemen) and the People's Democratic Republic of Yemen (South Yemen). A Unification Constitution was adopted in 1991 and amended in 1994 after the cessation of secessionist hostilities in the south and again in 2001. The form of a new Constitution was finalised by the country's Constitutional Drafting Committee in 2015, but it has not yet to be voted upon by Parliament.

12 Ballantyne (1980), *Legal Development in Arabia*, p. 27.

13 Bahrain, Constitution, art. 1; Jordan, Constitution of 1952, art. 2; Kuwait, Constitution, art. 2; UAE, Constitution, art. 7.

14 Qatar, Constitution, art. 1.

15 Oman, Basic Law of the State, art. 2.

16 Yemen, Constitution of 1990, as amended in 1994, art. 3. The 2015 draft Constitution retains the declaration of the 1991 Constitution in respect of the pre-eminence of Shariah Law.

17 Saudi Arabia, Basic Law of the Kingdom, art. 1.

Hence, only Saudi Arabia and Yemen, and to a slightly lesser degree Oman, make the *Shariah* undisputedly paramount.

As *a main source* of law, the *Shariah* has, at best, equal standing with other sources of law. It is neither the sole source nor even the main source of law and thus cannot take general precedence over other sources. The impact is twofold. First, the constitutional position facilitates the implementation of modern codified laws derived from non-Islamic sources. Second, their application replaces the *Shariah* and progressively reduces its general jurisdiction so that it becomes increasingly confined to matters involving personal relationships between Muslims. But absent from the Bahraini, Jordanian, Kuwaiti and Emirati constitutions is any direction or guidance as to when the judiciary should turn to either one source or another for application of the proper law. For this, direction must first be sought from specific legislation and then from general legislation. Only where existing legislation is incomplete shall the *Shariah* prevail.

The Qatari constitution declares that the *Shariah* is *the main source* of laws, though not the sole source. It is thus given more weight in this context than those of Bahrain, Jordan, Kuwait and the UAE, but still considerably less weight than the Yemeni constitution and the Saudi and Omani constitution equivalents. Although no further constitutional guidance as to the application of the *Shariah* is provided, the Oaths of Office of the Emir, the Advisory Council and the Cabinet reinforce the higher status of the *Shariah* in the daily operation of government. Each is required to swear to respect, in order, 'the Islamic *Shariah*, the Constitution, and the Law . . . and people's freedom and interests'.[18] The clear implication here is that, in the first instance, one must turn to the *Shariah.*

The Omani Basic Law of the State asserts that the *Shariah* is *the basis* of all legislation. It is also one of the fundamental pillars of national political policy. The government is required to maintain genuine consultation with the people, 'based on the national heritage, its values and its Islamic *Shariah*, while incorporating such contemporary manifestations as are appropriate'.[19] Hence, Oman's constitutional position is closer to Saudi Arabia than to the other States. However, notwithstanding the constitutional mandate, the degree of *Shariah* control is also being emasculated as Oman, too, moves to a greater codification of its laws.

In slightly stronger terms, the Yemeni constitution declares that Islamic *Shariah* is *the source of all* legislation. This wording was one of the more controversial of a number of constitutional amendments introduced in 1994, in order to reinforce the status of *Shariah* law. The constitution had previously declared the *Shariah* as merely 'the main source' of law, akin to the more liberal Qatari position. The Yemeni constitution further enhances the status of the *Shariah*, providing elsewhere that Islamic social justice is one of the key principles on which the

18 Qatar, Constitution, arts 74, 92 and 119.
19 Oman, Basic Law of the State, art. 10.

national economy is founded, that women have rights and duties guaranteed and assigned by the *Shariah* and stipulated by law, that inheritance is regulated by the *Shariah* and that defending the religion is a sacred duty. The Oath of Office of the President and other members of government requires them to 'swear by Allah Almighty to adhere to the *Qur'an* and his Prophet's *Sunna*'.[20]

The position of the Saudi Basic Law in respect of the *Shariah* stands in stark contrast to that in the Bahraini, Kuwaiti and Emirati constitutions. Although facing some erosion of its position with the introduction of modern codified laws, the *Shariah* is still paramount and is reiterated throughout the Basic Law as being the fundamental principle underlying the government, the law, the economy and society. The Basic Law in essence ties the very existence of the Kingdom to Islam, declaring that Saudi Arabia is a sovereign Arab Islamic state whose constitution is the Holy *Qur'an* and the *Sunnah* of the Holy Prophet.[21] The government derives its authority from the Holy *Qur'an* and the *Sunnah*, which are the ultimate sources of reference for the Basic Law and for all other laws of the state.[22] Governance must be based on the principles of justice, *Shura* (consultation) and equality in accordance with the Islamic *Shariah*. The state is required to protect Islam, implement its *Shariah* and order the people to do right and shun evil.[23] Property, capital and labour are personal rights which perform a social function in accordance with the Islamic *Shariah*.[24] Legislation, enacted by resolution of the Council of Ministers and ratified by royal decree, must be compatible with *Shariah* law.[25] Although the Basic Law provides for the separation of the branches of government, the King, in principle at least, is still the source of authority and thus the ultimate (mortal) power in the governance of the state.[26] However, the King's powers are not without limit since he is still obliged to observe the *Shariah* and other Saudi traditions in the execution of his office, among which is maintenance of *Shura* with the (both male and female) members of the Saudi royal family, the country's religious leaders and the leading members of the Saudi elite.[27]

20 Yemen, Constitution, art. 159.
21 Saudi Arabia, Basic Law of the Kingdom, art. 1.
22 Ibid., arts 7–8.
23 Ibid., art. 23.
24 Ibid., art. 9.
25 Ibid., art. 67.
26 The Saudi King is first 'The Custodian of the Two Holy Mosques', a responsibility and title which is perhaps akin, in principle if not in practice, to the British Monarch's awful responsibility as 'Defender of the Faith'. The two holy mosques referred to above are the sacred Islamic sites in Makah and Madinah.
27 See Saudi Arabia, Basic Law of the Kingdom, art. 43, which establishes the right of every citizen to have a consultation with the King in his capacity as the final arbiter on any complaint. The Omani Basic Law has similar provision.

In all GCC member States and Jordan, supreme executive, legislative and judicial authority is vested in the central government and ultimately the ruler and his family, although in the UAE authority is divided between the federal government and the seven constituent Emirates.[28] In Yemen, the authority is vested in the President.

28 *Bahrain*: The government comprises the King as Head of State and separate executive and legislative branches. The executive branch consists of the Prime Minister (as head of government) and the Council of Ministers (Cabinet), all of whom are appointed by the King. The legislative arm consists of a bicameral National Assembly with a partially elected lower house and an appointed upper house. In general, all legislation passes through both bodies and Cabinet for recommendation for royal assent. The King and the Cabinet may also promulgate legislation directly through royal, prime ministerial and ministerial decrees, all of which carry the force of law.

Jordan: Jordan is ruled by a hereditary monarchy and parliament, comprising a National Assembly and Senate. The King is Head of State and Commander in Chief of Jordan's Armed Forces. The King ratifies and promulgates laws, declares war and concludes peace, and ratifies treaties and agreements. However, treaties and agreements that involve financial commitments or that affect the public and private rights of Jordanians require approval of the National Assembly. The King convenes and prorogues the National Assembly and Senate, and appoints and may dismiss the Prime Minister and Speaker and members of the Senate.

Kuwait: The Constitution provides for the establishment of separate executive and legislative branches of government. Like Bahrain, the executive branch comprises the Amir (as Head of State), the Prime Minister (as head of government) and a Council of Ministers which serves as the Cabinet. The Amir appoints the Prime Minister who in turn appoints the Council of Ministers, the appointments still subject to Amiri approval.

Oman: The Cabinet, deriving its authority solely from the Sultan, is the highest administrative authority, with its members all appointed directly by the Sultan. The Cabinet considers matters related to administrative functions of the state, internal policies and foreign relations and submits its recommendations to the Sultan for approval. A popularly elected Consultative Council provides advice to the Cabinet on state policy and reviews draft legislation prepared by the ministries.

Qatar: The Qatari Constitution stipulates that the system of governance shall be based on the separation of authority; the Emir as Ruler holds the executive authority assisted by his Cabinet, while an Advisory Council holds the legislative authority. Since the Emir appoints the Cabinet and one-third of the Advisory Council, the division between the two branches of government is notional. The Constitution requires the Emir to rule in accordance with Islamic precepts.

Saudi Arabia: The Basic Law provides for a Council of Ministers as the executive arm of government and a Consultative Council as the legislative arm. The members of both bodies are appointed by the King. The Council of Ministers is led by the King in his capacity as Prime Minister. It is responsible for drafting and overseeing the implementation national policies and general affairs of state. The Consultative Council advises the King and Council of Ministers. The King has the power to restructure and to dissolve the Consultative Council as he deems necessary.

The UAE: The Chairman of the Supreme Council and thereby the President of the Federation is elected from among their own number – by unchallenged convention since independence in 1971, the Presidency has been held by the ruler of Abu Dhabi, the largest and wealthiest of the emirates, and the Prime Ministership by the ruler of Dubai.

Yemen: According to the 1990 Constitution as amended in 1994, Yemen is a republic with an executive arm and a bicameral legislature. The President is Head of State and the Prime Minister is head of government. The executive arm consists of the President and the Vice-President, Prime Minister and the Council of Ministers, all of whom are appointed by the President. The legislative branch consists of a Shura Council appointed by the

The States generally separate the executive and legislative branches of government, although the latter does not necessarily enjoy autonomy and independence. In most instances, the executive branch firmly cements in place the authority of the ruling family, since it predominately comprises the royal family's senior male members by virtue of both their blood lineage and the senior government offices they also hold. The distinction between the executive and the legislative branches of government exists more in the principle than in the practice. An amendment to the Jordanian constitution in 2015 gave the King the right to appoint and dismiss by royal decree, without the input of the legislative council, the strategically important positions of chief of the armed forces, chief justice of the courts, head of the intelligence services, as well as the Crown Prince and Regent.[29] Previously, his powers in this respect were limited to appointment of the Prime Minister.

2.3 The *Shariah* and the judicature

The States' constitutions generally mandate that the courts are independent and that judges shall not be subject to any authority or interference. The Saudi Basic Law, for example, provides that no control may be asserted over judges in the dispensation of their judgments except in the case of the Islamic *Shariah*.[30] Nevertheless, the state executives may still have leverage over the judicial power, since senior members of the judiciary are appointed by the exercise of executive authority through law or royal decree, and the laws that determine their prerogatives may be both initiated and issued by that same executive power. Apart from the UAE, where the constitution contains explicit conditions governing their removal from office, the executive authorities (that is, the rulers) retain power to appoint and dismiss members of the judiciary, notwithstanding constitutional provisions apparently to the contrary.

Although the principles derived from the *Shariah* are still a primary basis for all laws, most States have separate secular courts to deal with civil, criminal and commercial cases for which codified laws have been established or to which the *Shariah* cannot always be applied.

The Bahraini legal system is a mixed system based on English common law models and Sunni and Shia *Shariah* traditions, with influences from British India

President and an elected House of Representatives. However, Yemen has been in a state of political crisis since 2011, and outright civil war since 2015, which has caused this constitutional structure to become non-existent. Two main factions claim to constitute the legitimate authority, namely Houthi and other forces loyal to the former President Ali Abdullah Saleh, who was forced to step down in 2011 under popular pressure, and forces supporting current President Abdrabbuh Mansur Hadi who took over from Saleh in 2012. The Houthi forces control the capital Sana'a while President Hadi, supported by Saudi Arabia, controls the south and east. Al-Qaeda in the Arabian Peninsula (AQAP), with support from ISIL, control areas in the middle of the country and central coast.

29 Jordan, Constitution as amended in 2016, art. 40.

30 Saudi Arabia, Basic Law of the State, art. 46.

systems. The Judiciary Law of 1971 divides the judicature into two divisions – the civil courts and the *Shariah* courts with the Sunni and Shia (Jafari) jurisdictions. The civil courts are empowered to settle all commercial, civil and criminal cases and all matters related to the personal status of non-Muslims. The *Shariah* court system is limited to personal status cases of Muslims. It comprises a high court and a high court of appeal, both with Sunni and Jafari divisions. The Kuwaiti and Qatari legal systems are also based upon a number of diverse sources. Commercial and criminal laws derive from Ottoman and several modern Arab sources, notably Egyptian, and also reflect elements of the French legal code and the English common law. But unlike the Kuwaiti legal system, Qatari has maintained a *Shariah* court system which has full jurisdiction in all civil and criminal disputes over nationals and Muslims from other countries.

The Omani legal system is based primarily on the Islamic *Shariah* traditions of the Ibadi school. Custom, tradition and the *Shariah* still occupy important places as guides in judicial decision-making. Oman was the last of the GCC member States to overhaul its judicial system, with major changes in 1999 bringing the judiciary into line with the dictates of its Basic Law. A ternary courts system replaces the earlier separate *Shariah*, commercial courts and criminal courts. The *Shariah* courts, which formerly held competency in all civil and most criminal cases, have had their jurisdiction restricted to personal cases involving Muslims in both parties, and then as a court of first instance. Appeals against decisions of the *Shariah* court are made to the general courts of appeal.

The Saudi judicial system retains the traditional form of *Shariah* courts, with courts of first instance, courts of appeal and ultimately the High *Shariah* Court. Within this *Shariah system* there exists the Board of Grievances, which is effectively a civil court with jurisdiction over commercial matters which fall within the terms of reference of codified laws.

The UAE remains unusual for the Arab world because of its federated structure. The federal constitution permits each Emirate to have its own legislative body and judicial authority, thereby allowing the existence of both federal courts and local courts. Alongside this federal/local structure there exists another division between secular and *Shariah* judiciary, giving the UAE a fairly complex judicial structure. The UAE is essentially a civil law jurisdiction heavily influenced by the Egyptian legal system which in turn had its source in French and Roman law. It has also been influenced by Islamic law codified in the *Shariah* and embodied in the UAE civil, criminal and commercial codes. The Emirates of Abu Dhabi, Dubai and Ras Al-Khaimah have retained their own judicial structures, with Abu Dhabi and Dubai having a system of inferior, intermediate and superior courts. Ras Al-Khaimah possesses inferior and intermediate courts only, with final appeals going to the federal Court of Cassation.

The Jordanian constitution creates three categories of courts, namely civil, religious and special courts. The civil court system inherits its structure from the nineteenth-century Ottoman and Egyptian legal systems, which both used structure drawn from the French Napoleonic Code. It deals with all civil and criminal matters that do not fall under one of the special courts; it comprises magistrate courts, first instance courts, courts of appeal, high administrative courts and the Court of Cassation. The religious courts have jurisdiction only over issues of personal law, such as marriage, divorce or inheritance. They are further divided into the Sharia Court and Tribunals of Other Religious Communities. They draw their structure and jurisprudence from their respective religious tradition. Islamic religious courts are based on Islamic jurisprudence and legal tradition, whereas Christian religious courts and tribunals apply their own religious laws and systems. The special courts are limited to specific jurisdictions, such as a military court for offences involving crimes involving military personnel and national security, land settlement courts for claims of ownership over unregistered land, an income tax court for tax valuation disputes, and a primary and appellate court for customs disputes.

In Yemen, the *Shariah* and Islamic jurisprudence play a larger role in the legal and judicial structure than in most other Arab States, arguably except for Saudi Arabia. Yemen has a unified judicial structure, with courts of first instance, courts of appeal and ultimately the Supreme Court, all as courts of general jurisdiction. Separate specialised courts are prohibited by the constitution, hence the above courts can hear all civil, criminal, commercial and personal status matters. The Supreme Court also serves as a constitutional court. In addition to these established courts, a system of tribal adjudication applying customary law or tribal law exists outside the main urban areas for local issues.

In broad terms, the result is essentially a dual legal system (with lesser or greater degrees of seamless amalgamation) in which a civil law orientation exists in parallel with the Islamic *Shariah*. But in practice the *Shariah* courts and the body of *Shariah* law are becoming increasingly restricted to personal status matters of Muslims – family matters, divorce, inheritance, succession, property and charitable donations, some limited torts and a few criminal matters.[31]

The Kuwaiti and Saudi structures reflect the opposite ends of the judicial spectrum. At one end, Kuwait (which, it will be recalled, holds the *Shariah* as *a main* source of law) avoids the civil court–*Shariah* court dualism extant in some of the other States, having adopted a unified court structure approach rather than establish separate secular and *Shariah* courts. Hence, Muslim personal status cases are not assigned to a separate *Shariah* judiciary; instead, sections of the civil courts are designated for hearing personal status cases. The courts rule on the basis of codified Sunni law or Shia (*Jafari*) law, depending on the school of Islam to which the litigants adhere.[32]

Although the Kuwaiti constitution remains silent on the question of the precedence of the various sources of law, the law governing the conduct of

31 The Qatari Criminal Code, for example, stipulates that jurisdiction over certain crimes, such as intentional or unintentional homicide, and crimes of a sexual nature, such as sexual assault, homosexuality and prostitution, rests with the *Shariah* court if the accused is a Muslim and with the secular court in respect of non-Muslims.

32 Saif, op. cit., p. 14.

the judiciary moves to qualify that flexibility.[33] It requires a judge to proceed first by reference to the civil and commercial laws of the state, then to custom, and finally by reference to the *Shariah*:

(a) Legislative provisions apply to the matters to which such provisions relate both expressly and by implication.
(b) If there is no legislative provision, the judge gives judgment in accordance with custom. If there is no custom, the judge deduces his opinion taking guidance from the dictates of the Islamic jurisprudence (*fiqh*) most in accord with the reality and the interests of the country.[34]

Hence the order of priority of primary sources of Kuwaiti law is firstly constitutional, then legislative, customary and tribal, and lastly the *Shariah*.

In like manner, the Bahraini constitution provides the same degree of flexibility, and its law governing the judiciary also moves to qualify that flexibility.[35] But, unlike Kuwait, it requires that, in the absence of an express statutory legal provision, reference is directed first to the *Shariah*:

> In the event that a judge finds no provision of law capable of application, he shall deduce the bases of his judgment from the principles of the *Shariah* and the provisions thereof; in the absence of any such provision, custom shall be applied. A particular custom shall be preferred to a general custom. In the absence of custom, the tenets of national law and the principles of equity and good conscience shall be applied.[36]

Like Kuwait, Oman and Qatar also have largely unified systems, but both place a much greater emphasis on the importance of the *Shariah* in judicial decision-making. Both enjoy unified structures integrating the earlier systems of *Shariah* courts, commercial courts and criminal courts. In Oman's case, the former separate *Shariah* courts, which held competency in all civil and criminal cases, have had their jurisdiction restricted to the status of a court of first instance on personal status matters. Appeals against a decision of the *Shariah* court are now brought before general courts of appeal. Qatar has maintained *Shariah* divisions in both the primary and appellate jurisdictions, but retains a unified Court of Cassation, or Supreme Court. While these integration actions might be viewed as a weakening of the position of the *Shariah*, it could be equally argued that they constitute a strengthening of its position by keeping it in the mainstream of the judicial system instead of marginalising it.

33 Kuwait, Law No. 19 of 1959, the Judicial Code, as amended by Law No. 19 of 1990.
34 Ibid., art. 1; see also S H Amin (1991), *The Legal System of Kuwait*, p. 77.
35 Bahrain, Legislative Decree No. 13 of 1971, the Law of the Judiciary.
36 Ballantyne (1980), op. cit., p. 25.

However, this still raises the issue of whether the general dictates of the *Shariah* should apply in the first instance as general principles, or latterly in respect of the particular circumstances of the case being heard. Since both constitutions are not exclusive in their status of the *Shariah*, it may well have been the intention of the Omani and Qatari legislators to allow some degree of flexibility to avoid direct conflict between the *Shariah* and the secular codes. Where the civil or commercial laws or other laws or sources are silent on the matter of legislative application, there would be little question that it would be appropriate to turn in the first instance to the *Shariah* as the principal source of law. However, where the codes do give voice, they are generally comprehensive and their intentions are clearly prescribed, as the following extract from Qatar's civil commercial code illustrates:

1 The tenets of this law shall apply to all matters embraced expressly or by implication by the provisions hereof as well as to all commercial acts engaged in or by any person even if not a merchant.
2 In prescribing principles which apply to merchants and commercial acts, regard shall be had to contracts recognised by law . . .
3 If there is no contract, or if there is but it is silent as to a particular provision, or the provisions set out in the contract are void, the legislative provisions contained in this Law shall apply.
4 In the absence of the legislative provision which can be applied, the judge shall adjudicate in accordance with custom, special or local custom taking precedence over general custom, and in the absence of custom the principles of the Islamic Shari'a . . .[37]

The laws establishing the UAE federal Supreme Court and the federal courts of first instance require the courts to apply the provisions of the *Shariah* in the first instance:

> The Supreme Court shall apply the provisions of the Islamic Shari'a, federal laws, and other laws in force . . . conforming to the Islamic Shari'a. Likewise it shall apply those rules of custom and those principles of natural and comparative law which do not conflict with the principles of the Shari'a.[38]

Likewise, the courts of first instance are required to adhere to the following directive:

> The federal courts shall apply the provisions of the Islamic Shari'a, federal laws, and other laws in force, just as they shall apply those rules of custom and general legal principles which do not conflict with the provisions of the Shari'a.[39]

37 Qatar, Law No. 16 of 1971, the Civil and Commercial Code, arts 1–4.
38 UAE, Law No. 10 of 1973, Establishing the Federal Supreme Court, art. 75.
39 UAE, Federal Law No. 6 of 1978, Establishing the Courts of First Instance, art. 8.

Notwithstanding the fact they have retained separate judicial structures, the Emirates of Dubai and Ras Al-Khaimah provide that their respective courts shall exercise their powers, in order of priority, on the basis of the laws in force in the Emirate, on the provisions of the Islamic *Shariah*, on provisions of custom unless these contradict the law or public order or decency, and finally on the principles of natural justice, right and equity.[40]

These positions would appear to give precedence to the *Shariah* over all other sources of law and thereby, in effect, hold it as the principal source of law. As the courts would therefore appear to hold that any measure contrary to the *Shariah* would seem, by express provision, to be invalid, there arises the question of whether the laws establishing these courts contradict a constitutional position which has established that the *Shariah* is but one source of law among others.[41] Since the Federal Supreme Court also acts as a constitutional court and would thus rule on such question should it arise, it would presumably uphold the basic constitutional dictate.

At the other end of the above-mentioned spectrum is Saudi Arabia. As the most conservative and fundamentalist Islamic state in the region, Saudi Arabia maintains a stronger hold on the principles of the *Shariah* than the other States. The *Shariah* remains the fundamental basis of the legal system, and justice is administered according to the *Shariah* by a system of religious courts. Although traces of a hybrid dual system can be discerned in parts of the Saudi legal order by the existence of quasi-judicial administrative tribunals such as the Board of Grievances, the foundation of the Saudi judicial order is still wholly *Shariah*-based.

Having proclaimed the Holy *Qur'an* and the *Sunnah* as the basis of laws and as the constitution, the Basic Law requires the Saudi courts to apply the rules of the Islamic *Shariah*, in accordance with indications 'in the Holy *Qur'an* and the *Sunnah*, and then in accordance with the statutes of the Kingdom provided they do not contradict the *Qur'an* or the *Sunnah*'.[42] Thus, the *Shariah* is seen as superior to any positive legal or judicial order, a provision which assumes a unified, *Shariah*-based judiciary independent of the King. Since this system was well established when the Basic Law was introduced in 1992, the Basic Law does not so much establish a new judicial order as describe and codify the prevailing custom and practice.

Hence the Saudi *Shariah* courts have never lost their status as courts of general jurisdiction and there is no special personal status court structure or personal status code as exists in the other States under their dual or integrated systems. However, still within the *Shariah* judicial system, but operating at arm's length from the *Shariah* courts, are the quasi-judicial specialised tribunals which adjudicate on

40 Law Forming the Dubai Courts of 1970, art. 4; Law Forming the Courts of Ras Al-Khaimah, art. 1.

41 Ballantyne (1986), *Commercial Law in the Arab Middle East: The Gulf States*, p. 58.

42 Saudi Arabia, Basic Law of the State, art. 49.

matters which are essentially administrative in nature, or on disputes between government bodies and members of the public over government processes or decision-making (such as disputes over trademark registrations). Although the tribunals address matters which are governed by regulations which do not derive from the *Shariah* or are not easily covered by existing Islamic *fiqh*, they are still required to ensure that they do not conflict with their provisions. One outcome of this structure is that the pure essence of the *Shariah* can be better preserved without the constant diluting effects of introduced secular laws.

While Ballantyne saw the *Shariah* as a golden thread running through the legal and judicial systems of the Gulf and the Arab world beyond, he also suggested that the key characteristic of the *Shariah*'s position within these systems was one of uncertainty.[43] More than 30 years later, the uncertainty retreats progressively as the secularisation and codification of the laws within each State continues. With the possible exception of Saudi Arabia and Yemen, the *Shariah* may still intervene to a lesser or greater degree in most jurisdictions. The unknown factor in this progression exists outside the legal framework – namely the marked resurgence of Islam domestically and its growth internationally. As it attracts increasing numbers of new followers and appears to become increasingly fundamentalist, Islam may well have an as yet unforeseen impact on the domestic legal, judicial and societal structures – which in turn could stimulate somewhat of a reversal of status towards its former enhanced position within the constitutional, legal and judicial frameworks.

2.4 The *Shariah* and intellectual property protection

The situation of intellectual property law protection, a recent development in the legislative regimes of the States, illustrates this dichotomy between the *Shariah* and codified laws. The concept of intellectual property and its recognition and acceptability in *Shariah* law has been a subject of ongoing discussion among contemporary Muslim scholars.[44] Intellectual property as an intangible object, being the product of one's mental labours, is a recent concept not expressly mentioned in either the Holy *Qur'an* or the *Sunnah*, or in the early Islamic jurisprudence. Accordingly, its acceptability or otherwise must be inferred from general principles laid down by the *Shariah*. As the views of scholars and Islamic jurists differ on the issue of the application of these principles to new situations, it follows that there are differences of opinion in relation to the ownership and protection of intellectual property.

Some contemporary scholars reject the concept of intellectual property on the grounds that the concept of ownership in the *Shariah* is confined to tangible

43 Ballantyne (1986), op. cit., p. 64.

44 Mufti Taqi Usmani (undated), 'Copyright according to Islam', *Mufti Taqi Usmani Official page*, available at *Al-Balagh Webzine*, http://muftitaqiusmani.com/en/?p=11064, last accessed 26 May 2017.

objects only.[45] They contend that there is no precedent in the *Qur'an*, the *Sunnah* or the views of early Muslim jurists for an intangible object, such as knowledge, to be subject to private ownership or to sale and purchase. They would argue that, since it originates from or owes its origin to God, knowledge (and its expression in all its manifestations) is the common heritage of all mankind.[46] Knowledge cannot therefore become the exclusive property of one individual, nor be prevented from being acquired by others. Accordingly, a concept of intellectual property which leads to a monopoly over knowledge by an individual could not be acceptable by Islam.[47]

Yet other scholars have argued that intellectual property and its exclusive ownership is acceptable, since there is no express provision in the *Qur'an* or in the *Sunnah* which restricts the rights of ownership to tangible objects only.[48] Intellectual property protection does not necessarily hinder the acquisition of knowledge since an intellectual property law does not prevent an individual from accessing or utilising knowledge enjoying some form of protection as offered by that law. On the contrary, the law may prohibit a third party from gaining commercial advantage from the work without the permission of the individual who, by mental labour, has produced the work and is therefore most entitled to enjoy the commercial benefits that derive from it.

Jamar suggests that although the *Shariah* does not specifically address intellectual property matters, it does not prevent the enactment or enforcement of intellectual property laws, a view endorsed more recently by Malkawi.[49] Since intellectual property protection is neither prohibited nor mandated, its legal protection is therefore fully consonant with the *Shariah*. In the Islamic state, every citizen enters into an express or a tacit agreement to abide by its laws to the extent that they do not compel compliance with anything that is not permissible in the *Shariah*.[50] Accordingly, if the state promulgates a law in favour of intellectual property protection without violating a provision of the *Qur'an* and *Sunnah*, then that law is binding on all its citizens and must be respected. In this sense, intellectual property law is no different to criminal law or commercial law in its relationship to the *Shariah*.

Other proponents of this line of reasoning argue that ownership of intellectual property is justified on the basis of 'economic gain through labour'.[51] The creation

45 Ibid., p. 99.

46 Ida Abdul Ghani Azmi (1996), 'Basis for the Recognition of Intellectual Property in the Light of the *Shariah*', 27, *International Review of Intellectual Property and Competition Law*, p. 650.

47 Usmani, op. cit., p. 98.

48 See S H Amin (1993), op. cit., pp. 36–7.

49 Steven Jamar, 'The Protection of Intellectual Property under Islamic Law' (1992), 21, *Capital University Law Review*, p. 1082. See also Malkawi, op. cit., p. 88.

50 Usmani, op. cit., p. 99.

51 See, for example, Malkawi, op. cit., *passim*. See also Nadia Naim (2017), 'Intellectual Property Regimes in the GCC: Recommendations to Develop an Integrated Approach to

of intellectual property through the efforts of mental labour brings with it an entitlement to its exclusive exploitation. As is the case with movable and immovable property, any creative idea of a person expressed in written, technical or graphical terms should be respected in Islam.[52] Although it may be intangible, intellectual property may still be deemed to have a value quantifiable in a market context and therefore can be traded, transferred and transacted.[53] This is further borne out by writings of Muslim jurists who deal with the prohibition of unjust enrichment and the discouragement of certain types of commercial transactions such as those involving misrepresentation, fraud and trickery.[54]

According to Khoury, some commentators have gone so far as to contend that Islamic law comprises 'enough inconsistencies to [generally] make predictability in certain matters a serious concern'.[55] The disagreements thus arising cut across sectarian lines:

> The very nature of Islamic law as a jurist's law and differences of opinion even within individual schools means that it is not possible to provide firm answers to many of the questions that arise. As usual in the *Shariah*, which proceeds by way of example rather than principle, it is only possible to evaluate the general risks involved through isolation and investigation of the particular issues arising in [connection with the legal issue].[56]

It has been argued that the *Shariah* fails to keep abreast of the needs of increasingly complex economies and commercial practices, and that this failure constitutes a criticism against the functionality of the *Shariah* as a viable intellectual property regime.[57] Consequently, there exists a trend away from *Shariah* law towards modern western-derived law throughout the commercial laws in the Middle East. Indeed, one commentator suggests that the bulk of commercial law in the Middle East reads as a direct transportation of European law, while the case law is perceived as a direct translation of western terminology. This trend is also quite apparent with respect to intellectual property laws generally. The *Shariah* may provide basic principles and rules that promote the protection of intellectual property; however, in view of the lack of comprehensive certainty and agreement, the States appear to opt for a direct adoption of western legal norms and standards of protection.

Intellectual Property Rights', in David Price and Alhanoof AlDebasi, *Intellectual Property Rights: Development and Enforcement in the Arab States of the Gulf*, pp. 30–53.

52 According to the cardinal Islamic principle of *annasu musallatun als amwaliham*, 'People should be given recognition for the exclusive use of their property'. *Amwal* (labour) applies equally to intellectual property outputs; see S H Amin (1993), op. cit., p. 36.

53 Ibid. See also Azmi, op. cit., p. 671.

54 See S H Amin (1993), op. cit., p. 37.

55 Amir Khoury, 'Ancient and Islamic Sources of Intellectual Property Protection in the Middle East' (2003), 43, *IDEA*, p. 151.

56 Ballantyne (1986), op. cit., pp. 121–2.

57 Khoury, op. cit., pp. 193–5.

While some may argue that in reality there is a gulf between *Shariah* concepts and practice in Islam, their arguments, in Khoury's view, ignore the following:

- the *Shariah* includes clear norms and teachings concerning fair trade and rejection of unfair competition;
- while the *Shariah* law is an ancient law which does not provide clear-cut answers to modern legal issues such as those surrounding intellectual property, the answers to these modern questions may still be formulated by religious scholars through reasoning based on the underlying Islamic principles;
- the *Shariah* is not the only legal system not to have a binding precedent system – the civil law system does not have one – and therefore this should not pose an insurmountable hurdle to the development of consistent and fair rules relating to intellectual property protection;
- where conflict does arise, it is not in respect of inner conflicts between the principles within Islamic law but rather a balance between principles and conflicting interests.[58]

The *Shariah* may not directly address the issues relating to intellectual property rights, but the principles provided therein clearly indicate that the *Shariah* does not stand neutral on the question of intellectual property protection. Islamic legal and general principles of equity, prohibition of unjust enrichment and of misleading and dishonest representation can still be applied, particularly in respect of passing-off and trademark infringement. Where a state possesses and applies secular laws governing intellectual property protection, traditional Islamic principles would still feature prominently since constitutionally no legislation can be contrary to the provisions of the *Shariah*, and the interpretation of the secular law should be aided and supported in such a way as to support the Islamic legal culture.[59] Where the secular law of the west and the *Shariah* are philosophically opposed on this point is that the secular law is concerned with the rights of the intellectual property right holder and is designed to protect their exploitative interests. The *Shariah*, however, is concerned with obligations and aims at condemning dishonesty by the deceiver and protecting the consumer.[60]

Azmi suggests that the basis of intellectual property rights must be the principles of the *Shariah*, with the standards concerning the availability, scope and use of such rights measured by their compatibility with the *Shariah*.[61] However, some emerging areas of intellectual property do not easily fit with this fundamental criterion and may therefore result in conflict with religious tenets of the *Shariah* – notably patents arising out of biotechnological products and processes. Azmi

58 Ibid.
59 S H Amin (1993), op. cit., p. 40.
60 Ibid.
61 Azmi, op. cit., pp. 655–6.

draws a distinction between patents involving animals and plants and those involving human tissues, genes and body parts. Although man has domination over other creatures, this domination does not grant an absolute right to do anything desired without limit. Mankind must act with a sense of stewardship and ultimately be held responsible for its actions and their consequences. Islam still requires animals to be treated with due respect and without cruelty. Accordingly, experimentation on animals and the patenting of the outcomes may be allowed under the *Shariah* provided there is a balancing of the relative harm to the animals and the benefits to mankind. In respect of modification and manipulation of biological materials, the position is not quite so clear. The *Qur'an* reiterates that the universe and all its creations are created with a sense of order and proportion according to a set of laws of nature, which man cannot change. Yet it also recognises science's role in improving what exists in nature for the benefit of mankind. The issue comes to a head in respect of transgenic animals used as xenografts, which Azmi suggests are beyond the limits allowed by the advancement of science and the *Qur'anic* bounds on man's stewardship over other creatures.[62]

In respect of the exploitation of the human material, whether genetic material or body parts, Azmi argues such exploitation is *haram* (forbidden), according to the *Qur'an*.[63] He points out that classical scholars have long held that any transaction involving parts of the human body, whether by sale or donation, is *haram* on the grounds that it demeans the human dignity and the place of man in the fixed order of creation and function of living things. But modern scholars accept circumstances in which transplantation and donation of body parts may be acceptable, namely if:

- the transplant or donation constitutes the lesser of two evils, the benefits outweigh the risks and the potential donation does not cause harm to the donor;
- the process of donation or transplant is assured of success; and
- the transplant, donation or extraction does not impair the function of the human body.

Intellectual property is not the only area of law where the Islamic state needs to promulgate civil or secular laws. Indeed, the *Qur'an* is silent, or at least vague, on a wide range of commercial issues, including some modern commercial transactions, financing arrangements and limited liability commercial entities such as corporations. While the *Qur'an* addresses subjects of poverty, conventional commercial transactions, honest dealings, testimony and association, it does not provide systematic rules but rather exhorts the believer with words of wisdom, admonition and guidance amounting to mandatory injunction.

62 Ibid., p. 666.
63 Ibid., pp. 667–8.

2.5 Concluding remarks

While the *Shariah* is prescribed at the very least as a major source of law, the increasing codification of the regional secular law, particularly in respect of commercial relations, has acted to progressively reduce its former pre-eminence and will likely continue to do so in the future. As commercial law continues to develop along western lines, the position of the *Shariah* could well continue to be eroded and the customary laws and remnants of the common law systems will become extinguished.[64]

It could be argued that the *Shariah* need not necessarily hinder the transplantation of intellectual property laws of foreign origin with any great drama or conflict. The drama may arise when the application of the western-derived law conflicts with the principles of the *Shariah*. By incorporating in their intellectual property laws a qualification to the wholesale deference to western-based criteria by at least requiring the practical application of the law to be not inconsistent with the *Shariah*, some States have not resiled from this potential for conflict. For example, while they all exclude from patentability inventions which, among other conditions, are in violation of public order or morals, the GCC patent regulation extends that provision to also exclude inventions which conflict with or violate the principles of the Islamic *Shariah*.[65] The Saudi patent law includes a similar exclusion provision, but narrows it somewhat by confining the exclusion to inventions whose *commercial exploitation* (instead of the invention itself) violates the *Shariah*.[66] Thus the GCC and the Saudi positions would appear to be at odds with the western liberal philosophy established by the US Supreme Court generalisation that 'anything under the sun can be patentable'.[67]

Even more subtle, yet of much greater application, is the reflection of the *Shariah* exhortation against the consumption of alcohol by Muslims, which ultimately becomes manifest in most States in the prohibition of registration of trademarks and geographical indications relating to wines, spirits and other alcoholic beverages. Although the domestic intellectual property laws are generally silent on this matter, the universal practice is that such types of trademarks and geographical indications are not protectable.

One cannot assume that the bastion of *Shariah* preservation in the commercial context is not being continually eroded. The decision in 2003 of the Saudi Board of Grievances to rule against a longstanding *Shariah* prohibition on the registration of trademarks depicting pictures or drawings of living animals, despite strident opposition from the traditionalists, illustrates how that erosion continues on a

64 W H Ballantyne (1986), op. cit., p. 66.
65 GCC, Unified Patent Regulation 2000, art. 2.
66 Saudi Arabia, Royal Decree No. M/27 of 1425 AH (2004), art. 4.
67 See United States, *Diamond v Chakrabarty*, 447 US 303 (1980).

number of fronts.[68] In arriving at its decision, the Board ruled that the principles on which the original prohibition was based were disputable and, more importantly in this context, that the prohibition was against the public policy of Saudi Arabia and the interests of consumers and owners of the genuine trademarks. Some might suggest that the Board ruling reinforces the argument that the *Shariah* is irrelevant in the modern context when it confronts the commercial/legal imperative. They might also propose that it simply illustrates yet another anomaly pertinent to Ballantyne's conundrum of a generation or so ago concerning the irresistible and the irremovable. The real test is in the interpretation and application of these respective legal imperatives on the streets and in the courts.

Despite the paucity of formal rules within the *Shariah* on intellectual property protection, the *Shariah* has within its primary sources basic principles that do not discourage such protection. The analysis of the underlying principles of fair trade, prohibition of unfair competition and the importance of private property lead to the conclusion that Islam does not stand idle on issues pertaining to intellectual property rights and their protection.[69] Indeed, the underlying principles might appear to be not all that dissimilar to the rationales of intellectual property protection as perceived by modern western legal systems. In Malkawi's view, the best approach may to combine Islamic principles as found in the letter of the law as set out in religious texts and other sources of jurisprudence and other sources with a reasoning that captures the spirit of modernity.[70] *Shariah* maintains a dynamic and adaptable nature that allows rules to exercise flexibility to meet modern considerations while retaining core principles.

It is in this context that one needs to look at the development of intellectual property regimes in the States themselves.

68 Board of Grievances Decision No. 9/1424 of 23 August 2003. Reported in Abu-Setta & Co, Legal Attorneys Saudi Arabia, 'Letter to Clients', September 2003, available at www.smas-ip.com, last accessed 1 March 2017.

69 Ibid.

70 Malkawi, op. cit., p. 121.

3

PRE-TRIPS AND INTELLECTUAL PROPERTY PROTECTION IN THE ARABIAN PENINSULA

3.1 Introduction

The legal systems of the Arabian Peninsula States have undergone dramatic, radical and progressive change and development over the last 40 years or so, and that change is continuing. The major trend has been a greatly increased codification of law and administered regulation which entails increasing substitution of institutionalised procedures for the traditional informal, discretionary and often arbitrary exercise of authority.[1]

The pre-TRIPS history of the progressive formulation of intellectual property legislative regimes in the respective States illustrates a remarkable cycle of developments over an equally remarkably short period of time.[2] A generation or so ago, namely the mid-1970s, the level of effective intellectual property protection was virtually non-existent. None of the States possessed any laws in respect of copyright and neighbouring rights or subscribed to any international or regional convention in respect of protection of literary works or author's rights. The position in respect of trademarks, patents or other areas of industrial property was hardly brighter, although some limited legislation was in place in a few States.

Governmental concern and consequent legislative activity in respect of the protection of intellectual property rights existed primarily in relation to trademarks and trade descriptions, and then only in respect of commercial dealings with expatriate and foreign traders and businesses. There was little, if any, concern in

1 Nicholas Angell (2006), 'An Overview of Legal Structures in the GCC Countries', World Service Group (December), available at www.worldservicesgroup.com/publications.asp?action=article&artid=1649, last accessed 27 May 2017.

2 For an excellent background to the state of pre-TRIPS intellectual property protection in the Gulf region, see Alastair Hirst (1994), 'Developing IPR in the Gulf: Current Coverage, Problems, Post-Uruguay Round Trends', 17(2), *Middle East Executive Reports*, pp. 9–14.

respect of patent protection, and nil concern or activity in respect of author's rights and other areas of intellectual property such as plant varieties, geographical indications and the like.

Three distinct phases can be observed in the development of the States' intellectual property laws in this pre-TRIPS era:

- laws enacted before independence or during a period of effective foreign control, and which are an extension of or subordinate to those foreign sources – the prime examples being Jordan's Trademark Law of 1952, Bahrain's 1955 omnibus Patents, Industrial Designs and Trade Marks Regulation of 1955, and Kuwait's intended equivalent 1958 regulation;[3]
- laws which were developed as part of a post-independence codification of commercial and civil laws, led by Kuwait as the first of the British protectorates in the Gulf to achieve independence;
- more recent legislation in the late 1980s and early 1990s, generated by the States' recognition of the necessity to become part of the international trade community, and the obligations on compliance with international protection benchmarks that accompanied such membership.

The hallmark of the pre-independence laws was a subordination to, or transplantation of, laws or regulations already in existence in other jurisdictions. The Bahraini 1955 regulation providing protection for patents, industrial designs and trademarks, for example, borrowed much from the Indian pre-independence equivalent statute and was generally dependent upon UK laws and processes to be valid and operable.[4] The laws or regulations were not directed towards purely domestic operation at a local level, except to the extent that they impacted on foreigners' and expatriates' commercial relations with the local economy and populace.

By contrast, the post-independence laws were largely developed by the respective States with domestic needs and applications starting to come to the fore. However, they were still subject to external influences – but the influences were

3 Strictly speaking, none of the then Trucial States (Bahrain, Kuwait, Qatar and the seven Emirates that subsequently became the UAE – Abu Dhabi, Dubai, Ras Al-Khaimah, Sharjah, Ajman, Fujeirah, Umm al Quwain) was ever a colony or even a protected territory of the UK, although they were on occasion referred to as such in some laws (see Bahrain's Patents, Designs and Trade Marks Regulation of 1955, for example). Instead, they were recognised by the UK as sovereign states which, by virtue of various Agreements of Friendship, sought the protection of the UK against unfriendly intentions or acts by other countries, and which were accordingly deemed by the UK to be 'Protected States'. However, since their foreign relations and disposal of their lands were subject to UK approval, since resident UK subjects, foreigners and non-Muslims were subject to English law and authority under British extra-territorial jurisdiction, the States were subject to effective UK control. Hence the use of the term 'independence' to describe their newly acquired status in 1961 (Kuwait) and 1971 (Bahrain, Qatar and the seven Emirates) is appropriate.

4 Bahrain, Patents, Designs and Trade Marks Regulation, No. 1 of 1955. The Regulation was derived from the British Indian patents statutes.

becoming more regional in nature and possessing a greater degree of Arabic character. Sources of laws were also becoming increasingly regionalised – partly as a consequence of the States taking advantage of the opportunities to interact with their fellow Arab countries through their memberships of regional Arab bodies such as the League of Arab States and the GCC (from 1981). Kuwait's constitution and early laws, particularly its commercial code which incorporated provision for trademark protection, were largely based on Egyptian statutes, which in turn were based on French legal codes.[5] And since Kuwait's codes and laws were already in Arabic and had already undergone a period of extended testing in the context of common usage, it is not surprising that many of them became models for the equivalent laws required by the other States. The inconsistencies that could be observed in the equivalent laws across the other States largely arose as the States adapted the Kuwaiti models for their own perceived needs and use.

As the legislative regimes of the States became increasingly codified, secularised and sophisticated, and as the States themselves moved at their own separate pace towards membership of the international trade community, they were obliged to address the standards and obligations relating to intellectual property protection required by these bodies. New laws were introduced and enhancements were made to laws already in place, presaging the pending creation of the WTO and the introduction of TRIPS – for which WIPO was arguably the major source of influence by virtue of the legislative and other technical assistance it provided to the States. The suite of intellectual property laws enacted by Oman in 2000 is a prime example of this assistance. However, the developed countries with commercial interests in the region also endeavoured to bring considerable influence to bear upon the States to conform to international standards of protection, particularly in respect of trademarks and copyright and neighbouring rights.

3.2 Early regional initiatives on intellectual property protection

As Table 3.1 succinctly illustrates, the early 1970s saw little specific provision in respect of internally generated laws being in place for the protection of intellectual property rights *per se*, perhaps with the exception of trademarks. Saudi Arabia had introduced a trademark protection law more than 30 years earlier, in 1939, and Jordan followed with its own trademark law in 1952. But Kuwait was setting the regional benchmark in respect of protection standards, with the introduction in the early 1960s of its patent and industrial design statute, and with its civil, commercial and penal laws which also gave some measure of intellectual property protection. By the mid-1970s Kuwait and Bahrain had introduced and upgraded trademark protection laws, and Qatar had set plans in motion to introduce its own

5 The Kuwaiti constitution and the secular civil and commercial codes were drawn up largely under the guidance and influence of the eminent Egyptian jurist Abdul al-Rizzaq Al-Sanhouri; see Susan Rayner (1991), *The Theory of Contracts in Islamic Law*, p. 51.

trademark law. Oman and the UAE, meanwhile, lacked any specific intellectual property legislation and had little else by way of civil or commercial codes. None of the States had any copyright protection provisions, although, as is discussed later, other laws regulating publications and printing, and legal deposit of works, did enable some degree of protection – albeit by association rather than by design.

The Arabian Peninsula States were also conspicuously absent from the signatory lists of the major international bodies and the conventions on intellectual property rights. Kuwait became a signatory to the WTO's precursor, the General Agreement on Tariffs and Trade (GATT), soon after independence and remained the sole signatory from the region for more than 30 years until Bahrain, Qatar and the UAE also became signatories just prior to the creation of the WTO. Jordan was the first State to join WIPO, in 1972, and Qatar (1974) and the UAE (1976) joined soon after they each gained independence. Yet only Jordan was a signatory among the States to any of the international treaties and conventions administered by WIPO, and in particular the Berne, Paris and Rome Conventions, when it acceded to the Berne Convention in 1976. Nor had the States utilised any of the model laws for the protection of intellectual property rights that WIPO had devised specifically for developing countries and which encompassed:

- inventions and know-how;
- marks, trade names and acts of unfair competition;
- industrial designs;
- appellations of origin and indications of source.

All States were members of the League of Arab States, with Jordan, Saudi Arabia and Yemen joining in 1945 as foundation members, and the other States joining progressively as they achieved independence. The League, with the assistance of WIPO, had sponsored the development of two model laws for League members, one in 1972 addressing patent protection and the other in 1975 on trademarks, trade names, commercial indications and unfair competition.[6] Again, none of the States had taken advantage of the availability of this set of model laws to introduce or update their legislative regimes, although some of the other Arab countries, which were also members of the Arab League, had done so.

3.2.1 Trademarks

Trademarks have been the form of intellectual property most familiar to the States and to the business communities in the Arabian Peninsula region. Trademarks lie

6 The Model Law for Arab Countries on Patents (1972) and the Model Law for Arab Countries on Trade Marks, Trade Names, Commercial Indications and Acts of Unfair Competition (1975) were devised by the Industrial Development Centre for Arab States (IDCAS), the organisation within the League of Arab States responsible for industrial property matters. The model laws were drafted with assistance from WIPO.

TABLE 3.1 Intellectual property laws and international conventions in the Arabian Peninsula States in the mid-1970s

		Bahrain	*Jordan*	*Kuwait*	*Oman*	*Qatar*	*Saudi Arabia*	*UAE*	*Yemen*
National Laws	Copyright	–	–	–	–	–	–	–	–
	Trademarks		1952	1961	–	1978	1939	–	1940/76
	Patents	1955/77	–					–	
	Industrial designs		–	1962	–	–	–	–	–
	Plant varieties	–	–	–	–	–	–	–	–
	Geographical indications	–	–	–	–	–	–	–	–
	Integrated circuits	–	–	–	–	–	–	–	–
	Trade secrets	–	–	–	–	–	–	–	–
	Legal deposit of works	1975	–	–	–	–	–	–	–
	Printed matter	–	–	1961	1975	1968	–	1973	–
	Commercial codes	1971	1966	1961	–	1971	–	–	–
International Bodies	League of Arab States	1971	1945	1961	1971	1971	1945	1971	1945
	GATT	–	–	1963	–	–	–	–	–
	WIPO	–	1972	–	–	1976	–	1974	–
	– Berne Convention	–	–	–	–	–	–	–	–
	– Paris Convention	–	1972	–	–	–	–	–	–
	– Rome Convention	–	–	–	–	–	–	–	–
	– Other Conventions	–	–	–	–	–	–	–	–

Source: compiled by the authors

Notes: The emirate of Ras Al-Khaimah introduced a trademark registration statute in 1974 which, by virtue of the registration process, provided some degree of protection for registered marks.
In 1940, the British Government issued a simple statute covering the British Protectorate of Aden (southern Yemen); the independent Yemen Arab Republic (northern Yemen) issued a trademark statute in 1976.
Northern Yemen joined the League of Arab States in 1945; southern Yemen was still part of the British Protectorate of Aden.

at the heart of the system of commercial agencies that has dominated the nature and structure of regional and local business. For both practical and legal reasons, foreign merchants were nearly always required to appoint a local commercial agent (who also had to be a national) if they wished to do business in a sustained way in an Arab country. The agent thereby enjoyed, in effect, a local monopoly to import and distribute the foreign merchant's goods or services, and trademarks provided the means by which those goods and services were identified. Trademark protection was thus actively pursued by the local agent as an essential requirement in the protection of one's own trading territory. Local regulatory authorities, such as ministries of commerce or customs, helped to give practical effect to the local monopoly concept. In fact, many monopolies were (and still are) held by members of 'well-connected' families who often also held dual roles as senior members of the ruling elite. This was not necessarily construed as a conflict of interest, but more an appropriate and reasonable exploitation of position, capacity and available financial resources for the generation of both further wealth and employment for the local and wider community.

Attempts to parallel import goods bearing a foreign merchant's mark or goods which fell within the monopolistic control of the local commercial agent would be implacably opposed by the agent, irrespective of whether the goods in question were authentic or counterfeit. In this way, commercial agency legislation served indirectly as the main instrument whereby trademarks were protected. Trademark infringement cases in the civil courts were relatively rare occurrences. When they did appear, they focused on the protection of commercial rights and the elimination of the threat to monopoly rather than the recognition and protection of intellectual property rights. Hence early litigation arising out of the protection of these interests, such as the *Brylcreem*[7] case of 1981 in the UAE and the *Dettol*[8] case of 1992 in Saudi Arabia, were not lodged under the basic trademark laws as might have been in place but under the laws of commercial transactions.

However, rather than reliance merely on statute, the customary practice throughout the region to obtain some notional measure of protection for trademarks was through the publication of cautionary notices in the local Arabic and English-language daily press. Although the cautionary notices had no legal status *per se*, they served to establish and reinforce claims of prior ownership, which was useful in a dispute before a *Shariah* court or judicial or administrative authority on commercial conduct involving trademark ownership, rights of usage or commercial agency rights.

Saudi Arabia was the first State to introduce any form of statutory protection in any field of intellectual property with its trademark decree of 1939.[9] The decree

7 UAE, Court of Cassation Case No. 116/981 of 1981; the offending product being marketed as *Berylcream*.

8 Saudi Arabia, Board of Grievances Case No. 206/T/4 of 1992; the offending product being marketed as *Bettol*.

9 Saudi Arabia, Royal Decree No. 8762 of 1358 AH (1939), concerning Trade Marks.

provided for the local registration of trademarks and protection for a period of ten years with provision for renewal. Significantly, it also provided for both criminal and civil liability, for the ordering of provisional measures and for sanctions that must have been substantial for the region and the time – up to six months' imprisonment and between 5 and 50 guineas (being the official currency in circulation at the time). The decree did not address any other areas of intellectual property.

Bahrain, while still a protected state as part of the British Persian Gulf and Trucial States interests, provided limited trademark protection with the issuance in 1955 of an omnibus patents, industrial designs and trademarks statute.[10] The original form of the statute was made by the British government as a Queen's Regulation issued by its Political Resident in the Gulf (and resident in Bahrain), as part of the British government's extraterritorial jurisdiction in Bahrain.[11] The statute was subsequently translated into Arabic and issued by the Emir as a Bahraini statute.[12] This status was very much reflected in the statute, which was subordinate and supplementary to the then UK trademark law.[13] In effect, it enabled the local registration of trademarks (and industrial designs) which were already protected by virtue of registration in the UK, and extended to them the same level of protection locally as enjoyed in the UK. It also enabled the registration of trademarks of local origin, for which protection applied only in Bahrain, Kuwait and the other regional 'territories' of Qatar, Oman and Muscat (now Oman) and the Trucial States (now the UAE). Bahrain did not entirely remove its 1955 regulation from the statute books until 1991, although in 1977 it introduced a number of amendments to remove references to the UK and UK-related institutions.[14]

The Political Resident issued the equivalent regulation for Kuwait in 1958.[15] However, unlike his Bahraini counterpart, the Kuwaiti Emir did not translate and reissue it as a Kuwaiti local statute. Since Kuwait was moving towards independence in the near future and was well advanced in preparing a constitution and suite of post-independence statutes, it decided against bringing this colonial-era regulation into local effect. Instead, it incorporated trademark protection provisions within

10 See Husain Al-Baharna (1998), *British Extra-Territorial Jurisdiction in the Gulf 1913–1971*, for a concise analysis of British extra-territoriality and the pre-independence system of British courts in the British Protected States of the Persian Gulf.

11 The Political Resident was the senior representative of the British government in the Gulf region and was responsible for the implementation of British policy in the Gulf through a number of Political Agents resident in Bahrain, Qatar, Dubai and Abu Dhabi. The Political Resident enjoyed ambassadorial status. The British government appointed a Consul-General to Oman in recognition of its long-established sovereignty, but the Consul-General was administratively responsible to the Political Resident.

12 Bahrain, Patents, Designs and Trade Marks Regulation, No. 1 of 1955.

13 *Trade Marks Act 1938* (UK); *Registered Designs Act 1949* (UK).

14 Bahrain, Amiri Decree No. 22 of 1977, amending certain provisions of the Patents, Designs and Trade Marks Regulation of 1955.

15 Queen's Regulation No. 5 of 1958, the Patent, Industrial Designs and Trade Marks Regulation.

its new commercial code which, at the time and by regional standards, was well advanced and enlightened.[16]

In the four States (namely Bahrain, Jordan, Kuwait and Saudi Arabia) which possessed trademark laws in these early years, the examination of trademark applications was simple – the grounds for rejection being limited to procedural deficiencies or marks which were contrary to public policy or morality, or confusingly similar to armorial bearings and flags, and official signs and marks. Saudi Arabia extended its examination to include marks which were confusingly similar to international symbols or elements with a religious significance, marks contrary to the traditions or principles of Islam, and marks similar to marks already registered or under application.

Qatar enacted its first intellectual property law and first law on trademark protection late in the 1970s.[17] The law regulated the protection of trade and service marks, group marks, commercial indications, and indications of source and origin, but did not go so far as to encompass industrial designs. The law was largely derived from the League of Arab States' 1975 model law on trademarks, trade names, commercial indications and unfair competition, and was influenced by the corresponding sections of the Kuwaiti commercial code.

Trademarks still lacked any statutory form of protection in Oman and the UAE. Historically, Omani and UAE businesses and local authorities and courts have considered both States to be essentially free markets into which any licensed business may import goods without any form of regulatory control, such as restrictions on the sale of counterfeit merchandise. Accordingly, trademark owners had no real statutory means available to protect their interests from infringing marks. Ras Al-Khaimah, one of the smallest of the seven Emirates comprising the UAE, independently introduced a decree in 1974 which provided for a trademark registration and protection service administered by the Emirate's Chamber of Commerce, Industry and Agriculture. The protection afforded by registration did not extend outside the Emirate, but it did serve as a useful stratagem for reinforcing claims of ownership in the other Emirates and was therefore utilised by foreign merchants and their agents based in those other Emirates.[18]

The southern part of Yemen that constituted the British Protectorate of Aden reportedly offered a form of trademark protection from 1940, by way of regulation

16 Kuwait, Law No. 2 of 1961, the Commercial Code (arts 54–61 for trade names, arts 62–67 for protection against unfair competition and arts 69–92 for trademarks).

17 Qatar, Amiri Law No. 3 of 1978, the Trade Marks and Commercial Indications Law.

18 The Ras Al-Khaimah statute appears to have been largely based on the trademark provisions of the Kuwaiti Commercial Code, since with a few exceptions the order of the articles and their wording is near identical. The Ras Al-Khaimah statute had some deterrent potential insofar as it prescribed a penalty of up to one year's imprisonment and/or a fine of not more than 3,000 Emirati dirhams for persons found guilty of unlawfully using a registered mark, forging or imitating a registered mark, or using a counterfeit or forged mark, or selling goods with a forged mark. Articles 24–25 of the statute provided for the issuance of precautionary orders.

issued as part of the British government's extraterritorial jurisdiction, akin to the trademark protection available in Bahrain. The northern part of Yemen, then constituting the independent Yemen Arab Republic, enacted a simple trademarks and trade names law in 1976.

Information on the level of trademark registration activity in the region during these early years is patchy and uncertain. According to a survey conducted by WIPO and published in 1978 on intellectual property activity in the region, only Bahrain and Kuwait provided statistics on trademark applications and registrations.[19] The study reported that, for 1974, the latest year for which any statistics were recorded in the study, Bahrain granted 184 trademark registrations and Kuwait approved 372 applications. What is more telling is that only ten of the Bahraini applications and 13 of the Kuwaiti approvals were of Arab/local origin.[20] The pattern in Ras Al-Khaimah in respect of the predominance of trademarks of foreign origin was even greater than that in Bahrain and Kuwait; of the 800 marks registered in Ras Al-Khaimah during the period 1974–1978, only two were of Arabic origin.[21]

3.2.2 Patents

Until a pre-TRIPS flurry of legislative activity in the early 1990s, only Bahrain and Kuwait provided any measure of notional patent protection during the 1970s and 1980s. None of the other States possessed any patent protection statutes.

Bahrain's omnibus Patents, Designs and Trade Marks Regulation of 1955 also provided a form of protection for patents and industrial designs. Totally subordinate and supplementary to the then UK patents and industrial designs legislation,[22] it required prior registration of a patent with the UK Patent and Trade Marks Office as a precondition of eligibility for local registration, and granted local protection only for the duration of the UK period of protection. Bahrain amended the law in 1977 after independence to remove any reference to UK dependency.[23]

Kuwait, meanwhile, issued its original patent law (which also applied to industrial designs and models) in 1962.[24] The law provided for a period of protection of 15 years for patents and five years for designs and industrial models,

19 WIPO (1978), *Situation of Industrial Property in the Arab States*, WIPO, Geneva, p. 34. The Report warns that the absence of Saudi statistics in the report should be construed as a reflection on the difficulty of obtaining reliable statistical data from local Saudi sources and the paucity of local data-collection procedures rather than any indication of local trademark inactivity.

20 Ibid., p. 35.

21 Ras Al-Khaimah Chamber of Commerce and Agriculture Records, cited by Mohamed Al-Kamali, 'Development of Intellectual Property Law in the UAE', unpublished PhD thesis, University of Exeter, 1994, p. 151.

22 *Patents Act 1949* (UK).

23 Bahrain, Amiri Decree No. 22 of 1977 amending certain provisions of the Patents, Designs and Trade Marks Regulation of 1955.

24 Kuwait, Law No. 4 of 1962, governing Patents, Designs and Industrial Models.

from the date of application.[25] By virtue of this law, Kuwait was the first State to introduce its own patent law. Although only seven years apart, the Bahraini and Kuwaiti laws were markedly different, with the Bahraini law very much reflecting its then status as a British protected territory and Kuwait's 1962 law reflecting its newly acquired independence.

The level of service available in respect of patents was even more limited than it was for trademarks. Bahrain and Kuwait would accept patent applications, but would limit examination to matters of form and local application procedural requirements, since neither State possessed the means or expertise to carry out substantive or technical examinations. Hence the function of the respective receiving offices was in fact to serve as little more than a mailbox and a record of ownership – fulfilling a similar role to that of cautionary notices in the local media.

Available information on the amount of patent-related activity is even more difficult to identify than that for regional trademark activity. The aforementioned WIPO 1978 Report also recorded that, in 1974, 35 patent applications were filed for protection in Bahrain, all of which were of non-Arab origin, while for the same year 115 applications were filed in Kuwait, of which only four were of Kuwaiti origin.[26] However, there is no record of any of these patents having been granted. In any case, judging by the history of patent applications from the States in more recent times, it is more than likely that these few applications originated not from Kuwaiti nationals but from foreign expatriate workers in the oil industry and also claimed priority on the basis of another foreign patent.[27]

3.2.3 Copyright

None of the Arabian Peninsula States possessed any *sui generis* copyright protection legislation until 1989, when Saudi Arabia issued the region's first copyright law.[28]

Most States had in force laws which addressed the control and registration of published works, such as newspapers, journals, pamphlets and books.[29] The primary purpose of these laws was to ensure that all publishers were registered and that all material that they intended to publish or publicly distribute was first

25 Ibid., art. 12.

26 WIPO, op. cit., p. 36.

27 The US Patent and Trademark Office (USPTO) reports that, for the period 1977–1982, only four patent applications from the Gulf region were granted registration, all applicants from Saudi Arabia. However, the USPTO determines the origin of a patent according to the place of residence of the first-named inventor, as distinct from nationality. In each of the four cases, the application claimed priority on the basis of a US-origin patent. USPTO, *Patent Counts by Country/State and Year, January 1 1997–December 31 2001,* February 2002, available at www.uspto.gov/web/offices/ac/ido/oeip/taf/reports_stco.htm, last accessed 26 May 2017.

28 Saudi Arabia, Royal Decree M/11 of 1410 AH (1989) concerning the Protection of Copyrights.

29 Bahrain, Legislative Decree No. 20 of 1975 with respect to the Legal Deposit of Intellectual Works; Kuwait, Law No. 3 of 1961, the Press and Publications Law.

approved by the responsible ministry. Hence the laws' main objective was one of censorship and control. As part of the control mechanism, the laws generally required literary works to be lodged in a national repository, registered and approved by a central authority prior to their publication. They also required the publisher to provide written certification of the author's agreement to the publication of the work in the format presented for governmental approval. This was very much a control and censorship function rather than an acknowledgement of, and provision for, the protection of authors' rights. Saudi Arabia's printing and publishing law was one which specifically directed that, in addition to meeting the control and censorship elements of the law, publishers must respect the rights of the author, provided he was a Saudi national:

> Copyright of literary works, printing, translation and publishing are reserved for their Saudi owners, their heirs and persons whose works are printed . . .
>
> The Ministry must prevent every infringement of the rights stipulated in the above article; a committee . . . shall have jurisdiction to consider every infringement on said rights and award compensation to the interested party for the material and moral damages suffered.[30]

However, none of the publication and registration control laws offered a definition of an author or of a literary work. It is telling that responsibility for the control of publishing houses, and the printing and public circulation of material, rested with a ministry whose responsibilities also extended to the control and censorship of all material and information entering the public domain and often included the administration of justice and the *Shariah* as a public order and morality issue.

3.3 Examples of early regional intellectual property legislation

The Bahraini 1955 omnibus Patents, Designs and Trade Marks Regulation and the Kuwaiti 1962 Patents Law show in stark contrast the fundamentally different philosophical and structural attitudes between the subordinated pre-independence regulation and the emancipated post-independence statutes. The objective of the Bahraini regulation was to address and protect the commercial and industrial interests of the UK businesses trading in Bahrain and, by association, the interests of their local agents. The patents and designs provisions in particular, by virtue of the UK registration prerequisite, precluded any real opportunity for the encouragement and development of locally generated industrial property and its protection. The provision for a dual system of trademark registration, allowing for the protection of marks of local origin and usage, at least recognised the realities of regional trade.

30 Saudi Arabia, Royal Decree No. M/17 of 1402 AH (1982), the Printing Matter and Publications Law, arts 20–21.

3.3.1 The Bahraini Patents, Designs and Trade Marks Regulation of 1955

The subordinated status of the Bahraini regulation was established very clearly in the statute's opening definitions, which included the following:

> 'Comptroller-General' means the UK Comptroller-General of Patents, Designs and Trade Marks, and included any person authorised by him or the UK Board of Trade to issue certificates in respect of UK-registered patents, designs or trademarks.
>
> . . .
>
> 'Court' means the Joint Court.[31]
>
> . . .
>
> 'Patentee' means a person or persons for the time being entered on the UK Register of Patents as grantee or proprietor of the patent and the personal representative of a deceased grantee or proprietor.
>
> 'Registrar' means the person appointed jointly by the Political Resident and the Ruler of Bahrain to be Registrar of Patents, Designs and Trade Marks for the Territory . . .
>
> 'Territory' means the territory for which the 1955 law has been made applicable.'[32]

Bahrain was not specifically identified as the territory in question. However, some guidance was later provided by the description of the territory of a local trademark as constituting 'the territories of Bahrain, Kuwait, Qatar, Muscat and Oman, and the Trucial States'.[33] The law did not distinguish between local or otherwise in respect of the other areas of industrial property protected by the legislation.

To be competent to apply for local registration of a patent or design, the applicant was required to first have his right, title or interest entered on the UK Register of Patents and either be the patentee or designer or otherwise have legal title.[34] The law did not define a patent or describe its characteristics, the fundamental

31 The UK government envisaged the establishment of Joint Courts in Bahrain, Qatar and the Trucial States as part of the system of British extra-territorial jurisdiction to consider mixed cases – that is, matters between nationals of the individual states concerned and non-nationals. Although the jurisdiction of the Joint Court could encompass both civil and criminal cases, in practice it confined itself to civil matters only. The Joint Court was composed of a judge of the British Court in the Gulf States and the Ruler (Emir) or his representative. The system was only fully established in Bahrain, where the jurisdiction of the Joint Court was extended specifically to include matters under the Queen's Regulation and the Bahrain Regulation on Patents, Designs and Trade Marks Regulation of 1955. Joint Courts were not established for Kuwait; although they were planned for introduction in Qatar, they did not eventuate.

32 Bahrain, Patents, Designs and Trade Marks Regulation 1955, art. 1.

33 Ibid., art. 23.

34 Ibid., art. 17.

proposition being that an invention or article was a patent by virtue of its registration as such in the UK.

By contrast, the statute drew a distinction between trademarks already registered in the UK and trademarks of local origin and for local use only. In the former case, an applicant was required to first have his right, title or interest entered on the UK Register of Trade Marks and be either the owner or assignee of the mark.[35] In the case of an original local registration only, any person claiming to be the proprietor of a mark was entitled to seek registration.[36]

Some limited degree of protection was provided in respect of well-known marks in that a mark could not be registered if it was identical, or confusingly similar, to a mark already registered in either part of the local register in respect of the same goods or description of goods.[37] However, the Registrar might not refuse an application for registration solely on the grounds of being identical or very similar to a locally registered mark if the applicant could demonstrate that his mark was already registered in the UK or had been in regular local use for at least one year before the other mark was first used or locally registered.[38]

A local mark (but not a UK-registered trademark, to which the following conditions did not apply) could not be registered in whole or in part if it consisted of or contained:

- public or armorial bearings, crests, insignia or decorations of any state or nation, or official hallmarks or signs indicating an official warranty, unless properly authorised;
- marks identical with or similar to national flags, military or naval flags, medals or badges, or the signs of the Red Crescent or Red Cross, or emblems of exclusively religious significance;
- a geographical name or surname, or the name of a sect, castle or tribe in any of the territories;
- marks which were, or contained, the picture, name or trade name of a person, body corporate or association, without prior consent.[39]

35 Ibid., art. 17.

36 Ibid., art. 31.

37 Ibid., art. 13.1. Pursuant to art. 3, the Registrar of Patents, Designs and Trade Marks was required to maintain three separate registers – one for patents, one for designs and a third in two parts for UK-dependent (Part II) and marks of local origin for local use (Part III).

38 The Registrar of Patents, Designs and Trade Marks was appointed by the Political Registrar and notionally the Emir and was an officer of HM Government. It is interesting that the subordinate Supplementary Rules for the 1955 Regulation were issued by the Registrar on behalf of the Ruler of Bahrain and the UK's Political Resident in Bahrain jointly, instead of by a Bahraini government minister, department or authorised local official. In a subtle display of cultural sensitivity, the Supplementary Rules stipulated in art. 2 that trademark applications in respect of all goods in classes 32 (beer and stout) and 33 (wines and spirits) were to be published separately from the main Official Gazette (in which trademark registrations were normally publicly notified) and posted concurrently on the Registry noticeboard at 'Her Britannic Majesty's Political Agency, Bahrain'.

39 Ibid., art. 26.

The period of protection for a patent, design or UK-dependent trademark was not granted in terms of a stipulated period of time but existed only as long as the corresponding prerequisite UK registration remained current and valid. Where a term was extended in the UK, the local registration could also be similarly extended.[40] By contrast, the validity of a local origin and use trademark registration was seven years, with provision for renewal for periods up to a maximum of 15 years.[41]

A suit for infringement could be brought only by the registered owner or assignee and then only in respect of a duly registered patent, design or trademark. However, provision existed for the granting of injunctive relief, including the seizure and destruction of infringing goods and any associated materials and equipment, and the award of damages and costs.[42] The nature of the scale of penalties for different types of infringements reflected the commercial imperatives of the statute. Unauthorised use of the (British) Royal Arms or Arms or Emblems of the ruler of the Territory (that is, Bahrain) or of deceivingly similar arms or emblems, or using any sign or title to create the impression of being an employee of, or supplier to, either government carried a fine of only 300 Indian rupees.[43] In contrast, such acts as:

- applying a false trade description to articles or goods protected by a registered patent or trademark;
- forging or counterfeiting a registered trademark, patent or design or possessing equipment for such purpose;
- importing, selling or possessing any goods which infringed a registered patent;
- importing, selling or even possessing any goods which carried a counterfeit or misleadingly similar trademark, design or description, or which were so presented as to enable them to be passed off

carried penalties in each case of imprisonment for a period not exceeding two years, or a fine of up to 1,500 Indian rupees, or both. The court could also award damages of up to 1,500 Indian rupees for any losses which had been suffered as a direct result of the infringement and which had not already been otherwise compensated.[44]

The 1955 regulation remained unchanged until 1977, when a new law made sweeping changes to reflect and recognise Bahrain's change of status in 1971 from

40 Ibid., art. 22.
41 Ibid., art. 32.
42 Ibid., arts 46–47.
43 Ibid., art. 56.
44 Ibid., arts 55, 60. The use of Indian rupees as the legal tender for the purposes of the regulation was a legacy from the British Indian patents and trademarks regulation, on which the Bahraini regulation and the 1958 Kuwaiti regulation were based, from the period when the administration of the British Persian Gulf interests was under the control of the British Indian Office until India's independence in 1947. Control then moved to the British Foreign and Commonwealth Office.

a UK-administered territory to an independent sovereign state.[45] The effect of the 1977 amendments was, in general terms, to:

- remove any subordination or cross-reference to UK patents, design or trademark legislation, regulation or procedure;
- remove any reference to the UK or UK institutions such as the UK Patents Office or Trade Marks Registry, or 'Comptroller-General', and to any local offices or organisations which were part of Bahrain's former status as a UK-administered territory, such as the 'Joint Court', the 'Political Resident' and the 'Crown Prosecutor';
- expand the registrability of marks to include services;
- stipulate provisions and conditions in lieu of the former UK-dependent provisions and conditions for registered patents, designs and non-local trademarks;
- introduce provision for semi-independent review of administrative decision-making, by transferring the quasi-judicial discretionary authority of the Registrar of Patents, Designs and Trade Marks to a semi-independent committee formed by the Minister of Commerce and Agriculture.

The former UK-dependent term of protection for patents and designs was replaced by a period of 15 years for patents and five years for designs, with provision for renewal.[46] Patent protection could be renewed for another ten years if it could be shown that the patent was of special significance and had not returned a financial award proportional to the expenditure incurred by the inventor. Similarly, the former UK-dependent trademark term of protection was replaced by a period of five years with provision for further ongoing renewals for successive periods of five years each. Curiously, although all references to the UK were deleted throughout the new law, the former reference to a two-part Register of Trade Marks (Part II for UK registrations and Part III for local registrations) remained unchanged. Hence the original provision for a seven-year term for local trademarks remained unchanged, thereby creating a contradiction between the two provisions and confusion as to the proper and valid period of protection. Similarly, the description of a local trademark and the territories in which it was applicable, and the reference to trademarks which fell outside its bounds, was also overlooked in the 1977 amendments.

Nor did the 1977 amendments include any changes to either the description of the nature of infringements, or the nature or level of sanctions available. The relief and precautionary measures available to a court in respect of infringements remained unchanged, as did the use of the Indian rupee as the currency of the legislation, notwithstanding the fact that Bahrain since independence had adopted the dinar as the State's legal currency.

45 Bahrain, Amiri Decree No. 22 of 1977.
46 Ibid., art. 11.

3.3.2 The Kuwaiti Patents Law of 1962

By virtue of Law No. 4 of 1962, Kuwait was the second country after Bahrain among the Arabian Peninsula States to introduce its own patent legislation. The law also provided protection for industrial designs and models. National treatment was extended to non-Kuwaitis living in or who had an established business in Kuwait, other foreigners who were nationals of or lived in countries that gave Kuwait reciprocity, as well as companies, public institutions and other legal entities established in Kuwait or of countries which gave reciprocity to Kuwait.[47]

The Kuwaiti law provided for the grant of letters patent for 'any new invention which is utilisable in industry whether it concerns new industrial product, original industrial process and techniques or a new application of known industrial process or techniques'.[48] Excluded from protection by the granting of a patent were:

1 inventions whose utilisation results in a breach of morality or public policy;
2 chemical inventions relating to foodstuffs, medicines or pharmaceutical formula unless such products are made by special chemical methods or processes. In the latter event, the patent shall not be issued for the products themselves but for the method of their preparation.[49]

Protection was granted for 15 years from the date of filing of the application, with provision for a single renewal for a further five years. An application for a pharmaceutical patent, being a patent which fell within the scope of the above exemption from exclusion provision (that is, certain types of chemical inventions requiring special chemical methods or processes), could be protected for only ten years without provision for renewal.[50] Protection for a registered industrial design or model was valid for five years and renewable for two additional consecutive terms.[51]

Provision was also made for appeals to independent judicial authority, namely the Kuwait court of first instance, against decisions of the Trade Marks Control Office to reject an application or objection against an application, or non-renewal.[52] The jurisdiction of the court also extended to appeals against decisions of the Office in respect of compulsory licences and compensations and revocation of patent registrations.

Compulsory licensing could be granted in circumstances where the patented invention had not been utilised in Kuwait within three years from the date of grant of the patent, where the patent owner was unable to utilise it adequately to meet the needs of the country or where the utilisation of the invention had ceased for

47 Kuwait, Law No. 4 of 1962, the Law on the Control and Register of Trade Marks, art. 5.
48 Ibid., art. 1.
49 Ibid., art. 2.
50 Ibid., art. 12.
51 Ibid., art. 42.
52 Ibid., arts 22 and 31–32, and Implementing Regulations, art. 66.

at least two consecutive years.[53] Authority for granting the compulsory licence rested with the Trade Marks Control Office, provided the applicant could demonstrate that the invention would be utilised effectively and the patent owner had received suitable compensation. The decision of the Trade Marks Control Office in respect of a compulsory licence was also challengeable before the courts, but in the 50 years or so since this law was promulgated, no compulsory licences appear to have been issued in Kuwait.

If the invention was deemed to be of great national importance and its utilisation necessitated use of another invention for which a patent had already been granted, the Trade Marks Control Office could grant a compulsory licence to exploit both patents to either the applicant or to the owner of the previous invention, depending on which invention was of greater importance.[54] An invention could also be expropriated if such expropriation was deemed to be in the public interest or for national defence by the Minister of Finance and Economy.

Infringement of the rights of a patent, design or model holder was limited to the following:

- imitating the subject matter of a patented invention or duly registered design or industrial model;
- knowingly selling or offering for sale or circulation, or importing or acquiring with intent to trade, imitated products or materials bearing an imitated design or industrial model, if the invention or industrial model is registered in Kuwait;
- without right, placing on products, notices, trademarks or packing articles, particulars leading to the belief of his having obtained a patent of invention or a registration of a design or industrial model.[55]

Where a civil or criminal action had commenced, the right holder could request the court to issue provisional orders, particularly seizure of the infringing products or goods and any equipment or machinery used in the infringement. Penalties available to the court included a term of imprisonment for up to two years or a fine of not less than 10 Kuwaiti dinars and not more than 225 Kuwaiti dinars, or both, and seizure and destruction of the offending goods and any tools, machinery and equipment used as part of the infringing activity.

Law No. 4 of 1962 is remarkable for its longevity by regional standards, which stands as testimony to its enlightened and careful construction. Subject to amendments in 1991 and again in 2001, the law remained in force until as recently as April 2016. In recent years of the present TRIPS-plus era, however, it attracted criticism because of the flexibility and scope of its patentability exclusion provisions, the perceived gross inadequacy of its sanctions by modern standards, and because

53 Ibid., arts. 29 and 30.
54 Ibid., art. 31.
55 Ibid., arts 46–47. Article 47 provides that the owner is limited to seeking such relief 'during the hearing of a civil or criminal case'.

of the exclusion from protection of patentable pharmaceutical and agricultural products. Although Kuwait adopted the GCC Unified Patent Law as its domestic patent law in 2013, it was not until April 2016 that the necessary implementing regulations to bring the GCC Law into force were issued by the Kuwaiti Ministry of Trade and Industry.[56]

3.3.3 The Jordanian Trademark Law of 1952

Jordan's rich history has influenced its laws, starting from Ammon, Moab and Edom to the Nabataean Kingdom, the Roman Empire, and the Ottoman Empire, and finally with British occupation and control as a consequence of the British mandate over Palestine and Trans-Jordan granted by the League of Nations. During the term of the Ottoman Empire, Jordan had a number of laws regulating intellectual property matters. The first trademark law was the '1888 Regulation on Trademarks' concerning Industrial Products and Commercial Goods. Interestingly, some of the Ottoman-period laws remained in effect or in influence in some countries for many years after the demise of the Ottoman Empire. For example, Jordan did not replace its Ottoman-period copyright law until 1992.

Jordan gained its independence from the United Kingdom in 1946, and enacted its Constitution in 1952. Very soon thereafter it enacted Trademark Law No. 33 of 1952. This new law was not the first trademark statute that had been in place in Jordan; earlier regulations had been in force during the term of the British mandate, namely the trademarks law of 1930, which reflected the character of the UK trademark legislation. Also in place for some time was the Palestinian Trademarks Law No. 35 of 1938 (again, under the UK mandate). Because of this rather complicated history covering trademark protection and the fact that these laws were enacted during the British mandate, and generally in light of Jordan's involvement with Palestine, especially the West Bank, Jordan was keen to create its own law as soon as feasible after independence.

The 1952 trademark law was remarkably comprehensive and sophisticated for its time, no doubt reflecting the ongoing British influence in its construction and drafting. Article 2 defines a trademark as 'any mark used or is intended to be used upon goods or in connection therewith for the purpose of indicating that such goods are those of the proprietor of such trademark by virtue of having manufactured, selected, certified, traded in or offered them for sale'. The Law did not make any provision for or reference to protection of marks related to services (although subsequent amendments provided that all stipulated conditions and provisions related to marks distinguishing goods also applied equally to marks distinguishing services).[57]

56 Kuwaiti Law No. 71 of 2013 introduced the GCC Patent Law, while Law No. 115 of 2016 adopted the GCC Patent Law Implementing Regulations, coming into force on 4 April 2016.

57 Jordan, Law No. 33 of 1952, art. 31.

To be eligible for registration, a mark must also consist of characters, devices or marks or a combination thereof, which have a distinctive character sufficient to distinguish the goods to which they are attached from the goods of others.[58] Distinctiveness may be inherent or it may be acquired through use of the mark or the goods to which it is attached – such determination being able to be made by the Trademark Registrar or the courts.[59] In determining whether a trademark has a distinctive character as mentioned herein before, the registrar or the court may, in the case of a trademark in actual use, take into consideration the extent to which such use has rendered the trademark in fact distinctive for the goods in respect of which it is registered or is intended to be registered. Single colour or multi-colour trademarks are registrable.

The trademark law prohibited the following from being registered:

- marks resembling the Jordanian royal emblems, crests, the word 'royal', or any other words, characters or representations which created the impression of royal patronage;
- Jordanian emblem or medals or those of foreign states or countries unless authorised;
- marks indicating any official designation unless authorised or required;
- marks resembling the Jordanian national flag, military or naval banners, honours or decorations, or military insignia;
- marks which include the words and expressions 'patent', 'patented', 'by royal patent', 'registered design', 'copyright', 'counterfeiting is forgery', or similar words or expressions; and
- marks contrary to *ordre public* or morality, or which lead to deceiving the public, encourage unfair trading competition or contain false indications as to their real origin;
- marks indicating a geographical meaning, or surnames unless presented in a special manner;
- marks identical or similar to any emblem of religious significance;
- marks containing the picture, name of trade, person, or body corporate or association, without proper approval;
- a mark identical to, or resembling to such an extent as to deceive, a mark that is already registered for the same goods or class of goods;
- marks similar to or identical to the insignia of the Red Crescent or the Red Cross or the Cross of Geneva.[60]

Article 20 provided for a period of protection of seven years from date of registration with provision for ongoing renewal. However, this provision did not allow for any retrospectivity or concurrence. Hence it applied only to marks registered under

58 Jordan, Law No. 33 of 1952, art. 7(1)–(4).
59 Ibid., art. 7(3).
60 Ibid., art. 8(1)–(11).

this law subsequent to its enactment, and not to any trademark registered under any previous law. However, protection was subject to the principle of usage; a mark which had not been used in respect of the goods for which it was registered could be liable for cancellation on application by any third party.[61]

Article 38 provided for sanctions which, by contemporary standards could reasonably claim to carry a not insignificant deterrent value. It provided for fines of up to 100 Jordanian dinars and up to one year's imprisonment for persons who committed any of the following acts or incited others to do so:

- uses a trademark registered under this law or an imitation of such trademark applied to the same class of goods for which the mark is registered;
- sells, stores for the purpose of sale, or offers for sale, goods bearing a mark the use of which is an offence under this clause;
- uses a mark duly registered by another person under this law to promote goods of the same class as those for which registration has already been obtained by that other person;
- manufactures, engraves, embosses or sells any plate, block, seal or other representation of a duly registered mark or any other imitation thereof for the purpose of enabling any person other than the registered trademark owner, to make use of such mark or imitation in connection with goods of the same class as that for which registration has already been obtained;
- makes or causes to be made a false entry in the Trademark Register, or makes or causes to be made any written instrument falsely purporting to be a copy of any entry in that register, or produces or tenders or causes such instrument to be produced or tendered by way of supporting evidence, knowing that the entry or instrument is false.

Items which had been used in the commission of the infringing activity, such as equipment, materials, packaging, promotional material or any other items, could be subject to seizure and destruction.[62]

Article 46 stipulated that the Jordanian trademark law of 1930 and the Palestinian Trademarks Law No. 35 of 1938 and all their amendments were forthwith annulled. All other Jordanian and Palestinian laws promulgated before the enactment of this law shall be abrogated to the extent to which these legislations are repugnant to the provisions of this law.

The implementing regulations for Law No. 33 of 1952 were issued before the end of the same year, an impressive demonstration of bureaucratic efficiency and speed. The 1952 law remained in force, although subject to a number of amending actions, for many years and, like the early Kuwaiti patents law, is a remarkable for its longevity by regional standards.

61 Ibid., art. 22.
62 Ibid., art. 39.

3.4 Protection by association – non-intellectual property sources of protection

Notwithstanding the paucity of intellectual property law in the Arabian Peninsula States throughout most of the pre-TRIPS era, some degree of protection can be found in sources other than intellectual property-based laws, although the protection granted to rights holders was at times incidental and fortuitous.[63] The primary beneficiary was intended to be the local trader or agent or the consumer and not necessarily the owner or right holder of an intellectual property right. Hence the main objects of the protection were items of a commercial nature such as trademarks, trade names and indications of origin. While provisions existed for the punishment of infringers, the same degree of attention was not available for the award of financial compensation to the owner or right holder or for the payment of damages. In the application of these laws by the courts, the primary objective was to secure the cessation of the infringing activity rather than the imposition of deterrent sanctions.

The UAE Civil Transactions Code of 1985, for example, restates the principle drawn from the *Shariah* that, while an individual may exercise certain rights, it cannot be done so at the expense of the same rights that others are entitled to enjoy. In essence, a right is balanced by an obligation. Damage to, or infringement upon, the rights of others by one's actions must be compensated, but the original damage cannot be offset by another damage – in other words, 'two wrongs don't make a right'. The Code postulates three fundamental principles in respect of

63 The following represent just some of the laws enacted across the States from the 1970s onwards which included to a lesser or greater extent some degree of intellectual property rights protection. The list is by no means intended to be exhaustive, but does illustrate the range of laws then in force that could be utilised in the protection of intellectual property rights.

Bahrain: Law No. 12 of 1971, the Civil and Commercial Procedures Code; Law No. 20 of 1975, concerning the Legal Deposit of Intellectual works.

Jordan: Law No. 16 of 1960, the Criminal Law; Law No. 9 of 1961, the Law on Criminal Procedures; Law No. 43 of 1976, the Civil Law.

Kuwait: Law No. 2 of 1961, the Commercial Code; Law No. 3 of 1961, the Press and Publications Law; Law No. 67 of 1980, the Civil Code; Law No. 16 of 1960, the Penal Code; Law No. 56 of 1966, the Commercial Companies Code.

Oman: Royal Decree No. 7/1974, the Penal Code; Royal Decree No. 49/1984, concerning Printed Matter and Publications.

Qatar: Law No. 14 of 1971, the Criminal Code; Law No. 16 of 1971, Civil and Commercial Code; Law No. 8 of 1979 in respect of Printed Materials and Publications.

Saudi Arabia: Royal Decree No. M/17 of 1402 AH (1982), concerning the Control of Publications and Publishing; Royal Decree No. M/11 of 1404 AH (1984), for Combatting Commercial Deceit; Royal Decree No. M/49 of 1409 AH (1989), Law for Combatting Concealed Trading.

The UAE: Law No. 5 of 1973, concerning Press and Publications; Law No. 5 of 1985, the Civil Transactions Code; Law No. 3 of 1987, the Federal Penal Code; Law No. 18 of 1981, the Commercial Agencies Law; Law No. 4 of 1979, the Commercial Transactions Law.

Dubai: The Civil Wrongs Law of 1966 and Law No. 1 of 1970, the Penal Code.

causing damage to others in commercial transactions, which can equally be applicable to the protection of intellectual property:

1 A person shall be held liable for the unlawful exercise of his rights.
2 The exercise of a right shall be unlawful:

(a) if there is an intentional infringement of another's rights;
(b) if the interests which such exercise of right is designed to bring are contrary to the rules of the Islamic *Shariah,* the law, public order, or morals;
(c) if the interests desired are disproportionate to the harm that will be suffered by others; or
(d) if it exceeds the bounds of custom and usage.[64]

The UAE Penal Code of 1978 addresses misrepresentation in commercial transactions and provides a degree of protection for the consumer in respect of the true nature of goods offered for sale. The Code provides that any person who:

> resorts to deception or fraudulent means in contracting with another person and disseminates information contrary to the facts as to the nature or essential qualities of his goods or to the elements of its competition or as to the basic description or origin of his goods . . . shall be punishable . . . Any person who imports, purchases or promotes such goods for commercial gain with full knowledge of their reality shall also be liable.[65]

Similarly, the Oman Penal Code of 1974 provides a certain degree of protection for both the commercial agent and the consumer in respect of the use of imitated or confusing similar trademarks and trade names. The Code provides that a person who commits the following acts may be liable to a fine or term of imprisonment or both:

- imitates a registered mark belonging to a third party, or places such mark on any product, or knowingly offers for sale or sells a product bearing such imitated mark;
- uses a mark that is very similar to a registered mark to sell or offer for sale a product, with the intention of misleading a buyer;
- illegally uses, in any way, another person's trade name or a name which is very similar, with the intention of confusing or misleading or creating an association with that other trade name.[66]

Similar provisions can be found in the penal codes and commercial transaction codes of the other States.

64 UAE, Federal Law No. 5 of 1985, the Civil Transactions Code, art. 106.
65 UAE, Federal Law No. 3 of 1978, the Penal Code, art. 423.
66 Oman, Royal Decree No. 7/1974, the Penal Code, arts 305–307.

The laws governing the operation of commercial agencies generally recognise the exclusive right of a registered commercial agent to deal in the goods or products which are the subject of his agency. In establishing the commercial agent's monopolistic rights, the laws establish a limited form of protection for the marks and indications carried by those goods, providing that both the agency agreement and the associated marks are registered. The net effect of this protection is that other parties are prohibited from importing or trading in those goods, or in goods that are deceivingly similar or which carry deceivingly similar marks. Again, the law is directed at protecting the commercial rights of the agent and less so the rights of the owner of a trademark.

The role that the press and publications laws could play in providing some notion of copyright protection has been mentioned above. The fact that an application by a publisher to the government authority for approval to publish a work had to be accompanied by the author's agreement to publication at least provided the opportunity to clearly establish ownership of a literary work and thereby offered some degree of protection in limited circumstances. However, the approval requirement did extend to literary works that were not published in commercial quantities or works already published outside the state. By the same token, the laws requiring the lodgment of a published work in a repository holding may have established ownership, but the intellectual property protection they provided was almost accidental, where it did occur. Accordingly, the protection provided by the publishing laws and the lodgment laws was at best incidental and could not be considered to represent an unequivocal or adequate means of copyright protection.

The pursuit of the protection of intellectual property rights through the region's judicial systems had been a mixed success – in part due to the deficiency of qualified and experienced judges familiar with the concepts of intellectual property rights and the interpretation of the intellectual property laws.[67] The common law doctrine of *stare decisis* is not recognised under the *Shariah* and thereby is not adhered to in the *Shariah* courts or the civil courts. Consequently, the absence of accepted legal precedent also contributed to problems in respect of consistency in the application of judicial principles and interpretation of the statutes on intellectual property rights and their protection.[68] The following two cases from the Dubai courts illustrate this inconsistency.

In 1977, the owners of the trademark *Brylcreem*, an internationally well-known haircare product, brought an action in the Dubai courts against a local manufacturer of an identical product offered for sale under the trademark *Berylcream*. The Dubai court held that prior use and registration in a foreign country were persuasive elements in confirming ownership of a trademark and that fraudulent

67 Angell, op. cit., p. 4.

68 Ibid. See also Essam Al-Tamimi (2003), *Practical Guide to Litigation and Arbitration in the United Arab Emirates*, p. 5.

use of a well-known and original mark, irrespective of whether the original mark was also used in the UAE, constituted unfair competition. It further held that protection of the original mark should be provided according to the general laws against unfair competition and that the law should not turn a blind eye to the harm done to the rightful owner of the mark simply because of the absence of a law regulating the use of trademarks:

> Non-existence of a law regulating the registration of trademarks leads to the fact that this court cannot levy the penalties which are usually provided for in such laws, but that does not prevent the court from granting the necessary protection to the trademark on the bases of general principles of law and the principles of justice and equity.[69]

It further held that:

> as to proving damage and fraud to the public through the use of the imitation trademark, the Court is of the opinion that it is not necessary to prove the actual occurrence of misrepresentation, but it is sufficient to say that there is a probability of such an imitation misleading the public.

However, in an action brought by the owner of the *TIDE* trademark, against a local manufacturer of a similar product offered under the trademark *TIPE*, the Dubai appellate court held that, without a trademarks law in Dubai, imitating a trademark did not constitute an offence. It further held that, because Dubai was a trading community, it would be 'contrary to the principles of justice and equity' to impose any restriction upon free trade in the absence of government legislation.[70] In so ruling, it overturned the decision of the lower court that had been in favour of granting protection to the *TIDE* trademark. The Dubai Court of Cassation upheld the judgment of the appellate court on the grounds that, in the absence of any statutory trademarks law or customary law or Islamic law protecting trademarks, there was no basis for trademark infringement or unfair competition.[71]

In 1980, the Abu Dhabi Appeal Court held that an internationally known mark did not need to be registered locally in order to be entitled to local protection, since the property right to the mark was established by its first use and not by the act of registration.[72] Registration merely served to confirm rather than establish

69 Dubai Court of First Instance, Civil Division, Case No. 1378/1977, decided 24 June 1978; discussed in Al-Kamali, op. cit., p. 212, and S H Amin (1993), *Law of Intellectual and Industrial Property in Developing Countries: Muslim World*, pp. 41–2.

70 See Maren Hansen (1993), 'Taking a Realistic Approach to Trade Mark Protection in the Gulf Countries', 16, *Middle East Executive Reports*, p. 12.

71 Dubai Court of First Instance Case No. 3/1981, decided 10 January 1982; Dubai Court of Appeal Case No. 17/1982, decided 15 May 1982; discussed in Al-Kamali, op. cit., p. 180.

72 *McDonald's Corporation v Hassan Arzouni*, Abu Dhabi Court of Appeal, Case No. 240/1980, decided 18 March 1981; discussed in Al-Kamali, op. cit., pp. 143 and 177.

that right. The Court upheld the decision of the lower court that, although the *McDonald's* trademark was not at that time registered in the UAE, it was so well known internationally that local use of an identical or confusingly similar mark was likely both to be fraudulent and to cause confusion. This same principle was later endorsed by the Sharjah civil court in a similar action brought by the McDonald's Corporation (in fact, against the same defendant).[73] In the absence of any trademark laws in the UAE, the first law not being enacted until 1992, the decision in favour of McDonald's was based on the *Shariah*, the local civil codes and the general principles of justice and equity.

The case of *Reckitt and Colman v Al Jazirah* has been generally recognised as a landmark decision in controlling the production of locally manufactured counterfeit products in Saudi Arabia. The case, the first under the Saudi 1984 trademark law, was brought by Reckitt & Colman as the owners of the *Dettol* trademark against a local producer of *Bettol*, an imitation of Reckitt & Colman's *Dettol* disinfectant. On behalf of the company, the Saudi Ministry of Commerce had successfully appealed the original judgment in favour of the defendant, the local producer. The Ministry further appealed the appellate judgment, even though the decision was in its favour, on the grounds that the Ministry considered that the penalty was not commensurate with the gravity of the infringement. The Board of Grievances reversed the earlier decisions and ordered that the defendant be fined SR50,000, the maximum allowed under the trademark law.[74] It also ordered that all products and other labels, signs and materials bearing the imitation trademark *Bettol* be destroyed. Interestingly, though, the Board of Grievances did not order the defendant to pay any compensation, damages or costs. A civil case was reportedly settled satisfactorily out of court.[75]

However, apparently this was not the end of the matter for Reckitt & Colman in its protection of its *Dettol* trademark. According to one local report, more than 29 imitations of the *Dettol* trademark were found in Saudi Arabia in 1993, a year after the conclusion of the landmark decision in its favour.[76] The need to again

See also Stephen Bigger (1981), 'Notes from Other Nations', 71 *Trademark Reporter*, pp.657–9.

73 *McDonald's v Hassan Arzouni*, Sharjah Court of First Instance, Case No. 823/1985, decided 13 January 1986; discussed in Al-Kamali, op. cit., p. 143. In a landmark case in early 1996, McDonald's pursued six companies in Riyadh and Jeddah for violations of trademark legislation and filed suits against four of them. McDonald's had registered all its trademarks and promotional logos with the Ministry as soon as it entered into the Saudi market. McDonald's had settled its cases by the end of 1997 and is building further restaurants in Saudi Arabia, which suggests that it was satisfied with the outcome. See Stephen Bigger (1986), 'Notes from Other Nations', 76 *Trademark Reporter*, pp.354–5.

74 *Reckitt and Colman v Al Jazirah*, Saudi Board of Grievances Case No. 206/T/M of 27 June 1992. This final decision came after four years of legal proceedings. Discussed in Amin, op. cit., pp. 105–11. See also Amir Khoury, 'The Development of Modern Trademark Legislation and Protection in Arab Countries in the Middle East' (2000), 16, *Transnational Lawyer*, p. 325.

75 Hansen, op. cit., p. 8.

76 Ibid., pp. 14–15.

defend *Dettol* arose in Ras Al-Khaimah where a producer of allegedly counterfeit *Dettol* tried to register the trademark *Dollen*. The application for registration was rejected after the lodgment of an objection by Reckitt & Colman. The local producer reportedly simply moved production to Qatar and subsequently began exporting *Dollen* to the other States, including the UAE.

3.5 The pre-TRIPS status of intellectual property protection

3.5.1 Trademarks

By the mid-1990s and just prior to the establishment of the WTO and the appearance of TRIPS, all States had trademark laws in place – some of them long established and in a few instances second- and third-generation legislation. Bahrain, for example, issued a new trademark law in 1991 which eventually replaced entirely the 1955 regulation and the 1977 amendments, and thereby provided the opportunity to redress a number of the inconsistencies and contradictions which arose from an unsatisfactory and incomplete amendment of the original 1955 regulation.[77] Similarly, Kuwait over the years issued a number of enhancements to the trademark provisions of its longstanding commercial code.[78]

The most recent versions of the trademark laws of this period showed a high level of consistency and similarity, since most borrowed from the original Kuwaiti provisions, and thereafter continued to cross-fertilise each other as each round of new laws or amendments was introduced. However, most laws also relied quite heavily on the model laws on trademarks that had been prepared by the League of Arab States with the assistance of WIPO. Accordingly, they all contained similar provisions, particularly in respect of protection against counterfeiting and trademark infringement.[79] By the same token, they also all contained similar inadequacies in the eyes of the WTO and WIPO, and would require a number of changes to bring them into compliance with TRIPS, notably in respect of:

- protection for well-known marks, including foreign marks;
- provision for licensing;
- existence of sanctions of sufficient severity to act as a deterrent;
- expansion of provisional measures, remedies and relief;
- effective border-control measures;
- protection of trade secrets and protection from unfair competition;
- appeal provisions to independent judicial bodies on administrative decisions.

77 Bahrain, Legislative Decree No. 10 of 1991 in respect of Trade Marks, promulgated 25 June 1991.

78 Kuwait, Law No. 67 of 1980, Law No. 68 of 1980 and Ministerial Order No. 8 of 1995, for example.

79 WIPO, op. cit., p. 38.

The UAE was the last of the Arabian Peninsula States to provide some form of statutory trademark protection when it finally issued its first trademark law in 1992.[80] By mutual agreement, the law also superseded Ras Al-Khaimah's trademark registration statute of 1974. A unified Yemen issued a general intellectual property law in 1994, encompassing both copyright and industrial property and replacing the early trademark provisions of the former British Protectorate of Aden (southern Yemen) and the (northern) Yemen Arab Republic's trademarks and trade names law of 1974.

3.5.2 Patents and industrial designs

By the mid-1990s, all States except Jordan, Oman and Qatar had introduced their own domestic patent legislation, although implementation and administration systems and services varied from state to state. Oman and Qatar, meanwhile, intended to adopt the regional patent regulations recently approved by the GCC Supreme Council for their own domestic purposes and therefore did not introduce any patent legislation.[81] The major drawback with this strategy was that the GCC statute was intended to be supplementary to domestic laws. In particular, it did not contain any enforcement provisions or sanctions – this being deemed a matter for domestic laws to address.

Where patents laws were in place, the laws contained shortcomings which ensured that they would attract pressure for change. Kuwait's 1962 law as amended, for example, provided protection for only 15 years instead of the conventional 20 years and excluded certain chemical inventions involving foods, pharmaceuticals and medicines from protection.[82] By the same token, the UAE's patent law produced 30 years later contained a similar glaring deficiency – and one that attracted severe criticism from the United States – in that it did not provide any patent protection for pharmaceutical products and only a ten-year term of protection for pharmaceutical processes.[83] Yemen's comprehensive intellectual property law, which incorporated protection for patents, similarly provided protection for patents for only 15 years. Although these States provided for a conventional system of protection through registration and examination, they tended to operate as filing systems or

80 UAE, Federal Law No. 37 of 1992, in respect of Trade Marks. The law covered the seven Emirates of Abu Dhabi, Dubai, Sharjah, Ras Al-Khaimah, Ajman, Fujeirah and Umm al Quwain.

81 The GCC Unified Patent Regulations were approved by the GCC Supreme Council in September 1992 and issued in December 1992. At the same time the GCC Supreme Council approved the establishment of the GCC Patent Office, to be located in Riyadh, Saudi Arabia.

82 Kuwait, Law No. 4 of 1962 governing Patents, Designs and Industrial Models, as amended, arts 2 and 15.

83 UAE, Federal Law No. 44 of 1992 concerning the Organisation and Protection of Patents, Industrial Drawings and Industrial Designs, arts 6 and 14. See also USTR, *2001 National Trade Estimates, Gulf Cooperation Council Chapter*, available at https://ustr.gov/archive/assets/Document_Library/Reports_Publications/2001/2001_NTE_Report/asset_upload_file262_6571.pdf, last accessed 26 May 2017.

mailboxes only. Saudi Arabia alone provided for a working registration system that allowed for both formal and substantive examination.

Protection for industrial designs was achieved by the Yemeni law by a combination of specific and separate provision and by the application of the law's general provisions. In Kuwait and the UAE, the general provisions of their patent laws were extended to encompass industrial designs and models.

With the agreement of all its members, the GCC issued its regional patent regulations in late 1992. The regulations established a scheme for regional protection throughout all member States by allowing the lodgment of a single application with a regional patents office. However, the regional patent regulations were somewhat wanting in respect both of their effective operation and their compliance with TRIPS, because of their:

- exclusion of pharmaceutical and chemical inventions from any form of protection;
- protection commencing from date of grant, instead of date of application;
- protection for only 15 years, contrary to the forthcoming TRIPS Article 33 requirement of 20 years;
- absence of any effective enforcement provisions, or sanctions, remedies or relief;
- prohibition of concurrent applications to national patent offices and to the GCC Patent Office.[84]

The regional patent regulation specifically prohibited the simultaneous lodgment of a patent application, or even the enjoyment of concurrent protection, with the GCC regional office and a national receiving office.[85] The practical implications of this prohibition were that an application to the regional office was required to demonstrate that any former or simultaneous application to a national receiving office had been withdrawn, and any national protection already granted had been surrendered, prior to the GCC regional office accepting the application for regional protection. Also militating against the effective utilisation of the unified patent regulation was the delay by the GCC in issuing the corresponding implementing bylaws, which did not eventuate until some four years later, in 1996. Furthermore, the regional patents office did not come into operation and was not in a position to accept any patent applications until October 1999.

While Kuwait, Oman and Qatar all claimed to ascribe to the GCC unified patent regulations as their national patent law, only Oman enacted a decree prior to 1995 to formally recognise the regulation and to legitimise this arrangement.[86]

84 See WTO, Working Party on the Accession of the Sultanate of Oman, *Accession of the Sultanate of Oman: Additional Questions and Replies*, Document WT/ACC/OMN/22 (01-0140), 13 January 2000, 18–19.

85 GCC Unified Patent Regulations, September 1992, art. 15.

86 Oman, Ministerial Regulation No. 219/1993, adopting the GCC Unified Patent Regulations as the Patents Law of Oman.

In practical terms, patent infringement issues were less likely to arise in the Arabian Peninsula States than trademark or copyright issues, and patent protection would have been the area in which it would arguably have been easier for the States to satisfy demands from the industrialised countries to improve intellectual property protection. Indeed, since the amount of local and original patent generation was so small at that time, there was little pressure to test the efficacy of the local laws and organisational structures. The fact that the Kuwaiti patents office, established under its original 1962 patents law, was still not examining or publishing applications or granting patents 30 years after it was established did not appear to have attracted any great concern either locally or internationally (although the lack of provision of a satisfactory patents protection regime, particularly for pharmaceutical products, has still attracted criticism).[87] Even in the immediate pre-TRIPS period of the early 1990s, the primary purpose of the Kuwaiti patents office appeared to be that of a repository only, with the issuance by the office of reminder notices, for the renewal of applications to maintain protection, a common practice.

3.5.3 Copyright

The situation in respect of copyright was very different to that in respect of trademarks and patents, with little progress having being made throughout the region towards the provision of effective national protection regimes. All States were signatories to the League of Arab States' 1981 Agreement on the Protection of Author's Rights, but only Kuwait, Qatar and Saudi Arabia appear to have issued domestic regulations to formally recognise the provisions of the Agreement at home. This Agreement espoused many of the principles enshrined in the Universal Copyright Convention (UCC) and some elements of the Berne Convention. However, it limited the term of protection of literary works, performances or broadcasts to the life of the author or date of performance or broadcast plus 25 years. Protection was limited to the works of nationals of the Arab signatory countries and foreign nationals resident in those countries whose own governments provided reciprocal rights. Further, the Agreement relied entirely on the signatory countries to have in place their own national copyright laws to enable the effective implementation and enforcement of the rights enshrined in the Agreement. None of the above States at that time possessed the necessary domestic legislation and hence their adoption of the Agreement was largely symbolic.

By the mid-1990s, four States possessed their own copyright laws, namely Bahrain (1993), Saudi Arabia (1989), the UAE (1992) and Yemen (1994).[88] Saudi Arabia enhanced the copyright protection environment provided by its 1989 law

87 'Regional Update' (1989), 3, *World Intellectual Property Report*, p. 12.

88 Bahrain, Legislative Decree No. 10 of 1993; Saudi Arabia, Royal Decree No. M/11 of 1410 AH (1989); UAE, Federal Law No. 40 of 1992; Yemen, Law No. 19 of 1994.

by acceding to the UCC in 1994. The UAE introduced its first copyright law in 1992, reportedly after considerable and sustained pressure from the United States for the UAE to issue copyright and neighbouring rights protection legislation.[89]

These copyright laws were deficient in respect of complying with a number of the provisions and minimum standards of copyright protection required by the Berne Convention and which would soon be required by the impending TRIPS, particularly in respect of the following matters:

- inadequate, or in some instances absence of, provision for the protection of neighbouring rights;
- existence of compulsory licensing provisions;
- absence of detailed provision on rental rights, particularly in respect of computer programs and cinematographic works;
- absence of national treatment for the protection of foreign works that had already been published abroad;
- terms of protection of only up to 25 years, much less than the minimum period of 50 years that TRIPS would stipulate;
- little or no provision for independent judicial review of decision-making processes;
- inadequate or no border-control provisions;
- sanctions which were perceived as being inadequate and with little or no deterrent effect.

Protection of foreign works was a matter of particular concern to the developed countries and to the United States in particular. Generally speaking, both the Berne Convention and the UCC require member countries to protect foreign works on the same basis as they protect national works. In terms of actual standards of protection that all members undertake to provide, the UCC requirements are few in number, modest and vaguely worded;[90] the Berne Convention, however,

89 See Reema Ali and Loubna Haddad (1996), 'WTO Membership and Compliance in the Middle East Countries', 16(2), *Middle East Executive Reports*, p. 15; Rolf Meyer-Reumann (2001), 'The Endeavours of Gulf Countries to Meet WTO Requirements', 16(1), *Arab Law Quarterly*, p. 49; Amin, op. cit., pp. 112, 126, 129.

90 The Universal Copyright Convention (UCC) comprises 25 articles, only ten of which really address substantive issues of copyright protection, and two accompanying protocols and resolutions. The UCC was developed by UNESCO as an alternative to the Berne Convention for those states which disagreed with aspects of the Convention but still wished to participate in some form of multilateral copyright protection. These states included developing countries and the Soviet Union, which thought that the strong copyright protections granted by the Berne Convention overly benefited western copyright-exporting nations, the United States and most of Latin America. The United States and Latin America were already members of a Pan-American copyright convention, which was weaker than the Berne Convention. The Berne Convention states also became party to the UCC, so that their copyrights would exist in non-Berne Convention states. Berne Convention states were concerned that the existence of the UCC would encourage parties to the Berne Convention to leave that convention and

prescribes a much more fully articulated scheme of mandatory minimum standards of protection. Adherence could therefore permit a significantly lower level of protection for foreign works than would be allowed under Berne. None of these four States with domestic copyright legislation had acceded to the Berne Convention, and, in any case, their domestic laws did not meet its standards.

Effective implementation of the above laws was hampered by the ongoing non-appearance of the necessary implementing regulations – a pattern of extended delay which often repeats itself throughout the region. Saudi Arabia's implementing regulations for its copyright law of 1989, for example, did not appear until some three years after the law was enacted. Yemen's implementing regulations for its 1994 intellectual property rights law (which included the provisions for copyright) were not issued until 2007.

This disinterest or disinclination to embrace copyright and neighbouring rights protection can be explained in part by the entrenched attitude by officialdom that copyright was still essentially a mechanism for the control of local press and publications. This attitude is reflected by the prepublication approval and registration lodgment provisions contained in the Bahraini, Saudi, Emirati and Yemeni copyright laws which, in the case of Bahrain and Saudi Arabia, were still compulsory and carried provision for the imposition of fines for non-compliance.[91]

Other areas of intellectual property for which the forthcoming TRIPS would require WTO members to provide protection – notably plant varieties, geographical indications, layout designs of integrated circuits, undisclosed information and trade secrets – remained largely ignored or overlooked and without targeted or specific protection provisions.

In respect of membership of the multilateral trading system, Kuwait became a contracting party to GATT in 1963, soon after its independence, and remained the only member from the region for many years. Thirty years later, Bahrain became a contracting party to GATT in 1993, and Qatar and the UAE both followed suit in 1994. Saudi Arabia applied to contract to GATT in 1993, enjoyed observer status at the Uruguay Round of meetings on the new WTO, and continued to seek membership of the WTO. Oman had not expressed any formal interest in contracting to GATT and was not inclined to initiate an application for membership of the WTO until 1996.

adopt the UCC instead. So the UCC included a clause stating that parties which were also Berne Convention parties need not apply the provisions of the Convention to any former Berne Convention state which renounced the Convention after 1951. Thus any state which adopts the Berne Convention is penalised if it then renounces it in favour of the UCC, since its copyrights might no longer exist in Berne Convention states (extracted from Wikipedia Encyclopaedia, available at http://en.wikipedia.org/wiki/Universal_Copyright_Convention, last accessed 26 May 2017.

91 Bahrain, Law No. 10 of 1993 concerning the Protection of Copyright, art. 35; Saudi Arabia, Royal Decree No. M/11 of 1410 AH (1989) Law on the Protection of Copyright, arts 26 and 27; UAE, Federal Law No. 40 of 1992 concerning Copyright, arts 33–36. The lodgment had to be made by the publisher and not by the author.

Jordan, Qatar, Saudi Arabia, the UAE and Yemen were members of WIPO, Jordan (1972) being the first to join and soon followed by the UAE (1974). The Yemen Arab Republic (northern Yemen) joined in December 1978, while the southern People's Democratic Republic of Yemen acceded to the WIPO convention in December 1989. After unification, WIPO recognition of the two former states was withdrawn and a unified Republic of Yemen was recognised as a member in lieu in December 1990.

None of the States had yet expressed any intention of acceding to the major international intellectual property protection agreements, such as the Berne, Paris and Rome Conventions. It has been suggested that the long-term reluctance of the States to accede to the major intellectual property conventions was not so much due to a policy of commercial isolationism or ignorance of intellectual property protection but rather an indication of their full appreciation of the commercial implications of intellectual property and its protection, and an understanding of the restrictions upon their current commercial practices that accession to the international conventions would bring.[92] The States had always been aware that their domestic production of the various forms of subject matter amenable to legal protection as intellectual property, although growing, was still far outweighed by the volumes of foreign production that they imported for local use. Accession to the international conventions was perceived as being more likely to restrict that growth than to accelerate it.[93]

One curious anomaly in this picture of general disinterest in the international intellectual property conventions is the accession by Oman (1986) and Qatar (1983) to the Nairobi Treaty on the Protection of the Olympic Symbol (see Table 3.2).[94] In Oman's case, accession took place more than a decade before it achieved membership of WIPO and almost 15 years before it acceded to any of the core intellectual property protection conventions. However, in both cases, accession could be construed more as a reflection of the keenness of the two States to become involved in the Olympic movement, for which adoption of the Nairobi Treaty was an essential political prerequisite in the absence of an international sporting pedigree, than as a commitment to intellectual property protection.

92 Hirst, op. cit., p. 10.

93 Ibid.

94 Oman, Royal Decree No. 7/1986. Qatar is listed by WIPO as having become a party to the Nairobi Treaty in July 1983, but Qatar does not appear to have issued any domestic decree or ministerial regulation, as it normally would have done, authorising this action. Saudi Arabia enacted Royal Decree No. M/2 of 1406 AH (1986), approving accession to the Nairobi Treaty, but does not appear to have lodged the instruments of accession with WIPO, which does not record it as being party to the Treaty.

TABLE 3.2 Intellectual property laws and international conventions in the Arabian Peninsula States in the early 1990s

		Bahrain	*Jordan*	*Kuwait*	*Oman*	*Qatar*	*Saudi Arabia*	*UAE*	*Yemen*
National laws	Copyright	1993	1992	–	–	–	1989	1992	1994
	Trademarks	1991	1952	1980	1987	1978	1984	1992	1994
	Patents	1977	–	1962	–	–	1989	1992	1994
	Industrial designs	1997	–	1962	–	–	–	1992	–
	Plant varieties	–	–	–	–	–	–	–	–
	Geographical indications	–	–	–	–	–	–	–	–
	Integrated circuits	–	–	–	–	–	–	–	1994
	Undisclosed information	–	–	–	–	–	–	–	1990
	Legal deposit of works	1975	1994	–	–	1982	1989	1993	
	Printed matter and publication	1979	–	1961	1984	1979	1982	1980	
Bodies	Arab Agreement on Author's Rights	–	–	1986	–	1986	1985	–	–
	GCC patent regulation	–	–	–	1993	1996	–	–	–
	League of Arab States	1971	1945	1961	1971	1971	1945	1971	1945
	GCC	1981	–	1981	1981	1981	1981	1981	–
	GATT	1993	–	1963	–	1994	–	1994	–
	WIPO	–	1990	–	–	1976	1982	1974	–

Conventions	Berne	–	–	–	–	–	–	–	–
	Paris	–	–	–	–	–	–	–	–
	Rome	–	–	–	–	–	–	–	–
	Nairobi (Olympic symbol)		–	–	1986	1983	–	–	–
	Universal Copyright Convention		–	–	–	–	1994	–	–

Source: compiled by the authors

Notes: The League of Arab States (LAS) formally adopted the Arab Agreement on Author's Rights at the Conference of LAS Ministers of Culture held in Baghdad on 5 November 1981. The Agreement was prepared with assistance and guidance from UNESCO. However, the Agreement did not come into force until 1985, when ratification by the required number of states was achieved. Accession to the Arab League did not necessarily also require formal adoption of the Agreement. It is worth noting that none of the three acceding Gulf states possessed their own copyright laws to enable them to locally implement the limited protection to copyright provided by the Agreement.

Although all GCC member states had endorsed the GCC Unified Patent Regulation, and had at various times declared that they recognised its validity, only Oman had enacted a statute formally adopting the Regulation as the Patent Law of Oman (Ministerial Regulation No. 219/1993, September 1993). In 2003, Qatar eventually enacted a similar law (Law No. 12 of 2003).

3.6 Some external influences

3.6.1 The Gulf Cooperation Council (GCC)

The Gulf Cooperation Council (GCC) has been portrayed by its advocates as the means for the fulfilment of the aspirations of the citizens of the Gulf States for some form of Arab regional unity. Accordingly, they exhort that the decision to create the GCC was not a product of the moment but an institutional embodiment of an historical, social and cultural reality reflecting the deep religious and cultural ties that link the six member States and the strong kin relations that prevail among their citizens.[95] From a more pragmatic perspective, it was also a response to a perceived threat from an Islamic fundamentalist Iran, a Ba'athist Iraq, the state of civil war in Yemen and the 1979 Soviet intervention in Afghanistan – all of which threatened to destabilise the ruling dynasties in the Arabian Peninsula and to involve their States in wider conflicts.[96]

The GCC's advocates further argue that the GCC established a cooperative framework for mutual coordination and integration in many fields in order to achieve a strong degree of regional unity.[97] According to the GCC Charter, the underpinnings for this framework are the special relations, common qualities and similar systems founded on the creed of Islam, faith in a common destiny and the sharing of one goal. These noble sentiments have not been mere hollow words; in fact, parallels might be drawn between the movement towards regional integration and the early character of the European Union before the latter reached its current highly homogeneous state.

While the GCC member States established common regional positions on such international political issues as regional security, support for Palestine and the Arab boycott of Israel, and the Iraqi invasion of Kuwait, they also had differences of opinion on these same issues. Differences of opinion and position also existed in respect of the regional protection of intellectual property rights. Apart from the issuance of its regional unified patent regulations in 1992 (later amended in 2000), and the establishment of a regional patent office in Riyadh, Saudi Arabia, the GCC as a regional body did not produce much in the way of effective contribution to the development of intellectual property protection regimes in its member States during the pre-TRIPS period. It took the regional patent office, for example, over six years from the time of its approval before it was able to commence operations and receive patent applications from October 1998. Even then, it was not able to undertake any substantive examination of the applications.

95 Gulf Cooperation Council, 'About the GCC: Objectives', p. 1, available at http://gcc-sg.org/en-us/AboutGCC/Pages/StartingPointsAndGoals.aspx, last accessed 13 June 2017.

96 See R K Ramanazi (1988), *The Gulf Cooperation Council: Record and Analysis.*

97 Gulf Cooperation Council, 'About the GCC: Charter', Preamble, available at http://gcc-sg.org/en-us/AboutGCC/Pages/Primarylaw.aspx, last accessed 13 June 2017.

A much more effective contribution to the development of intellectual property protection regimes was the ongoing willingness and practice of the government officials with responsibilities for certain elements of intellectual property matters to network with their counterparts in the other GCC member States. The networking generally focused on emerging practical issues relating to intellectual property rights such as legislative drafting, administration and systems, and enforcement practices. There is no doubt that the GCC framework facilitated this regional networking, but that is not to say that the GCC itself proactively created or fostered this networking process.

From its earliest years, the GCC also discussed a proposed regional trademark regulation, the genesis of which predated its sister unified patent regulations. The proposed regional regulation suffered from frequent review – which in part explains its non-appearance as a formal statute, but also illustrated the fluid state of regional trademark protection perceptions and regional differences of opinion. The proposed regulation did not emerge in agreed form prior to the WTO and TRIPS coming into existence. In fact, it was not concluded and agreed upon by GCC members until mid-2007, well after each state had constructed its own TRIPS-based trademark law. It is perhaps not all that surprising, then, that in terms of its contribution towards shaping the character and direction of its member States' intellectual property laws and protection regimes the GCC was overshadowed by the contributions of other regional organisations, such as the League of Arab States, and by WIPO. In particular, WIPO has had a major influence on the States' intellectual property laws, with input ranging from policy development and legislative drafting through to infrastructural capacity building, systems, staff training and public awareness education.

3.6.2 The Arabian Peninsula States and the WIPO relationship

The contribution of WIPO, and in particular its Bureau for Arab Countries, which then existed, to the development of the States' intellectual property laws during the pre-TRIPs era ranged from policy development and legislative drafting through to infrastructure development, staff training and public awareness education. As mentioned earlier, WIPO had input into the early models of intellectual property laws developed by the League of Arab States.

However, WIPO did (and does) have a particular agenda. In relation to the preparation of intellectual property legislation for the implementation of TRIPS, assistance was given in the following ways:

- preparation and submission of draft laws on all areas of intellectual property;
- preparation and submission of draft provisions to amend and update existing intellectual property laws;
- preparation and submission of comments and suggestions on draft laws prepared by (and received from) governments of developing countries.

WIPO constructed a number of draft or model laws and utilised these laws in providing legislative advice to countries which sought its assistance.[98] The laws took into account developments in intellectual property at the international level as reflected in meetings of the various WIPO committees, and WIPO used these model laws as its preferred way of implementing the provisions of the various international treaties in each particular field of intellectual property.[99]

The WIPO assistance to the Arabian Peninsula Sates included input into the creation and construction of their intellectual property laws and all States took advantage of this input. But it has also included assistance with the preparation of responses to questions from members of the WTO Council of TRIPS, both in the pre-accession examination process and in the reviews that the Council conducted of WTO developing country members which had utilised the TRIPS five-year transition period. Bahrain, Kuwait, Qatar and the UAE went through this review process. So did Oman, even though its intellectual property laws had received close scrutiny from WTO members just a year earlier as part of its WTO accession process.[100]

What stands out is that the States maintained good working relations with WIPO and its Bureau for Arab Countries. They relied on the Bureau for the formal roles stipulated above as part of the Bureau's brief on technical assistance. The other side of this positive relationship is that the laws prepared and presented by WIPO to these States as their domestic intellectual property protection regimes enshrined the formal position of WIPO as an international organisation 'dedicated to helping to ensure that the rights of creators and owners of intellectual property are protected worldwide'[101] – that is, a protectionist policy. WIPO's position, perhaps not unreasonably so from its perspective and charter, is that the incorporation of these higher standards on intellectual property protection into the States' laws at the earliest possible point – that is, at their drafting – will 'resolve problems for the developing countries before they arise'.[102]

98 WIPO's current model laws (which it also describes as 'draft laws') address the major areas of intellectual property enshrined in TRIPS, namely, Copyright and Related Rights; Geographical Indications; Trademarks; Industrial Designs; Patents; Layout-Designs (Topographies) of Integrated Circuits; Protection Against Acts of Unfair Competition, including protection of secret information.

99 See WIPO document 'Legislative Assistance Provided by the World Intellectual Property Organization (WIPO) in Relation to the Implementation of the Agreement on Trade-Related Aspects of Intellectual Property Rights (the TRIPS Agreement) and the Doha Declaration', 8 July 2003, available at www.wipo.int/ip-development/en/legislative_assistance, last accessed 26 May 2017.

100 Interview by the author with officials of the Oman Ministry of Commerce and Industry, December 2004.

101 WIPO, *General Information*, 1 (WIPO Publication No. 400(E)).

102 See Peter Drahos (2002), 'Developing Countries and International Intellectual Property Standard-setting', 5, *Journal of World Intellectual Property*, 777.

3.7 Concluding remarks – a prelude to TRIPS

TRIPS constitutes Annex IC of the Marrakesh Agreement Establishing the World Trade Organisation (WTO), which was concluded on 15 April 1994 and entered into force on 1 January 1995. In accordance with the requirements of Article II.2 of the Marrakesh Agreement, TRIPS is binding on all members of the WTO. In terms of its coverage, TRIPS is still the most comprehensive multilateral agreement on intellectual property rights, encompassing most types of rights with the particular exception of breeders' rights, utility models and traditional knowledge. It establishes minimum standards of protection in respect of:

- copyright and related rights, including computer programs and databases;
- trademarks, including service marks;
- geographical indications, including additional protection for geographical indications for wines and spirits;
- industrial designs;
- patents, including new plant varieties;
- layout designs of integrated circuits;
- undisclosed information, including trade secrets, and control of anti-competitive practices in contractual licences.

It has been suggested that TRIPS was successfully advocated by the governments of the industrialised world in order to obtain worldwide protection for the innovations and technologies generated by their corporations.[103] Industrialised countries forced developing countries to negotiate an agreement on TRIPS with a clear objective of universalising the standards of intellectual property protection that they had incorporated in their domestic legislation once they had obtained a high level of technological and industrial capacity. Correa suggests that a number of factors that converged during the 1980s and 1990s explain the priority given by some countries, notably the United States, to a far-reaching enhancement of the intellectual property system worldwide, namely:

- the growing importance of technology as a factor in international competition;
- elimination or reduction of trade barriers in developing countries, which increased both the opportunity for direct exports from those countries and their attractiveness to multinational companies to gain access to those markets without the obligation for local investment or technology transfer;
- the erosion during the 1980s of US supremacy in manufacturing and technology by Japan and subsequently Asian 'tiger economies', attributable to too-open policies in respect of technology transfer and innovation imitation.[104]

103 Carlos Correa (1998), 'Implementing the TRIPS Agreement in the Patent Field: Options for Developing Countries', 1, *Journal of World Intellectual Property*, p. 75.

104 Ibid.

The perception that this declining American competitiveness was in large part due to losses from overseas piracy and counterfeiting was effectively promoted by US industry lobbies, particularly the pharmaceutical, software and recording industries, which convinced the US government of the need to link trade and protection of intellectual property rights to preserve US technology supremacy and the consequent economic advantage. Thus TRIPS was not conceived merely as an instrument to combat counterfeiting and piracy but also as a component of a policy of 'technological protectionism' by establishing international rules to counter a declining competitive position in world markets.[105] The adoption of TRIPS represented a major victory for industrialised countries and for their most active industry lobbies. It mirrored the standards of intellectual property rights protection that were suitable for industrialised countries at their then prevailing level of development. It thus had several serious and adverse implications for developing countries, as many of its protectionist provisions could place higher obstacles in the path of these countries in their endeavours towards technological achievement.

The economies of the Arabian Peninsula States were largely driven by products outside the remit of the WTO, namely oil and gas. However, the States also saw that membership of the WTO would give them the potential to exert influence on some areas of international trade, whereas outside the WTO they would have no such ability. Yet the States also realised that they would have little choice but to join the international community that the WTO represents and to become part of the north–south argument, particularly as they tried to broaden and develop their national economic bases. The perceived significance to the States of membership of the WTO and the requisite intellectual property legislative framework as a key national political and economic strategy is illustrated by Oman's reaction to achieving WTO membership. The options before the Sultanate were perceived to be somewhat limited; it was, in effect, either accede to the WTO or face global trade isolation.

Despite a somewhat lukewarm attitude towards the WTO and the vehement criticism of its policies in some quarters, it was widely accepted that remaining outside the WTO would not be in the interests of any country, particularly a developing country. And membership of the WTO brought with it a number of other agreements and a requirement to adopt and establish laws and systems to comply with the requirements of TRIPS. While the Arabian Peninsula States may well have viewed membership of the WTO as a necessity in an international context, TRIPS was more likely perceived as just part of a total package. Even if there were misgivings in some quarters concerning its new minimum protection standards, TRIPS may well have been viewed as being largely irrelevant domestically and hence having little practical impact in the internal marketplace.

Reporting in early 1995, and just after the introduction of TRIPS, the United States Trade Representative reported that the GCC as a whole, as well as its member

105 Ibid., p. 82.

States, lacked comprehensive sets of laws and regulations to ensure effective intellectual property protection, although some progress had been made in recent years.[106] While all three major areas of intellectual property – namely trademarks, patents and copyright – received critical attention, the report was particularly scathing of the inadequate levels of protection for literary works of foreign origin, for sound and video recordings, and for a wide range of foreign goods imported for domestic consumption. It added that in no case was protection adequate for US works. The report was particularly critical of the absence of patent protection for pharmaceutical products, and of inadequate terms of protection for pharmaceutical processes in Kuwait and the UAE, lack of protection for US copyright works and sound recordings in Bahrain and the UAE, and the widespread copyright and trademark violations in Oman and Qatar. At the same time, the report acknowledged that Bahrain had strong patent and trademark laws, that Saudi Arabia had a complete and adequate patent law, and that the UAE had taken very effective steps to eliminate copyright piracy in video products. However, the report focused on the inadequacy of levels of protection for US interests and not on the degree of compliance with TRIPS requirements. In so doing, the report reveals the major US corporate influences behind the direction the report takes, namely the pharmaceutical industry and the film, recording and video industry.

Also writing on the status of intellectual property protection in the region at the time of the establishment of the WTO, one expert commentator and long-term expatriate resident of one of the States showed considerable foresight when he suggested that the pre-TRIPS period of the Uruguay Round of negotiations represented 'an era of resurgent bilateralism'. He predicted that 'the Gulf states can expect to remain under continuing pressure . . . for legislative and enforcement activity in intellectual property matters'.[107] In fact, the States would enjoy little respite from the US bilateralism for the next five years of the transitional period for TRIPS compliance and beyond. If the writer was short of the mark in his forecast, it was only in respect of an underestimation of the timing and duration of the period of US resurgent bilateralism, which continued under the banner of President George W Bush's Middle East Free Trade Area (MEFTA) strategy.[108] The States would experience the effects of the increased 'ratcheting up' of US policy in using bilateral trade agreements in the post-TRIPS climate to establish the MEFTA as one of its objectives in attempting to establish a dominating diplomatic and economic influence in the region as part of its broader international political strategy.

As this chapter has attempted to explore, the history of intellectual property protection in the Arabian Peninsula States in the pre-TRIPS era shows that foreign

106 As reported in 'USTR's Annual Report: GCC Trade and Investment Barriers' (1995), 18(5), *Middle East Executive Report*, pp. 13–17.

107 Hirst, op. cit., p. 12.

108 The US bilateral trade strategy is discussed in further detail in Chapter 8.

influences have continually made their presence felt on intellectual property protection legislation. Sometimes the foreign influences were obvious and intrusive, as in the case of the Bahrain pre-independence omnibus regulation, and at times the influences have been subtle but even more effective, as illustrated by Kuwait's post-independence introduction of commercial and civil laws based on Egyptian and French foundations. The foreign influences have been of both western and Arabic origin.

However, the next major influence of foreign origin on the development of the intellectual property regimes of the Arabian Peninsula States, and which would soon confront them, would be the creation of the WTO and the introduction and implementation of TRIPS – as Chapters 4 and 5 discuss.

4

TRIPS AND COPYRIGHT AND THE NATURE OF COMPLIANCE IN THE ARABIAN PENINSULA

Notwithstanding the passage of time, and even though it has been in force for over 21 years, TRIPS is still the primary and universally recognised multilateral agreement on global intellectual property protection. Hence it is appropriate that it is used here as the minimum standards benchmark for examining the development of the Arabian Peninsula States' intellectual property protection regimes. Because of the dimension of this task, it is undertaken over two chapters. This chapter examines the general structure and requirements of TRIPS – its Preamble, Principles and Objectives, national treatment, and most-favoured-nation (MFN) treatment. The chapter then examines the Agreement's provisions in respect of the major area of copyright and neighbouring rights and nature of the States' compliance. Chapter 5 then examines TRIPS and regional compliance in respect of the group of rights universally known as industrial property – namely, trademarks and geographical indications, patents, industrial designs, integrated circuits, plant breeder's rights and trade secrets.

4.1 Introduction – the context of TRIPS and its conventions

TRIPS was created not with the view of establishing an entirely new regulation but with the intention of supplementing and developing some sense of cohesion with the then existing major international conventions on intellectual property protection, namely the Berne, Paris and Rome Conventions, and the Washington Treaty. TRIPS is based upon and supplements these conventions by providing additional obligations and a higher level of protection. The supplemented provisions become compulsory, even for WTO member countries that have not ratified the above conventions, by virtue of their WTO membership. However, nothing in TRIPS may derogate from any existing obligations that members may have to each other under the Paris, Berne or Rome Conventions or the Washington Treaty.[1]

The general goals of TRIPS, as enunciated in its Preamble, include the reduction of distortions and impediments to international trade, the promotion of effective and adequate protection of intellectual property rights, and ensuring that measures and procedures to enforce intellectual property rights do not themselves become barriers to legitimate trade. Although the Preamble recognises that intellectual property rights are private rights, the underlying public policy objectives of national systems for the protection of intellectual property, including developmental and technological objectives, are also recognised. The Preamble also acknowledges that least-developed countries require maximum flexibility in the domestic implementation of their laws and regulations in order to enable them to create a sound and viable technological base.

The Agreement's public policy objectives are further enunciated in Part I by a declaration on the fundamental objective of TRIPS and on the equally fundamental principles by which WTO members should be guided in formulating their laws relating to the Agreement. Article 7 *Objectives* provides that:

> The protection and enforcement of intellectual property rights should contribute to the promotion of technological innovation and to the transfer and dissemination of technology, to the mutual advantage of producers and users of technological knowledge, and in a manner that is conducive to social and economic welfare, and to a balance of rights and obligations.

Article 8 *Principles* recognises that members have the right to adopt measures necessary for the protection of public health and other public interest reasons in sectors of vital importance to their socio-economic and technological development. However, such measures must still be consistent with TRIPS provisions.

TRIPS Part I (Articles 1–8) sets out further general provisions and basic principles governing the protection of intellectual property rights. It establishes minimum standards to be applied by all WTO members, these same standards also being the maximum standards that they are obliged to adopt. However, members are not constrained from adopting more extensive protection than that required by TRIPS, provided that such protection does not contravene the TRIPS provisions.

1 Specifically, members are obliged to comply with:

- Articles 1–12 and 19 of the Paris Convention, generally in respect of TRIPS Parts II, III and IV, and specifically in respect of TRIPS' provisions on trademarks, geographical indications and undisclosed information;
- Articles 1–21 (except Article 6*bis*) of the Berne Convention and its Appendix in respect of TRIPS Part II, Section 1, copyright and related rights;
- Articles 1–6, 10, 12–15 and 19 of the Rome Convention in respect of permitted exceptions to the rights of performers, producers and broadcast organisations;
- Articles 2–7 (other than Article 6.3), Article 12 and Article 16 of the Washington Treaty.

Members are also free to determine the appropriate method of implementing the TRIPS provisions within their own legal systems and practices. Articles 3–5 stipulate the fundamental obligations on national and MFN treatment of foreign nationals, which are common to all categories of intellectual property covered by the Agreement. These obligations cover not only the substantive standards of protection but also matters affecting the availability, acquisition, scope, maintenance and enforcement of intellectual property rights as well as those matters affecting the use of intellectual property rights specifically addressed in the Agreement.

TRIPS Part II (Articles 9–40) addresses each intellectual property right in succession and sets out the minimum standards of protection to be provided by each member.[2] Each of the main elements of protection is defined, namely the scope of the subject matter to be protected, the rights to be conferred and permissible exceptions to those rights, any particular special provisions (such as the reversal of burden of proof in respect of process patents), and the minimum duration of protection. TRIPS sets these standards by requiring compliance with the substantive obligations of the major pre-existing conventions and by adding a number of obligations on matters where the pre-existing conventions are silent or where they are seen by their proponents as being inadequate.

Part III (Articles 41–61) requires members to have in place enforcement procedures which permit effective action against infringements, with remedies that constitute an effective deterrent to further infringements. The procedures apply equally to all fields of intellectual property covered in Part III. The procedures must be equitable and fair, and must not be unnecessarily complicated, costly or involve unreasonable time limits or unwarranted delays, but their application must not create a barrier to legitimate trade. However, a member is not obliged to put in place a special judicial system for the enforcement of intellectual property rights distinct from that for the enforcement of law in general, nor is a member required to make a preferential allocation of resources to intellectual property enforcement at the expense of the law in general.

Part IV (Article 62) addresses the acquisition and maintenance of intellectual property rights and related *inter partes* procedures. Members may require compliance with certain procedures as a condition of enjoying intellectual property rights within that member's national boundaries, but such procedures and formalities must be reasonable and must not create an unwarranted curtailment of the period of protection of a right. Final administrative decisions in any of these procedures must be subject to review by a judicial or quasi-judicial authority.

2 TRIPS Part II, Standards Concerning the Availability, Scope and Use of Intellectual Property Rights addresses the seven intellectual property rights of Copyright and Related Rights (Articles 9–14), Trademarks (Articles 15–21), Geographical Indications (Articles 22–24), Industrial Designs (Articles 25–26), Patents (Articles 27–34), Layout Designs of Integrated Circuits (Articles 35–38), Undisclosed Information (Article 39) and Anti-competitive Practices in Contractual Licences (Article 40).

Part V (Articles 63 and 64) provides for the establishment of a multilateral mechanism for the settlement of disputes between members, in accordance with the provisions of Articles XXII and XXIII of GATT (1994) as elaborated and applied by WTO's Dispute Settlement Understanding (DSU) – a provision sought in particular by developing countries to counter the perceived likelihood of unilateral action by developed countries in respect of enforced adherence to TRIPS or greater standards.[3] Retaliatory action by one member against another may be taken only after the existence of a violation or non-compliance has been established by the WTO's Dispute Settlement Body. This mechanism is aimed at preventing unilateral actions, such as those undertaken by the United States under Section 301 of its Trade and Tariffs Act.[4]

Part VI (Article 65–67) establishes transitional arrangements for the implementation of the obligations of TRIPS. Developed countries are granted a one-year period to bring their legislation and practices into conformity with TRIPS. Developing countries and countries in the process of transformation from a centrally planned into a market economy are granted a five-year transition period, and least-developed countries are granted 11 years (except for obligations concerning national and most-favoured-nation treatment, to which the standard one-year transition applies). In addition, a further transitional period of five years is allowed for countries which are bound to introduce product patent protection in areas of technology not so protected in their territory on the general date of application of TRIPS for those countries. However, patent applications for pharmaceutical and agricultural chemical products must be accepted for filing from the very beginning of the transition period. Although granting of the patent could be deferred until the end of this period, the novelty of the invention is preserved as of the date of filing the application. If authorisation for the marketing of the relevant pharmaceutical or agricultural chemical product is obtained during the transitional period, the developing country concerned is required to offer an exclusive marketing right for the product for five years, or until a product patent is granted, whichever is the lesser period.

The final provisions and institutional arrangements, as described in Part VII (Articles 68–73), include the establishment of a Council to monitor the operation of TRIPS and, in particular, members' compliance with their TRIPS obligations. The Council was specifically directed to act in cooperation with WIPO. The Council was also required to review the implementation of TRIPS after the expiry of the five-year transitional period granted to developing countries and again at subsequent two-year intervals.

3 Carlos Correa (1998), 'Implementing the TRIPS Agreement in the Patent Field: Options for Developing Countries', 1, *Journal of World Intellectual Property*, p. 75.

4 Ibid., p. 3. United States activity under Section 301 of its Trade and Tariffs Act is examined in further detail in Chapter 8.

4.2 TRIPS and the Arabian Peninsula States

All Arabian Peninsula States have adopted TRIPS by virtue of their WTO membership. Kuwait became a contracting party to GATT, the predecessor to the WTO, in 1963, just two years after it gained its independence. Thirty years later, Bahrain, Qatar and the UAE became contracting parties to GATT, just prior to the introduction of the WTO. As such, they became foundation members of the WTO and signatories to TRIPS, and any scrutiny of their intellectual property regimes by other WTO members was notional. Jordan, Oman, Saudi Arabia and Yemen were treated differently, since all four were required to undergo a full scrutiny of their intellectual property protection regimes as part of their WTO accession processes. Oman's accession process took just four years to complete, from 1996 to 2000, while Jordan's took six years. Saudi Arabia, meanwhile, required more than 12 years of political and diplomatic wrangling before its bid for accession was successful. Saudi Arabia was finally admitted to WTO membership in November 2005, just after it finally signed a bilateral trade agreement with the United States, the last WTO member to agree to Saudi membership.

Yemen's membership campaign was even more protracted, being finally admitted in June 2014. Yemen joined the WTO in June 2014 after 14 years of difficult negotiations over the terms of its membership. As part of its accession, Yemen became signatory to TRIPS. Consequently, the Yemeni intellectual property regime faced major changes in order to be in compliance with TRIPS requirements.

Shortly after Jordan started negotiations to join the GATT in January 1994 its application was transferred to the WTO working party because of the impending establishment of WTO in 1995. Jordan sought to accede to the WTO by 1999

> because the 'Millennium Round' would raise the bar and the terms of entry would be enormous. As a result, Jordan set a self-declared deadline of 1999. Jordan succeeded in meeting the deadline as the General Council voted for Jordan's accession package on December 1999. It became a member in April 2000.[5]

4.2.1 National treatment and most-favoured-nation treatment

The national treatment provision of TRIPS forbids discrimination between a member's own nationals and the nationals of other members, and requires the member to accord treatment no less favourable than that accorded to its own nationals. The MFN treatment obligation forbids discrimination between the nationals of other members by requiring that any advantage a member grants to the nationals of another member must be extended immediately and unconditionally to the nationals

5 Bashar Malkawi (2005), 'Jordan and the World Trading System: A Case Study for Arab Countries', American University Washington College of Law, SJD dissertation, pp. 156–8.

of all other members, even if such treatment is more favourable than that which the member gives to its own nationals.

Specific provision for both the national treatment and MFN treatment obligations of TRIPS Articles 3–5 is the exception rather than the rule and appears to be somewhat inconsistently applied within the States' various laws. While most provide a general statement addressing national treatment, few make similar provision for MFN treatment.

Kuwait's new copyright law makes a declaration on MFN, stipulating that protection is extended to works published in a state that is a member of international agreements of which Kuwait is a member.[6]

Qatar also allows the protection of its copyright law to include works protected by international agreement to which Qatar is a party.[7] The Qatari trademark law of 2002, which is now overtaken by Qatar's adoption of the GCC Unified Trade Mark Law, included a slightly different provision, granting MFN on a reciprocal basis – that is, extending MFN rights to citizens of foreign countries to the same extent that those countries treated the citizens and residents of Qatar.[8]

Saudi Arabia's 2003 copyright law extends protection to works copyrighted under international agreements to which the Kingdom is a party. Yet its later industrial property law of 2004 does not make any reference to either national treatment or MFN treatment.[9]

The UAE's original trademark and patents laws of 1992 made stated provision for reciprocal treatment, the patents law also providing for the application of international treaties to which the State is a signatory (these provisions remaining unchanged in the respective 2002 amending legislation); the copyright law makes no reference to either national treatment or MFN treatment.[10]

Bahrain and Oman, no doubt reflecting the imperatives of their recent free trade agreements with the United States, adopt a slightly different approach. Rather than placing weight on the inclusion of simple declarations on national treatment or MFN treatment, they incorporate throughout their laws a significantly greater degree of detail on prerogatives, conditions and restrictions relating to rights holders which effectively ensures that equal treatment exists regardless of country of origin. Oman's copyright law alone makes any specific reference to national treatment or MFN treatment, extending such provisions in accordance with any multilateral and bilateral international treaties and conventions, to which it is a party or may become a party in the future.[11]

Likewise, the States whose laws make only passing reference to either national treatment or MFN treatment would argue, as Oman has done before the WTO,

6 Kuwait, Law No. 22 of 2016, art. 2.
7 Qatar, Law No. 7 of 2002, art. 5(4).
8 Qatar, Law No. 9 of 2002, art. 2.
9 Saudi Arabia, Royal Decree No. M/211423 (2002), art. 4; Royal Decree No. M/41 of 1424 (2003), art. 18.
10 UAE, Federal Law No. 44 of 1992, art. 2; Federal Law No. 37 of 1992, art. 5.
11 Oman, Royal Decree No. 65/2008, art. 57(f).

that the brevity of any specific provision in their laws does not necessarily preclude the enjoyment of such treatment equally by both nationals and foreign rights holders.[12] They would contend that, since their laws do not impose any nationality conditions or limitations in respect of rights holders to whom the protection of the laws might be extended to the detriment of non-nationals, national treatment and MFN treatment may be assumed; accordingly, they hold that they comply with their obligations under TRIPS Articles 3–5. In any case, brevity or absence of specific provision is more than offset by the increasing degree of obligation by the States to international conventions which themselves require commitment to national treatment and MFN treatment between the convention signatories.

Jordan's copyright law extends protection of published or unpublished works to any country that is a party to international agreements related to copyrights to which Jordan is a party; it also provides for reciprocal treatment. The copyright law also details persons who must comply with the law's provisions – for example, if the performer is a Jordanian or if the performance is done by an artist whose country has a bilateral or international agreement with Jordan in this field; or if the performance was consolidated in an audio recording protected by the Jordanian copyright law; or if the live performance was broadcast within a program protected by the law.[13] Jordan's trademark law extends protection to nationals and foreigners whose country is signatory to an international convention for mutual protection of trademarks, to which Jordan is a party.[14]

Even Yemen's pre-TRIPS law of 1994 provided a succinct declaration on national treatment to the effect that the rights relating to a work, invention, trademark or design of foreign origin shall be recognised to the extent that the foreign country concerned accords the same treatment to Yemeni works, or accords treatment in accordance with international agreements to which Yemen is a party.[15] Yemen continues on the same path with its new laws. The 2010 trademark and geographical indications law[16] and the 2011 patents, utility models, layout designs of integrated circuits and undisclosed information law extend protection to foreigners, who choose to base their effective activities in the Republic, or in a state or entity which is linked by an international agreement on intellectual property, or which has relations based on the principle of reciprocity.[17] The copyright law of 2012 provides for the protections enshrined in the law to be extended

12 WTO Council for Trade-Related Aspects of Intellectual Property Rights, *Review of Legislation: Oman*, WTO Document IP/Q/OMN/1 (03-1675), 24 March 2003.
13 Jordan, Law No. 22 of 1992, as most recently amended to Law No. 23 of 2014, art. 57.
14 Jordan, Law No. 33 of 1952 on Trademarks, as most recently amended to Law No. 15 of 2008, art. 41.
15 Yemen, Law No. 19 of 1994, arts 6, 64 and 120.
16 Yemen, Law No. 23 of 2010 on Trademarks and Geographical Indications, art. 53.
17 Yemen, Law No. 2 of 2011 on Patents, Utility Models, Layout Designs of Integrated Circuits and Undisclosed Information, art. 42.

to nationals of countries which are members of international treaties and conventions of which Yemen is also a member.[18]

4.3 Copyright and neighbouring rights

Copyright law is a form of intellectual property rights. It is considered one of the oldest and most important forms of intellectual property. The wide attention that was given to copyrights by the international community shows the level of commitment to protect copyrights and neighbouring rights. Since 1886, when the Berne Convention for the Protection of Literary and Artistic Works was created, developed countries have been working on enhancing the level of protection of copyrights in their respective countries and in developing and least-developed countries; especially with the advance of technology and the variety of works now being created.

4.3.1 TRIPS copyright provisions and obligations (Articles 9–14)

TRIPS utilises and adds to the substantive provisions enshrined in the Berne Convention, as the foundation for its copyright protection standards. TRIPS does not fully elucidate the nature of literary or artistic works entitled to protection, but instead obliges members to comply with Articles 1–21 (except Article 6*bis*) and the Appendix of the Convention, which address issues of protectable subject matter, minimum terms of protection, rights to be conferred and permissible limitations to those rights.[19] The Convention Appendix allows developing

18 Yemen, Law No. 15 of 2012 on Copyright, art. 3(b).

19 TRIPS, art. 9.1. Article 2 of the Berne Convention lists the main group of artistic and literary works which is entitled to receive protection. This group includes the following:

(1) The expression 'literary and artistic works' shall include every production in the literary, scientific and artistic domain, whatever may be the mode or form of its expression, such as books, pamphlets and other writings; lectures, addresses, sermons and other works of the same nature; dramatic or dramatico-musical works; choreographic works and entertainments in dumb show; musical compositions with or without words; cinematographic works to which are assimilated works expressed by a process analogous to cinematography; works of drawing, painting, architecture, sculpture, engraving and lithography; photographic works to which are assimilated works expressed by a process analogous to photography; works of applied art; illustrations, maps, plans, sketches and three-dimensional works relative to geography, topography, architecture or science.

. . .

(3) Translations, adaptations, arrangements of music and other alterations of a literary or artistic work shall be protected as original works without prejudice to the copyright in the original work.

. . .

(5) Collections of literary or artistic works such as encyclopaedias and anthologies which, by reason of the selection and arrangement of their contents, constitute intellectual creations shall be protected as such, without prejudice to the copyright in each of the works forming part of such collections.

countries, under certain conditions, to make some limitations to author's rights in respect of the translation and reproduction of copyright works. The provisions for the protection of moral rights, as enshrined in Article 6*bis* of the Convention, are specifically excluded from TRIPS and therefore receive neither acknowledgement nor protection. However, TRIPS Article 2.2 and Article 9.1 still require members to comply with other Convention provisions which address some moral rights elements – namely, Article 10(3) (right of attribution in quotations of the author's work), Article 11*bis*(2) (moral rights in broadcasting and public communication) and Appendix Article IV(3) (right of attribution in the case of translations or reproductions produced under licence).

TRIPS Article 9.2 confirms that copyright protection shall extend to expressions, but not to ideas, procedures, methods of operation or mathematical concepts as such. Computer programs, whether in source or object code, shall be protected as literary works under the Berne Convention and hence only those limitations that apply to literary works may be applied to computer programs.[20] Databases and other compilations of data or other material, whether in machine-readable or other form, are similarly protected, provided that they constitute intellectual creations by reason of the selection or arrangement of their contents.[21] Such protection does not extend to the data or material itself and is without prejudice to any copyright otherwise subsisting in the data or material.

TRIPS Article 11 establishes the existence of rental rights for computer programs and of cinematographic works in certain circumstances. Authors shall be provided with the right to authorise or to prohibit the commercial rental of originals or copies of their copyright works. In the case of cinematographic works, the exclusive rental right is subject to the so-called impairment test: a member is excepted from the obligation unless such rental has led to widespread copying of such works which is materially impairing the exclusive right of reproduction conferred on authors. In the case of computer programs, the obligation to provide rental rights does not apply where the program itself is not the essential object of the rental.

The related rights pertaining to performers, producers of phonograms and broadcasting organisations are stipulated in TRIPS Article 14. Rather than simply refer to the Berne Convention, as it has done in respect of literary and artistic works, TRIPS reproduces the substantive rights recognised by the Rome Convention, albeit in a simplified form. Performers may prevent the unauthorised fixation of their live performance, the reproduction of such fixation and the unauthorised broadcasting and the communication to the public of their live performance, although the right covers only aural and not audiovisual fixations. Producers of phonograms are entitled to an exclusive reproduction right and an exclusive rental right, while broadcasting organisations have the right to prohibit the unauthorised fixation, reproduction and rebroadcasting of broadcasts, as well as any other public communication of their television broadcasts.

20 TRIPS, art. 10.1.
21 Ibid., art. 10.2.

TRIPS addresses the question of terms of protection by referring back to the Berne Convention or by reproducing the provisions of the Rome Convention. In the case of an artistic or literary work, photograph or work of applied art, TRIPS defers to the Berne Convention provisions.[22] TRIPS also provides that, except for a photographic work or a work of applied art, where a minimum term is calculated on a basis other than the life of a natural person, the term shall be not less than 50 years from the end of the calendar year in which the work was published or otherwise made.[23] However, TRIPS restates the terms of protection stipulated in Article 14 of the Rome Convention for performances, phonograms and broadcasts, and extends them to 50 years for works by performers and producers of phonograms and 20 years for broadcasting organisations, calculated from the end of the year in which the performance, recording or broadcast took place.[24]

Where members permit limitations or exceptions to exclusive rights, they are required to confine them to certain special cases which do not conflict with a normal commercial exploitation of the work and which do not unreasonably prejudice the legitimate interests of the right holder. In any case, any such limitations or exceptions must remain within the extent permitted by the Berne or Rome Conventions.

4.3.2 Current regional copyright legislation

Although the Arabian Peninsula States generally have long provided some limited degree of protection to a narrow range of published artistic, literary and scientific works through laws dealing with proper commercial practice and the control of publications and publishing houses, the introduction of regional copyright protection legislation has been a recent phenomenon. The catalyst for the introduction of specific copyright laws arose more from external pressures from developed countries for frameworks to protect their copyrightable works in the region, rather than a proactive local appreciation of the imperatives for comprehensive copyright protection. As discussed earlier, not all States had copyright laws in force when TRIPS was introduced, and those laws that were in existence fell some way short of the TRIPS minimum protection standards. Hence, most were required to revisit their copyright laws with a view to bringing them at least up to the standard of TRIPS and the other major international conventions, and somewhat closer to the standards of protection being demanded by the major developed countries.

All States have undergone the process of initially enacting copyright laws and subsequently substantially amending or replacing them, in each case since 2000.

22 The Berne Convention, art. 7 provides that a literary work shall be protected for the life of the author plus 50 years, while the minimum term of protection for a photograph or work of applied art shall be 25 years.

23 TRIPS, art. 12.

24 Ibid., art. 14.5.

Oman underwent this process as part of its WTO accession process, introducing its first copyright law in 1996 at the time of its initial application but subsequently replacing it as a consequence of the WTO legislation examination process, just prior to acceding to the WTO Protocol in October 2000. It introduced further change in 2008 with Royal Decree No. 67/2008, as a consequence of its free trade agreement with the United States.

The Saudi law has been through similar scrutiny as part of its WTO membership campaign also. Its earlier decree on copyright of 1989 was replaced by an upgraded decree in 2003, prior to its accession to the WTO.

Kuwait replaced its long-standing law of 1999 in 2016. The 1999 law was deficient in the sense that it lacked basic articles and was not sufficient for today's intellectual property and societal environment. Kuwait represents the 'Hollywood' of the GCC member States because it is the hub for performers, musicians and moviemakers and all arts forums in the region. The fact that a country like Kuwait did not have an adequate law for the protection of copyrights and neighbouring rights was disappointing. However, this changed with the new law of 2016, since it is more developed insofar as it covers many topics and targets several issues which the old law lacked.

Jordan has been amending its copyright law approximately every ten years, introducing a new law in 1992 and amending it in 2005 and again in 2014. The amendment of 2014 contains major changes to the original copyright law in 1992, since it touches on the protection of neighbouring rights and folklores as well as providing for the enforcement of injunctions and other provisional measures against infringers.

The UAE's 2002 law retains levels of protection previously provided by its copyright law of a decade earlier, but strengthens the nature of the protection for computer programs and redefines the rights of performers, producers of sound recordings and broadcast organisations. The law reflects a dramatic shift in attitudes towards the protection of all copyrightable material within the UAE government, business and community environments since the original law was implemented.

Yemen modelled its new copyright law of 2012 on the WIPO model copyright law.[25] The law covers neighbouring rights, the protection of folklore for the same term of protection as for other kinds of works, which were not included or described in detail in the older 1994 version of the law.[26]

Qatar introduced its current copyright law in 2002, replacing an earlier law enacted in July 1995. It is reportedly in the process of upgrading the 2002 law.

Kuwait, Jordan and Oman represent the benchmark for regional copyright protection, both in terms of the standards and the comprehensive nature of their respective laws. Jordan and Oman have recently upgraded their laws to give effect to the substantially increased levels of copyright protection arising from their

25 Yemen, Law No. 15 of 2012 on the Protection of Copyright and Related Rights.
26 Yemen, Presidential Law Decree No. 19 of 1994 in respect of Intellectual Property.

obligations under their respective free trade agreements with the United States. Particular attention has been given to protection and enforcement of copyright in the digital environment. Consequently, they each possess the most advanced and comprehensive copyright laws in the region.

All States have now acceded to the Berne Convention, although this does not necessarily greatly enhance the level of copyright protection they provide – with the exception of the protection of an author's moral rights, the standards of the Berne Convention have already been largely incorporated into TRIPS. More recently, most of the States, with the exception of Kuwait, Saudi Arabia and Yemen, have also acceded to the WIPO Internet Treaties, namely the WIPO Copyright Treaty (WCT) and the WIPO Performances and Phonograms Treaty of 1996 (WPPT), both of which aim at providing enhanced levels of protection for technological and internet-based copyright material.

4.3.3 The subject matter of copyright protection

Among the copyright laws of the States, an author is variously defined as:

> except as proven otherwise, any person who publishes a work and claims authorship either by stating his name on the work or by using any other means to claim authorship of the work.[27]

Or elsewhere, quite simply as 'the natural person who creates the work'.[28]

The declared purpose common to all the copyright laws is to protect the authors of creative works which are of a literary, scientific, artistic and cultural nature in general regardless of the nature of such works, or the type thereof, or the method of expression used therein, or the purpose of writing or creation.[29] The laws generally replicate the range of protectable works as listed in the Berne Convention Article 2, including derived works with creative elements and translated works. As stipulated by the Bahraini, Kuwaiti and Omani laws (in virtually identical lists), created works of literature, arts and science enjoy protection regardless of their value, type, form of expression or purpose of production. The protected works include:

- books, booklets, articles, pamphlets and other written works;
- computer programs and databases, whether in the source or object code;

27 Kuwait, Law No. 22 of 2016, art. 1 and UAE Federal Law No. 7 of 2002 both include almost identical definitions.

28 Bahrain, Legislative Decree No. 22 of 2006, art. 1; Oman, Royal Decree No. 65/2008, art. 1; Qatar, Law No. 7 of 2002, art. 1; Saudi Arabia, Royal Decree No. M/48 of 1424 (2003), art. 1.

29 Bahrain, Legislative Decree No. 22 of 2006, art. 2; Oman, Royal Decree No. 65/2008, art. 2; Qatar Law No. 7 of 2002, art. 2; Saudi Arabia, Royal Decree No. M/41 of 1424 AH (2003), art. 2; UAE, Federal Law No.7 of 2002, art. 2.

- works that are delivered orally such as lectures, speeches, sermons and other oral works of a similar nature;
- dramatic and dramatico-musical works, dances, pantomimes and other works created for theatrical performance;
- musical compositions with or without words;
- audiovisual works such as cinematographic works and works for television;
- line or colour drawings, sculptures, engravings, lithography, printing on fabric, wood or metals, and any similar works in the field;
- photographic works and works analogous to photography;
- works of applied and plastic arts either handcrafted or industrial;
- illustrations, geographical maps, designs, sketches and three-dimensional works related to geography, topography, architecture or science;
- the title of the work if creative.[30]

Also protected are derivative works, such as translations, adaptations and orchestrations, as well as collections of works and expressions of folklore, such as encyclopedias and anthologies, provided there is creativity in the selection or the arrangement of the contents of such works.[31]

By the same token, the copyright laws replicate the Berne Convention's list of works to which protection is commonly not extended, such as legislation, court judgments and administrative determinations, international agreements and treaties, official documents and their translations, or news which is published, broadcast or otherwise placed in the public domain. However, they also generally make provision for the protection to be extended to folklore or works of national culture, which are not mentioned in either TRIPS or the Convention.

The States provide an added measure of protection for software, with specific attention given to infringements, and penalties in particular being increased in respect of technology-related offences. In respect of the requirement of TRIPS Article 10, computer programs and software are generally included in those works to which protection is extended, and described in sufficiently broad terms to give some degree of flexibility to allow for technological advances. Databases are also protected if they are creative in the arrangement and selection of their subject matter. The extent of the exception to this provision is very limited – such as the Saudi provision for the production of 'one reserve copy of computer programs . . . for the purpose of protecting the original, whilst keeping the original with the user, to show upon request'.[32] The Emirati law covers even more ground than the other States by allowing for further discretion to be granted to the responsible

30 As stipulated in Bahrain, Legislative Decree No. 22 of 2006, art. 2; Oman, Royal Decree No. 65/2008, sect. 2.

31 Bahrain, Legislative Decree No. 22 of 2006, art. 3; Kuwait, Law No. 22 of 2016, art. 3; Oman, Royal Decree No. 65/2008, sect. 3.

32 Saudi Arabia, Royal Decree No. M/41 1424 AH (2003), art. 15(12).

minister to determine what may constitute computer programs and applications, databases and works analogous to them, to which protection may be later extended as further technological advances may require.[33]

Kuwait goes further than the other States. It addresses and provides special attention to computer programs, software and data. It provides that the economic rights are protected and may be transferred with regard to the licensing agreement that is listed on the program. It also provides a term of protection of 50 years. Moreover, in the case of an infringement in which technology or software is used to violate the rights of a right holder, the sanctions are increased to two years' imprisonment and/or a maximum fine of KD50,000.[34]

In accordance with the exception provision of TRIPS Article 13, the laws allow for a limited range of circumstances and situations in which protected works may be used without the permission of the author or right holder. They generally include limited reasonable use by libraries and educational institutions, use for teaching and research, use in news or current affairs in print or broadcast media, and personal use. Kuwait adds to the TRIPS exceptions by providing that a person may use a work without the approval of the right holder to promote that work to an audience, or to present in a convention or workshop as long as it is not used for a commercial reason. In addition, a person can show part of a work of another for the purpose of obtaining opinions and criticism about it. [35]

Jordan and Kuwait distinguish the right of ownership to a work in case of employment contracts. As a general rule, if a person creates a work for the account of another, the copyright is accorded to the author, unless agreed otherwise in writing. This situation happens in biographies and memoirs. However, if an employee creates during the term of his employment contract a work related to the activities or businesses of his employer or utilises the employer's expertise, data, tools, equipment or materials placed at the employee's disposal, the copyright of such works belongs to the employer after taking into consideration the intellectual effort of the employee. On the other hand, if the creation is not related to the businesses of the employer, and the employee did not utilise any of the employer's expertise, data, tools or primary material for the creation, the intellectual property rights belong to the employee unless agreed otherwise in writing.[36]

4.3.4 Terms of protection

Except for Bahrain and Oman, the States generally adhere to the requirements of TRIPS Articles 12 and 14.5, and the Berne Convention Articles 7 and 7*bis* in

33 UAE Federal Law No. 7 of 2002, art. 2(2).

34 Kuwait, Law No. 22 of 2016, arts 12, 21 and 41.

35 Kuwait, Law No. 22 of 2016, art. 29.

36 Jordan, Law No. 22 of 1992 on Copyright, as most recently amended to Law No. 23 of 2014, art. 6; Kuwait, Law No. 22 of 2016, art. 2.

TABLE 4.1 Current copyright laws and international conventions in the GCC member States

Bahrain	Legislative Decree No. 22 of 2006 with respect to the Protection of Copyright, as amended by Law No. 50 of 2014
	Legislative Decree No. 19 of 2005 ratifying Bahrain's accession to the WIPO Performances and Phonograms Treaty (WPPT) and the WIPO Copyright Treaty (WCT)
	Legislative Decree No. 1 of 2005 approving Rome Convention for the Protection of Performers, Producers of Phonograms and Broadcasting Organizations
	Legislative Decree No. 30 of 1996 ratifying the Bahrain's accession to the Berne Convention for the Protection of Literary and Artistic works
Kuwait	Law No. 22 of 2016 governing Copyrights and Neighbouring Rights
	Law No. 35 of 2014 ratifying Kuwait's accession to the Berne Convention for the Protection of Literary and Artistic Works
	Law No. 16 of 1986 acceding to the Arab Agreement for the Protection of Author's Rights
Oman	Royal Decree No. 65/2008, the Law of Copyrights and Neighbouring Rights
	Royal Decree No. 53/2005 ratifying Oman's accession to the WIPO Performances and Phonograms Treaty (WPPT) and the WIPO Copyright Treaty (WCT)
	Royal Decree No. 63/1998 ratifying Oman's accession to the Berne Convention for the Protection of Literary and Artistic Works and the Paris Convention for the Protection of Industrial Property
Qatar	Law of July 2005 in respect of Qatar's accession to the WIPO Performances and Phonograms Treaty (WPPT) and the WIPO Copyright Treaty (WCT)
	Law No. 7 of 2002 in respect of Copyrights and Neighbouring Rights
	Law No. 31 of 2001 in respect of Qatar's accession to the Berne Convention for the Protection of Literary and Artistic works
	Law No. 50 of 1986 in respect of Qatar's accession to the League of Arab States Agreement for the Protection of Author's Rights
Saudi Arabia	Royal Decree No. M/41 of 1424 AH (2003) concerning Copyright
	Royal Decree No. M/48 of 1424 AH (2003) ratifying Saudi Arabia's accession to the Berne Convention for the Protection of Literary and Artistic Works and the Paris Convention for the Protection of Industrial Property
	Royal Decree No. M/12 of 1414 AH (1994) assenting to the Universal Copyright Convention
UAE	Federal Law No. 10 of 2005 ratifying the UAE's accession to the WIPO Performances and Phonograms Treaty (WPPT)
	Federal Law of October 2004 ratifying the UAE's accession to the International Convention for the Protection of Performers, Producers of Phonograms and Broadcasting Organizations (Rome Convention)
	Federal Law of April 2004 ratifying the UAE's accession to the WIPO Copyright Treaty (WCT) and the Berne Convention for the Protection of Literary and Artistic Works
	Federal Law No. 7 of 2002 concerning Copyright and Neighbouring Rights

Source: compiled by the authors

TABLE 4.2 Current copyright laws and international conventions in Jordan and Yemen

Jordan	Law of 1992 with respect to the protection of Copyright, as amended up to Law 3 of 2014
	Law of 2004 ratifying Jordan's accession to the WIPO Performances and Phonograms Treaty (WPPT) and the WIPO Copyright Treaty (WCT)
	Law of 1999 ratifying Jordan's accession to the Berne Convention for the Protection of Literary and Artistic Works
Yemen	Law No. 15 of 2012 in respect of Copyright and Related Rights
	Law No. 14 of 2008 ratifying Yemen's accession to the Berne Convention for the Protection of Literary and Artistic Works

Source: compiled by the authors

respect of minimum terms of protection granted to copyrightable works, with provision commonly existing as follows:

- for works of a sole author, the lifetime of the author plus 50 years;
- in respect of the works of joint authors, the lifetime of the last surviving author plus 50 years;
- for works published under a pseudonym, anonymously (unless the identity of the author becomes known) or posthumously, 50 years from first publication;
- for cinematographic works, works of applied articles and photographic works, 50 years from first publication;
- for works of performers, 50 years from the first recording of the performance or, if no recording was made, from the first performance;
- for works of producers of sound recordings, 50 years from the first production, publication or fixation (if not published) of the sound recording;
- for works whose ownership is vested in a legal entity, 50 years from the first publication or production;
- for broadcasts, 20 years from the date of first broadcast.

The period of protection is generally calculated from the beginning of the year following the year in which the death of the author occurred, or the first publication, production, recording, fixation or broadcast took place, although some exceptions do exist.

The Kuwaiti law provides a term of protection for encyclopedias and anthologies, in which each chapter or a book of the encyclopedia is published separately, of 50 years, calculated from the release date of the chapter or book. The law also provides a period of protection of 50 years for computer programs and software.[37] The Saudi copyright law distinguishes between the main corpus

37 Kuwait, Law No. 22 of 2016, art. 25.

of artistic works and photographs and works of applied arts. It extends to photographs and works of applied arts a period of protection of only 25 years, which is actually consistent with the standards set by TRIPS Article 12 and Berne Convention Article 7(4).[38] Similarly, the Jordanian law distinguishes between cinematic and television production works and works of applied arts by setting the protection of the latter for 25 years and the former for 50 years, thereby being consistent with TRIPS Article 12. [39] Other States do not bother to make the Saudi or TRIPS/Berne distinction between these and other literary or artistic works, thereby neatly avoiding the necessity of otherwise defining works of applied articles and distinguishing them from other works.

The Bahraini and Omani laws, meanwhile, offer significantly increased periods of protection, to reflect their obligations under the intellectual property protection provisions of their recent free trade agreements with the United States. Hence, Bahrain has extended protection for the above categories for a further 20 years to a total of 70 years, with the exception of broadcasts which still enjoy the limited 20 years' protection.[40]

Oman provides an even further extensive period of protection and in so doing has established a whole new benchmark for the region. In accordance with the terms of its free trade agreement, literary works are protected for the life of the author plus 70 years, while joint works enjoy protection for 70 years following the year of the death of the last surviving author.[41] However, audiovisual works and collective works, anonymous and pseudonymous works, performances and sound recordings are all now protected for 95 years following the year of first publication.[42] Furthermore, if such works are not published or otherwise made public within their first 25 years, protection exists for 120 years following their creation. Broadcasting programmes retain the commonplace 20-year period of protection.

4.3.5 Moral rights and economic rights

Although TRIPS specifically excludes any provision for the protection of an author's moral rights *per se*, they receive attention in the Berne Convention and are addressed in the copyright laws of all the Arabian Peninsula States. The laws all draw a distinction between an author's moral rights and economic rights and, in some cases, between those of the performer. The laws generally provide that the author's moral rights are inalienable and include the right to decide whether his work should be published and the manner of its publication; while the economic rights encompass the right to utilise his work commercially or to

38 Saudi Arabia, Royal Decree No. M/41 of 1424 AH (2003), art. 19(1)(6).

39 Jordan, Law No. 22 of 1992 on Copyright, as most recently amended to Law No. 23 of 2014, arts 31–32.

40 Bahrain, Legislative Decree No. 22 of 2006, Chapter 7, arts 37–44.

41 Oman, Royal Decree No. 65/2008, arts 26–27.

42 Ibid., arts 28–33.

authorise others to do so.[43] The scope of the author's moral rights includes the right to:

- have his/her name or pseudonym indicated on his/her work;
- object to any alteration, deformation or any modification of his/her work;
- object to any distortion and to prohibit any other use of the work which would be prejudicial to the author's honour or reputation;
- withdraw the work from publication, under certain circumstances.

Jordan provides authors with the right to prevent others from altering, deforming or any modifying their work; however, Jordan limits this right to the extent that does not cross or interfere with someone else's rights. Hence, an author has no right to prevent any alteration or modification in a translated work unless 'the translator fails to note the places of such modification or should the translation prejudice the author's reputation and cultural or artistic standing or distorts the content of the work'.[44]

Economic rights include the exclusive right of the author to commercially exploit the work by carrying out, or authorising others to carry out, any of the following acts:

- reproduction of the work;
- translation of the work;
- making excerpts, musical arrangement or other transformation of the work;
- distribution to the public of the work through sale;
- rental to the public of audiovisual works or computer programs;
- public performance of the work;
- communication of the work to the public.

Jordan also adds that the author has the exclusive right to publish his personal letters. However, the copyright law prevents the author from exercising this right unless they obtain a prior approval from the original recipient or successors of those letters, especially if publication of those letters will harm the recipient.[45]

The economic rights are transferable to other parties. Such transfer must generally be in writing and be registered and lodged with the relevant ministry for it to be valid and have legal standing. The rights are also transferable wholly or in part by inheritance or by legal action. The Jordanian, Kuwaiti, Qatari, Saudi and Yemeni laws also stipulate that, where an author dies intestate, the rights

43 Bahrain, Legislative Decree No. 22 of 2006, art. 5; Kuwait, Law No. 22 of 2016, arts 6–7; Oman, Royal Decree No. 65/2008, art. 5; Qatar, Law No. 7 of 2002, arts 7–14; Saudi Arabia, Royal Decree No. M/41 of 1424 AH (2003), arts 8–9; UAE, Federal Law No. 7 of 2002, arts 5, 7–8; Yemen, Law No. 19 of 1994, arts 12–13 and 18–19.

44 Jordan, Law No. 22 of 1992, as most recently amended to Law No. 23 of 2014, art. 8(D).

45 Jordan, Law No. 22 of 1992, as most recently amended to Law No. 23 of 2014, art. 10.

devolve to the persons entitled to receive them, according to the provisions of the *Shariah* in respect of inheritance.[46] The Jordan and Yemen laws go a little further by regulating the persons entitled to economic rights of a deceased author by stating that when an author passes away without any heirs, any co-authors will have the exclusive rights over the joint work.[47]

> It is important to note that the distinction in the treatment between economic and moral rights reflects the balance within the copyright laws of the members of the GCC for accommodating natural rights theories and utility theories for copyright. The utility of copyright justifies the protection of copyright for as long as the protection constitutes an incentive to create and no more. Economic rights are the means for benefiting from a work and therefore provide an incentive for the author to create. Moral rights on the other hand extend from the relationship between the author and the work and are not meant to provide an incentive for the author to create. Their perpetual protection also does not unreasonably limit the ability of society to benefit from a work, even after the expiry of the copyright term over the economic right, and therefore do not obstruct the utility aspect of copyright protection.[48]

The notion of providing any form of protection for neighbouring rights was largely unknown in the region and was therefore conspicuously absent from the States' copyright laws until first incorporated by Oman into its law of 2000.[49] The current laws now generally provide an enhanced level of protection for performers, producers of sound recordings and broadcasting organisations. Saudi Arabia, however, generally defers the specification of such rights to its corresponding responsible authorities to detail through ministerial regulation. The laws differentiate between the respective rights of the performer, producer and broadcaster, bringing these laws more into line with the requirements of TRIPS Article 14. They generally provide for performers to have the moral right to be identified with respect to their performances and to object to any distortion, mutilation or any modification of their performances. They also enjoy economic rights to:

- fix or record their unfixed performances;
- broadcast or communicate to the public their unfixed performances;

46 Qatar, Law No. 7 of 2002, art. 29; Jordan, Law No. 22 of 1992 as most recently amended to Law No. 23 of 2014, art. 21; Kuwait, Law No. 22 of 2016, art. 9; Saudi Arabia, Royal Decree No. M/11 of 1410, art. 17; Yemen, Law No. 15 of 2012, art. 7.

47 Jordan, Law No. 22 of 1992 as mostly recently amended to Law No. 23 of 2014, art. 22; Yemen, Law No. 15 of 2012, art. 17.

48 Riyadh Al Balushi, Noora Al Lawati, and Muluk Mohsin (2017), 'The Term of Protection of Economic Rights under the Copyright Laws of the GCC', in David Price and Alhanoof AlDebasi (eds) *Intellectual Property Rights: Development and Enforcement in the Arab States of the Gulf*, p. 72.

49 Alastair Hirst (2002, 'A Comprehensive Reform of the UAE Copyright Law', 1, *Middle East Executive Reports*, p. 17.

- reproduce sound recordings containing an unauthorised fixation of their performances;
- rent sound recordings containing their performances;
- make recordings of their performances available to the public.[50]

The Jordanian copyright law states that the performer retains the moral right of attribution in respect of a live performance or an audio recording, even when the economic rights are transferred to other parties. However, if the actual making use of the work prevents attribution to the performer, the right may not apply. However, the performer still enjoys the moral right of integrity and may object to any infringement to their rights and to prohibit any distortion or perversion or any other alteration to the performance if it harms their reputation.[51]

Producers of sound recordings and broadcast organisations, meanwhile, enjoy only economic rights, such rights being the exclusive right to carry out or authorise the direct or indirect reproduction of their recordings or broadcasts in any form, the rental or sale to the public of copies of the recording, or the rebroadcasting of the original broadcast.[52] Jordan, Kuwait, Qatar, the UAE and Yemen place limits on these rights. Qatar restricts the rental right of performers and producers to sound recordings only, without recognising the rental rights of broadcasters; Jordan, the UAE and Yemen extend the rental right of performers to audiovisual works, but do not recognise rental rights for broadcast organisations. Kuwait recognises rental rights to performers, producers of sound recordings and broadcasters, but does not extend this right to audiovisual works unless agreed otherwise.[53] The Jordanian copyright law states that:

> Any broadcasting entity shall have exclusivity of the rights in regard to its programs:
>
> - Consolidate its programs or record or reproduce these recordings. This shall apply to direct and indirect reproduction.
> - Rebroadcast its programs and transfer it to the public.[54]

50 Bahrain, Legislative Decree No. 22 of 2006, arts 14–15; Jordan, Law No. 22 of 1992, as most recently amended to Law No. 23 of 2014, art. 23(a); Kuwait, Law No. 22 of 2016, art. 8; Oman, Royal Decree No. 65/2008, art. 15; Qatar, Law No. 7 of 2002, art. 40; UAE, Federal Law No. 7 of 2002, art. 16.

51 Jordan, Law No. 22 of 1992, as most recently amended to Law No. 23 of 2014, art. 23(b).

52 Bahrain, Legislative Decree No. 22 of 2006, arts 16–17; Jordan, Law No. 22 of 1992, as most recently amended to Law No. 23 of 2014, art. 23(c); Kuwait, Law No. 22 of 2016, art. 16–18; Oman, Royal Decree No. 65/2008, arts 16–17; Qatar, Law No. 7 of 2002, arts 41–42; UAE, Federal Law No. 7 of 2002, arts 18–19; Yemen Law No. 15 of 2012, arts 25–30.

53 Qatar, Law No. 7 of 2002, art. 40(2); UAE, Federal Law No.7 of 2002, art. 17; Yemen, Law No. 15 of 2012, arts 26–28.

54 Jordan, Law No. 22 of 1992, as most recently amended to Law No. 23 of 2014, art. 23(d).

The distinction between the respective rights of the various contributors to joint and collective works receives somewhat briefer attention than that devoted to rights of performers, producers and broadcasters.[55] Where the respective contributions in respect of joint works can be identified and separated, each contributor enjoys his moral and economic rights in respect of his part separately to the other contributors and may exploit his own part provided that this does not prejudice the exploitation of the jointly owned work. But where the respective contributions cannot be separated, all are considered equal partners in the ownership of the whole work, unless they have otherwise agreed, and no partner may solely exercise any rights without the agreement of the other partners.

In the case of a joint musical composition, the composer retains the exclusive right to the public performance, execution, publication or copying of the whole work, but without prejudice to the right of the lyricist to separately publish his own created part.[56] Where the joint musical production involves choreography which has special predominance or elements, such as opera or ballet, the choreographer may utilise a public performance of the whole work, while the composer may utilise the musical element provided that he does not use it as a basis for another musical work, unless otherwise agreed.

In the case of a joint work for cinema, radio, television or other broadcast, contributing partnership includes the scenarist or author, the scriptwriter, the editor or adaptor, the composer, the director and the original author if the joint work is an adaptation or extraction from another prior work.[57] Also, if an author refuses to complete the assigned work for any reason, the co-authors can continue on the work and the author's moral and economic rights are restricted to the individual contribution only.[58] The scenarist, scriptwriter, editor and director are jointly entitled to produce the adapted work, notwithstanding any objections from the author of the original work or musical composer but without prejudice to the rights of these two resulting from their participation in the joint composition. The author and composer are still entitled to publish their respective parts of the work in any other manner, unless otherwise agreed.

Where the respective contributions cannot be distinguished or identified and the work was created under the direction of a natural person or legal entity who also undertakes responsibility for publication, that person or legal entity is

55 Bahrain, Legislative Decree No. 22 of 2006, art. 32; Oman, Royal Decree No. 65/2008, art. 21; Qatar, Law No. 7 of 2002, art. 46; UAE, Federal Law No. 7 of 2002, art. 25.

56 Bahrain, Legislative Decree No. 22 of 2006, arts 31–32; Jordan, Law No. 22 of 1992, as most recently amended to Law No. 23 of 2014, art. 11; Kuwait, Law No. 22 of 2016, art. 24; Oman, Royal Decree No. 65/2008, art. 25; Qatar, Law No. 7 of 2002, art. 35; Saudi Arabia, Royal Decree No. M/41 of 1424 AH (2003), art. 5(3); UAE, Federal Law No. 7 of 2002, art. 27; Yemen, Law No. 15 of 2012, arts 16–23.

57 Bahrain, Legislative Decree No. 22 of 2006, art. 35; Kuwait, Law No. 22 of 2016, art. 25; Oman, Royal Decree No. 65/2008, art. 24; Qatar, Law No. 7 of 2002, art. 36; Saudi Arabia, Royal Decree No. M/41 of 1424 AH (2003), art. 5; UAE, Federal Law No. 7 of 2002, art. 27.

58 Yemen, Law No. 15 of 2012, art.24.

entitled to enjoy both the moral and the economic rights involved in creating the collective work.[59]

4.3.6 Translated works and compulsory licensing

Some States take advantage of the provision in respect of the translation of foreign works, as allowed by TRIPS Article II, which provides *inter alia* that a member may grant to one of its nationals a licence to translate and publish a foreign-language work which has not been translated and published in that member State within three years of the original publication of the work. This provision, which amounts to a form of compulsory licensing, continues to meet with opposition from some developed countries and particularly the copyright exporting countries, which see it as a form of potential encroachment on the monopolistic nature of their copyright rights and a potential loss of income generation. It is an area which has been discussed in the United States free trade agreements with both Bahrain and Oman. Perhaps not surprisingly, therefore, Bahrain and Oman have removed such provisions from their current copyright laws. However, it is surprising that Jordan, having also signed a free trade agreement with the United States in 2001, has revised its copyright law several times since with no change to the compulsory licensing provisions.

While an author's right to translate their work (or to authorise others to do so) is generally acknowledged, Jordan, Qatar, Saudi Arabia, the UAE and Yemen make provision for the responsible minister to grant a non-exclusive and non-assignable licence for translation of foreign-language works. Such a licence allows translation into Arabic and/or the domestic publication of an Arabic translation of a foreign-language work if the author of the original work fails to exercise translation rights within a specified period of time (generally 3–5 years) after its original publication.[60] As a general principle, the ministerial authority is restricted to foreign works which may be desirable or necessary for educational or research purposes, but it may also be exercised where it would be in the public interest to do so. Saudi Arabia extends this right to works that have already been translated and published in Arabic in the Kingdom, but which have gone out of print and the author or translator has failed to authorise further publication.[61] Kuwait allows for the responsible office to grant a non-exclusive and non-assignable licence to translate as long as it is for educational reasons and in the public interest. The

59 Bahrain, Legislative Decree No. 22 of 2006, arts 33 and 35; Kuwait, Law No. 22 of 2016, art. 23; Oman, Royal Decree No. 65/2008, arts 22–23; Qatar, Law No. 7 of 2002, art. 34; Saudi Arabia, Royal Decree No. M/41 of 1424 AH (2003), art. 6(3); UAE, Federal Law No. 7 of 2002, art. 26.

60 Qatar, Law No. 7 of 2002, art. 27; Jordan, Law No. 22 of 1992, as most recently amended to Law No. 23 of 2014, art. 11(c); Saudi Arabia, Royal Decree No. M/41 of 1424 AH (2003), art. 16; UAE, Federal Law No. 7 of 2002, art. 21; Yemen, Law No. 15 of 2012, art, 48.

61 Saudi Arabia, Royal Decree No. M/41 of 1424 AH (2003), art. 16.

licensee must still provide a fair compensation to the right holder. The law does not prevent the right holder from also exploiting the work. The law does not specify a certain period of time in order to grant the licence, which provides more flexibility for the responsible author to decide when to grant the licence.[62]

4.3.7 Management of collective rights

The principle of collective-rights management and practice of creating copyright collection and protection societies goes beyond TRIPS and the Berne Convention. Although the principle and practice is now common in developed countries, it has only recently started to gain wide acceptance and recognition in the Arabian Peninsula States.

Bahrain, Kuwait, Oman and the UAE have taken some steps towards copyright protection management by including provision for the collective administration of copyright and the neighbouring rights. They give specialised collection societies legal status and enable the holders of copyright and the neighbouring rights to assign their economic rights to them to commercially exploit and administer on the right holders' behalf.[63] The collection societies are forbidden to discriminate between the right holders with whom they enter into management contracts. They must keep registers including the names of their members, their positions and the jobs they contracted, indicating the type of job, duration and the agreed licensing fees. The societies must be registered and annually licensed by the responsible ministry and must inform the ministry of any change in these registers.

One likely impact of the Bahraini, Kuwaiti, Omani and UAE provisions is that collective management organisations already established in developed countries may well be encouraged to establish operations or set up regional associations. Such activity would not only improve the enforcement of domestic copyright and neighbouring rights protection but also spearhead the spread of collective management societies to the other States. Such activity would also benefit the right holders and serve as another effective mechanism for the control of unauthorised and counterfeit copyrightable works of all descriptions. Currently, effective copyright collection agencies do not operate in the Arabian Peninsula region.

4.3.8 Infringements

The nature of copyright infringement provisions in the earlier copyright laws of the GCC member States dealt mainly with the traditional form of unauthorised reproduction of print material. In the more recent laws, there has emerged a pattern of increasing complexity in the nature of the infringing acts, accompanied by a shift

62 Kuwait, Law No. 22 of 2016, art. 32.

63 Bahrain, Legislative Decree No. 22 of 2006, arts 57–61; Kuwait, Law No. 22 of 2016, art. 33; Oman, Royal Decree No. 65/2008, arts 35–39; UAE, Federal Law No. 7 of 2002, arts 30–33.

in emphasis away from the more conservative or conventional forms of infringement involving print-based or hard-copy material towards infringing acts within an electronic/digital context.

Although the States still recognise the traditional or conventional infringements against a right holder's moral rights, they also recognise infringements against economic rights, such as unlawful alteration, publication, reproduction, translation, performance and broadcast, and importation or promotion of any imitated or forged works. The newer laws of Bahrain, Jordan, Kuwait and Oman now include fairly extensive provisions in respect of infringing acts in the digital context, notably relating to technological protection measures, rights management information and the responsibilities and liabilities of internet service providers.

There is a strong common element across the description of unlawful acts (which are also described as unlawful, prohibited, infringements or offences) across the States. These common elements enable the unlawful acts to be generally categorised into two broad groups. The first broad group encompasses any act that constitutes an infringement on the moral and/or economic rights of the right holder, such as:

- exercising any of the right holder's exclusive rights without the right holder's approval;
- making a copyrighted work available to the public or displaying the work, performance, audio recording or radio programme through computers or software and programs or telecommunications networks or other methods or other means;
- publishing, selling or renting or otherwise trading in a copyrighted work or sound recording, broadcast or audiovisual work without authorisation;
- amending a work, its nature, subject or title without the knowledge of the author and prior written consent.

The second broad group encompasses acts relating to satellite broadcasts, technological protection devices or systems and rights management information, such as:

- deactivating any devices or instruments preventing or limiting the reproduction of a copyrighted work;
- removing, modify or falsely adding any electronic data relating to copyright administration and rights;
- importing, selling or otherwise trading in equipment, systems or software that enables unauthorised reception or download of satellite programmes.

This second group is more commonly seen as the more serious of unlawful acts and therefore attracting more severe penalties. Kuwait's copyright law, for example, provides for a maximum term of imprisonment of two years and/or a fine of no less than KD500 and no more than KD50,000 for the first group above, but provides for a maximum term of imprisonment of two years and/or a fine of no less than KD1,000 and no more than KD100,000 for the second group relating to satellite broadcasts, technological protection devices and rights management information.[64]

Oman's copyright law provides a sound example of the common range of unlawful acts, although it should be noted that its list and descriptors are somewhat more comprehensive than most of the other States. This arises mainly from its obligations under its FTA with the United States, as well as the recent appearance of its law:

> 1 – Sells, leases, or transacts a copy of work protected in accordance with the provisions of this law, without the consent of the right holder.
> 2 – Intentionally violates any of the protected moral or economic copyrights or neighbouring rights protected by the provisions of this law.
> 3 – Intentionally violates any of the protected moral or economic copyrights or neighbouring rights protected by the provisions of this law for the purpose of realising commercial benefits or achieving private financial gains, or intentionally violates any of the author's rights even without meaning to, directly or indirectly realising financial gains.
> 4 – Intentionally violates the economic right of a work in the Sultanate of Oman by its publication abroad, or offering it for further distribution, or export.
> 5 – Commits any of the prohibited actions prescribed in paragraphs (1, 2, 3) of Article (40) of this Law with the purpose of realising commercial profits or private financial gain, unless the perpetrator was a non-profit public library, a document-keeping agency, educational or scientific or cultural institution, or a non-commercial governmental broadcasting corporation.
> 6 – Knowingly traffics in counterfeit labels affixed or designed to be affixed to: a sound recording, a copy of a computer program, documentation or packaging for a computer program, or an audiovisual work.
> 7 – Knowingly traffics in counterfeit documentation or packaging for a computer program.
> 8 – Intentionally imports or exports goods infringing the provisions of this law.
> 9 – Manufactures, assembles, modifies, imports, exports, sells, leases, or otherwise distributes a tangible or intangible system or device, knowing or having reason to know that the device or system is primarily used in decoding an encrypted program-carrying satellite signal without the written authorisation of the lawful distributor of such signal.
> 10 – Intentionally receives or further distributes an encrypted program-carrying satellite signal if he knowing or having reasons to know that it has been decoded without the written authorisation of the lawful distributor of such signal.[65]

64 Kuwait, Law No. 22 of 2016, arts 41 and 42.
65 Oman, Royal Decree Law No. 65/2008, art. 52.

It should be noted that the Omani law draws a distinction between strict liability and an accidental or infringing act, and requiring most of the above acts to have been committed knowingly or intentionally – in other words, in application of the common law *mens rea* principle. Hence, in these instances it would be necessary for the authorities to establish that the infringing party "knew or ought reasonably to have known" that their action or article with which they were dealing was an infringing act or infringing copy.

Bahrain also recognises unlawful acts that are deliberate or "wilful", and in doing so draws a distinction between simple acts and acts for with a financial gain element:

> Wilfully infringes copyright or related rights on a commercial scale, including, but not limited to, (i) significant wilful infringements that have no direct or indirect motivation of financial gain, and (ii) wilful infringement for purposes of commercial advantage or private financial gain.[66]

A few States also include acts that go a little further than the range of acts in the above Omani copyright law. The Bahraini law recognises as an unlawful act the 'using expressions of folklore in a manner that violates Article (68) of this law'.[67] Article 68 provides that expressions of folklore, which reflect the traditional popular heritage originating, developed and consistently preserved in the Kingdom, are the property of the State. They may be used in an appropriate manner provided that such use shall not mutilate them and that their source is stated. In similar fashion, the Yemeni copyright law prohibits improper use of expressions of folklore, including their distortion or mutilation.[68]

The copyright laws of all States provide a limited range of permitted exceptions to the stipulated exclusive rights enjoyed by the holder of the copyright, to ensure that certain social objectives are not obstructed. However, variations exist between the various laws. All laws provide a number of exceptions to facilitate education by permitting copying for the purpose of illustration, permitting the performance of works for face-to-face instruction, and permitting copying to satisfy the needs of a researcher. There are permitted exceptions designed to ensure that the exercise of copyright does not become a barrier to the preservation of culture by permitting libraries and archives to make copies for use if the original is damaged or lost. There are also exceptions to ensure that freedom of expression and dissemination of information are not obstructed by allowing news outlets to copy for the purpose of reporting news and current events and to make full or partial copies of written pieces that discuss issues concerning society. Some of the copyright laws also have specific exceptions that permit non-profit public performances at religious ceremonies or by state army bands.

66 Bahrain, Law No. 22 of 2006, art. 65(1)(a).
67 Bahrain, Law No. 22 of 2006, art. 65(1)(g).
68 Yemen, Law No. 15 of 2012, art. 77(5).

It is worth noting that the scope of available exceptions differs from one State to the next. For example, the exception for permitting the non-profit public performance of a work at religious ceremonies is available under the copyright laws of Bahrain and Oman but not the others.[69] Some exception may appear to be available across the whole region at first instance, but the scope of their application may vary greatly. For example, the exception for permitting media outlets to reproduce articles relating to current issues that concern the public allows reproducing the 'whole' written article in Kuwait, Qatar, Saudi Arabia and the UAE, and only a 'part' of the written article in Bahrain and Oman.

The scope of the private use exception varies greatly across the different copyright laws among the States. This difference in scope highlights the fact that many of these laws do not reflect the reality of how users interact with copyright works in the digital environment and makes abidance of the law impossible by the public. Violation of copyright law through private use is extremely difficult to prove and is unlikely to lead to prosecution. This does not mean that this exception is not important. The unavailability of an exception to permit many of the legitimate activities that users perform nonetheless, without any fear of prosecution, gives a message to users that the law has no value, is not realistic and is incapable of being enforced. There is certainly a problem that needs to be addressed when the law becomes irrelevant to the daily lives of people in society.

The 'fair dealings' and 'fair usage' allowances that exist in many western-based copyright laws really constitute defences against alleged infringement instead of private use exceptions to exclusive rights. Copyright laws that incorporate such allowances, such as the 'fair use' provisions under the American copyright law, enable a court to examine each allegation of infringement on its own merits and unique set of facts and circumstances, without the need for the use to be specifically mentioned in the law, to decide whether that use is not an infringement.[70] None of the copyright laws of the States has fair use or fair dealing style exceptions; instead, they provide an exhaustive closed list of permitted uses. Under the closed-list system, any use that is not explicitly included in the law would be considered an infringement of copyright regardless of the circumstances under which the use is carried out.

4.4 Copyright in the digital environment

4.4.1 Background

The Middle East has not been immune or protected from the global digital revolution that the world has undergone over the last decade or so. The digital revolution has had a significant impact on every intellectual property regime and none more

69 Bahrain, Law No. 26 of 2002, art. 27(a); Oman, Royal Decree No. 65/28, art. 20(6)(a).
70 See Riyadh Al Balushi, Noora Al Lawati, and Muluk Moh, op. cit.

so than copyright protection. It has required, and will continue to require, fundamental changes to copyright law to attempt to keep pace with new technologies and communications development infrastructures and practice. Digitisation and information communications technology (ICT) has exponentially increased the ease of creation, modification, distribution and particularly access to information. It has created a new medium in which works of an artistic, literary, dramatic and musical nature can be accessed and distributed to the public in a virtual, instantaneous and real-time fashion.

Arab business increasingly expects and demands latest ICT strategies and infrastructure to both effectively integrate and compete in the global and regional markets. Society expects and also demands that social media and the internet be available, accessible and subject to minimum restriction as the new-age means of communication. And governments are contributing to these expectations and demands by moving more and more towards e-commerce and e-government operations – and this extends to areas of intellectual property activity. For example, a number of States provide for online registration of copyrightable work of lodgment of trademark applications, but Saudi Arabia and the UAE have taken this initiative one step further by announcing in early 2016 that they will be only accepting trademark registration applications online.[71]

As this online and internet access increases, the capacity to monitor and control copyright protection reduces in an equally dramatic fashion. For example, as demonstrated in the recent upheavals in Syria and Iraq, the new weapon of the terrorist, dissident or revolutionary is no longer the spy network or inflammatory pamphlet, but information search and dissemination via the internet, the mobile phone and SMS, and satellite reception facilities.

Hence protection of copyright can be extremely difficult, if not at times impossible, to enforce in relation to digital communications, particularly over the internet and at the end-user level, since there are so many avenues for, and instances of, alleged infringement. However, what is detected by copyright holders is necessarily the tip of the iceberg. Furthermore, the current regional copyright legislation and its TRIPS benchmark is now more than 21 years old in its primary form, and is not equipped to adapt easily and smoothly to the digital and internet revolutions. The digital era has created new modes of expression that flawlessly, inexpensively and instantaneously reproduce and distribute creative works through various data bases, websites and programs. Complicating any statutory adaptation is the fact that ICTs can bring together rather disparate forms of copyrightable material and modes of expression into a uniform digital expression or language, and into a largely uniform access and distribution system. Internet technology is developing faster than the laws that govern it or protect the information it transmits can keep pace.

71 As reported in the Saba Monthly Bulletin (2006), 15 February, available at www.sabaip.com/en/News/Saudi-Arabia-Trademark-Renewal-Going-Online, last accessed 29 May 2017.

To be effective and to achieve its core objectives, copyright law needs to continuously adapt in response to the introduction of emerging industries, technologies and the creation of new materials. As new ways of expressing and exploiting creative materials have developed, the rights have expanded and been reformulated. As technology has advanced, legislation has become increasingly focused on proprietary interests and financial gain rather than creative artistic development. A few regional copyright laws have evolved and been modified, in an attempt to adapt in the face of new creative expressions and technology. But in so doing they have become increasingly complex and arguably unwieldy. The movie, music and games industries are the three main areas that, from their perspective, have been presented with dramatic opportunities for growth and promotion of their respective genres. At the same time, they face challenges of some significance in terms of the protection and exploitation of their proprietary interests and copyright assets. The digital environment requires a closer assessment of some long-established conventions commonly taken for granted.

The fundamental difficulty with copyright protection in relation to digital music is that anyone with internet access – whether via computer or mobile phone – can easily and freely upload or download copyright music. Software protocols that facilitate access regularly come and go. Napster, Kazaa and Grokster are examples of protocols that existed just a decade or so ago that have since been superseded. LimeWire, Bit-Torrent and Netflix are examples of services that currently do allow the free downloading of music files. Accessing, distributing and reproducing music via the internet have become increasingly popular among internet users of all ages. This raises the key issue of whether the law of copyright in its current guise is sufficiently adequate to protect the rights of the creative songwriter and/or performer author, or whether the time may have come for *sui generis* legislation to be enacted.

The film industry experiences issues akin to those facing the music industry. Under the laws, 'cinematographic films' include feature films, television programmes, documentaries, short films, home videos, animated films, television commercials and some multimedia products, such as computer games. The production and dissemination of pirated movies and the infringement of copyright laws represent the greatest difficulties faced by the film industry. The change in technology has increasingly caused problems for the industry as a perfect copy of the original image can now be duplicated and the increased bandwidth in broadband internet allows individuals to quickly download full-length feature films.

The Arabian Peninsula region has seen an absolute explosion in internet usage over the last 15 years or so, and this has had an impact on issues of copyright and other areas of intellectual property rights protection. According to industry statistics, internet penetration into the region's domestic markets over the period 2001 to 30 June 2016 – in other words, the percentage of the population of a State that uses the internet – has ranged from Yemen's fairly modest growth rate of 0.1 per cent to 24.7 per cent, in contrast to Qatar's 3.8 per cent to a staggering 97.4 per cent.[72]

72 'Internet World Stats Middle East' (2016), available at www.internetworldstats.com/middle.htm, last accessed 29 May 2017.

The common response of the States to this phenomenon in terms of incorporating provision into their respective copyright laws appears to be mainly limited to incorporating provisions in their scale of infringements and offences in respect of the marginally related areas of technological protection measures and rights management information. Although very important in their own right, neither really addresses the growing issues of internet piracy. In the case of those States that have not made specific provision for the unique nature of transmission of copyright material over the internet, it would appear that there is undue reliance or hope that the language of their copyright laws is sufficiently technologically neutral to cope with internet-based or ICT-based infringements.

4.4.2 Technological protection measures and rights management

Reflecting the changing nature of infringing activity away from traditional print-based acts to electronic and broadcast-based acts of an increasingly technical sophistication, the more recent laws now take cognisance of acts which facilitate or enable the commission of infringements relating to the manufacture or import of electronic deactivation devices and satellite decoding devices, or the illegal modification or removal of such devices or information concerning transmission broadcast rights. These new clauses are directly aimed at confronting the global and sophisticated industries concerned with the production of counterfeit computer software, games, pirated music, video recordings and downloads. They are also aimed at more recent internet-based material, counterfeit smart cards and decoders/descramblers for the multitudinous satellite TV channels for which the Arabian Peninsula region in general is squarely placed within the transmission footprints.

The region's laws now generally recognise, to a lesser or greater degree, the illicit removal or alteration of any technical protection or rights information intended to regulate or limit public access to any work, performance, recording, broadcast or transmission as an infringing activity. Each in very similar language, the current Bahraini, Jordanian, Kuwaiti, Omani, Qatari and Saudi laws now include provision for the prohibition of the following acts related to technological protection measures, rights management information and the retransmission of television signals:

- circumventing without authority any effective technological measure that controls access to a protected work, performance, phonogram or other subject matter;
- manufacturing, importing, distributing or otherwise dealing in any devices, products, components or services which are promoted as being able to circumvent any effective technological measure, or have only a limited commercially significant purpose or use other than circumvention, or are primarily designed, produced or performed for the purpose of enabling circumvention;

- committing any of the following without authority, and knowing or having reasonable grounds to know that it would induce, facilitate or conceal an infringement of any copyright or related right:
  - o knowingly removing or altering any rights management information;
  - o importing or distributing rights management information knowing that the rights management information has been removed or altered without authority; or
  - o importing or distributing, broadcasting or making publicly available copies of works, performances or phonograms, knowing that rights management information has been removed or altered without authority;
- manufacturing, marketing or otherwise distributing a tangible or intangible device or system, knowing or having reason to know that it is primarily of assistance in decoding an encrypted program-carrying satellite signal;
- receiving or further distributing a program-carrying signal that originated as an encrypted satellite signal knowing that it has been decoded without proper authorisation.[73]

Qatar's somewhat limited provisions in its 2002 copyright law are nevertheless reinforced by the provisions relating to the improper digital transmission of information, including copyrightable material, in its Law No. 14 of 2014, on the Prevention of Cybercrime.

The UAE's copyright law of 2002 does not make specific reference to either technological protection measures (TPMs) or rights management information (RMI) systems, but nevertheless provides a degree of protection arguably equivalent to that provided by Bahrain and the other above States. In language more general and thus technologically neutral reliant, it includes the following offences:

- manufacturing or importation without having a right, for the purpose of sale or rental of any equipments, instruments or apparatus designed or prepared for the purpose of fraud against any technology used by the author or the holder of the neighbouring right to arrange or administer such rights or for preservation of specific standard of quality of the copies;
- delaying or disgracing, without having a right, any technological protection or electronic information meant to arrange and administer the rights stipulated in this law;
- loading or storing any copy of the programs, applications or databases in the computer before having a licence from the author, the right holder of their successor.[74]

73 See Bahrain, Legislative Decree No. 22 of 2006, art. 45; Kuwait, Law No. 22 of 2016, arts 42 and 43; Oman, Royal Decree No. 65/2008, art. 41; Qatar, Law No. 7 of 2002, art. 51; Saudi Arabia, Royal Decree No. M/41 of 1424 AH (2003), art. 21.

74 UAE, Law No. 7 of 2002, art. 38.

Yemen's copyright law does not make any specific reference to the existence of technological protection measures or rights management information, even though it was crafted and enacted in 2012 as part of its WTO membership drive. Not surprisingly, then, it also does not make any acknowledgement of the existence of the internet and copyright protection for right holders or liability of internet service providers, even though the law was drafted in collaboration with WIPO.

4.4.3 Liability of internet service providers

Reflecting their obligations enshrined in their free trade agreements with the United States, both Bahrain and Oman incorporate into their recent copyright laws extensive (by regional standards) provisions that address the obligations of internet service providers in providing, facilitating or not preventing acts amounting to unauthorised downloading of copyrighted material.[75]

Bahrain goes a step further than the other States by including detailed provisions concerning the proper conduct of internet service providers, reflecting, again, its obligations under its free trade agreement. The law provides that a service provider shall be held to be a contributory infringer where it is established that the provider knowingly caused, induced or materially contributed to, through its system or network, an infringement of the rights of a copyright holder by another party. However, a service provider who complies with certain conditions shall not be held liable for any damages for infringements that may occur in the course of normal service provision business.[76] The conditions require that the service provider:

- does not receive any financial benefit directly attributable to the infringement;
- does not make any modification to the content of the material during transmission through its network;
- does not select the recipients of the electronic copy of the material, except as an automatic response to a third-party request;
- expeditiously removes or disables access on its network to the material upon receipt of notification of an infringement;
- ensures that, where the material is subject to conditions on user access at the originating site, access is limited to authorised users;
- complies with international standards concerning the refreshing, reloading or other updating of material when specified by the party making the material available online in accordance with widely internationally accepted standards in respect of data communications protocol for the system or network through which that person makes the material available; and
- does not interfere with technology that is consistent with widely internationally accepted standards on information governing use of the material.

75 See Bahrain, Law No. 22 of 2006, arts 46–56.

76 Bahrain, Legislative Decree No. 22 of 2006, arts 48–49 and 51–54.

Where a service provider satisfies or complies with these requirements, the injunctive relief which a court may grant against the service provider for infringing activity is limited to orders to disable access to infringing material, link or online location, or to terminate a specified account. The service provider shall then be exempted from liability for any resulting claims. A copyright office is authorised, on complaint by a copyright or related right holder of an alleged infringement, to require a service provider to make available to both the office and the right holder any information in its possession as to the identity of the alleged infringer.

Those laws which give particular attention to infringements in the digital/technological environment also draw a distinction between the scale of penalties that may be imposed in respect of infringing acts across the broad copyright spectrum, with provision for the more severe penalties to be applied to the infringements in the digital/technological environment.[77]

The UAE's copyright law does not make any specific provision in respect of internet-based copyright offences and the role and liability of internet service providers. However, its Federal Decree No. 5 of 2012, on Combating Cyber Crimes, warrants attention as providing the potential for internet-based copyright crimes to be interpreted as coming within the scope of, and being prosecuted under, the Cyber Crimes law. First, it defines such key expressions as electronic information, computer network, information technology and internet protocol address.[78] It then declares, among others, the following offences:

- gains access to a website, an electronic information system, computer network or information technology means without authorisation or in excess of authorization or unlawfully remains therein (Article 2(1));
- deletion, omission, destruction, disclosure, deterioration, alteration, copying, publication or re-publishing of any data or information (Article 2(2);
- uses a fraudulent computer network protocol address by using a false address or a third-party address by any other means for the purpose of committing a crime or preventing its discovery (Article 9);
- wilfully and without authorisation runs a software on the computer network or an electronic information system or any information technology means, and caused them to stop functioning or being impaired, or resulted in destruction or alteration of the program, system, website, data or information (Article 10);
- prepares, designs, produces, sells, buys, imports, displays for sale or make available any computer program or any information technology means, or promotes by any means links to websites, computer program or any information technology means designed for the purposes of committing, facilitating or abetting in the commission of the crimes specified in this Decree-Law (Article 14);

77 The nature of sanctions across all intellectual property laws of the Arabian Peninsula States is discussed in greater detail in Chapter 6.

78 UAE, Federal Decree No. 5 of 2012, on Combating Cyber Crimes, art. 1

- without authorisation, deliberately receives or intercepts any communication through any computer network (Article 15);
- any owner or operator of a website or computer network who deliberately and knowingly saves or makes available any illicit content or if he fails to remove or blocks access to this illicit content within the period determined in the written notice addressed by the competent authorities indicating the illegal content and being available on the website or the computer network (Article 39).

The sanctions for the above offences in some instances far exceed the maximum sanctions of Dh500,00 and minimum three months' imprisonment available under the copyright law, the cyber law sanctions ranging from Dh750,000 and minimum six months' imprisonment to Dh3million and five years' imprisonment.[79] The generalised nature of the above descriptions of offences give this law wider application (and facilitates greater understanding by rights holder, prosecutorial authorities and the judiciary) than Bahrain's very detailed and specific provisions in its copyright law as crafted from its FTA with the United States.

4.5 Concluding remarks

The laws of copyrights and neighbouring rights in the Arabian Peninsula are very similar to each other. However, this does not mean that the laws are identical, since minor differences exist between them. Following or modelling the TRIPS Agreement does not guarantee that the laws will have the same set of standards. TRIPS provides the contracting countries with the flexibility to structure and implement a law that suits their vision and society as long as they provide the minimum standards of protection which are mentioned in TRIPS. For example, the duration of the copyright term in which the work enters the public domain[80] differs from one State to another because of the different analysis that these countries have applied to TRIPS. This has an effect on the rights that a right holder enjoys and the length in which he can monopoly his economic rights.

> For those, who rely on the expiry of the copyright term and re-use the works in their entirety, or through an adaptation, will not be able to publicly perform, or make their works available, in the members of the GCC where the term has not expired.[81]

Although such differences do not conflict with international agreements, it creates an imbalance in the GCC and between the GCC member States and Jordan and Yemen as prospective members.

79 UAE, Federal Decree No. 5 of 2012, on Combating Cyber Crimes, art. 10.
80 Riyadh Al Balushi, Noora Al Lawati, and Muluk Mohsin, op. cit., p. 81
81 Ibid., pp. 82–84.

Unifying a copyright law among the GCC member States, current and future, is becoming a crucial issue. First, the region's laws are becoming somewhat outdated and do not confirm with today's needs, especially with the advances in new technologies; second, new works are appearing that did not exist before. One example of the latter is the mobile application, or 'App', which demonstrates how inconsistent and dissimilar the GCC members are in protecting it. Some of the States entitle Apps to legal protection under copyright law, rationalising their approach by highlighting that Apps are basically software that runs in a phone. Others consider that Apps should be protected through patent law because the technology that they use can often be the subject matter of a patent.[82] Although this specific question – can an App be copyrighted or patented? – has been debated for a long time, it is a question that all States have to answer, in order to establish a more stable environment in the region, to reduce conflict and to achieve mutual compatibility.

As the second part of the assessment of the States' compliance with their obligations under TRIPS, the next chapter examines the States' legislative protection regimes in respect of the broader group of intellectual property collectively and universally described as industrial property rights.

82 Manel Ben Said, 'Protection of IP rights for Mobile Apps' (2008), available at www.tamimi.com/en/magazine/law-update/section-11/may-8/protection-of-ip-rights-for-mobile-apps.html?utm_source=Mondaq&utm_medium=syndication&utm_campaign=View-Original, last accessed 29 May 2017.

5

TRIPS AND INDUSTRIAL PROPERTY AND THE NATURE OF COMPLIANCE IN THE ARABIAN PENINSULA

5.1 Introduction

This chapter explores the Arabian Peninsula States' progress in respect of the protection of industrial property – namely, trademarks, geographical indications, industrial designs, patents, layout designs for integrated circuits, trade secrets and new plant varieties. TRIPS is again taken as the minimum standards benchmark against which this progress is assessed.

As already discussed in the previous chapter on copyright and neighbouring rights, the general structure and requirements of TRIPS – its Preamble, Principles and Objectives, national treatment and most-favoured-nation (MFN) treatment provisions – apply equally to all fields of industrial property rights.

5.2 Trademarks

5.2.1 TRIPS provisions and obligations (Articles 15–21)

The fundamental principle of trademark protection provided by TRIPS is that any sign, or any combination of signs, capable of distinguishing the goods and services of one undertaking from others must be eligible for registration as a trademark, provided that it is visually perceptible. Such signs may take the form of particular words, including personal names, letters, numerals, figurative elements and combinations of colours as well as any combination thereof. Where signs are not inherently capable of distinguishing the relevant goods or services, members may require, as an additional condition for eligibility for registration, that distinctiveness be acquired through use. Members are free to determine whether to allow the registration of signs that are not visually perceptible, such as sounds or smells. Certain limited exceptions to the rights conferred by a trademark, such as fair use of descriptive terms, may be permitted, provided that such exceptions take account of the legitimate interests of the owner of the trademark and of third parties.

The owner of a registered trademark must be granted the exclusive right to prevent all third parties not having the owner's consent from using, in the course of trade, signs for goods or services that are identical or similar to those in respect of which the trademark is registered, where such use would result in a likelihood of confusion. In case of the use of an identical sign for identical goods or services, a likelihood of confusion must be presumed.

TRIPS takes the provisions of Article 6*bis* of the Paris Convention in respect of prohibiting the registration or use of a mark which is confusingly similar to a well-known mark that is either already registered or in use for identical or similar goods, and extends them, *mutatis mutandis*, to marks in respect of services. It further takes these provisions and applies them to marks for goods and services which are not similar to goods and services for which a well-known trademark is used or registered if their use would indicate a connection between those goods or services and those of the owner of the well-known mark, to the detriment of the owner's interests.

Initial registration, and each subsequent renewal, of a trademark shall be for a term of not less than seven years, while registration shall be renewable indefinitely. Where use is required as a condition of registration, cancellation on the grounds of non-use can occur only after three years of uninterrupted non-use, unless valid reasons based on the existence of obstacles to such use are shown by the trademark owner. Use of a trademark by another person, when subject to the control of its owner, must be recognised as use of the trademark for the purpose of maintaining registration status.

5.2.2 Trademark laws in the Arabian Peninsula States

Trademark laws are the longest-standing intellectual property protection laws in the Arabian Peninsula States. They have faced scrutiny from both regional and international sources and consequently been subject to review processes which have given them the best opportunity of all intellectual property laws in the States to reach TRIPS compliance. The fact that they also address an area of commercial endeavour which has been long-standing, locally active and financially lucrative for local traders and businesses means that they have also had the opportunity to be tested in respect of their efficacy and practicability.

All States have enhanced or entirely replaced their early trademark laws since the introduction of TRIPS, while some have pursued even more recent upgrades with their adoption of the GCC Unified Trade Mark Law of 2013. The first set of enhancements were carried out after the expiration in 2000 of the TRIPS-permitted transitional period for developing countries and have thereby brought them generally into compliance with TRIPS requirements.

The second set of enhancements has been marked by the recent adoptions of the GCC Unified Trade Mark Law. The foundations for the Trade Mark Law were laid down over 30 years ago, when the GCC Supreme Council embarked on a regional trademark single-registration scheme. In December 2006, the Supreme Council adopted the long-awaited GCC Unified Trademark Regulation, a statute that was over 20 years in the making. In 2013, the Regulation was amended, to be reintroduced as the GCC Unified Trade Mark Law (hereinafter the GCC Law). The primary objective of the GCC Law is to replace the trademark laws of the GCC member States, thereby introducing a degree of consistency and harmonisation in regional trademark protection. The main features of the Law include provision for:

- extension of the definition of a trademark to include single colours, combinations of colours, sound and smell marks;
- collective marks;
- translation of a trademark;
- filing multiclass applications in the GCC;
- claims of priority based on prior foreign applications;
- rejection of a trademark due to similar or confusingly similar goods/services even where the previous application was filed under a different class;
- cancellation of a mark for non-use over a period of five consecutive years after registration;
- protection for marks well known in the GCC, even if not registered;
- duration of protection stipulated;
- 60-day appeal period following the rejection of an application;
- civil and criminal action by right holders against infringing parties;
- strengthened sanctions, including terms of imprisonment of up to five years, and fines of up to 1 million Saudi riyals ($US270,000) or local currency equivalent.

The above penalties are consistent with those prevailing in the Saudi trademark law, but are significantly different from those stipulated in the trademark laws of the other States.

However, the GCC Law does not offer a unified filing system as was intended to be the case with the unified patent regulation scheme that the GCC also established in 2007. Hence, trademark applications will need to continue to be filed separately in each State for protection.

The GCC Law provides that the protection of a trademark is not only extended to any national and foreigners residing in any of the GCC member States and who are authorised to carry out any commercial, industrial, handicraft or services activity in any of those States. It is also extended to foreigners who belong to any state that is a member of a multilateral convention in which a GCC member State is a party or who resides in such State.[1] The GCC Law offers protection based on the national treatment (unlike the Qatari trademark law of 2002, which based the protection on a reciprocity treatment).

1 Qatar, Law No. 7 of 2014, adopting the GCC Unified Trade Mark Law as the trademark law in Qatar, art. 5.

The GCC Law needs to be approved and ratified domestically by each GCC member State by a decree or a law in order to come into force domestically.[2] Most GCC member States –namely, Bahrain, Kuwait, Qatar and Saudi Arabia – have ratified and implemented the GCC Law to be the applicable trademark law in their respective countries; Oman and the UAE have yet to approve the GCC Law (although they approved the GCC Unified Trademark Regulation of 2007).

Bahrain introduced a new trademark law in 2006 law to replace its long-standing and conservative trademark law, namely its pre-TRIPS law of 1991. This 1991 law had been created by the excision of the trademark provisions from the original pre-independence omnibus regulation of 1955, as amended in 1977 into a new and specific trademark law. Consequently, the law still contained some specific elements from the 1955 law and the 1977 amendments. More importantly, it was strikingly deficient in respect of crucial elements such as protection for well-known marks. The new law has provided the opportunity to redress a number of the inconsistencies and contradictions which arose from the past incomplete restructurings of the original 1955 legislation. However, in 2014, Bahrain replaced its 2006 law with the GCC Law as the only applicable trademark law in the country.

Kuwait and Saudi Arabia replaced their original laws in 2001 and 2002, and again in 2015 and 2016 when they also ratified the GCC Law as their only applicable trademark laws. Kuwait has previously attracted critical attention from within the WTO, and from the United States in particular through its Special 301 Reports, for the perceived inadequacy, laxity and non-deterrent character of its trademark protection, of the nature of infringements and the level of sanctions. That situation should no longer exist with its adoption of the GCC Law. Saudi Arabia adopted the GCC Law in 2014, and subsequently brought it into force in September 2016, when it enacted the necessary implementing regulations. However, it has yet to issue a decree to revoke or cancel its 2002 trademark law. Accordingly, it would appear the 2002 law may still be in force and an active law in the LKingdom alongside the GCC Law. Interestingly, according to some anecdotal information from sources within the government, the 2002 law is deemed to be no longer the applicable trademark law, and Saudi authorities are currently relying solely on the GCC Law as the official trademark law. The real test as to the validity of this assertion and the applicable law will arise when charges of infringement come before the judicial authorities.

Qatar, on the other hand, has adopted the GCC Law to operate alongside its 2002 trademark law, subject to the requirement that any provision of the 2002 law that is inconsistent with the GCC Law shall be void. Therefore, the 2002 law must conform with provisions of the GCC Law, thus harmonising the domestic and regional laws in this respect.

2 Omar Obeidat and Sadaf Nakhaei (2016), 'GCC Unified Trademark Law: Key Provisions and Challenges', *Al-Tamimi Law Update* (February), available at www.tamimi.com/en/magazine/law-update/section-14/february-8/gcc-unified-trademark-law-key-provisions-and-challenges.html, last accessed 26 May 2017.

In 2000, Oman replaced its original 1996 law with a new trademark law as part of its WTO accession process, as part of a suite of seven *sui generis* intellectual property laws together encompassing the major areas of TRIPS. It has since incorporated trademark protection into a single comprehensive law encompassing all areas of industrial property.[3] This was a logical and sensible move, since the year 2000 suite of laws contained many identical provisions, particularly in respect of enforcement and sanction.

The UAE was content to retain its law of 1992, but introduced a range of amendments – sweeping amendments – in 2000 and 2002.

Oman and the UAE have not yet ratified the GCC Law but indications suggest that they are in the process of issuing the necessary law or decree to ratify and formally adopt the Regulation domestically.

Yemen formerly relied on its pre-TRIPS omnibus intellectual property law of 1994, which required substantial changes to bring it into TRIPS compliance as part of Yemen's eventual WTO accession. In 2010, Yemen enacted a *sui generis* law on Trademarks and Geographical Indications. The law is in compliance with TRIPS standards especially in regard to protecting well-known marks.

When Jordan enacted a trademark law in 1952, it became the first country in the region to introduce a legal framework for the protection of trademarks, instead of relying on an inherited framework from another era. The 1952 law was amended several times to reflect the rapid changes in the trademark world and keep the law up to date, the first amendment occurring in 1999. This amendment was more on a domestic level; it introduced collective marks as well as well-known marks. The law was again amended in 2007, when the focus this time was more on an international level by devoting provisions to cover the registration of trademarks internationally. The most recent amendment occurred in 2008. This brief amendment, which consists of just four articles, amends the rights to license a trademark and modifies the definition of well-known trademarks to highlight that a national treatment is provided for these kinds of marks.

In the last few years, all States have also shown increasing willingness to commit to or at least follow some of the WIPO-administered international agreements that complement the TRIPS trademark provisions. Hence, all States have now acceded to the Paris Convention, Jordan being the first to do so in July 1972 and Kuwait being the most recent when it joined in December 2014. By the same token, most States have either formally acceded to the Nice Agreement Concerning the International Classification of Goods and Services, or declared that they adhere to the Nice Agreement without going through the accession process, or at least generally use its classifications for the purpose of categorising goods and services for their domestic trademark registrations, as discussed further below. Bahrain, Jordan and Oman have been the most active in this regard, formally

3 Oman, Royal Decree No. 67/2008, the Law on Industrial Property Rights, Title II, Part 1, arts 36–47.

acceding to the Berne Convention, the Nice Agreement, the Protocol Relating to the Madrid Agreement for the International Registration of Marks and the WIPO Trademark Law Treaty, although accession to the latter three agreements has been as a direct consequence of their obligations under their recent free trade agreements with the United States. Table 5.1 shows current trademark laws and conventions in the GCC member States, and Table 5.2 shows current trademark laws and conventions in Jordan and Yemen.

5.2.3 Scope of protection for trademarks

The trademark laws of the 1990s lacked provision for protecting well-known marks; a well-known mark could be refused registration and protection if the same or similar mark was already under application. The post-TRIPS laws and the GCC Law have come a long way in addressing shortcomings such as well-known marks, as well as clarification of licensing and transfer provisions and appeal provisions to independent judicial bodies on administrative decisions. In respect of the nature of protectable subject matter, the descriptions of each State are generally consistent with the minimum requirements of registrable matter outlined by TRIPS Article 15.

The GCC Law and the Omani law provide the leading definitions of what may constitute a mark, the primary characteristic being the ability to be graphically represented. This is an advance on the lesser TRIPS minimum standard of a mark being 'visually perceptible'.[4] The GCC Law provides that a trademark shall:

> mean everything that takes a distinctive form such as names, words, signatures, letters, figures, drawings, logos, titles, hallmarks, seals, pictures, engravings, packs or any other mark or group of marks if used or intended to be used either to distinguish goods, products or services of a facility or other facilities or to indicate the rendering of a service or the control of inspection of goods or services. The sound or smell shall be considered as part of the trademark.[5]

Oman goes one step further, including:

> words (including personal names), designs, letters, colours or combinations of colours, numerals or the shape of goods or their packaging, holograms, geographical indications, sounds, scents and tastes. Slogans, where they are not long enough to be protected by copyright, shall be protected as marks.[6]

Since Bahrain, Kuwait, Qatar and Saudi Arabia have ratified the GCC Law, they allow the registration of sound and smell marks when having a distinctive form or

4 TRIPS, art. 15(1).
5 GCC Unified Trade Mark Law of 2013, art. 2.
6 Oman, Royal Decree No. 67/2008, art. 1.

TABLE 5.1 Current trademark laws and conventions in the GCC member States

Bahrain	Law No. 30 of 2014 approving the GCC Unified Trade Mark Law of 2013.Legislative Legislative Decree No. 18 of 2007 ratifying Bahrain's accession to the Trademark Law Treaty Legislative Decree No. 18 of 2005 ratifying Bahrain's accession to the Protocol Relating to the Madrid Agreement for the International Registration of Marks Legislative Decree No. 17 of 2005 ratifying Bahrain's accession to the Nice Agreement Concerning the International Classification of Goods and Services for the Purpose of the Registration of Marks Decree No. 31 of 1996 ratifying Bahrain's accession to the Paris Convention for the Protection of Industrial Property
Kuwait	Law No. 13 of 2015 ratifying the GCC Unified Trade Mark Law of 2013 Law No. 36 of 2014 ratifying Kuwait's accession to the Paris Convention for the Protection of Industrial Property
Oman	Royal Decree No. 67/2008, the Law on Industrial Property Rights Royal Decree No. 37 of 2007 promulgating the Sultanate's accession to the Protocol Relating to the Madrid Agreement for the International Registration of Marks and to the Trademark Law Treaty Royal Decree No.63/1998 promulgating the Sultanate's accession to the Paris Convention for the Protection of Industrial Property and the Berne Convention for the Protection of Literary and Artistic Works
Qatar	Decree No. 7 of 2014 adopting the GCC Unified Trade Mark Law of 2013 as the Trademark Law of Qatar Law No. 9 of 2002 in respect of Trade Marks, Business Names and Data, Industrial Designs and Geographical Indications Decree No. 31 of 2001 in respect of Qatar's accession to the Paris Convention for the Protection of Industrial Property
Saudi Arabia	Royal Decree No. M/51 of 1435 AH (2014) approving the adoption of the GCC Unified Trade Mark Law of 2013 Royal Decree No. M/48 of 1424 AH (2003) ratifying Saudi Arabia's accession to the Paris Convention for the Protection of Industrial Property and the Berne Convention for the Protection of Literary and Artistic Works Royal Decree No. M/21 of 1423 AH (2002), the Law of Trademarks
UAE	Federal Decree No. 52 of 2007, adopting the GCC Unified Trademark Law of 2013 in the UAE Federal Law No. 37 of 1992 concerning Trade Marks, as amended by Federal Law No. 8 of 2002 Federal Decree No. 20 of 1996 concerning the UAE's accession to the Paris Convention for the Protection of Industrial Property
GCC	GCC Unified Trade Mark Regulation of December 2006, as amended in 2013 as the Trademark Law

Source: compiled by the authors

TABLE 5.2 Current trademark laws and conventions in Jordan and Yemen

Jordan	Law No. 33 of 1952 on Trademarks as amended up to Law No. 15 of 2008
	Law of 2008 ratifying Jordan's accession to the Nice Agreement for International Classification of Goods and Services for the Purposes of the Registration of Marks
	Law of November 2008 ratifying Jordan's accession to the Vienna Agreement Establishing an International Classification of the Figurative Elements of Marks
	Law of 1972 ratifying Jordan's accession to the Paris Convention for the Protection of Industrial Property
	Law No. 23 of 2010 on Trademarks and Geographical Indications
Yemen	Law No. 23 of 2010 on Trademarks and Geographical Indications
	Law of February 2007 ratifying Yemen's accession to the Paris Convention for the Protection of Industrial Property

Source: compiled by the authors

can otherwise be 'graphically represented'; whereas the UAE allows sounds to be registrable under the same condition but not smells.[7] 'Graphically represented' is not defined but, based on convention elsewhere, could include, for example, musical scores or recordings for sound marks, or formulae and ingredient listings or industry standard descriptors for smells.

Jordan has not updated its trademark definition since the first amendment of 1999. The definition is short and basic compared with other laws in the region. The law only permits the registration of visual marks which are able to distinguish goods or services by stating: 'Any visually perceptible sign used or to be used by any person for distinguishing his goods or services from those of others.' By mentioning visual marks, it excludes sound and smells marks from protection.

The Yemeni Trademark and Geographical Indications Law does not include any mention of unusual marks such as sound and smell marks. Even though the law was enacted recently in 2010, its definition of trademark is basic as well. The mark has to be visible to the eye. The law defines a trademark as:

> anything of distinctive form which is visible to the eye, including names, words, letters, numbers, signatures, drawings, symbols, seals, pictures or embossment, or a particular arrangement of colour or set of colours, or any group of these features, if used or intended to be used to distinguish the products or services of a commercial, industrial, agricultural, professional or service enterprise.[8]

TRIPS Article 17 permits limited exceptions from registrability provided that a balance is maintained between the legitimate interests of the trademark owner and

7 UAE, Federal Law No. 37 of 1992, art. 2.
8 Jordan, Law No. 24 of 1999, art. 2; Yemen, Law No. 23 of 2010, art. 3.

those of third parties, without providing further guidance as to the nature or limits of those limitations. The States commonly allow that the grounds for exclusion of a sign from recognition as a trademark or from registrability generally include the following:

- marks devoid of any distinctive feature, or which consist of merely generic names or ordinary images on goods, products or services;
- marks identical or confusingly similar to the public emblems, flags and other symbols related to the State, Arab or international organisations or any institutions thereof, or any foreign country;
- symbols of the Red Crescent or the Red Cross and other similar symbols as well as any confusingly similar forms of those symbols;
- marks which are identical or similar to symbols of a purely religious nature;
- geographical names and indications where the use thereof may be misleading as to the origin of the goods or services;
- names, photographs or emblems of a third party, unless with prior consent;
- degrees or awards to which an applicant is not lawfully entitled;
- marks which may mislead the public or which contain false data as to the origin of products or services, or their other characteristics, as well as marks containing an imaginary, imitated or forged trade name;
- marks owned by natural or legal persons, dealing with whom is forbidden;
- marks containing the words or phrases: 'Privilege', 'Privileged', 'Registered', 'Registered drawings', 'Copyright' or 'Imitation is forgery' or similar words and phrases;
- national and foreign decorations, as well as currency coins and bank notes;
- the mark whose registration for some categories of products or services results in undervaluing other products or services distinguished by such mark;
- a mark which is an imitation, reproduction of an essential feature or translation of a well-known trademark or other prior registered mark if this will cause public confusion as to identical or similar, or even dissimilar, goods covered by the mark.[9]

The GCC Law has extended the subject matter of the mark to include sound and smell marks, yet it does not go any further to include the other non-traditional marks. The law specifically mentions the marks that are protected and the marks that are excluded; however, it keeps silent in regard to other non-traditional marks such as textile marks, taste marks, motion marks and hologram marks. These marks are unusual marks which cause some difficulties in determining their functions and distinctiveness. The GCC is reluctant to expand its trademark protection to include these non-traditional trademarks.

Jordan adds an interesting point to the previous list; a mark cannot be registered in Jordan if it offends the values of Arab and the old Islamic values.[10] This exclusion

9 As prescribed by the GCC Unified Trade Mark Law of 2013, art. 3.
10 Jordan, Law No. 24 of 1999, art. 8.

can only be found in Jordanian law as the GCC Law does not mention marks that offend Arab culture or Islamic values. However, the GCC Law prevents the registration of marks which are identical or similar to symbols of a religious nature.

All States affirm that any sign which is offensive to or a violation of public morals, or is contrary to *ordre public*, shall not be considered to be a mark and may not be registered as a trademark.

The exclusion from registration in the above listing of 'marks owned by natural or legal persons, dealing with whom is forbidden' applies in particular to marks owned by Israelis or Israeli companies, as part of the boycott of Israel adopted and implemented by members of the League of Arab States as a by-product of the support of Arab countries for Palestine in the Israel–Palestine conflict.[11] The earlier trademark laws of Kuwait, Qatar and Saudi specifically excluded from registration 'marks which the boycott of Israel Office decides is identical or similar to an Israeli, mark, symbol or emblem', while those of Oman included an exclusion similar to that above. The GCC Law does not make any reference to the non-registration of trademarks in the context of the boycott of Israel.

5.2.4 Well-known marks

Article 16 of TRIPS requires WTO members to provide a level of protection that prevents third parties from taking commercial advantage of the goodwill associated with well-known marks, irrespective of whether those marks are registered or in use locally. The recently updated trademark laws have paid particular attention to this area, and the protection of well-known marks and signs, particularly foreign signs, has now been considerably strengthened. As a general rule, the laws provide that a mark or sign may not be registered if:

- it is identical with, or confusingly similar to, or constitutes a translation of, a mark or trade name which is well known in the country for identical or similar goods or services of another enterprise; or
- it is not identical with or similar to a well-known mark, but its use would indicate a connection between those goods or services and the owner of the well-known mark and the interests of the owner of the well-known mark would likely be damaged by such use.[12]

11 Of which all eight States are members. The boycott, which is still officially in force, operated on three levels: primary level, which prohibited direct business dealings with Israel; secondary level, which prohibits dealing with blacklisted firms which do business with Israel, which may include registering a trademark in Israel; and tertiary level, which prohibits dealing with firms which deal with blacklisted firms. In 1994, the States decided to end the secondary and tertiary levels of the boycott, while notionally continuing with the primary level.

12 Jordan, Law No. 34 of 1999, art. 8; GCC Unified Trade Mark Law of 2013, art. 3; Oman, Royal Decree No. 67/2008, art. 36(2); UAE, Federal Law No. 37 of 1992 as amended by Federal Law No. 8 of 2002, art. 4; Yemen, Law No. 23 of 2010, art. 6.

A well-known mark does not need to be registered to gain this protection, but it must be well known outside its country of origin - that is, internationally or at least regionally. TRIPS Article 16.2 requires members to take account of knowledge of the trademark in their own country, including knowledge obtained as a result of promotion of the trademark, even if in advance of actual use.

Jordan follows TRIPS in respect of protecting well-known marks. It provides that a mark is well-known as long as its reputation surpasses the country of origin where it has been registered. The Jordanian law also requires that a mark has to be famous in the relevant sector among consumers in the country. Hence, a well-known mark will be entitled to legal protection under the law regardless if it is registered in Jordan or not. The owner of the well-known mark has the right to prevent third parties from using identical or similar goods or services, and has a further right to prevent third parties from using the mark for different good or services if such use indicates a connection between those goods or services and the well-known mark. Further, the law provides that a likelihood of confusion shall be assumed if an identical well-known mark is used on identical goods. [13]

The GCC Law provides a protection against infringements for a trademark that has an international goodwill beyond the boundaries of its country of origin. The well-known mark may not be registered in the GCC unless the owner or a representative of the owner has requested the registration. The well-known mark and its goodwill can be identified by the public's awareness, whether by promotions or long period of registration as well as the number of countries in which the trademark is registered or renowned. It can also be determined by the value of trademark and its effect on promoting the goods or services distinguished by the trademark.

Some further advantage is given to marks deemed to be well known by the provision of a right of applicants to claim priority on the basis of an earlier application for registration filed either with a state that is a member in a multilateral international convention to which a GCC member State is a party.[14] The GCC Law makes a specific provision on national treatment in respect of trademarks.[15]

5.2.5 Rights of ownership

The basic right to be protected by the registration of a trademark is the exclusive right to use the mark and to prevent other parties from using the mark without consent.[16] The owner of the registered mark can also prevent others from using identical or similar marks on similar or dissimilar goods, including geographical indicators or services, if such use may give grounds for confusion by the public.[17]

13 Jordan, Law No. 34 of 1999, art. 26.
14 GCC Unified Trade Mark Law of 2013, art. 11.
15 GCC Unified Trade Mark Law of 2013, art. 5.
16 Jordan, Law No. 34 of 1999, art. 26; GCC Unified Trade Mark Law of 2013, art. 17; Oman, Royal Decree No. 67/2008, art. 39; UAE, Federal Law No. 37 of 1992 as amended by Federal Law No. 8 of 2002, art. 17; Yemen, Law No. 23 of 2010, arts 22 and 23.
17 GCC Unified Trade Mark Law of 2013, art. 17.

All States provide that the person who registers the mark is deemed to be the owner of the mark, unless there is proof to the contrary.[18] However, any claim of ownership cannot be disputed if the owner of the registered mark has used it continuously for five years since registration, and no claim has been made against the validity of the original registration during this period. For the purposes of this provision, continuous use includes use by a licensee or assignee.

Saudi Arabia's early trademark law of 1984 established the precedent for a period of protection of ten years for a registered trademark, and the other States have since followed suit. All accommodate unrestricted renewal, commonly for recurring ten-year periods – thus exceeding by some margin the minimum period of seven years specified in TRIPS Article 18. However, since TRIPS requires, and all States provide, indefinite renewal, the distinction is largely academic.

Arising from concerns expressed in WIPO and the WTO in respect of the inadequacy or absence of licensing and transfer provisions in the earlier trademark laws of the States, provisions addressing licensing and transfers have been strengthened and are now extant across the States' laws. In general terms, the owner of a mark may grant a non-exclusive and non-assignable licence to any natural person or legal entity in respect of some or all of the products or services for which the mark is registered.[19] The licensing agreement must be in writing, specify the terms, conditions and duration of the licence, and be registered with the responsible ministry to have any legal effect. Jordan, for example, permits a trademark owner to license his mark for one or more persons to use the mark for all or some of the goods. The owner may continue to use the mark unless agreed otherwise. The licensing agreement must be in writing and must not exceed the protection period of the registered mark. Interestingly, Jordan allows trademark owners to license goods but not services.[20]

The UAE provides that

> a contract licensing the use of a trade mark shall be recorded in the Trade Marks Register of marks. Such licensing shall have no effect in respect of third parties except after being recorded in the register and announced in the manner determined in the Executive Regulations.

The UAE requires that the licensing agreement be registered in the Trade Mark Register to have legal effect; however, this is not the case in Jordan as the parties can register the contract.

18 Jordan, Law No. 34 of 1999, art. 26; GCC Unified Trade Mark Law of 2013, art. 7; Oman, Royal Decree No. 67/2008, art. 36; UAE, Federal Law No. 37 of 1992 as amended by Federal Law No. 8 of 2002, art. 17; Yemen, Law No. 23 of 2010, art. 7.

19 Jordan, Law No. 34 of 1999, art. 26; GCC Unified Trade Mark Law of 2013, arts 30–31 Oman, Royal Decree No. 67/2008, arts 24–26 and 45; UAE, Federal Law No. 37 of 1992, arts 30–32; Yemen, Law No. 23 of 2010, art. 25.

20 Jordan, Law No. 15 of 2008, art. 3.

None of the States permits compulsory licensing of trademarks, in accordance with the exclusion stipulated by TRIPS Article 21, although Oman does permit the responsible minister to declare a trademark exhausted and to authorise other parties to use that mark or import goods bearing that mark in instances of unmet demand, anti-competitive practices and unreasonably low-quality standards of goods.[21]

The ownership of a registered trademark may be transferred or assigned with or without the goodwill of the commercial business. Where the marks are deemed to have an established relationship with the business, the transfer of ownership of the business is deemed to include the transfer of the trademarks registered in the name of the transferor, unless specifically agreed otherwise. If the ownership of the business is transferred without the trademark, the transferor may continue to use the mark in connection with the products or services in respect of which the mark was originally registered.[22]

5.2.6 Classifications system for goods and services

Only Bahrain and Jordan among the States are signatories to the Nice Agreement on the International Classification of Marks for Goods and Services, having adopted the eighth edition of the Agreement in February 2005 and November 2008 respectively. Both States have since adopted the tenth edition. The others either generally follow the Nice Agreement classifications or at least refer to them as the starting point for categorising goods and services for domestic trademark registrations. The advantage of this strategy is that they can retain the flexibility to ignore or prohibit certain classification categories, as suits their domestic needs and prerogatives. This strategy is not inconsistent with the Paris Convention Article 6*quinquies* allowing signatory states to deny registration to marks that are deemed to be contrary to public order or morality, and the Nice Agreement Article 2 permitting signatory states to reserve the right to use the Nice Classification merely as a subsidiary system. Jordan follows the 11th edition (which came into effect on 1 January 2017), while Kuwait, Saudi Arabia and the UAE reportedly follow the Nice tenth edition; Yemen follows the eighth edition and Qatar the seventh.

All States conform to a lesser or greater extent with the Agreement's classification system. The majority provide for the registration of marks for both goods and services in classes in accordance with an 'international classification' system (without specifying the Agreement) as well as in accordance with their respective implementing regulations, thereby allowing some discretion at the ministerial level

21 Oman, Royal Decree No. 67/2008, art. 41(1), the responsible minister being the Minister for Commerce and Industry.

22 Jordan, Law No. 34 of 1999, art. 19, and Law 15 of 2008, art. 3; GCC Unified GCC Trade Mark Law of 2013, art. 28; Oman, Royal Decree No. 67/2008 art. 45(3); UAE, Federal Law No. 37 of 1992, art. 28; Yemen, Law No. 23 of 2010, art. 25.

on the exclusion or otherwise of certain classes of goods or services. Classes commonly subject to possible exclusion are notably class 32 (beer and stout, as well as mineral and carbonated waters, other non-alcoholic beverages, syrups and other products used to make non-alcoholic beverages) and class 33 (wines and spirits). Generally, there are no restrictions on classes of registration or goods within individual classes in the laws themselves, but the laws make additional allowance for ministerial discretion as to the classes in which marks may or may not be registered. Each stipulates that a trademark may be registered for one or more classes of goods or services as prescribed (which includes the provision to prohibit) by their respective responsible ministers in the corresponding implementing regulations. The Bahraini, Jordanian and Omani implementing regulations allow that applications for the registration of marks shall be submitted in accordance with the international classification of goods and services, including classes 32 and 33, without qualification. The Kuwaiti and Saudi regulations both exclude class 33 in its entirety, and restrict class 32 to 'mineral and aerated water and other non-alcoholic beverages – syrup and other preparations for making drinks', thereby deleting any reference to beers, spirits or alcoholic beverages.[23] Saudi Arabia also prohibits the registration of marks in respect of Christmas trees and related products.[24] Qatar still follows the rather outdated seventh edition of the Nice Classification of 42 classes, with the exception that class 33 and alcoholic goods in class 32 cannot be registered. The Qatari Trademark Office is reportedly now accepting applications in classes 43, 44 and 45, although it is not clear whether it will follow the tenth or the most recent 11th edition of the Classification.[25]

However, what may appear to be allowed, or at least not disallowed, in one place may be prohibited in another. Since the consumption of alcohol is generally prohibited in the *Qur'an*, it follows that the registration of marks related to alcohol products would be contrary to public morals. Accordingly, the position commonly espoused both by the respective responsible ministries and by regional trademark registration agents alike is that trademarks in class 32 and class 33, as well as class 29 (meat products) in respect of pork-based products, are not registrable in any of the States on the grounds that they are contrary to the teaching of Islam, to *Shariah* law and to the respective States' trademark laws.[26] Saudi Arabia, when

23 See 'Kuwait: Adopting the Tenth Edition of the Nice Classification' (2016), *SABA Intellectual Property Bulletin*, 13 October 2016, available at www.sabaip.com/en/documents/fe_bulletin/Saba-IP-Bulletin--November-2016.pdf, last accessed 26 May 2017.

24 Ibid.

25 As reported in 'NICE Classification 11th Edition' (2017), *SABA Intellectual Property Bulletin*, 14 February, available at www.sabaip.com/en/documents/fe_bulletin/Saba-IP-Bulletin--February-2017.pdf last accessed 26 May 2017.

26 See Rawan Makram Sunna (2003), 'Bridging the Gulf: Harmonisation of Trade Mark Laws in the Gulf Cooperation Council Countries', 1, *Trademark World*, Supplement, p. 29. See also the respective country entries in the following regional legal attorneys and trademark and patents agents: AGIP, op. cit.; ST&P, Attorneys and Agents at http://stplegal.com/read-news.aspx?title=kuwait-adopts-nice-10th-classification, last accessed 1 March 2017; NJQ &

acceding to the Paris Convention, expressed its objection to and concern with the stipulation of Article 7 of the Convention that 'the nature of the goods to which a trademark is to be applied shall in no case form an obstacle to the registration of the mark', on the grounds that some goods such as alcoholic and pork-based products were prohibited under Islamic law.[27] On an issue of such fundamental religious and social significance to Saudi Arabia, reliance alone on the generality of public order and morality provisions of the Paris Convention and TRIPS to prohibit the registration of offending marks was clearly inadequate.

5.2.7 Infringements

Some States draw a clear distinction between acts of infringement against the private rights of the trademark owner and those against the public rights in respect of representation of the status of a mark. The GCC Law, Jordan, the UAE and Yemen deem infringements against the private rights of the trademark owner, and thereby potentially or actually causing commercial loss, to be the more serious offences. Hence such acts as counterfeiting a registered mark, fraudulently using another person's registered mark or knowingly and misleadingly imitating a registered mark may attract the severest penalties. Use of an unregistered mark or mark excluded from registrability (except for those marks excluded solely for want of distinctive features), or falsely claiming or indicating that a mark has been registered, may be punishable by penalties that are a fraction of those which can be applied to the former type of infringement.

The GCC Law provides for a simple but comprehensive list of infringing acts as follow:

- misrepresenting or imitating a mark registered under the provisions of the Law or imitating it in a manner misleading or confusing the public, or using in bad faith any misrepresented or imitated mark;
- identifying his goods or services in bad faith with a mark owned by others.

Associates at http://njq-ip.com/country/bahrain/trademarks/general-information, last accessed 1 March 2017; Saba & Co Group at www.sabaip.com/en/Resources/IP-Tables, last accessed 1 March 2017.

Kuwait reported to the WTO Council of TRIPS, that 'since acquiring, marketing or importing wines and spirits is prohibited, protection of such marks may be rejected for resulting in a breach of morality and public order', WTO Document IP/Q4/KWT/1 (01-6322), 13 December 2001, 15. Saudi Arabia also reportedly prohibits registrations in class 28 for 'Christmas trees and related products' (reported by Saba & Co Group, above).

The rules of the GCC Customs Union, which entered into force on 1 January 2003, recognise and categorise pork, alcoholic products and tobacco products as 'special goods' and further recognise that the GCC member States may import or prohibit them at their own discretion.

27 Reported in the Al-Tamimi *Law Update* April 2004, 31, available at www.tamimi.com/catalog/1998_2004/pdf/april%20LU.pdf, last accessed 6 January 2008.

The GCC Law also recognises the following acts as offences:

- knowingly selling, offering for sale or trading, or possessing with the intention of trading any goods bearing false or imitated marks; or unlawfully uses such marks or offers services under them;
- using a non-registered mark from the list of prohibited marks to register;
- using an unregistered trademark or unlawfully indicating on a mark or commercial document that such mark is registered;
- using a forged or imitated mark in bad faith;
- knowingly possessing tools or material intended to be used in the imitation of registered or famous trademarks.[28]

Jordan took a simpler approach than the GCC Law, with the following deemed to be infringements or offences (without distinction):

1 Whoever counterfeited a trademark registered under this law, imitated it in any other way that misleads the public, or affixed a counterfeit or imitation mark on the same goods for which the trademark has been registered.
2 Whoever illegally used a trademark owned by another on the same class of goods or services for which that trademark is registered.
3 Whoever sold or possessed for the purpose of selling or offered for sale goods bearing a trademark.[29]

Oman adopts an even simpler position, stating that any act that is reserved under the law as the exclusive right of the trademark owner or licensee that is done by a third party without the approval of the owner or licensee is an infringement.[30]

5.3 Geographical indications

5.3.1 TRIPS provisions and obligations (Articles 22–24)

TRIPS Section 3 on the protection of geographical indications (hereinafter GIs) is different to the rest of TRIPS; it balances the obligations for protection with the exceptions to protection, whereas the rest of TRIPS is weighted heavily in favour of protection of the intellectual property right holder. The GI provisions represented at the time of its negotiation a delicate balance between conflicting European interests seeking high levels of protection, particularly for wines and spirits, and North American interests which are more interested in limiting protection than extending it.

28 GCC Unified Trade Mark Law 2013, art. 42; Yemen, Law No. 23 of 2010, art. 47.
29 Jordan, Law No. 34 of 1999, art. 38.
30 Oman, Royal Decree No. 67/2008, art. 67.

TRIPS Article 22 defines a GI as one which identifies a good as originating in the territory of a member, or a region or locality in that territory, where a given quality, reputation or other characteristic of the good is essentially attributable to its geographical origin. Thus, the quality, reputation or other characteristics of a good can each be a sufficient basis for eligibility as a GI, where they are essentially attributable to the geographical origin of the good. WTO members are required to provide interested parties with the legal means to prevent use of any designation or presentation which may mislead the public as to the geographical origin of a good, and use which constitutes an act of unfair competition within the meaning of Article 10*bis* of the Paris Convention. Members are also required to refuse or invalidate the registration of a trademark which uses a GI for goods not originating in the territory indicated, if the indication is used in such a manner that it may mislead the public as to the true place of origin of the goods.

TRIPS Article 23 requires WTO members to provide an additional level of protection to wines and spirits, and in particular to provide the legal means for preventing use of a GI identifying wines or spirits not originating in the place indicated by that GI, even where the true origin is indicated, or where the indication is given in a translated form, or where it is qualified. Accordingly, unlike the status in respect of other GIs, those for wines and spirits are to be protected even where use by a third party would not mislead the public and unfair competition would not exist. While a multilateral system of notification and registrations of GIs, albeit for wines only, is mooted, members are obliged to enter into negotiations on such a system, but are not committed to the outcomes.

Limits are established to obligations for wholesale protection. As described by one commentator, these limits represent the other half of the delicate balancing act of conflicting interests, in favour of those with 'acquired rights' or 'sins of the past', by allowing for a number of exceptions to protection.[31] Members availing themselves of the use of these exceptions are, again, obliged to at least enter into negotiations aimed at increasing the protection for wines and spirits, but are not committed to any outcomes. However, the exceptions cannot be used to diminish the protection of GIs that existed prior to TRIPS' entry into force.

5.3.2 Geographical indications (GIs) in the Arabian Peninsula

The attention given to GIs by the Arabian Peninsula States is slight and mainly as a corollary to trademarks. The prevailing position is to provide only the briefest passing reference to them within the scope of the respective trademark laws, to the limited extent of merely prohibiting the registration as a mark of a geographical name or indication that is liable to mislead or cause confusion as to the origin of the goods or services in respect of which registration is sought. Kuwait, Saudi

31 Ibid., p. 176.

TABLE 5.3 Current geographical indications laws in the Arabian Peninsula States

Bahrain	Legislative Decree No. 16 of 2004 with respect to Geographical Indications, as amended by Legislative Decree No. 16 of 2006
Jordan	Law No. 8 of 2000 on Geographical Indications
Kuwait	Law No. 13 of 2015 approving the GCC Unified Trade Mark Law of 2013
Oman:	Royal Decree No. 67/2008, the Law on Industrial Property
Qatar:	Decree No. 7 of 2014, adopting the GCC Unified Trademark law of 2013.
	Law No. 9 of 2002 in respect of Trade Marks, Business Names and Data, Industrial Designs and Geographical Indications
Saudi Arabia:	Royal Decree No. M/51 of 1435 AH (2014) approving the adoption of the GCC Unified Trade Mark Law of 2013
UAE	Federal Law No. 37 of 1992 concerning Trade Marks, as amended by Federal Law No. 8 of 2002
Yemen	Law No. 23 of 2010 on Trademarks and Geographical Indications

Source: compiled by the authors

Arabia and the UAE have adopted this simple approach.[32] However, the approach does not give GIs *per se* any measure of protection. Although it may restrict registration for the offending marks, it does not necessarily prevent the exploitative use or misuse of a GI outside the trademark context, nor provide a form of protection as envisaged by TRIPS Article 23 – that is, where there is no misleading use or unfair competition. In 2013, Saudi Arabia circulated a draft for GIs law. The purpose of the draft is to have professional input on the proposed law before enacting it. Currently, there is no form of legal protection for GIs in the Kingdom, which leaves GIs unprotected domestically and internationally.

Bahrain, Jordan, Oman and Yemen, meanwhile, make more comprehensive provisions, with Bahrain, Jordan and Yemen having a discrete GIs law and Oman including a dedicated GIs section within its comprehensive law on industrial property. The States also offer some complementary protection under their respective trademark provisions by continuing to recognise the above-mentioned exclusion of GIs from trademark registrability.

Table 5.3 includes those intellectual property laws which include some substantive provision for the protection of GIs.

32 Kuwait, Law No. 1 of 2001, art. 62(6) and (7); Saudi Arabia, Royal Decree M/21 of 1423 AH (2002), art. 2(f); UAE, Federal Law No. 37 of 1992, as amended by Federal Law No. 8 of 2002, art. 3(6).

5.3.3 Nature and scope of a geographical indication

For those States whose laws define a GI, the definitions generally include the following characteristics (which also closely follow TRIPS Article 22.1):

> Any expression or sign indicating the geographical name of a country, region, locality or place which serves to designate a product originating therein, the quality, characteristics and reputation of which are due exclusively or partly to the geographical environment, the natural or human factors of such origin.[33]

The nature of the protection provided by Bahrain, Jordan, Oman and, to a lesser degree, Qatar and Yemen take three forms – namely, prohibitions on registration of offending marks, systems of registration for GIs and legal means for interested parties to oppose registration of a mark or indication.

First, the laws of these States prohibit the registration as a trademark, and use in designating goods in the course of trade, of a GI presented in a manner which:

- misleadingly suggests or implies that the goods originate in a geographical area other than their true place of origin, even where the GI used is literally correct; or
- by virtue of its use, would constitute an act of unfair competition, including the use of a false GI of the true place of origin, and the use of a GI in translation.[34]

Second, in recognition of the implications of TRIPS Article 24.9, which removes any obligation upon a member to protect a GI which is not or is no longer protected in its own country, Bahrain, Jordan, Qatar and Oman all make provision for the creation of national registers for the eventual possible registration, protection and recognition by other TRIPS signatories of their own GIs. Entitlement to register a GI is limited to natural persons or legal entities carrying on an activity as a producer in the geographical area, or any competent authority.[35] Creation of these national registers is indicative of a small but growing appreciation in these States of the developing enterprise for GIs of local origin, and the necessity to formalise recognition through local registration, if the indications are to obtain recognition internationally. Interestingly, the Yemeni law does not mention any requirement to register a GI. It suggests that a GI can be registered as a trademark in the country and follow the requirements of trademarks.

Third, Bahrain, Jordan, Oman and Yemen enable any interested party, whether they are individuals, producers or consumers, to oppose registration or to institute legal proceedings to prevent, in respect of GIs:

- the use of any designation or presentation of a good that indicates or suggests the good originates in a geographical area other than the true place of

33 As expressed by Qatar, Law No. 9 of 2002, art. 1; Oman, Royal Decree No. 67/2008, art. 49.
34 As expressed by Bahrain, Legislative Decree No. 16 of 2004, art. 2.
35 See, for example, Oman, Royal Decree No. 67/2008, arts 52 and 53.

origin in a manner which misleads the public as to the geographical origin of the good;

- any use which constitutes an act of unfair competition within the meaning of Article 10*bis* of the Paris Convention;
- use of a registered GI identifying goods not originating in the place indicated by the indication, even where the true origin of the goods is indicated or the GI is used in translation or accompanied by expressions such as 'kind', 'type', 'style', 'imitation' or the like; or
- the use of a GI in a manner that may form public confusion in terms of the source of the product, even if the indication is literally correct.[36]

The Qatari and Yemeni laws permit:

> persons who reside in a place especially reputed for the production of certain goods to prevent those who trade in similar goods produced in other places from affixing to their goods marks which would mislead the public as to the origin of those similar goods.[37]

However, limitations apply. The Bahraini, Jordanian and Omani laws provide that a GI shall not be registered or protected if the indication is:

- identical to a domestic customary term or common name of a good or service used in good faith;
- also the name of a person or business used in a manner which is not misleading;
- (or may be) confusingly similar to marks currently registered or under application;
- otherwise refused registration as a trademark pursuant to trademarks law;
- not protected or used (or has ceased to be protected or used) in its country of origin; or
- contrary to public order or morality.[38]

Jordan goes a little further by stipulating that certain acts when committed will not be considered an infringement against a right holder, namely, to:

- own a trademark being similar or identical to a GI through the *bona fide* use before the effectiveness of the provision of such law, or before granting protection to the GI in the place of origin;
- submit a trademark registration application in Jordan being identical or similar to a GI or to register thereof in *bona fide*;
- use a GI in any manner indicating another country, if being identical to Arabic familiar expression of a common name of any product or service;

36 Jordan, Law No. 8 of 2000, art. 3.
37 As expressed by Qatar, Law No. 9 of 2002, art. 39; Yemen, Law No. 23 of 1010, art. 35.
38 Bahrain, Legislative Decree No. 16 of 2004, art. 9; Oman, Royal Decree No. 67/2008, art. 51.

- a person using his/her name or ancestor's name in a commercial activity in a manner that does not mislead public;
- use a GI which has no protection, or its protection was terminated in its place of origin, or is no longer used in this country.[39]

The Qatari law defers to implementing regulations to clarify the nature of such protection and the distinctions, if any, between registered and non-registered geographical indications.[40]

5.3.4 Additional protection for wines and spirits

The notion of providing protection, let alone additional protection, for alcohol-related goods or services would be anathema to most States, notwithstanding their general obligations under TRIPS Article 23.1 to provide protection for GIs for wines and spirits. However, the States will exercise their exception prerogatives under Article 23.2, which allows a WTO member to refuse or invalidate a trademark which carries a wine or spirit GI if that member's legislation so permits. And, as already mentioned, each State's trademark law makes provision for a trademark application that is contrary to *ordre public* or morality to be refused registration. It is not surprising, therefore, that the States devote little attention to the protection of GIs, let alone those relating to wines and spirits.

On the contrary, trademarks related to wines and spirits, irrespective of whether they also contain a GI, are not registrable in most of the States. Applications for the protection of marks and/or GIs relating to wines and spirits will invariably be rejected on the grounds that the marketing, sale or importation of the goods which they identify constitute a breach of public order and morality and are therefore prohibited. The sale of wines and spirits (and all alcoholic products) is prohibited in Saudi Arabia and some of the UAE Emirates, according to Islamic law.

Oman adopts a slightly more liberal stance to the sale of alcohol products than the other States, but not necessarily to the protection of GIs relating to them. Unlike some of its neighbours, Oman permits the sale of alcohol products, as a rather lucrative commercial activity, to non-Muslim resident expatriates under strictly regulated and controlled conditions.[41]

The Omani industrial property law does not make any specific reference to either a higher level of protection to GIs relating to wines and spirits or, indeed, their inclusion or exclusion in respect of protection under the law. Oman has previously advised the WTO that its law grants protection to all GIs including those

39 Jordan, Law No. 8 of 2000, art. 7.

40 Qatar, Law No. 9 of 2002, art. 38.

41 Non-Muslim expatriates who earn above a prescribed minimum monthly wage may buy a licence fee and registration book from the Muscat police headquarters enabling them to purchase specified amounts of alcohol at specially designated (and discreetly disguised) shops.

relating to wines and spirits.[42] In practice, as previously indicated, trademarks and GIs relating to alcohol products are most likely to be refused registration under the public morality provisions of the industrial property law.

Jordan has taken a different approach with GIs relating to wine and spirits. The law provides a higher level of protection for wine and spirits which represent GIs. The law clearly prevents the registration of such GIs if it 'indicates or suggests that the goods in question originate in a geographical area other than the true place of origin including the use of a GI in translation or accompanied by (kind), (imitation) or the like'.[43]

The trademark registrar, in which GI are registered, may reject the registration of any trademark which contains or consists of a GI with respect to goods not originating from the place of origin that may mislead the public. The registrar may also reject the registration if a GI is literally true, but misleads the public in respect of the product's real place of origin. The law also highlights the fact that the period of protection (ten years) for trademarks may be cancelled by the registrar at any time if such trademark consists of a GI to goods not originating from the place of origin.

5.4 Industrial designs

5.4.1 TRIPS industrial designs provisions and requirements (Articles 25–26)

In addition to its general standards of protection, TRIPS devotes just two articles to protection of industrial designs, less than the attention given to the additional protection for GIs attached to wines and spirits.[44] However, TRIPS requires members to also comply with the Paris Convention's provisions relating to patents generally and to the specific industrial design provisions of Articles 4E, 5B, 5*bis* and 5*quinquies*. Article *5quinquies* states simply that industrial designs shall be protected. TRIPS Article 25.1, meanwhile, obliges WTO members to provide for the protection of independently created industrial designs that are new or original; a member may deem a design not to be new or original if it does not significantly differ from known designs or combinations of known design features, and may decline to extend protection to designs dictated essentially by technical or functional considerations.

Members are required to grant the owner of a protected industrial design the right to prevent third parties not having the owner's consent from making, selling or importing articles bearing or embodying a design which is a copy, or substantially a copy, of the protected design, when such acts are undertaken for commercial purposes. As with other intellectual property rights, some limited exceptions may

42 WTO Council for Trade-Related Aspects of Intellectual Property Rights, *Review of Legislation: Oman*, Document IP/Q/OMN/1 (03-1675), 24 March 2003, p. 6.

43 Jordan, Law No. 8 of 2000, art. 3.

44 J Phillips (1998), 'Protecting Values in Industrial Designs', in Correa and Abdulqawi (eds), *Intellectual Property and International Trade: The TRIPS Agreement*, p. 179.

be allowed, provided that such exceptions do not unreasonably conflict with the normal exploitation of protected industrial designs, do not unreasonably prejudice the legitimate interests of the owner of the protected design and take account of the legitimate interests of third parties. The period of protection shall amount to at least ten years, the prescription 'amount to' providing some flexibility in respect of initial and renewal terms that might be established.

Textile designs, which come within the scope of industrial designs, receive a special mention. In order to take account of the short life cycle and sheer number of new designs in the textile sector, requirements for securing protection of such designs, in particular in regard to any cost, examination or publication, must not unreasonably impair the opportunity to seek and obtain such protection. Members are free to meet this obligation either through industrial design law or through copyright law.

5.4.2 Industrial design laws in the Arabian Peninsula

The Arabian Peninsula States address their TRIPS obligations by incorporating some degree of protection for industrial designs either into their patents laws (Kuwait, Saudi Arabia and the UAE), their trademark law (Qatar), inserting a separate chapter in a comprehensive industrial property law (Oman), or by enacting a *sui generis* industrial designs law (Bahrain, Jordan and Yemen). Notwithstanding these different approaches, the nature of the protection in each State is quite similar, although the scope of the respective laws varies. Again, Bahrain and Oman offer the most comprehensive provisions, which go beyond addressing the TRIPS minimum standards.

Until the introduction of its industrial designs law in 2006, Bahrain originally provided protection for industrial designs within its 1955 Regulation which encompassed patents, designs and trademarks. As part of an overall strategy to adopt discrete laws in each of the main areas of intellectual property, Bahrain removed the trademark provisions into a *sui generis* law in 1991 and followed suit with a new patent and utility models law in 2004. As a consequence, any remnant of the original law was rescinded, thereby removing any reference to, and therefore any protection for, industrial designs. The 2006 law has rectified this oversight.

Oman has taken the opposite path to Bahrain and incorporated protection into a separate chapter in its comprehensive industrial property law. In so doing, it has rescinded its *sui generis* industrial designs law of 2000.

By way of contrast, Kuwait is still reliant upon legislation originally enacted in 1962, but which has been subjected to amendment (rather than total replacement) in 1999 and again in 2001.[45] The only changes of any real substance made to the 1962 law in respect of industrial designs in the amending legislation have related to period of protection, and fees and charges.

45 Originally, Kuwait, Law No. 4 of 1962, the Law of Patents, Designs and Industrial Models, as amended by Law No. 4 of 1999 and Law No. 3 of 2001.

Qatar has incorporated industrial design protection in four brief articles within its current trademark law. Because of their brevity and consequent omissions, the industrial designs provisions will likely require further enhancement in the future. Specific reference to industrial designs is limited to acknowledging the right of a person to register a design and to prevent others from exploiting it, to stipulating a period of protection, and a simple statement applying the general provisions of the law to industrial designs, provided that such application 'is without prejudice to its special character'.[46] What is meant by 'its special character' is not explained.

Saudi Arabia and the UAE have, for the first time, incorporated provision for the protection of industrial designs into their patents laws.[47] However, the attention given to designs in the Saudi law is still very slight – namely, just two articles referring to the nature of an industrial design necessary to qualify for protection and the right of the owner of an industrial design to take action against any infringements of those rights. The UAE law goes into a little greater detail, encompassing both industrial designs and models, as well as extending to them the general provisions within the law.

The Jordan and Yemen laws provide more comprehensive laws than the other States. Both countries give special attention to industrial designs and models by each enacting a discrete law which is in compliance with TRIPS. Jordan first enacted an industrial designs law in 2000, which is still in force.. Yemen amended its industrial property law of 1994 by enacting a separate law for industrial designs in 2010.

5.4.3 Character and scope of an industrial design

Except for Qatar's law, the various descriptions of an industrial design are very similar in their essential elements and generally encompass most of the elements of the following description as detailed in the Omani law:

> Any composition of lines or colours or any three-dimensional form, whether or not associated with colours, provided that such composition or form gives a special appearance to a product of industry or handicraft . . . and is judged by the eye.[48]

The Jordan and UAE descriptions go somewhat further and distinguish between an industrial design and an industrial model, the former defined as 'any innovative creation or composition of lines or colours, which generates a product that can be used in industry or craft' and the latter as 'any innovative three-dimensional

46 Ibid., arts 42–45.

47 UAE, Law No. 17 of 2002, specifically arts 43–53; Saudi Arabia, Royal Decree M/27 of 1425 (AH) (2004), arts 59–60. Prior to the introduction in mid-2004 of this omnibus law on patents, layout designs of integrated circuits, new plant varieties and industrial models, industrial designs were not protectable or registrable in Saudi Arabia, due to the absence of a dedicated design statute or any provision in its other intellectual property legislation.

48 Oman, Royal Decree No. 67/2008, art. 1.

TABLE 5.4 Current industrial designs laws and conventions in the Arabian Peninsula States

Bahrain	Legislative Decree No. 6 of 2006 with respect of Industrial Designs Legislative Decree No. 31 of 1996 ratifying Bahrain's accession to the Paris Convention for the Protection of Industrial Property
Jordan	Law No. 14 of 2000 on Industrial Designs and Models Law of 1972 ratifying Jordan's accession to the Paris Convention for the Protection of Industrial Property
Kuwait	Law of 36 of 2014 ratifying Kuwait's accession to the Paris Convention for the Protection of Industrial Property Law No. 4 of 1962 concerning Patents, Designs and Industrial Models, as amended by Law No. 4 of 1999, and Law No. 3 of 2001
Oman:	Royal Decree No. 67/2008, the Law on Industrial Property Royal Decree No.63/1998 promulgating the Sultanate's accession to the Paris Convention for the Protection of Industrial Property
Qatar:	Law No. 9 of 2002 in respect of Trade Marks, Business Names and Data, Industrial Designs and Geographical Indications Decree No. 31 of 2001 in respect of Qatar's accession to the Paris Convention for the Protection of Industrial Property
Saudi Arabia:	Royal Decree No. M/27 of 1425 AH (2004) in respect of Patents, Layout Designs of Integrated Circuits, Plant Varieties and Industrial Models Royal Decree No. M/48 of 1424 AH (2003) ratifying Saudi Arabia's accession to the Paris Convention for the Protection of Industrial Property
UAE:	Federal Law No. 31 for the Year 2006 Pertaining to the Industrial Regulation and Protection of Patents, Industrial Drawings and Designs Federal Decree No. 20 of 1996 concerning the UAE's accession to the Paris Convention for the Protection of Industrial Property
Yemen	Law No. 28 of 2010 on Industrial Designs Law of February 2007 ratifying Yemen's accession to the Paris Convention for the Protection of Industrial Property

Source: compiled by the authors

shape that can be used in industry or craft'.[49] Kuwait retains a more conservative definition, omitting reference to any three-dimensional form. An industrial design or model is defined as follows:

> Any arrangement of lines or any type of figure, whether coloured or uncoloured, designed for use in industrial production by a mechanical, manual or chemical process shall be considered as a design or industrial model.[50]

49 Jordan, Law No. 14 of 2000, arts 2 and 4; UAE, Federal Law No. 17 of 2002, art. 1.
50 Kuwait, Law No. 4 of 1962 as amended by Law No. 4 of 1999 and Law No. 3 of 2001, art. 35.

By contrast, and possibly by a drafting oversight, Qatar does not offer any description of an industrial design in its current law, although it offers definitions of the other areas of industrial property covered by the law.

As permitted by TRIPS Article 25.2, none of the States allows protection to extend to designs dictated essentially by technical or functional considerations. An industrial design cannot be registered if it lacks originality or has entered the public domain through publication or use prior to the filing of an application for registration or the priority application date. A common exception to the public domain qualification applies generally in respect of industrial designs which are displayed at international exhibitions or scientific conferences, for which temporary protection may apply.

Commonly excluded from protection are designs which may be contrary to *ordre public* or morality, while Saudi Arabia goes one step further by also excluding designs which are contrary to the *Shariah*.[51] Yemen goes a little further by excluding an industrial design that includes 'religious slogans or symbols, or seals or flags belonging to the Republic, other states or regional or international organisations'.[52] Yemen and Jordan exclude from protection an industrial design or model if it is dictated by technical or functional considerations of a product.[53]

Jordan identifies the right holder of an industrial design or model as the creator or their heirs. A right holder can be more than one person if all participated in the creation of the design or model as result of their joint effort, unless agreed otherwise. But if they created the design or model independently, the creator is deemed to be the first one who files an application for registration. If the creation is a result of an employment contract, which requires the employee to accomplish such a creation, the right holder is the employer, unless agreed otherwise.[54]

The nature of protection generally accords to the right holder the exclusive right to prevent any third party from using the industrial design in the manufacture of any product, or importing or otherwise possessing any product related to the industrial design or model for the purpose of using or offering for sale. All States require an industrial design to be registered to qualify for protection.[55] They enshrine the principle of 'first to register', registration being a presumption of ownership. While some allowance can be made for exceptions to this principle where 'the contrary is established', the absence of implementing regulations or judicial authority in each case does not provide any guidance as to what may constitute 'the contrary'. In the case of the Qatari law, the general application of the trademark provisions may by implication extend some protection to industrial designs, in the absence of any specific reference to an obligation for registration.

51 Saudi Arabia, Royal Decree No. M/27 of 1425 AH (2004), art. 4.
52 Yemen, Law No. 28 of 2010, art. 4(2).
53 Jordan, Law No. 14 of 2000, art. 4; Yemen, Law No. 28 of 2010, art. 4(3).
54 Jordan, Law No. 14 of 2000, art. 5
55 Oman, Royal Decree No. 67/2008, art. 20; Saudi Arabia, Royal Decree No. M/27 of 1425 AH (2004) arts 2 and 59; UAE, Federal Law No. 17 of 2002, arts 1 and 4.

Jordan has established a separate registration office, namely, the 'The Industrial Designs and Models Register'. The office is responsible for maintaining all information related to industrial designs and models, and any changes such as any assignment, transfer of ownership, or licence granted by the owner of the industrial design or model to others, and, also, any restriction on its use.[56]

Consistent with TRIPS Article 26.3, the period of protection is universally at least ten years from date of application or priority filing, with provision for an extension for an additional five years. Curiously, the Qatari law still provides for only five years' protection, albeit with opportunity for extension for two further similar periods but nonetheless subject to renewal application deadlines and payment of the requisite fees.[57] As the total period of Qatar's possible protection available amounts to more than ten years, it can be argued that Qatar still complies with TRIPS Article 26.3 in outcome if not entirely in spirit. Jordan goes beyond TRIPS standards for the term of protection of an industrial design or model, by providing a term of 15 years from the date of filing the application.[58]

The laws of Jordan, Saudi Arabia, the UAE and Yemen make particular reference to the protection of textile designs, which are generally acknowledged as being within the scope of industrial designs and therefore are accorded the same degree of protection.[59] They provide no other special protection or treatment for textile designs, other than this acknowledgement, and none makes reference to the requirements of TRIPS Article 25.2 in respect of the non-impairment of the opportunity for protection.

5.4.4 Infringements

The nature of an infringement against an industrial design right is described very briefly and succinctly. It is described variously as:

- any act of exploitation reserved exclusively for the design right holder undertaken without the prior approval of the right holder (Oman, Saudi Arabia and the UAE);[60]
- imitating a registered industrial design, knowingly using a registered industrial design with intention to mislead, and falsely claiming an industrial design is registered (Qatar, the UAE and Yemen);[61] or

56 Jordan, Law No. 14 of 2000, art. 3
57 Qatar, Law No. 9 of 2002, art. 44.
58 Jordan, Law No. 14 of 2000, art. 11.
59 Saudi Arabia, Royal Decree No. M/27 of 1425 AH (2004), art. 1; UAE, Federal Law No. 17 of 2002, art. 2.
60 Oman, Royal Decree No. 67/2008, s. 68; Saudi Arabia, Royal Decree No. M/27 of 1425 AH (2004), art. 34; UAE, Federal Law No. 31 of 2006, art. 51.
61 Qatar, Law No. 9 of 2002, art. 12; UAE, Federal Law No. 31 of 2006, art. 51; Yemen Law No. 28 of 2010, art. 34(a).

- knowingly selling, offering for sale, importing or otherwise trading in products or materials on which there appears an imitation of a registered industrial design, or falsely claiming that a design is registered (Bahrain, Jordan, Kuwait and Yemen).[62]

5.5 Patents

5.5.1 TRIPS provisions and obligations (Articles 27–34)

TRIPS Article 27 requires WTO members to make patents available for any invention, whether for a product or process, in all fields of technology without discrimination, provided that the invention is new, involves an inventive step and is capable of industrial application. It also requires that patents be available and patent rights be enjoyable without discrimination as to the place of invention, or whether products are imported or locally produced. Three exceptions are permitted to this basic rule on patentability, namely:

- inventions contrary to *ordre public* or morality, including inventions dangerous to human, animal or plant life or health or seriously prejudicial to the environment;
- diagnostic, therapeutic and surgical methods for the treatment of humans or animals;
- plants and animals other than micro-organisms and essentially biological processes for the production of plants or animals other than non-biological and microbiological processes.

However, any member excluding plant varieties from protection under patent provisions must provide an effective *sui generis* system of protection.

The exclusive rights that must be conferred by a product patent are those of making, using, offering for sale, selling and importing for these purposes. Process patent protection must extend rights not only over use of the process but also over products obtained directly by the process.[63] Patent owners shall also have the right to license, assign or transfer the patent. The term of protection available shall extend for a period of 20 years from the date of filing of the application.[64]

WTO members shall require that an applicant for a patent shall disclose the invention in a manner sufficiently clear and complete for the invention to be carried out by a person skilled in the art. They may also require the applicant to indicate the best

62 Bahrain, Legislative Decree No. 6 of 2006, art. 30; Jordan, Law No. 14 of 2000, art. 10; Kuwait, Law No. 4 of 1962 as amended by Law No. 4 of 1999 and Law No. 3 of 2001, art. 46; Yemen, Law No. 19 of 1994, art. 114.

63 TRIPS, art. 28.1.

64 Ibid., art. 33.

mode for carrying out the invention known to the inventor at the filing date of the application or, where priority is claimed, at the priority date of the application.[65]

Limited exceptions to the exclusive rights conferred by a patent may be allowed, provided that such exceptions do not unreasonably conflict with a normal exploitation of the patent and do not unreasonably prejudice the legitimate interests of the patent owner, and take account of the legitimate interests of third parties. Members may allow compulsory licensing and government use without the authorisation of the right holder, provided the latter's interests are still protected.[66] Compulsory licensing may be permitted only where the right holder has already refused to grant a voluntary licence on reasonable terms and within a reasonable period of time, although this requirement can be dispensed with in times of national or other extreme urgency or in cases of public non-commercial use.[67] Use of a compulsory licence provision should also be limited to the supply of the domestic market, although this requirement and the above condition on use may be waived to remedy anti-competitive practices.

TRIPS Article 34 provides for the reversal of the burden of proof in civil cases involving process patents, whereby the defendant may be required to prove that the process used to obtain an identical product is different from the patented process. Members are obliged to apply this presumption in the following circumstances:

- when the product obtained by the patented process is 'new'; or
- when there is a 'substantial likelihood that an identical product was made by the process and the owner of the patent has been unable through reasonable efforts to determine the process actually used'.

5.5.2 Patent laws in the Arabian Peninsula

As with copyright and neighbouring rights, the development of formal patent-protection regimes within the Arabian Peninsula States is a fairly recent event. Except for Bahrain and Kuwait, which both introduced patent legislation in 1955 and 1961, patent-protection laws did not appear until the late 1980s/early 1990s. The concern of the States for a strong patent-protection regime has not been particularly strong, simply because the environment to foster local invention and technology transfer has never really been strongly established. Hence there has been neither the generation of patent applications of local origin of any dimension, nor the opportunity for, or the existence of, a thriving patent infringement industry (as exists in the case of copyright). The issue of standards of patent-protection performance in the region has not generated any great concern from the developed countries, except perhaps from those governments and industry

65 Ibid., art. 30.

66 The term 'compulsory licence' does not appear in TRIPS, although it is used in the Paris Convention. The term used is 'other use without authorisation'.

67 TRIPS, art. 31.

lobby groups representing the interests of the international pharmaceutical conglomerates. The relatively few patents which have originated from within the States in recent times have mostly come from the energy industries in Saudi Arabia and the UAE. They have mostly been lodged by expatriate residents rather than nationals, been owned by a foreign company and have included a claim for priority based on an earlier foreign patent application.[68]

Although the principles enshrined in the various laws follow very similar themes and display a high degree of regional common ground, the laws differ quite significantly in terms of their breadth and attention to detail.

Bahrain was the first State to introduce a patent law with its pre-independence law of 1955 encompassing patents, trademarks and industrial designs. That law was subsequently upgraded in 1977 and entirely replaced in 2004 with a law which in turn was substantially modified in 2006 to reflect its intellectual property protection obligations under its free trade agreement with the United States. Kuwait issued its original patent law in 1962 and upgraded it in 1999 and again in 2001. The law was replaced in 2013 by Kuwait adopting the GCC Unified Patent Regulations of 1992 as amended in 2000 (hereinafter the GCC Patent Regulations).

The Supreme Council of the GCC issued its first GCC Patent Regulations and statute establishing the GCC Patent Office in Riyadh, Saudi Arabia, in December 1992. These were subsequently amended in late 1999 and reissued in April 2000. The main benefit of the GCC Patents Regulations is that it allows a GCC member State to obtain protection across all other members by the lodgment of a single patent application with the GCC Patent Office.[69]

Oman issued its first patent legislation in 2000, previously having preferred to adopt and adhere to the GCC Patents Regulations. It has since combined this law and a number of other related laws issued at the same time into a comprehensive

68 See WIPO, 'Statistical Country Profiles', available at www.wipo.int/ipstats/en/statistics/country_profile/#B, last accessed 26 May 2017. The statistical country profiles cover the period 2001 to 2015 inclusive, and provide information on patents, utility models, trademarks and industrial designs. They include information on applications from within the country, applications from outside the country, and applications which have already been lodged with another office claiming priority. It should be noted that the data is not necessarily complete, relying on WIPO members' IP offices to report annual figures and activity in the various WIPO industrial property classification and registration treaties which members have utilised. The data nevertheless provide a useful comparative basis for assessing industrial property activity.

69 Under the 1992 GCC Regulations, duplication of application or registration with the GCC Patent Office and with any GCC member State national patent office was not permitted. The GCC Patent Office would not accept any patent application if a separate application had already been lodged or a patent granted in a member State, unless the applicant undertook to first relinquish the national application or patent or as soon as a patent was provisionally granted by the GCC Patent Office (GCC Unified Patent Regulations, art. 29; Patent Office Guidelines, para. 11). The force of this cumbersome restriction was never effectively tested, since none of the GCC member States issued a patent in its own right and originating from its own nationals (as distinct from an international patent) by the time this restriction was deleted by the year 2000 amendments.

industrial property law, issued in 2008. Notwithstanding the existence of its own patent legislation, Oman continues to recognise the validity of the Regulations.

Qatar did not issue a domestic patents law until 2006, relying previously on the provisions of the GCC Patent Regulations to meet its TRIPS obligations in respect of patent protection. It should be noted, however, that the Regulations are essentially a registration statute and include very little by way of enforcement provisions, notably in respect of infringements, precautionary measures and sanctions. The Regulations defer these matters to each member State to establish within their own domestic laws. Although Qatar has now introduced a domestic patent law, it seems that it still needs to issue the necessary implementing regulations to bring the law into effect.

Saudi Arabia issued its original patent law in 1989, but replaced it in 2004 with a new law which also encompasses layout designs of integrated circuits, plant varieties and industrial models.

The UAE repealed its original 1992 law with Law No. 17 of 2002 which was amended in 2006. The law of 2002 and its amendments reflect the enhanced commercial environment and address the large number of TRIPS obligations in which the original law was deficient. The 1992 law suffered from a number of shortcomings, not least of which was the exclusion of pharmaceutical products from protection, although pharmaceutical processes were still protected. However, the subordinate implementing regulations still need to be issued before the law comes into effective use.

All States except Yemen are contracting parties to the Patent Cooperation Treaty (PCT), with the UAE the first State to accede in March 1999; Bahrain, Oman, Qatar, Saudi Arabia and Kuwait all followed suit in December 2006, July 2001, May 2011, May 2013 and June 2016 respectively. Jordan is the most recent party to the PCT, having lodged its instruments of accession with WIPO on 9 March 2017. The Treaty is expected to enter into force in Jordan on 9 June 2017.[70]

Jordan first enacted a patent law back in 1999, and then substantially amended it in 2001 and 2007. A new amended patent law is reportedly due to be approved by the Cabinet during 2017. The new amendment will accept online submission for patent applications. It will also allow the public to view rejected applications which were rejected based on the subject matter of the invention only. The underlying reason for this permission is to spread knowledge and the techniques that were used in the rejected patent, and also to prevent any kind of infringements. The new amendment will give the applicant the right to withdraw his application before granting the patent. In addition, the amendment touches on the rights of the patentee in regard to transferring the ownership, mortgaging the patent and cancelling it.

Yemen replaced its general intellectual property law of 1994 in 2011 by a comprehensive law for Patents, Utility Models, Layout Designs of Integrated Circuits and Undisclosed Information.

70 As reported in the *Saba Bulletin*, 20 December 2016, available at www.sabaip.com/en/News/Jordan-Accession-to-the-PCT, last accessed 13 March 2017.

TABLE 5.5 Current patent laws and conventions in the GCC member States

Bahrain	Legislative Decree No. 6 of 2012 ratifying Bahrain's Accession to the Budapest Treaty on the International Recognition of the Deposit of Microorganisms for the Purposes of Patent Procedure (August 2012)
	Legislative Decree No. 1 of 2004 in respect of Patents and Utility Models, as amended by Law No. 14 of 2006
	Legislative Decree No. 44 of 2005 ratifying Bahrain's accession to the Patent Cooperation Treaty
	Legislative Decree No. 19 of 2005 ratifying Bahrain's accession to the Patent Law Treaty
	Legislative Decree No. 12 of 2004 adopting the GCC Unified Patents Regulations in Bahrain
	Legislative Decree No. 31 of 1996 ratifying Bahrain's accession to the Paris Convention for the Protection of Industrial Property
Kuwait	Law No.11 of 2016 ratifying Kuwait's accession to the Patent Cooperation Treaty
	Law No. of 36 of 2014 ratifying Kuwait's accession to the Paris Convention for the Protection of Industrial Property
	Law No. 71 of 2013 ratifying the GCC Unified Patents Regulations
	Law No. 4 of 1962 as amended by Law No. 4 of 1999 and Law No. 3 of 2001 concerning designs and industrial models
Oman	Royal Decree No. 67/2008, the Law on Industrial Property Rights
	Royal Decree No. 37/2007 ratifying the Sultanate's accession to the Budapest Treaty on the International Recognition of the Deposit of Microorganisms for the Purposes of Patent Procedure, and the Patent Law Treaty
	Royal Decree No. 37/2001 ratifying the Sultanate's accession to the Patent Cooperation Treaty (PCT)
	Ministerial Decision No. 14/2000 recognising the GCC Unified Patents Regulations (1992) as the Patent Law of Oman
	Royal Decree No. 63/1998 ratifying the Sultanate's accession to the Paris Convention for the Protection of Industrial Property
Qatar	Law No. 21 of 2015 ratifying Qatar's accession to the Budapest Treaty on the International Recognition of the Deposit of Microorganisms for the Purposes of Patent Procedure
	Law No. 36 of 2011 ratifying Qatar's accession to the Patent Cooperation Treaty
	Law No. 30 of 2006 concerning Patents
	Law No. 12 of 2003 adopting the GCC Unified Patents Regulations as the Patent Law of Qatar
	Ministerial Decree No. 31 of 2001 in respect of Qatar's accession to the Paris Convention for the Protection of Industrial Property
Saudi Arabia	Royal Decree No. M/27 of 1434AH (2013) ratifying Saudi Arabia's accession to the Patent Cooperation Treaty and to the Patent Law Treaty
	Royal Decree No. M/27 of 1425 AH (2004), the Law of Patents, Layout

(continued)

TABLE 5.5 Current patent laws and conventions in the GCC member States *(continued)*

	Designs of Integrated Circuits, Plant Varieties and Industrial Models
	Royal Decree M/48 of 1424 AH (2003) acceding to the Paris Convention for the Protection of Industrial Property, and the Berne Convention for the Protection of Literary and Artistic Works
	Royal Decree No. M/28 of 1422 AH (2001) recognising the GCC Unified Patents Regulations
UAE	Federal Law No. 31 for the Year 2006 Pertaining to the Industrial Regulation and Protection of Patents, Industrial Drawings and Designs
	Federal Decree No. 84 of 1998 concerning the UAE's accession to the Patent Cooperation Treaty (PCT)
	Federal Decree No. 20 of 1996 concerning the UAE's accession to the Paris Convention for the Protection of Industrial Property
GCC	GCC: Unified Patent Regulations of 1992, as amended in 2000

Source: compiled by the authors

TABLE 5.6 Current patent laws and conventions in Jordan and Yemen

Jordan:	Accession of March 2017 to the Patent Cooperation Treaty
	Accession of November 2008 to Budapest Treaty on the International Recognition of the Deposit of Microorganisms for the Purposes of Patent Procedure
	Law No. 32 of 1999 on Patents, as amended in 2001 and 2007
Yemen	Law No. 2 of 2011 on Patents, Utility Models, Layout Designs of Integrated Circuits and Undisclosed Information
	Law of February 2007 ratifying Yemen's accession to the Paris Convention for the Protection of Industrial Property

Source: compiled by the authors

5.3 Patentability scope and criteria

In accordance with the requirements of TRIPS Article 27, the laws of the States and the GCC Patent Regulations generally provide that a patent may be granted for any new invention that is the result of a new idea or an innovative improvement on an invention which may be already patented, in any area of technology. The invention must be scientifically based and useful in industry, whether this entails new industrial products, the development of new industrial techniques, methods or processes, or new ways of applying well-known industrial techniques, methods or processes.[71] An

71 Bahrain, Legislative Decree No. 1 of 2004, art. 1; Jordan, Law No. 32 of 1999, as amended, art. 3; Kuwait and GCC Patents Regulation of 2000, art. 2; Oman, Royal Decree No. 67/2008, art. 2; Qatar, Law No. 30 of 2006, art. 2; Saudi Arabia, Royal Decree No. M/27 of 1425

invention can be considered as industrially applicable if it can be used in any kind of industry in the broadest sense of the word – which variously includes agriculture, fishing, handicraft or services. Yemen may have the most recent patent statue, but the Omani patent law has the best prescription on what may be 'new', 'inventive' and 'industrially applicable':

1 (1)(b) An invention is new if it is not anticipated by prior art.
Prior art shall consist of everything disclosed to the public, anywhere in the world, by publication in tangible form or by oral disclosure, by use or in any other way, prior to the filing or, where appropriate, the priority date, of the application claiming the invention.
. . .
2 An invention shall be considered as involving an inventive step if, having regard to the differences and similarities between the claimed invention and the prior art . . . the claimed invention as a whole would not have been obvious to a person skilled in the art at the filing date or, if applicable, at priority date of the claimed invention.
3 An invention shall be considered industrially applicable if it can be made or used in any kind of industry or if it has specific, substantial and credible utility. The term 'industry' shall be understood in its broadest sense, as any human economic activity leading to the production of goods and services; it shall cover, in particular, handicraft, agriculture, fishery and services.[72]

Bahrain, Kuwait, Oman, the UAE and Yemen make provision for the registrability and protection of a utility model, provided it is new, involves an inventive step and is industrially applicable. They describe a utility model as an invention which is not sufficiently inventive or creative to obtain a patent but which otherwise meets the requirements of the patent law in terms of being new and of practical application in industry.[73] Jordan, Qatar and Saudi Arabia do not make any distinction between patents and utility models, omitting from their respective laws any reference to the latter. It is worth noting that, while TRIPS does not make any reference to utility models, protection afforded to utility models by Articles 1(2), 4 and 5 of the Paris Convention is still binding on WTO members. Article 1(2) of the Convention stipulates that the protection of industrial property includes utility models.

Commonly excluded from patentability is any invention (or the exploitation thereof) which may represent a violation of *ordre public* or morality, or which may

AH (2004), art. 43; UAE, Federal Law No. 31 of 2006, art. 4; Yemen, Law No.2 of 2011, art. 5.

72 Oman, Royal Decree No. 67/2008, art. 3.

73 Bahrain, Legislative Decree No. 1 of 2004, art. 30; Oman, Royal Decree No. 65/2008, arts 1 and 15; Kuwait, Law No. 4 of 1962 as amended by Law No. 4 of 1999, art. 34*bis*; UAE, Federal Law No. 31 of 2006, art. 1; Yemen, Law No. 2 of 2011, art. 5.

be harmful to human, animal or plant life, to health, or to the environment. Saudi Arabia, Yemen and the GCC Regulation add a further condition which specifically excludes from patentability any invention which may conflict with the principles of Islamic *Shariah* or which affects national security.[74] Yemen and the GCC Patent Regulations add an exception to the registration – namely, mathematical discoveries, theories and procedures such as methods of doing business and performing purely intellectual activity or playing games.[75] The UAE recognises that inventions which may have national security implications may still be protected but directs that they will be dealt with in accordance with special procedures to be stipulated in the implementing regulations.[76] Besides these possible special exclusions, the common exclusions from patentability reflect the limitations prescribed by TRIPS Article 27.3, namely:

- diagnostic, therapeutic and surgical methods for the treatment of animals or humans (but not the products used in these methods);
- plants and animals other than micro-organisms, and essentially biological processes for the production of plants or animals (other than non-biological and microbiological processes);
- discoveries, scientific theories and principles, mathematical and business methods, computer programs, pure mental activities and game playing.

In addition to the above, Oman excludes from protection natural substances and known substances for which a new use has been discovered, but extends protection to:

- process inventions which consist of steps performed or directed by a computer program; and
- product inventions consisting of elements of a computer-implemented invention, including in particular machine-readable program code stored on a tangible medium and a general-purpose computer whose novelty arises primarily from its combination with a specific computer program.[77]

Bahrain maintains by far the narrowest range of inventions excluded from possible patentability. Besides the above general *ordre public* and morality exclusion provisions, the only inventions for which patents shall not be granted have been confined to those relating to:

74 Saudi Arabia, Royal Decree No. M/27 of 1425 AH (2004), art. 4(a); GCC Unified Patent Regulations, art. 2; Yemen, Law No. 2 of 2011, art. 6.
75 GCC Unified Patent Regulations, art. 3; Yemen, Law No. 2 of 2011, art. 6.
76 UAE, Federal Law No. 31 of 2006, art. 6.2.
77 Oman, Royal Decree No. 67/2008, art. 2(1)(c) and 2(2).

- animals;
- diagnostic, therapeutic and surgical methods necessary for the treatment of humans and animals, with the exception of products used in any of these methods.[78]

Jordan covers in its exclusion from patentability a wide range of inventions including TRIPS exceptions as follows:

- inventions whose exploitation is detrimental to public order or public morality;
- inventions whose non-exploitation is necessary to protect the life and health of humans, animals and plants or to avoid severe damage to the environment;
- discoveries, scientific theories and mathematical methods;
- diagnostic, therapeutic and surgical methods necessary for the treatment of humans or animals;
- plants and animals other than micro-organisms;
- biological methods for the reproduction of plants and animals other than non-biological and microbiological methods.[79]

Adequate protection for patented pharmaceutical and agricultural chemical products in the States has been a matter for concern for the major multinational pharmaceutical companies and has caused their national governments to scrutinise the States' patent laws. The pre-TRIPS patent laws of Bahrain, Kuwait, Saudi Arabia and the UAE specifically excluded patent protection for chemical inventions relating to foodstuffs, medicines or pharmaceutical formulae. However, these States would argue that pharmaceutical and agrochemical products now receive full patent protection by virtue of their non-inclusion in the above list of exclusions from patentability. Kuwait, Saudi Arabia and the UAE, for example, each originally excluded from protection:

> chemical inventions relating to foodstuffs, medical drugs or pharmaceuticals unless those products are manufactured in special chemical methods. In this case, the protection shall be for the methods of manufacture not the products themselves[80]

but have since removed this particular reference in their current laws to bring their lists of patentability exclusions into line with TRIPS Article 27.3.

The Yemeni pre-TRIPS law of 1994 prohibited from patentability any invention which violates the Yemeni social system and the provisions of the Islamic jurisprudence.[81] It further excluded from patentability non-chemical inventions

78 Bahrain, Legislative Decree No. 1 of 2004 as amended by Law No. 14 of 2006, art. 3(a).
79 Jordan, Law No. 32 of 1999 as amended by Regulation No. 97, art. 4.
80 Kuwait, Law No. 4 of 1962, art. 2(2); UAE, Federal Law No. 44 of 1992, art. 6(ii).
81 Yemen, Law No. 19 of 1994, art. 65.

related to foodstuff, medicines or pharmaceuticals (except for any special chemical processes or methods used in their manufacture); new methods for the treatment of diseases; and biological methods for the production of new type of animals or plants.

However, since its accession to the WTO, the Yemeni law has been replaced by Law No. 2 of 2011 to better suit the TRIPS requirements and standards. Hence, the exceptions to patentability are:

- inventions the use of which would violate *Shariah* law, public order or public morals, or the national security; or inventions harmful to the environment, or to the life or health of humans, animals or plants;
- mathematical discoveries, theories and procedures; the rules, regulations and procedures for carrying out commercial activity, for performing pure intellectual activity, or for playing games;
- methods of diagnosis, cure or surgery for either humans or animals;
- plants or animals, or the methods used to produce plants or animals with the exception of micro-organisms, non-biological methods and microbiological processes;
- living organs, tissues and cells, natural biological materials, DNA, blood, hormones or genes.[82]

5.5.4 Rights conferred by a registered patent

The patent laws provide the right holder with the exclusive rights to enjoy and explore his invention. Yet it is important to determine who the lawful right holder of an invention might be, since the inventor may not necessarily be the right holder. The Jordanian law provides a clear description of the right holder/s, as follows:

- if the invention is a result of joint efforts of several people, all of them will be equal partners in the ownership, unless agreed otherwise;
- if several people invent the same invitation at the same time separately and independently, the rights shall belong to the applicant who files it;
- the rights will be accorded to the employer if the invention is conducted by the employee during the course of employment and relates to the activities or business of the employer, or if the employee in making the invention uses the experience, business, information, instruments or the articles of the employer under his own disposal, unless otherwise agreed in writing;
- the rights will be accorded to the employee, if the invention does not relate to the activities or business of the employer and the employee in making the invention did not use the experience, information, instruments or raw materials

82 Yemen, Law No. 2 of 2011, art. 6.

of the employer, under the employee's own disposal, unless otherwise agreed in writing.[83]

Omani patent law provides more detail in regard to inventions that are invented as a result of an employment contact. An employer is obligated to increase the employee's salary when the economic gain of the invention is disproportionately high compared with the salary. This obligation to pay remuneration arises from the making of the invention and the exploiting of it. Even if the employer fails or neglects to register a patent, it does not exempt him from paying the remuneration. And if he fails or neglects to file for a patent application within one year from the date on which the employee reported the invention, the employee shall have the right to the patent. However, if the employee files an application within one year after the expiry of the employment contract and that the invention falls within the scope of the former employer's main business, it will be presumed that the invention has been made under the expired contract, unless the employee produces evidence to the contrary.[84]

The patent laws generally provide that the owner of a patent has the exclusive right to exploit the invention by manufacturing, using such invention and importing what is manufactured thereof, selling and offering it for sale, irrespective of whether the subject of the patent is a product or a process.[85] The owner is also protected against the importation and offering for sale of a patented invention by a third party. Where the patent has been granted for a process, the owner enjoys the right in respect of the process and in respect of any product directly obtained by means of that process. The owner also has the right to transfer his patent and its title with or without compensation and may grant it to others by inheritance.[86]

Consistent with the requirements of TRIPS Article 33, all States provide for a period of protection of 20 years from the date of filing of the application.[87] Of those that recognise utility models, namely Bahrain, Kuwait, Oman and the UAE, protection is generally provided for a period of ten years from date of filing.

83 Bahrain, Legislative Decree No. 1 of 2004, arts 8–10; Jordan, Law No. 32 of 1999 as amended in 2001, art. 5, GCC Unified Patent Regulations, art. 2; Oman, Royal Decree No. 67/2008, art. 4; Qatar, Law No. 30 of 2006, art. 3; Saudi Arabia, Royal Decree No. M/27 of 1425 AH (2004), arts 5 and 6; UAE, Federal Law No. 31 of 2006, art. 9; Yemen, Law No. 2 of 2011, arts 7 and 8.

84 Oman, Royal Decree No. 67/2008, art. 4.

85 Bahrain, Legislative Decree No. 1 of 2004, art. 11.2; Jordan, Law 32 of 1999, as amended, art. 21; Kuwait, pursuant to GCC Regulations of 2000, art. 12; Oman, Royal Decree No. 67/2008, art. 11; UAE, Federal Law No. 31 of 2006, art. 15; Yemen, Law No. 2 of 2011, art. 17.

86 Jordan, Law No. 32 of 1999, as amended, art. 27.

87 Bahrain, Legislative Decree No. 1 of 2004, art. 14; Kuwait, Law No. 4 of 1962 as amended by Law No. 4 of 1999, art. 12; Oman, Royal Decree No. 67/2008, art. 12(1); Qatar, Law No. 30 of 2006, art. 11; Saudi Arabia, Royal Decree No. M/27 of 1425 AH (2004), art. 19; UAE, Federal Law No. 31 of 2006, art. 14.

However, Kuwait's 'patents for models of use' may receive protection for only seven years from date of application, with no provision for renewal.[88]

All States allow for claims of priority under certain conditions in respect of a patent application first lodged in another country. Generally, claims of priority are allowed if the original application is lodged in a country which is a WTO member or is party to an international agreement or treaty to which the State has also acceded. Jordan allows for claim of priority of a national, regional or international application previously filed in any country with a bilateral or multilateral agreement for industrial property protection with Jordan, within a period of 12 months from the filing of the first application. Oman and Yemen take a similar approach.

By virtue of their PCT accession, the States further provide for claims of priority on the basis of an application first submitted in any of the other PCT member countries. The period of time for claiming priority is 12 months from date of first filing.

Bahrain and Oman provide for the protection period to be extended for a further period of up to four (Bahrain) or five (Oman) years to allow for delays in granting patent approval where such delays are not attributable to conduct on the part of the patent applicant.[89] They further provide for extension of protection where delays occur in the marketing approval process on product safety and efficacy. Bahrain limits eligibility for such extensions to pharmaceutical products, but sets the maximum possible period as 'sufficient to compensate the patent holder for any justified reduction in actual protection period', while Oman limits such extended period to up to two years, but does not specify any particular products to which the extension provision applies.

Jordan, Oman and Saudi Arabia alone make provision for the reversal of the burden of proof in respect of process patents, to the extent required by TRIPS Article 34: namely, when the product obtained by the patented process is new, or when there is a 'substantial likelihood that the identical product was made by the process and the owner of the patent has been unable through reasonable efforts to determine the process actually used'.[90]

Bahrain and Yemen acknowledge the need to include such provision, but only in respect of the second of the two conditions stipulated in TRIPS Article 34.1: that is, where there is a substantial likelihood that the identical product was made by the patented process and the patent owner has been unable to reasonably determine the process actually used.[91]

The fact that provision for the reversal of the burden of proof has been considered by some of the other States would seem to indicate that the issue has

88 Kuwait, Law No. 4 of 1999, art. 34*bis*(a).

89 Bahrain, Legislative Decree No. 1 of 2004, as amended by Legislative Decree No. 14 of 2006, art. 14(b)–(c); Oman, Royal Decree No. 67/2008, art. 12.

90 Jordan, Law No. 32 of 1999, as amended, art. 34; Oman, Royal Decree No. 67/2008, art. 74(3); Saudi Arabia, Royal Decree No. M/27 of 1424 AH (2004), art. 48.

91 Bahrain, Legislative Decree No. 1 of 2004, as amended by Legislative Decree No. 14 of 2006, art. 12; Yemen, Law No. 2 of 2011, art. 40.

been put to one side rather than forgotten. The UAE had considered the inclusion of an appropriate clause at a late stage in the drafting process for its 2006 law, but for some unexplained reason did not include any such provision in the final promulgated version.[92] Such omission by the States may not be entirely accidental or unintentional. Retention of the burden of proof upon the complainant, being the right holder of the patent and thus most likely of foreign origin, would work in favour of local industry and against the likelihood of successful 'strategic litigation' by the foreign right holder.[93]

5.5.5 Compulsory licensing

All States and the GCC itself take advantage of provisions for compulsory licensing as permitted by TRIPS Article 31. Generally, the laws provide that a non-inclusive non-transferable compulsory licence may be granted by the responsible minister in circumstances where the patent or utility certificate has not been utilised actively and seriously within two (Qatar) or three years from being awarded, or where the patent holder's refusal to grant a licence to utilise it may impact upon the establishment or development of industrial or commercial activities within the State concerned.[94] Jordan, Saudi Arabia and Yemen stipulate a period of four years from the date of lodgment of a patent application or three years from date of grant, whichever is the later, provided the patent holder has not exploited the invention or done so inadequately. Jordan also may grant a compulsory license to use a patent if it is a necessity for national defence or emergency or if the patent holder has exercised his rights in such a way as to prevent others from competing fairly. In addition, approval of the patent holder is not required if the issuance of the compulsory licence is for export to a country suffering a pandemic or other national health emergency.[95]

The party seeking the award of a compulsory licence must be able to demonstrate that efforts were made to obtain a licence from the patent holder under reasonable commercial terms and conditions, and that the applicant has the

92 In June 2002, the UAE reported to the WTO Council of TRIPS, in response to questions from members, that the draft amendments to its patent law provided that 'in the case of litigation concerning process patents, the court shall have the authority to order a defendant to prove the manufacturing process which he has used is different from the process protected by the Patent'. However, this provision does not appear in the settled law, which was enacted later that year. See WTO Document IP/C/W/291/Add.2 (02-1093), 5 March 2002, p. 3.

93 Fred Warshovsky, as quoted by Carlos Correa in Correa and Abdulqawi (eds) (1998), op. cit., p. 217.

94 Bahrain, Legislative Decree No. 1 of 2004, art. 25; Kuwait, Law No. 4 of 1962 as amended by Law No. 4 of 1999, art. 29; Oman, Royal Decree No. 67/2008, art. 13; Qatar, Law No. 30 of 2006, art. 15; Saudi Arabia, Royal Decree No. M/27 of 1425 AH (2004), art. 24; UAE, Federal Law No. 31 of 2006, art. 24.

95 Jordan, Law No. 32 of 1999, as amended, art. 22; Saudi Arabia, Royal Decree No. M/27 of 1425 AH (2004), art. 24; Yemen, Law No. 2 of 2011, art. 33.

means and capacity to sufficiently exploit the invention. Conditions attached to the issuance of a compulsory licence, which largely reflect those stipulated by TRIPS, require that:

- the patent or utility certificate holder is entitled to receive fair compensation;
- the compulsory licence is non-transferable, except where the ownership of the establishment of the licensee or the part thereof utilising the patent has been assigned;
- the issuance of the compulsory licence is intended to satisfy the needs of the local market only (the assumption being that local market means national market); and
- the right holder may still exploit the patent or license others to do so.

In the case of semi-conductor technology, Bahrain, Jordan, Oman, Saudi Arabia, the UAE and Yemen provide that the compulsory licence may be granted only for public, non-commercial use, or to remedy a practice determined after judicial or administrative process to be anti-competitive or an act of unlawful competition.[96]

Notwithstanding the requirements of TRIPS Article 27.1 that 'patents shall be available and patent rights enjoyable without discrimination as to the place of invention . . . and whether products are imported or locally made', Qatar and the UAE stipulate that importation is not deemed to be 'working' a patent and therefore does not constitute justification for precluding the granting of a compulsory licence to another party.[97] This would appear to be in direct contradiction of TRIPS Article 27.1 and the GCC Unified Patent Regulations Articles 12.1 and 12.2, all of which recognise importation as working the patent and thereby a ground for precluding the issuance of a compulsory licence. It would also appear to be discriminating against patents on the grounds of origin, again contrary to TRIPS Article 27.1, but it is a discrimination that works in favour of the States concerned.

Both Oman and the UAE have separately confirmed that import of the product shall not be deemed a legitimate reason to prevent the issue of the obligatory authorisation (compulsory licence).[98] In response to questioning from WTO's

96 Bahrain, Legislative Decree No. 1 of 2004, art. 25; Jordan, Law No. 32 of 1999, as amended, art. 23; Oman, Royal Decree No. 67/2008, s. 13(9); Saudi Arabia, Royal Decree No. M/27 of 1425 AH (2004), art. 24(b); UAE, Federal Law No. 31 of 2006, art. 24.1(h); Yemen, Law No. 2 of 2011, art. 34.

97 Qatar, Law No. 30 of 2006, art. 15; UAE, Federal Law No. 31 of 2006, art. 24.2.

98 In the case of the UAE, WTO Council for Trade-Related Aspects of Intellectual Property Rights, *Review of Legislation: the United Arab Emirates*, Document IP/C/W/291 (01-3419), 10 July 2001, 5. The UAE has also clouded the issue on importation. It originally advised the Council of TRIPS that 'in defending his position, the owner of the patent cannot introduce imported product as a valid ground. It does not present a legitimate reason for avoiding compulsory licensing if one or more of the reasons referred to in the above-mentioned Article 23 of the Patent Law are met.' When the UAE was further questioned on

Council of TRIPS on this apparent contradiction, Oman has offered the following explanation of its position:

> [I]t has become clear that Article 27/1 of TRIPS do [sic] not contradict with Article 15/c of the Patent Law as Article 27/1 deals with the Patent Law and the patentable materials in general while the Article 15/c of the Patent Law deals with obtaining the compulsory licence in exploiting the patent and the importation is not considered as legal reason to grant the compulsory licence.[99]

The Omani response would appear to simply add to the contradiction, or at least to confuse the issue; in any case, the response was not pursued further within the Council of TRIPS. The UAE has similarly confirmed before the Council that importation does not satisfy the requirements of working a patent, but again has also clouded the issue.[100] The WTO developed-country members appear to have seen little point in lodging a dispute against (or 'seeking consultations with') any of the three States under the WTO's Dispute Settlement procedures over the States' respective stances on patent working.[101]

Authority for granting and revoking compulsory licences generally rests with the responsible minister (or minister-equivalent in the case of Saudi Arabia).[102]

this point, it advised that 'the approved amendment of the Article 23 of the Patent and Designs Law doesn't stipulate any more that the importation of the product is not considered legal justification for the owner to avoid compulsory licence. Therefore, the Patent law related provisions are now in conformity with Article 27 and 31 of the TRIPS Agreement' (WTO Document IP/C/W/291/Add. 3 (02-3461), 24 June 2002). However, when the settled law was issued a few months later, it retained the provision of the earlier law that excluded importation as working the patent.

99 WTO Council for Trade-Related Aspects of Intellectual Property Rights, *Review of Legislation: Oman*, Document IP/Q/OMN/1 (03-1675), 24 March 2003.

100 WTO Council for Trade-Related Aspects of Intellectual Property Rights, *Checklist of Issues on Enforcement: Responses from Qatar*, Document IP/C/W/291/Add 3 (02-3461), 24 June 2002.

101 There would have been little point in the United States bringing such a dispute to the WTO's Dispute Settlement Body (DSB), since it had already 'covered the ground' on this issue with its dispute against Brazil in May 2000 (DS199 of 30 May 2000) in respect of the provisions on the local working of a patent in Article 68 of Brazil's industrial property law. The position already taken by Brazil was very similar to that adopted by Bahrain, Oman and the UAE. In what was more or less a face-saving win for both sides, the US agreed to withdraw the dispute and settle its differences with Brazil outside the formal WTO DSB forum. It also acknowledged that its dispute related to the potential use by Brazil of its Article 68 rather than any actual application. In return, Brazil, while asserting that its patent law did not contravene TRIPS Article 27, agreed to hold prior consultation with the US if it ever decided to impose a compulsory licence on a US-held patent in Brazil. See WTO Dispute Settlement: *Dispute DS199: Brazil – Measure Affecting Patent Protection* and WTO Dispute Settlement: *Dispute DS224: United States – US Patent Code*, Documents WT/DS199/1 and 3 (01-0093 and 01-506).

102 Namely, the President of the King Abdul Aziz City for Science and Technology (KACST), the national centre responsible for patents, and all other industrial property, policy and administration. See Royal Decree No. M/27 of 1425 AH (2004), arts 27–28.

The UAE law, however, requires such decisions to remain within the jurisdiction of the courts, although the responsible minister may grant the compulsory licence where the exploitation of the patent is deemed to be in the national interest.[103] The Bahraini, Jordanian, Omani, UAE and Yemeni ministerial decisions are still subject to possible judicial appeal.[104]

Although the GCC Unified Patent Regulation prescribes the grounds for issuing compulsory licences, it generally defers to State laws in respect of provision for compulsory licensing. However, the GCC Patent Office may still grant a compulsory licence to a government agency of a GCC member State to exploit a patent, albeit still subject to the conditions that prevail in the domestic legislation.[105] The GCC Patent Office claims (although it is not specified in the regulations or subordinate bylaws) that the prior consent of all six GCC member States must be given for the Office to issue a compulsory licence, which constitutes an additional assurance against any abuse in the compulsory licensing regime.[106] In practice, however, the granting of compulsory licensing has never been exercised by the GCC Patent Office in order to test this requirement.

5.5.6 Infringements

The patent laws of the States reveal a fair degree of common ground in their descriptions of the nature of the infringement of patent rights, although the remedies and level of sanctions available can differ markedly. The laws are also rather succinct, perhaps overly so, when compared with the infringement descriptions contained in the corresponding copyright laws. The laws offer only the broadest definition of acts which may constitute an infringement, as generally being 'any act of exploitation of rights provided for in the provisions governing each of the patented subject matters . . . without the written consent of the registered patentee'.[107] Acts of exploitation in essence include the making, importing, offering for sale, or storing for such purposes, in respect of goods the subject of a patent or goods produced directly by a process the subject of a patent. Oman and the UAE, in almost identical terms, both add the act of providing false information or documents to obtain a patent or utility certificate as an infringing act.[108]

103 UAE, Federal Law No. 17 of 2002, arts 28 and 29.1.
104 Bahrain, Legislative Decree No. 1 of 2004, as amended by Law No. 14 of 2006, art. 36; Jordan, Law No. 32 of 1999, as amended, art. 26; Oman, Royal Decree No. 67/2008, art. 14; UAE, Federal Law No. 31 of 2006, art. 29.2; Yemen, Law No. 2 of 2011, art. 11.
105 GCC Unified Patent Regulations as amended 2000, art. 20.3.
106 See GCC Patent Office news, available at www.gulf-patent-office.org.sa/Regulationframe.htm, last accessed 30 November 2010.
107 As stipulated by Saudi Royal Decree No. M/27 of 1425 AH (2004), art. 34.
108 Oman, Royal Decree No. 67/2008, art. 66(1); UAE, Federal Law No. 31 of 2006, art. 62.

The Bahraini, Jordanian and Yemeni laws, again in very similar language, stipulate that a person who knowingly and unlawfully commits any of the following acts infringes the rights of the patent owner:

- imitates an invention or utility model for which a patent was granted pursuant to the law;
- labels products, advertisements, marks, packaging or wrapping materials or the like in a manner indicating that he has obtained a patent or utility model patent;
- produces, sells, displays for sale or distribution, imports, or obtains for trading purposes a product protected by a patent in the State.[109]

As occurs in respect of the other major areas of intellectual property, all States make provision for precautionary measures to be sought in instances of threatened or actual infringements

5.5.7 Yemen's 'right to a discovery'

The Yemeni intellectual property law of 1994 had an interesting feature not seen in the other industrial property laws of the region. It provided for formal recognition and registration of a 'discovery'. The old law defines an act of 'discovery' as 'obtain[ing] knowledge of an existing matter previously unknown in the fields of laws, characteristics and phenomena related to the material world, including the discovery of materials or living things'.[110] The Act provided that a Yemeni who obtained knowledge of an existing matter previously unknown in the fields of 'laws, characteristics and phenomena related to the material world' may be deemed to have made a discovery and shall be entitled to enjoy certain rights, including the following:

- naming rights over the discovery;
- the grant of an 'incentive remuneration . . . determined by a resolution by the Council of Ministers, and . . . paid to the discoverer as a lump sum'; and
- a certificate attesting to the discovery and granting priority over the discovery.

The law further provided that after the remuneration was paid, the discovery would enter the public domain and becomes the right of all citizens. However, where the discovery is within the field of industrial or agricultural development, the discoverer may still enjoy exploitation rights under the patent or industrial designs provisions of the law, as appropriate.

109 Bahrain, Legislative Decree No. 1 of 2004, as amended by Legislative Decree No. 14 of 2006, art. 41; Jordan, Law No. 32 of 1999 as amended, art. 32; Yemen, Law No. 2 of 2011, art. 36.

110 See Yemen, Law No. 19 of 1994, arts 49–57.

In 2011, Yemen entirely replaced its law of 1994 to be more in compliance with TRIPS standards. Hence, the section covering the Right of Discovery was deleted. The section was a unique provision of the old law, but clearly did not fit with the current thinking of an invention and patent.

5.6 Layout designs (topographies) of integrated circuits

5.6.1 TRIPS provisions and obligations (Articles 35–38)

TRIPS requires members to provide protection on the basis of certain provisions of the Washington Treaty on Intellectual Property in Respect of Integrated Circuits (Washington, 1989).[111] These provisions deal, *inter alia*, with the definition of an 'integrated circuit' and 'layout-design (topography)' requirements for protection, exclusive rights and limitations, as well as exploitation, registration and disclosure. TRIPS adds to the Washington Treaty provisions on four points:

- the minimum term of protection shall be ten years, instead of the eight years stipulated in the Washington Treaty (Article 38.1);
- the rights must extend to articles incorporating infringing layout designs (Article 36);
- unwitting infringers must be allowed to use or sell stock already acquired or ordered at the time of being advised of their infringement (Article 37.1); and
- the conditions of TRIPS Article 31 in respect of compulsory licensing or government use without the authorisation of the right holder apply *mutatis mutandis* to layout designs, instead of the more generous corresponding provisions of the Washington Treaty (Article 37.2).

In essence, TRIPS excludes provisions of the Treaty (notably those on compulsory licensing) that had been rejected by the United States and Japan during the negotiations on the Treaty and supplements the latter with the stricter provisions that those countries had failed to obtain at the Washington Diplomatic Conference.[112]

111 Washington Treaty on Intellectual Property in Respect of Integrated Circuits, arts 2–7 (except art. 6(3)), art. 12 and art. 16(3). The Washington Treaty was opened for signature in May 1989, but has never come into force. Articles 2(i) and (ii) of the Treaty define an integrated circuit and layout design (topography) as follows:

- an 'integrated circuit' means a product, in its final form or an intermediate form, in which the elements, at least one of which is an active element, and some or all of the interconnections are integrally formed in and/or on a piece of material and which is intended to perform an electronic function;
- a 'layout design (topography)' is defined as the three-dimensional disposition, however expressed, of the elements, at least one of which is an active element, and of some or all of the interconnections of an integrated circuit, or such a three-dimensional disposition prepared for an integrated circuit intended for manufacture.

112 Carlos Correa, 'Layout Designs of Integrated Circuits', in Correa and Abdulqawi (eds) (1998), op. cit., pp. 234–5.

The TRIPS obligation to protect layout designs applies to such layout designs that are original in the sense that they are the result of their creators' intellectual effort and are not commonplace among creators of layout designs and manufacturers of integrated circuits at the time of their creation.[113] The exclusive rights include the right of reproduction and the right of importation, sale and other distribution for commercial purposes. WTO members are required to consider unlawful the unauthorised sale, importation or distribution for commercial purposes of a protected layout design or integrated circuit incorporating such design or an article incorporating such integrated circuit if it contains an unlawfully reproduced layout design.[114] The minimum period of protection is ten years from the date of filing for registration, or from the date of first commercial exploitation where a member does not require registration as a condition for protection; in any case, protection may lapse 15 years after the creation of the layout design.[115]

5.6.2 Layout-design laws in the Arabian Peninsula

As is the case with plant varieties, the protection of layout designs of integrated circuits is not an issue generating any great concern or attention with either the Arabian Peninsula States or developed countries operating, or with interests, in the States. As Correa has pointed out, the semi-conductor industry is highly concentrated in a few industrialised countries, and technological advancement is an interactive, cumulative process in which improvements are directly based on the pre-existing stock of carefully guarded knowledge.[116] Developing countries are most unlikely to have the technological skills and knowledge capacity to manufacture counterfeit products that incorporate chips and chip technology products; they are net importers of such products. The impact of TRIPS in respect of layout designs is likely to be felt mainly in respect of the importation of these products, which, in any case, will be slight. While software piracy has been an ongoing problem of some dimension in the States, counterfeit chip technology production or importation involving the States does not appear to have ever arisen as an issue as far as the chip technology industry is concerned. It is not surprising, therefore, that the States have either largely ignored the issue of protection of layout designs (the UAE) or have simply added brief reference to them in the general provisions of their other intellectual property laws (Kuwait, Oman, Saudi Arabia and Yemen).

Bahrain, Jordan and Qatar, however, have discrete laws in place. The Bahraini law in particular is very comprehensive by regional standards. The law includes substantive issues not seen in the other States' laws in respect of the creator's rights

113 TRIPS, art. 35, and Rome Convention, art. 3.2.

114 TRIPS, art. 36.

115 Ibid., art. 38.2–3.

116 Carlos Correa, 'Layout Designs of Integrated Circuits', in Correa and Abdulqawi (eds) (1998), op. cit., p. 234.

in the employment context, expiry of rights and grievance procedures.[117] It also contains a fairly comprehensive level of detail relating to registration procedures that would perhaps be normally deferred to implementing regulations. The Jordanian law goes as far as the Bahraini law. The law includes the creator's rights in the employment context as well as licensing and exploiting the design and the precautionary measures and sanctions in case of infringement.[118]

Kuwait's provision for the protection for layout designs of integrated circuits in its other intellectual property laws is token, to say the least. It has argued that protection has been provided by extending to them the protection already given to industrial designs and models in its patent and industrial designs law.[119] It has achieved this by the simple strategy of inserting the words 'and integrated circuits' after the words 'designs and industrial models' wherever the latter appears throughout the patents and designs law, by amendments in 1999. Accordingly, the period of protection, the nature of infringements and the sanctions and relief that apply in respect of designs and industrial models also apply to layout designs. For example, a layout design must therefore be registered to obtain protection, and protection is provided for a period of ten years from date of application. However, the Kuwaiti industrial design law as it currently stands does not provide any definition or description of what may constitute a layout design or integrated circuit (as it does for a design and an industrial model). This strategy has had the effect of creating by implication an inappropriate description of an integrated circuit as being the same as that for a design or industrial model – namely, 'any arrangement of lines or any type of figure, whether coloured or uncoloured, designed for use in industrial production by a mechanical, manual or chemical process'.[120]

Oman introduced discrete legislation for the protection of layout designs in 2000, the first State to do so, but has since incorporated such provisions into its comprehensive industrial property rights law of 2008, and rescinded the integrated circuits law of 2000.[121]

The Yemeni law on patents, utility models, layout designs of integrated circuits and undisclosed Information and the Saudi law on patents, plant varieties, industrial models and layout designs both dedicate just five articles to the protection of layout designs, but extend general provisions throughout the respective laws to apply equally to layout designs.[122]

The nature and authoritative source of any protection for layout designs within the UAE intellectual property regime are confused and they appear, therefore, to receive protection more by implication than by specific provision. In July 2001,

117 See Bahrain, Legislative Decree No. 5 of 2006, arts 7–9.
118 Jordan, Law No. 10 of 2000 on the Protection of Layout Designs of Integrated Circuits.
119 See WTO Council for Trade-Related Aspects of Intellectual Property Rights, *Review of Legislation: Kuwait*, Document IP/Q4/KWT/1 (01-6332), 13 December 2001, p. 28.
120 Kuwait, Law No. 4 of 1999, art. 1.
121 Oman, Royal Decree No. 67/2008, arts 27–35.
122 Saudi Arabia, Royal Decree No. M/27 of 1425 AH (2004), arts 49–53.

the UAE advised the WTO that layout designs were protected under its patent law and specifically that the law's provisions relating to industrial designs and models applied equally to integrated circuits – a similar strategy to that adopted by Kuwait, but without the legislative formalisation.[123] The basis for such claim in the patent law was unclear, and the relationship between industrial designs or models and layout designs was equally unclear. In March 2002, the UAE again advised the WTO that topographies were classified among the works protected under its copyright law.[124] The period of protection was the same as that available to other forms of copyrightable material, very much greater than that provided by the corresponding patent legislation. The WTO appeared to have been satisfied with the UAE response since there is no record of the contradictory explanations having been pursued further.

Since the UAE Ministry has not received any applications for registration of layout designs of integrated circuits at the time of writing, the veracity of the above claims has not yet been tested. Nor have there been cases on infringements of right holder's rights in respect of layout designs or integrated circuits to come before the UAE federal or local courts to clarify under which law a prosecution for infringement of the right the owner of a layout design might proceed. In 2010, the UAE reportedly advised that it was considering the introduction of layout designs for integrated circuits law, which would bring the UAE to compliance with TRIPS. The proposed law would cover the registration process and the standards or requirement of registering a layout design, as well as a term of protection of 15 years.[125] However, seven years on, there has not been any sign of such legislation.

Table 5.7 shows the current protection of layout designs of integrated circuits in the Arabian Peninsula States.

5.6.3 Nature and scope of a layout design

The Bahraini, Jordanian and Qatari laws, and the Omani, Saudi and Yemeni layout-design sections within their comprehensive laws, base their layout-design provisions on the corresponding WIPO model law.[126] They borrow directly from

123 WTO Council for Trade-Related Aspects of Intellectual Property Rights, *Review of Legislation: The United Arab Emirates*, Document IP/C/W/291 (01-3419), 10 July 2001. UAE Federal Law No. 44 of 1992, arts 43–51, applied specifically to industrial designs and models and does not make any reference to layout designs.

124 WTO Council for Trade-Related Aspects of Intellectual Property Rights, *Review of Legislation: The United Arab Emirates*, Document IP/C/W/291.Add.2 (02=1093), 3 March 2002, p. 3.

125 Rob Deans and André Human (2010), 'United Arab Emirates: Major Changes to UAE IP Laws Announced', available at www.mondaq.com/x/95168/Patent/Major+Changes+To+UAE+IP+Laws+Announced, last accessed 26 May 2017.

126 See WIPO, 'Draft Act on the Protection of Layout Designs (Topographies) of Integrated Circuits', available at www. www.wipo.int/treaties/en/text.jsp?file_id=295136, last accessed 13 June 2017.

TABLE 5.7 Current laws on layout designs of integrated circuits in the Arabian Peninsula States

Bahrain	Legislative Decree No. 5 of 2006 concerning Layout Designs of Integrated Circuits
Kuwait	Law No. 4 of 1962 concerning Patents, Designs and Industrial Models, as amended by Law No. 4 of 1999 and Law No. 3 of 2001
Jordan	Law No. 10 of 2000 on the Protection of Layout Designs of Integrated Circuits
Oman	Royal Decree No. 67/2008, the Law on Industrial Property Rights
Qatar	Law No. 6 of 2005 on Protection of Layout Designs of Integrated Circuits
Saudi Arabia	Royal Decree No. M/27 of 1425 AH (2004), the Law of Patents, Layout Designs of Integrated Circuits, Plant Varieties and Industrial Models.
UAE	—
Yemen	Law No. 2 of 2011 on Patents, Utility Models, Layout Designs of Integrated Circuits and Undisclosed Information

Source: compiled by the authors

Article 1(i) and (ii) of the model law for their definitions of a layout design and integrated circuit:

- integrated circuit: a product, in its final form or an intermediary form, which consists of interconnections or elements at least one of which is active and which is intended to perform an electronic function;
- layout design: any three-dimensional disposition of interconnections or elements of an integrated circuit, at least one of which is active, which is intended for manufacture.[127]

Originality is a fundamental criterion for protection.[128] Yemen and Jordan add more requirements for granting protection to an integrated circuit layout. It must be new, it has to be a result of an intellectual effort, and it is not commonly and widely known among experts in the industrial sector concerned. A design can be registered if application for registration is presented within two years of its first commercial exploitation anywhere worldwide.[129]

127 Bahrain, Legislative Decree No. 5 of 2006, art. 1; Oman, Royal Decree No. 67/2008, art. 1; Qatar, Law No. 6 of 2005, art. 1; Saudi Arabia, Royal Decree No. M/27 of 1425 AH (2004), art. 2.

128 Bahrain, Legislative Decree No. 5 of 2006, art. 2; Oman, Royal Decree No. 67/2008, art. 27; Qatar, Law No. 6 of 2005, art. 6; Saudi Arabia, Royal Decree No. M/27 of 1425 AH (2004), art. 49.

129 Jordan, Law No. 10 of 2000, art. 4; Yemen, Law No. 2 of 2011, art. 24(B).

Hence, excluded from registrability is any layout design which has already been commercially exploited locally or overseas more than two years ago.

Registration is a prerequisite for protection; at the same time, registration presumes ownership. Unless the contrary is established, the registrant is deemed to be the right holder of the layout design and thereby its creator. The right holder alone has the right to commercially exploit the layout design and to transfer the right in whole or in part.[130] The right holder is entitled to protection against unlawful importation, sale or other commercial exploitation of the layout design or other articles in which it is incorporated.[131] The emphasis here is on protecting commercialisation; the laws still allow use of a layout design without authorisation for research or teaching purposes, for personal or non-commercial use, or where the responsible minister deems such use is in the public interest. Jordan adds another exception to explore the layout design without the approval of the right holder when the reproduction of the design is for a non-authentic part of the design.[132]

Jordanian law provides more detail in regard to the lawful right holder depending on several factors. As a rule, the right holder for the design is the inventor. However, if the design is a result of a cooperation of more than one person, all of them shall be on an equal footing and be right holders. But if the invention was invented by more than one independently, the right holder is the first to apply for registration. If the design was a result of an employment contract, the employer shall be the right holder, unless agreed otherwise.[133]. Moreover, the law allows public access to the information and data on layout designs registered with the Office of Integrated Circuits Designs.[134]

The term of protection for layout designs is provided from the date of filing an application for registration, or from the date of its first local or foreign commercial exploitation, whichever is the earlier. The Bahraini, Jordanian, Qatari, Saudi and Yemeni laws all provide for a period of protection of ten years; the Bahraini and Saudi laws also include the qualification of Article 6(3) of the Washington Treaty and Article 38.3 of TRIPS (but omitted from the WIPO model law), that in all cases the term of protection expires 15 years after the creation of the layout design (thereby allowing an extension to the original ten-year period).[135] Jordan differentiates between domestic and foreign layout designs in regard to the date at which the protection becomes effective; for a domestic design, protection begins from the date of the application, whereas the term of protection of a foreign design starts from the date of first commercial exploitation anywhere

130 Jordan, Law No. 10 of 2000, art. 14.

131 Bahrain, Legislative Decree No. 5 of 2006, arts 6, 10, 12 and 15; Oman, Royal Decree No. 67/2008, art. 29; Qatar, Law No. 6 of 2005, arts 3–4; Saudi Arabia, Royal Decree No. M/27 of 1425 AH (2004), arts 49–53.

132 Jordan, Law No. 10 of 2000, art.10.

133 Jordan, Law No. 10 of 2000, art. 5.

134 Jordan, Law No. 10 of 2000, art. 3.

135 Bahrain, Legislative Decree No. 5 of 2006, art. 13; Qatar, Law No. 6 of 2005, art. 8; Saudi Arabia, Royal Decree No. M/27 of 1425 AH (2004), art. 19(b).

worldwide.[136] But very strangely, the Omani law, in what can only be a drafting oversight, provides for protection to commence from date of filing or exploitation, but does not stipulate any term for period of protection *per se*.[137]

The Bahraini, Omani, Saudi and Yemeni laws provide for a system of compulsory licensing as included in the Washington Treaty (but for which neither TRIPS nor the WIPO model laws make any provision). In brief, a non-exclusive, non-assignable compulsory licence may be granted by the responsible minister in circumstances where:

- the layout design is not locally available;
- the layout design is available but with unreasonably low quality standards, or in quantities insufficient to meet local demand, or at prices that the appropriate minister deems abusive; or
- other reasons of public interest, including remedying anti-competitive practices, so require,[138] or in the case of national security and emergencies.[139]

To preclude compulsory licensing, the Bahraini, Saudi and Yemeni laws require the layout design to be utilised by the original right holder within four years of the date of application or three years from grant, whichever is the longer period. Jordan and Oman do not stipulate any such requirement. Conditions attached to the issuance of a compulsory licence, which largely reflect those stipulated by TRIPS, require that:

- exploitation under the licence is limited to satisfying the needs of the local market only (the assumption being that local market means national market);
- exploitation cannot exceed the scope and purpose for which the licence was originally granted;
- the original right holder is entitled to receive fair compensation.

The right holder may continue to exploit the layout design, as it is not restricted to the licensee only. The licensee may not assign the licensing agreement to third parties; otherwise, the license will be void.[140]

5.6.4 Infringements

The laws provide, in very similar fashion to each other, a simple description of an infringement as being an act without authorisation that includes copying a layout design in whole or part, or knowingly importing, selling or distributing

136 Jordan, Law No. 10 of 2000, art. 12.
137 Oman, Royal Decree No. 67/2008, art. 31.
138 Bahrain, Legislative Decree No. 1 of 2004, art. 23; Saudi Arabia, Royal Decree No. M/27 of 1425 AH (2004), art. 24.
139 Jordan, Law No. 10 of 2000, art. 17; Yemen, Law No. 2 of 2011, art. 33.
140 Jordan, Law No. 10 of 2000, art. 18.

a layout design or the integrated circuit of which it may be part.[141] Saudi Arabia adds that falsely claiming or indicating that a layout design is registered also constitutes an infringement.

5.7 Undisclosed information, trade secrets and anti-competitive practices

5.7.1 TRIPS provisions and obligations (Articles 39–40)

TRIPS provides that undisclosed information and trade secrets are deemed to be protectable under the rules of unfair competition. The protection does not confer any exclusive right, but provides the right (and the obligation) to prevent practices contrary to honest commercial practices with respect to both the disclosure and acquisition of undisclosed information. TRIPS Article 39 requires members to ensure effective protection against unfair competition as provided in Article 10*bis* of the Paris Convention by protecting undisclosed information.[142] Persons and legal entities must be able to prevent information lawfully within their control from being acquired by, or disclosed to, others without their consent in a manner contrary to honest commercial practices, provided that such information:

- is secret in that it is not generally known, either as a whole or in its various parts, to persons who would normally deal with that kind of information;
- has commercial value because of its secret state; and
- has been subject to reasonable steps by its owner to keep it secret.[143]

TRIPS Article 39.3 makes a particular requirement to provide protection against unfair commercial use of undisclosed test or other data submitted as a condition for gaining market approval for new pharmaceutical or agricultural chemical products or for products which utilise new chemical entities. It requires members

141 Bahrain, Legislative Decree No. 5 of 2006, art. 10; Oman, Royal Decree No. 67/2008, art. 29(1); Saudi Arabia, Royal Decree No. M/27 of 1425 AH (2004), art. 51.

142 The Paris Convention, art. 10*bis*, requires countries to provide effective protection against unfair competition. Any act of competition contrary to honest practices in commercial or industrial matters is an act of unfair competition. In particular, the following are prohibited:

- all acts which create confusion by any means in respect of the establishment, goods, or activities of a competitor;
- false allegations in the course of trade which discredit the establishment, goods or activities of a competitor;
- indications or allegations the use of which is liable to mislead the public in respect of the nature, manufacturing process, characteristics, suitability of purpose, or quantity of goods.

143 A note to TRIPS Article 39 describes 'a manner contrary to honest commercial practices' as, at least, 'practices such as breach of contract, breach of confidence and inducement to breach, and includes the acquisition of undisclosed information by third parties which knew, or were grossly negligent in failing to know, that such practices were involved in the acquisition'.

to protect such data against disclosure, except where it is necessary to protect the public or unless steps are taken to ensure that the data are protected against unfair commercial use.

In respect of the control of anti-competitive practices, TRIPS Article 40 requires members to recognise that some licensing practices pertaining to intellectual property rights which restrain competition may have adverse effects on trade and impede the transfer and dissemination of technology. Members may adopt, consistent with other TRIPS provisions, appropriate measures to prevent or control practices in the licensing of intellectual property rights which are abusive and anti-competitive. TRIPS also provides for a mechanism allowing for consultation and exchange of relevant confidential information between members in situations where companies from those members are involved in a dispute over anti-competitive practices.

5.7.2 Current regional undisclosed information and anti-competitive practices provisions

The positions taken by the States in respect of the provision of protection for undisclosed information and trade secrets within the prescription of TRIPS Article 39 are fairly evenly balanced between either largely ignoring the matter (Kuwait and Saudi Arabia), incorporating some provision within the scope of other intellectual property laws (Oman and the UAE) and providing discrete laws for the protection of trade secrets and acts contrary to honest commercial practices (Bahrain, Jordan, Qatar and Yemen). However, the UAE has included some provision for 'know-how', as it is thus described, in its patents and industrial designs law of 2002. In respect of anti-competitive practices in contractual licences, as outlined by TRIPS Article 40, only Bahrain and Oman make specific acknowledgement of the requirement to control such practices, although all States can also refer to, and rely on, the extensive provisions that already exist outside the intellectual property protection regime. All States can justifiably argue that protection of undisclosed information and anti-competitive practices, being essentially commercial matters, are addressed in detail in their respective commercial codes, civil codes and penal codes.

Kuwait and Saudi Arabia would acknowledge that they do not provide any specific legislative protection of undisclosed information or trade secrets in the intellectual property context, but would claim that some levels of protection are already included elsewhere within their legislative frameworks governing commercial conduct, or that the introduction of appropriate legislation is being examined. Kuwait, for example, has argued that its copyright law guarantees protection of undisclosed information in the copyright context since the owner of a copyright has exclusive right to determine publication of his work.[144]

144 WTO Council for Trade-Related Aspects of Intellectual Property Rights, *Review of Legislation: Kuwait*, Document IP/Q4/KWT/1 (01-6322), 13 December 2001.

Accordingly, anyone who discloses such information without prior consent from the rightful owner commits an infringement under copyright law. However, this line of argument does not take account of the fact that copyright deals with rights of attribution and economic exploitation but does not encompass rights or obligations in respect of disclosure or non-disclosure. It also ignores the freedom-of-use provisions in respect of copyrighted works which can bring a work into the public domain. More importantly, it ignores the fact that TRIPS Article 39 and Paris Convention Article 10*bis* address a requirement for the protection of proprietary information that is not otherwise protected by patents, copyrights or industrial designs and models laws.

Saudi Arabia has claimed that some protection for undisclosed information of a proprietary nature already exists under the Regulation for the Protection of Confidential Commercial Information and with other laws outside the intellectual property context. It has asserted that rights relating to the protection of undisclosed information are covered by the Islamic *Shariah* and by existing laws such as the commercial code, commercial transactions code, unfair competition law and the Regulation for the Protection of Confidential Commercial Information.[145] Having a regulation governing confidential commercial information is a step forward in protecting undisclosed information. However, a law needs to emerge to regulate this area as it is crucial part for business and a regulation is not enough to protect undisclosed information.[146]

Bahrain's law for the protection of trade secrets was originally rather brief. It consisted of just nine clauses, only four of which dealt substantively with trade secrets and dishonest commercial practice (the other five addressing matters relating to enforcement, administration and due process). However, it was expanded rather significantly in 2006 following the completion of Bahrain's free trade agreement with the United States to add fairly extensive clauses on the protection and confidentiality of undisclosed safety and efficacy data relating to the market approval for new pharmaceutical and agrochemical products. The additions also guarantee exclusive market access against new or similar products using test data already used for marketing efficacy in another country.[147] The additions also incorporate and expand upon the requirements of TRIPS Article 39, including protection of test data submitted to government authorities for obtaining marketing approval of pharmaceutical or agricultural products. Oman now provides similar exclusive marketing provisions for pharmaceutical and

145 WTO Working Party on the Accession of the Kingdom of Saudi Arabia, *Additional Questions and Replies*, Document WT/ACC/SAU/6/Add.3 (96-4561), 30 October 1996. The Saudi Companies Law, Article 22, for example, provides for sanctions against any government official who improperly or without authorisation divulges company secrets to which he has, or has had, access by reason of his duties.

146 The Minister of Commerce and Industry's Decision No. (3218) dated 25/03/1426H (4 May 2005) Regulations for the Protection of Confidential Commercial Information.

147 Bahrain, Legislative Decree No. 12 of 2006, arts.2*bis*, 2A*bis* and 2B*bis*.

TABLE 5.8 Current trade secrets laws in the Arabian Peninsula States

Bahrain	Legislative Decree No. 7 of 2003 in respect of Trade Secrets, as amended by Law No. 12 of 2006
Jordan	Law No. 15 of 2000 on Unfair Competition and Trade Secrets
Kuwait	—
Oman	Royal Decree No. 67/2008, the Law on Industrial Property
Qatar	Law No. 5 of 2005 concerning Trade Secrets
Saudi Arabia	The Minister of Commerce and Industry's Decision No. 3218 of 25/03/1426H (4 May 2005) Regulations for the Protection of Confidential Commercial Information
UAE	Federal Law No. 17 of 2002 for the Industrial Regulation and Protection of Patents, Industrial Drawings and Designs
Yemen	Law No. 2 of 2011 on Patents, Utility Models, Layout Designs of Integrated Circuits and Undisclosed Information

Source: compiled by the authors

agrochemical products, but includes them in an expanded section on protection against unfair competition in its new comprehensive law on industrial property.[148]

Jordan was among the first to provide a legal form of protection for trade secrets. Its brief law on trade secrets and unfair competition, comprising just nine articles, was enacted in 2000 at the same time as its accession to the WTO. Qatar's trade secrets law of 2002, which is slightly longer at 14 articles, borrows significantly from the Bahraini former law and from a model law prepared by WIPO. In addition to rather brief and general provisions for protection of commercial secrets, the law specifically extends protection in particular to confidential information concerning marketing approval of pharmaceutical and agrochemical products.[149] Penalties for infringements are substantial in comparison with Qatar's other intellectual property laws. Qatar claims that this law is compatible with TRIPS.[150]

Yemen has made its first provisions for any form of legal protection for trade secrets with its incorporation of four brief articles on undisclosed information in its new Law No. 2 of 2011 on Patents, Utility Models, Integrated Circuit Layouts and Undisclosed Information. The four articles do not really go beyond laying down some basic conditions and requirements for trade secrets.

148 Oman, Royal Decree No. 67/2008, ss 60–65.

149 For a comparative review of Qatar's trade secrets law and those of the other GCC member States, see Mohamed Salem Abou El Farag, 'The Protection of Trade Secrets in Qatar', in David Price and Alhanoof AlDebasi (eds) (2017), *Intellectual Property Rights: Development and Enforcement in the Arab States of the Gulf*, pp. 173–91.

150 WTO Council for Trade-Related Aspects of Intellectual Property Rights, *Minutes of Meeting*, 27–28 November 2001, Document IP/C/M/34 (01=6407), 20 December 2001.

5.7.3 Nature of protection of undisclosed information

Bahrain, Jordan, Oman, Qatar, Saudi Arabia, the UAE and Yemen, borrowing directly from TRIPS Article 39, all provide that undisclosed information, or 'know-how', must be protected if:

- it is unknown, or not available among, or readily accessible, to persons who normally deal with such kind of information;
- it draws its commercial value from its confidentiality or secrecy;
- the owner or person lawfully in control of the information has taken reasonable steps to keep it secret.[151]

Jordan and Saudi Arabia include an exception to protected trade secrets. A commercial secret shall not be protected if it is inconsistent with the *Shari'ah*, *ordre public* or morality.[152]

There is no specified period of protection. Rather, the obligation to protect remains in effect as long as the undisclosed information's value is unknown and it remains secret. Know-how acquired through one's own means or through legal means may be used or disclosed or transferred to another party, but that other party may not use, disclose or communicate any element of know-how without consent of its owner. Disclosure without approval of the owner of the know-how constitutes an infringement, provided that the person committing the act was aware of the confidential nature of the know-how or could not have ignored such nature.

Unlike the other States, Jordan defines the person who is lawfully in control of the trade secret and who has the right to prevent any person from misusing the protected trade secrets. The person in control may claim compensation for the damages caused as a result of such secrets being misused. The person who enjoys such right is any person who has the right to disclose the trade secret, or to use it and to keep it from the public.[153]

The Yemeni law lists situations in which it will not be in conflict with the protection of a trade secret, namely:

- obtaining the information from publicly available sources such as offices (including patent offices), open government archives and published research,

151 Bahrain Legislative Decree No. 7 of 2003, art. 2; Jordan, Law No. 15 of 2000, art. 4; Oman, Royal Decree No. 67/2008, art. 65(2) 34; Qatar, Law No. 5 of 2005, art. 7; Saudi Arabia, the Minister of Commerce and Industry's Decision No. (3218) dated 25/03/1426H, art. 1; UAE, Federal Law No. 17 of 2002, arts 39–40; Yemen, Law No. 2 of 2011, art. 29; Saudi Arabia, Minister of Commerce and Industry Decision No. (3218) dated 25/03/1426H, art. 7.

152 Jordan, Law No. 15 of 2000, art. 4.

153 Jordan, Law No. 15 of 2000, arts 5 and 7.

studies and reports or as a result of independent research, innovation, invention, development, modification or enhancement;

- if both parties arrived at the same information as a result of spontaneous and independent efforts involving testing, experimentation and analysis of products which circulate on the market and which incorporate the undisclosed information;
- possessing and using information which is known and available, and which circulates among practitioners of the industrial activity in the scope of which the information falls.[154]

5.7.4 Protection of information relating to pharmaceutical products

The Bahraini, Jordanian, Qatari and Omani, Saudi and Yemeni laws all make some limited provision for the protection of undisclosed test or other data submitted by an applicant for market authorisation of a pharmaceutical or agricultural chemical product which utilises new chemical entities. In language that is virtually identical to the TRIPS Article 39.3 text, the prohibition on disclosure in the laws:

> shall extend to undisclosed tests or data which were the outcome of considerable effort, and which are submitted to the competent authorities for the purpose of obtaining approval for marketing of pharmaceutical or agricultural chemical products utilising new chemicals entities.[155]

The laws also provide, as required by TRIPS Articles 70.8 and 70.9, that the government authority in receipt of the tests or data must protect them against disclosure for as long as they remain secret. It must also prohibit their unfair commercial use by preventing any third party from using the data without approval in the marketing of similar drugs or products for five years following the date of marketing approval of the drugs or products.

The UAE position on protection of pharmaceutical and agrochemical products realises an equally strong level of protection. It enables inventions dealing with the chemistry of drugs or pharmaceutical compounds to be protected by patents or utility certificates if they meet the conditions required by the law and its implementing regulations as of 1 January 2005.[156] However, some degree of protection has already been in place through Ministerial Decree No. 404 of 2000, which stipulates that no drug or new pharmaceutical compound shall be registered unless it has been granted a patent – thereby extending to the drug or compound the protection and confidentiality applicable to patents. The decree also requires

154 Yemen, Law No. 2 of 2011, art. 32.

155 Bahrain, Legislative Decree No. 7 of 2003, art. 2; Oman, Royal Decree No. 67/2008, art. 65(3).

156 UAE, Federal Law No. 17 of 2002, arts 70–71.

the secrecy of information attached to an application for registration of a drug or pharmaceutical compound to be protected. The issuance of this ministerial decree was a direct response to pressure brought to bear by US pharmaceutical industry groups through the Office of the US Trade Representative.[157]

Saudi Arabia provides that during the period of protection of a trade secret, the registration office can permit third parties to use the undisclosed data of secret tests which is submitted by another applicant if the product first registered in the Kingdom has not been subject of trading within a reasonable period of time determined by the registration authority, after approving its marketing and if it is for necessary to protect the public.[158]

5.7.5 Control of anti-competitive practices in contractual licences

Oman has extensively expanded its provisions for control of anti-competitive practices and protection against unfair competition. An act or practice that is contrary to 'honest practices' now includes, but is not limited to, the following:

- breach of contract, breach of confidence and inducement to breach;
- acquisition of undisclosed information by third parties who knew, or were grossly negligent in failing to know, that such practices were involved in the acquisition;
- breach of legal duties in general when their purpose or consequence is to obtain illicit advantages over competitors, such as the breach of environmental or labour law;
- any act or practice, in the course of industrial or commercial activities, that may cause confusion or mislead with respect to another's enterprise or its activities, in particular its products or services;
- any similar act or practice that may damage the goodwill or reputation of another's enterprise, regardless of whether such act or practice causes confusion;
- any false or unjustifiable allegation that may be likely to discredit another's enterprise or its activities, in particular its products or services;
- any act or practice that results in the disclosure, acquisition or use by others of undisclosed information without the consent of the person lawfully in control of that information and in a manner contrary to honest commercial practices.[159]

Bahrain's law provides that the following constitute acts which are contrary to honest commercial practices:

157 See Chapter 8 for further discussion on the UAE's experiences with the USTR's Special 301 Reports.
158 Saudi Arabia, Ministerial Decision No. 3218 of 25/03/1426H, art. 6.
159 Oman, Royal Decree No. 67/2008, arts 61–64.

- disclosure of secret information acquired by a party to a 'confidentiality agreement';
- disclosure of, or inducement to disclose, secret information in breach of a duty of trust;
- misappropriation of information by unlawful means including fraud, espionage, theft or other improper means;
- acquiring trade secrets from another person while knowing, or being capable of knowing, that such other person has acquired the trade secrets unlawfully.[160]

As a rather curious and awkward inclusion for a law of this nature – which indicates that the law was largely and loosely constructed by borrowing from Bahrain's other intellectual property laws – provision is included for a person whose rights have, or appear to have, been infringed to seek provisional relief. Such relief includes the cessation of the infringement, the provisional seizure of articles and goods including imported goods on arrival, and the seizure of infringing machinery and tools and related evidence.[161]

However, Jordan takes a different approach from Bahrain and Oman by stating that any provision in a licence contract that may restrict competition related to any of the intellectual property rights which may have negative effect on commerce, or may hinder the transference or dissemination of the technology, shall be deemed void and null, and in particular to:

- prohibit the licensee from transferring modifications done on the technology included in the licence contract except for the licensor (back transferring of technology);
- prevent the licensee from arising juridical or administrative disputes in respect of the licensed intellectual property right;
- compel the licensee to accept the license with a number of rights instead of one right only.[162]

5.8 New plant varieties

5.8.1 TRIPS provisions and obligations

Protection of new plant varieties as a distinct and separate intellectual property right falls outside the scope of TRIPS, which confines the treatment of their protection to being a patent matter. TRIPS Article 27.3(b), in addressing patentable subject matter, provides that inventions which include plants and essentially biological processes for the production of plants, other than non-biological and microbiological

160 Bahrain, Legislative Decree No. 7 of 2003, art. 4.
161 Ibid., art. 6.
162 Jordan, Law No. 15 of 2000, art. 9.

processes, may be excluded from patentability. However, it still requires members to provide for the protection of plant varieties either by patents or by an effective *sui generis* system or by a combination of both.

It has been suggested that this flexibility reflects the lack of consensus on the form that protection of plant varieties should take – that is, whether they should be protectable under the European approach of breeder's rights, or the United States and Japanese approach of protection under a patents regime.[163] These different approaches lead to a different scope and extent of protection. Although the breeder's rights regime permits protection of a plant variety as determined by a specific combination of genes, it does not allow for the protection of particular genes, a possibility instead allowed under patent law.

Outside of the TRIPS patent-protection approach, the international standard of protection is that established by the Convention of the International Union for the Protection of New Plant Varieties (1999) (UPOV Convention).[164] The Convention grants protection of a new plant variety to the breeder – the breeder being defined as the person who breeds, or discovers and develops, and registers, a new plant variety. The bounds or characteristics of 'discovers and develops' are the subject of intense international debate. However, 'breeding' may include the isolation and propagation of a naturally occurring mutation or variation. To be deemed protectable, a plant variety must meet the conditions of being:

- new, by virtue of not being the subject of prior commercial acts;
- distinct, by being clearly distinguishable from any other variety;
- uniform or homogeneous in its relevant characteristics;
- stable, after a cycle of propagation or repeated propagation;
- variety denominated, having a denomination under which it may be commercialised.[165]

The breeder's basic right in respect of a particular plant variety encompasses the production, reproduction and conditioning for propagation, together with the selling, marketing, importing or exporting and stocking of the new variety. The scope of the right includes not only the plant variety or propagated material itself but also the harvested material and may extend to products made directly from the harvested material.[166] The breeder's rights do not prohibit use by others of

163 Carlos Correa, 'Patent Rights', in Correa and Abdulqawi (eds) (1998), op. cit., p. 197.

164 'UPOV Convention' being the Act of the International Convention for the Protection of New Varieties of Plants of 2 December 1961, as revised at Geneva on 19 March 1991. Although UPOV is an autonomous international body, its association with the WTO and WIPO in particular is close, the WIPO Director-General being *ex-officio* UPOV Secretary-General. WIPO has prepared a Plant Breeder's Rights Bill, which serves as its *sui generis* alternative to the TRIPS patent-protection approach. The Bill is based on the 1991 UPOV Convention.

165 UPOV Convention, arts 5–9.

166 Ibid., arts 14–15.

protected propagation material for non-commercial or private purposes, for experimental purposes or for the purpose of breeding other varieties. But this is a limited use, in effect confined to research and experimental uses. The use-by-others provision does not automatically extend to include farmers or recognise their rights to use farm-saved or own-harvested propagating material or seed for replanting. The existence and possible application of a farmer's right, if any, is left to the Convention signatories to decide, depending on their own circumstances or interests, or to the bargaining outcomes of multilateral or bilateral agreements.

5.8.2 Current regional provisions for new plant varieties

As is the case with layout designs of integrated circuits, statutory protection of new plant varieties or plant breeder's rights has received little attention or action from the States, and there is little indication of external pressure upon them within the context of the WTO to comply with their TRIPS obligations at this stage. The States either largely ignore the issue of protection of new plant varieties (Bahrain, Kuwait, Qatar and Yemen), add specific provisions on the protection of new plant varieties to the general provisions of their patent laws (Saudi Arabia), or enact very brief *sui generis* laws for the protection of new plant varieties (Jordan, Oman and the UAE).

Bahrain, Kuwait, Qatar and Yemen do not make any substantive provision, either in their respective patent laws or other intellectual property laws, for the protection of new plant varieties, although Bahrain has removed plants from the types of inventions excluded from patent protection. Kuwait and Yemen have stipulated in their patent laws that patent protection shall not be extended to plant varieties and essentially biological ways for producing them (excluding microbiological processes or the products thereof), but have not developed any alternative protecting legislation.[167] The GCC Patent Regulations also excludes plant species and varieties from patent protection in the same manner as these individual States.[168] Although Bahrain has reportedly had in local circulation for a number of years a draft law in respect of new plant variety protection, there are no indications of it being enacted in the near future. Bahrain, Jordan and Oman have acceded to the UPOV Convention as part of their respective free trade agreements with the United States; Bahrain's draft *sui generis* law will now need to be enacted, or its patent law updated, to enable local implementation of the Convention's provisions.[169]

167 See the discussion on patentability in Sections 5.5.3 and 5.5.4 above.

168 In June 2002, Qatar was advising the WTO Council for TRIPS that the GCC Council was currently examining a separate form of regulation on plant-variety protection and that this legislation, once approved, would apply in Qatar. However, the GCC Council has yet to draft, let alone issue, such a law. See WTO Council for Trade-Related Aspects of Intellectual Property Rights, *Review of Legislation: Responses from Qatar to the questions posed by Australia, Canada, the European Communities and their member states, Switzerland and the United States*, IP/C/W/346 (02-3101), 5 June 2002, pp. 1, 6.

169 The UPOV Convention came into effect in December 2005 in Bahrain, in October 2004 in Jordan, and in October 2007 in Oman.

Saudi Arabia, meanwhile, has adopted a hybrid approach that borrows both from the patent-protection approach and the *sui generis* option. It dedicates five articles within its patent law specifically to the protection of new plant varieties, but also provides for the general patent provisions to apply equally to new plant varieties.

Oman originally followed the *sui generis* alternative offered by TRIPS Article 27.3(b) by enacting specific legislation for the protection of new plant varieties in 2000. The 2000 law follows the plant breeders' regime for the protection of new plant varieties enshrined in the UPOV Convention and draws upon some (but not all) elements of the UPOV Model Law on the Protection of New Plant Varieties, from which it draws much of its text. However, in 2009, Oman issued a *sui generis* law covering a plant breeder's rights, which replaced the 2000 law and is in line with the UPOV Convention.[170]

Jordan did not have any form of protection for new plants varieties until 2000, when it enacted a new law. A registration office at the Ministry of Agriculture was established to examine applications for new varieties of plants as well as handle the accession to the UPOV Convention.[171] The law defines a variety and the conditions in which it can be registered, along with the process of the registration and the requirements in which a compulsory licence can be granted without the approval of a breeder. The law did not forget the rights conferred on the breeder, including the right to prevent others from using the registered variety.

The UAE, on the other hand, did not join the UPOV Convention, but enacted a federal law for the protection of new varieties in 2009. Much like Jordan, a registration office was established under the Ministry of Environment and Water to examine and register new varieties.

5.8.3 Scope of protection for new plant varieties

The Jordanian, Omani, Saudi and UAE laws provide that to qualify for protection, a plant variety, or its propagation types or elements, must be new or novel, distinct, homogeneous and constant or stable.[172] A variety is new or novel if it (or its propagating material) has not been marketed within the country for more than one year or marketed elsewhere for more than six years in the case of trees or vines or four years in the case of all other plant varieties. A variety is deemed to be distinct if it is distinguishable from other known varieties by at least one characteristic, is uniform if the differences between its elements are within generally accepted limits,

170 Oman, Royal Decree No. 49/2009, the Law on the Protection of Breeder's Rights in New Varieties of Plants.

171 Bassam Al-Tarawneh and Ali Al-Zubi (2006), 'The Impact of Joining Jordan to the International Agreement for the Protection of New Varieties of Plants (UPOV)', 6(9), *International Journal of Humanities and Social Science*, p. 143.

172 Jordan, Law No. 24 of 2000 on the Protection of New Varieties of Plants, art. 5; Oman, Royal Decree No. 49/2009, arts 5–9; Saudi Arabia, Royal Decree No. 1425 AH (2004), arts 54–55; UAE, Federal Law No. 17 of 2009 on the Protection of New Plant Varieties, arts 5–9.

TABLE 5.9 Current laws on protection of new plant varieties in the Arabian Peninsula States

Bahrain	Legislative Decree No. 12 of 2005 ratifying Bahrain's accession to the International Convention for the Protection of New Plant Varieties (UPOV Convention)
Jordan	Council ministers No 648 ratifying Jordan's accession of October 2004 to the International Convention for the Protection of New Plant Varieties (UPOV Convention) Law No. 24 of 2000 on the Protection of New Varieties of Plants
Kuwait	—
Oman	Royal Decree No. 49/2009 promulgating the Law on the Protection of Breeders' Rights in New Varieties of Plants Royal Decree No. 67/2008, the Law on Industrial Property Royal Decree No. 37/2007, ratifying Oman's accession to the International Convention for the Protection of New Plant Varieties (UPOV Convention)
Qatar	—
Saudi Arabia	Royal Decree No. M/27 1425 AH (2004) in respect of Patents, Layout Designs of Integrated Circuits, Plant Varieties and Industrial Models
UAE:	Federal Law No. 17 of 2009 on the Protection of New Plant Varieties
Yemen	—

Source: compiled by the author

and is stable if its main characteristics remain unchanged after repeated propagation. The UAE adds another condition to grant a protection: a variety should not harm the environment or human health and shall not contradict the *Shariah* or the laws of the country.[173]

The right of protection by registration is granted to the breeder of the plant variety or his successors in title, the breeder being commonly defined as the person who breeds, discovers or develops a plant variety. Registration grants to the breeder, being the right owner, the right of:

- sole utilisation of propagating types and elements for the commercial plant production;
- transfer of all or part of the utilisation right, with or without financial consideration;
- preventing third parties from utilising the right, and seeking precautionary relief;

173 UAE, Federal Law No. 17 of 2009, art. 5.

- legal compensation against infringements;
- requiring any person offering for sale or marketing the plant variety or its propagating elements to use the registered designation or name for that plant variety.[174]

However, exceptions to this right permit use of the protected plant variety for experimental or research activities and personal non-commercial use.

Unlike Jordan, Oman and the UAE, the Saudi law does not recognise or even acknowledge the right of the farmer to further propagate and use plant material which is the product of a harvest on his own holding, but which may otherwise be patent-protected plant material. In fact, the Saudi law in effect excludes any provision for farmer's rights by stipulating that such acts as producing or propagating patented plant material, adapting it for the purposes of propagation, or storing it for such purposes, constitutes an infringement of the rights of the plant patentee.[175] Such rights extend to harvested material in whole or in part.

As for the term of protection for a variety, Jordan, Oman, Saudi Arabia and the UAE all provide the same term of protection for a plant variety – namely, 20 years and 25 years for trees and vines (Saudi Arabia omitted vines as a plant that receives a longer term of protection). The difference is the date at which the protection begins. In the Saudi and Jordanian laws, the protection starts from the date of filing the application, whereas the Omani and UAE laws set it from the date of the grant of the breeder's right.[176]

The Jordanian, Omani, Saudi and UAE laws also provide for a system of compulsory licensing to be available for plant varieties, as is permitted under the TRIPS patent provisions, but for which no provision is made in the UPOV Convention and the WIPO model law.[177] The responsible minister may grant a non-exclusive compulsory licence where the owner of the plant variety has not made sufficient use of the plant variety within three years from registration and has not otherwise agreed to grant a licence on reasonable terms to the applicant, or where the award of the compulsory licence is necessary to protect the public interest. The issuance of a compulsory licence does not prejudice the right of the right holder to reasonable compensation.

174 Jordan, Law No. 24 of 2000, art. 15; Oman, Royal Decree No. 49/2009, art. 14; Saudi Arabia, Royal Decree No. 1425 AH (2004), art. 56; UAE, Federal Law No. 17 of 2009, art. 15.

175 Saudi Arabia, Royal Decree No. M/27 of 1425 AH (2004), art. 56(a) and (b). These provisions in essence replicate the breeder's rights as detailed in the WIPO Model Law, art. 14.

176 Jordan, Law No. 24 of 2000, arts 8 and 18; Oman, Royal Decree No. 49/2009 art. 19; Saudi Arabia, Royal Decree No. 1425 AH (2004), art. 19; UAE, Federal Law No. 17 of 2009, art. 19.

177 Jordan, Law No. 24 of 2000, art. 21; Oman, Royal Decree No. 49/2009, art. 17; Saudi Arabia, Royal Decree No. M/27 of 1425 AH (2004), arts 24–31; UAE, Federal Law No. 17 of 2009, art. 31.

5.9 Concluding remarks

The picture that emerges from the foregoing examination of the Arabian Peninsula States' industrial property legislative regimes is that, at the global level, the regimes have a thread of common purpose and generally a broad strategic direction. However, at the lower level of individual laws, there exist instances of both considerable similarity and significant deviation in their content and structure. In some instances, laws share common material, and it is apparent that there has been wholesale borrowing in a number of cases – to the extent that their texts (in the English-language translations at least) are virtually identical. However, some laws also retain their own peculiar idiosyncrasies in other instances; they reveal glaring omissions and are notable for their brevity and lack of sophistication when compared with the corresponding statutes of their sister States. This is particularly the case in respect of some of the region's copyright laws.

What also emerges from a scrutiny of the States' performance in respect of their adoption of the latest international standards on intellectual property protection is that those which currently lead the vanguard in this regard – namely Bahrain and Oman – have done so outside the multilateral context. Instead, their latest suites of laws have developed from the context of their free trade agreements with the United States. Although these agreements have often incorporated a requirement for adherence to multilateral conventions sponsored by the WTO or WIPO, they have also incorporated higher standards of intellectual property protection, but only in areas of particular concern to the United States. Developed in a bilateral context, they are then utilised in subsequent bilateral agreements as the new international standards.

It should be no surprise that the intellectual property laws which are the most comprehensive and sophisticated are those relating to copyright and neighbouring rights and trademarks, since these are the two areas which have most concerned the developed countries in ensuring that their own rights and investments in the region are protected. The protection of patent rights may have lagged somewhat behind copyright and trademarks, but an increased regional recognition of their crucial importance in national development and technology transfer has seen the patents laws in most States and the GCC significantly enhanced in recent years. The remaining rights enshrined in TRIPS, in which there is not the same imperative for preservation of interests and investments, either have gained some degree of protection by laws noticeable for their brevity or by association, or have been largely passed over.

At a more pragmatic level, a greater degree of harmonisation of the region's intellectual property laws may well lead to an enhanced understanding of the laws themselves at the operational level and facilitate the collectivisation of locally nurtured talent and expertise that is emerging in the States' various ministries, judiciaries and enforcement agencies. But a paucity of strategic regional direction also leaves the individual States susceptible to the external unilateral pressures to conform to the intellectual property laws of the industrialised countries rather than local laws which more appropriately address national and regional needs.

The protection of industrial property has come a long way in the Arabian Peninsula. In recent years, the States have realised the importance and the benefits that protecting industrial property has on the economy – especially in achieving their new objectives domestically and in achieving a new vision for the region. The protection arose first as a result of the multilateral agreements revolving around membership of the WTO. The protection was subsequently enhanced by activity in the bilateral contexts of which the EU and United States were part – both directly and indirectly. The interest in industrial property increased as the States became more aware of the power and the need for such a set of laws.

However, having the requisite laws, irrespective of whether they have TRIPS-related shortcomings, are TRIPS-compliant or include TRIPS-plus provisions, is one thing; being able to effectively enforce them and achieve the desired national objectives is another matter – as Chapters 6 and 7 explore.

6

TRIPS AND INTELLECTUAL PROPERTY ENFORCEMENT

6.1 Introduction

The TRIPS enforcement regime is addressed in Part III of the Agreement and applies equally to all intellectual property rights covered in Part II. The regime is primarily self-contained, but is also based in part on the Berne and Paris Conventions. The Berne Convention provides reference in respect of the right to enforce protected works (art. 15), seizure of infringing copies (art. 16) and application of the Convention (art. 36), while the Paris Convention includes articles in respect of seizures (arts 9 and 10) and appropriate remedies (art. 10*ter*). Neither the Rome Convention nor the Washington Treaty contains any enforcement or sanction provisions. The principal features of Part III are the existence of adequate norms and minimum standards for the protection of intellectual property, the effective enforcement of those norms and standards, both domestically and at state borders, and an effective dispute-resolution settlement mechanism to ensure that WTO members comply with their obligations to provide those adequate norms and standards for their effective enforcement.

TRIPS Part III requires WTO members to provide under their domestic laws a comprehensive regime that ensures that the rights established in TRIPS Part II can be effectively enforced, both by their own nationals and by foreign right holders. As part of that regime, members are required to make provision for:

- fair and equitable civil and administrative procedures;
- independent judicial review of final administrative decisions on appeal;
- provisional measures;
- border control measures on application and *ex officio*;
- damages and indemnification;
- criminal procedures and remedies.

The Arabian Peninsula States have achieved only partial success in meeting the TRIPS Part III requirements. They have generally succeeded in establishing the necessary legislative regimes and judicial frameworks that address the above TRIPS requirements (although not necessarily exclusively within intellectual property frameworks). However, they have not been as successful in creating and bringing to a state of operational effectiveness the essential infrastructural and administrative strategies and processes. All States now allow for matters relating to rights to be pursued in civil and criminal jurisdictions. They also enable aggrieved right holders to seek provisional measures against actual or potential infringements. In some States and in some laws, enforcement provisions have been strengthened by increases in the nature and scale of sanctions and by the introduction of sanctions which provide for seizure of infringing goods and material, closures of infringing premises, compensation and increased penalties for repeat offences. In respect of the issue of independent judicial review, the post-2000 laws generally have moved to reduce administrative discretionary authority in intellectual property matters by transferring more of the officials' discretionary powers and functions to the civil courts or by requiring administrative decision-making to be subject to at least semi-independent, quasi-judicial appeal or final judicial review.

The majority of the States' intellectual property laws have benefited from an extensive input into their creative development and legislative drafting by WIPO through its International Bureau. They have also been subject to frequent cross-fertilisation, exchanges of views and borrowings from within each other. It is not surprising, therefore, that in most cases the laws generally conform to the thrust of the TRIPS enforcement obligations, the main exception in this regard being Jordan's group of minor intellectual property laws issued as part of its accession to WTO membership in 2000.[1] However, they still fall well short of the TRIPS-plus standards in respect of deterrent levels of sanctions being increasingly demanded by the developed nations and pursued through regional and bilateral trade agreements. This has caused the States to continue to attract critical attention from developed countries and particularly the international watchdog organisations and lobby groups representing the major global producers and exporters of the main forms of intellectual property.

1 Namely, Jordan, Law No. 8 of 2000 on Geographical Indications, Law No. 10 of 2000 on Integrated Circuits, Law No. 14 of 2000 on Industrial Designs, Law No. 15 of 2000 on Unfair Competition and Trade Secrets, and Law No. 24 of 2000 on New Plant Varieties, The laws are discussed further in section 6.2.5 following.

6.2 TRIPS enforcement obligations[2] and the response of the Arabian Peninsula States

6.2.1 General obligations and civil and administrative procedures (TRIPS Articles 41–49)

TRIPS Article 41 requires WTO members to have in place enforcement procedures which permit effective action against infringements and remedies that constitute an effective deterrent to further infringing activity. The enforcement procedures must be equitable and fair; they must not be unnecessarily complicated or costly or involve unreasonable time limits or unwarranted delays. Nor must their application create a barrier to legitimate trade. However, a member is not obliged to put in place a special judicial system for intellectual property rights enforcement distinct from that for the enforcement of law in general; nor is a member required to make a preferential allocation of resources to enforcement at the expense of the law in general. Members are required to make provision for parties to a proceeding to have opportunity for judicial review of final administrative decisions, and, subject to jurisdictional provisions in a member's law concerning the importance of a case, of at least the legal aspects of initial judicial decisions.

Members are required to make civil judicial procedures available to right holders to enforce their intellectual property rights established by TRIPS, including procedures that will provide:

- timely and detailed written notice of the basis of any claims;
- representation by independent legal counsel;
- the right to present evidence and to substantiate their claims;
- protection from 'overly burdensome requirements concerning mandatory personal appearances';
- protection of confidential information, unless contrary to constitutional requirements.[3]

Judicial authorities must be given the authority to order parties in control of evidence which may substantiate another party's claim to produce such evidence.[4] Where a party refuses or otherwise does not do so, judicial authorities must be empowered to make any preliminary and final determinations, affirmative or negative, on the basis of the information presented to them, provided that all parties have had the opportunity to be heard on the allegations and the evidence. Discretion is granted to members to authorise judicial authorities to order the

2 The following summaries of the salient features of TRIPS Part III are taken from the WTO website description, available at www.wto.org/english/tratop_e/trips_e/intel2b_e.htm#enforcement last accessed 30 May 2017.

3 TRIPS, art. 42.

4 Ibid., arts 43 and 47–48.

infringer to inform the right holder of the identity of third persons involved in the production and distribution of the infringing goods or services and of their channels of distribution. The exercise of such authority must not be 'out of proportion to the seriousness of the infringement', although no guidance is provided as to the benchmarks for 'proportion' or 'seriousness'. To militate against the frivolous or abusive use of enforcement provisions, judicial authorities are to have the authority to order a party who has abused enforcement procedures to provide adequate compensation for the injury suffered because of such abuse to a party wrongfully enjoined or restrained. This provision extends to government officials, whose exemption from liability to appropriate remedial measures exists only to the extent that their actions are taken or intended in good faith in the course of administration of a particular law.

The provisions within the States for civil and administrative processes in relation to the enforcement of rights as required by TRIPS tend to be prescribed in statutes other than their intellectual property laws. All States possess long-standing statutes relating to civil and commercial procedures, the judiciary and judicial procedures, and penal codes which include extensive provisions on the conduct of criminal investigation, evidence and prosecution.[5] The long-standing existence of Islamic

5 Some of the major codifications relating to the region's legal and judicial systems and procedures, and which address in part the above requirements of TRIPS, include the following:

Bahrain: Decree No. 13 of 1971, the Judiciary Act; Civil Procedures Code (1971, as amended 1990), Law of Commerce (1971, as amended 1990), Criminal Code (1987), Code of Criminal Procedure (1966).

Jordan: Law No. 16 of 1960, the Penal Code, as amended; Law No. 43 of 1976, the Civil Code, as amended; Law No. 22 of 1997, the Companies Code, as amended.

Kuwait: Law No. 19 of 1959, the Judiciary Law, as amended by Law No. 19 of 1990; Law No. 16 of 1960, the Penal Code; Law No. 17 of 1960, the Criminal Procedure Code; Law No. 38 of 1980, the Code of Civil Procedure, as amended by Law No. 47 of 1994; Law No. 67 of 1980, the Civil Code; Law No. 68 of 1980, the Commercial Code, as amended by Law No. 45 of 1989; Law No. 17 of 2011 on Border Issues.

Oman: Law No. 7/1974, the Penal Code; Commercial Code (1990); Royal Decree 90/99 the Judicial Structure of Oman; Royal Decree No. 91/1999 establishing the Administrative Court; Royal Decree No. 92/1999, the Public Prosecution Authority; Royal Decree No. 93/1999 establishing the Supreme Judicial Council.

Qatar: Law No. 14 of 1972, the Criminal Code; Law No. 16 of 1971, the Civil and Commercial Code; Law No. 6 of 1999, the Law of the Judiciary.

Saudi Arabia: Royal Decree No. M/64 of 1395 AH (1975), regulating the Judiciary; Ministerial Ordinance No. 109 of 1332 AH (1959), the Administrative Rules of Procedure of Judicial Bodies.

UAE: Federal Law No. 10 of 1973, establishing the Federal Supreme Court; Federal Law No. 6 of 1978, establishing the Courts of First Instance; Federal Law No. 3 of 1987, the Penal Code; Law No. 11 of 1992, the Code of Civil Procedure; Federal Law No. 35 of 1992, the Code of Criminal Procedure.

Yemen: Law No. 1 of 1990, the Judicial Authority Act; Law No. 1 of 1991, the Judicature Act; Republican Decree Pertaining to Law No. 12 of 1994 on Crimes and Penalties; Republican Decree Pertaining to Law No. 13 of 1994 on Criminal Procedures; Law No. 14 of 2002, the Civil Code.

jurisprudence with a complexity and sophistication that compares favourably with western legal systems, together with a comprehensive codification of civil and commercial regimes, ensured that the States enjoyed well-established civil and administrative review procedures in judicial proceedings prior to TRIPS-related laws coming into effect. However, one conspicuous element which has been given some attention in the TRIPS-related laws is the degree of discretionary administrative final decision-making. This has been progressively curtailed by the emergence of provisions for judicial authority to have the powers to review such decision-making, although such inclusions are still not uniform across the States' intellectual property laws.

Where the exceptions arise because of the absence or inadequacy of such judicial provision, they generally appear as curious variations to the norm. It would seem that their occurrences are more likely to be due to continuing adherence to the conservative position or oversight, rather than a deliberate stratagem to avoid independent review. Some of the more recent laws, such as the suite of various industrial property laws of Bahrain of 2006, the comprehensive industrial property law of Oman of 2008, and the more recent industrial property law of Yemen of 2011, each introduce into the appeals process an additional level of administrative authority through the creation of quasi-judicial appeals committees.[6] Although the committees generally enjoy a degree of independence, they are still appointed by the minister responsible for that particular area of intellectual property. This additional process has two benefits – first, it acts somewhat as a facilitator, providing a filter for a judicial system already overburdened with largely trivial or procedural matters; second, it retains the decision-making in the area in which the main expertise in the practical issues relating to rights is likely to reside. Where the appeals committee strategy falls short of the standard required by TRIPS is that the effective source of higher authority still rests with the minister concerned. Although the committee may in certain instances contain external or independent members, its constitution and membership still falls largely within the gift of the minister concerned to make or recommend the appointment of its members, and thus be able to influence outcomes. However, it must be stressed that, notwithstanding the role of the minister and the appeals committee, further provision still exists in most laws in most States for final appeal to rest with an independent judicial authority through the civil courts.

Like Bahrain and Oman, Kuwait, Qatar and the UAE provide for the ministerial appeals committee process. The UAE goes to some lengths to emphasise the committee's independence. In respect of patent and industrial designs and models,

6 See, for example, Bahrain, Legislative Decree No. 6 of 2014 (GCC trademark law), art. 12, and Law No. 14 of 2006 (patent and utility model law), art. 36; Oman, Royal Decree No. 67/2008 (copyright), as amended by Royal Decree No. 131/2008, art. 98; Yemen, Law No. 2 of 2011 (patents, utility models, layout designs of integrated circuits and undisclosed information), arts 2 and 39.

the committee is 'headed by a judge nominated by the Minister of Justice and Islamic Affairs and Awqaf and two persons with experience in relation to industrial property rights regulated by this Law from outside the Department'.[7] The corresponding trademark law provides for a committee, again appointed by the Minister of Economy and Commerce but which comprises the Ministry Under-Secretary as chairman, two representatives of the Ministry and one representative of each Emirate chosen by the competent authority. Even so, decisions of both committees may still subsequently be appealed to the civil court in accordance with the Civil Procedures Code.

Saudi Arabia's industrial property laws provide that appeals against administrative decisions may be made to the quasi-judicial Board of Grievances.[8] In the case of trademark matters, the Board serves as the first and only forum for appeal against administrative decisions, whereas in the case of patents and industrial models, a standing committee of five members plays an intermediate role. The committee is vested with the power to initially hear all disputes and contests of administrative decisions, with appeals against decisions of the committee being heard by the Board of Grievances.

The GCC Unified Patent Regulations, which have been recognised *de jure* by Bahrain, Kuwait and Saudi Arabia, and at least *de facto* by the other GCC member States, as constituting or complementing their domestic patent laws, provide for the establishment by the GCC Ministerial Council of a 'Grievance Committee' to consider appeals against decisions of the GCC Patents Office.[9] But such decisions relate only to matters in respect of filing, examination, grant of patent and compulsory licensing, and do not relate to infringements and enforcement. However, the GCC also acknowledges that the final authority in respect of appeals must still rest with the respective GCC member States themselves, by stipulating that such final appeal shall be made in accordance with the laws of the State concerned.[10]

Although the copyright laws do not provide the same scope as the industrial property laws for discretionary administrative decision-making, some provision still exists in limited instances – notably in respect of the granting of local licences for the translation into Arabic of foreign works. The Kuwaiti and Saudi laws allow

7 UAE, Law No. 17 of 2002, art. 66.

8 The Saudi Board of Grievances was established in 1955 by Royal Decree No. 17/13/8759 of 1374 AH, as a quasi-judicial review body for government and administrative decision-making. It has been restructured a number of times over the years, to now become an independent entity directly responsible to the Saudi Council of Ministers. The Board consists of a president with the rank of minister, deputy president and two directors, legal advisers on *Shariah* law and other legal matters, and an unspecified number of magistrates according to specific need. Members of the Board are statutory appointments; the president is appointed by the King on the recommendation of the Council of Ministers.

9 GCC Unified Patent Regulations, 2000, arts 25 and 28. The Committee comprises 12 members, two drawn from each member State, and maintains a balance between legal and technical expertise.

10 Ibid., art. 25.

appeals against administrative decision-making to be made directly to the courts of first instance (Kuwait) or the equivalent Board of Grievances (Saudi Arabia).[11] No specific provision exists in the copyright laws of Qatar, Jordan and, rather unusually, in the recent copyright laws of Bahrain and Oman for appeal to independent judicial authority against decisions of administrative bodies or the responsible minister, although the extent of discretionary authority available to administrative bodies is considerably less than that available under the industrial property laws.

6.2.2 Provisional relief (TRIPS Article 50)

TRIPS Article 50 requires WTO members to provide their judicial authorities with authority to prevent an infringement of an intellectual property right from occurring or to stop an infringement in progress, preserve relevant evidence in regard to an alleged infringement, and in particular prevent goods, including imported goods, from entering the commercial market, by the ordering of injunctive relief. The measures may be adopted *inaudita altera parte*, particularly where any delay is likely to cause irreparable harm to the right holder or poses a demonstrable risk of evidence being destroyed. The judicial authorities can require an applicant for *ex parte* orders to provide any reasonable evidence in order to establish that an infringement has occurred or is imminent, and to supply other information necessary for the identification of the goods concerned to assist the authority which will enforce the provisional measure. The judicial authorities must also be authorised to require, at their discretion, that the applicant provide a security or equivalent assurance sufficient to protect the defendant and to counter abuse of provisional measures. If proceedings have not been initiated within a reasonable period, the defendant may request that the provisional measures be revoked or cease to have effect. Where provisional measures are revoked or lapse, or where no infringement is subsequently found, the judicial authorities may order the applicant upon request of the defendant to compensate the defendant for any injury caused by the provisional measures.

Common to the intellectual property laws of all Arabian Peninsula States are provisions for a range of precautionary measures and provisional relief against threatened or actual infringements of intellectual property rights. There are some instances, as mentioned below, where the precautionary measures in a few individual laws fall somewhat short of the standard required by TRIPS Article 50. Again, where these deficient laws are disparate from the provisions enshrined in other domestic laws, it would appear that the deficiency lies more with drafting or translation issues than a deliberate stratagem on the part of the legislators. Notwithstanding these few instances, the intentions at least of the prescribed measures are generally very similar across all States and across all areas of intellectual

11 Kuwait, Law No. 22 of 2016 (copyright), arts 34, 35; Saudi Arabia, Royal Decree No. M/41 of 1424 AH (2003) (copyright), arts 16, 23.

property law. Perhaps again not surprisingly, arguably the most comprehensive statements of precautionary measures are to be found in the recent Bahraini and Omani copyright and industrial property laws. They both stipulate that a court may generally order the following measures:

- direction that the alleged infringement cease or not take place;
- appointment of an expert to prepare a detailed description of the alleged infringing activity, work, goods or material, together with the materials, equipment and devices suspected of being used in the infringement;
- orders for the preservation of related evidence;
- attachment on the alleged infringing versions or copies of the work, goods or material and the materials, equipment, implements and devices suspected of being used in the infringement together with the proceeds generated from the suspected infringement;
- prevention of the entry into the channels of commerce of suspected infringing goods, including imported goods immediately after customs clearance.[12]

Oman's subsequent Plant Breeder's Rights Law of 2009, in an exercise of economy and internal harmonisation, simply states that 'the provisional, civil, customs and criminal measures provided in the Law of Industrial Property Rights issued by Royal Decree 67/2008 shall apply'.[13] In similar fashion, the other States do not see an imperative to be so comprehensive. Saudi Arabia, for example, makes provision in its law in respect of patents, industrial models, layout designs and new plant varieties for the Board of Grievances to take such emergency action as it deems appropriate in respect of an actual or threatened infringement. However, the law does not provide any prescription or make any specific mention of provisional measures *per se* or the consequent warranty and succeeding substantive action, deferring such detail to the subordinate implementing regulations. The law provides simply that 'the Committee may take the necessary prompt measures it deems necessary to prevent the damages resulting from the infringement'.[14] In like terms, the Saudi copyright law simply stipulates that '[the committee] may take any temporary measure it finds necessary to protect the copyright till a final decision is reached regarding the complaint or grievance'.[15]

The measures for the preservation of related evidence are in essence the local equivalent of the common-law Anton Piller orders, in that they may

12 See, for example, Bahrain, Legislative Decree No. 22/2006, arts 62–63, and Legislative Decree No. 11 of 2006, art. 45; Oman, Royal Decree No. 67/2008, art. 73.

13 Oman, Royal Decree No. 49/2009, art. 25.

14 Saudi Arabia, Royal Decree No. M/27 of 1425 AH (2004) arts 34–35. The relevant Saudi committee in this case being a committee established by the King Abdul Aziz City for Science and Technology (KACST) as the statutory authority responsible for the oversight of patents and related areas.

15 Saudi Arabia, Royal Decree No. M/41 of 1424 AH (2003), art. 23.6.

be taken as conservatory measures where delay may prejudice the right holder beyond compensation or where there is an established risk that material which constitutes evidence related to the infringement will be lost. The measures may be taken without prior notification to the defendant, although the defendant must be notified of the measures as soon as they are implemented. The defendant may appeal the orders within a prescribed period of time after notification or implementation, and the court may confirm, amend or withdraw the measures at its discretion.

As a countermeasure against abuse of the availability of provisional measures, or frivolous complaints of alleged infringement, most laws require applications for relief to be accompanied by a surety as determined by the court and which must be lodged with the court at the time that the provisional measures are sought. The issuance of any orders must be followed by a substantive action brought before the court by the complaining right holder within a stipulated and limited period of time. The required time frames vary significantly and illogically between the States and between the classes of laws, ranging from eight days to 31 days, and must form at least an obstacle if not a deterrent, in initiating litigation against an infringing party. Some of the variations, for example, include the following:

- 8 days: the UAE generally; Jordan in respect of copyright, patents, designs, trademarks, trade secrets only; Qatar in respect of patents; and Yemen in respect of copyright, trademarks, designs and GIs only;
- 10 days: Qatar in respect of trademarks;[16]
- 15 days: Bahrain and Oman and Qatar in respect of copyright;[17]
- 20 working days: Bahrain in respect of trademarks and Oman in respect of industrial property;[18]
- 31 calendar days: Oman as an alternative to 20 working days, whichever is the longer, in respect of industrial property.[19]

Failure to bring such action may cause the provisional measures to be revoked and leaves the complaining right holder open to a counter-action for damages by the respondent. Failure to do so causes the orders to cease to have effect and leaves the complainant liable to claims for compensation by the party against whom the orders were sought.

The GCC Trademark Law provides for a period of 20 days,[20] whereas the earlier GCC Patent Regulation does not include any provisions for provisional measures, or other judicial enforcement measures, presumably relying on the

16 Qatar, Law No. 9 of 2002, art. 46(4).
17 Bahrain, Law No. 22 of 2006, art. 62(5); Oman, Royal Decree No. 65/2008, art. 42; Qatar, Law No. 7 of 2002, art. 47(d).
18 Bahrain, Law No. 22 of 2006, art. 62(7); Oman, Royal Decree No. 65/2008, art. 42
19 Oman, Royal Decree 67/2008, as amended by Royal Decree No. 131/2008, art. 73(5).
20 GCC Unified Trademark Law of 2013, art. 40(7).

domestic laws of the acceding GCC member States to determine whether such measures may apply.

The Saudi copyright law does not specifically mention provisional measures other than referring to the copyright regulation, which provides that a surety may be lodged at the request of the committee.[21] The regulation provides a period of 31 days to file a complaint against alleged infringers.[22] The Saudi patent law and the Kuwaiti laws, in general, do not require lodgment of a surety by the complaining party. The newest Kuwaiti (copyright) law requires that a case must be launched within 15 days from the day of issuance of orders for provisional measures.[23]

6.2.3 Special requirements relating to border measures (TRIPS Articles 51–60)

The special requirements relating to border measures constitute a significant proportion of the TRIPS enforcement obligations. They establish a scheme for suspension of the release into circulation of suspected counterfeit trademark or pirated copyright goods, either on application by a right holder or by *ex-officio* action by border authorities.[24]

The strategy of utilising border seizure to control the trade in infringing goods is foreshadowed in the Paris Convention, which provides that 'all goods unlawfully bearing a trademark or trade name shall be seized on importation into those countries of the Union where such mark or trade name is entitled to protection'.[25] WTO Members are required to make provision for the holder of an intellectual property right to make application to administrative or judicial authorities for customs authorities to suspend the release of goods into free circulation where grounds exist for suspecting that the importation of counterfeit trademark or pirated goods may occur.[26] Such provision need not apply in respect of goods in transit, or where a particular border is subject to a customs union between two members. Members may permit the competent authorities to act upon their own initiative in

21 Saudi Arabia, Royal Decree No. M/41 of 2003, art. 22(7), and Ministerial Decision No. 16888/1 of 2004, art. 27.

22 Ibid., art. 27.

23 Kuwait, Law No. 22 of 2016, art. 34.

24 TRIPS, art. 51. As a footnote to this article, the term 'counterfeit trademark goods' is defined as 'any goods, including packaging, bearing without authorisation a trademark which is identical to the trademark validly registered in respect of such goods, or which cannot be distinguished in its essential aspects from such a trademark, and which thereby infringes the rights of the owner of the trademark in question under the law of the country of importation'. The term 'pirated copyright goods' is defined as 'any goods which are copies made without consent of the rights holder in the country of production and which are made directly or indirectly from any article where the making of that copy would have constituted an infringement of a copyright or a related right under the law of the country of importation'.

25 Paris Convention, art. 9(1).

26 TRIPS, art. 51.

suspending the release of goods where *prima facie* evidence exists that an intellectual property right is being infringed. Members may order the destruction or disposal of infringing goods outside the channels of commerce, but shall not allow the re-exportation of counterfeit goods in an unaltered state or subject them to a different custom procedure, other than in exceptional circumstances.[27]

The right holder may be required to lodge a bond or surety in order to protect the defendant and the competent authorities, and to prevent abuse.[28] Payment of such surety shall not prejudice any other remedy available to the right holder. The surety shall be released if the right holder fails to pursue the right of action within the prescribed period of time.

Suspended goods must be released if customs authorities are not informed within a prescribed period that provisional measures have been ordered prolonging the suspension or that judicial proceedings have been initiated.[29] Where suspension of the release of goods is carried out or continued in accordance with a provisional measure, the suspension shall be revoked or cease to have effect if proceedings are not initiated. Where an importer has suffered injury because of the wrongful detention of goods, or where the goods are released because the right holder does not initiate an action within the prescribed period, authorities shall be empowered to order the right holder to pay compensation to the importer, consignee and owner of the detained goods for any injury suffered.

The attention given by most States within their copyright and trademark laws, or generally within their intellectual property laws to the special border control requirements of TRIPS was rather slight and almost incidental during the first decade of the post-TRIPS period. This might in part be attributable to the eventual establishment of the customs union between the GCC member States in January 2003, after a very long gestation period. A footnote to TRIPS Part III, Section 4 allows that a member shall not be required to apply the provisions of Section 4 at borders with other members with which it has formed a custom union and among which all controls over movement of goods across these borders have been substantially dismantled. However, reliance on this provision by the States as grounds for inaction ignores the fact that the amount of intra-GCC trade represents a small percentage of the total trade of each member State. In any case, they might well argue, as Oman has done before the Council of TRIPS, that the provisions relating to infringements of an intellectual property right and to the remedies and provisional relief apply equally to infringing imported and exported goods.[30] They would also argue that a right holder can obtain orders on the suspension of customs clearance of allegedly

27 Ibid., art. 59.
28 Ibid., art. 53.
29 Ibid., arts 55–56.
30 WTO Council for Trade-Related Aspects of Intellectual Property Rights, *Review of Legislation: Oman*, 16; Document IP/Q4/OMN/1 (03-1675), 24 March 2003.

counterfeit goods as part of the provisional measures and relief generally available, and that these provisions by and large correspond to TRIPS Articles 51–60. Customs have the legal authority to act *ex officio* to detain and/or seize suspected goods at ports of entry, to confiscate and destroy infringing goods and to suspend the release of imported counterfeit and pirated goods, as required by TRIPS.[31]

However, the apparent slight appearance of customs and border provisions within specific intellectual property laws may also be due to the fact that a number of States have deferred such provisions to separate customs laws – some which directly address intellectual property issues and others which have a wider application. Kuwait, for example, issued in 2011 a law on border issues which encompass the treatment of fraudulent trademarks and counterfeit goods; and a decade earlier Jordan had already issued a ministerial regulation on border measures for the protection of rights.[32]

Over the last decade or so, the attention given to substantial provision in respect of border measures to protect intellectual property rights has grown significantly. At one end of the spectrum, Kuwait and Jordan do not make specific reference to border or customs measures in any of their laws. The UAE, in addition to its border control law, and Yemen provide brief substantive provision in their copyright and trademark laws for border control authorities to act to suspend the release of suspected infringing goods, but only on application from a right holder, and not *ex officio* or on their own cognisance.[33]

Saudi Arabia was the first State to make provision for measures that arguably come close to addressing the border measure obligations enshrined in TRIPS Articles 51–60. No doubt driven by the external scrutiny of its intellectual property regimes arising from its campaign for WTO membership, Saudi Arabia has enshrined these provisions in a ministerial order on border measures in respect of trademarks and copyright.[34] Bahrain and Oman have followed suit in respect of including similar provisions. Bahrain, however, has limited such provisions to its copyright law, but has not extended them to any areas of industrial property.

Oman provides a comprehensive prescription of border control measures, including similar principles and processes in both its copyright law and its general industrial property law. While its copyright law offers a succinct description of border measures, the industrial property law devotes a whole part to providing a comprehensive and detailed exposition of measures both in respect of right-holder complaint and *ex-officio* action.[35] The Plant Breeder's Rights Law defers generally to the provisions

31 Ibid., 25.

32 Kuwait, Law No. 17 of 2011 on Border Issues; Jordan, Regulation No. 7 of 2000 on Border Measures for the Protection of Intellectual Property Rights.

33 UAE, Federal Law No. 7 of 2002, art. 36; Yemen, Law No. 15 of 2012, Sect. II arts 70–76.

34 Saudi Arabia, Ministerial Decision No. 1277 of 1425 AH (2004), Regulations for Border Procedures for Protection of Intellectual Property Rights of Trademarks and Copyright.

35 See Oman, Royal Decree No. 65/2008 (Copyright) art. 41, Royal Decree No. 67/2008 (Industrial Property) Part V arts 79–92, and Royal Decree No. 49/2009, art. 25(2).

of the industrial property law. Hence Oman's border control provisions apply equally across the broad spectrum of intellectual property with equal force.

All three States provide that customs authorities, acting either *ex officio* or on complaint from the right holder, may suspend the clearance of suspected infringing goods upon obtaining *prima facie* evidence of infringement. Alternatively, the courts, or the Board of Grievances in the case of Saudi Arabia, may issue *ex parte* orders suspending clearance on application of the right holder. When acting on the application of the right holder, the courts or the customs authorities may require lodgment of a security bond before issuing the order or seizing the goods. Orders for suspension on application must be followed with the initiation of civil or criminal proceedings within a specified period of time; failing such proceedings, the goods shall be released. Seized infringing goods may be disposed of through non-commercial channels, but they are not allowed to be re-exported or allowed to enter the local market under another customs procedure. While the Saudi regulation permits the parties concerned to challenge the decisions of the customs authority before the Board of Grievances, there is no indication in the ministerial order whether a decision of the Ministry or the Board can be similarly challenged.

Qatar has taken a similar approach to that of Saudi Arabia in respect of border measures primarily to target counterfeit and pirated goods. Instead of including separate provisions in each of its intellectual property laws, it has promulgated a separate law on border measures, namely Law No. 17 of 2011 for the Protection of Intellectual Property Rights. In so doing it establishes a consistent set of provisions and sanctions across all its IP laws, although the sanctions in this Law are without prejudice to any greater sanction provided by other laws. Article 1 of the Law provides that the 'rights under protection' refers to rights under the protection of Laws No. 7 of 2002 (copyright), 9 of 2002 (trademarks and geographical indications, industrial designs and business names), 5 of 2005 (trade secrets), 6 of 2005 (layout designs of integrated circuits) and 30 of 2006 (GCC patents). Law No. 17 of 2011 provides border authorities with the rights to seize alleged counterfeit goods or goods bearing counterfeit marks either *ex officio* or on complaint by the rights holder. However, the Law does not apply to suspect goods that are in transit or from a country which is a member of a customs union with Qatar.[36] The momentum continued with the issuance in September 2014 of Law No. 14 of 2014 Concerning Cybercrime Prevention. While the law is broadly based, applying to Qatar's commercial, criminal, penal, telecommunications and even terrorism codes, it also provides both general and specific application to intellectual property rights.[37]

36 Qatar, Law No. 17 of 2011 on Border Measures to Protect Intellectual Property Rights, art. 8.

37 Qatar, Law No. 14 of 2014 Concerning Cybercrime. Chapter 5 is entitled 'Violation Intellectual Property Rights', but the general provisions also refer to download of unauthorised or illegal material..

6.2.4 Damages, indemnification and other remedies (TRIPS Articles 45–46)

TRIPS Articles 45 and 46 require members to accord to their judicial authorities the capacity to award damages adequate to compensate for any injury suffered because of the infringement, as well as expenses and legal costs. Recovery of profits and/or payment of pre-established damages may be ordered, even where the infringer did not knowingly engage in the infringing activity. Judicial authorities must have the capacity to order infringing goods to be destroyed or otherwise disposed of outside the channels of commerce without any compensation to the infringer and in such manner as to avoid any harm to the right holder. To ensure that the risk of further acts of infringement is minimised, the authority extends to orders for the disposal in similar fashion of materials and implements that have been used predominantly in the creation of the infringing goods, again without compensation to the infringer. However, account must be taken of proper proportion between the seriousness of the infringement and the remedies ordered, as well as the interests of third parties. In the case of counterfeit trademarks, the simple removal of the unlawfully affixed trademark will not normally be sufficient to enable the goods to be released back into channels of commerce.

As is the case with the availability of provisional measures, the statutory provision for judicial authority in respect of the award of damages and the application of other remedies is likewise inconsistent – both across the States and within the respective intellectual property laws of each State. Bahrain, for example, has provision for the award of damages in its copyright law and by virtue of its adopted GCC Trademark Law, but not in its patent law; Kuwait has provision in its copyright, adopted GCC trademark and patent laws; Saudi Arabia has provision in its copyright and adopted GCC Trademark Law, but not its patent, designs, integrated circuits and plant varieties law. The UAE, in contrast, has provision for award of damages in its trademark law but not in its copyright or patent laws. Qatar allows for damages in its earlier copyright, trademark and geographical indications laws, but not in its later patent and layout-designs laws. Oman, Jordan and Yemen make provision across their respective full suite of laws for the award of damages.

In their simplest form, the nature and dimension of available damages that may be awarded are confined to simple statements, in essence to compensate the aggrieved right holder for the damage suffered, being subject to determination by the courts on a case-by-case basis. But a number of States and laws are more comprehensive. The GCC Trademark Law, adopted or being adopted by Bahrain, Kuwait, Qatar and Saudi Arabia, makes additional provision for the award of pre-established damages at the request of the right holder. Article 41 of the Regulation stipulates:

1 The court determines the compensation so as it deems redressing the damage, to be considered by the court the value of a good or service – that is subject of infringement – in accordance with what is determined by the plaintiff on the retail price or any other licit criterion required to apply or by experience.

2 The owner of the right, instead of a compensation claim redressing the damage including profits earned by the infringer in accordance with the provisions of the preceding paragraph, may request at any time and before the deciding on the claim to judge in his favour an adequate compensation if it is proved that the infringement was by using the trademark in the intention a limitation of commodity or was in any other manner.
3 Obligating the infringer to provide the court of jurisdiction or to the owner with the information in his possession on all those persons or entities that contributed in any aspect of the infringement, and on the methods of production and distribution channels of such goods or services, including the identity of all those who participated in the production or distribution of goods or services and determining his own distribution channels.

The Oman Copyright Law goes even further, providing for the following to be included in any judicial damages calculation:

- compensations sufficient enough to cover for the damages to the right holder attributed to the infringement;
- amount of profits gained by the infringer and attributed to the infringement, and which was not taken into consideration when estimating the above compensations;
- when estimating the compensations, taking into consideration the value of the infringed good or service, as estimated at the retail price determined by the right holder, or according to any other criterion he determines, provided that it is fair;
- as an alternative, and upon request of the right holder, the previously estimated compensation, provided it does not exceed 10,000 Omani rials for each act of infringement;
- when estimating the amount of compensation, the Court must consider the court fees and lawyers' charges incurred by the right holder, except in exceptional circumstances as seen by the Court in view of the compensation demanded by the right holder.[38]

In respect of costs, the common convention throughout the region in respect of civil cases is for either party to bear its own legal costs, irrespective of outcome and notwithstanding the provisions of Article 45.2 of TRIPS. Hence the States' intellectual property legislation is singularly quiet on the issue of authority to award costs – with two exceptions. Both the Omani and Yemeni copyright laws authorise the courts to either make a specific award in respect of costs and legal fees or to include such costs in and fees in their calculation and award of damages.[39]

38 Oman, Royal Decree No. 65/2008 (Copyright), art. 41.
39 Oman, Royal Decree No. 65/2008 art. 43(5), as amended by Royal Decree No. 13/2008, art. 41; Yemen, Law 15 of 2012, art. 79.

All States make some provision across virtually all their intellectual property laws for offending goods, and any tools, machinery and equipment used in the commission of the infringement, to be confiscated, destroyed or otherwise disposed of in such other way as a court or administrative authority may deem appropriate. The provisions appear to be generally consistent with only a few minor variations. For example, the seizures may be limited to criminal proceedings at the particular's court's discretion, as the Bahraini copyright law provides.[40] Kuwait's trademark and patent laws both authorise the court upon the request of the right holder to order the destruction of the infringing work or goods and the materials and equipment used.[41] The trademark law further allows the court to decide in special circumstances to dispose of the infringing goods outside the commercial channels only if the destruction results in a great harm to public health or the environment.[42] The copyright law permits the confiscation of the pirated works and the equipment used in the infringement, but does not mention or provide for the destruction of the infringing goods, as did the old copyright law. The one exception to this general seizure convention appears to be Jordan's singularly brief trade secrets law, which has omitted any seizure provision.[43]

The UAE courts may also order offending goods to be confiscated, destroyed or otherwise disposed of in such other way as they deem appropriate, as well as the tools, machinery and equipment used as part of the infringing activity.[44] Infringing premises may be closed for a period of up to six months in respect of copyright and trademark infringements, but not in the case of patents and industrial design infringements. Neither the copyright law nor patents law makes provision for compensation, while the trademark law retains such provision from its predecessor law of 1992.[45]

Closure of the infringing premises is not common in respect of first offences. The few instances of such closure provisions include Qatar's copyright law minimum of one month to a remarkable maximum og three years' closure and its trademark law six-month maximum closure.[46] There does not appear to be any instances of maximum closure under the copyright law. The Saudi and UAE copyright laws also allow for closure for a few months for first offences. Most of the region's laws limit closure of an infringing establishment to being one of the options available in respect of repeat offences, and even then practices vary marginally. Where closure is available, they generally exist within the range of six months to nine months.

40 Bahrain, Law 22 of 2006, art. 65(3)–(4).

41 Kuwait, Law No. 1 of 2015 (GCC trademarks), art. 41(4); Law No. 3 of 2001 (patents, industrial designs and utility models), art. 48.

42 Kuwait, Law No. 1 of 2015 (GCC trademarks), art. 41(4).

43 Jordan, Law No. 15 of 2000. The Law consists of just ten brief articles, mainly concerned with the description of a trade secret.

44 UAE, Federal Law No. 7 of 2002 (copyright), arts 38 and 40; Federal Law No. 8 of 2002 (trademarks), arts 39–40; Federal Law No. 17 of 2002 (patents), art. 63.

45 UAE, Federal Law No. 8 of 2002 (trademarks), art. 41.2.

46 Qatar, Law No. 7 of 2002 (copyright), art. 52, Law No. 9 of 2002 (trademarks), art. 52(1).

6.2.5 Criminal procedures and sanctions (TRIPS Article 61)

TRIPS Article 61 requires WTO members to make provision for criminal procedures and penalties to be applied at least in cases of willful trademark counterfeiting or copyright piracy on a commercial scale. Remedies, which include imprisonment and/or fines, must be sufficient to provide a deterrent and must be consistent with penalties applied for crimes of corresponding gravity. Remedies may also include seizure, forfeiture and destruction of the offending goods and any materials, tools or equipment predominantly used in the commission of the infringement. Since these are minimum requirements, members may provide criminal procedures and penalties for other cases of intellectual property right infringement.

All States provide for criminal proceedings to be available across the broad range of intellectual property rights, notably in cases of willful infringing activity and/or activity on a commercial scale. Notwithstanding the existence of a fair degree of common ground between the various types of national intellectual property laws in respect of the nature of offences, the penalties that they attract still vary markedly between them and even between the laws in each State. One exception is Oman, which has applied the same sanctions and scale of penalties across its laws. The marked differences have left certain States open to accusation from some developed countries that the perceived inadequate levels of sanctions still engender an environment which is tantamount to fostering unchecked piracy and counterfeiting and which is providing safe haven for illegal importers, traders and manufacturers. However, as one senior government official from one State in the region wryly described life in a local prison: 'There are no single cells, weekly linen changes, basketball games, movies or even regular meals in a local prison.' A similar statement could be made about prison conditions in the other States.

The adoption and intended implementation of the GCC Trademark Law by Bahrain, Kuwait, Qatar and Saudi Arabia will bring a greater degree of consistency and harmonisation of sanctions across the region, when the Regulation comes into full effect across these GCC member States – current and prospective. The other States will need to make substantial increases in respect of their trademark sanctions if they are to approach anywhere near the scale of the GCC Law. For example, the GCC Law provides for sanctions of up to one million Saudi riyals (SR) or equivalent currency and up to one year's imprisonment. Oman's maximum sanctions are currently equivalent to SR97,000 plus one year's imprisonment, Jordan's to SR32,000 plus one year's imprisonment, the UAE's to a mere SR10,200 plus one year's imprisonment, and Yemen's to a similarly mere SR15,000 plus two years' imprisonment.[47]

Bahrain's other sanctions, which were formerly the most lenient among the GCC member States, have increased only marginally. In 2003 and 2004 it issued

47 Bahrain, Law No. 6 of 2014, art. 42(b); Kuwait, Law No. 15 of 2008, art. 38; UAE, Federal Law No. 37 of 1992, as amended by Law No. 8 of 2002, art. 37; Yemen, Law No. 23 of 2010, art. 47.

new geographical indications and trade secret laws which carried penalties for infringements of up to 3,000 Bahraini dinars (BD) and two years' imprisonment.[48] Laws issued in 2006 for patents, designs and integrated circuits actually carry reduced sanctions of up to BD2,000 and one year's imprisonment.[49] The copyright law of 2006 fares a little better, with a maximum BD4,000 and one-year imprisonment provision.[50] It is uncertain what impact, if any, the intellectual property provisions of Bahrain's free trade agreement with the United States may continue to have on further increasing the level of sanctions across all of Bahrain's intellectual property laws. What is clear is that some Bahraini sanctions are still very lenient even by regional standards, but the free trade agreement requires Bahrain to provide strong deterrence against piracy and counterfeiting.

Kuwait's copyright law of 2016 provides for a maximum fine of 100,000 Kuwaiti dinars (KD) – the highest financial penalty of any regional IP law by a wide margin – and/or imprisonment for up to two years.[51] Kuwait's increased financial penalty from KD500 to KD100,000 illustrates the interest the government has in protecting copyright and neighbouring rights. This is a significant shift from providing the lowest financial penalty for copyright violations within the region to providing one of the highest in regard to intellectual property. However, its patent law does not provide similarly strong penalties, providing just KD5,000 and one year's imprisonment.[52]

Qatar's penalties, at least in respect of copyright infringements, are reasonably substantial by regional standards, even though they are largely unchanged from earlier legislation. However, they remain at the lower end of the regional spectrum in industrial property areas. Penalties range up to QR100,000 and imprisonment for up to 12 months for copyright infringement acts, but are as low as QR10,000

48 Bahrain, Legislative Decree No. 16 of 2004 (geographical indications), art. 6; Legislative Decree No. 7 of 2003 (trade secrets), art. 7.

49 Bahrain, Legislative Decree No. 14 of 2006 (patents), art. 41; Legislative Decree No. 11 of 2006 (trademarks), art. 48; Legislative Decree No. 6 of 2006 (designs), art. 30; Legislative Decree No. 5 of 2006 (integrated circuits) art. 35. The standard Bahraini, Kuwaiti and Omani currency unit is worth just under ten Qatari, Saudi and Emirati units. The currencies of all the Arabian Peninsula States are linked, formally or effectively, to the US dollar. The exchange rates (as at 30/01/2017) are as follows:

BD (Bahraini dinar)	= US$2.65	US$1.00 = BD0.38
JD (Jordanian dinar)	= US$1.41	US$1.00 = JD0.71
KD (Kuwaiti dinar)	= US$3.28	US$1.00 = KD0.31
OR (Omani rial)	= US$2.6	US1$.00 = OR0.38
QR (Qatari riyal)	= US$0.27	US$1.00 = QR3.67
SR (Saudi riyal)	= US$0.27	US$1.00 = SR3.67
AED (UAE dirham)	= US$0.27	US$1.00 = AED3.67
YER (Yemeni rial)	= US$0.004	US$1.00 = YER250.35

50 Bahrain, Legislative Decree No. 22 of 2006, art. 65.

51 Kuwait, Law No. 22 of 2016, art. 42.

52 Kuwait, Law No. 71 of 2013, art. 3.

and two years for patents infringements.[53] However, rather curiously, acts relating to manufacture or import of electronic deactivation or satellite-decoding devices, or their illegal modification or removal, do not have a monetary penalty specified and carry a maximum term of imprisonment of only one year.[54] While a logical presumption may be that the financial sanctions relating to other copyright offences shall apply, the fact that different types of offences carry differing minimum and maximum financial penalties would militate against this presumption. Also noteworthy is the fact that the more recent of the laws, namely the patents law of 2006, carries the most lenient penalties, while the longest-standing current law, namely the copyright law, carries the most severe.

The UAE's laws are also internally inconsistent, but at least reasonable standards have been set in some cases. The patents and industrial designs laws carry maximum penalties of up to AED100,000 and two years' imprisonment for patents and design infringements, but the copyright law has provision for penalties up to an impressive AED500,000 and an unspecified maximum period of imprisonment.[55] Penalties for manufacturing or importing means to commit a technological fraud, to delay or discredit technological anti-fraud or anti-copy software, or to load or store computer programs and databases without authorisation – for which no provision existed in the earlier copyright law – are now recognised as the most serious of copyright violations and accordingly may attract the above maximum penalties. But in stark contrast, and at the other end of the spectrum, penalties for trademark infringements, such as use of a counterfeit trademark or improper use of a registered trademark, may attract a penalty of up to 12 months' imprisonment and/or a fine of between AED5,000 and AED10,000.[56] However, the fine for fraudulent use has in effect been lessened in impact by being altered from a previously uncapped minimum amount to a capped maximum amount.

Saudi Arabia has established the new regional benchmark in terms of the deterrence value of its sanctions by increasing them dramatically from their previous levels and by applying them across all intellectual property laws. In particular, harsher penalties for infringements in respect of information technology-based intellectual property and for repeat offences are introduced. These penalties stand in stark contrast to those extant in neighbours Bahrain, Jordan and Kuwait. But the penalties also illustrate the impact of the greater degree of critical scrutiny and pressure that Saudi Arabia received from the United States and from international business and watchdog organisations previously as part of its drive for WTO membership and currently as the largest and most diverse economy in the Middle East. Any unlawful act of exploitation of a patented subject matter

53 Qatar, Law No. 7 of 2002 (copyright), arts 50–51; Law No. 30 of 2006 (patents), art. 24.

54 Qatar, Law No. 7 of 2002, art. 51.

55 UAE, Federal Law No. 17 of 2002 (patents), art. 62; Federal Law No. 7 of 2002 (copyright), arts 38–39.

56 UAE, Federal Law No. 8 of 2002 (trademarks), arts 37–38.

carries a financial penalty of up to SR100,000, while violation of any provision of the copyright law may be subject to a fine of up to SR250,000, a dramatic increase on the maximum fine of SR10,000 (without any imprisonment provision) available under its 1989 law.[57] Fraudulent use of a registered trademark has attracted the most dramatic increases in financial penalty, with the fine having increased from a maximum of SR50,000 under the 1984 equivalent law to SR1 million.[58] The maximum term of imprisonment remains unchanged at 12 months in respect of patents and trademark violations, but has been reduced from 12 months to six months in respect of infringements of copyright and neighbouring rights.

Oman has taken a different approach to the other States. It initially achieved consistency by adopting a common scale of penalties across the full suite of seven intellectual property laws introduced during the year 2000, providing for imprisonment for up to two years and/or a fine of up to OR2,000 or both. Hence the maximum allowable penalties for counterfeiting or a trademark infringement are the same as those for infringements in respect of trade secrets or new plant varieties. The general severity of the sanctions was increased fivefold from 2008 in respect of the financial penalties, with maximum fines of OR10,000 now available.[59] The Omani strategy of standardised sanctions attracted criticism from some quarters, notably the United States, on the grounds that its sanctions were too lenient and are not in accordance with the TRIPS Article 61 requirement that sanctions should be sufficiently effective to act as a deterrent.[60] Indeed, the United States, on more than one occasion, had accused Oman of being a haven for copyright piracy in the region because of the apparent laxity of the sanctions in its copyright law.[61] Oman's response was that the sanctions are sufficiently severe to meet the deterrence objective of TRIPS Article 61, particularly the term of imprisonment.

Until its introduction of a new suite of intellectual property laws between 2010 and 2012 as part of its campaign for WTO membership, Yemen arguably had the most lenient sanctions in the region. Its single intellectual property law provided for maximum sanctions of 10,000 Yemeni rials (YER) and up to six months' imprisonment for infringements,[62] the financial sanction equating to just US$50 on then prevailing exchange rates. And on the basis of the largely anecdotal information available on levels of penalties imposed by Yemeni courts for infringements, maximum fines were not imposed. However, since 2010, its sanctions have been dramatically increased by local standards to a *minimum* of YER500,000 and/or a

57 Saudi Arabia, Royal Decree No. M/27 of 1425 AH (2004) (patents), art. 34; Royal Decree No. M/41 of 1424 AH (2003) (copyright), art. 22.

58 Saudi Arabia, Royal Decree No. 21 of 1423 AH (2002), art. 43.

59 Oman, Royal Decree No. 65/2008 (copyright) art. 43, Royal Decree No. 67/2008 art. 93.

60 Interviews conducted by the author with officials of the Oman Ministry of Commerce and Industry, December 2008.

61 Ibid.

62 Yemen, Law No. 19 of 1994 (intellectual property), art. 124.

minimum of one month's imprisonment (without a stipulated maximum) for copyright offences.[63] Industrial property-related offences now may carry fines of up to YER1 million and/or two years' imprisonment for trademark, geographical indications and industrial designs offences, and up to YR1 million with no imprisonment term for patents, trade secrets and integrated circuits offences.[64]

Jordan's range of sanctions across its suite of intellectual property laws appears somewhat uneven and curious, and warrants closer scrutiny. On the one hand, its copyright and trademark laws carry sanctions of up to 6,000 Jordanian dinars (JD) and up to one year's imprisonment, being at the lower end of the regional scale.[65] Its patents law, however, provides for even lower sanctions of a maximum mere JD3,000 and one year's imprisonment.[66] But, most surprisingly, none of its five laws encompassing geographical indications, industrial designs, new plant varieties, integrated circuits and trade secrets appears to make any provision for fines or terms of imprisonment or any other criminal sanctions.[67] The conclusion that seems inevitably to be drawn is that criminal proceedings are not an option for violations of the respective rights protected by these laws, and that rights holders may only take action through civil proceedings, with damages and seizures the only relief available to them.

National attitudes towards recidivism also vary among the States and are reflected in their respective laws, although most make some provision within the broad spectrum of their intellectual property laws. In respect of trademarks, the GCC Trademark Law provides for sanctions to be doubled and the offending establishment to be closed for up to six months. However, the Law qualifies this extra sanction by holding that an offence would only be deemed to be a 'repeat offence' if committed within three years from the date on which the sentence for the previous offence was imposed.[68]

The most common recidivism maximum provision is generally a doubling of the original sanctions and closure of the offending establishment for periods ranging between three and six months. Variations from this common regional convention include Oman's and Qatar's general doubling only of both the original sanctions, and Saudi Arabia and Yemen doubling the fine only in respect of patents violations. Kuwait generally allows for a 50 per cent increase in the maximum penalties to be imposed if the recurrence occurs within five years of the first offence, while Qatar and Saudi Arabia generally allow for a doubling of penalties for repeat offences

63 Yemen, Law No. 15 of 2012 (copyright and related rights), art. 77.
64 Yemen, Law No. 23 of 2010 (trademarks and geographical indications), art. 47, Law No. 28 of 2010 (industrial; designs), art. 34, Law No. 2 of 2011 patents etc.), art. 39.
65 Jordan, Law No. 22 of 1992 (copyright) as amended, art. 51; Law No. 33 of 1952 (trademarks) as amended, art. 38.
66 Jordan, Law No. 32 of 1999 (patents) as amended, art. 32.
67 Jordan, Law No. 8 of 2000 (geographical indications), Law No. 10 of 2000 (integrated circuits), Law No. 15 of 2000 (trade secrets), Law No. 14 of 2000 (industrial designs), Law No. 24 of 2000 (new plant varieties).
68 GCC Trademark Law, art. 43.

without time limitations from the initial offence. The UAE generally does not make any provision for increasing penalties for repeat offences, except in the case of copyright infringements, where a repeat offence attracts a minimum fine of between AED30,000 and AED200,000 and imprisonment for at least nine months, the level of severity of the penalty depending on the nature of the repeated offence.[69]

Jordan does not make any recidivism provisions within its intellectual property laws except within its copyright law, which requires just the maximum original sanctions to be applied and closure of the offending establishment for one year.[70] However, the financial provisions would seem to carry the assumption that maximum penalties would not have been applied for the first violation.

Table 6.1 (and Table 6.2 in respect of Jordan and Yemen) summarises the provisional measures, damages, remedies and sanctions that are available under the respective intellectual property laws of the Arabian Peninsula States. To place them into a meaningful perspective, and to facilitate comparison between them and between their respective laws, the monetary penalties have been listed in both the respective local currencies and in US dollars in brackets. The table highlights the differences between the States in respect of the range and nature of the various elements of their available sanctions. Where anomalies do appear – for example, in respect of the different seizure provisions between Bahrain's laws, and Jordan's omissions – it is suggested that the difference could be explained by accidents of drafting design by different initiating bodies rather than by deliberate intent.

However, what stands out most markedly is the significant spread in the range of financial penalties now extant across the States, ranging from the minute and minimal to the impressive – in this latter case, such as those embraced by the States that have adopted the GCC Trademark Law and by the UAE in respect of its copyright law. In the latter cases again, recidivism provisions can significantly increase these penalties – doubling them in the case of the Saudi laws. Saudi Arabia and the UAE have been under the greatest pressure from developed countries, and especially the United States, to introduce sanctions that will serve as effective deterrents, and Table 6.1 illustrates the success of that concerted pressure. Saudi Arabia across all intellectual property laws and the UAE in some instances now provide for financial penalties which are severe by local economic standards and which are arguably well within the scope of being effective deterrents. What is surprising is that Bahrain and Jordan appear to have managed to emerge relatively unscathed from US pressure in respect of their very lowly penalties for trademark infringements. But this clearly illustrates that copyright and trademark violations through counterfeiting and piracy, and patent violations, particularly in respect of pharmaceutical products, are the key concerns for the United States in terms of rights protection. The other States will probably continue to attract criticism for the perceived inadequacy of their financial penalties.

69 UAE, Federal Law No. 7 of 2002, arts 37.2 and 38–39.
70 Jordan, Law No. 22 of 1992 as amended, art. 51(a)(2).

TABLE 6.1 Sanctions for intellectual property infringements in the GCC member States

	Statute	*Provisional relief*	*Maximum sanctions*		*Seizures etc.*	*Closures*	*Damages available*	*Recidivism sanctions*	*Border measures*
			Fine	*Jail*					
Bahrain	Copyright 05/14		BD4,000 ($10,610)	1 year	yes				yes
	GCC Trademarks 6/14		SR1,000,000 ($266,620)	3 years			yes		
	Patents etc 14/06	yes			no				
	Designs 6/06					no		both sanctions doubled and6 months' closure	
	Trade secrets 12/06		BD2,000 ($5,305)	1 year	*yes*		*no*		no
	Integrated circuits 5/06								
	GIs 16/04								
Kuwait	Copyright 22/16		KD100,000 ($32,7914)	2 years		yes	yes	fine increased 50% and permanent closure	
	GCC Trademarks 13/15	yes	SR1,000,000 ($266,620)	3 years	yes	no	yes	both doubled and 6 months' closure	no
	Patents, Designs, integrated circuits 03/01		KD5,000 ($16,395)	I year		no	yes	no	

Oman	Copyright 65/08	yes	OR10,000 ($25,975)	3 years	yes	no	yes	both doubled	yes
	Industrial property 67/08, Plant breeders' rights 49/09								
Qatar	Copyright 07/02	yes	QR100,000 ($27,464)	1 year	yes	3 years	yes	both doubled	yes[i]
	GCC Trademarks 07/14		SR1,000,000 ($266,620)	3 years		no		both doubled and 6 months' closure	
	Patents 30/06		QR10,000 ($2,746)	2 years			no	no	
	Integrated circuits 06/05		QR50,00 ($13,732)	1 year				both doubled	
	Trade secrets 05/05						yes		
	Designs, GIs 09/02								
Saudi Arabia	Copyright 41/03	yes	SR250,000 ($66,660)	6 months	yes	2 months	yes	both doubled	yes[ii]
	GCC Trademarks 51/14		SR1,000,000 ($266,620)	3 years		no		both doubled and 6 months' closure	
	Patents, designs, integrated circuits, plant varieties 276/04		SR100,000 ($26,662)	nil			patents only	fine doubled	no

(continued)

TABLE 6.1 Sanctions for intellectual property infringements in the GCC member States *(continued)*

	Statute	*Provisional relief*	*Maximum sanctions*		*Seizures etc.*	*Closures*	*Damages available*	*Recidivism sanctions*	*Border measures*
			Fine	*Jail*					
	Trade secrets 50/05	no	no	no	no		yes	no	
UAE	Copyright 07/02		Dh500,000 ($136,132)	<3 months			yes	minimum $200,000 and 9 months' closure	yes
	Trademarks 8/02	yes	Dh10,000 ($2,722)	1 year	yes	6 months	yes	6 months' closure	
	Patents, designs, know how 31/06		Dh100,000 ($27,226)	2 years		no	no	no	no
	New plant varieties 17/09	no	Dh250,000 ($68,046)	>2 months	no	6 months	no	both doubled	

Source: compiled by the authors

Notes:

[i] Per Qatar, Law No. 17 of 2011 on Border Issues.

[ii] Per Saudi Arabia, Ministerial Decree No. 1277 of 1425 AH (2004) on Regulation for the Border Procedures for the Protection of Intellectual Property rights for Trademarks and Copyrights (issued 3 July 2004).

TABLE 6.2 Sanctions for intellectual property infringements in Jordan and Yemen

<table>
<tr><th rowspan="2"></th><th rowspan="2">Statute</th><th rowspan="2">Provisional relief</th><th colspan="2">Maximum sanctions</th><th rowspan="2">Seizures etc.</th><th rowspan="2">Closures</th><th rowspan="2">Damages available</th><th rowspan="2">Recidivism sanctions</th><th rowspan="2">Border measures</th></tr>
<tr><th>Fine</th><th>Jail</th></tr>
<tr><td rowspan="8">Jordan</td><td>Copyright 23/14</td><td>yes</td><td>JD6000 ($8,470)</td><td>3 years</td><td>yes</td><td>no</td><td>yes</td><td>maximum penalties and 1 year closure</td><td rowspan="8">yes[i]</td></tr>
<tr><td>Trademarks 15/08</td><td>yes</td><td>JD6000 ($8,470)</td><td>1 year</td><td>yes</td><td>no</td><td>no</td><td>no</td></tr>
<tr><td>Patents 28/07</td><td>yes</td><td>3000 ($4,235)</td><td>1 year</td><td>yes</td><td>no</td><td>yes</td><td>no</td></tr>
<tr><td>GIs 8/00</td><td rowspan="5">yes</td><td rowspan="5">nil</td><td rowspan="5">nil</td><td rowspan="4">yes</td><td rowspan="5">no</td><td rowspan="5">yes</td><td rowspan="5">no</td></tr>
<tr><td>Designs 14/00</td></tr>
<tr><td>New plant varieties 24/00</td></tr>
<tr><td>Integrated circuits 10/00</td></tr>
<tr><td>Trade Secrets 15/00</td><td>no</td></tr>
<tr><td rowspan="4">Yemen</td><td>Copyright 15/12</td><td rowspan="4">yes</td><td>YR500,000 minimum ($,1998)</td><td>1 month minimum</td><td rowspan="4">yes</td><td>yes</td><td rowspan="4">yes</td><td>both sanctions doubled and 6 months’ closure</td><td>yes</td></tr>
<tr><td>Trademarks and GIs 23/10</td><td rowspan="3">YR1,000,000 ($3,996)</td><td rowspan="2">2 years</td><td rowspan="3">no</td><td rowspan="2">both doubled and 3 months’ closure</td><td rowspan="2">yes</td></tr>
<tr><td>Industrial designs 28/10</td></tr>
<tr><td>Patents, trade secrets, integrated circuits 2/11</td><td>nil</td><td>fine only doubled</td><td>no</td></tr>
</table>

Source: compiled by the authors

Note:

[i] By virtue of Law No. 7 of 2000 on Border Measures for the Protection of Intellectual Property Rights.

6.3 Concluding remarks

Having the requisite intellectual property laws, even if they are not fully TRIPS-compliant, is one thing; being able to effectively enforce them and achieve the outcomes desired by rights holders is another matter. The most challenging element of the post-TRIPS period, as perceived by both the Arabian Peninsula States themselves and the developed industrial countries, is the regional enforcement of their protection obligations consistent with the standards enshrined in TRIPS, the TRIPS-plus treaties and bilateral agreements to which the States have acceded. Notwithstanding the presence of comprehensive sets of laws and treaty commitments, there exists a disjunct between the principle of intellectual property protection as enshrined in the various legislative regimes and its practical application as exemplified by the degree of effective enforcement action. On the one hand, the States now enjoy comprehensive statutory regimes and are progressively initiating the consequential structural, judicial and institutional reforms to give the regimes full and proper effect. On the other hand, the effectiveness of enforcement actions against infringing activities, particularly in respect of piracy and counterfeit goods, the nature and frequency of judicial actions and the severity of penalties available, has yet to reach the standards required by the developed nations which constitute the major global exporters of intellectual property. It also needs to be said, however, that there also exists a difference of opinion between the various States and the industrialised countries which constitute the primary exporters of intellectual property to the region as to what constitutes 'effective enforcement'.

The barriers to the elimination of intellectual property infringements, which lie at the heart of this dichotomy, do not rest solely in the domain of the administering and enforcement authorities or the judiciary; entrenched local societal, cultural and commercial attitudes and practices are also major contributing factors, as the next chapter discusses.

7

POST-TRIPS AND THE ENFORCEMENT CHALLENGE

7.1 Introduction – the challenges for effective enforcement

The most challenging element of TRIPS, as perceived by both the Arabian Peninsula States themselves and the developed countries with established commercial interests in the region, has been that of the enforcement of the States' intellectual property protection obligations consistent with the standards enshrined in TRIPS Parts II and III. Notwithstanding the fact that most have taken significant strides in recent years in setting in place comprehensive legislative regimes for the protection of intellectual property rights, and most already have laws that are largely TRIPS-compliant, they face an ongoing challenge to address the continuing disjunct that appears between the principle of enforcement as enshrined in the various legislative regimes and the practice as exemplified by the degree of effective action. In all States, the practical application of compliance obligations through effective enforcement has been, and continues to be, the most difficult area with which to contend.

According to a WIPO survey conducted in 2002 on counterfeiting and piracy, the ineffectiveness of enforcement systems can be attributed, in many cases, to:

- legislation not being drafted effectively or extensively;
- lack of human resources, funding and practical experience in the enforcement of intellectual property rights;
- insufficient knowledge on the part of right holders and the general public, concerning their rights and remedies;
- a general lack of training of enforcement officials, including the judiciary; and
- systemic problems resulting from insufficient national and international coordination, including a lack of transparency.[1]

1 As enunciated in a survey conducted in 2002 by WIPO among its member states and reported in WIPO (2002),'Synthesis of Issues Concerning Difficulties and Practices in the Field of

These shortcomings are not necessarily the exclusive confine of just the States themselves, or even of other developing countries. But they do apply to, and are a succinct exposition of, the challenges facing the States with respect to their enforcement obligations.[2] To the above list, however, should be added the challenges posed by the clash of alien cultural and economic mores with entrenched local societal attitudes.

With most of the States, the principal barriers to the elimination of infringement of intellectual property rights do not subsist so much in the substantive law as in the practical application of the remedies and sanctions available (or not available, as the case may be) to deter counterfeiting and piracy and other infringements. For those States which still have in force laws that are essentially pre-TRIPS by virtue of the nature and standards of their enforcement provisions, the negative impact of the barriers is exacerbated by the presence of sanctions which are both inadequate and incomplete in scope and scale. But irrespective of these inadequacies of scope and scale in a few older laws, the sanctions available to the authorities across the broad spectrum of the region's intellectual property laws are not being fully exploited. The reasons do not rest solely with the enforcement authorities or the judiciary; entrenched local societal, cultural and commercial attitudes also contribute to the development of this enforcement challenge.

7.2 Societal attitudes – 'an honest trade'?

The leaderships of the States generally recognise that being part of the world trading community through membership of the WTO and adherence to its terms of membership through the adoption and implementation of its multilateral agreements, such as TRIPS, is crucial for their respective national economic growth and health.[3] Accordingly, they also recognise that the obligations that accompany such membership must be enforced domestically. By contrast, there still exists throughout the States a widespread lack of public awareness of the

Enforcement', *WIPO Consultation Meeting on Enforcement, Geneva, 11-13 September*, WIPO Document WIPO/CME/3, pp. 4–5.

2 The survey was addressed to all WIPO member countries, including the Arabian Peninsula States. None of the States, nor any other Arab country, responded to the survey, which in itself could be construed as an indicator of deep-seated systemic deficiencies and infrastructural shortcomings in intellectual property enforcement in the region. It also illustrates the difficulty that faces any researcher in obtaining reliable, periodic and comparative data for any of the States on intellectual property enforcement practices and performance.

3 The Saudi Minister of Commerce and Industry, Hashim Bin Abdullah Yamani, when interviewed on Saudi Arabia's admission to the WTO in December 2005, suggested that the Kingdom had little choice: 'The idea of seeing Saudi Arabia outside the WTO, isolated from the developments in international trade, would result in it being unable to compete internationally . . . if Saudi Arabia did not join the WTO it would lose any chance to defend its important economic and trade interests' (as quoted in the *Gulf News*, 30 October 2005). See also an interview with Hamoud Al-Najar, Yemen Ministry of Trade and Industry, on Yemen's membership of the WTO, in 'Joining the Club', *Yemen Times*, 23 January 2014, at www.yementimes.com/en/1749/business/3384/Joining-the-club.htm, last accessed 26 May 2017.

western concept of intellectual property rights – what they mean, what constitutes an infringement and the wider implications of infringing activity. This lack of public awareness is particularly prevalent within the older generations, among whom the everyday use of the English language with its subtle complexities is still not widespread; the lack of public awareness is shared by local merchants, as well as some small-scale infringers and end-users of potentially infringing material.[4]

Even where an awareness or understanding of intellectual property rights does exist, there nevertheless also still prevails a conservatism that questions the desirability and necessity to comply with international and national intellectual property protection obligations, which may seem so removed and irrelevant at the local community level or in the local *souk* (marketplace). Commonplace is a deep-rooted societal attitude that holds that ownership of a good confers an unlimited right of use and disposal, including copying and resale, while imitation is deemed to be legitimate practice.[5] No harm is held to have been done to the owner of the original good if the resale is on a reasonable scale and if it is conducted in a different – in either a geographic or economic sense – market. The sale of counterfeit versions of luxury western goods in the local *souk* at a fraction of the genuine products' retail price is not perceived as disadvantaging the owner of the luxury goods, since the buyer would still not have purchased the much more expensive genuine product if the counterfeit versions were no longer available. The claim of 'genuine imitation', frequently offered in the *souks* and on the street stalls as an unwritten assurance as to the quality and value of the counterfeit and pirated goods on offer, is still asserted with candour and with a certain degree of conviction that such claim is a positive marketing ploy. Hence, external attempts to fetter this *laissez-faire* and perceived non-competing micro-economy are neither welcome nor fully comprehended in the local environment. This common sentiment, as expressed by an illegal trader in response to a raid on his shop by government officials, is that anti-piracy measures are 'not fair'. 'We pay money for these [disks] and we sell them. This is an honest trade,' the trader protested.[6]

Also widespread is the perception that the protection of intellectual property rights, particularly in respect of software and audiovisual copyrights, foreign trademarked consumer goods and pharmaceutical patents, represents a protection of western (and particularly US and European) commercial interests at the expense

4 Interviews conducted by the author with officials, Oman Ministry of Commerce and Industry, and Qatar Ministry of Economy and Trade, December 2008. See also M. Sadiq Sohail (2012), 'Consumer Influences on Pirated Software Purchases: Perspectives from an Emerging Gulf Nation', 5(1), *International Journal of Trade and Global Markets*; 'Super Dupers! Fake items in Oman's markets' (2014), *Times of Oman*, 5 June 2014, available at http://timesofoman.com/article/35427/HI/Super-Dupers!-Fake-items-in-Oman's-markets, last accessed 26 May 2017.

5 S H Amin (1993), *Law of Intellectual and Industrial Property in Developing Countries: Muslim World*, pp. 1–2.

6 *Times of Oman*, p. 2, 27 August 2002.

of technology transfer and industrial development for the benefit of the local markets and communities. This perception is reinforced by the cynical view that western countries, formerly imperial overlords in living memory, are now continuing their exploitation as political and commercial bullies. Trade with western countries is desired, but the perceived imposition of a new western-style commercial colonialism, bolstered by western intellectual property protection regimes, may well be an unpalatable consequence.[7] It is not surprising, then, that attitudes develop to justify the use of infringing, counterfeit or pirated material or goods. This justification can be seen in the following reasons offered by locals in response to a Saudi local media survey conducted a decade ago on using pirated software:

- the software is priced too high;
- the company that has created the software is already very rich, so stealing the software doesn't really matter;
- the morality or business practices of the company that has created the software are questionable, so it is acceptable to steal their software;
- the people using the pirated software are poor, so it is acceptable for them to steal from the rich company;
- the software is defective so paying full price is silly;
- the software is only for personal private use;
- the software has poor local support so the company shouldn't expect people to pay for it;
- buying one copy of an application (and then sharing) is good enough.[8]

Hence, attempts by western companies to wean locals away from counterfeit or pirated products by a positive reinforcement strategy can sometimes produce an unexpected and negative result. For example, an offer by a leading global operating systems and software manufacturer to educational institutions and students of discounts of up to 90 per cent off the normal retail price of some of its leading products, in an attempt to steer consumers and end-users away from pirated versions of its leading software, was not received with wholesale enthusiasm. In some quarters, the reaction to the offer was a cynical one – along the lines that the normal pricing structure of the software to members of the public must be exorbitant to allow such a generous discount to educational institutions and students. Acceptance of the discount offer was legitimising the original pricing structure and endorsing the commercial practices of a major foreign yet global company that was still over-exploiting the local markets.[9]

7 John Carroll (2001), 'Intellectual Property Rights in the Middle East: A Cultural Perspective' (2000–2001), 11, *Fordham Intellectual Property, Media and Entertainment Journal*, p. 590.
8 As published in 'A Window into the World of Anti-Piracy', *Arab News*, 11 October 2005.
9 *Gulf News*, 16 July 1998, p. 3. The local reaction in some quarters to the offers reported above is also based on the author's own experiences and discussions with some regional educational institutions at the time of the offer.

Further contributing to an environment of enforcement less rigorous than that sought by western countries is a perception by the more conservative sections of the populations of the States that the Middle East is being subjected to an ongoing cultural penetration by western countries that contributes to an erosion of Islamic beliefs, values and local culture at every turn. Western culture is seen as often immoral and corrupt, and so the enforcement of intellectual property rights for goods and services that are largely western in origin constitutes governmental and religious sanction of these immoral and corrupting influences.[10] Enforcement of intellectual property protection by the governments of the region on behalf of predominantly western right holders not only reinforces these corrupting influences but also provides the governments with powerful tools for controlling cultural content and eliminating the 'informal' but commonplace and socially acceptable cultural distribution mechanisms that have long been in place (in other words, the uncontrolled copying and duplication that the west would describe as counterfeiting and piracy).[11] This cynicism and resentment towards the west in respect of the latter's protected goods is reinforced by some local attitudes towards the western expatriate populations, who in most States represent a significant proportion of the population and who lead a very visible, comfortable and often culturally insensitive lifestyle.

There also prevails a cultural dilemma in the local populations of some States insofar as the necessity to resort to public judicial processes for the resolution of a dispute, as distinct from the utilisation of informal and private mediation, is perceived by many as a negative reflection on both parties. One characteristic of an Arab community is the confidential treatment of local disputes. Public disclosure of those disputes through court proceedings, particularly those relating to family companies, is liable to prejudice the personal and professional standing of the family, the family company and the traditions of the immediate community of which the family is a part. Accordingly, there appears to be a widespread disinclination to pursue a dispute or infringement through the judicial system, other than as a last resort. The paramount consideration for all parties is to achieve a mutually satisfactory resolution in which the acknowledged direct commercial losses of the aggrieved party are compensated, while still allowing for some saving of 'face' by both sides. Punishment of the infringing party by the imposition of the financial or custodial sanctions available in legislation may stop the infringing act, but does not necessarily benefit the aggrieved party; in fact, imprisonment of a family breadwinner may simply create a burden for the local community.

Hence, where a local complaint concerning infringement of intellectual property rights is formally raised with the local authorities or the responsible ministry, common practice throughout the States is for local officials or ministry officials to act as mediator between complainant and infringing party in order to attempt

10 Carroll (2001), op. cit., pp. 596–7.
11 Ibid., p. 594.

to engineer a solution satisfactory to both parties. The solution may include an 'appropriate gesture' to the complainant. The nature of the 'appropriate gesture' depends on the circumstances and extent of the alleged offence, but may consist of a financial payment by way of compensation and cessation of the offending activities. Hence, what may appear to western eyes as inaction in the face of infringing activity actually constitutes an alternative dispute resolution that locals would argue is more effective in achieving a better possible outcome than that which might be achieved by following the slow and tortuous path of civil and/or criminal litigation.[12]

The issue of transparency arises in this context. Many of the leading business organisations in every State in the region are close-knit, family-run enterprises whose principals, by virtue of being members of either the extended royal families or the societal and commercial elite, also hold considerable political and economic influence. There can exist a reluctance to comply with either public disclosure of commercial and financial information customarily required under western laws or laws of western origin which counteract the profit-making imperative of past, *laissez-faire* practices. The continued lack of transparency springs from some political and government practices that are still beyond successful attempts at legal reform.[13]

To offset these conservative values, a pro-western youth culture fuelled by a domestic population that is predominately under the age of 25 is growing in numbers and influence in each State. A further offsetting factor is that the native-born nationals constitute the minority of the domestic populations in all but two States. Accordingly, the rate of regional internet connectivity and growth in computer hardware and software market penetration is dramatic, and the regional market for pirated western goods, and particularly western music, Hollywood and Bollywood movies, and computer applications, software and games, continues to grow apace.[14]

12 These semi-official processes of alternative dispute resolution (ADR) may often result in satisfactory outcomes, but little other than the outcome is recorded. Use of the ADR approach is officially supported, with all states having mediation and arbitration legislation and systems in place. Oman and the UAE, for example, require all civil cases to be offered the arbitration and mediation process associated with the courts before the cases come before the courts.

13 Howard Stovall (2000), 'Arab Commercial Laws – Into the Future', 34, *The International Lawyer*, p. 844.

14 The impact of the youth culture and expatriate populations has generally been overlooked by the few commentators on intellectual property in the region, but is worth further study, unfortunately beyond the scope of this work. However, three points of significance need to be borne in mind. All the States have very young populations, with more than half of the indigenous population in each State being under 21 years of age. Further, except for Saudi Arabia and Oman, expatriates make up the majority of the total populations, comprising over 85 per cent thereof in the case of the UAE. In Oman and Saudi Arabia, the expatriate numbers are considerably lower, but still comprise 35–40 per cent of the total population. Expatriates are predominately at either end of the socio-economic spectrum – the lower end comprising low-paid workers from the Indian and Asian subcontinents and the upper end mainly

Complicating, or rather reinforcing, the growing societal attitude towards non-compliance with enhanced standards of intellectual property protection is the existence of a large and dynamic expatriate population, which in most States can contribute to an environment of evasion rather than compliance. The combination of government enforcement strategies which still target end-sellers rather than consumers and the existence in all States of lengthy court lists that can result in delays of years for both civil and criminal cases means that the likelihood of expatriates who knowingly and willingly participate in illegal activities being caught and prosecuted is remote. Hence, participation in counterfeiting or piracy activities and possible prosecution are worth the risk when weighed against the financial savings that counterfeit or pirated goods or services can provide over their genuine counterparts. Government officials in some States have complained that the expatriate participation in infringing activity is particularly prevalent in respect of mobile phones, computer software and illegal reception of TV cable and satellite transmission. Of even greater concern is the widespread and growing industry in life-threatening counterfeit automobile parts and pharmaceuticals.[15]

Even if there is a full understanding of intellectual property rights, there is a perception that certain people, mostly religious people, are socially protected from acts of infringements. Hence, society may presume that they are immune from suit for infringement cases. In 2013, the Saudi Ministry of Culture and Information ruled in favour of a Saudi female writer against a well-known sheikh for plagiarising

comprising very well-paid (certainly by local indigenous standards) western expatriates from the developed countries. Caught between these two groups are the local youth – among whom high unemployment is endemic – being unwilling to undertake the menial, lowly paid jobs carried out by the former expatriate group and unable to secure the highly paid executive contracts enjoyed by the latter expatriate group. These three elements create a regional environment in which the demand for 'best-price' latest fashion consumer goods and cheapest entertainment through pirated audio and video items is high and the market for illegal goods flourishes. See UNDP, *Arab Human Development Report 2016* in respect of population demographic, available at www.arabstates.undp.org/content/rbas/en/home/library/huma_development/arab-human-development-report-2016--youth-and-the-prospects-for-/, and Gulf Research Centre (2016), 'Nationals and non-nationals in GCC countries population', available at http://gulfmigration.eu/total-population-and-percentage-of-nationals-and-non-nationals-in-gcc-countries-latest-national-statistics-2010-2015, last accessed 26 May 2017.

15 Ibid. See also, for example, 'Shadowy Traders, Shady Deals . . . the Piracy Business Continues', *Bahrain Tribune*, 16 October 2003, p. 2 (hard copy with the authors). See also 'Counterfeit software public market', *Arab News*, 25 June 2008, available at www.arabnews.com/node/313231, last accessed 26 May 2017; "'Raising the Stakes', *Business.com*, 16 December 2008, available at www.arabianbusiness.com/raising-stakes-42023.html, last accessed 26 May 2017; 'TV piracy is not a "victimless crime"', *Khaleej Times*, 26 April 2016, available at www.khaleejtimes.com/nation/general/tv-piracy-is-not-a-victimless-crime-says-osn-ceo, last accessed 26 May 2017; 'Merchants of death', Editorial, *Arab News*, 15 February 2013, available at www.arabnews.com/editorial-merchants-death, last accessed 26 May 2017; 'Dh6.7m in counterfeit goods seized by Dubai Customs in 2014 Q1', *Gulf News*, 27 April 2014, available at http://gulfnews.com/news/uae/government/dh6-7m-in-counterfeit-goods-seized-by-dubai-customs-in-2014-q1-1.1324982 last accessed 26 May 2017.

more than 75 percent of her book. He was ordered to pay SR330,000 in compensation to the writer and his book removed from Saudi markets and banned from entering the country.[16] This case is considered a landmark case – first, because a woman filed a lawsuit against a sheikh; second, because it changed the perception of religious people (sheikhs) from being socially protected to being people who make mistakes; and third, because it brought more awareness to the need to educate people about intellectual property and the legal ways to protect it.

7.3 Regional piracy and the enforcement response

The challenges for the effective enforcement of intellectual property rights throughout the region are exacerbated by the fact that counterfeiting and piracy, particularly of software, video and music, are still widespread and lucrative businesses. All States experience a ready supply of illegal vendors, mainly low-paid expatriate workers from the Indian subcontinent and East Asia, for whom the chance of quick reward far outweighs the risks of seizure and possible deportation. There is also a constant demand for access to pirated goods which are much cheaper, more easily available and often more up to date than their legitimate equivalents. Copyright violations dominate, and range from the illegal extensions of satellite TV subscriptions to non-subscribers, unauthorised publishing and sale of copyrighted books, ripped music, pirated software, downloaded bootlegged movies and television broadcasts, and taped regional shows.

The nature and *modus operandi* of an end-selling operation at the grassroots level was well described in the following report from the Kuwaiti News Agency (KUNA) on the operation of a prevalent activity involving the sale of counterfeit DVDs and videos on the streets of Kuwait City. While the KUNA report focused on a typical small-scale street-vendor activity, it also made pointed reference to what would appear to be a well-organised infrastructure for producing the counterfeit goods and organising distribution networks, with links that would appear to reach high into Kuwaiti society. It also helped to illustrate the dimension of the problem in combating counterfeit material and the concern and response of manufacturers and distributors to the problem. The report came after years of reports in KUNA of action by government officials in conducting raids, confiscating infringing material and closing infringing establishments for violations of Kuwait's intellectual property laws:

> Vendors selling bootlegged merchandise can be seen on the corners of many shopping malls.
>
> A young man lays his rug on the pavement in front of a shopping mall . . . and lays out more than 50 video tapes of movies on the rug . . . several of

16 Abdullateef, L.(2012) "تغريم الشيخ عائض القرني ٣٣٠ الف ريال في قضية الكاتبة سلوى العضيدان". (Translated by Alhanoof AlDebasi) *Almadina* newspaper, available at www.al-madina.com/node/353477, last accessed 26 May 2017.

> the movies are still in theatres while others are not released yet. He says he constantly worries about authorities confiscating his merchandise. The . . . stock he carries belongs to his ambiguous "boss", who pays [the young man] 100 fils for each item he sells.[17] He . . . has no information pertaining to the centre of operations or who supplies him, he meets his boss in a public place, settles accounts and leaves, and the next delivery is scheduled over the phone.'
>
> 'Selling bootlegged (video) tapes in Kuwait is a business that generates incredible revenues for its owners; four or five individuals in all of Kuwait . . . the "business" is, in essence, an oligopoly operated by several individuals through an ambiguous yet intricate network of production, warehousing, and distribution . . . all one needs to pull off a similar operation is 12 video recorders and one video player, costing no more than 450 Kuwaiti Dinars all together . . . the cost of video tapes range from 100 to 120 fils per tape, mounting the total production cost for a single video tape of the latest Hollywood movie to around 250 fils which then sells for one Kuwaiti Dinar. The utilities are stored in a secure secret place, known only to one person, trusted by the owner, and most of the persons who work at the copy-production centres are women. Once the women copy the tapes, the owner transports them to the head distributor, who on his part transports the merchandise to several other distributors who then supply the vendors.[18]

While the report is describing a scenario in Kuwait, the picture that it paints is similar to scenes that can still be found on the streets, outside the shopping malls and in the *souks* of cities in the other States.

For years after the above media report appeared, the local media was continuing to report that Kuwait still carried a proliferation of pirated material which was available from street vendors, within the souks and from merchants within the numerous shopping malls. Hence, it is not surprising that Kuwait's performance in curbing copyright piracy continued (and still continues) to come under particular attack from the United States Trade Representative (USTR) though its annual Special 301 Report and the industry lobby organisations which have input into the USTR reporting process. Although the USTR reports need to be read with reservation in respect of their balance and equity because of their declared bias in favour of promoting the self-interest of US business, they still illustrate why the USTR argues that it has good reason to continue to be concerned over what it sees as the Kuwaiti lack of apparent success with its enforcement effort.

Media reports abound of similar well-organised merchandising activities of counterfeit goods in other States. Half a dozen years after the above KUNA report on street-side sale of pirated goods, the *Arab News* was reporting on a comparable and well-established counterfeit software public market in Riyadh:

17 1,000 fils = 1 Kuwaiti dinar (= US$3.27 as at 1 March 2017).

18 *Kuwait News Agency* (KUNA), 4 July 2002, p. 1.

> The computer software market in the Al-Ulaya district of Riyadh is a computer-geek's heaven. This is the place where counterfeit software – such as Windows and Photoshop – is available at next-to-nothing prices . . . The market is well organized. Salesmen use subtle methods to sell counterfeit goods without attracting the attention of local officials. Both sellers and buyers cannot care less about breaking copyright laws.
>
> Both Saudis and expatriates are involved in the sale of copied software. Expatriates generally hide their CDs under the counter and are careful when showing them to prospective customers. Saudis set up tables in the streets and are more open about what they are doing.
>
> The market is open seven days a week from morning till midnight. On sale are brilliant copies of expensive software. The copied items come with professionally designed covers and cases . . .
>
> The Kingdom's counterfeit business generates a huge profit. Blank CDs only cost SR1, and a copied CD can sell for anything between SR10 to SR20. Sellers also deceive customers by offering them CDs that do not work.
>
> Customers say low prices attract them to come to the market. [One customer] said he is able to buy software, which would normally cost SR1,000, for only SR15. 'It's ideal for me to buy counterfeit software as I can't afford original software.'
>
> . . . [A] nother customer said the prices in this market are very appealing. 'The very high price of genuine CDs makes us look for cheap counterfeit ones. At the end of the day, fake CDs do the same job, as we can't afford genuine software.'
>
> . . .
>
> 'Without these counterfeit CDs, we wouldn't even know what Windows looks like.'
>
> [T]he sale of counterfeit goods thrive due to the high price of original programs. 'The prices of software programs are higher than the price of a computer itself. SR250 is the average price of a computer while a program like Photoshop costs SR3,000. The only way to stop this illegal practice is to reduce the price of the original CDs to make them affordable for people like me.'[19]

Regional and domestic media have regularly carried reports of raids and confiscations, with pirated software, video and audio material, printed material, brand-name sportswear, cigarettes and cosmetic lines being the more common targets. The raids are generally targeted at small-scale participants towards the end of the distribution line – wholesalers, resellers, street and *souk* traders, and end-user businesses (although reports occasionally appear of raids, in the UAE in particular, on

19 'Counterfeit software public market', *Arab News*, 25 June 2008, available at www.arabnews.com/node/313231, last accessed 3 February 2017.

importers and distributors involving large-scale confiscations). The raids are often conducted on a regular basis and often with prior public warning, when they are also meant to serve as part of a public awareness campaign on intellectual property rights. According to Omani government officials, and generally confirmed by their Bahraini counterparts, the following strategy is commonplace in respect of raids and inspections and can also be observed in the other States:[20]

- Pre-raid: businesses in a certain shopping district or area are given warning of the impending raid and are warned to dispose of or surrender any possible infringing product.
- First infringement: usually confiscation of the offending goods and a formal warning against re-offending; a future inspection is listed to check against any re-offending. Notice is generally given of an impending follow-up inspection.
- Second infringement: further confiscation and fine imposed by the Ministry; premises may be closed for at least a few days, or until the fine is paid, or even longer.
- Third infringement: further confiscation, fines and longer closure of the premises.
- Fourth infringement: formal criminal prosecution is launched; possible permanent closure of the premises.

More often than not, raids serve both as an enforcement action and as part of a public awareness/education strategy. Hence, local press and electronic media frequently form an integral part of a police/ministry raiding party, and the detail and success of the raid are reported at length. Presence of the media is also useful for displaying to regional watchdog bodies and to the key authorities in western countries, such as the USTR, that the local authorities are sincere and active in their attempts to stamp out piracy and counterfeiting. Also present on appropriate occasions are representatives of the right holder or the regional watchdog body. Hence the nexus between enforcement authorities and media is a deliberate one; it is noticeable, for example, that the intensity of the reporting in the local press of enforcement activities increases immediately prior to or after the introduction of a new intellectual property law, only to ease soon thereafter.

Nevertheless, the raids can, and do, occur without warning, particularly when a major international company or the regional office of an influential industry watchdog organisation, such as the Arabian Anti-piracy Alliance (AAA) or the Business Software Alliance (BSA), is the right holder or initiator of the formal complaint. The infringements are then likely to be referred to the public prosecutor's office for initiation of a criminal action. However, since the court lists

20 Interview conducted by the author with officials, Oman Ministry of Commerce and Industry, December 2008.

in most Arabian Peninsula States are very full, it may be a matter of years before the case is listed and then heard.

A commonly repeated accusation from government officials in the States is that counterfeiting, piracy and the associated smuggling of counterfeit goods are not conducted by locals but instead mainly by expatriates, notably from the Asian and Indian subcontinents, in collaboration with foreign importers who are their fellow countrymen.[21] And this subtle ethnic distinction is often highlighted in the media reports of raids.[22] A report in the Saudi press on the seizure of more than 200,000 imported pirate optical disks asserted that the vast majority of the disks originated from Indonesia and that more than 75 per cent, or more than 150,000, were 'hand carried' by couriers.[23] In view of the fact that all States still require foreign merchants to have a local partner or commercial agent, and in light of the general commercial astuteness of local businessmen and traders, the accusations do not stand up to scrutiny. This is borne out by the above-quoted Kuwaiti media report which clearly points to local involvement at the highest levels, and also by the following reports on enforcement activity which indicate counterfeiting and piracy of such magnitude that would not seem feasible without active local organisation and involvement:

- seizures by Dubai Authorities of almost 2,500,000 fake products representing AED51.7million (US$14million), after a series of raids around the Emirate of Dubai during 2016. The fake products included car parts and accessories, cosmetics, handbags, accessories, phones and chargers, as well as sport products;[24]
- Jordanian Customs Department seizure of more than 922 cartons of counterfeit cigarettes in October 2016;[25]

21 Interview conducted by the author with officials, Oman Ministry of Commerce and Industry and Qatar Ministry of Economy and Trade, December 2008. See also, for example, Bassam Al Azzeh, 'Copyright Violation can Lead to Deportation from the UAE', *Al Tamimi Law Update*, May 2016, available at www.tamimi.com/en/magazine/law-update/section-14/may-9/copyright-violation-can-lead-to-deportation-from-the-uae.html, last accessed 26 May 2017.

22 See, for example, *Times of Oman*, 5 October 2005, p. 1, in which it was reported that a number of Asian nationals were arrested in a raid in which thousands of pirated classified arts and pornographic CDs were confiscated. The report mentioned more than once that the 'culprits' were Asian nationals. A subsequent report of further raids in which those arrested were all expatriates appeared in the *Times of Oman*, 5 December 2005, p. 4; see also 'Why the fight against fake goods is important to economic growth', Opinion, *Times of Oman*, 29 October 2016, available at http://timesofoman.com/article/95326/Opinion/Columnist/Why-the-fight-against-fake-goods-is-important-to-economic-growth, last accessed 26 May 2017.

23 Al-Tamimi & Co., Legal Advocates (UAE), *Law Update*, Issue No. 136, July 2002, p. 9.

24 'Dubai confiscate counterfeit products in amount of 51.7 million dirham', 16 February 2016, *Emarat Alyoum Newspaper*, available at www.emaratalyoum.com/business/local/2016-02-16-1.870124, last accessed 30 May 2017.

25 'The Jordan Customs Department (JCD) Foiled an Attempt to Smuggle Cigarettes in a Large Amount', *Jordan Customs News*, 17 January 2017, available at www.customs.gov.jo/ar/CMS_content_View.aspx?Key=10462, last accessed 13 June 2017.

- seizure of 123 million items of counterfeit goods by Saudi customs authorities across Saudi ports during 2015;[26]
- seizures by the Bahraini Information Affairs Authority of 87,000 pirated works during a series of 309 raids conducted during 2014;[27]
- seizure and destruction by Yemeni authorities in November 2014 of more than 6 tons of counterfeit medications and pills;[28]
- seizures by Saudi Ministry of Commerce officials of more than 1.7 million fake watches in Jeddah, in June 2004. The watches, which had come by road from Dubai, had already been allocated for distribution to 37 regional retail outlets;[29]
- seizure by Dubai police in January 2002 of more than 120 million counterfeit cigarettes, including 90 million counterfeit Marlboro cigarettes, having a reported street value of Dh27 million (US$7.5 million) and representing one of the largest seizures of its kind anywhere in the world at the time.[30]

The above reports illustrate that the counterfeiting and piracy operations which have surfaced in the States are becoming increasingly international in character, are growing in their level of sophistication and are occurring on a much greater scale than previously. As some States already acknowledge, it would appear that organised crime is becoming increasingly involved in the production, distribution and marketing of counterfeit and pirated goods. Counterfeit goods sourced from China have become a problem of major dimension, particularly in Saudi Arabia as the region's major economy and consumer market.[31] As one regional response to this emerging trend, the Saudi Ministry of Commerce and Industry recently moved to establish a national investigation group responsible for large-scale piracy, the role of which will include research into the nature of organised crime activities and intelligence gathering, as well as specialised enforcement.[32]

26 '123m fake goods seized in 2015', *Arab News*, 19 March 2016, available at www.arabnews.com/saudi-arabia/news/897461, last accessed 26 May 2017.

27 *AlMenara Newspaper*, 'Bahrain: 87 Thousand Pirated Works Were Confiscated in 6 Months', 8 September 2014, available at www.menara.ma/ar/2014/08/09/1302077--مخالف-بصري-سمعي-منتوج-ألف-87-مصادرة-البحرين-أشهر-ستة-خلال-للقانون.html, last accessed 26 May 2017.

28 'Consumer protection: more than 6 tons of pills enters the country', *Yemen Association for Consumer Protection Newsletter*, 30 November 2014, available at www.consumeryemen.org/index.php?option=com_content&view=article&id=455:2014-12-01-14-31-13&catid=1&Itemid=3, last accessed 26 May 2017.

29 *Arab News*, 8 June 2004, available at www.arabnews.com/?page=1&section=0&article=46470, last accessed 20 January 2006.

30 Reported in 'Largest seizure of counterfeit cigarettes ever in UAE' (2002), *Al-Tamimi, Law Update*, Issue No. 131, February 2002, p. 1.

31 See 'Exporters of fake Chinese goods to be blacklisted', *Arab News*, 16 March 2014, available atwww.arabnews.com/news/541006, last accessed 26 May 2017.

32 Ibid.

7.4 Judicial processes

In its 2002 Report, the UK Commission on Intellectual Property Rights and Development Policy argued that the 'private' nature of intellectual property rights suggests the importance of disputes between parties being resolved either out of court or under civil law, rather than through the criminal justice system.[33] It further argued that, since state enforcement of intellectual property rights was a resource-intensive activity, there was a strong case for developing countries to adopt intellectual property legislation that emphasised enforcement through a civil rather than a criminal justice system. This would reduce the enforcement burden on the government in the case of counterfeiting on a large scale, although the state enforcement agencies would still be required to intervene. The Commission noted that developing countries had come under pressure from industry which advocated enforcement regimes based on state initiatives for the prosecution of infringements.[34] It suggested that such pressures should be resisted and that right holders should assume the initiative and costs of enforcing their rights. Intellectual property rights were essentially private rights and, as with any other kind of private right, the enforcement of those rights was primarily a matter for the individual owners of those rights.

However, others have rightly argued that enforcement of intellectual property rights often cannot be done in any meaningful or effective way in developing states without the support of governmental authorities[35] and this is particularly the case in the Arabian Peninsula States. Where there is significant intellectual property infringement at street level, as is ongoing throughout the region, government must take the initiative through the public prosecutor to bring criminal cases and thereby commit its authority to the elimination of widespread infringement. Without such support, it is difficult for private right holders, using civil remedies alone, to bring the situation under control. More will be gained for right holders by well-publicised raids on suspected premises, convictions of individuals and their punishment with meaningful levels of fines or imprisonment, destruction of infringing goods and the equipment used to produce them, and the closure of premises, than would be gained by proceedings with the object of obtaining for the right holders compensation for the loss and expense suffered by them as a result of the infringement. It is only

33 UK Commission on Intellectual Property Rights, *Integrating Intellectual Property Rights and Development Policy* (2002), p. 147. The Preamble to TRIPS recognises that intellectual property rights are private rights.

34 Ibid.

35 See Michael Blakeney, 'Enforcement of Intellectual Property Rights: Challenges, Remedies and Public Awareness', *WIPO National Seminar on Intellectual Property for Faculty Members and Students of Ajman University*, May 2004, p. 32, WIPO Document WIPO/IP/UNI/DUB/04/7. See also Alastair Hirst (1999), 'The Role of the Government Authorities in the Enforcement of Intellectual Property Rights', *WIPO Workshop on the Enforcement of Intellectual Property Rights for Judges*, Beirut, December, p. 3, WIPO Document WIPO/IPR/JU/BEY/99/5B.

when street-level piracy has been largely eliminated and intellectual property has become widely recognised as a permanent feature of the state's legal order that civil litigation, as opposed to criminal prosecutions, can become the norm in intellectual property matters.[36]

Both approaches are not necessarily mutually exclusive, and the States have tended to follow elements of both approaches in their judicial aspects of intellectual property enforcement. Hence, one can find instances of the resolution of disputes between parties being achieved outside the court system, of civil and criminal actions proceeding both jointly and separately, and of numerous reports of well-publicised raids accompanied by seizure and destruction of infringing goods and business closures. However, while reports of raids against infringing individuals and establishments for copyright piracy or trademark infringements are numerous, it is very difficult to assess the extent to which the outcomes of these raids are being pursued within the judicial system. It is this perceived lack of connectivity and continuity between policing actions and judicial proceedings that generates much of the criticism from developed countries on the climate of intellectual property enforcement in the States. It may also create the impression to the casual observer (or, indeed, the not-so-casual observer such as the IIPA) that courts are doing little to enforce intellectual property rights.

Some States, notably Saudi Arabia, Oman and the UAE, have drastically overhauled and restructured their judicial systems in recent years as part and parcel of their constitutional, political and administrative reforms. The UAE has gone as far as introducing regulations to establish dedicated courts to handle intellectual property rights disputes and small claims.[37]

These overhauls, while crucial to the establishment of effective and modern judicial systems, may also have a negative impact on the enforcement of the intellectual property regime in the medium term. The necessary changes and the rate of change have largely outstripped the capacity of the system to integrate them, and the community's capacity and willingness to understand, adopt and respond properly to them. The UAE Justice Ministry acknowledges that it will need to provide specialised training to judges to help them understand the procedures and technicalities associated with intellectual property rights cases when it establishes its specialised courts.[38]

Contributing to the negative impact of the legislative changes and judicial reforms is the unfamiliar nature in a jurisprudential sense of some of the legal concepts enshrined in the new laws. Some of the TRIPS enforcement procedure concepts and mechanisms, for example, have no natural place in a civil law system and their terminology has no natural counterpart in the lexicon of modern legal

36 Hirst, ibid.

37 UAE, Ministry of Justice, Ministerial Resolution No. 137 for 2016.

38 As reported in *AGIP Bulletin*, 24 March 2016, available at www.agip.com/News.aspx?id=6367, last accessed 30 May 2017.

Arabic. For example, the new enforcement standards provide judicial authorities with the power to make provisional orders so as to prevent the occurrence of infringement even when it is merely threatened and to preserve relevant evidence in regard to the alleged infringement. However, judges who are unfamiliar with the legislation under which the required substantive case may proceed may be unwilling to make such an order so early in a case. The evidence would need to be very compelling to convince them that the damages threatened by infringement could not be made good by monetary compensation. Also unfamiliar to local judges and officials is the nature of intellectual property itself, as may be the nature of the adversarial legal process as envisaged in TRIPS. Hence it is not uncommon to find that prosecutions of actions that constitute an infringement against a right of an intellectual property nature may proceed under other laws, such as the commercial agency or criminal/penal codes, with which the judiciary is more familiar. For example, the Omani media in 2005 reported that charges then currently pending against a number of Asian nationals arrested for counterfeiting 'classified arts' and pornographic CDs would be laid under Royal Decree No. 65/1987, the much older law governing the printing and distribution of published works, rather than Royal Decree No. 37/2000, the then current copyright law, notwithstanding the fact that infringements detailed in the copyright act addressed the alleged offences under prosecution.[39]

The common law principle of *stare decisis* or legal precedent is not recognised in Islamic States. As discussed earlier, the guiding source for legal judgment can be either the *Shariah* or statute law, depending on the particular jurisdiction. Insertion of an opinion from a secular judge as a legal precedent would be to deny or usurp the authority of the *Shariah* and to place the opinion of a judge above Islamic law. The extent to which previous judicial decisions might at least be taken into account or even consulted varies from State to State and will in part depend on the degree of Islamic conservatism within that State. Hence in Saudi Arabia, adherence will be strictly to the *Shariah*, whereas in the UAE, decisions of a superior court, while not binding on the lower courts, might at least be persuasive.

However, a consequence of the absence of the principle of *stare decisis* in the judicial system is that one imperative for the explanation and careful recording of legal argument and explanation of the basis for judicial decision-making is absent. The quality of records of judicial proceedings and judgments across the States varies markedly, but in any case does not approach the standard assumed in western countries. Legal practitioners complain that court records are often incomplete or even missing.[40] Judgments often record the decision without

39 As reported in the *Times of Oman*, 5 October 2005.

40 Essam Al-Tamimi (2003), *Practical Guide to Litigation and Arbitration in the United Arab Emirates*, p. 5; see also 'UAE legal experts welcome court changes', *The National, UAE*, 16 September 2013, available at www.thenational.ae/uae/uae-legal-experts-welcome-court-changes, last accessed 26 May 2017.

reference to any reasoning or argument, are not always publicly available and are at best published haphazardly. In Bahrain, for example, only judgments made by the Court of Cassation are publicly available and then only in the Official Gazette and, of course, only in Arabic, while *Shariah* court judgments are not (officially, at least) publicly available. In Kuwait, court proceedings and judgments may be made publicly available, but then only at the discretion of the courts. In Jordan, only judgments made by the Cassation Court and the Supreme Court of Justice are publicly available, but then only in Arabic. However, it must be remembered that almost all intellectual property laws (with the exception of those of the UAE) provide for the court's judgment to be published in a local Arabic daily paper, at the expense of the guilty party, and this publication, albeit incomplete and non-authoritative, forms a public record of sorts. This practice, which is often followed, can also serve as a form of public awareness-raising of the nature of the offence and public admonition of the guilty party.

Because of the very full court lists which all States currently face, alternative dispute-resolution procedures take on increasing importance and play a greater role than they would otherwise in resolving disputes. Accordingly, government officials would argue that on-the-spot confiscation of infringing goods and equipment, financial penalties which are realistic in light of the economic circumstances of the infringing parties and closure of the infringing premises are very effective, and even arguably more effective than the threat of a possible prison sentence after a lengthy process of litigation.[41] If, however, organised crime continues to encroach on the territory of the petty infringer, as suggested earlier, then the customary methods of control and enforcement which target the tail of the supply chain and the end-seller will become totally ineffective.

All Arabian Peninsula States make extensive use of alternative dispute-resolution strategies, both within and outside the judicial structure, and all have in place formal processes for the utilisation of alternative dispute-resolution and mediation processes and reconciliation committees.[42] The purpose of the committees is to encourage and facilitate the amicable settlement of commercial and civil disputes of whatever value, and, if possible, to obviate the necessity for the matter to proceed to formal litigation. A party to a dispute is not obliged to defer to the alternative dispute-resolution process, but the courts generally may not hear a case unless the matter has been before the relevant reconciliation committee or a party has been given the opportunity to utilise the process but has expressed its prerogative not to so proceed. The reconciliation committees do not have authority over summary matters or matters at which the attendance of the public

41 Interviews conducted by the author with officials in the Bahrain Ministry of Commerce, Qatar Ministry of Economy and Trade, and Oman Ministry of Commerce and Industry, December 2008.

42 UAE Federal Law No. 4 of 2001 provides for the appointment by the Minister of Justice of one or more reconciliation committees at the federal courts of first instance. This law is not applicable in Dubai or Ras Al-Khaimah.

prosecutor may be required – that is, in respect of criminal cases. These alternative dispute-resolution processes, which occur within the context of legislative authority and an extra-judicial framework, reinforce the informal mediation processes undertaken proactively by local authority and ministry officials.

Omani government officials have acknowledged that few cases involving the infringement of intellectual property rights ever reach the courts, notwithstanding the legislative provisions and the number of raids that are undertaken, particularly in respect of copyright and trademark infringements.[43] But this scenario is as much due to the widespread practice of alternative dispute-resolution options as to any shortcomings in judicial structures and processes. In the opinion of the officials, the notion that the law and its penalties should be used as a first resort to punish the wrongdoer is inconsistent with Omani (and Muslim) values and commercial practices. Accordingly, the officials would assert that the fact that only a few civil cases, and no criminal cases, on intellectual property rights infringements have come before the Omani courts is not necessarily a negative reflection on the judicial system; instead, it is an indicator that the alternative dispute-resolution processes are working effectively. Where a case, mainly involving a foreign right holder, goes to court, the court tends to play a similar role as the government officials, namely that of a mediator in reaching a settlement acceptable to all parties, albeit within the parameters of the legislation under which the dispute is proceeding. On occasion, the ministry official who may have attempted (unsuccessfully) to resolve the dispute that has become the subject of the court hearing will appear before the court as an expert in the case.[44]

7.5 Prosecution and punishment

A combination of weak measures of criminal sanctions and civil damages and the inability to recover the costs of enforcement can actually serve to encourage infringement and discourage civil enforcement by right holders. These weak measures, often based on a formulation of lost profit to the right holder, encourage infringers to anticipate that the sanctions imposed through a criminal action together with damages recoverable through civil litigation would amount to only a fraction of the wholesale price for resale, and an even smaller fraction of the retail price for commercial or personal use, particularly if amortised over a number of infringing operations. Under such circumstances, infringement becomes a calculated business risk that can still leave an infringer with a handsome profit from the proceeds of the infringing activity, even if caught and punished. This is best illustrated by the status of deterrent capability of the Jordanian eight intellectual property laws and the Qatari patents law. The Jordanian copyright, trademarks and patents laws, which

43 Interviews conducted by the author with officials in the Oman Ministry of Commerce and Industry, December 2008.

44 Interviews conducted by the author with officials in the Oman Ministry of Commerce and Industry, December 2008.

provide for maximum sanctions ranging from JD3,000 ($4,325) (patents) to JD6,000 ($8,470) (copyright and trademarks) and maximum terms of imprisonment of one year (trademarks and patents) to three years (copyright), are the most lenient among the States. However, its other intellectual property laws, namely geographical indications, designs, new plant varieties, integrated circuits and trade secrets do not specify any criminal sanctions such as fines or imprisonment at all. In effect, there is no deterrent capability.

The former Kuwaiti copyright law of 1999, which was in force for a number of years until replaced in 2016 by Law No. 22 of 2016, had a statutory maximum fine of KD10,000 ($2,746) and imprisonment for up to two years. These sanctions were the most lenient sanctions of all the GCC member States. The administration by the courts of laws already lenient became even more lenient, with the courts reportedly imposing fines of only KD100 (US$327), a token financial penalty even by local and regional standards.[45]

The earlier-mentioned seizure by Dubai authorities of 90 million counterfeit cigarettes worth some US$7.5 million in January 2002 reportedly eventually resulted in the imposition of fines of up to US$2,750 upon each of the accused in the criminal case, and $56,000 in compensation to the cigarette manufacturer in the civil proceedings.[46]

A ‘fear factor’ survey conducted by the Arabian Anti-piracy Alliance produced some striking results in respect of local attitudes towards the deterrence impact among traders and members of the public of sanctions within Saudi intellectual property laws. While the survey is somewhat dated, having been conducted in 2005–2006, the survey results indicate that the deterrence impact of the sanctions in the current Saudi copyright law are insignificant – notwithstanding the fact that the law provides for the imposition of fines of up to SR250,000 (US$66,650) and up to six months’ imprisonment, both of which may be doubled for repeat offences. The survey found that:

- 79 per cent of respondents believed that an employee convicted of selling non-original software, games or movies/music would not be imprisoned;
- 89 per cent felt that the owner of the establishment would not be imprisoned;
- 70 per cent considered that the establishment would not be closed;
- 85 per cent felt that a non-national infringer would not be deported;
- 72 per cent believed that financial penalties would be imposed, but 54 per cent of those believed that the penalty would be less than SR10,000.[47]

45 As reported in Al-Tamimi & Co, Legal Advocates (UAE), *Law Update*, Issue No. 163, October 2004, p. 22.

46 As reported in the *Gulf News*, 24 January 2008.

47 As reported in the IIPA Submission to the USTR, Saudi Arabia: Special 301 Out-of-Cycle Review, August 2006, Appendix C, and the IIPA Submission for the 2007 Special 301 Report, available at www.iipawebsite.com/rbc/2007/2007SPEC301SAUDIARABIA.pdf, last accessed 26 May 2017.

Interestingly, though, financial penalties rather than imprisonment were considered to be the most effective deterrent by a margin of some significance – 87 per cent as against 67 per cent. The survey results demonstrate that there is little fear that infringers would be punished to any great degree if caught and convicted. But it could also be argued that the survey indicates that, in light of the perceived already substantial levels of financial sanctions, education and awareness-raising is likely to be a more effective strategy in reducing infringing activity rather than further increases in local penal sanctions.

Those States that are perceived as being committed to reducing the incidence of intellectual property infringements to internationally accepted levels – and Saudi Arabia and the UAE are arguably the leaders in this respect – place a greater reliance on, and utilisation of, the criminal justice system. As the most active and vigorous of the States in enforcing intellectual property rights by this strategy, the UAE has experienced the most dramatic decreases in copyright piracy and trademark violations for the region, and has also established a number of precedents for the region in terms of judicial determinations.[48] But even this level of commitment does not ensure that maximum or even severe sanctions are fully, comprehensively and consistently utilised. Even where courts of first instance may have imposed sentences perceived locally as being severe, there appears to be a fairly common tendency for appellate courts to act in the defendant's favour in ameliorating the severity of the sentence by reducing or dismissing one or more of their elements.

The following case from Saudi Arabia was reported in the local media at the time as a leading case because of the enforcement standards it established.

In March 2012, the Saudi Board of Grievances handed down its judgment on a counterfeit goods case that was heralded at the time as a landmark case because of the perceived severity of the penalty meted out by the Board.[49] The shop owner was prosecuted for copying and selling counterfeit DVDs in violation of the Kingdom's Copyright Law of 2003. The Violation Review Committee had recommended a fine of SR150,000 and a ten-day prison sentence. The Board found the charges established and imposed a fine and closure of his shop. However, it appears that, in light of the shop owner's continuing offending after sentence had been passed, the Board determined to add a further sentence of ten days' imprisonment and closure of his shop for 60 days.

The sentence has been lauded as the first time that a term of imprisonment has been handed down for a copyright infringement case in Saudi Arabia. Commenting on the judgment, Scott Butler, CEO of the AAA for the GCC, said that 'the adjudication of the case is a very important victory for anti-piracy advocates as it

48 See USTR, '2005 Special 301 Report', p. 5.

49 'Court verdict sets new precedent in anti-piracy fight', *Arab News*, 1 March 2012, available at www.arabnews.com/node/407587, last accessed 26 May 2017. See also 'Piracy blues', *Gulf News*, 19 September 2010, available at http://gulfnews.com/business/technology/piracy-blues-1.683896, last accessed 26 May 2017.

is the first-ever court judgment in the Kingdom resulting in imprisonment'.[50] He added that the judgment is a strong deterrent to prevent such criminal activities from proliferating in the country, knowing the Saudi judiciary is prepared to apply the full force of the law in trying cases related to piracy.

But the case is also enlightening in respect of the nature of enforcement of copyright infringements. Article 22 of the Saudi copyright law, in force for almost a decade by the time the judgment was handed down, provides for the following penalties:

1 A fine not exceeding two hundred and fifty thousands riyals.
2 Closing the violating establishment or the one which participated in the violation of the copyright, for a period not exceeding two months.
3 Confiscation of all copies of the work along with the materials used or intended for use in the infringement on the copyrights.
4 Imprisonment for a period not exceeding six months.

Article 23 provides for the maximum penalties to be imposed and the period of closure doubled. Accordingly, the penalties imposed were well short of those available to the Board.

It emerged during the course of the hearing that the convicted shop owner's retail outlet and warehouse had been raided seven times since 2006, resulting in the seizure of more than 100,000 counterfeit products and several pieces of reproduction equipment. Each of the first six offences resulted in escalating fines and shop closures by the Violation Review Committee, eventually totalling SR300,000 in fines and 100 days of closure. It is also noteworthy that the case was commenced in mid-2010, but was not concluded until March 2012.

In a case heard prior to the introduction of the UEA's 2002 amendments to its intellectual property laws, the Dubai Court of First Instance convicted a dealer for illegally copying satellite pay-television smart cards, which permitted access without subscription payment to encrypted pay-television. The Court fined the dealer AED50,000, sentenced him to one month's imprisonment and ordered that he be subsequently deported. The court further ordered that the offending material and equipment used in its manufacture be confiscated. This particular case was heralded at the time as a landmark case in the UAE in respect of its subject matter and the perceived severity of the penalty imposed, thereby illustrating the seriousness with which the UAE regarded intellectual property infringement matters – notwithstanding the fact that the financial penalty imposed was the minimum specified under the then Emirati copyright law.[51] It

50 'Court verdict sets new precedent in anti-piracy fight', *Arab News*, 1 March 2012, available at www.arabnews.com/node/407587, last accessed 3 February 2017.

51 Dubai Court of First Instance Judgment No. 6106 of 26 February 2001; as discussed in Al-Tamimi & Co, Legal Advocates (UAE), *Law Update*, Issue No. 120, March 2001, p. 9.

is interesting to note that the convicted dealer, by virtue of the deportation order, was not an Emirati national.

However, to illustrate the inconsistency that can still exist across the UAE in the application of enforcement action against intellectual property infringements, a local court in Ajman, the neighbouring Emirate, soon thereafter considered a similar case against the owner of a local satellite receiver and electronics shop, but merely fined the owner and his salesman AED10,000 each and ordered confiscation of the infringing material.[52] No reference was made in the court's judgment to any closure of the premises or to any other sanctions being imposed.

But even the UAE, which has been considered to have one of the best regulatory structures as well as the best enforcement record, can still err too much on the side of leniency, according to some local legal practitioners. It would appear that, as a general rule, financial penalties commonly tend to be towards the bottom rather than the top of the statutory range, and the imposition of prison terms is infrequent – notwithstanding the substantial penalties available under its main intellectual property laws and the very occasional and heralded court case in which the maximum available penalties are applied.

The following case in Abu Dhabi, in which the Court of Appeal (Criminal Division) reduced the sentences imposed by the primary court upon a local merchant for the unauthorised copying and installation of computer software on a number of computers being offered for sale, illustrates the nature of judicial leniency.[53] A software company and the Abu Dhabi Public Prosecutor had separately brought actions against the merchant for illegally copying the company's software and installing it on a number of computers. The merchant admitted the offence and entered into a restitution settlement with the software company, which withdrew its complaint as a consequence. However, the Public Prosecutor continued with the criminal charges. On the basis of the admission, the primary court sentenced the merchant to three months' imprisonment and imposed a fine of AED50,000 on one charge and AED10,000 in respect of a second charge. The court also ordered that the infringing software and the computers on which it had been loaded be confiscated, that the merchant's establishment be closed for one month and that the court's decision be published in a local daily newspaper at the merchant's expense. The court also ordered a stay of execution for three years on the jail sentence subject to successful execution of the restitution settlement.

The merchant appealed the primary court's judgment, seeking annulment of the lesser fine and all other orders. The appellate court held that the primary court had erred in imposing two separate penalties when the charges originated from one and the same act. Accordingly, the appellate court cancelled the lesser fine of

52 As reported in Al-Tamimi & Co, Legal Advocates (UAE), *Law Update*, Issue No. 133, April 2002, p. 3. In both the Dubai and the Ajman case, penalties were reportedly imposed pursuant to UAE Federal Law No. 40 of 1992, the Copyright Law, arts 42 and 45.

53 Abu Dhabi Court of Appeal, Case No. 874/2004, 6 June 2004; as discussed in Al-Tamimi & Co, Legal Advocates (UAE), *Law Update*, Issue No. 162, September 2004, pp. 20–1.

AED10,000. It confirmed the primary court's order regarding the stay of execution but extended it to include both the prison sentence and the greater fine of AED50,000, in accordance with the provisions of Article 83 of the Penal Code in light of the restitution settlement.[54] The court further held that the primary court's orders directing the confiscation of the computers carrying the infringing software were without basis, since Article 40 of the UAE copyright law stipulated that confiscation may only be directed against machinery specifically designed and used for the purpose of infringement. This description did not apply to the seized computers even when they carried infringing software since they could be used for legitimate purposes after the software was removed. In respect of the primary court's order for closure of the business, the appellate court held that closure was a mandatory provision under the copyright law, for which execution could not be stayed. However, it reduced the period of closure to one week from the original one month imposed by the primary court. In the final analysis, the convicted merchant was merely required to close his business establishment for just one week.

However, one should not assume that, although the States may appear to have been reluctant to act forcefully in respect of criminal prosecutions, they have been on more solid ground and correspondingly more active in respect of their role in civil proceedings and in judicial review of decisions by administrative bodies. One can find numerous instances of long-standing practice among them (albeit with lesser or greater degrees of activity), but particularly in the UAE in establishing some judicial parameters in respect of the interpretation of statutes. This has occurred particularly in such areas of trademark law as the protection of well-known marks, deceptively misleading marks, passing off and, more recently, the registrability requirements of non-conventional marks, such as colour marks.

In Qatar, the courts have affirmed established principles in respect of the protection of well-known marks, including well-known marks that are not registered locally. The Court of First Instance ruled in favour of Escada AG, owner of the trademark ESCADA, in an action brought by the company against a local chain of barber shops trading under the name ESCADA.[55] The court held that Escada AG had established an international reputation and the services denoted by the mark were recognised regionally and locally. The court found that the use of the identical trade name by the local company would cause the public to reasonably assume an association between the two marks and contravened the provisions of Articles 8(8), 36 and 37 of the Trademarks Law No. 9 of 2002. The court ordered that the registration of the local mark be cancelled and that the local company cease all usage of the infringing mark.

In a rather different trademarks matter, the UAE Trademarks Office established a precedent in trademark registrability when it accepted and registered a single-colour trademark. Mars Inc. succeeded in registering the colour orange in class

54 UAE Federal Law No. 3 of 1987, the Penal Code. Article 83 allows a court to order a stay of execution of a jail sentence and a non-proportional fine.

55 Ibid., July 2007.

30 for its Uncle Ben range of rice products.[56] Mars was able to demonstrate that its use of the colour in its packaging of the rice products had established distinctiveness through use and a clear association in the marketplace between its products and the colour orange. It should be noted that Mars had been successful in securing registration in other jurisdictions for the colour orange and did not face any opposition to its application for local registration of the colour mark.

In Yemen, the Court of First Instance considered an appeal by the French tyre company Michelin against a decision of the Registrar of Trademarks to allow registration of the local mark 'M-MICHELIN INTERNATIONAL' and to disallow Michelin's opposition to the registration.[57] The court noted that Michelin is a well-known trademark with an established international reputation and had been registered in Yemen since 1983 in classes 9 and 12 for tyres and car parts. Registration was sought for the local mark in class 4. The court held that the local mark was deceptively similar to the appellant's mark to the extent that the public would be misled and thereby contravened the provisions of Yemen's intellectual property law article 89(g) and the Commercial Law article 63. The court ordered that the decision of the Registrar be set aside and that registration of the M-MICHELIN INTERNATIONAL be cancelled.

But the issuance of a court ruling does not necessarily mean that the case is concluded and the matter resolved. In 1999, a large US-based multinational firm won a trademark infringement case in a Yemeni court. More than ten years later, the ruling was still technically under appeal and the infringer continued to infringe on the trademark despite the court ruling.[58] In a second case involving a US company's trademark, a Yemeni appeals court handed down a final ruling in April 2001 in favour of the US company. In August 2003, the Yemeni Supreme Court rejected the appeal of the infringing company and ordered it to cease production and destroy the infringed trademark. By July 2012, the ruling reportedly still had not yet been enforced.[59]

In a more recent case before the UAE Federal Supreme Court in April 2016, the Court considered the complex issue of registrability of foreign trademarks in their original form and the issue of translation and transliteration of marks. The Court rejected an appeal by a producer of Chinese herbal medicines against a decision of the Ministry of Economy to reject an application for registration of its mark in Chinese characters.[60] The appellant had claimed in its registration

56 As reported by Al-Tamimi & Co, Legal Advocates (UAE), Law Update, Issue No. 194, May 2007, p. 20.

57 As reported in Saba & Co, op. cit., April 2007.

58 US Department of State, Bureau of Economic and Business Affairs, '2012 Investment Climate Statement', June 2012, available at www.state.gov/e/eb/rls/othr/ics/2012/191265.htm, last accessed 26 May 2017.

59 Ibid.

60 The report above is summarised from the case report by Peter Hansen (2016), 'UAE Federal Supreme Court says Chinese and English trademarks are the same but different', *Hogan*

application that its mark was a well-known mark internationally and was registered in a number of countries. The Ministry had rejected the application for registration of the Chinese character mark on the basis of a prior registration for the same mark in Latin (English) characters by another party. The courts of first instance and appeal both ruled in favour of the Ministry's determination.

The applicant argued that the prior mark was improperly registered because it was no more than a Latin character version of its Chinese mark. The Court found no evidence that the appellant had used the Latin character version of the mark anywhere in the world before the UAE registration by the other party.

In rejecting the appeal, the Supreme Court confirmed that a Chinese character mark and the same mark in Latin characters should be considered to be relevantly similar in transliteration – the pronunciation of the Latin characters and the Chinese characters being similar. In so doing, the Court reinforced the position taken by the Saudi Board of Grievances in respect of the action brought by INTEL in respect of a confusingly similar Arabic character mark, as discussed earlier.

And in what may well have been a rather rare case for the region, the Jordanian Trademark Office ruled for the protection of the Basmati name as a geographical indicator for rice originating from the Indian subcontinent.[61] PUSA BASMATI 1121, a well-known variety from India, is widely referred to as '1121'. A Jordanian manufacturer applied for the registration of '1121' as a trademark for coffee, tea, sugar and rice among other goods. Upon publication of the mark in the Jordanian Official Gazette, the Indian Ministry of Commerce filed for an opposition on the basis that the mark in question evoked a connection to Basmati rice and led to unfair competition and consumer deception. The Jordanian Trademark Office found that the registration of the trademark '1121' in class 30 for rice would create a false impression that products bearing that mark originated from the region where Basmati rice is being grown. The Trademark Office ruled that rice be removed from the list of goods as a pre-condition for approving the registration of the mark '1121'.

7.6 Structural and legislative processes

When described in layman's terms, the fundamental elements of the various areas of intellectual property protection encompassed by TRIPS may appear relatively easy to comprehend. But the translation of the layman's description into national legislation is a different matter, since TRIPS itself and its related international

Lovells Lime Green IP News, 12 April 2016, available at www.limegreenipnews.com/2016/04/uae-federal-supreme-court-says-chinese-and-english-trademarks-are-the-same-but-different, last accessed 26 May 2017.

61 As reported in 'Jordan: TMO Sets Precedent for the Protection of Geographic Indicators' (2014), *SABA Intellectual Property Bulletin*, 1 December, available at www.sabaip.com/en/documents/fe_bulletin/Saba--Co.-IP-Bulletin--December-2014.pdf, last accessed 26 May 2017.

conventions set requirements and standards which are very complex and sophisticated. The reality, as asserted by the UK Commission on Intellectual Property, is that in developing countries, intellectual property is a relatively new and specialist area of public policy.[62] Accordingly, the developing countries lack experienced and well-qualified officials to provide the necessary expertise, requiring them to have an inordinate dependence on technical assistance provided by WIPO and other bodies – including developed countries with their own agendas. The problem can be particularly acute in the case of intellectual property since there are few people who possess both the specialised technical skills of legislative drafting and expertise in intellectual property law. From a technical perspective, it can be difficult to incorporate into the national laws the very specific requirements of TRIPS Part III relating to enforcement. As mentioned above, some of the procedural concepts and mechanisms provided for in TRIPS Part III are of Anglo-American common law origin: they have no natural place in a civil law system and their terminology has no natural counterpart in the lexicon of modern legal Arabic.

The legislative drafting, therefore, requires expertise, skill and care in law, language and technical translation. In some respects, the States have endeavoured to address the difficulties identified by the UK Commission by virtue of the technical assistance they have sought and received from WIPO in the form of legislative advice, drafting assistance and expert commentary in the creation of their intellectual property laws. These endeavours have not been entirely successful, since a number of incongruities and structural inconsistencies still exist in the laws (and upon which comment has earlier been made). However, the challenge re-emerges at the domestic secondary level, as the States tackle the task of drafting procedural statutes and regulations which create the necessary implementation mechanisms and processes, and yet are still comprehensible to both the local administrators and the general public.

An inherent weakness in the legal structures of the States is the inadequacy and at times absence of procedural laws and subordinate regulations to give practical effect to a substantive law. This is particularly the case in respect of the timeliness of the production of enabling regulations following the enactment of a substantive intellectual property law. The substantive law generally comes into effect either on its publication in the Official Gazette or at a specified period of time thereafter (commonly 30 or 90 days) or upon issuance of the subordinate implementing regulations.

Almost all intellectual property laws require the drafting, approval and introduction of the corresponding subordinate implementing regulations before they can come into practical effect. Implementing regulations address a broad range of issues, not least among them being scales of registration fees and other charges, administrative structures, registration requirements, composition of review committees, authorisations and delegations – without which any implementation of the

62 UK Commission on Intellectual Property Rights, op. cit., pp. 138–9.

substantive laws in question cannot proceed. Although some intellectual property laws establish the authority for ministry officials to carry out enforcement activities, the implementing regulations generally define the bounds of that authority.[63] An inordinate period of time, measured in years, can, and often does, exist between gazettal of the substantive law and issuance of the necessary implementing regulations to bring the laws into effect, thereby creating an imponderable impediment to effective enforcement. This may not be a matter of great import in areas of little or no local activity, such as protection of new plant varieties or integrated circuits, but it can have significant ramifications in respect of the daily administration of copyrights, trademarks and patents. Oman, for example, issued a new suite of intellectual property laws between May and October 2000, but five years later only some of the corresponding implementing regulations had just started to emerge.[64] The reasons offered for the delay in issuing the other implementing regulations included delays by WIPO in its preparation of the regulations, delays by the other GCC member States which Oman felt obliged to consult on the nature and content of the regulations as part of its GCC membership, or obstacles thrown up by other government departments which were a necessary part of the regulation issuance process. Similarly, the implementing regulations for its 2009 law on plant breeder's rights did not appear until late 2015.[65]

At this time of writing, it appears that Qatar may still be awaiting implementing regulations for its trademarks and copyright laws enacted in 2002 (but which have now been replaced by Qatar's adoption of the GCC Unified Trademark Regulation as its new trademarks law). Article 53 of the trademark law of 2002 required the implementing regulations to be issued within three months of the law coming into effect (which occurs on publication in the Official Gazette). The common practice in such circumstances is to continue to use the implementing regulations for the now repealed prior law, thus exacerbating the confusion and uncertainty in the minds of the administrators and the public as to which law is in force. Some GCC member States in recent times have been in the situation of having repealed an intellectual property law without it ever having been brought into effect.

At one end of the spectrum for timeliness is the case of the introduction of the implementing regulations for Yemen's former patent protection provisions.

63 See, for example, Kuwait, Law No. 64 of 1999 (copyright), art. 45; Oman, Royal Decree No. 38/2000 (trademarks), art. 44; Qatar, Law No. 7 of 2002 (copyright), art. 55; Saudi Arabia, Royal Decree No. M/41 of 1424 (copyright), art. 24; UAE, Federal Law No. 17 of 2002 (patents), art. 65.

64 The first implementing regulations to appear, in May 2004, were those for Royal Decree No. 92/2000 (protection of new plant varieties). The implementing regulations for Royal Decree No. 38/2000 (trademarks, geographical indications and trade secrets) appeared in July 2005, and those for Royal Decree No. 82/2000 (patents) appeared in September 2005. On 17 December 2005, the Ministry announced that it was then able to start accepting patent applications for filing purposes only, since the fees and charges for such filing had just been issued – more than five years after the patents law had been gazetted.

65 Oman Royal Decree No. 49/2009; Ministerial Regulation 103/2015, the Implementing Regulations for Royal Decree No. 49/2009.

The provisions were issued as part of a comprehensive copyright, trademarks and patents law in 1994; the implementing regulations for the patents provisions eventually appeared in July 2007. They have since been replaced by the series of new industrial property laws in 2010 and 2011 (for which implementing regulations were issued soon after), and a new copyright law in 2012. Consequently, uncertainty can and does exist as to the extant validity of a particular law and the extent to which it should or can be enforced. In such circumstances, the common reaction is to do nothing, or at best act conservatively. In May 2004, for example, the Directorate of Industrial Property at the Bahrain Ministry of Commerce publicly announced that it would cease accepting patent applications for filing because the implementing regulations for its new patent law enacted in January 2004 had not yet been issued.[66] The announcement advised that the cessation would stay in place until such time as the implementing regulations, which were to stipulate the required lodgment processes and fees structure, were issued. The implementing regulations were eventually issued in May 2006.[67] In July 2006 the Directorate announced that it would begin accepting the filing of patent and utility model applications, consequent upon the recent issuance of the implementing regulations.[68] However, the filing exercise was not for the purpose of conducting examination but for recordal purposes and for noting priority dates only. A saving grace in this confusion is the fact that, up to mid-2006, the Directorate had not received any patent applications of local origin for filing or examination.[69]

By contrast, its sister government agency responsible for copyright protection, the Directorate of Publications and Press in the Ministry of Information, was reportedly already conducting raids, seizing alleged counterfeit or pirated material, instituting fines, ordering closures and initiating prosecutions for infringements in accordance with the provisions of the proposed new copyright law, even though the law had not yet been enacted.[70] This Directorate believed that retrospective application of the new law, which it anticipated would be in force by the time the prosecutions came to court, should not be a major issue for either the public prosecutor or the judiciary and should not therefore prejudice the conduct of the case under the old or new rules as appropriate at the time.

However, this is not to say that, on occasion, the issuance of laws and subordinate regulation cannot be effectively coordinated and occur in rapid succession following

66 See 'Filing of Patent Applications Ceased in Bahrain' (2004), *Abu Ghazaleh Intellectual Property Newsletter*, 1 May, available at www.agip.com/bulletin_news.aspx?id=200&month=5&year=2004, last accessed 26 May 2017.

67 By Ministerial Decision No. 54 of 2006, published in Official Gazette No. 2783 of 10 May 2006.

68 See 'Patent and Utility Model Applications Now Accepted in Bahrain' (2006), *Abu Ghazaleh Intellectual Property Newsletter*, 14 June, available at www.agip.com/News.aspx?id=1008, last accessed 26 May 2017.

69 Interviews conducted by the author with the Bahrain Ministry of Commerce, December 2008, and subsequent personal correspondence.

70 Interviews conducted by the author with Bahrain Ministry of Information, December 2008.

the enactment of the substantive law. Saudi Arabia, for example, issued implementing regulations for its new law on Patents, Layout-Designs of Integrated Circuits, Plant Varieties and Industrial Models on 26 December 2004, within the prescribed three-month period since the law's promulgation and within two months of the law coming into effect. Kuwait adopted the GCC Trademark Regulation as its new trademark law on 22 March 2015, pursuant to Law No. 13 of 2015. The corresponding implementing regulations were gazetted on 27 December 2015 and came into effect the following day.[71]

However, sometimes the issuance of the implementing regulation can have a different effect to that intended. Qatar's ministerial regulation, substantially increasing the scale of fees for trademark registrations, is an example at hand. The regulation increased the fees by at least 100 per cent, and even 12-fold for the registration of a licensing agreement, leading to a reported 'scandalous upheaval in the IP community' and a downturn in registration activity.[72]

7.7 Administrative structures

In terms of the institutional structures and frameworks in place in the States for the administration and enforcement of intellectual property rights, a number of common elements can be seen, although each State retains some elements of its own distinctive individual organisational features to best suit its particular needs. The more common model is for responsibility to be vested across two ministries (or three ministries if one includes police and security forces involved in conducting raids and other statutory enforcement provisions), although in some States their administration and enforcement may require the involvement of agencies across five discrete government ministries (if public prosecutorial offices in justice ministries are also included in this count). Typically, responsibility for the administration of industrial property rights encompassing trademarks and patents (and notionally other areas such as geographical indications, trade secrets, unfair competition and new plant varieties) resides within a ministry whose terms of reference may include some or all of commerce, finance, industry or trade. Copyright and neighbouring rights often reside within a ministry whose description and terms of reference may encompass some of cabinet affairs, national heritage and culture, and information – the latter in some respects being a logical extension of the earlier censorship function and control of publications and publishing houses. Customs and border control matters relating to the movement of goods generally lie within the purview of a ministry for the interior or ministry of trade, while internal enforcement involving police actions requires the authority of the ministry of internal affairs or internal security.

71 Kuwait, Ministerial Regulation No. 500 of 2015, published in Official Gazette No. 1268 on 27 December 2015.

72 Qatar, Ministerial Regulation No. 47 of 2005. Reported in Saba & Co, op. cit., June 2005.

Qatar and the UAE offer the simplest and most integrated organisational structure. They both incorporate all responsibility for the implementation and administration of intellectual property within the portfolio of a single Ministry of Economy and Commerce (Qatar) or Ministry of Economy (UAE). Within the Ministry, subordinate departments administer trademarks, patents and copyright affairs. Bahrain, Kuwait and Yemen pursue the more common and logical structure of a Ministry of Information or Ministry of Culture (in the case of Yemen) being responsible for copyright matters, and ministries of commerce, trade and/or industry having general responsibility for industrial property rights, including registration and licensing matters. Oman and Jordan pursue a similar model, with a complicating variant that stipulated that matters and responsibility pertaining to plant breeder's rights reside with the Ministry of Agriculture.

Table 7.1 illustrates the organisational structures and division of primary responsibilities for protection of industrial property and copyright across the Arabian Peninsula States.

The Kuwaiti Ministry of Information, in which responsibility for copyright and neighbouring rights is vested, also monitors the government press and the radio and television broadcasting stations. All literature, audio, video and any other media material coming into Kuwait from abroad must still pass through the Censorship Department of the Ministry of Information for approval.

Saudi Arabia has a 'four-ministry' model for the administration of intellectual property rights, in structures that are both undergoing change and development, namely in each case:

- a commerce ministry, primarily responsible for implementing the trademarks law, but also responsible for ensuring compliance with national standards in respect of products and goods that come within the purview of the trademark, patent and copyright laws;
- an information and culture ministry, which is primarily responsible for implementing the copyright law, but which also administers the printing and publications laws;
- a finance and economy ministry, which supervises the respective customs authority which is charged with implementing the customs laws;
- a quasi-ministry, the King Abdul Aziz City for Science and Technology (KACST), which is primarily responsible for implementing the patents law and the industrial designs law.[73]

73 According to its own website (www.kacst.edu.sa/en/about.asp), the King Abdul Aziz City for Science and Technology is an independent scientific organisation of the Saudi Arabian government, established in 1977 as the Saudi Arabian National Center for Science and Technology (SANCST) and later in 1985 renamed as King Abdul Aziz City for Science and Technology. KACST is governed by a Supreme Committee, chaired by the Prime Minister (the King) and composed of the ministers of the major ministries to which science and technology are of greatest relevance, the President of KACST, and three other members

TABLE 7.1 Intellectual property administrative frameworks in the Arabian Peninsula States

	Copyright and neighbouring rights	*Trademarks and other IP*	*Patents and designs*	*Plant varieties*	*Border control*
Bahrain	Ministry of Information – Directorate of Press and Publications – Copyright Protection Office	Ministry of Industry, Commerce and Tourism – Industrial Property Directorate – Commercial and Company Affairs Directorate – Registry of Patents, Designs and Trade Marks – Industrial Property Tribunal			Ministry of Interior – Customs Affairs
Kuwait	Ministry of Information – National Council for Culture, Arts and Letters – National Library	Ministry of Commerce and Industry – Patents and Trademarks Office			Finance Ministry – General Administration of Customs
Oman	Ministry of Commerce and Industry	Ministry of Commerce and Industry – Commerce Directorate – Intellectual Property Department – Copyright Section		Ministry of Agriculture and Fisheries – Plant and Animal Research Directorate	Royal Oman Police – Inspectorate General of Police and Customs
Qatar	Ministry of Economy and Commerce Intellectual Property Directorate – Trademarks, Industrial Designs, Geographical Indications Office – Patents and Integrated Circuits Office – Copyright Protection Office				Ministry of the Interior
Saudi Arabia	Ministry of Culture and Information – General Administration of Copyright	Ministry of Commerce and Industry – General Administration of Trademarks	King AbdulAziz City of Science and Technology – General Directorate of Patents		Finance Ministry – Customs Directorate

(continued)

TABLE 7.1 Intellectual property administrative frameworks in the Arabian Peninsula States *(continued)*

<table>
<tr><th></th><th>Copyright and neighbouring rights</th><th>Trademarks and other IP</th><th>Patents and designs</th><th>Plant varieties</th><th>Border control</th></tr>
<tr><td>UAE</td><td colspan="4">Ministry of Economy
– Industrial Property Directorate
– Trademarks Office
– Patents Office
– Copyright Department</td><td>Federal Customs Authority
– Customs Directorates of each Emirate</td></tr>
<tr><td>GCC</td><td>n/a</td><td colspan="2">GCC General Secretariat</td><td colspan="2">n/a</td></tr>
<tr><td>Jordan</td><td>Ministry of Culture– National Library
– Copyright Protection Office</td><td colspan="2">Ministry of Trade and Industry
Industrial Property Directorate
– Patents Registrar
– Trademarks Registrar
– Integrated Circuits Registrar
– Industrial Designs Registrar</td><td>Ministry of Agriculture
– New Plant Varieties Registrar</td><td>Minister of the Interior?</td></tr>
<tr><td>Yemen</td><td>Ministry of Culture
– Copyright Office</td><td colspan="3">Ministry of Industry and Trade
– General Administration of Industrial Property</td><td>Finance Ministry
– Customs Authority</td></tr>
</table>

Source: compiled by the authors

Perhaps 'dynamic' is an apt description of the organisational infrastructures responsible for intellectual property governance and administration among the States, particularly as the structure of government is constantly changing and developing. As part of the new vision for 2030, the Saudi Council of Ministers approved in March 2017 the formation of the Saudi Intellectual Property Commission. The Commission, which will be financially and administratively independent, will handle trademark matters (instead of the Ministry of Commerce and Investment), copyright matters (instead of the Ministry of Culture and Information) and patent matters (instead of KACST), thereby unifying all types of intellectual property under the one administration. As can be seen in the case of the Qatari and UAE experiences, the assignment of ministerial responsibilities for intellectual property rights is shifting away from being based on traditional notions of control towards an economic rationalism and exploitation. Consequently, organisational structures at the operational levels are still evolving. By the States' own admissions, effective enforcement of intellectual property rights is hampered by a shortage in the ministries, enforcement agencies and the judicial system of personnel expert in the interpretation and understanding of intellectual property legislation and trained in enforcement strategies and practice. Oman, for example, indicated to the WTO just prior to its accession in 2000 that it would take a full transitional period of five years to effectively implement the minimum standards of TRIPS, and particularly its enforcement provisions, because the country did not have appropriate and effective enforcement laws, procedural laws, the institutional machinery for their enforcement or the trained and experienced personnel to implement them.[74]

The divisions of authority and responsibility for the national management of intellectual property, as outlined in Table 7.1, was not always viewed with satisfaction by those developed countries with regional commercial interests or ambitions. The involvement of multiple ministries in the management and enforcement structures is perceived as a fundamental cause for inadequate enforcement performances. Developed countries have been prompted to pressure some of the States to legislate for a single law for comprehensive intellectual property rights enforcement and to establish a single administration, monitoring and enforcement agency under the supervision of one government ministry.[75] The pressure has been resisted

nominated by the Prime Minister. KACST is responsible for promoting the developmental sciences and technology in the Kingdom.

74 See WTO Working Party on the Accession of the Sultanate of Oman, *Accession of the Sultanate of Oman: Communication from the Sultanate of Oman*, Document WT/ACC/SPEC/OMN/5 (98-0272), 26 January 1998; see also WTO Working Party on the Accession of the Sultanate of Oman, *Accession of the Sultanate of Oman: Additional Questions and Replies*, document WT/ACC/OMN/9 (98-3054), 3 August 1998.

75 UK Commission on Intellectual Property Rights, op. cit., pp. 151–2. See also Mart Leesti and Tom Pengelly, 'Institutional Issues for Developing Countries in Intellectual Property Policymaking, Administration and Enforcement', UK Commission on Intellectual Property Rights Study Paper 9, pp. 32–4. The developed countries have also suggested to some GCC

to date by all States, although some States have established inter-ministry coordination agencies – not always with complete success, it appears. Both the IIPA and the USTR on occasion in the past urged the establishment of inter-ministry specialist departments focusing on intellectual property protection and rights enforcement, as well as the creation of specialist courts to deal with intellectual property cases. To impose such a requirement, however, would be contrary to Article 41.5 of TRIPS, which provides that 'nothing in this Part creates any obligation with respect to the distribution of resources as between enforcement of intellectual property rights and the enforcement of law in general'.

While the governmental structures that have been adopted, or have been allowed to evolve, have contributed to some of the coordination and performance issues that they experienced, they are not the only key issues. In each case, one ministry at least appears to be gaining a leading, even dominant role in the administration of the laws and the enforcement of intellectual property rights. As with the judicial system, the key problem confronting the respective ministerial departments involved in intellectual property management and enforcement has been the lack of expert human resources and institutional capacity.

While processes for the registration and administration of trademarks are generally well established, having been in operation for a number of years, the same cannot be said of patents. While all States maintain patent offices, they generally serve as filing or recordal offices only, with none of the States carrying out searches and substantive and technical examinations without some form of external collaboration. The consequence of this scenario is that protection provided by the respective patent laws in principle may not be extended in practice to the patents themselves because required examination and other statutory procedures have not been carried out. By way of example, in June 2016, it was reported in the local professional press that the UAE Patent Office would start substantive examination of patent applications filed between 1994 and 2009.[76] If the conventional rule of 20 years' protection from date of filing applies, then most of these applications would not receive any protection if eventually granted letters patent.

Hence, agreements for technical examinations to be undertaken in collaboration with, or by, foreign patents offices recognised as international examination authorities has become common practice. The Oman Patent Office, for example, signed an agreement with the Egyptian Patents Office in 2014 for the development of capabilities at the Oman Patents Office. The Egyptian Patent Office would also act as the examining office for all pending and new patent applications filed in

member States on occasion that specialist intellectual property courts should be established for the civil and criminal prosecution of intellectual property rights infringements.

76 Sarah Holder (2016), 'GCC countries – review of patent developments', *Rouse, The Magazine*, 28 June 2016, available at www.rouse.com/magazine/news/gcc-countries-review-of-patent-developments, last accessed 26 May 2017.

Oman.[77] The UAE signed a similar agreement with the South Korean Intellectual Property Office. In April 2016, the Kuwaiti Patent Office announced that, following the issuance of implementing regulations for Kuwaiti Law No. 71 of 2013 adopting the GCC Patent Regulation as the patent law of Kuwait, it has stopped accepting new patent applications.[78] Applicants seeking patent protection in Kuwait were directed to utilise the GCC Patent Office.[79]

The GCC Patents Office already has in place an agreement with the Chinese Intellectual Property Office and, to a lesser extent, the Austrian Patent Office for those offices to conduct examinations of patent applications lodged with the GCC.

It is uncertain whether further evolution in the relevant governmental structures and organisations may occur in the near future in respect of those GCC member States that have adopted the GCC Unified Trademark Law as their respective trademark laws. The trademark offices of each GCC member State will remain as the receiving offices and registration and renewal offices for trademarks on a national basis. Registering a trademark across the six GCC members will still require filing six separate national trademark applications. The announcements by the four adopting States were accompanied by notices of significant increases in fees, indicating a possible expanded function for each office.

7.8 Concluding remarks

It is rather challenging to obtain reliable longitudinal data from authoritative sources within and between the Arabian Peninsula States on their, and the region's, performances in enforcing their intellectual property laws and protecting individual rights. It is also difficult to obtain reliable data on the success of raids and judicial activity in controlling the prevalence of counterfeiting and piracy and other forms of illegal intellectual property activity in the region. There are four fundamental reasons for this situation, namely:

- the absence of reliable, independent and longitudinal data-collection structures and processes in and across the region, and the absence of public access to such data if and where they are collected;
- laxity or uncertainty in procedures and practices in the secure control, monitoring and destruction of infringing goods and equipment, thereby allowing confiscated illegal and counterfeit goods to remain in or return to the marketplace (and in a sense be subject to double-counting by being on occasion the subject of subsequent seizures);

77 As reported in 'Oman: Patent Official Fees Due', *SABA Intellectual Property Bulletin*, 10 October, available at www.sabaip.com/en/documents/fe_bulletin/Saba-IP-Bulletin--November-2016.pdf, last accessed 26 May 2017.

78 Kuwait, Law No. 115 of 2016, the Implementing Regulations for Law No. 71 of 2013, adopting the GCC Patent Regulation as the patent law of Kuwait.

79 As reported in 'Kuwait: Final GCC Country with PCT Membership', *Saba Bulletin*, 30 May 2016.

- where raids are publicly reported, they are often linked to another political agenda or strategic objective process and are thus often presented in a manner best suited for that particular agenda or initiative; an example of such an agenda might be the issuance of a new intellectual property law and a consequent public awareness campaign;
- competition between ministries for resources and status – governmental departmental reports, which are often on restricted circulation, concentrate on the positives and do not always portray the global picture.

Where information does appear, it is quite often based on unofficial sources and reports, or is secondhand, anecdotal and lacking any consistency or format that easily allows comparative analysis across sectors or years. For example, in April 2014, the *Arab News* cited sources from the Saudi Ministry of Culture and Information to report that during the previous year the Ministry's Copyright Violations Committee had imposed fines of SR5.8 billion on 667 copyright violators and seized 3,000 computers used for violating copyrights – an average fine of SR8.7million per violator, and many times the maximum fine of SR250,000 permitted under the Saudi copyright law.[80] Of course, this curious statistic may just be an error in translation rather than an exaggeration, but it nevertheless demonstrates the challenge in securing reliable and verifiable data and reports on enforcement measures. Hence, such reports that do appear still should be read in the context of the political environment in which they appear. This is not to say that they should be discarded; rather that recognition should on occasion be given to a symbiotic association between local colour and hard facts. It has also been suggested that there is another, more sinister, explanation for the inherent difficulty in obtaining reliable statistics, namely the 'clandestine and mobile nature of the facilities used to manufacture pirate and counterfeit goods, and of the persons involved in producing and distributing such goods', the apparent implication being that such persons are likely to be 'well connected'.[81]

However, it should not be assumed that, in the absence of authoritative and verifiable reports and statistical data, the States are not making progress in their fights against counterfeiting, piracy and other intellectual property rights enforcement. Media sources report regularly on enforcement actions and seizures of goods that are counterfeit or that carry infringing trademarks or which constitute copyright violations. In early March 2016, for example, the Saudi press was carrying that the Saudi customs authorities seized:

80 '72 Riyadh stores closed for copyright violations', *Arab News*, 12 April 2014, available at www.arabnews.com/news/554456, last accessed 26 May 2017.

81 Saba & Co, op. cit., April 2005.

- 400,000 fake auto spare and 372,000 fake medications during 2015;[82]
- 123 million pieces of counterfeit items at the ports across the Kingdom during 2015.[83]

And during a similar period, Dubai media was reporting that Dubai authorities seized fake goods worth AED38.4million in 95 raids during seizures of fake products that were carried out in the first half of 2016.[84] The seized goods included fake watches, sunglasses, electronics, auto spare parts, textiles, bags and footwear. Dubai Customs also reported in January 2016 that smuggling of counterfeit goods had dropped by almost 58 per cent between 2014 and 2015.[85] The counterfeit goods seized covered a wide range of products from clothes, mobile phones and accessories to cigarettes and auto spare parts. The estimated value of the seizures in 2015 was AED14.85 million in 2015 compared with more than AED36 million in 2014.

A few years earlier, in mid-2013, the *Yemen Times* reported that over 57 tons of expired, counterfeit goods had been destroyed in the first six months of the year.[86] The goods consisted mainly of counterfeit food products, cosmetics and medicines. The newspaper added that there had been 581 documented violations, of which 522 had been referred for prosecution. The media reports continue that during the previous year the Ministry of Industry and Trade had destroyed over 80 tons of expired and counterfeit goods, reported more than 1,200 violations and referred 732 cases for prosecution.[87] Penalties varied from shop closures to prison sentences.

In March 2017, the Saudi Ministry of Trade and Investment announced that it had closed more than 75 accounts on social media, including Twitter, Facebook, Instagram and Snapchat, for allegedly posting thousands of ads for fake goods;[88] At the same time, the Dubai Department of Economic Development reported

82 'Fake products boom in Saudi Arabia's markets', *Al-arabiya*, 11 December 2015, available at https://english.alarabiya.net/en/variety/2015/12/11/Fake-products-boom-in-Saudi-Arabia-s-markets.html, last accessed 26 May 2017.

83 '123m fake goods seized in 2015', *Arab News*, 19 March 2016, at www.arabnews.com/saudi-arabia/news/897461, last accessed 26 May 2017.

84 'Dubai customs seizes fake goods worth Dh38.4m', *Gulf News*, 3 August 2016, available at http://gulfnews.com/news/uae/society/dubai-customs-seizes-fake-goods-worth-dh38-4m-1.1873048, last accessed 26 May 2017.

85 As reported in 'Decline in smuggled counterfeits, Dubai Customs says', *Gulf News*, 19 January 2016, available at http://gulfnews.com/news/uae/society/decline-in-smuggled-counterfeits-dubai-customs-says-1.1656085, last accessed 26 May 2017.

86 'Over 57 tons of expired, counterfeit goods destroyed', *Yemen Times*, 8 July 2013, available at www.yementimes.com/en/1692/report/2602/Over-57-tons-of-expired-counterfeit-goods-destroyed.htm, last accessed 26 May 2017.

87 Ibid.

88 'Saudi Trade Ministry closes 75 social media accounts for promoting fake goods', *Arab News*, 12 March 2017, available at www.arabnews.com/node/1067061/saudi-arabia, last accessed 26 May 2107.

that it had ordered closure of 8,894 social networking accounts that were used to allegedly peddle counterfeit goods in 2016.[89] The number closed down in 2016 was 200 per cent higher compared with 2015.

The States have attracted recognition from some international quarters for the progress they made to date, in what has been a remarkably short period of time by global standards, in constructing comprehensive and TRIPS-compliant intellectual property protection regimes. The USTR's Annual Special 301 Report is not really an international benchmark of domestic intellectual property protection standards and measure, but rather a measure of how the United States views the compliance of conduct of its trading partners to its intellectual property imperatives and advancing its own trade objectives. Nevertheless, it provides an interesting perspective on the States' progress. In 1995, when the GCC member States were first examined by the USTR and included in its Annual Report, the USTR placed them all on either its Priority Watch List or its Watch List. Jordan later appeared briefly on the Report's Watch List for three successive years in 1997 to 1999, and then disappeared. By contrast, in its most recent 2016 report, the USTR has retained Kuwait alone, placing it on the Priority Watch List from the Watch List in the previous year. The elevation of Kuwait to the Priority Watch List may be justifiable in light of its outmoded intellectual property laws that then existed, which were still in essence of a pre-TRIPS standard, and its less than committed enforcement performance.[90]

The Business Software Alliance (BSA) Global Study on software piracy, which has been conducted for more than 20 years, also serves as an interesting reflection on the States' performances in respect of software piracy management. However, like the USTR Special 301 Report, it also needs to be viewed and qualified as representing the interests of largely US-based computer software producers. As a longitudinal study, the BSA's reports are useful, insofar as they reveal that over the period 1996–2016 local enforcement strategies have led to a period of ongoing reduction among the States in software piracy – particularly over the first decade since the introduction of TRIPS.[91] The BSA, which is also a member of IIPA,

89 'DED closes down 8,894 social network accounts for peddling counterfeits', *Arab News Gazette*, 11 March 2017, available at http://arabnewsnetwork.ae/ded-closes-down-8894-social-network-accounts-for-peddling-counterfeits, last accessed 26 May 2017.

90 The USTR and the operation of its annual Special 301 Reports in respect of the Arabian Peninsula States is discussed in greater detail in Chapter 8.

91 The Business Software Alliance (BSA) is an international organisation representing the leading software and e-commerce developers in 65 countries around the world. Promoting itself as the voice of the international software industry, BSA interacts with governments and consumers on the promotion of the role of software in global development and in relation to its fight against software piracy and internet theft. The following description was taken directly from BSA's website (www.bsa.org) in 2012:

> The Business Software Alliance is the foremost organization dedicated to promoting a safe and legal digital world. BSA is the voice of the world's commercial software industry and its hardware partners before governments and in the international marketplace. Its members represent one of the fastest-growing industries in the world. BSA programs foster technology innovation through education and policy initiatives that promote

claims to be the leading global computer software protection lobby organisation and asserts that its Annual Global Study is the premier survey on international software piracy. The 1996 Report for the year 1995 stated that the GCC member States together with Jordan had an average software piracy rate of 89 per cent, with Saudi Arabia being the best performer with a rate of 77 per cent and Oman being the poorest performer with a rate of 96 per cent.[92] Yemen was not included in the BSA Survey until 2007.

By 2005, piracy rates had increased in 67 countries, remained unchanged in 33 countries and decreased in only eight countries.[93] The average global piracy rate had increased by three percentage points to 38 per cent; in more than half the countries studied, the piracy rate exceeded 75 per cent. Only a third of the countries studied had a piracy rate below 50 per cent. The GCC member States and Jordan had improved their piracy rates from 89 per cent to 53 per cent, mainly due to the performance of the UAE, which achieved a greater than 50-point decrease, and Oman which achieved a 33 per cent decrease. The UAE achievement placed it on a par with Japan, South Africa and Western Europe overall, and retained it the top 20 countries in terms of lowest global piracy rates. Not far behind the UAE was Saudi Arabia, which managed to reduce its piracy rate to 51 per cent, a result that was still not of sufficient significance to enable it to be removed from the USTR 2008 Special 301 Listing.

By the 2016 Report for the year 2015, the steady improvements of the previous decade have slowed to the extent of now reaching something of a plateau.[94] The GCC member States together with Jordan and Yemen (since 2007) show a piracy rate of 56 per cent. However, Yemen with a piracy rate of 87 per cent distorts the averages somewhat – if the Yemen figure is omitted, the percentage rate for the rest of the States reduces to just over 50 per cent. To some extent, the slow-down

copyright protection, cyber security, trade and e-commerce. . . . Since 1995, the Business Software Alliance (BSA) has commissioned an annual study on global trends in computer software piracy, the studies since 2004 having been conducted by International Data Corporation (IDC), on behalf of BSA. IDC and previous studies conducted for BSA used the following basic research architecture to measure piracy rates and dollar losses:

- determine how much packaged software was put into use in 2004.
- determine how much packaged software has been paid for during the year.
- then subtract one from the other to get the amount of pirated software.

Once the amount of pirated software is known, the piracy rate is determined as the percentage of total software installed that was pirated.

92 Business Software Alliance, *Sixth Annual BSA Global Software Piracy Study 2008*, available at http://globalstudy.bsa.org/2008/studies/globalpiracy2008.pdf, last accessed 13 June 2017.

93 Business Software Alliance, *Third Annual BSA and IDC Global Software Piracy Study 2006*, available at www.bsa.org/~/media/Files/Research%20Papers/GlobalStudy/2005/IDC_Global_Software_Piracy_Study_2005.pdf, last accessed 13 June 2017.

94 Business Software Alliance, *Global Software Survey*, May 2016, available at http://globalstudy.bsa.org/2016/downloads/studies/BSA_GSS_US.pdf, last accessed 26 May 2017.

TABLE 7.2 1996–2016 BSA piracy study results – Arabian Peninsula piracy rate (%)

	1996	*1998*	*2000*	*2002*	*2004*	*2006*	*2008*	*2010*	*2011*	*2013*	*2015*
Bahrain	92	89	80	76	62	60	57	54	54	53	54
Kuwait	91	88	80	73	68	66	62	60	59	58	58
Oman	96	93	78	70	64	63	61	62	61	60	60
Qatar	91	87	81	76	62	60	54	49	50	49	48
Saudi Arabia	77	73	59	50	52	52	51	52	51	50	49
UAE	86	49	44	36	34	34	35	36	37	36	34
Jordan	87	80	71	64	64	63	58	57	57	57	56
Yemen	–	–	–	–	–	–	89	90	89	87	87
Gulf Total	89	80	71	64	57	57	58	57	57	56	56
North America total	28	26	25	24	22	22	21	21	21	19	17
Western Europe total	43	36	34	35	35	34	33	31	31	29	28

Source: compiled by the author from the BSA and BSA & IDC Annual Global Piracy Studies 2001–2016. Surveys appear not to have been conducted for 2012 and 2014.

of the improvement rate over the last decade is offset by the dramatic increase in market penetration in the region for computer and electronic hardware and software.

Table 7.2 details the piracy rate in the Arabian Peninsula region between 1995 and 2015. The years listed refer to the year in which each Report was published.

There is no doubt that the States have yet more work to do in the construction of their intellectual property protection regimes. Enforcement and infrastructure issues will continue to require attention in the mainstream areas of trademarks, copyright and patents as the complexity of their non-energy economies continue to develop and mainly external forces continue to pressure them to conform to the ever-enhancing international 'norm' of TRIPS-plus standards. Saudi Arabia and the UAE constitute the largest of the Arabian economies and enjoy the greatest profile in terms of intellectual property activity and need for effective enforcement strategies and performance. However, they are arguably the two States that have been the most successful in curbing infringing activity. Bahrain, Jordan, Oman and Qatar represent the middle position, in respect of both activity and performance. Kuwait is arguably the least compliant of the GCC member States and will continue to attract critical attention and pressure to improve on its performance. Yemen trails the other States; having recently achieved WTO membership, it will likely experience similar scrutiny of its intellectual property protection regime as did Saudi Arabia, and will no doubt be required to introduce a regime that is consistent with the current best international standards of protection and thereby exceeds current TRIPS standards.

In the past, one of the key driving forces for change and for the States to move to TRIPS-plus levels of intellectual property protection has been generated by the developed countries. The strategy has operated through adherence to a web of international conventions and commitment to bilateral trade agreements which contain a comprehensive compendium of requirements for enhanced levels of intellectual property protection that far exceed the TRIPS-required standards. The USTR Special 301 Reports have been an important weapon in driving that change.

More recent times have seen the emergence of a more influential role in regional intellectual property agenda setting being taken on board by the GCC itself, as evidenced by the adoption of both the GCC patent regulations and the GCC trademark law by a number of GCC members – both of these drivers are discussed in the next chapter.

8

TRIPS-PLUS AND 'RAISING THE BAR'

8.1 Introduction

Previous chapters have charted the progression of the Arabian Peninsula States' intellectual property protection regimes through the era prior to the establishment of the WTO and appearance of TRIPS (pre-TRIPS), the era of achieving membership of the WTO and compliant intellectual property regimes (TRIPS), and the era of challenges of TRIPS implementation and enforcement (post-TRIPS). This chapter considers some external influences that have had an impact upon the respective States' intellectual property protection environments during the post-TRIPS era, and the extent to which those influences may have contributed to enhanced or upgraded protection standards – in other words, the TRIPS-plus environments.

Having come to terms with the dimension of the transformation of their respective intellectual property protection regimes as required by the terms of their WTO membership, the States have had to face the prospect of a new round of imposed changes as they enter a TRIPS-plus environment. The term 'TRIPS-plus' lacks precise definition, but has come into increasingly common usage in the debate on contemporary intellectual property rights and their protection standards. It has been described, in a general sense, as 'commitments which go beyond what is already included or consolidated in the TRIPS Agreement', and more specifically as

> both those activities aimed at increasing the level of protection for right holders beyond that which is given in the TRIPS Agreement and those measures aimed at reducing the scope or effectiveness of limitations on rights and exceptions under the TRIPS Agreement.[1]

1 David Vivas, 'Regional and Bilateral Agreements and a TRIPS-plus World: The Free Trade Area of the Americas', TRIPS Issues Papers No. 1, p. 4, available at www.wto.org/english/

In common with other developing and least-developed countries, the States have faced additional pressures from the major developed countries, and from the United States in particular, to adopt more comprehensive and higher standards of intellectual property protection that go well beyond those required by TRIPS – in other words, TRIPS-plus standards. This pressure to adopt TRIPS-plus standards of intellectual property protection can be applied by two different strategies, namely:

- directly, through bilateral trade agreements, investment framework agreements, and free trade agreements (FTAs) which include extensive and detailed intellectual property protection chapters or provisions, and which require accession to or compliance with a number of TRIPS-plus international intellectual property protection conventions;[2]
- indirectly, through the coercive use of a threatened or actual withdrawal of preferential trade provisions or imposition of trade-related sanctions or retaliation to 'persuade' trading partners to adopt TRIPS-plus intellectual property protection standards.

An example of the application of the first strategy, which the chapter examines, is evidenced in the TRIPS-plus elements of the intellectual property chapters of the FTAs concluded by the United States with Jordan, Bahrain and Oman. An example of the second strategy, which the chapter also examines, is the role of the Office of

tratop_e/region_e/sem_nov03_e/vivas_eugui_paper_e.pdf, last accessed 26 May 2017. Sisule Musungu and Graham Dutfield, for example, have also described post-TRIPS as a 'concept which refers to the adoption of multilateral, plurilateral, regional and/or national IP rules and practices which have the effect of reducing the ability of developing countries to protect the public interest'. See Sisule Musungu and Graham Dutfield, 'Multilateral Agreements and a TRIPS-plus World: The World Intellectual Property Organisation', TRIPS Issues Papers No. 3, p. 3, available at www.iprsonline.org/ictsd/docs/WIPO_Musungu_Dutfield.pdf, last accessed 26 May 2017. See also Mohammed El-Said (2005), 'From TRIPS-minus to TRIPS to TRIPS-plus: Implications of IPRs for the Arab World', 8, *Journal of World Intellectual Property*, p. 53.

2 The international conventions which commonly form part of the US bilateral treaty negotiating agenda, for example, include WIPO's Copyright Treaty (WCT) and Performances and Phonograms Treaty (WPPT) in particular, but also generally include the following:

- Patent Cooperation Treaty (PCT);
- Convention Relating to the Distribution of Programme-Carrying Signals Transmitted by Satellite (1974) (Brussels Convention);
- Protocol Relating to the Madrid Agreement Concerning the International Registration of Marks (1989) (Madrid Protocol);
- Budapest Treaty on the International Recognition of the Deposit of Microorganisms for the Purposes of Patent Procedure (1980);
- Hague Agreement Concerning the International Registration of Industrial Designs (1999);
- International Convention for the Protection of New Varieties of Plants (1991) (UPOV Convention);
- Trademark Law Treaty (TLT);
- Patent Law Treaty (PLT).

the United States Trade Representative (USTR) and its use of the Special 301 provisions as a tool to pressure states to adopt standards of protection much higher than those required by TRIPS. These two strategies, however, should not be perceived as alternatives, but rather as complementary to each other – as is demonstrated later in this chapter.

Bilateral trade and investment agreements, particularly FTAs, are the most common medium for imposing TRIPS-plus provisions. They typically contain extensive intellectual property protection provisions, which the major industrialised countries use to establish standards which exceed those enshrined in TRIPS, or to remove or reduce the flexibilities provided by or permitted in TRIPS, or to even establish protection in new areas of intellectual property rights which go beyond the parameters of TRIPS.

The process of utilising bilateral trade and investment agreements to impose TRIPS-plus intellectual property protection has been described as a process which constitutes a 'raising the bar' or a 'global ratcheting' of intellectual property protection minimum benchmarks.[3] This process, which is seeing certain national intellectual property norms globalise upwards to those higher standards at a remarkable rate, is dependent upon the following key elements:

- forum shifting, in which the standard-setting agenda is moved from one forum in which difficulties are encountered in imposing TRIPS-plus standards (such as the WTO) to another forum in which success is more likely to be achieved (such as bilateral and regional agreements);
- coordinated bilateral and multilateral intellectual property protection strategies;
- entrenchment in bilateral agreements of the principle of ever-increasing minimum protection standards; and
- Investor-state dispute settlement (ISDS) provisions which enable an aggrieved foreign investor to sue the state in private international arbitration rather than though domestic or international judicial channels.

The two major protagonists in this process of global integration are the United States and the European Union, although the United States has been the lead player in respect of the Middle East region. Utilised as a key element of the US bilateral strategy is the tactic of reward and coercion – the former illustrated by the application of its Generalised System of Preferences (GSP) and the promise of preferential access and tariff treatment to US markets, and the latter by the use of its USTR Annual Special 301 Listings and the threat of trade retaliation.

The intellectual property provisions of the FTAs that the United States have concluded with Jordan (Jordan FTA), Bahrain (Bahrain FTA) and Oman (Oman FTA) pointedly illustrate how it continually strives to raise protection standards

3 Peter Drahos (2001), 'BITs and BIPs – Bilateralism in Intellectual Property', 4, *Journal of World Intellectual Property*, 6, pp. 798–9.

and mostly (but not always) succeeds. While the United States stated after the conclusion of the Oman negotiations that it was pleased with the strengthened protection of intellectual property rights in its recent FTAs (including those with Morocco and Australia, as well as those with Jordan and Bahrain), it also stated at the commencement of subsequent negotiations and discussions, including those with the UAE, Kuwait and Qatar, that it would be seeking even higher levels of protection and enforcement.[4] However, negotiations on these particular FTAs soon slowed considerably and ground to a halt.

8.2 Bilateralism – 'multilateralism by the backdoor'

Bilateral trade and investment agreements are promoted by their advocates as being stepping stones towards full integration of their participants into a global free-market economy by ensuring that governments implement the liberalisation, privatisation and deregulation measures of the globalisation agenda.[5] They argue that the introduction of free trade and the removal of regulations on investment that the bilateral agreements generate will lead to economic growth, the reduction of poverty, increased living standards and employment opportunities.

The critics of bilateral agreements, however, argue that there is ample evidence to show that, on the contrary, the agreements merely allow transnational corporations more freedom to exploit workers and to shape the national and global economies of the junior partners to suit the corporations' interests.[6] They further posit that these binding international agreements severely constrain future governments in their policy options and help lock in existing economic reforms which may have been imposed by the International Monetary Fund, the World Bank or the Asian Development Bank, or are pursued by national governments of their own volition. Some commentators have argued at length that the self-interest mechanisms which are particular to the US-sponsored bilateral agreements, such as the conditions relating to the protection of intellectual property rights, their enforcement and the control or check mechanisms for managing the agreements, are tantamount to an intrusion into domestic lawmaking.[7]

Bilateral agreements have been critically painted as part of an insidious fast-expanding and bewildering web, popping up like a hydra's heads throughout the

4 Office of the United States Trade Representative (USTR), *2005 Special 301 Report*, p. 2.

5 Aziz Choudry (2004), 'Bombarded by Bilateral Trade and Investment Agreements', *Bilaterals.org*, March, p. 3, available at www.bilaterals.org/IMG/pdf/Bombarded_by_Bilatera_92909-2.pdf, last accessed 26 May 2017. See also Peter Drahos and John Braithwaite (2002), *Information Feudalism: Who Owns the Global Economy?* and Carlos Correa (2004), 'Bilateral Investment Agreements: Agents of New Global Standards for the Protection of Intellectual Property Rights?', *GRAIN*, August, available at www.grain.org/article/entries/125-bilateral-investment-agreements-agents-of-new-global-standards-for-the-protection-of-intellectual-property-rights, last accessed 26 May 2017.

6 Choudry, ibid.

7 See Peter Drahos (2001), op. cit., p. 798.

world, and constructing in patchwork fashion what the developed nations have not been able to impose through such international forums as the WTO, or through multilateral negotiations.[8] They are also seen as insidious because they are invariably conducted in unequal contest in closed session between unequal partners – mainly a developed country and a developing or least-developed country. With the stronger partner having an established objective to protect its own economic and trade interests, and having little or no interest in making allowance for the divergent or conflicting national and developmental interests of the weaker partner, the resultant agreement is both inevitable and predictable. As two expert commentators on bilateralism so colourfully, yet accurately, describe the outcome of such a scenario, 'bilateralism is like cooking an elephant and rabbit stew: however you mix the ingredients, it ends up tasting like elephant stew'.[9]

It has been suggested that, on intellectual property issues that really matter to it, the United States has been able to utilise webs of coercion.[10] One of those webs of coercion is its strategy of establishing bilateral agreements which include the introduction of TRIPS-plus standards of intellectual property protection. Developing countries operate within an intellectual property paradigm dominated by the United States and the European Union, and by international business. TRIPS sets minimum standards, while bilateral arrangements raise them. Developing countries can expect very few concessions on intellectual property issues, but are prepared to sign the bilateral agreements containing TRIPS-plus provisions in intellectual property rights in order to gain access to US and EU markets or to avoid losing access to them.

However, critics of bilateralism tend to concentrate on the policies and practices of the United States and the European Union, and appear to overlook the fact that many developing countries also enter into bilateral trade and investment treaties with each other and with least-developed countries. These 'south–south' bilateral agreements can often include the same essential features as the north–south agreements, particularly in respect of a broad definition of investments which encompass intellectual property rights, restrictions on and compensation for expropriation, and dispute resolution, although not to the same degree of complexity as the US-sponsored or EU-sponsored agreements.[11]

8 Aziz Choudry (2003), 'Bilateral Trade and Investment Deals a Serious Challenge to Global Justice Movements', *GRAIN*, December, p. 1, available at www.grain.org/article/entries/3620-bilateral-trade-and-investment-deals-a-serious-challenge-to-global-justice-movements, last accessed 26 May 2017.

9 Drahos and Braithwaite, op. cit., p. 194.

10 Peter Drahos, 'Developing Countries and International Intellectual Property Standard-Setting' (2002), 5, *Journal of World Intellectual Property*, p. 781.

11 See United Nations Conference on Trade and Development (UNCTAD) (20006), 'Investment Provisions in Economic Integration Agreements', 114–6, Document UNCTAD/ITE/IIT/2005/10. See also UNCTAD (2016), 'UN System Task Team on the Post-2015 UN Development Agenda', available at www.un.org/en/development/desa/policy/untaskteam_undf/thinkpieces/22_thinkpiece_trade.pdf, last accessed 26 May 2017.

8.3 Bilateral agreements between the United States and the Arabian Peninsula States

Under the administrations of Presidents Bill Clinton and George W Bush, the United States developed its bilateral strategy to expand and deepen control over its economic ties with countries in the Middle East through a series of graduated steps encompassing a range of bilateral agreements which either created a protection framework for intellectual property rights or contained specific protection provisions.[12] They include:

- establishing Trade and Investment Framework Agreements (TIFAs), to initiate trade liberalisation within the target state and to 'promote the establishment of legal protections for [US] investors, improvements in intellectual property protection, more transparent and efficient customs procedures and greater transparency in government and commercial regulations';[13]
- establishing Bilateral Investment Treaties (BITs) to introduce common rules for investment in each state, by incorporating international (that is, US) business rules and norms into the domestic laws;
- establishing the more comprehensive FTAs, as the principal process by which US intellectual property rights industries are able to ensure that their required and sought-after standards of protection keep pace with new developments;
- expanding these FTAs by bringing other regional or neighbouring states into them, and eventually weaving these 'subregional FTAs' into a greater US–Middle East Free Trade Area (MEFTA);
- supporting applications for WTO membership for those 'peaceful countries in the region that seek it';[14]

The Pan-Arab Free Trade Area Agreement, sponsored by the Arab League and signed at the League's Economic and Social Council Meeting on 19 February 1997, included provisions on trade, investments, intellectual property rights and dispute settlement, available at http://archive.is/u3kTk, last accessed 31 May 2017. For examples of south–south agreements involving the GCC member States, and with similar investment and intellectual property provisions, see the agreements between Bahrain and Jordan, Kuwait and Pakistan, Oman and India, Qatar and Turkey, Saudi Arabia and Korea, and UAE and Lebanon, all available at http://unctad.org/en/Docs/iteiit20053annex_en.pdf and http://unctad.org/en/docs/iteiit20053_en.pdf, last accessed 31 May 2017.

12 See USTR Fact Sheet (2004), 'Middle East Free Trade Initiative', 23 June, available at https://ustr.gov/archive/Document_Library/Fact_Sheets/2004/Middle_East_Free_Trade_Initiative_US_Regional_Plan_to_Spur_Economic_Growth.html, last accessed 26 May 2017.

13 USTR Trade Facts (2004), 'Middle East Free Trade Initiative: US Regional Plan to Spur Economic Growth', 2 March, available at https://ustr.gov/about-us/policy-offices/press-office/fact-sheets/archives/2004/march/middle-east-free-trade-initiative-us-regional-, last accessed 26 May 2017.

14 In this case, Saudi Arabia, Yemen and Lebanon being the main applicants in this context. Saudi Arabia applied for accession to GATT (1947) on 23 June 1993 and reaffirmed its intention to accede to the WTO in December 1995. The original GATT Working Party on Saudi Arabia's accession continued as the WTO Accession Working Party. It is worth noting

- providing financial and technical assistance and training to assist states develop the capacity to take part in negotiations, implement trade agreements and build legal and entrepreneurial infrastructures;[15]
- using the US GSP programme and the USTR's Special 301 provisions as positive and negative reinforcement to control trade ties with eligible and/ or recalcitrant states.

The United States leads the European Union in the installation of its bilateral agreements in the Middle East region, and in the Gulf in particular, with its bilateral agreement strategy a small part of a much bigger picture.

8.3.1 The Middle East Free Trade Area (MEFTA)

While the United States had concluded a number of bilateral trade and investment agreements (BITs and TIFAs) with Middle East and North African (MENA) countries during the late 1990s, the impetus to sign new agreements with MENA countries increased after the terrorist attacks on the World Trade Centre on 11 September 2001 ('9/11'). In May 2003, the United States proposed the creation of a Middle East Free Trade Area (MEFTA), a plan of graduated steps for the Middle East countries, and the GCC member States in particular, to individually enter into trade and investment agreements with the United States, with the eventual goal of a regional free trade agreement by 2013. MEFTA was a key element in the US Middle East Peace Initiative, and its war against international terrorism. The United States envisaged the creation of a US–MEFTA agreement complementing and extending its already significant economic and military involvement in the region.[16] Accordingly, US trade and investment relations with the countries of the Middle East had (and still have) considerable potential importance and urgency in terms of both US political and economic interests.

The United States repeatedly declined to negotiate collectively with the Arabian Peninsula States as a regional or GCC bloc, insisting instead on separate individual

that the United States sponsored an application from Iraq for accession, but opposed applications from Iran and Syria.

15 The USTR describes 'technical assistance' as including the review of, and drafting assistance on, laws concerning intellectual property and enforcement. 'Training' usually covers the substantive provisions of TRIPS, including enforcement. Such assistance is provided by a number of US government agencies, including the US Patent and Trademark Office, the Copyright Office, Department of State, the US Agency for International Development, Customs and Border Protection, Department of Justice and Department of Commerce. US industry is also actively involved in providing specific enforcement-oriented training in key markets. The United States expects progress in the near term, but where this is not achieved, it will consider other means of encouraging implementation, including the possibility of dispute-settlement consultations. See USTR, *2016 Special 301 Report*, pp. 67–9.

16 See Kenneth Katzman (2006), 'The Persian Gulf States: Post-War Issues for US Policy', *CRS Report for Congress*, No. RL31533, The Library of Congress, January 2006, Executive Summary, available at www.dtic.mil/get-tr-doc/pdf?AD=ADA476192, last accessed 31 May 2017.

negotiations and agreements to be initiated and concluded with each of the States. It justified this state-by-state approach on the grounds that it recognised the differing levels of development across the region and was thereby pursuing a step-by-step approach tailored to individual States' particular needs.[17] However, this argument cannot be sustained in view of the fact that the bilateral agreements which the United States has entered into with the States, and other developing countries, are all based on a model agreement whose objective is to achieve standardisation with minimal deviation. Change is permitted to the extent that such change constitutes refinement of the model. Hence the intellectual property chapter of the Oman FTA is almost identical to those of the earlier Bahrain FTA, but with additional provisions added. Similarly, the Bahrain FTA is in turn closely aligned with the Jordanian, the Moroccan and even the Australian agreements. Critics would argue that this step-by-step approach enables the United States to implement a divide-and-conquer strategy and to prevent the creation of opposition alliances of the kind that it has encountered in the multilateral forums of the WTO and WIPO.[18] It also allows the United States to maximise its immense political and economic bargaining power to extract the most favourable trading terms and intellectual property protection regimes terms from its agreement partners, and this tactic is being used in its implementation strategy for the MEFTA.

In contrast, the European Union has consistently refused to enter into separate bilateral discussions with the individual States and has chosen instead to negotiate its proposed FTA with the GCC as a bloc. The European Union has pushed for human rights and a greater degree of economic integration between the GCC member States as key issues in the continuation of negotiations; the establishment of a GCC Customs Union was an EU precondition for eventually signing an FTA. The European Union also views GCC integration as a step toward greater regional stability and mutual prosperity. Yet negotiations with the European Union have taken a considerable time, and have still yet to be concluded. Negotiations have recently stalled again after the European Union presented conditions and tried to introduce issues such as those relating to terrorism and human rights, which appeared to the GCC to be well removed from the economic agenda and into the political arena. Dispute still exists over EU insistence upon including in negotiations such issues as human rights, national government systems and GCC member States' restrictions on foreign ownership – issues which the States see as being irrelevant to the FTA, but which are also central to the US negotiations with the individual States. The States view the EU insistence on including these issues in negotiations as interference in their domestic affairs and criticisms of their systems of government.

Because of the stalled nature of EU–GCC negotiations over an extended period of time, the European Union impact on intellectual property protection

17 USTR Robert Zoellick, as reported in 'Sultanate, US Hold Joint Meeting on Free Trade Pact', *Times of Oman*, 15 October 2004.

18 See Choudry (2003), op. cit., p. 1.

regimes of the GCC member States in the context of a bilateral strategy has not been significant and has been put to one side for the purposes of this work.

8.3.2 The US–Jordan FTA

Negotiations between the United States and Jordan on a proposed bilateral FTA commenced in June 2000, and the completed agreement was signed on 24 October 2000. The United States–Jordan Free Trade Agreement (Jordan FTA) was the first FTA the United States signed with an Arab country, and the third US FTA overall after Israel and Canada/Mexico (NAFTA). Being negotiated and concluded prior to the 9/11 attacks and thus pre-dating the US MEFTA initiative, it did not carry the same geopolitical and strategic imperative as the post-2001 agreements. Hence it is much briefer than the other two region FTAs that followed. The intellectual property provisions of the Agreement comprise just one article consisting of 29 fairly brief sub-articles extending over five pages of text. The following is not meant to be a comprehensive analysis of the intellectual property provisions of the Jordan FTA, but instead focuses on those TRIPS-plus elements of the Agreement. Some of those elements include:

International treaties and conventions

Each Party is required to give effect to the provisions contained in the following agreements (although they are not necessarily required to accede to the agreements):

- WIPO/Paris Union Joint Recommendation Concerning the Protection of Well-Known Marks (1999), articles 1–6;
- International Convention for the Protection of New Varieties of Plants (1991) (UPOV Convention), articles 1–22;
- WIPO Copyright Treaty (1996) (WCT), articles 1–14;
- WIPO Performances and Phonograms Treaty (1996) (WPPT), articles 1–22;

and to make best efforts to ratify or accede to the Patent Cooperation Treaty (1984) (PCT), and the Protocol relating to the Madrid Agreement Concerning the International Registration of Marks (1989) (Madrid Protocol).

Trademarks

In respect of trademarks, Article 4(6) and 4(7) of the Jordan FTA reinforces a clear trademark/geographical indications hierarchy – with geographical indications (GIs) being in the subordinate position – that reflects the established North American position at the expense of the European position on GIs. It thus endeavours to reverse, in some respects, what is clearly perceived by the United States as the overly elevated protection status given to GIs in TRIPs. Article 4(6) provides that trademarks shall include service marks, collective marks and certification marks and may include GIs. A footnote to Article 4(6) states in effect that a GI shall be considered a trademark if it meets the TRIPS Article 22 definition of a GI. Article 4(7) gives the owner of a registered trademark the right to prevent third parties from using a mark which is identical or similar to the registered mark if there is a likelihood of confusion. Since a GI is thus deemed to be a trademark, this right extends over GIs. This same right is extended to owners of well-known marks, even if they are not registered in Jordan.

Copyright and neighbouring rights

The copyright and related rights protection provisions go beyond TRIPS and provide substance and detail to the general provisions of WIPO Internet Treaties, namely, the WIPO Copyright Treaty (WCT) and the WIPO Performances and Phonograms Treaty (WPPT). They focus upon enhanced protection, extended control and effective exclusion mechanisms.

While the WCT and WPPT already provide authors, performers and producers with the exclusive rights to make their works available by transmission or online, the FTA draws a significant distinction between authorisation and prohibition, and adds the exclusive right of right holders to prohibit the availability of their works. The right to authorise or to prohibit applies to all reproductions of their works in any manner or form, whether it be permanent or temporary (including temporary digital storage form).[19] The exclusive right to prohibit, which also applies equally to performances, recordings, broadcasts and the retransmission of broadcast signals,[20] effectively prevents the works or signals from being subject to the imposition of any form of compulsory licensing.

The Jordan FTA reinforces the control aspects of the WCT and the WPPT by placing severe limitations on the general provision afforded in those treaties and TRIPS for countries to mandate within their national laws certain limitations or exceptions to protection, by incorporating the limits and exceptions into the FTA, along very similar lines to the provisions in the US Digital Millennium Copyright Act 1998.[21] Technological control measures are given a very broad description, encompassing any technology, device or part that, in the normal course of operation, controls access to a protected work, performance or recording, notwithstanding any other purposes, functions or applications. A prohibition, both civilly and criminally, is placed upon the manufacture, sale, import or export, or general dealing of any product or service that could be used for circumvention but which has only a limited commercially significant purpose, irrespective of whether such limited use may be entirely legitimate or due to unrelated factors, such as a high degree of specialisation.[22]

19 Jordan FTA, art. 4(10).
20 Ibid., art. 4(12), art. 4(13).
21 Ibid., art. 4(13).
22 Ibid.

The FTA also recognises the right of free transfer of economic rights held by contract or other agreement, including contract of employment involving protected subject matter. It also requires government agencies to commit to using only authorised or legitimate software, and to manage such use. Finally, it provides exceptions and limitations to the exclusive rights of copyright holders, but requires such exceptions to be confined to cases that do not conflict with the normal exploitation of the work and do not unreasonably prejudice the legitimate interests of the right holder.[23]

However, the copyright provisions do not include any reference to a possible extension of the terms of protection for any category or form of copyrightable works.

Patents

Article 4(18) of the Jordan FTA provisions extend and strengthen the patent protection standards of TRIPS and at the same time reduce the TRIPS flexibilities. It removes the national discretion permitted by TRIPS Article 27.3(b) for excluding from patentability plants and animals other than micro-organisms and essentially biological processes for the production of plants or animals. The requirement for Jordan to ratify the UPOV Convention further removes the discretion afforded by TRIPS Article 27.3(b) for a WTO member to provide for the protection of plant varieties either by a patents system or by an effective *sui generis* system of its own construction or by any combination thereof.

The FTA imposes a very restricted usage of the patent subject matter without the authorisation of the right holder, and in so doing severely restricts the flexibility provided in TRIPS Article 31. Use without right-holder authorisation, or in other words the government's capacity to approve compulsory licensing, is restricted to just three circumstances as detailed in TRIPS Article 31(l), namely:

- to remedy a practice determined to be anti-competitive;
- for public non-commercial use or in the case of a national emergency or other circumstances of extreme emergency; and
- a failure to meet working requirements.

However, the FTA removes the other use without approval provisions of TRIPS Article 31 subsections (a) through to (k).

Measures relating to certain regulated products

The so-called 'regulated products' of the Jordan FTA Article 4 refer to pharmaceutical products. Article 4(22) provides strict data exclusivity provisions

23 Ibid., art. 4(16).

in respect of test data submitted for marketing approval purposes, to ensure that 'unfair commercial use' does not occur. The impact of this provision, which does not exist in TRIPS, is to prohibit the use of such test data by governments on behalf of third parties, competitors or generic drug manufacturers, for the purposes of testing the market efficacy of similar or competing pharmaceutical products. Such prohibition is unlimited and hence applies even after the patent protection term of the 'regulated' pharmaceutical product has expired. This provision is squarely aimed at preserving the competitive monopoly of the 'regulated' product and preventing the potential entry of similar generic products into the market.

The competitive advantage is further enhanced by making mandatory an extension of the patent protection term to compensate the patent owner for unreasonable delay in the market approval process.[24] Again, this is a requirement that is not provided in TRIPS. The FTA does not distinguish between the causes of the unreasonable delays – that is, those that might have been caused by the government agency or those that might have been caused by the right holder as a strategy to increase the protection term. The FTA is unclear as to whether this might be a one-off extension or whether there could be multiple extensions driven by perceived multiple instances of delay.

Article 4(23)(b) gives further advantage to the patent right holder by also making mandatory the right holder being notified of the identity of any third party requesting marketing approval (which could be for its own pharmaceutical product) for an identical or similar product during the term of the 'regulated' pharmaceutical patent, even if such third party does not rely in any way upon the first product's marketing test data.

Enforcement

The Jordan FTA strengthens the principle of adhering to a standard in both civil and criminal procedures and remedies that will be sufficient to act as a deterrent to further infringements. Introduced into the FTA is the long-established US regime of statutory or pre-established damages, thereby obviating the inherent difficulties in establishing actual damages in a piracy or counterfeiting case. At the same time, some elements of judicial discretion are also removed. For example, Article 4(24) includes provision for the aggrieved right holder to enjoy the prerogative to decide whether to elect between relying on statutory damages or proving actual damages.[25] It requires the courts to use the suggested retail price of the legitimate product being infringed upon as a measure of the loss to the right holder, or some other equivalent measure established by the right holder, rather than merely allowing the court to consider using this measure at its discretion or only upon request.

24 Ibid., art. 4(23)(a).
25 Ibid., art. 4(24).

Provision for the award of monetary damages, again of sufficient severity to deter piracy even where actual economic harm cannot be determined, significantly extends TRIPS discretionary provisions for the award of damages adequate to compensate for injury suffered.

Criminal procedures and penalties are to be applied in respect of trademark or copyright or related rights piracy on a commercial scale, with the definition of 'commercial scale' encompassing both willful infringements for commercial advantage or private financial gain and willful infringements that may have no direct or indirect motivation of financial gain.[26] While TRIPS requires that penalties must be of sufficient severity to act as a deterrent, it leaves it to individual countries to determine and give expression according to their own circumstances as to what may constitute sufficient deterrence. It also places some qualification on the level of severity of sanctions that may be imposed by requiring that they be consistent with the level of penalties applied to crimes of a corresponding gravity. However, such matters of detail, normally falling within the competence and authority of local legislators or judicial authorities to address or determine, are overridden by the FTA. The Memorandum of Understanding to the intellectual property provisions of the FTA require Jordan to 'raise its criminal penalties to JD6,000 so as to meet its obligations to ensure that statutory maximum fines are sufficiently high to deter future acts of infringement'.[27]

Transition periods

The Jordan FTA was signed on 20 October 2000, and entered into force on 17 December 2001. The FTA sets certain time periods for Jordan to implement its intellectual property obligations, ranging from:

- with immediate effect in respect of the pharmaceutical products and data exclusivity provisions of paragraph 22;
- six months in respect of paragraph 1(b);
- 12 months in respect of acceding to the UPOV Convention;
- two years in respect of acceding to the WCT and WPPT and the copyright obligations (paragraphs 10–16); and
- three years for all other obligations.

The various transitional periods were unrealistic, particularly those requiring immediate or very soon implementation. The short time frames were also inconsistent with TRIPS and other WTO treaty and general provisions for special and differential treatment being allowed for developing countries in respect of meeting their treaty obligations.

26 Ibid., art. 4(28).

27 Jordan FTA, 'Memorandum of Understanding on Issues Relating to the Protection of Intellectual Property Rights', para. 3.

8.3.3 The US–Bahrain FTA

On 29 May 2004, the United States and Bahrain announced the signing of an FTA between their two countries. Like the Jordan FTA, this Agreement was concluded in less than six months of negotiations, a remarkably short period of time in the context of free trade agreement negotiations.

The Bahrain FTA was greeted with general positive enthusiasm on both sides.[28] The Bahraini Prime Minister, Shaikh Khalifa bin Salman Al Khalifa, described it as a reflection of the respect and appreciation which the Kingdom had gained as a consequence of its constant development, which in turn had boosted the safety and success of the country's political, economic and social policies.[29] With somewhat different emphasis, the USTR's Robert Zoellick declared the FTA to be a:

> high quality, comprehensive agreement that will provide American workers, consumers and businesses unprecedented economic opportunity in Bahrain. Bahrain will substantially open its services market, streamline digital trade, protect intellectual property. . .[30]

The Bahrain FTA is based on a model agreement that the United States developed over the course of negotiations on other FTAs, including those with Jordan and Morocco. It derives its basic detail from the Jordan FTA of four years earlier, but greatly extends a number of the Jordan FTA characteristics and provisions. The intellectual property provisions alone have grown from some four pages of text in the Jordan FTA to 24 pages with accompanying side letters in the Bahrain FTA. Being the first of a number of FTAs that the United States was originally determined to negotiate with the GCC member States in order to establish its MEFTA, the Bahrain FTA was seen at the time of its signing as therefore the most crucial. The standards achieved and concessions gained in the Agreement were

28 The Bahrain FTA consists of 21 chapters incorporating market access, textiles and apparel, rules of origin, customs administration, sanitary and phytosanitary measures, technical barriers to trade, safeguards, government procurement, cross-border trade in services, financial services, telecommunications, electronic commerce, intellectual property rights, labour, environment, transparency, agreement administration and dispute settlement. Chapter 14 addresses intellectual property rights and represents a significant component of the FTA. The final version of the FTA text is available at https://ustr.gov/trade-agreements/free-trade-agreements/bahrain-fta/final-texts, last accessed 1 March 2017. The Bahraini King issued a decree ratifying the FTA on 21 July 2005, after it was passed by the Bahraini parliament and the Shura Council earlier that month. US President George W Bush signed the FTA into law on 11 January 2006, after Congress passed the Agreement by an overwhelming majority in December 2005.

29 As quoted in the *Bahrain Tribune*, 30 May 2004, p. 4.

30 USTR Press Release (2004), 'US and Bahrain Conclude Free Trade Agreement', 27 May, at https://ustr.gov/about-us/policy-offices/press-office/press-releases/archives/2004/may/us-and-bahrain-conclude-free-trade-agreement, last accessed 26 May 2017.

meant to establish a precedent and the new enhanced benchmark for future agreements among the GCC member States, just as Jordan's did in the wider Middle East.

The United States can justifiably claim to have been very successful in achieving its negotiation objectives. According to the USTR's Industry Trade Advisory Committee tasked with providing expert comment and advice to the US President and the USTR on the intellectual property provisions of the Agreement, the Bahrain FTA meets most of the negotiating goals and objectives contained in the US Trade Act of 2002 and the goals of the US intellectual property-based industries, creators and innovators.[31] The Committee, commonly known by the acronym 'ITAC-15', asserts that the intellectual property chapter of the FTA requires Bahrain to make a number of significant concessions and commitments which go considerably beyond the level of protection already provided by its national legislation and which markedly exceed TRIPS standards.

Notwithstanding its length, the intellectual property chapter of the Bahrain FTA still does not constitute a comprehensive agreement encompassing all areas of intellectual property protection. Instead, it addresses only those particular areas of concern to the USTR and US business in terms of their own intellectual property investments and exports, and their keenness to ensure that intellectual property rights involving the new technologies in the digital environment are fully protected while that environment is still in the fledgling stage.

According to the USTR, the following outcomes in respect of the protection of intellectual property rights were achieved with the successful completion of the Bahrain FTA:

31 As part of the consultative process with US industry and stakeholders, the USTR has established a group of industry advisory committees to advise and recommend on each chapter of an FTA. The advisory group overall is made up of more than 700 carefully selected stakeholders, comprising senior members of major US industries or their legal counsel, government officials and business, academic experts and consumer groups. The advisory group provides advice on both proposed and ongoing USTR activities and is kept informed on developments in both agreement negotiations and Special 301 reviews, available at https://ustr.gov/archive/Document_Library/Press_Releases/2005/November/Trade_Advisory_Committees_Support_US-Oman_FTA.html, last accessed 31 May 2017. For a concise description of the modus operandi of the USTR's expert advisory committee structure, see also 'Mission of the USTR', at https://ustr.gov/about-us/about-ustr, last accessed 1 March 2017.

The members of ITAC-15, the committee responsible for advising on the intellectual property provisions of the Bahrain FTA, include persons who have a particular vested interest in ensuring that the highest possible standards of intellectual property protection for US rights holders are incorporated into any FTA. They include IIPA, as chairman of ITAC-15, PhRMA, the Recording Industry Association of America and other major US corporations. See ITAC-15 (2004), 'Report on the Bahrain FTA', pp. 2 and 22, available at https://ustr.gov/archive/assets/Trade_Agreements/Bilateral/Bahrain_FTA/Reports/asset_upload_file822_5528.pdf, last accessed 26 May 2017.

International treaties and conventions

Each Party is required to ratify or accede to the agreements that formed part of the Jordan FTA, as well as the following additional agreements:

- Patent Cooperation Treaty, as revised and amended (1970) (PCT);
- Convention Relating to the Distribution of Programme-Carrying Signals Transmitted by Satellite (1974) (Brussels Convention);
- Budapest Treaty on the International Recognition of the Deposit of Microorganisms for the Purposes of Patent Procedure (1980);
- Trademark Law Treaty (1994) (TLT).

Both parties are also required to make their best efforts to ratify or accede to the Patent Law Treaty (2000) (PLT), and the Hague Agreement Concerning the International Registration of Industrial Designs (1999). The obligation to ratify or adopt the above treaties applies equally to both parties and therefore might appear to be a balanced obligation. In fact, the United States had already adopted most of the treaties and so the treaty adoption obligations in reality represent a somewhat uneven imposition upon Bahrain of the US status quo.[32]

Trademarks

The trademarks and GI provisions attract succinct but significant attention. Both parties are required to accede to the TLT, but since the TLT applies only to visually perceptible signs, the FTA again broadens the scope of available protection by stipulating that a trademark need not be visually perceptible to be registrable and that registration shall not be denied on the grounds that a mark or sign is composed of a sound or includes a scent.[33]

The precedence of trademarks over GIs, clearly established in the Jordan FTA, is further reinforced.[34] It goes further by including specific provision to prohibit the protection or recognition of a GI that is confusingly similar to a prior mark, thereby unequivocally protecting prior marks against later GIs. This stance is consistent with US law and policy in the relationship between trademarks and GIs, and in direct opposition to the European position. Further subversion of the GI status is generated by the inclusion of specific provision for the rejection of a GI application or the cancellation of a registered GI if the GI may cause confusion with either a trade mark application or registered mark.[35]

32 The US joined the above-mentioned treaties on the following dates: WCT (6 March 2002), WPPT (20 May 2002), PCT (24 January 1978), Brussels Convention (7 March 1985), Madrid Protocol (2 November 2003), Budapest Treaty (19 August 1980), UPOV (8 November 1981), TLT (12 August 2000). At the time of writing it has not yet acceded to the Hague Agreement. See WIPO, 'Contracting Parties to Treaties Administered by WIPO', 15 July 2008.

33 Bahrain FTA, arts 14.2.1 and 14.2.6.

34 Ibid., arts 14.2.4 and 14.2.13.

35 Ibid., art. 14.2.13

Further TRIPS-plus provisions in respect of trademarks that were not present in the Jordan FTA include:

- extension of the TRIPS limitation for marks to be visually perceptible for registrability to include scent and sound marks or signs (graphically representable);
- a minimum ten-year registration period (as distinct from TRIPS' seven-year minimum period).

Domain names on the internet

Domain names on the internet, which do not receive any mention in the Jordan FTA, also receive only brief but important mention. Provision is included for the introduction of uniform procedures for domain-name dispute resolution for each country's top-level domains (TLDs), and for public access to a reliable and accurate database of contact information for domain-name registrants.[36] However, these provisions relate only to trademark cyber piracy.

Copyright and neighbouring rights

The copyright and related rights protection provisions constitute the predominant part of the Bahrain FTA intellectual property chapter (Chapter 14), reflecting the concern of the USTR and the US copyright industry with the extent of global copyright piracy in general and the Gulf region in particular, and their determination to ensure that such piracy in the digital environment is eliminated before it can become too entrenched. The copyright and related rights protection provisions go well beyond TRIPS and the Jordan FTA, and provide substance and detail to the general provisions of the WIPO Internet Treaties. They focus upon enhanced protection, extended control and effective exclusion mechanisms.

As with its predecessor, the Bahrain FTA draws a significant distinction between authorisation and prohibition, and adds the exclusive right to right holders to prohibit the availability of their works. The right to authorise or to prohibit applies to all reproductions of their works in any manner or form, whether it be permanent or temporary (including temporary digital storage form).[37] The exclusive right to prohibit, which also applies equally to performances, recordings, broadcasts and the retransmission of broadcast signals,[38] effectively prevents the works or signals from being subject to the imposition of any form of compulsory licensing.

But where the Bahrain FTA differs from the Jordan FTA is that it provides for an extension of the minimum period of protection for a copyright work,

36 Ibid., arts 14.3.1 and 14.3.2.
37 Ibid., art. 14.4.1.
38 Ibid., arts 14.4.10(b), 14.5 and 14.6.2.

performance or recording, to become the life of the author or date of performance or recording plus 70 years, significantly exceeding both TRIPS and Berne Convention 50-year provision.[39] The United States for some years has been using its bilateral agreements as an alternative route outside the WTO/WIPO forum to achieve this higher standard (which is nevertheless still less than the 95 years which the US copyright industry sought to have included in the FTA).[40] Photographic works (and, by reasonable inference, works of applied art), which TRIPS and the Berne Convention deferred to national legislation to determine any period of protection in excess of their stipulated minimum period of 25 years, will also enjoy this new extended period of protection.[41]

The Bahrain FTA adopts the same control aspects of the WCT and the WPPT by incorporating limits and exceptions along very similar lines to the provisions in the US Digital Millennium Copyright Act 1998, which were also included in the Jordan FTA.[42]

In respect of the circumvention of technological measures controlling access to protected works, a very limited and circumscribed list of exception circumstances is permitted. Technological control measures are given a very broad description, encompassing any technology, device or component that, in the normal course of operation, controls access to a protected work, performance or recording, notwithstanding any other purposes, functions or applications.[43] Even more embracing and draconian is the prohibition placed upon the manufacture, sale, import or export, or general dealing of any product or service that could be used for circumvention but which has only a limited commercially significant purpose, irrespective of whether such limited use may be entirely legitimate or due to unrelated factors, such as a high degree of specialisation.

The FTA requires the implementation of measures contained in the WCT and WPPT prohibiting the removal or alteration of electronic rights-management information systems. Both criminal and civil remedies apply in respect of their removal or alteration, as well as in respect of importing, distributing, transmitting, broadcasting or generally dealing in material from which rights-management information has been removed.[44] The nature of an infringement of intellectual property rights enshrined in TRIPS generally requires the existence of elements of willful activity and commercial gain. The FTA language broadens the scope of possible infringing activity by replacing the willfulness and commercial gain standards for liability with the lesser standards of knowing or having reason to know, and private financial gain. The latter may be interpreted as any activity which bypasses the payment of copyright fees to a collection agency and thus may include

39 Ibid., art. 14.4.4.
40 ITAC-15 (2004), op. cit., p. 11.
41 Ibid.
42 Ibid.
43 Bahrain FTA, art. 14.4.7(a)–(b).
44 Ibid., art. 14.4.8–9.

the download of a transmission or electronic recording or performance, irrespective of whether such download is for commercial use or for private use.

In respect of the protection of encrypted programme-carrying satellite signals, the Bahrain FTA draws a distinction between the contents of a transmission or signal and the transmission or the signal itself, establishing that each owner has separate rights of equal standing and is therefore entitled to compensation where those rights are infringed.[45] It makes the manufacture, sale, import or export or otherwise possession of any device that could be primarily of assistance in decoding an encrypted signal a criminal offence, irrespective of whether the device has legitimate applications or is being legitimately used. The FTA also restricts local retransmission by similarly criminalising the further distribution or receipt of a transmission, knowing that it has been decoded without the authorisation of the lawful distributor of the signal. At the same time it again reduces the degree of willfulness requirement for an act to become unlawful.[46]

According to ITAC-15, except for a few shortcomings, the substantive copyright text achieves all that the US copyright industry sought in the FTA negotiations.[47]

Patents

In respect of patents, protection becomes virtually unassailable once granted. Bahrain's discretion to refuse or limit patentability, challenge a patent application or revoke a patent is severely limited. Pre-grant opposition, or provision to challenge a patent application, is removed, any opposition permitted only after the patent has been granted.[48] To impose further limitation on the chances for a successful challenge, the FTA stipulates that revocation may be permitted only on grounds that would have justified refusal to grant the patent in the first place – that is, because of its lack of patentability or because of fraud, misrepresentation or inequitable conduct in respect of the patent application.[49]

Protection is extended to any new uses or methods of using a known product, including products to be used for particular medical conditions, thereby encouraging the practice of 'evergreening' or allowing defensive patents to essentially extend the life span of the original patent.

The FTA acknowledges the right of either party to provide limited exceptions to the exclusive rights conferred by a patent, provided that such imposition does not unreasonably conflict with normal exploitation of the patent or does not unreasonably prejudice the legitimate interests of the patent owner – a restatement of

45 Ibid, art. 14.7.

46 Ibid, art. 14.8(a). By article 14.8(a), the 'willfulness' requirement as contained in TRIPS is reduced to 'knowing' or 'having reason to know'.

47 ITAC-15 (2004) op. cit., p. 12.

48 Bahrain FTA, art. 14.8.4.

49 Ibid., art. 14.8.4.

TRIPS Article 30.[50] However, the FTA neither specifically prohibits nor acknowledges Bahrain's right to impose compulsory licensing requirements, as permitted by TRIPS Article 31, and enshrined in the patent laws of a number of the States and the GCC Patent Regulation. This prompted ITAC-15 to express its disappointment that the FTA did not confine the possibility of compulsory licensing to explicit situations that are needed to remedy antitrust violations, national emergencies or other circumstances of extreme urgency, and to govern situations of public non-commercial use[51] – confining it to the limited circumstances of TRIPS Article 31(b) only. This creates some uncertainty as to whether an application for or granting of a compulsory licence may be challengeable on the grounds that it is an action tantamount to investment expropriation. However, since the list of permitted exceptions is meant to be exclusive, any act not specifically included in the list would automatically be deemed to be unlawful.

Pharmaceuticals

The Bahrain FTA includes provisions similar to those in the Jordan FTA in respect of data exclusivity for marketing approval, but extends the breadth and depth of those earlier provisions considerably, now including complex and extensive requirements in respect of protection for patents and their related test data that essentially amounts to extended terms of protection. It imposes an obligation of non-reliance on either the pioneer approval or the pioneer data package itself for a period of at least five years from the date of approval for a pharmaceutical product and ten years for an agricultural product.[52] As with the Jordan FTA, and reinforcing the same provision introduced in respect of patents generally, the same level of protection provided for new pharmaceutical products is extended to new products incorporating a previously approved chemical entity or new uses for current protected products.

The Bahrain FTA imposes measures that explicitly restrict Bahrain from terminating the data-protection period with the expiration of the underlying patent and prohibits generic drug approvals during the term of the patent covering a pharmaceutical product.[53] These measures go a considerable way to preventing parallel importing or local production of cheaper generic pharmaceutical or agricultural products, by excluding market access to products with the same or similar applications. Approval of generic pharmaceutical products is further effectively blocked by the requirement that the state shall implement approval processes that prevent third parties from marketing a product covered by the patent or its approved method of use, and by the requirement that the owner of

50 Ibid., art. 14.8.3.

51 ITAC-15 (2004), op. cit., p. 15.

52 Bahrain FTA, arts 14.9.1 and 14.9.2(c)–(d).

53 Ibid., arts 14.9.3 and 14.9.4.

a patent shall be notified of the identity of any other person seeking market approval to enter the market during the term of the patent.

Enforcement

The Bahrain FTA significantly strengthens the principle enshrined in the Jordan FTA of adhering to a standard in both civil and criminal procedures and remedies sufficient to act as a deterrent to further infringements – perceived by the United States as a key element of any effective enforcement system.[54]

In recognition that piracy and counterfeiting 'industries' are becoming increasingly complex and organised, the FTA mandates that courts have the authority to order an infringer to identify other persons or parties involved in any aspect of the infringement, including distribution, and to provide this information to the right holder.[55] Failure to comply renders the infringer liable to a fine or imprisonment. Provision for the award of monetary damages, again of sufficient severity to deter piracy even where actual economic harm cannot be determined, significantly extends TRIPS' discretionary damages provisions to compensate for injury suffered. Judicial authorities may order the seizure of all suspected counterfeit or pirated goods, any related materials and equipment used in the commission of the offence, as well as any traceable assets and any documentary evidence which may be relevant to the offence. The items subject to seizure need not be individually identified as long as they fall within general categories specified in the seizure order. Importation or exportation of counterfeit or pirated goods is to be treated as criminal activity to the same extent as if the goods were for trade in the domestic market.

The Bahrain FTA authorises courts to order, at the conclusion of the civil proceedings concerning copyright, trademark or patent infringements, that the prevailing party be awarded payment of court costs or fees and reasonable attorneys' fees by the losing party.[56] In civil judicial proceedings, materials and implements used in the manufacture or creation of pirated or counterfeit goods may be destroyed or disposed of outside the channels of commerce without compensation, as may the pirated or counterfeit goods at the right holder's request.[57]

While TRIPS requires that penalties must be of sufficient severity to act as a deterrent, it leaves it to individual countries to determine and give expression according to their own circumstances as to what may constitute sufficient deterrence. It also places some qualification on the level of severity of sanctions that may be imposed by requiring that they be consistent with the level of penalties

54 ITAC-15 (2004), op. cit., p. 18.
55 Bahrain FTA, art. 14.10.11.
56 Ibid., art. 14.10.8
57 Ibid., art. 14.10.10.

applied to crimes of a corresponding gravity. However, matters of detail which would normally fall within the competence and authority of local legislators or judicial authorities to address or determine, taking account of domestic legislation, judicial precedent or societal norms and standards, could be overridden by FTA supplementary or consequential provisions which may dictate the new level of penalties within Bahrain's intellectual property laws.

While the enforcement provisions are generally viewed favourably by ITAC-15, it nonetheless advocated stronger language in the FTA in respect of the deterrent effect of sentencing guidelines and broader discretionary powers in respect of search and seizures.[58]

The FTA introduces new provision for the liability of internet service providers (ISPs), but also limitations on the extent of that liability. It includes legal incentives for service providers to cooperate with copyright owners in deterring the unauthorised storage and transmission of copyrighted materials.[59] It establishes the basic functional equivalent of the concepts and provisions embodied in US law as found in S.512 of the US Digital Millennium Copyright Act 1998. Where ISPs do so cooperate, particularly in respect of removal of allegedly infringing material and provision of information on sources of the material, the FTA limits the remedies available against ISPs for copyright infringements that they do not control, initiate or direct but which occur through their systems or networks.[60]

Transitional provisions

With two exceptions, all obligations in respect of intellectual property protection, including adherence to international conventions and treaties, must be implemented upon entry into force of the Bahrain FTA.[61] The FTA overall, and the intellectual property protection provisions specifically, placed a significant burden upon Bahrain, considering that it had yet to fully implement TRIPS some four years after the deadline for developing countries.

The implementation arrangements applying generally to the FTA as a whole provide that the United States will give targeted assistance to Bahrain in implementing the high level of commitments achieved in areas such as 'modifying its current laws and regulations to meet its FTA obligations'.[62] Thus the United States can ensure that its requirements and standards for the maximum protection of its own interests can be incorporated where necessary, and in the most suitable form, into amendments or additions to Bahraini intellectual property legislation.

58 ITAC-15 (2004), op. cit., pp. 19–20.

59 Bahrain FTA, art. 14.10.29.

60 Ibid. The two exceptions are adherence to the Brussels Satellite Convention and the Budapest Treaty on the International Recognition of Micro-organisms, both of which require adherence within one year of the FTA coming into force.

61 Ibid., art. 14.11.

62 USTR Trade Facts, 'Free Trade with Bahrain', op. cit., p. 91.

The first impression is that US participation with Bahrain in revising its current laws or introducing new laws to meet its obligations under the FTA seems reasonable and sensible, since Bahrain readily acknowledges that it is severely lacking in the legislative, administrative and judicial expertise necessary to fast-track its intellectual property protection regimes to a standard comparable with developed countries. However, this US strategy also can ensure that the current Bahraini laws will be amended or written according to the US formula. The United States, through the USTR and its system of trade-specific advisory committees, can draw upon a complex and sophisticated infrastructure with numerous levels of legal and technical expertise, which Bahrain cannot hope to come anywhere near to matching in the defence and protection of its own interests.

8.3.4 The US–Oman FTA

Following completion of the Bahrain FTA, the USTR quickly notified Congress (in November 2004) of its intention to negotiate with Oman and the UAE on their respective FTAs. The USTR subsequently announced that negotiations would commence in March 2005, and that:

> These FTAs [with Bahrain and Oman] will build on those that we already have with Jordan and Morocco, as well as the FTA that we have recently signed with Bahrain . . . these FTAs will directly benefit the United States . . . a comprehensive FTA with Oman and the UAE will generate job opportunities for US companies, farmers and ranchers, help create jobs in the United States, and help American consumers save money while offering them more consumer choices.[63]

Because of the negative reaction among some of the GCC member States to the way that the Bahrain FTA was conducted and presented as a *fait accompli* to the GCC, a degree of reluctance initially appeared to develop in Oman and the UAE about entering into an FTA as willingly as did Bahrain. In December 2004, after the differences emerged within the GCC member States over Bahrain's FTA, the Omani Minister for Economy was reported in the local press as saying that it was too soon to say whether it would seek a free trade agreement with the United States.[64]

However, these early misgivings and expressions of cynicism did not stand in the way of the negotiations, which commenced in March 2005 and proceeded apace. The FTA took just seven months to negotiate and conclude, marginally longer than

63 Acting USTR Allgeier (2005), 'United States to Begin Free Trade Negotiations This Week with the United Arab Emirates and Oman', USTR Press Release, 8 March 2005, p. 2. See also 'Oman–US FTA: What's the Deal?', *Oman Economic Review Online*, March 2005, available at www.oeronline. com/php/2005_march/cover.php, last accessed 26 May 2017.

64 'Oman cautious on US Trade Talks', *Arab News*, 30 November 2004, available at www.arabnews.com/search/site/Oman%20Cautious%20on%20US%20Trade%20Talks%E2%80%99%2C, last accessed 13 June 2017.

the Jordan and Bahrain FTAs.[65] The Omani Minister of Commerce and Industry, H E Maqbool bin Ali Sultan, stated that the agreement 'will consolidate, slowly define and further strengthen the existing economic and trade relations between our two countries'. His use of the qualifier 'slowly' in respect of redefining the relationship between Oman and the United States was perhaps expressing a note of caution and reservation about the FTA and its overall benefits to Oman.[66]

The intellectual property chapter (Chapter 15) of the Oman FTA builds on its regional predecessors, to the extent that, with the exception of a few key provisions discussed below, it replicates the Bahrain text. Oman's Chapter 15 reproduces virtually word for word the text of the intellectual property chapter in the Bahrain FTA; of the 88 clauses in the Oman chapter, 76 are identical to the corresponding Bahrain FTA chapter. Of the remaining 12 clauses, only seven include changes of any substance, namely those dealing with:

- public availability of information on trademark applications (art. 15.2.12);
- precedence of trademarks over similar GIs (art. 15.2.13);
- protection for well-known marks against other trademarks and GIs (art. 15.2.14);
- extension of copyright periods of protection (art. 15.4.4);
- exclusion of animals from patentability (art. 15.8.20);
- omission of explicit provision for patentability of plants (art. 15.8);
- maintenance of inventories of seized infringing goods and materials (art. 15.10.27).

The Oman FTA requires both parties to accede to the same international protection treaties representing TRIPS-plus standards, as required by the Bahrain FTA. However, there are a few crucial areas where the two FTAs are not identical – where, on the one hand, the Oman FTA provisions go beyond those achieved by the Bahrain FTA, and where, on the other hand, it has not adopted further enhanced standards as enshrined in the Bahrain FTA.

Trademarks and geographical indications (GIs)

ITAC-15 considered that, at the time of its completion, the Oman FTA provided the greatest degree of protection for well-known marks yet provided in an FTA.[67]

65 The Oman FTA consists of 21 chapters covering the same subject areas as the Bahrain FTA. Chapter 15 addresses intellectual property rights and again represents a significant component of the FTA.

66 'Washington Seals Trade Agreement with Oman', as reported in the *Financial Times* (London), 4 October 2005.

67 ITAC-15 (2005), 'The U.S.–Oman Free Trade Agreement (FTA) The Intellectual Property Provisions', November 15, available at https://ustr.gov/archive/assets/Trade_Agreements/Bilateral/Oman_FTA/Reports/asset_upload_file124_8402.pdf, last accessed 26 May 2017.

It includes provision for owners of well-known marks to prohibit or cancel registrations of marks that are identical or similar to the well-known mark. This protection extends not only to the registration of conflicting marks but also to the use of such marks. It also extends protection for well-known marks so as to prevent infringement by GIs as well as other trademarks, a provision that is not included in the Bahrain FTA. The Oman FTA reinforces the US position on trademarks and GIs, and squarely subordinates the latter in relation to the former. In so doing it removes the special status or provision for a preferential system of protection, as advocated vigorously by the European Union collectively and most European states individually, and enshrined in TRIPS Articles 22 and 23, but which has been opposed by the United States.

While the Morocco, Jordan and Bahrain FTAs all include provision for improving the protection of trademarks at the expense of GIs, the Oman FTA takes this protection even further by introducing additional provisions in favour of trademarks. The FTA introduces an obligation to refuse to protect or recognise a GI where it is likely to cause confusion with a trademark which is already registered or under application for registration, or which is already in use in good faith, or which has already become well known.[68] Further, the FTA extends the definition of a GI, for the purposes of the FTA, to include signs which apply to marks generally and geographical indicia in addition to the actual names of geographical places.[69] In so doing, it increases the scope of geographically related names or terms susceptible to non-protection or to trademark precedence, and thereby even further protects the priority status of trademarks over GIs. In some respects, Jordan, Oman and Bahrain have become pawns in the ongoing differences of opinion between the United States and the European Union over the nature of protection for GIs. It is most likely that the United States will argue, as it is now doing with other areas of intellectual property protection, that these provisions as enshrined in its FTAs with a number of countries represent the modern international standard in respect of GIs and their relationship to trademarks and their consequent restricted degree of protection.

Copyright

The major advance of the Oman FTA over the Jordan and Bahrain FTAs is that it further extends the term of protection of a work (including a photographic

68 Oman FTA, art. 15.2.13(a).

69 The footnote to the FTA, art. 15.2.4 describes geographical indications for the purpose of Chapter 15 as 'indications that identify a good as originating in the territory of a Party, or a region or locality in that territory, where a given quality, reputation, or other characteristic of the good is essentially attributable to its geographical origin. Any sign or combination of signs (such as words – including geographical and personal names, as well as letters, numerals, figurative elements and colors, including single colors), in any form whatsoever, shall be eligible to be a geographical indication.'

work), performance or phonogram. While it retains the same term as exists in the Bahrain FTA for a natural person, it extends beyond the Bahrain FTA provisions by providing for a term:

(a) not less than 95 years from the end of the calendar year of the first authorised publication of the work, performance or phonogram; or
(b) failing such authorised publication within 25 years from creation of the work, not less than 120 years from the end of the calendar year of the creation of the work, performance or phonogram.[70]

Both these terms far exceed the term of protection as provided in TRIPS, and also exceed the 70-year term included in the Bahrain FTA. They also exceed the terms for which the IIPA argued in its submission to the USTR prior to the start of the FTA negotiations. The IIPA argued that, given developments in communications media which were making cross-border transmissions the norm, it was essential that all countries further harmonise the term of protection on a global basis; accordingly, it sought the same terms of protection that it had sought for the Bahrain FTA – namely, not less than 70 years and 95 years respectively.[71] The USTR clearly took heed of the IIPA's arguments, but pushed for further concessions from Oman in the negotiations.

Patents

ITAC-15 comments that the Oman FTA generally provides strong patent protection. However, Oman has not retained the express provision in the Bahraini and Moroccan Agreements to the effect that each party shall make patents available for plant inventions, much to the marked disappointment of ITAC-15. Instead, Oman has simply reaffirmed the general statement of TRIPS Article 27.1 – that is, that patents shall be available for all inventions in any field of technology which are new, inventive and industrially applicable.[72] It also confirms that patents will be available for new uses of or methods of using known products.

Although this strategy may give Oman some discretionary provision in respect of future patents on plant varieties or form, or plant-derived inventions, it still tends to continue a shift of emphasis on patentable inventions from an exclusive focus to an inclusive focus – that is, an invention may be presumably deemed patentable unless there is express provision to the contrary. Nevertheless, extending the parameters of patentability to be as inclusive as possible by providing both general statement and express provision was an important issue for the United States in the

70 Oman FTA, art. 15.4.4.

71 IIPA testimony before the 'Public Hearing Concerning Proposed United States–Oman Free Trade Agreement, Friday January 14, 2005, Before the Trade Policy Staff Committee', Washington, DC, pp. 5–6, available at www.iipawebsite.com/rbi/2005_Jan5_Oman.pdf, last accessed 26 May 2017.

72 Oman FTA, art. 15.8.1.

FTA negotiations. Oman's stand caused ITAC-15 to express its serious concerns, describing the stand as 'a disappointing trend'.[73] To minimise further damage to the US position, it urged the USTR to pressure Oman to reform its patents system to meet its commitments under the FTA as soon as possible.

The removal of the express provision in respect of plants either from patentability or from patentability exclusion also maintains the status quo of providing protection within a *sui generis* framework of its discrete UPOV-based law, as permitted by TRIPS.

Enforcement

In respect of patent infringements, the Oman FTA requires the parties to provide its judicial authorities with the power to award damages of up to three times the actual damages, unless there exceptional circumstances that should be taken into account. This provision, which appeared in the Morocco FTA but was omitted from the Jordan and Bahrain FTAs, meets with the approval of ITAC-15[74] in that it both increases the range of options available to the judicial authorities and increases the deterrent value of the sanction options available.[75]

The Oman FTA adds a new (and welcome, in the view of ITAC-15) provision which does not appear in the Bahrain FTA and other earlier FTAs. It requires each party to maintain an inventory of goods and equipment proposed to be destroyed, and permits the delay in the destruction of these goods and equipment so that they may be used as evidence in civil and administrative cases.[76] Hence the provision constituting the preservation of evidence adds another element of deterrence to the enforcement system.

Transitional arrangements

The intellectual property chapter of the Oman FTA does not include any transitional arrangements. Hence, the FTA was due to come into immediate effect after it has been approved by both governments.

With only minor exceptions, the Oman FTA now represents the highest standards of protection in the areas of copyright, trademarks, GIs and enforcement, and will no doubt be held up as the new international standard for future FTAs. It is not surprising, therefore, that the US Advisory Committee for Trade and Policy Negotiations urged the Administration to ensure that the Oman FTA was signed into law as quickly as possible so that American farms, factories, service providers and consumers could begin to receive the benefits of the FTA at the earliest possible time.[77]

73 ITAC-15 (2005), op. cit., p. 15.
74 Ibid., p. 19.
75 Oman FTA, art. 15.10.27(d).
76 Ibid, art. 15.10.27(d). See also ITAC-15 (2005), op. cit., p. 22.
77 ITAC-15 (2005), op. cit., Report Covering Letter.

8.3.5 The US FTA negotiations with the other GCC member States

Negotiations on a US–UAE FTA commenced in March 2005 – at around the same time as the Oman negotiations. As the Oman FTA negotiations were being concluded, significant differences were emerging between the negotiating teams, with the UAE indicating that US insistence on a range of labour, intellectual property and human rights issues, even at so early a stage in the negotiations, warranted a call for a cautious approach. But these early misgivings and expressions of cynicism did not stand in the way of the two sets of negotiations proceeding apace. However, by early 2006, the UAE negotiations had stalled.

Although neither negotiating team would admit as much, a significant factor in the stalled UAE negotiations appears to have been the furore over the acquisition by a UAE company, Dubai Ports World, of the British Company P&O Ports, which brought with it infrastructure ownership of six US ports. The acquisition, which was consistent with Dubai Ports World's global development and acquisition activity, generated an intense degree of hysteria in some sectors of US government and business that the UAE's ownership of these US ports would constitute a grave risk to US security.

More than three years later and after five major rounds of talks, both sides were still unable to reach agreement on an FTA. The UAE declared in the local Arab press that it would resist pressure by the United States to immediately open its telecommunications sector to foreign investors. In remarks published in the Dubai-based Arab-language paper *Emarat Al Yom*, the UAE Minister for Public Sector Development, Sultan bin Said Al Mansuri, stated in respect of the US telecommunications demand that 'this is rejected, we will not give up one of our rights. We must give the current operators the chance to develop before we allow new ones in.'[78]

Soon thereafter both parties announced that they were unable to complete FTA negotiations under the existing time frame for the US Administration's fast-track trade promotion authority. Nevertheless, in a display of diplomatic cordiality, the United States announced that both sides agree that they remain committed to completing FTA negotiations at some later date.[79]

In similar vein to the UAE reluctance to concede to unacceptable US demands, Qatar took a firm stance in respect of its negotiations. The Qatari local press reported that Qatar had frozen bilateral free trade talks with the United States because Washington was imposing preconditions that were not in Qatar's interests. In particular, the Qatari FTA negotiators raised objections to US demands for full access for US investors to Qatar's services and energy industries and 100 per cent foreign ownership of Qatari companies. The then Qatari Ambassador to the United States, Nasser bin Hamad al Khalifa, suggested that the WTO agreements were sufficient

78 Ibid.

79 Shakir Husain, 'Informal US–UAE Trade Talks to Go On', *Gulf News*, 12 March 2007, available at www.uaeinteract.com/docs/Informal_US-UAE_trade_talks_to_go_on/24368.htm, last accessed 26 May 2017.

for mutual trade and investment between any two member countries. The Ambassador also suggested that Qatar 'does not need a free trade agreement with the US'.[80]

The Qatari government's stance at the time was that, with one of the strongest global economies and one of the highest per capita income rates in the world, it did not need either US financial support or preferential treatment for entry into US markets to enable its economy to continue to grow. It could therefore take a strong bargaining position in respect of US negotiating points, to the extent of walking away from the negotiating table if it was not satisfied – a situation which the United States may well feel unused to in recent times.

8.4 Other GCC FTAs

The concluded United States and proposed EU Agreements stand in stark contrast to the other agreements entered into or currently being negotiated by the GCC, in respect of raised intellectual property protection provisions and standards.

By early 2017, the GCC has concluded just two FTAs, namely with Singapore and the EFTA group of European states (Iceland, Liechtenstein, Norway and Switzerland). The GCC–Singapore FTA was signed in Doha, Qatar, on 15 December 2008. It is seen as a milestone agreement, particularly since it is the first FTA signed by the GCC with a non-Arab country.[81] It is described as a comprehensive agreement[82] that encompasses trade in goods and services, rules of origin, customs procedures and government procurement among others. However, it does not contain any specification or even mention of intellectual property rights. In fact, the Singapore government website on the FTA, as an indication of design rather than oversight, advises: 'Intellectual Property – This chapter is currently not covered under this Agreement.'[83]

The GCC's FTA with the EFTA states was signed in June 2009, and came into force on July 2014. The Agreement covers a broad range of areas including trade in goods, trade in services, government procurement and competition, and provides for dispute settlement through arbitration. One of the stated objectives of the FTA is 'to ensure adequate and effective protection of intellectual property rights, pursuant to Chapter 5'.[84] The parties essentially confirm the application of TRIPs provisions, and commit to concluding negotiations on an intellectual

80 As quoted by *Kuwait News Agency*, 'US–Qatari negotiations on free trade agreement frozen', 29 April 2006, at www.kuna.net.kw/ArticlePrintPage.aspx?id=1656345&language=en, last accessed 26 May 2017.

81 See Singapore Government, 'Overview of the Gulf Cooperation Council (GSFTA)', at www.iesingapore.gov.sg/-/media/IE-Singapore/Files/Publications/Brochures-Free-Trade-Agreements/FTAs_GCCGSFTA_FA.ashx, last accessed 26 May 2017.

82 Ibid.

83 Ibid.

84 Free Trade Agreement between the EFTA States and the Member States of the Co-Operation Council for the Arab States of the Gulf, art. 1.2(d), available at <http://www.efta.int/media/documents/legal-texts/free-trade-relations/gulf-cooperation-council-GCC/EFTA-GCC%20Free%20Trade%20Agreement.pdf, last accessed 26 May 2017.

property-related Annex not later than two years after the entry into force of the Agreement.[85] In the meantime, a special consultation mechanism is foreseen in case of problems in the area of intellectual property rights affecting trade conditions between the Parties. It appears that there have been some difficulties with its practical application, with some GCC member States countries not yet implementing the Agreement due to what has been termed 'some technical issues'.[86]

The GCC is currently in negotiations with Japan, Australia and China over potential FTAs, and has concluded FTA negotiations with New Zealand. The negotiations with Japan commenced in May 2006, but have been suspended since mid-2007. The negotiations with Australia commenced in 2007, with intellectual property issues being included in the initial negotiation areas. These negotiations halted in June 2009, but recommenced in mid-2014.

As both these agreements have not yet progressed beyond the negotiation stages, there is little guidance or information (official or otherwise) on the positions of each of the parties. However, the Australian Government commentary on the early-stage negotiations with the GCC included the remark: 'A detailed exchange of views on how intellectual property rights should be reflected in the FTA revealed considerable differences in our respective approaches.'[87] Both parties have expressed their desire to conclude and sign an FTA during 2017.

The negotiations with New Zealand were concluded in 2009, and the draft agreement has been reportedly undergoing technical and legal formalisation ever since. However, it appears that intellectual property rights were not one of the agreed key negotiating planks.[88]

8.4.1 The proposed China–GCC FTA

The nature and significance of a China–GCC should not be underestimated. China has overtaken the United States as the largest exporter to the GCC, with exports growing to $60 billion a year in the last decade. *The Economist* Intelligence Unit predicts that by 2020, China will be the GCC's most important economic partner.[89] Similarly, the interest of both parties in reaching a mutually satisfactory agreement should also receive close consideration.

The GCC and China concluded a Framework Agreement on Economic, Trade, Investment and Technology Cooperation in July 2004. The Agreement provided

85 Ibid., art. 5.1(1).

86 European Free Trade Association, 'GCC FTA, General', available at www.efta.int/free-trade/free-trade-agreements/gcc, last accessed 26 May 2017.

87 Australian Government Department of Foreign Affairs and Trade (2017), 'Australia–Gulf Cooperation Council (GCC) FTA', at http://dfat.gov.au/trade/agreements/agccfta/Pages/australia-gulf-cooperation-council-gcc-fta.aspx#about, last accessed 26 May 2017.

88 See New Zealand Government Foreign Affairs and Trade (2017), 'NZ Inc Gulf Cooperation Council (GCC) strategy', available at www.mfat.govt.nz/assets/_securedfiles/NZ-Inc-stategy/NZ-Inc-GCC/NZInc-Strategy-GCC-09-2013.pdf, last accessed 26 May 2017.

89 'The GCC in 2020: Outlook for the Gulf and the Global Economy', *The Economist* Intelligence Unit, March 2009, p. 13, available at www.graphics.eiu.com/marketing/pdf/Gulf2020.pdf, last accessed 26 May 2017.

for the launching of negotiations on the creation of a China–GCC Free Trade Area.[90] A number of negotiating rounds were held intermittently over the next five years. However, negotiations were suspended during 2009 as part of the GCC's decision to halt all its ongoing FTA talks with countries and regional organisations. It is not known whether intellectual property figured in these rounds of negotiations, either in its own right or as a subset of negotiations in respect of trade in goods. However, it seems that intellectual property protection was an issue at least with some sectors from the GCC side. The *Gulf News*, a leading Gulf newspaper, was reporting in late 2006 that Chinese products were already flooding Gulf markets, many of which were counterfeit products brought in by Dubai-based Chinese traders.[91] The paper questioned how the GCC–China FTA would deal with the issue.

Negotiations recommenced in early 2014 according to Chinese media services.[92] At the same time, the negotiations agreed on cooperation for the period 2014 to 2017, which includes cooperation in politics, trade, energy, environmental protection and climate, culture, education, health and sports. However, intellectual property still does not seem to be included – in its own right, at least.

In light of the previous history of China's FTAs, the absence of any real history in respect of GCC FTAs, and the early China–GCC FTA negotiations, the likely position that each party might take in respect of intellectual property protection and the agreed outcome as enshrined in the eventual text are rather difficult to assess. The proposed China–GCC FTA negotiation agenda covers trade in goods and services, investment, and economic and technical cooperation. Intellectual property issues rank highly in a number of these broad areas, and are generally an indispensable part of a contemporary FTA. Hence, it is reasonable to presume that their provisions in the proposed China–GCC FTA should accord with current generally accepted standards and requirements.

But, largely based on China's FTA profile, a number of inferences can still be drawn. First, in the absence of a GCC profile, the nature of the form of the agreement (as distinct from its substantive content) is likely to be more influenced by the Chinese side. And two particular features of the China FTA profile are the diversity of the agreements in terms of their respective coverage and format, and the concise nature or brevity of the agreements when it comes to intellectual property references. And this could be reflected in the proposed China–GCC FTA.

The importance that both parties attach to intellectual property rights and their protection in the proposed FTA may be demonstrated by whether they are stipulated in the FTA's objectives. Inclusion in the Agreement's objectives will mean

90 Chen Mo (2011), 'Exploring Economic Relations between China and the GCC States', 5(4), *Journal of Middle Eastern and Islamic Studies (in Asia)*, pp. 88–105.

91 Saifur Rahman (2006), 'GCC-China free trade deal by 2007', *Gulf News*, 8 September (online), at http://gulfnews.com/business/economy/gcc-china-free-trade-deal-by-2007-1.254236, last accessed 26 May 2017.

92 Mu Xuechan, 'China, Gulf states outline 2014-2017 cooperation', *Xinhua*, 17 January 2014, available at http://news.xinhuanet.com/english/china/2014-01/17/c_126023632.htm, last accessed 26 May 2017.

that both parties perceive them as enjoying a higher priority which will warrant a greater level of commitment to their effective introduction, implementation and ongoing maintenance. The core objectives of the proposed Agreement may be trade in goods and services, energy and foreign investment, but these issues involve and are interwoven with intellectual property at both the micro and macro level. But this might also be viewed as meaning intellectual property thus does not required its own specific reference in the objectives.

One type of intellectual property rights that could feature in the proposed FTA could be those encompassing traditional knowledge and cultural heritage – areas which do not fit into the general contemporary multilateral intellectual property protection framework. They are not addressed in TRIPs or in the current WIPO treaties, but they involve copyright, genetic resources, geographical indications, plant varieties, and more. Both China and all the GCC member States possess rich, complex and diverse cultural heritages developed over many centuries but still current and active. They have established comprehensive statutory and cultural regimes to record, protect and preserve their cultures and have joined a range of international conventions. Traditional knowledge and cultural heritage recognition and protection figure in a number of China FTAs, namely those with New Zealand, Peru, Costa Rica, Korea and Australia. China and the GCC have the opportunity through their proposed FTA not only to provide an appropriate level of protection for their own cultures to be acknowledged and protected, but also to make a strong contribution to the development of the 'contemporary international standard' of protection for traditional knowledge and cultural heritage. This requires not only a strong statement on protection but also a comprehensive one. This strategy is akin to that followed by developed countries striving for highest possible levels of protection for copyright works with FTAs that provide for all-encompassing protection with reduced exceptions, greatly increased sanctions and longer terms of protection.

Both China and the GCC appear keen to conclude an Agreement within the near future. Media speculation suggests that the will on both sides to come to a successful conclusion could mean that such agreement could be finalised sometime in 2017. Charles Freeman, former US Ambassador to Saudi Arabia, has commented on the nature of the relationship between the GCC member States and China, which helps to explain this keenness, as follows:

> The Arabs see a partner who will buy their oil without demanding that they accept a foreign ideology, abandon their way of life or make other choices they would rather avoid. They see (in China) a country that is far away and has no imperial agenda in their region, but which is internationally influential and likely in time to be militarily powerful.[93]

93 R. Bailey (2013), 'Is China set to become the GCC's most important economic partner by 2020? And what does this mean for the region?', *Gulf Business*, 16 April, available at http://gulfbusiness.com/china-and-gcc-growing-ties/#.ViEQUi6gyoM, last accessed 26 May 2010.

8.5 The role of the USTR and the Annual Special 301 Report

As mentioned earlier, pressure to adopt TRIPS-plus standards of intellectual property protection can be applied indirectly through the coercive use of a threatened or actual withdrawal of preferential trade provisions or imposition of trade-related sanctions or retaliation to 'persuade' trading partners to adopt TRIPS-plus intellectual property protection standards. And an example of this indirect application is the role of the USTR and its use of the Special 301 provisions as a tool to pressure states to adopt standards of protection much higher than those required by TRIPS.

The US trade and investment policy, which encompasses intellectual property standards, is the responsibility of the Office of the United States Trade Representative (USTR). Created by the US Congress in the 1962 Trade Expansion Act, the Office is authorised to set and administer overall trade policy, including all matters in respect of the WTO, bilateral and multilateral trade and investment issues, trade-related intellectual property protection issues and administrative responsibility for the Generalised System of Preferences (GSP) in respect of tariffs on imports, and Section 301 (including Special 301) complaints against foreign trade practices which the USTR considers to be unfair to its own interests.

As a key part of its international monitoring of the activities of the nation's trading partners, the USTR reports annually on the conduct of different countries in respect of their treatment of intellectual property rights which are owned by US business or citizens, or in which they have an interest. The Annual Special 301 Report on intellectual property rights represents the coercive element in the US bilateral strategy. The Report is conducted pursuant to Section182 of the Trade Act 1974, as amended by the Omnibus Trade and Competitiveness Act 1988 and the Uruguay Round Agreement Act (URAA) 1994. Under the Special 301 provisions of Section 182, the USTR identifies those countries that it considers deny adequate and effective protection for intellectual property rights, or deny fair and equitable market access for US businesses that rely on intellectual property protection. The Special 301 provision was amended in the URAA to clarify that a country could be found to deny adequate and effective intellectual property protection even if it was in compliance with its obligations under TRIPS.[94] This clarification meant in effect that the USTR could take unilateral trade action against a trading partner which it deemed to have inadequate (by US standards) national intellectual property laws, even where the WTO Dispute Settlement Body had absolved the trading partner of any liability under international trade law.[95]

Under the Special 301 provisions, the USTR has created three levels of 'egregious activity' in respect of US intellectual property rights, namely the Priority Foreign Country, Priority Watch List and Watch List. Countries that are

94 USTR, *2003 Special 301 Report*, 'Statutory Authority', p. 9.

95 Douglas Rosenthal (1998), 'A Comment on the Special 301 Annual Review', 1, *Journal of World Intellectual Property*, p. 743.

deemed to have the most onerous or egregious acts, policies or practices, resulting in the greatest adverse impact (actual or potential) on US products, are designated as a Priority Foreign Country and could potentially be faced with a unilateral withdrawal of US trade benefits or the lodgment of a complaint by the United States for resolution through the formal WTO Dispute Settlement process. Placement on the Priority Watch List or Watch List indicates that the USTR considers that particular problems exist with respect to the protection or enforcement of US intellectual property rights or market access for US interests. Countries placed on the Priority Watch List also become the focus of increased bilateral attention in respect of the areas of US concern. The Watch List indicates that countries have practices that meet some of the US requirements but still need close monitoring in implementing their commitments with regard to intellectual property protection and market access for US products and interests.

A Special 301 listing may not necessarily lead directly to some form of retaliatory action, but the coercive influence and impact of a listing, particularly when associated with an out-of-cycle country review, can be such that it may still lead to a TRIPS-plus consequence without the necessity for the threatened action to take place.

However, a certain degree of caution should be observed in trying to establish too close a causal association between these events above, since other factors – not least of which are those arising from international strategic alliances and rewards for 'friends' in the war against international terrorism – can also impact on the appearance, reappearance or disappearance of a state from the Special 301 listings. While it may be easy to establish an obvious causal association between a Special 301 listing and the subsequent commitment to a bilateral agreement, promulgation of a national intellectual property law or accession to a post-TRIPS convention, a Special 301 listing can still play a role in achieving a less obvious but desirable outcome in the greater political context.[96]

The undue influence of the US intellectual property industry lobby groups upon the USTR and upon the direction of US trade policy and intellectual property

96 Perhaps not entirely coincidental in this regard was Bahrain's removal from the Special 301 Listing in 1999 and the completion of the transfer of the command base for the US Navy Fifth Fleet from Saudi Arabia to the southern part of Bahrain. In August 2001, the United States designated Bahrain as a 'major non-NATO ally', an indication not only of a strong desire by the United States to strengthen military ties with Bahrain but also the importance of Bahrain in the US global military strategy. Similarly, Qatar's removal from a Special 301 Listing in 2003 coincided with the transfer in early 2003 of the US Combined Air Operations Center from the Prince Sultan Air Base in Saudi Arabia to Qatar, after Saudi Arabia directed that a strong US air force presence on Saudi air bases was no longer necessary following the lifting of the no-fly zones in southern Iraq and the Saudi refusal to allow the bases to be used for possible air strikes against Iraq after 9/11. 'US pulls out of Saudi Arabia' (2003), *BBC News*, 29 April, available at www.news.bbc.co.uk/2/hi/world/middle_east/2984547.stm, last accessed 26 May 2017.

protection strategy has been extensively documented and debated.[97] They are intimately involved in the Special 301 assessment process (as well as the bilateral agreement and FTA process) and exert considerable influence on the nature and direction of the Report and their recommendations – their views are often reflected in the final decisions on Special 301 listings. They actively lobby the USTR and Congress. Some are also particularly influential in the Gulf States and maintain an active regional presence, operating local infringement 'hotlines', initiating prosecutions and participating in local enforcement and business re-education activities. Foremost among these lobby groups are the aforementioned Business Software Alliance (BSA), the International Intellectual Property Alliance (IIPA) and particularly the Pharmaceutical Researchers and Manufacturers of America (PhRMA), all of which interact directly with the Gulf national governments at the most senior levels.[98] At times they appear to assume pseudo-state authority in their dealings with the States, making representations direct to State rulers, ministers and authorities.

The USTR started reviewing the Arabian Peninsula States in 1989, with Saudi Arabia appearing in the Priority Watch List in that year, followed by the UAE on the Watch List in 1993, and the other States (with the exception of Jordan) making their first appearances in 1995. Yemen has not been reviewed by the USTR and so does not appear on any listing.

Table 8.1 shows the record of the Gulf States in being included, or otherwise, in the Special 301 Annual Report since 1995.

Bahrain was first placed on the USTR Special 301 Watch List in 1995 and was retained there until 1998 because the USTR considered that its intellectual property laws were not consistent with its international obligations under TRIPS, and because high piracy levels continued while enforcement was weak. However, because of what it considered to be concerted enforcement actions throughout 1998 and into 1999, the USTR removed Bahrain in 1999. Bahrain was the first of the GCC member States to succeed in being removed, and has not reappeared on any list since.

At first glance, Bahrain's removal and non-reappearance is hard to fathom and difficult to justify, if viewed in the narrow context of domestic standards of

97 See, for example, Assafa Endeshaw, 'The Paradox of Intellectual Property Lawmaking in the New Millennium: Universal Templates as Terms of Surrender for Non-industrial Nations; Piracy as an Offshoot', available at https://papers.ssrn.com/sol3/papers.cfm?abstract_id=291692, last accessed 26 May 2017. See also Sangeeta Shashikant, 'The Politics of United States Free Trade Agreements', 167–168, *Third World Network*, available at www.ghwatch.org/sites/www.ghwatch.org/files/freetrade.pdf, last accessed 26 May 2017.

98 According to its website, 'PhRMA, the Pharmaceutical Research and Manufacturers of America represents the country's leading innovative biopharmaceutical research companies. Our members are devoted to discovering and developing medicines that enable patients to live longer, healthier and more productive lives.' Its members include the world's leading pharmaceutical companies. It represents the interests of both US and other pharmaceutical multinationals from the UK, Switzerland and France in the Gulf. See www.phrma.org/about, last accessed 31 March 2017.

TABLE 8.1 US Special 301 Listings of the Arabian Peninsula States 1996–2016

	1995	*1996*	*1997*	*1998*	*1999*	*2000*	*2001*	*2002*	*2003*	*2004*	*2006*	*2008*	*2010*	*2016*
Bahrain	Watch	Watch	Watch	Watch	–	–	–	–	–	–	–	–	–	–
Jordan	–	–	Watch	Watch	Watch	–	–	–	–	–	–	–	–	–
Kuwait	Watch	Watch	Priority Watch	Priority Watch	Priority Watch	Watch	Watch	Watch	Priority Watch	Priority Watch	Watch	Watch	Watch	Priority Watch
Oman	Watch	Watch	Watch	Watch	Watch	–	–	–	–	–	–	–	–	–
Qatar	Oo	Oo	Watch	Watch	Watch	–	Watch	–	–	–	–	–	–	–
Saudi Arabia	Watch	Watch	Watch	Watch	Watch	Watch	Watch	Watch	Watch	Watch	Watch	Watch	–	–
UAE	Watch	Watch	Watch	Watch	Watch	–	Watch	–	–	–	–	–	–	–
Yemen	Not assessed by USTR under Special 301													

Source: compiled by the authors from USTR Annual Special 301 Reports, 1995–2016

Note: 'Oo' – other observation. Generally used for initial entries, as an informal listing, where the 'egregious activity' is not quite to the Watch level

intellectual property protection and when compared with the performance of the other Arabian Peninsula States. When the USTR last included Bahrain in its Special 301 Listing in 1998, Bahrain's copyright and trademark laws still dated from the early 1990s and had not been brought into TRIPS compliance, and patent protection for pharmaceutical products was only available in practice through re-registration of patents filed in the UK (a legacy of its 1955 pre-independence law). Furthermore, end-user business software piracy was still almost 90 per cent according to US industry estimates, giving Bahrain the second-worst piracy rate of any Gulf state after Oman.[99] Even in 2003 its software piracy rate was still only marginally better than then worst-performing Kuwait. Nevertheless, its removal coincided with the commencement and successful conclusion of negotiations with the United States for a bilateral investment treaty, the second regional State to enter into such an agreement after Jordan (1997). Its removal further coincided with the emergence, albeit only in draft form, of a comprehensive suite of individual intellectual property laws, which had been prepared with the assistance of WIPO and some of which were largely based on the WIPO model laws.[100] Yet it took another six to seven years before the new copyright and trademarks laws in particular appeared – while the respective pre-TRIPS (and thereby TRIPS non-compliant) 1991 and 1993 laws remained in force.

Jordan first appeared in the Special 310 Watch List in 1997 and remained there until 1999. The 2000 Report does not give any guidance as to Jordan's removal from any listing, although it does advise that Jordan joined the Berne Convention during 1999. The 2000 removal coincides with the commencement of negotiations for the Jordan FTA.

Since its first appearance in the Special 301 Listings in 1995, Kuwait has moved regularly between the Priority Watch List and the Watch List, mainly because of ongoing USTR concerns about the lack of proper copyright legislation and software piracy. Kuwait was elevated from the Watch List to the Priority Watch List in 1998 and remained there in 1999. The 1999 Report described Kuwait as the worst pirate market in the Gulf region and the only WTO country without a copyright law, and threatened to elevate it to Priority Foreign Country status.[101] Kuwait's performance the following year improved sufficiently for it to be removed to the Watch List, where it remained until 2004, when it was again elevated to

99 The data for the 1998 year are available in the BSA, *Eighth Annual Global Piracy Study*, June 2003, p. 7, available at www.bsa.org/country/Research%20and%20Statistics/~/media/Files/Research%20Papers/GlobalStudy/2003/IPR_GlobalStudy2003.ashx, last accessed 26 May 2017.

100 See WTO, Document IP/Q4/BHR/1 (01-6218), 6 December 2001, 2.

101 USTR, *2001 Special 301 Report*, as quoted in the IIPA, '2005 Special 301 Report on Global Copyright Protection and Enforcement', Appendix E, p. 28, available at www.iipawebsite.com/pdf/2001_SPEC301HISTORY.pdf, last accessed 1 March 2017. Also reported in 'Results of 1999 "Special 301" Provisions of 1974 Trade Act Regarding Intellectual Property Protection' (1999), 13, *World Intellectual Property Report*, p. 216.

the Priority Watch List. Kuwait was retained on the Priority Watch List in 2005, because of its continuing high rates of copyright piracy, lack of progress in amending its copyright law to meet international obligations and failure to fully implement the work plan which it had agreed with the United States in 2002 to increase intellectual property rights enforcement. In what the aforementioned critics of the US bilateral strategy would no doubt consider as intrusion into or interference with internal administration of domestic policy, the Report urged Kuwait to make public declarations that piracy would not be tolerated, increase the frequency of raids on suspected infringers, prosecute offenders and impose deterrent sentences, publish the outcomes of raids to deter others and amend its copyright law in the near future to correct its deficiencies.

Kuwait reverted to the Watch list in 2006, and remained there until 2014. The following year it returned to the Priority Watch List and remains there for 2016 because of its failure to make progress on amending its outdated intellectual property laws and because of ineffective enforcement against copyright and trademark infringement.[102] The 2016 Report states that:

> Although Kuwaiti officials initially took steps to resume enforcement following the announcement of the 2014 OCR, effective enforcement actions have reportedly significantly decreased since June 2015, particularly against trade in counterfeit goods. The United States awaits improvements in copyright and trademark enforcement and the passage of long-overdue copyright legislation that is consistent with Kuwait's international commitments. The United States stands ready to work with Kuwait toward resolving these important issues.[103]

Oman was examined by the USTR for the first time in 1995 and raised to the Watch List in 1996, the USTR describing the country's intellectual property protection regime as 'minimal and stagnant'.[104] The USTR retained Oman on the Watch List for the following three years after accusations from US copyright industry lobby groups that Oman's market was 'dominated by piracy' and was 'a haven for pirates fleeing less hospitable neighbouring states'.[105] But within just a few years, and in a remarkable turnaround, Oman progressed from being the worst of the States in terms of intellectual property protection to becoming the best-performing in comparative terms. It reduced its software piracy rate as measured by the BSA

102 USTR, *2016 Special 301 Report* (2016), April 16, p. 46, available at https://ustr.gov/sites/default/files/USTR-2016-Special-301-Report.pdf, last accessed 1 March 2017.

103 Ibid.

104 See IPA (2005), '2005 Special 301 Report on Global Copyright Protection and Enforcement', p. 36, available at www.iipawebsite.com/special301_TOCs/2005_SPEC301_TOC.html, last accessed 26 May 2017.

105 As reported in 'Results of 1998 'Special 301' Provisions of 1974 Trade Act Regarding Intellectual Property Protection' (1998), 12, *World Intellectual Property Report*, p. 201.

from 96 per cent in 1996 to 78 per cent in just five years.[106] During 2000 it promulgated a suite of intellectual property laws which, at that time, was the most comprehensive, modern and TRIPS-compliant among all the States, achieved membership of the WTO and acceded to TRIPS in September of that year. It also acceded to the Patent Cooperation Treaty in February 2001. Accordingly, Oman was removed from the Special 301 List in 2001 and subsequently has not reappeared on any listing.

The USTR first reported on Qatar in 1995 and accorded it a 'Special Mention', a listing repeated in 1996 and 1997, because of the perceived shortcomings in its intellectual property regime. The USTR raised Qatar to the Watch List in 1998 because of US industry concerns that Qatar was becoming a potential 'haven of piracy', and called upon it to legalise the software used in government offices, improve copyright enforcement and implement its TRIPS obligations.[107] Qatar remained on the Watch List for the next two years because of its failure to enact TRIPS-consistent legislation and perceived serious enforcement problems. Despite US copyright industry concerns, the USTR removed Qatar from all lists in 2001, but returned it to the Watch List in 2002 for failure to sign and implement a promised new copyright law. Qatar's removal from any listing in 2003 coincided with the issuance of new copyright and trademark laws during 2002, and the USTR's view that it had instituted improved, sustained enforcement actions against copyright infringement. According to the BSA, Qatar's software piracy rate fell dramatically between 2002 and 2003, from 76 per cent to 63 per cent, arguably one of the better improvements in performance of any Gulf state for those years.[108]

Saudi Arabia was first reviewed by the USTR in 1989 and was immediately placed on the Priority Watch List. It moved regularly between the Priority Watch List and the Watch List between 1989 and 1995 and remained on the Watch List since 1995. The USTR retained Saudi Arabia on the Watch List for several years in the late 1990s, despite recommendations from the US copyright industry that it be elevated to the Priority Watch List for continued piracy, lack of effective and deterrent enforcement actions and a TRIPS-incompatible copyright law. In its report for 2003, the USTR expressed concern over reports that a Saudi company in 2002 had attempted to register unauthorised copies of patented US pharmaceutical products with the Saudi Ministry of Health.[109]

The USTR retained Saudi Arabia on the Watch List for 2005 because it considered that its 2003 copyright law lacked some basic minimum standards required by both TRIPS and the WIPO Internet Treaties, including provision for

106 BSA, *First Annual BSA and IDC Global Software Piracy Study*, July 2004, op. cit., p. 8.
107 See IIPA, '2005 Special 301 Report on Global Copyright Protection and Enforcement', op. cit., p. 37.
108 See BSA, *Eighth Annual BSA Global Piracy Study*, June 2003, op. cit., p. 7.
109 USTR, *2003 Special 301 Report* (2003), April, Saudi Arabia Appendix, available at https://ustr.gov/sites/default/files/2003%20Special%20301%20Report.pdf last accessed 31 May 2017.

destruction of seized goods, materials and machinery, and failure to provide for recovery of litigation costs.[110] It asserted that the US copyright industry reported that piracy rates remained high due to the absence of deterrent penalties and lack of transparency in the enforcement system. The Report also noted that Saudi Arabia's patent registration system was seriously deficient, with a backlog of thousands of applications, a comment it also made in the previous year's report. However, the Report did also acknowledge that Saudi Arabia had been protecting intellectual property rights relating to pharmaceutical products and that there had been no major instances of patent infringement over the last year. As it did with Kuwait, the USTR maintained pressure on Saudi Arabia to comply with its demands by warning that it would also work on these issues through the WTO accession process, the clear implication being that Saudi Arabia would need to accede to US demands in respect of intellectual property protection standards if it wished its accession to the WTO to be approved.

The extent of influence of the intellectual property industry lobby groups is illustrated by the following situation in respect of Saudi Arabia's copyright law. Saudi Arabia introduced extensive changes to the law in 2003, bringing it largely into TRIPS compliance. The law was constructed with the technical and drafting assistance of WIPO's then International Bureau and included deterrent penalties of up to SR500,000 (for repeat offences). Even so, IIPA, which criticised the 1993 law, argued to the USTR that the new 2003 law still 'fails to meet the basic minimum standards of [TRIPS] and fails to fully meet the standards set by the two WIPO "digital" treaties'.[111] IIPA went on to state that 'Saudi Arabia must live up to commitments to bring its copyright system up to adequate standards – both substantive and enforcement – before they should be rewarded with favourable trade treatment and WTO accession'. In similar vein, PhRMA roundly criticised Saudi Arabia's patent enforcement practices as 'having become impossible' and 'Alice in Wonderland', and urged the US Administration to seek comprehensive patent reforms as a condition of Saudi WTO accession.[112] As a consequence, whether directly or indirectly attributable to the pressures brought to bear by IIPA and PhRMA on the US Administration, Saudi Arabia for the time

110 USTR, *2005 Special 301 Report* (2005), p. 46, available at https://ustr.gov/sites/default/files/2005%20Special%20301%20Report.pdf, last accessed 26 May 2017. In fact, the Saudi Copyright Law art. 22.1(4) provides for confiscation of all copies of the infringing work as well as all materials used or intended to be used in the infringements, while art. 22.4 provides for the award of financial compensation. The Saudi authorities have also shown their willingness to seize and destroy infringing material, as evidenced by a series of publicised destruction events in late 2004 and early 2005.

111 IIPA submission on Saudi Arabia to the USTR for the *2004 Special 301 Report*, available at www.iipawebsite.com/rbc/2004/2004SPEC301SAUDIARABIA.pdf, last accessed 26 May 2017.

112 PhRMA (2004), Submission on the USTR *2004 Special 301 Report*, available at www.phrma.org/international/resources/13.02.2004.600.cfm, last accessed 20 December 2010 (hard copy on file with authors).

being remained unfulfilled in respect of its aspirations for WTO membership and continued to be listed on the Special 301 Report Watch List. Saudi Arabia eventually achieved WTO membership in December 2005.

The USTR retained Saudi Arabia on the Watch List until 2009. In 2009, the USTR noted that a locally based US–Saudi Intellectual Property Rights Working Group had commenced working, which had resulted in progress on certain intellectual property rights issues. Saudi Arabia had also made progress in enforcement by increasing the number of raids and prosecutions, and improving transparency through the Ministry website. However, Saudi Arabia still needed to make further improvements to its enforcement system by encouraging courts to impose deterrent-level sentences, including jail sentences.[113] The 2010 Report noted that Saudi Arabia had significantly improved its intellectual property rights protection and enforcement regime and as a result had been removed from the Watch List in February 2010.[114]

The UAE's experience with the Special 301 Listings not only strikingly illustrates the nature of the USTR's strategy and operation in respect of individual countries but also is a prime example of the undue influence that certain industry lobby groups exert in contributing each year to the direction of the USTR Report. Throughout the UAE's period of inclusion in the Special 301 Listing, it has experienced ongoing pressures to comply with US requirements, first in respect of copyright protection and then for patent protection and marketing exclusivity for pharmaceutical products, which at times has more than offset the progress that it has made in other areas of intellectual property protection. Despite being generally considered to have had the best performance in the Middle East since 1995 for tackling copyright piracy, the UAE was on the Special 301 Watch List almost continuously since its first review in 1991 until 2001.

In 1997, the BSA recommended that the UAE be removed from any Special 301 Listing because of the UAE's record of reducing software piracy, according to the BSA's benchmark annual piracy review, from 86 per cent to a remarkable 50 per cent over the preceding triennium. The USTR acknowledged that piracy of motion pictures and sound recordings had been largely eliminated in the UAE and efforts to reduce software piracy had increased with considerable success.[115] However, it retained the UAE on the Watch List on the recommendation of PhRMA because its patent law exempted medicines and pharmaceutical compounds from protection and contained compulsory licensing provisions which

113 USTR (2009), *2009 Special 301 Report*, April 30, available at https://ustr.gov/sites/default/files/2009%20Special%20301%20Report%20FINAL.pdf, last accessed 26 May 2017, p. 31.

114 USTR (2010), *2010 Special 301 Report*, 30 April, p. 6, available at https://ustr.gov/issue-areas/intellectual-property/special-301/2010-special-301-review, last accessed 2 2017.

115 As quoted in IIPA, '2005 Special 301 Report on Global Copyright Protection and Enforcement', Appendix E, op. cit., pp. 56–7, available at www.iipawebsite.com/pdf/2005SPEC301HISTORICALSUMMARY.pdf, last accessed 13 June 2017.

the USTR deemed to be onerous, notwithstanding the fact that these exemptions and provisions were consistent with TRIPS.

Between 1998 and 2001, despite the US copyright industry and IIPA recommendations that it be removed, the USTR kept the UAE on its Watch List. The USTR noted that efforts to reduce software piracy had 'not been sufficient to reduce the level of illegal activity' (1998), that there remained deficiencies in the area of patents, particularly in respect of protection for pharmaceutical products subject to patent protection, and that little progress had been made towards enactment of a new patent law.[116]

In early 2000, PhRMA urged that the UAE be placed on the Priority Watch List because of its continued failure to protect patented pharmaceutical products and commercially valuable confidential data as required by TRIPS.[117] PhRMA subsequently withdrew its request following assurances that the UAE would provide adequate and effective protection for patented pharmaceutical products and requested that it even be taken off the Watch List. The UAE was finally removed from the Watch List following a written commitment to take specific measures to ensure adequate and effective protection of patented products, including specific commitments on the implementation of TRIPS, data protection and the withholding of marketing approval for unauthorised copies of patented products.[118] In December of that year, PhRMA accused the UAE of express violations of bilateral and multilateral commitments to protect intellectual property rights for patented pharmaceutical products and confidential data, and failure to live up to written commitments and its WTO obligations, and sought an immediate USTR out-of-cycle review of the UAE and its designation as a Priority Foreign Country.[119] It also urged the UAE government to de-register all unauthorised copies submitted for marketing approvals, on the grounds that they were derived from patented pharmaceutical products of PhRMA-member companies and other pharmaceutical multinationals, or directly or indirectly relied on, referred to or used original protected clinical and laboratory data of PhRMA regional members.

The UAE Ministry of Health dismissed the PhRMA claims that it had abrogated its WTO obligations. It argued that all medicines registered in the country complied with UAE federal laws, including a ministerial decree banning the registration of any drug or pharmaceutical compound which was not already the subject of patent protection in its country of origin.[120] The impact of the ministerial order was to effectively counter the inflow into the UAE, and thereby the other

116 Ibid.

117 USTR (2001), *2001 National Trade Estimate Report on Foreign Trade Barriers*, p. 152, available at https://ustr.gov/archive/Document_Library/Reports_Publications/2001/2001_NTE_Report/Section_Index.html, last accessed 26 May 2017.

118 Ibid.

119 Ibid. See also 'Pharma Group Again Putting Pressure on UAE for IP Violations' (2000), *PhRMA Newsletter*, 117, December, p. 20.

120 UAE, Ministerial Order No. 404 of 2000, arts 1 and 2.

States, of generic drugs, a matter of considerable concern to PhRMA and its members. The Ministry also correctly countered that it was still within the WTO's grace period for developing countries in respect of patented pharmaceutical products (the grace period not expiring until 1 January 2005).

The USTR accordingly re-listed the UAE for 2001, despite the fact that its efforts in reducing copyright piracy had been widely praised, even by the USTR. According to the USTR:

> the UAE was removed from the Watch List last year [2000] in recognition of its commitment to not provide marketing approval to unauthorised copies of patented pharmaceutical products . . . however, the UAE subsequently granted marketing approval for a number of unauthorised copies of patented pharmaceuticals.[121]

The USTR finally removed the UAE from the Watch List in 2002, mainly as a result of specific provision in its new patent law of 2002 for immediate transitional protection and marketing exclusivity for patented pharmaceutical and agrochemical products – the only regional State to have included such a provision.[122] The UAE also had agreed to allow the United States to review and have input into a draft of its new patent law, in order to ensure compliance with TRIPS. The UAE's success in finally being removed from a Special 301 Listing also coincided with its introduction during 2002 of updated TRIPS-compliant laws in respect of copyright and neighbouring rights, trademarks, and patents and industrial designs, and the signing of a TIFA with the United States early the following year.

However, the pressure continues: even though the UAE has not since returned to the Special 301 Listings, it has still been the subject of submissions to the USTR. The IIPA, for example, recently requested the USTR to re-list the UAE on the 2016 Report's Watch List because of its perceived failure to allow the establishment and operation of a collecting society for copyright royalties, and because of the amount of pirated and counterfeit products in malls outside the cities and in the burgeoning free trade zones.[123] The USTR declined to act on the IIPA's recommendation, and the UAE was not listed.

121 USTR (2001), *2001 Special 301 Report, Office of the United States Trade Representative*, April, p. 18, available at https://ustr.gov/sites/default/files/2001%20Special%20301%20Report.pdf, last accessed 26 May 2017. By 'unauthorised', the USTR meant generic pharmaceuticals.

122 UAE, Federal Law No. 17 of 2002, art. 71.

123 IIPA (2016), 'Special 301 Report on Global Copyright Protection and Enforcement', UAE Appendix, p. 1, available at www.iipawebsite.com/rbc/2016/2016SPEC301UAE.PDF, last accessed 26 May 2017. Abu Dhabi, Dubai, Sharjah and Ras Al-Khaimah are all in the process of establishing free trade zones, Dubai's Jebel Ali zone in particular being on a significant scale.

8.6 Concluding remarks

Where TRIPS and the Berne and Paris Conventions establish general levels of intellectual property protection, the Jordan, Bahrain and Oman FTAs significantly raise those levels and establish new parameters; and where the international conventions allow limitations or exceptions to that protection, the FTAs reduce or confine those limitations and exceptions. Further, the Bahrain and Oman FTAs introduce into the national and regional environments the protection of copyrights and neighbouring rights in the digital context, particularly in respect of the internet and satellite transmission where TRIPS has been overtaken by the march of technological progress.

For Jordan, Bahrain and Oman, this may not be a real issue. The fact that the negotiations on each of the three FTAs were successfully concluded in what could be deemed record time is a clear indication of both US determination to adopt an aggressive bargaining stance and obvious keenness by these States to reach an agreement. The rapid progression and conclusion of negotiations for the Bahrain FTA, for example, took even the USTR by surprise.[124] However, notwithstanding speedy conclusions, it was some time before these FTAs were given full practical effect and the benefits or otherwise to both parties became realised and can be assessed. In any case, the real measure of success will lie in the administration of the new standards on the ground by the local police, judicial and administrative agencies responsible for enforcement and implementation of the enhanced protection regime of the FTA.

Although these three FTAs were meant to set progressive precedents or increasingly raise the bar for the Arabian Peninsula by allowing national interests and bilateral agreements to override regional collective interests and multilateral talks, the three States' desires to raise their economic profile internationally, expand their economic bases by gaining greater access to the lucrative US markets and attract increased foreign investment are no doubt major reasons behind each deal. All three States appear to have enjoyed significant, or at least positive, economic gains since their FTAs became operational; the USTR has reported that since the implementation of the Jordan FTA in December 2001, the two-way goods trade has grown over 350 per cent, from $568 million in 2001 to more than $2 billion in 2016. Similarly, since the Bahrain FTA's implementation in 2006, two-way goods trade reached $1.2 billion, up 61 per cent over the same period, while Oman exported goods worth $882 million to the United States and imported goods worth $1.2billion.[125] Local commentators have also suggested that the FTAs can be viewed as a political reward for the close strategic support that Jordan, Bahrain and Oman have consistently provided the United States in the region.[126]

124 USTR Press Release, 'US and Bahrain Conclude Free Trade Agreement', op. cit.

125 U.S. Department of State, 'Outcomes of Current U.S. Trade Agreements', available at www.state.gov/e/eb/tpp/bta/fta/c26474.htm, last accessed 26 May 2017.

126 *Khaleej Times* (UAE), 20 December 2004, available at www.khaleejtimes.com/Displayarticle.asp?section=middleeast&xfile=data/middleeast/2004/december/middleeast_december743.

The national treatment and MFN obligations enshrined in the Bahrain and Oman FTAs may mean that, notwithstanding any otherwise limiting provisions in their national laws, Jordan, Bahrain and Oman will be required to extend to US investors conditions no less favourable than those already extended to its regional partners. This situation may well be to the detriment of the particular regional and economic benefits that the States have so far developed among themselves for their mutual regional benefit and advancement. In so doing, the erosion of particular preferential regional provisions may adversely affect the unity of the GCC itself. Some of the GCC member States, chiefly Saudi Arabia, raised strong objections to the Bahrain FTA on the grounds that it violated the basic tenets of the economic agreement signed by the GCC Supreme Council in 2001, which stipulates that 'no member state may grant to a non-member state any preferential treatment exceeding that granted herein to member states, nor conclude any agreement that violates provisions of this agreement'.[127] Saudi Arabia's initial strong opposition to independent bilateral deals by GCC member States eventually softened – one possible reason being its own (then still impending) WTO membership.

As events came to pass, the Jordan, Bahrain and Oman FTAs were concluded and have come mainly, if not entirely, into effect, while FTA negotiations between the United States and the UAE, Qatar, and Kuwait commenced but soon stalled. FTA negotiations with Saudi Arabia and Kuwait didn't even commence. With all but one of the Arabian Peninsula States removed from the Special 301 Reports (although the possibility of reinstatement is always present), the impact of those Reports as a vehicle for change with intellectual property protection standards has lessened. A change in US Presidents and Administration in 2009 also brought a change in directions for US geopolitical imperatives, policy and strategy.

The greater significance of the intellectual property provisions of the Jordan, Bahrain and Oman FTAs may lie not so much in the conditions and requirements that they impose individually on the three States, but rather in the precedents which they establish for the other Middle East countries. The FTAs establish new regional benchmarks for intellectual property protection to which the other States may be pressured to accede, not necessarily by the United States but by other countries seeking to establish bilateral or multilateral agreements with TRIPS-plus obligations.

xml, last accessed 1 March 2017. See also Emilie Rutledge and Janardhan (2004), 'Bahrain–US FTA Exposes GCC Chinks', *Bilaterals.org*, December, available at www.bilaterals.org/?us-bahrain-trade-deal-exposes-gcc&lang=fr, last accessed 26 May 2017.

127 Unified Economic Agreement Between the Countries of the Gulf Cooperation Council, art. 31, available at http://www.gcc-sg.org/ar-sa/CognitiveSources/DigitalLibrary/Lists/DigitalLibrary/ 1111318748548/الاقتصاد.pdf (in Arabic), last accessed 13 June 2017.

9

TRIPS-MINUS AND PROTECTION STILL PENDING

9.1 Introduction

The multilateral intellectual property protection framework, as exemplified by TRIPS, has been constructed to best deliver the protection on those intellectual property rights that the major players – the developed countries – have sought to have protected. The multilateral framework is given further substance by the network of TRIPS-plus treaties and bilateral agreements, in which the same developed countries figure prominently. The dominant characteristic of this framework is that, to be protectable as intellectual property, a right must be private in nature, identifiable, ascribable and commercially exploitable. Issues or rights that do not fit within this framework – notably traditional knowledge and cultural heritage in the broadest sense – enjoy little, if any, of the protection offered by TRIPS, the TRIPS-plus treaties and the bilateral agreements. The absence of protection on an international mutually agreed scale for these issues has witnessed them subject to potential and actual encroachment by the multilateral protection framework on terms dictated by that framework. In essence, they suffer a TRIPS-minus protection environment.

Although a number of descriptions for traditional knowledge and cultural heritage have been in widespread circulation, as yet there is no universal agreement on the terminology or the definitions or even agreed parameters in the major multilateral forums as to what might or should be included in their deliberations. Although traditional knowledge seems to be the most commonly used term, others frequently arise – such as cultural heritage, folklore, traditional cultural expressions, indigenous knowledge. This is as much a reflection of the broad scope of what may be encompassed within their bounds as uncertainty on what might constitute 'traditional' or 'knowledge', or even 'protection' and its purpose. It has been suggested, for example, that the term 'folklore' is quite inappropriate in this context since it presumes matter of a historical nature only and suggests that 'expressions of culture', being current self-expressions of living functional traditions, should be used instead.[1] 'Folklore' was, and still is, the term used most commonly in international discussions and is found in many national laws, including those of the Arabian Peninsula States. What seems a common consensus is that 'protection' in the narrow and conventional intellectual property sense does not address the needs or scope of these concepts, even allowing for differences in their possible definitions.

WIPO currently prefers to mainly use in a fairly generic way the terms 'traditional knowledge' (TK) and 'traditional cultural expressions' (TCE), with 'folklore' being used less widely. It draws a distinction between these two major terms. It uses 'traditional knowledge' to refer to tradition-based literary, artistic or scientific works, performances, inventions, scientific discoveries, designs, marks, names and symbols, undisclosed information and all other tradition-based innovations and creations resulting from intellectual activity in the industrial, scientific, literary or artistic fields.[2] Although there is no formal definition for traditional knowledge that WIPO would adopt, traditional knowledge is best described as 'a living body of knowledge that is developed, sustained and passed on from generation to generation within a community, often forming part of its cultural or spiritual identity'.[3]

'Traditional cultural expressions' encompass productions consisting of characteristic elements of the traditional artistic heritage developed and maintained by a community or by individuals reflecting the traditional artistic expectations of such a community, in particular:

- verbal expressions, such as folk tales, folk poetry and riddles, signs, words, symbols and indications;
- musical expressions, such as folk songs and instrumental music;
- expressions by actions, such as folk dances, plays and artistic forms or rituals, whether or not reduced to a material form; and
- tangible expressions, such as productions of folk art (in particular, drawings, paintings, carvings, sculptures, pottery, terracotta, mosaic, woodwork, metalware, jewellery, basket weaving, needlework, textiles, carpets, costumes), crafts, musical instruments and architectural forms.[4]

1 WIPO (2015), *Intellectual Property and Genetic Resources, Traditional Knowledge and Cultural Expressions*, WIPO Publication No. 933, p. 16, available at www.wipo.int/edocs/pubdocs/en/tk/933/wipo_pub_933.pdf, last accessed 1 June 2017.

2 WIPO International Bureau, 'Intellectual Property and Traditional Knowledge: Our Identity, Our Future', WIPO International Forum on Matters Concerning Intellectual Property and Genetic Resources, Traditional Knowledge and Folklore, Oman, 21–22 January 2002, WIPO Document IPTK/MCT/02/INF.11 November 2002.

3 WIPO (2015), op. cit., pp. 14–18.

4 Ibid.

Also included within WIPO's broad lexicon of traditional knowledge is the term 'genetic resources' (GRs) to encompass plant, animal or microbial origin, such as medicinal plants, agricultural crops and animal breeds that constitute genetic material of value. Some traditional knowledge is closely associated with genetic resources through the utilisation and conservation of the resource, often over generations, and through their common use in modern scientific research.[5]

9.2 The protection of traditional knowledge and expressions of culture

Many developing countries, holders of traditional knowledge, expressions of culture and cultural heritage, and non-governmental and civil society organisations are advocating for greater protection to be made available. Within both the WTO and WIPO, extended debate has taken place on the nature of the appropriate system to protect traditional knowledge and expressions of culture and cultural heritage within the international sphere. Central to the debate is the question of whether they can be protected under the current multilateral intellectual property protection system and, if not, what *sui generis* system might be adopted.

Proponents of the current system would argue that it has adequate flexibility to provide a reasonable degree of balance between the holders of non-conventional intellectual property rights within the established framework, the entitlement of society to enjoy the benefits of exploitation of those rights, and the imperative of those with the capacity to commercially exploit those rights. In instances where the nature of those rights is not contemplated within the conventional framework, voluntary contractual arrangements between right holder and exploiter should be adequate to compensate and address the inadequacies of the framework.

It can be argued that the very attributes of traditional knowledge prevent it from being included into the conventional intellectual property system. Traditional knowledge seeking protection under conventional copyright provisions runs afoul of the requirement for identification and attribution. In the area of patent protection, traditional knowledge does not meet the patentability requirements of novelty, inventive step and industrial application. Some countries have decided that the existing intellectual property framework is inadequate to protect traditional knowledge and are pursuing their own *sui generis* systems of protection.[6] However, calls for the creation of an international *sui generis* system are increasing.

WIPO asserts that it recognises the importance of protecting traditional knowledge and traditional cultural expressions as intellectual property rights. The purpose is to ensure that they do not disappear and are promoted and protected. In order to do that, a process of identification, documentation, transmission, revitalisation

5 Ibid., p. 18.

6 See Surinder Verma (2004), 'Protecting Intellectual Property: Is a Sui Generis System an Answer?', 7, *Journal of World Intellectual Property*, p. 770.

and promotion of traditional knowledge and traditional cultural expressions is a must.[7] Therefore, there are two forms of protection, which are a positive and a defensive protection. Positive protection grants intellectual property rights in the subject matter of traditional knowledge and traditional cultural expressions. By granting such rights, third parties are prevented from using traditional knowledge and traditional cultural expressions. Positive protection also permits communities to commercially exploit and use traditional knowledge and traditional cultural expressions.[8] Defensive protection does not grant any rights over the subject matter of traditional knowledge and traditional cultural expressions. Its purpose is to prevent third parties who are not part of the community from acquiring exclusive rights by documenting it and making it available to the public.[9]

In 1998 and 1999, WIPO undertook a number of global fact-finding missions 'to identify and explore the intellectual property needs and expectations of new beneficiaries, including the holders of indigenous knowledge and innovations, in order to promote the contribution of the intellectual property system to their social, cultural and economic development'.[10] These missions were intended to enable the 'study of current approaches to, and future possibilities for, the protection of intellectual property rights of holders of indigenous knowledge, innovations and culture'. During the subsequent WIPO-sponsored conferences to discuss the missions' findings in respect of the linkages between intellectual property and traditional knowledge and their implications, three primary issues which were of universal concern to the countries involved in the studies emerged, namely:

- the protection of traditional knowledge, innovations and creativity, whether or not associated with those resources;
- the protection of expressions of folklore, including handicrafts; and
- access to genetic resources and benefit-sharing.[11]

7 WIPO (2016), *Developing a National Strategy on Intellectual Property, Traditional Knowledge and Traditional Cultural Expressions*, WIPO Publication No.3, p.3, available at www.wipo.int/edocs/pubdocs/en/wipo_pub_tk_3.pdf, last accessed 26 May 2017.
8 Ibid.
9 Ibid.
10 WIPO (2001), 'Intellectual Property Needs and Expectations of Traditional Knowledge Holders', *WIPO Report on Fact-Finding Missions on Intellectual Property and Traditional Knowledge (1998–9)*, WIPO Publication No. 768(E), p. 17. The fact-finding missions were carried out in the following areas: South Pacific (Australia, New Zealand, Fiji and Papua New Guinea), South Asia (Bangladesh, India and Sri Lanka), Southern and Eastern Africa (Uganda, United Republic of Tanzania, Namibia and South Africa), North America (United States of America and Canada), West Africa (Nigeria, Ghana, Mali and Senegal), the Arab countries (Oman, Qatar, Egypt and Tunisia), South America (Peru and Bolivia), Central America (Guatemala and Panama) and the Caribbean (Trinidad and Tobago, Guyana and Jamaica). The reports of the Missions are available at www.wipo.int/edocs/pubdocs/en/tk/768/wipo_pub_768.pdf, last accessed 1 June 2017.
11 Ibid., p. 217.

The missions and the subsequent forums made a number of observations and recommendations to the member states themselves, to the international community and to the international organisations with an interest in the protection of traditional knowledge. The recommendations included that WIPO, UNESCO and the other international organisations should work towards the creation of a *sui generis* international convention for the protection of expressions of folklore. Most of the forums also commented on the WIPO–UNESCO model law for the national protection of expressions of folklore from illegal exploitation of 1982 as a relevant basis for national laws.

The missions also included an examination of traditional knowledge in selected Arab countries. The subsequent consultative forums made a number of pertinent observations and recommendations. They observed that:[12]

- Arab countries are rich with one of the most precious cultural and civilisational heritages in the world, which constitutes an important pillar for human civilisation and an integral part of the world patrimony.
- Arab folklore (Arab popular heritage) is a strong means of bringing together the Arab peoples. However, this common aspect does not exclude or diminish the importance of the local variations specific to each people.
- Arab folklore (Arab popular heritage) and traditional knowledge are subject to various dangers, including negligence, disappearance, piracy, mutilation and illegal exploitation; therefore, there is a need for the provision of legal protection at national, regional and international levels.
- Currently, there is no legal framework available for the protection of expressions of Arab folklore at either national or international levels.

The missions and forums recommended to the Arab countries that they should:

- create specialised institutions or centres as a national and cultural necessity for the collection, classification, conservation, documentation and dissemination of folklore (Arab popular heritage) and develop a specialised environment;
- work together on their national legislation for the provision of measures aiming at the protection of expressions of folklore;
- (each) prepare an open list of expressions of folklore and traditional knowledge, the preservation and protection of which is considered necessary;
- rely, when reviewing and amending their legislation, on the WIPO model provisions set, as adapted to recent developments in the field.

At the same time, they recommended to international organisations that WIPO, UNESCO and the specialised international organisations intensify their efforts in

12 Ibid., pp. 325–6.

order to provide greater assistance to Arab countries in particular and developing countries in general by:

- providing training and technical and legal cooperation to Arab countries;
- elaborating an international convention on the protection of expressions of folklore;
- establishing a standing committee on expressions of folklore and traditional knowledge in both WIPO and UNESCO.

Since the WIPO missions, however, little progress has been achieved in respect of the key issue of the creation and universal acceptance of a *sui generis* international protection convention. WIPO established a senior committee, as recommended above, in 2001, and the Arabian Peninsula States have taken some steps towards the creation of national protection schemes and the identification, documentation and preservation of their cultural heritages. WIPO's committee, the Intergovernmental Committee on Intellectual Property and Genetic Resources, Traditional Knowledge and Folklore, is charged with examining the feasibility of establishing *sui generis* or other systems of protection for expressions of traditional knowledge, but its work so far has largely revolved around establishing the parameters and meanings of key terms, such as what is meant by tradition, knowledge, culture and heritage. It has yet to agree on a draft legal document as a basis for a convention.

In 2007, the United Nations General Assembly adopted the United Nations Declaration on the Rights of Indigenous Peoples. Article 2 of the Declaration recognises that

> indigenous peoples and individuals are free and equal to all other peoples and individuals and have the right to be free from any kind of discrimination, in the exercise of their rights, in particular that based on their indigenous origin or identity.

Article 31 provides that indigenous peoples 'have the right to maintain, control, protect and develop their Intellectual Property over such cultural heritage, traditional knowledge and traditional cultural expressions'.

The two global forums responsible for intellectual property rights, namely the WTO and WIPO, have not yet been able between them to translate these declarations into a suitable form of treaty or convention binding upon their members.

9.3 Copyright and traditional knowledge and folklore in the Arabian Peninsula

Whatever terminology is used, traditional knowledge, folklore and cultural heritage are characterised by the fact that, generally, they are not produced systematically but in accordance with the individual or collective creators' responses to and interaction with their cultural environment. Being representative of cultural values, they may constitute elements that integrate a vast and mostly coherent complex of beliefs and knowledge. More than likely they will be held collectively, being vested in the community rather than in individuals (although individuals as leaders or elders may hold them in trust). Furthermore, traditional knowledge and cultural heritage are usually transmitted orally from generation to generation and thus remain largely undocumented. They are also dynamic in the sense that they are current, possess everyday relevance and are subject to processes of constant evolution. Accordingly, existing intellectual property mechanisms, which are intended to function in a trade-related, private protectionist context and are governed by a predetermined and static time frame, do not fully respond to the essential nature of traditional knowledge, folklore and cultural heritage.

A major problem with the effective and just protection of indigenous knowledge is that the creative work or knowledge must still fit in with western ideas of intellectual property in general and copyright in particular, and the legislative structure which develops from it – that is, an intangible personal property right expressed in a tangible way. But conventional mechanisms based on western ideas which are intended to function in a trade-related, private protectionist context do not adequately respond to the essential nature of traditional knowledge and cultural heritage. The international treaties, such as TRIPS and the Berne and Paris Conventions, and the domestic intellectual property laws based upon them, still require a copyrighted work, a trademark or a patentable invention to be in material or reproducible form, to belong to an identifiable individual, group of individuals or legal entity, to be original and to be independently created rather than derived or copied.

Even though the Berne Convention, for example, actually makes reference to traditional knowledge, it still requires a work to meet certain criteria if it is to gain copyright protection. These requirements mean that some important forms of traditional knowledge have not gained intellectual property protection. For example, the traditional custodians of areas in which cave or rock art occurs cannot assert copyright over the art because they cannot and should not identify an individual creator or artist; because the art was created so long ago, it no longer fits within copyright protection time frames. By the same token, orally transmitted folklore or heritage passed down over generations find it difficult to gain copyright protection because they have not been reduced to fixed, material or reproducible form. Other issues arise where the process of reducing the traditional knowledge to material form was done by a third party. The operation of copyright law may provide some protection for traditional knowledge custodians where they are also owners of copyright in the work, but copyright law can also operate to create difficulties over ownership of traditional knowledge. The act of recording in written form or fixation of an oral tradition may create for the recorder a legally enforceable right to the copyright of that recording as a producer or publisher, but it may well create further problems where such a fixation or transmission may be contrary to tradition and practice or where the producer has no traditional right of access to such tradition.

Nevertheless, the use of recordings, databases and registers for creating a permanent record or digital repository of expressions of traditional knowledge is gaining increasing attention. The documentation or fixation of traditional knowledge is also crucial to protecting it. Conversely, there are some negative aspects to recording and documenting traditional knowledge. First, because traditional knowledge is oral, performative, expressive and multidimensional, the documentation or fixation causes it to lose those distinct elements. Second, once in fixed form, the knowledge becomes vulnerable to exploitation and unlawful use.

Some of the Arabian Peninsula States have moved to include, to a lesser or greater degree, formal recognition of expressions of culture and traditional knowledge in their respective copyright laws. Although this inclusion provides some form of legal standing for traditional knowledge, it still does not fully address the dilemmas of protection in a conventional intellectual property context. On occasion, it appears that the references may be more of a token gesture than a conscious and determined effort to provide or enhance protection.

Bahrain and Qatar adopt the strongest positions on the protection of traditional knowledge and folklore among the States, insofar as their copyright laws make particular detailed references to the position of national folklore and give the broadest illustration of the range of folkloric expressions which may be protected.

The Bahraini copyright law extends its protection to all creative works, including those of a cultural nature irrespective of the nature of such works and their form of expression. It uses the WIPO-discarded term of 'folklore'. It includes in the scope of expressions of folklore all productions of a community heritage, whether verbal, musical, expressed by movement, or tangible as represented by distinctive elements reflecting traditional heritage that originated or were developed and preserved in a particular geographic area and which cannot be attributed to a known author.[13] They include the following expressions in particular:

- folk tales, proverbs, puzzles and popular poetry;
- folk songs with musical accompaniment;
- folk dances and performances;
- traditional products such as line or colour drawings; sculptures, pottery and ceramics;
- engravings on wood, metal or ornaments;
- needlework, textiles, carpets and clothes;
- musical instruments; and
- architectural shapes.

'Performers' include actors, singers, musicians, dancers and other persons who act, sing, deliver, declaim or perform in any way works that are protected or unprotected pursuant to the provisions of this law, or that have fallen into the public

13 Bahrain, Legislative Decree No. 22 of 2006, art. 1.

domain after their protection period has expired, as well as expressions of folklore. Performances to a wider public audience outside the immediate community context receive specific attention, public performance being any activity 'in a place where persons other than family members and friends may be present'.

Recognised among the infringements listed in the law is the use of expressions of folklore in a manner that violates certain other provisions in the act, namely a requirement that the use must be in an appropriate manner that respects the integrity of the expressions and acknowledges their source.[14] In many respects this requirement is a restatement for expressions of folklore of the general moral rights of attribution and integrity. While expressions of folklore may be used, such use must be in an appropriate manner and must not mutilate the expressions, and their source should be mentioned.

As is the case with the other States, the Bahraini copyright law stipulates that expressions of folklore which reflect the traditional popular heritage of the State and which originated and were developed and consistently preserved in the Kingdom shall be the property of the State.[15] The law also provides for rights management, requiring that associations or organisations managing rights of authors and neighbouring rights be licensed by the responsible ministry and subject to the supervision and control of the ministry.[16]

The Qatari copyright law defines national folklore as follows:

> Any expression which consists of distinctive elements of the traditional artistic heritage, originating or developed in the State of Qatar and reflects its artistic heritage, shall be considered as national folklore, including in particular the following expressions:
>
> (1) oral expressions such as tales, popular poetry and riddles;
> (2) musical expressions such as popular songs accompanied by music;
> (3) motion expressions such as popular dances, plays, artistic forms and rituals, whether or not incorporated into material form;
> (4) tangible expressions such as:
>
> (a) products or popular art particularly drawings with lines and colours, engravings, sculptures, ceramics, pottery, woodwork, mosaic, metal, jewellery, hand-woven bags, knitting, carpets, textiles, (b) musical instruments; and (c) architectural forms.[17]

'Performers' include those who perform expressions of folklore, while collections of works and expressions of folklore are protected as derived works – although,

14 Ibid.
15 Ibid., arts 65(1)(g) and 68.
16 Ibid., arts 58–60.
17 Qatar, Law No. 7 of 2002, art. 1.

again, this protection does not necessarily extend to the folklore itself. Collective works where individual authorship cannot be distinguished can also be protected.

Again, the Qatari copyright law declares that national folklore is the public property of the State and the State is charged with the responsibility of protecting the national folklore by all legal means and methods. It is empowered to exercise the author's rights – in fact, to act as the author of works of folklore with respect to any acts of distortion, alteration or commercial utilisation.[18]

Jordan's position on protection for folklore and national heritage in its copyright law of 1992 is a little confusing. Interestingly, the law in its original form did not provide any protection. A subsequent amendment provided that Article 7, entitled 'Works not subject to Protection', makes a curious statement. It states that:

> The protection provided for under this law shall not include the following works unless collections of these works are distinguished with personal effort . . .
>
> . . .
>
> c) works that have become public property. National folklore shall be considered public property for the purposes of this Article, provided that the Minister shall exercise the copyrights of such works to counter distortion, alteration or damage to cultural interests.

The default position would thus seem to be one of uncontrolled use, unless post-use distortion, alteration or damage is subsequently established. With the latest amendment of 2014, the legislators recognise the importance of defining the scope of protection as well as imbuing the State with a guardianship right and responsibility. However, the new amendment falls short by not setting any penalties or sanctions in cases of using Jordanian folklore or its national heritage without authorisation.[19]

Kuwait's earlier copyright law of 1999 did not make any specific reference to folklore or other works falling within the ambit of traditional knowledge. It enacted a new copyright law in 2016, but this new law still does not make any substantive provisions for the protection of folklore and national heritage. Folklore and national heritage is defined by listing the acts that are considered national heritage. The law also states that 'the national heritage of Kuwait society is a public property of the State. And the State, acting through the Ministry of Information, has the right to exercise the author's literary and financial rights for him.'[20] It still requires attribution to an individual for protection to be able to have effect, or for the State to act on the individual's behalf to protect that individual's private rights.

Oman makes a much stronger and comprehensive statement of intent on protection. The copyright law recognises expressions of folklore and includes

18 Ibid., art. 32.
19 Jordan, Law No. 23 of 2014, art. 56.
20 Kuwait, Law No. 22 of 2016, arts 1, 3 and 5.

them in those works to which the protection of the law extends. It defines expressions of national folklore as:

> any expression or production of distinguishable elements reflecting the traditional popular heritage that was originated, developed and maintained in the Sultanate of Oman to express the traditional cultural identity which is communicated through generations, including particularly the following expressions:
>
> - Oral expressions such as popular stories, anecdotes, sayings, mysteries, poems and other folklores.
> - Musical expressions such as folk songs accompanied by musical instruments.
> - Movement performances such as dances, popular artistic presentations and traditional popular rituals.
> - Concrete expressions such as drawings or paintings, sculptures, pottery, porcelain, carving, sculpture, mud, engraving on wood and metals, jewellery, needlework, textiles, clothing, carpets, traditional musical instruments, architectural forms and all products of plastic folk art.[21]

The Royal Decree also includes in its definition of works of applied arts any artistic creation of useful function or integrated into tools for producing traditional or industrial crafts.[22] Performers include persons who 'act, sing, orate, recite, play, dance or otherwise perform other works and national folklore expressions'.[23] Protection of the law extends to expressions of these cultural forms in general, whether they come within the parameters of oral, musical or concrete expressions, or performances. While the notion of private ownership is still a central theme, provision exists for the State to assume ownership of the moral rights, but only where no natural right of succession occurs.[24]

Saudi Arabia goes a little further than Yemen, Kuwait and the UAE. Its copyright law adopts a slightly stronger position on the protection of folklore, which is acknowledged as including:

> all literary, artistic or scientific works which are assumed to have been created on Saudi territory and transmitted from one generation to the next and constitute part of the traditional Saudi cultural and artistic tradition.[25]

21 Oman, Royal Decree No. 65/2008, art. 1.12.

22 Ibid., art. 1.10.

23 Ibid., art. 1.19.

24 Ibid., art. 5. The competent authority in this context being the Minister of Commerce and Industry, with whom most intellectual property protection responsibility resides, notwithstanding the existence of the Ministry of Heritage and Culture and an independent Public Authority for Craft Industries.

25 Saudi Arabia, Royal Decree No. M/41 of 1424 AH (2003), art. 1.

Compilations of expressions of folklore enjoy protection of the law as derived works. The law also provides that the national folklore shall be considered the public property of the State, the relevant copyrights for which are exercised by the Ministry of Information as the responsible ministry.[26] Arguably, as an initiative to preserve the internal integrity of, and to maintain some control over, works deemed to be Saudi folklore, the importation or distribution of copies of classified works of folklore or copies of translations or reproductions of folklore produced outside the Kingdom is prohibited, except with the permission of the Ministry.

The UAE copyright law contains a definition of folklore as:

> every expression of people's heritage, oral, musical, dynamic, or tangible in distinct elements which reflects the artistic traditional inheritance, developed or endured in the State and which cannot be attributed to an author.[27]

The law also acknowledges derived work as being any expression of a people's heritage, whether oral, musical, dynamic or tangible (in distinct elements that reflect the artistic traditional inheritance), which has developed or survived in the State and which cannot be attributed to an author. Folklore is not included among the range of works or activities entitled to protection, but provision does exist for moral rights to revert to the State once the economic rights expire. However, there is no guidance as to the nature of the protection that the law might provide other than by implication.[28]

The Yemeni copyright law of 2012 provides provisions for the protection of traditional knowledge and folklore. It is noticeable that the law gives greater attention to traditional knowledge and folklore than some of the other States, devoting a discrete chapter of five articles to the protection of expressions of folklore.[29] The law defines the terms, drawing the scope of protection along with the exceptions. Article 55 states that traditional knowledge and folklore include:

> *al-mathurat* and popular or folklore expressions, each expression is the distinct elements that reflect traditional folklore that originated in the Republic and in particular:
>
> § Verbal expressions, such as folk tales, folk poetry and riddles, songs and poetry.
>
> § Musical expressions, such as folk songs, accompanied by music and music tracks.
>
> § Kinetic expressions, such as folk dances, plays and artistic forms or rituals, whether embodied in a material form or not.

26 Ibid., art. 7(1)–(2).
27 UAE, Federal Law No. 7 of 2002, art. 1.
28 Ibid., art. 42.
29 Yemen, Law No. 15 of 2012, arts 55–61.

§ Tangible expressions, such as:

- products of folk art, in particular drawings, lines or colours on wood or mosaic, or mother-of-pearl, metal or jewels, hand-woven bags, needlework, embroidery, fabrics, carpets and clothing;
- musical instruments; and
- architectural forms.

Traditional knowledge and folklore are deemed to belong to the State, which has responsibility for both moral rights and economic rights – on the one hand protecting them from exploitation, distortion or modification, and on the other hand controlling their performance and copying through licensing arrangements.[30] Article 61 prohibits the importation or distribution of copies of works of folklore or copies of translations of national folklore without prior authorisation from the Ministry. The sanctions for infringements of the folklore protection are severe, amounting to

> a fine of not less than 500,000 rials or imprisonment of not less than one month, according to the gravity of the offence anyone who commits . . . contravention of the provisions of articles (57, 58) of this law or distortion, mutilation of expressions of folklore.[31]

The problem with all the above laws, to the extent that they provide differing degrees of protection for traditional knowledge and expressions of culture, is that they still operate with the paradigm of the global convention of copyright as a private economic right. Notwithstanding any recognition of the particular character of traditional knowledge or expressions of culture, the laws are still based on the premise that ownership can be attributed to a person, a discrete group or a legal entity. They extend protection to an author, performer, publisher or broadcaster rather than to an item, work or performance itself; hence, works which cannot be clearly attributed to an owner or defined group of owners may not be protectable. The laws also still assume a limited period of protection – for example, the life of the author plus a specific number of years.

Furthermore, the bilateral agreements which Jordan, Bahrain and Oman have settled tend to militate against the provision that exists in the national copyright laws to extend protection to traditional knowledge. Both the Bahrain and Oman FTAs include in their definitions of performers 'actors, singers, musicians, dancers, and other persons who act, sing, deliver, declaim, play in, interpret, or otherwise perform literary or artistic works *or expressions of folklore*' (emphasis added).[32] But,

30 Ibid., arts 56–58.
31 Ibid., art. 77.
32 Bahrain FTA, art. 14.6.5; Oman FTA, art. 15.6.5.

at the same time, the FTAs create two problems: first, in the context of their provisions on copyright, 'performance' means a performance fixed in a phonogram unless otherwise specified.[33] The specific rights granted to performers are limited to the authorisation or prohibition of the broadcast or fixation of their unfixed performances – they do not extend to protection of the cultural heritage enshrined in the performance. The rights, being private rights, must belong to the individual and do not cover the situation where individual ownership cannot be attributed. Second, both FTAs restate the position of TRIPS Article 70.3, to the effect that neither party shall be required to restore protection to subject matter that has fallen into the public domain in its territory on the date that the FTA comes into force. This exclusion applies equally to all traditional knowledge, including knowledge relating to genetic material and the pharmacological properties of plants and their medicinal applications. The Jordan FTA does not make any reference to traditional knowledge or folklore.

Outside the conventional intellectual property protection regime, all States have laws to protect certain elements of traditional knowledge. In fact, in many instances these laws pre-date intellectual property laws, an indication in itself of the better understanding on the part of the States and the higher priority that they place on the protection of their national heritages. All States are very sensitive to and very proud of their respective rich cultural heritages, and are mindful of the need, particularly in recent years, to protect them. The States have in place laws for the protection of artifacts and historical sites, but these relate to the physical protection of these objects, their preservation and the prevention of their illicit export, as distinct from protection from copying or similar expropriation or unfair commercial exploitation by third parties.[34] But these laws tend to focus on protection of past cultures and heritages, rather than current expressions of culture.

Oman has been pre-eminent among the Gulf States in its efforts to protect and preserve its cultural heritage. Oman's primary law for the protection of its cultural heritage, the National Heritage Protection Law, was promulgated in 1976. The law's principal objectives are the physical preservation of the integrity of cultural property of the State and the prohibition or restriction of export of any property or object of historical significance. It encompasses all kinds of monuments as well

33 Bahrain FTA, art. 14.4.1; Oman FTA, art. 15.1.

34 Just one example each of a national heritage-type law introduced by each State include the following:

Bahrain – Legislative Decree No. 5 of 1986, the National Council for Culture, Arts and Literature.
Jordan – Antiquities Law No. 21 of 1988, as amended by Law No. 55 of 2008.
Kuwait – Law No. 11 of 1960, the Law of Antiquities, as amended by Law No. 9 of 1994.
Oman – National Heritage Protection Law, 1976.
Qatar – Law No. 2 of 1980 on Antiquities.
Saudi Arabia – Law No. M/26 of 23/6/1392 AH (1972), the Law on Antiquities.
UAE – Law No. 8 of 1970 on Archaeological Heritage.
Yemen – Archaeology Protection Law of 1994, as amended in 1997.

as 'chattels of cultural properties'.[35] Oman has also taken steps to document and preserve some aspect of its traditional knowledge and cultural heritage, as illustrated by these few examples:

- The Public Authority for Craft Industries, established in 2003 and responsible for preserving every aspect of Oman's traditional craft industries, is undertaking a census of all Omani crafts, including geographical sources and spread, tools and machinery used, social, cultural status of the craftsman and the product, significance and traditional Arabic names.
- The Oman Centre for Traditional Music, established in 1983 to document, conserve and promote traditional Omani music, has documented and digitised since its inception more than 80 per cent of Oman's musical traditions including photographs and audiovisual and sound recordings.
- At the Omani Traditional Medicine Clinics, established in 1988 with the aim of conserving Omani national heritage in the field of traditional medicine, traditional healers from different regions of Oman provide to the public free-of-charge medical treatment based on plant medicines. Each healer keeps his specialised medicinal knowledge secret.

In 1982, the GCC member States established 'the GCC Folklore Centre' in Doha, Qatar.[36] The main objectives of the centre were to:

- document and classify expressions of folklore in the GCC member States;
- protect Gulf folklore from misuse and illicit exploitation and preserve the rights of GCC member States to sue and to prevent these illegal acts;
- publish studies on Arab Gulf folklore;
- raise awareness importance of folklore in the Gulf region; and
- establish a central database for Gulf folklore.

Sadly, the Centre closed its doors in 2005 because of financial issues.

As a consequence, Qatar established the Qatar Heritage and Identity Centre in 2009, in part to continue some of the work of the GCC Folklore Centre.[37] One of the main objectives of the Centre is to preserve the assets that were documented

35 'Chattels of cultural property' are defined as including archaeological fossils, rare archetypes of flora and fauna, fragments of manuscripts, ancient books, documents and printed matter of special historical, artistic, scientific or literary value or interest, as well as traditional-style furniture items, painted earthenware, musical instruments, jewellery, precious stones and weapons.

36 See Daniel Martin Varisco (1989) 'The Arab Gulf States Folklore Centre: A Resource for the Study of Folklore and Traditional Culture', 23(2), Cambridge Journal of Review of Middle East Studies, pp. 157–167.

37 QHIC: Qatar Heritage and Identity Center, History of the QHIC, available at www.networkqatar.com/clients/_/qhic/history.php, last accessed 1 June 2017.

and left after the closure of the GCC Folklore Centre. The Qatari Centre is focusing on promoting, protecting and documenting Qatari heritage. It is raising awareness and investing in the younger generation to protect Qatari culture and traditional knowledge.[38]

All States participate to a lesser or greater degree in the international forums for protection of elements of traditional knowledge, to the extent that they have each ratified a number of conventions addressing aspects of traditional knowledge, expressions of culture, heritage estates and symbols and folklore. The following is just a sample of some of the conventions to which the States have acceded:

- Nagoya Protocol on Access to Genetic Resources and the Fair and Equitable Sharing of Benefits Arising from Their Utilisation to the Convention on Biological Diversity (2010) (except Bahrain, Kuwait, Oman and Saudi Arabia);
- Convention on Protection and Promotion of the Diversity of Cultural Expressions (2005) (except Bahrain, Saudi Arabia and Yemen);
- Convention on the Safeguarding of the Intangible Cultural Heritage (2003);
- Convention on the Protection of the Underwater Cultural Heritage (2001) (except Kuwait, Oman, Qatar, UAE and Yemen);
- Convention on Biological Diversity (1992);
- International Treaty on Plant Genetic Resources for Food and Agriculture (2001) (except Bahrain);
- Convention on the Protection of the World Cultural and Natural Heritage (1972);
- Convention on the Means of Prohibiting and Preventing the Illicit Import, Export and Transfer of Ownership of Cultural Property (1970) (except the UAE and Yemen);
- Convention for the Protection of Cultural Property in the Event of Armed Conflict (1954) (except the UAE).

All States have listed a number of sites on the World Heritage List with the exception of Kuwait which has tentatively identified sites for potential listing.[39]

38 QHIC: Qatar Heritage and Identity Center, Goals and objectives of the center, available at www.networkqatar.com/clients/_/qhic/mission_vision.php, last accessed 1 June 2017.

39 *Bahrain*: Pearling, Testimony of an Island Economy (2012) and Qal'at al-Bahrain – Ancient Harbour and Capital of Dilmun (2005).

Jordan: Baptism Site 'Bethany Beyond the Jordan' (Al-Maghtas) (2015), Petra (1985), Quseir Amra (1985) and Um er-Rasas (Kastrom Mefa'a) (2004).

Oman: the Archaeological Sites of Bat, Al-Khutm and Al-Ayn (1988), Bahla Fort (1987), Land of Frankincense in Dhofar governorate (2000) and the Aflaj irrigation system of Oman (2006).

Qatar: Al Zubarah Archaeological Site (2013).

Saudi Arabia: Al-Hijr Archaeological Site (Madâin Sâlih) (2008), At-Turaif District in ad-Dir'iyah (2010), Historic Jeddah, the Gate to Makkah (2014) and Rock Art in the Hail Region of Saudi Arabia (2015).

9.4 Patents, biodiversity and access to genetic resources

The issues confronting the protection of rights in respect of copyright-aligned traditional knowledge exist in similar degree with rights related to the exploitation of genetic resources and biodiversity. Issues arise in respect of ethics, preservation, respect for the rights of traditional users, continuing access, conservation and equitable sharing of benefits of the genetic resources. The award of patents on purely legal grounds generate underlying concerns in communities concerning biological resources which are common heritage and which should not be patented. A major issue in the debate on traditional knowledge is the relationship between intellectual property protection and the ownership and rights pertaining to the knowledge on which the intellectual property right has been based. It has been suggested that applicants for rights consisting of or developed from genetic resources should identify the source of these resources; provide proof that they were acquired with the prior informed consent of the country or region concerned; and share any benefits from the commercialisation of the patent with the country or region.[40]

The issue of protection of traditional knowledge also arises in the context of the TRIPS-mandated provisions concerning patentable products and processes, particularly in respect of genetic resources, biodiversity and inventions derived from native flora and fauna. The issue arose in the WTO in 1999 during the review of Article 27(3)(b) of TRIPS, which requires WTO members to protect new plant varieties either by a patent or by an effective *sui generis* system, or any combination thereof.

Developing countries have been seeking clarification of the exclusion provisions of TRIPS Article 27(3)(b). At the same time, they have expressed concern at the ongoing shrinkage in matters protected from patentability and therefore open to exploitation by multinational business. They have long argued that life forms in the broadest sense should be excluded from patentability, that information relating to the origins of a biological invention should be enshrined in the patent application process, and that the principle of prior informed consent should be incorporated into TRIPS.[41] In particular, they have expressed concern about the granting of patents and other intellectual property rights in respect of traditional knowledge to parties other than the indigenous peoples/communities who own and control it. They are further concerned that their traditional knowledge is being exploited without their prior knowledge or authorisation and without a sharing of the benefits that accrue from such exploitation and use. In some instances, the commercial harvesting of the indigenous flora, as in the case of the

UAE: Cultural Sites of Al Ain (Hafit, Hili, Bidaa Bint Saud and Oases Areas) (2011).
Yemen: Old Walled City of Shibam (1982), Old City of Sana'a (1986), Historic Town of Zabid (1993), Socotra Archipelago (2008).

40 Dina W. Kariodimedjo (2017), 'Traditional Knowledge and Cultural Heritage Protection in the Arabian Gulf and Indonesia: A Comparative Study' in David Price and Alhanoof AlDebasi (eds) Intellectual Property Rights: Development *and Enforcement in the Arab States of the Gulf*, p. 282.

41 See Verma, op. cit., p. 780.

Hoodia cactus plant of southern Africa to extract the valuable patented material, has threatened the very survival of the plant.

The strong position taken by the developing countries on the protection of traditional knowledge led to its inclusion in the Doha Ministerial Declaration in November 2001. Paragraph 19 of the Declaration instructed the Council for TRIPS – as part of its review of TRIPS Articles 27.3(b) and 71.1 – to consider the relationship between TRIPS and the Convention on Biological Diversity, and the protection of traditional knowledge and folklore. The Convention on Biological Diversity, which was agreed in 1992, seeks to promote the conservation of biodiversity and the equitable sharing of benefits arising out of the utilisation of genetic resources.[42] It asserts the sovereign rights of nations over their national resources and their right to determine access according to national legislation with the aim of facilitating the sustainable use of these resources, promoting access and their common use. It notes that access to genetic resources should be on the basis of prior informed consent and on mutually agreed terms that provide fair and equitable sharing of the results of R&D and the benefits of commercialisation and utilisation.[43] The Convention calls for the fair and equitable sharing of the benefits derived from the use of traditional knowledge and states that access and transfer of genetic resources should be consistent with the 'adequate and effective protection of intellectual property rights'.[44]

As of early 2017, 196 parties have ratified the Convention, including Jordan and Yemen. However, it is noticeable that the United States has not ratified the Convention; it signed the treaty in 1993 but has not ratified it. The United States remains firmly opposed to the Convention on the grounds that it does not see any conflict between the Convention and TRIPS. It argues that patent-disclosure requirements would be ineffective with respect to prior informed consent and access to benefit-sharing goals, as well as adding a burden to the patent system.

The Nagoya Protocol of 2010 constitutes a supplementary agreement to the Convention on Biological Diversity, and provides a legal framework for the effective implementation of

> the fair and equitable sharing of the benefits arising from the utilization of genetic resources, including by appropriate access to genetic resources and by appropriate transfer of relevant technologies, taking into account all

42 Convention on Biological Diversity (CBD), art. 1, available at www.cbd.int/convention/text/default.shtml, last accessed 1 June 2017.

43 Ibid., art. 15.

44 Article 8j of the CBD provides that 'Members should respect, preserve and maintain knowledge, innovations and practices of indigenous and local communities embodying traditional lifestyles relevant for the conservation and sustainable use of biological diversity and promote their wider application with the approval and involvement of the holders of such knowledge, innovations and practices and encourage the equitable sharing of the benefits arising from the utilization of such knowledge, innovations and practices'.

> rights over those resources and to technologies, and by appropriate funding, thereby contributing to the conservation of biological diversity and the sustainable use of its components.[45]

The Protocol explicitly mentions that the provisions listed therein shall not affect the rights and obligations of any contacting party deriving from any existing international agreement such as TRIPS, except where the exercise of those rights and obligations would cause serious damage or threat to biological diversity.[46] The parties also have the right to draft and ratify any international agreements relating to access and benefit-sharing, as long as these agreements are supportive of and do not run counter to the objectives of the Convention and the Protocol.[47]

The scope of the Protocol applies to genetic resources and the traditional knowledge associated with genetic resources that are covered by the Convention and the benefits arising from utilisation.[48] It obliges each country to adopt legislative, administrative or policy measures, concerning the benefits arising from the utilisation of genetic resources which are held by indigenous and local communities and the traditional knowledge associated with genetic resources in accordance with domestic legislation. The Protocol also obliges countries to assign rights for these indigenous and local communities over these genetic resources, which are shared in a fair and equitable way with the communities concerned.[49]

By early 2017, 89 countries had joined the Nagoya Protocol, including Jordan (2012), the UAE (2014) and Qatar (2017). Yemen signed the Protocol in 2011 but it has not yet become a party. Bahrain, Kuwait, Oman and Saudi Arabia have not expressed any views about joining the Protocol.[50]

The United Nations Food and Agriculture Organisation (FAO) adopted the International Treaty on Plant Genetic Resources for Food and Agriculture in November 2001.[51] The main objectives of the treaty is to establish a global system to provide farmers, plant breeders and scientists with access to plant genetic materials, to share knowledge about the benefits they derive from the use of these materials with the country of origin, and to recognise the efforts and contributions that farmers invest to diversify crops.[52] With the exception of Bahrain, all States have acceded to or ratified the Treaty, with Jordan being the first to do so in 2002,

45 Nagoya Protocol on Access to Genetic Resources and the Fair and Equitable Sharing of Benefits Arising from Their Utilization to the Convention on Biological Diversity, opened for signature 29 October 2010, entered into force 12 October 2014, art 1.

46 Ibid., art. 4(1).

47 Ibid., art. 4(2)

48 Ibid., art. 2.

49 Ibid., art.5.

50 Convention on Biological Diversity, 'parties to the Nagoya Protocol', available at www.cbd.int/abs/nagoya-protocol/signatories/default.shtml, last accessed 1 June 2017.

51 FAO, 'International Treaty on Plant Genetic Resources for Food and Agriculture', available at www.fao.org/plant-treaty/overview/en, last accessed 1 June 2017

52 Ibid.

followed by Kuwait in 2003, then Oman and UAE in 2004, Saudi Arabia in 2005, Yemen in 2006 and Qatar in 2008. It is not clear if Bahrain will accede to the treaty.

As a result of the International Treaty, the League of Arab States established the Arab Network of Plant Genetic Resources (ANPGR) in 2011.[53] The purpose of the ANPGR is to ensure that the Arab countries cooperate and contribute with their local centres and programmes to preserve and sustain utilisation of plant genetic resources as well as the fair and equitable sharing of the benefits arising out of their use, in harmony with the Treaty.[54] To date, only 15 Arab countries have joined the ANPGR, including Jordan, Oman, Qatar and Saudi Arabia.[55]

Oman, Jordan, UAE and Yemen have established their own Plant Genetic Resources centres to act as national platforms for ANPGR to share information and knowledge for research and development for target groups such as farmers. The UAE also established 'the Plant Genetic Resources Centre' in 2017, to document the State's genetic resources and biodiverse plant species, and to study and conserve them.[56] The Centre also focuses on improving the capacity to access and exchange plant genetic resources information, and to preserve plant genetic resources by:

- maximising use of the results of other projects and database applications;
- preventing redundancy and duplication of data and efforts; and
- ensuring maximum coordination among various agricultural institutes, programmes and personnel for the benefit of agricultural development and food security.[57]

With the recent and rapid changes in the plant genetic resources, many of the indigenous plants that are in common usage for therapeutic and medicinal purposes among the States are granted protection. The following are just a few examples of plant varieties used for medicinal purposes in the region and currently the subject of scientific research in the UAE:

- seeds of the senna plant, *Cassia italica*, used as a laxative and for stomach pains;
- seeds of the desert squash, *Citrullus colocynthi*, highly acclaimed as a cure for diabetes;

53 The Arab Organization for Agricultural Development, 'The Arab Network of Plant Genetic Resources', available at www.aoad.org/gb/AboutSystem.aspx, last accessed 26 May 2017.

54 Ibid.

55 Ibid.

56 'Abu Dhabi will set up the Plant Genetic Resources Centre', *Gulf News*, 24 November 2014, available at http://gulfnews.com/news/uae/environment/abu-dhabi-to-set-up-plant-genetic-resources-centre-1.1417330, last accessed 26 May 2017.

57 Emirates Plant Genetic Resources Knowledge Network, available at http://emirates.plantgenetic.com/Pages/About.aspx?lang=EN&DId=0&I=0&CId=0&CMSId=5002852#sthash.zZ0Ksavy.dpuf, last accessed 1 June 2017.

- the bitter sap of the milkweed, *Calotropis procera*, dried and used to treat toothache; poultices made from the leaves are applied to joints to heal rheumatism;
- *Salsola imbricata* and several *Suaeda* species, dried and powdered, used as snuff to clear the sinuses;
- poultices of the henna plant used to soothe headaches; henna is also extensively used as a hair dye and particularly to decorate hands and feet in intricate designs for special occasions such as weddings and *Eid* celebrations;
- the poisonous plant, *Rhazya stricta*, used in small quantities to settle gastric upsets;
- the fragrant herb, *Teucrium stocksianum*, a member of the sage family, used for combating fevers;
- the seeds of garat, *Acacia nilotica*, ground to a powder and used to dry out second-degree burns.[58]

Notwithstanding these individual scientific and cultural initiatives, the States have not taken strong legislative steps to protect their biodiversity and genetic resources in the intellectual property context. Perhaps this is not surprising in view of the fundamental differences in the international forums over the issue of protection of traditional knowledge and genetic resources and the form that the protection, if any, should take. And perhaps also contributing to this situation is the relatively low level of domestic-initiated patent activity in the Arabian Peninsula region, particularly patent activity involving indigenous genetic resources. Much of the regional patent application activity originating in the region arises from the oil and gas industries. Accordingly, the patent laws or plant protection laws of the States generally follow a conventional format and show a common WIPO-sourced heritage.

However, these fledgling efforts are being undermined by external pressures aimed at reinforcing their TRIPS-plus protective environment. The Bahrain and Oman FTAs limit the grounds on which a patent may be revoked to those that would have justified a refusal to grant a patent – that is, where the application does not satisfy the tests of being new (or a new use), involving an inventive step and being capable of industrial application.[59] The FTAs also provide that only fraud, misrepresentation or inequitable conduct may be the basis for revoking a patent or holding it unenforceable, and opposition to the grant of a patent may not proceed until after the patent has been granted. Since disclosure of any genetic material in respect of the patent is not a condition for granting the patent, its non-disclosure would not come under the classification of either fraud or misrepresentation and would not be grounds for revoking a patent.

58 See *UAE Interact*, 'Traditional Uses of Plants', at www.uaeinteract.com/history/trad/trd10.asp, last accessed 13 June 2017.

59 Bahrain FTA, art. 14.8.4; Oman FTA, art. 15.8.4.

9.5 Trademarks and geographical indications

The States' trademarks and geographical indications (GI) laws offer some limited opportunity or potential for the protection of traditional knowledge, cultural expressions or folklore. In the case of trademarks, the ongoing unlimited registration allows marks of cultural heritage to be utilised to protect indigenous cultural material for longer periods of time, even beyond the copyright period – this feature of trademarks law makes it more flexible than copyright law. However, a major limitation is that the protection comes only in respect of goods and services in the *course of trade*, a requirement of TRIPS and a requirement enshrined in the trademark laws of all the States. Commercialisation of a culturally sensitive mark or symbol may be both prohibited and anathema to many societies. However, there is a growing trend to utilise such marks or symbols before third parties and foreign organisations secure registration of seemingly exotic-sounding indigenous words, designs and themes.

In the case of GIs, there is a greater degree of protection potential, notwithstanding considerable ongoing contention within the WTO and other international forums on the nature of protection that should be extended to GIs. The original negotiations on the GI provisions of TRIPS were among the most difficult to resolve, because of the fundamental differences between the two main protagonists of the Agreement, namely the United States and the European Union. Accordingly, in recognition of the compromises that had to be made to finalise the negotiations, TRIPS has created an artificial distinction by providing a basic standard of protection for all GIs and a higher standard specifically for those relating to wines and spirits.

Two issues have been debated in the TRIPS Council under the Doha mandate, namely the extension of the higher level of protection of TRIPS Article 23 beyond wines and spirits, and the creation of a multilateral register for wines and spirits. In respect of the issue of extending the levels of protection beyond wines and spirits, some WTO members have been seeking to initiate negotiations to amend TRIPS, while other members oppose the move.[60]

Those advocating extension argue that the higher level of protection enables them to improve the marketing of their products by differentiating them more effectively from their competitors. A proposal by the European Union calls for TRIPS to be amended so that all products would be eligible for the higher level of protection of Article 23 and for inclusion on the multilateral registration system

60 Paragraph 18 of the Doha Declaration notes that the Council of TRIPS will handle work on extension under the Declaration's paragraph 12 on implementation issues. Paragraph 12 states that 'negotiations on outstanding implementation issues shall be an integral part' of the Doha work programme and that implementation issues 'shall be addressed as a matter of priority by the relevant WTO bodies'. Many developing and European countries argue that the outstanding implementation issues are already part of the negotiation and its package of results (the 'single undertaking'). Others argue that these issues can become negotiating subjects only if the Trade Negotiations Committee decides to include them in the talks.

currently being negotiated for wines and spirits. Those opposing extension argue that the existing level of protection, under TRIPS Article 22, is adequate. They posit that extending the additional protection to other products would impose extra financial and administrative burdens on all WTO members, and most heavily on developing countries, and that these burdens would outweigh any trade benefit.

Protection of GIs in the context of the above-mentioned debates on an extension of protection and a multilateral register creates something of a conundrum for the Arabian Peninsula. With the exception of Jordan, the States may have considerable difficulty in endorsing a proposal which advocated an extension of protection beyond wines and spirits if such proposal presupposed any degree of commitment to also protecting wines and spirits. The States are also unlikely to be supportive of the proposal for a register which includes wine and spirits because of the religious, legal and bureaucratic issues domestically. Yet the issue of broadening the scope of GIs may be attractive since the States realise that they themselves have products that are indigenous to their own territories and to the region and which may be worthy of protection. These products include certain blends and brews of coffee, traditional Arabic clothing, ceremonial weapons, woven products and methods, sweets, perfumes and fragrant oils, to mention just a few. It could also be argued that domestically the States inadvertently provide a form of protection to geographical indications for wines and spirits and pork-derivative products by not allowing any trademarks directly related to these products to be registered and/or protected – irrespective of whether those marks originate from the original owners or from foreign or domestic competitors or counterfeiters.

The States may perceive that the need for a formalised system of protection does not arise as much domestically as it does abroad. Domestic protection can call upon a combination of custom and cultural traditions, as well as provisions of domestic trademark laws and commercial conduct codes. However, adequate protection overseas for domestic geographical indications will require protection at home as well as local protection for the other country's GIs.

As mentioned earlier, only Bahrain, Jordan, Oman and Yemen have specific GI laws or substantive provisions in force, while the other States incorporate some notional reference or slightly stronger provision within their trademark laws. The Bahraini and the Yemeni GI laws require a GI to be protected in its country of origin to obtain local protection.[61] To enable local protection to occur, it requires the designated Ministry (usually of Commerce and Industry) to maintain a GI register. The Omani GI law and the GI provisions of Qatar's trademark law do not require registration as a precondition for local protection, notwithstanding the fact that they both also provide for the existence of a register.[62] The Omani law also restricts protection to those GIs that remain protected or which are still used in their country of origin.

61 Bahrain, Legislative Decree No. 16 of 2004, art. 3; Yemen, Law No. 23 of 2010, art. 32.
62 Oman, Royal Decree No. 40/2000, art. 4; Qatar, Law No. 9 of 2002, arts 38 and 40.

There are a number of local products in these States which could qualify for protection, and should be protected, under local laws. For example, some of the Jordanian local products that are protected under its GI law are *Albulquaoui Ghee*, *kafaraat olive oil*, *Jdita pomegranate* and *jerashi labna*. However, the case is a little different for the other States with the unresolved question being which particular laws might most appropriately and effectively provide protection – that is, trademark laws or GI laws. Just a few of the products that have been suggested as suitable for some form of protection include:

- UAE 'Masafi' mineral water, as well as a number of mineral/spring waters from other States;
- western Yemen Mocha coffee;
- Arabic *karwa* and other local and regional blends of Arabic coffee and cardamom;
- perfumes, particularly those which utilise frankincense, myrrh and other indigenous plant derivatives, such as *Amouage* from Oman;
- Omani *halwa*, a date-based sweet traditionally and still customarily served with *karwa* to visitors and as a mark of Gulf hospitality;
- other date-based food and handicraft/artisan products;
- eastern Yemen 'Doan' honey from the Hadramout region;
- Saudi Arabia Sukary al-Qasim – special types of dates from the Qasim area;
- Qatar pearls and pearl-shell products;
- Jordan Dead Sea soup and scrubs.

Some of these products have well-established international reputations, but others do not yet enjoy an international market warranting a high degree of protection of their GI elements. What is still unclear is whether commitment to any of the three major proposals expounded will lead to protection of local GIs in foreign markets, or whether it will be primarily geared to protecting foreign GIs in domestic markets. A number of foreign GIs are already excluded from protection in the region on moral or religious grounds and would continue to be so.

The recent movement by some of the GCC and other States towards closer trade relationships with other countries through bilateral agreements may also militate against the generation of benefits by their adoption of an enhanced protection regime for geographical indications. In the absence of any clear and identifiable benefit, it is most unlikely that the States would commit to an enhanced protection regime that extends beyond the current status quo. But they may also hold that a more compelling reason for maintaining the status quo is the inability of the WTO's and WIPO's major players to agree among themselves as to the nature that an enhanced level of protection, if any, should take. The States may see little need to travel any further in respect of protection for geographical indications in an intellectual property protection context.

9.6 Concluding remarks

Despite the involvement of several intergovernmental bodies working on the protection of traditional knowledge and an impressive body of literature and documents produced by international, national and non-governmental bodies, the progress achieved in this respect is not very impressive so far. In fact, the major achievement to date has been the provision of a sustained and active debate over a number of years, which has enabled the developing countries to ensure that the issues surrounding the appropriate protection of traditional knowledge, biodiversity and access to genetic resources continue to maintain a high profile and undergo intense public scrutiny.

As they have done previously with other areas of intellectual property, the Arabian Peninsula States are likely to stand back and observe the negotiating and positioning of the major representatives from both the developed nations and the other developing countries. Since the major players cannot yet resolve their diametrically opposed positions on protection of traditional knowledge in an intellectual property context, the States would no doubt consider that refraining from becoming too heavily involved might be an appropriate course of action. In the meantime, the States will continue with their own national initiatives to identify, record, register and protect the abundant elements of their national cultures and heritages, until the appropriate mode for the protection of the intellectual property aspects of those cultures and heritages is clarified in the multinational forums. They will no doubt become involved if the benefits, potential and actual, to them are abundantly clear, or if their obligations in the international context require them to support a particular position of commitment.

Where this strategy breaks down, however, is in the context of negotiation and conclusion of regional and bilateral trade agreements with intellectual property provisions and obligations that limit the discretionary authority of signatories to protect their traditional knowledge or genetic resource potential. This scenario particularly occurs in respect of provisions relating to the preservation of monopolistic rights through the maximisation of patentability and the minimisation of patentability exclusions for pharmaceutical and agrochemical products and processes.

However, the issue of how to maximise protection of the region's various forms and expressions of traditional knowledge, traditional cultural expressions, genetic resources, folklore, or other terms that the States might be inclined to use, offers another opportunity for them to act collaboratively to establish a broad regional framework for the development, management and preservation of this crucial area of TRIPS-minus non-protection. The collaboration might occur through a degree of harmonisation of national laws, while still maintaining their individual integrity, or through the sponsorship of a set of initiatives by an expanded GCC.

10

TRIPS ANEW – AND POSSIBLE FUTURE DIRECTIONS

10.1 Introduction

The primary objective of this work has been to examine the endeavours of the Arabian Peninsula States – namely the GCC member States of Bahrain, Kuwait, Oman, Qatar, Saudi Arabia and the UAE, and Jordan and Yemen as prospective GCC members – in establishing national intellectual property protection regimes which both meet their international treaty obligations and are also congruent with their domestic policy objectives and needs. The minimum standards benchmark for this examination has been the WTO's TRIPS Agreement of 1995 (TRIPS), since all these States needed to accede to and fully comply with TRIPS as a condition of WTO membership. The work encompasses the status of intellectual property protection prior to the introduction of the WTO and TRIPS (the 'pre-TRIPS stage'), the States' response to their obligations to meet TRIPS requirements ('TRIPS and post-TRIPS stage'), the impact of external influences through bilateral trade agreements ('TRIPS-plus stage') and areas which fall outside the TRIPS protection spectrum ('TRIPS-minus stage').

The work argues that, since the late 1960s/early 1970s, when they either gained their independence or emerged from sustained periods of international isolationism, these Arabian Peninsula States have undergone a transformation of their intellectual property legislative regimes at a very rapid rate – virtually in the time frame of one or two generations. This period of transformation has been marked by three major but very different phases of development of the regimes. Each phase has been characterised by degrees of foreign intervention which have directed or influenced to greater or lesser extent the construction of the States' intellectual property laws. But this foreign intervention has not necessarily caused the creation of laws that have been congruent with the States' needs or have achieved their objectives in terms of enforcement effectiveness.

The first of these phases, namely the pre-TRIPS period that continued through to the mid-1990s, is notable for the dearth of *sui generis* intellectual property laws in existence; the laws that were in force were few in number and existed mainly in the fields of trademarks and patents. But even these laws were subject to foreign design; Jordan's trademark law of 1952 was based on the Palestinian law promulgated during the British mandate of Palestine and Trans-Jordan, and hence was based on English trademark law. Bahrain's 1955 law on patents, industrial designs and trademarks was almost entirely and directly subordinate to the corresponding UK laws and processes. The Kuwaiti trademark and patent laws of 1961 and 1962 respectively were based on Egyptian models, which in turn derived much from corresponding continental civil codes. However, this dearth of *sui generis* laws does not mean that protection for certain types of intellectual property rights was not available; it existed in an overarching perspective in the divine laws of social and moral conduct laid down in the *Qur'an* and the *Sunna* of the Prophet. In a more corporeal and secular sense, and in the absence of any mainstream intellectual property framework, it also existed in the form of laws governing commercial activity and conduct. However, even these commercial laws were generally subject to foreign influence and secular codification. In addition, the national frameworks for the control of publishing and public dissemination of printed material, which all States possessed and actively enforced, also provided some limited protection for certain types of copyrightable material.

The second developmental phase is marked by the establishment of the WTO and the consequential introduction of TRIPS in 1995, and a flurry of legislative activity by the Arabian Peninsula States as they attempt to meet their statutory obligations to make their intellectual property laws TRIPS-compliant and their enforcement effective. In so doing the States took advantage of the five-year discretionary period granted by the WTO Charter to developing countries to reach compliance with TRIPs and other WTO agreements – on occasion stretching that discretionary period well beyond the intentions of the Charter's creators. TRIPS heralded a major shift in the multilateral intellectual property environment and treatment of intellectual property rights by establishing unprecedented levels of protection for global implementation. However, the shift took shape by reference largely to the needs of the leading industrialised nations (and, to a lesser extent, those of the other developed countries). WIPO, which had already been a significant influence on the States' pre-TRIPS intellectual property laws, continued to play a crucial role in guiding the States in the compilation of their TRIPS-compliant laws and the judicial, structural and administrative capacity-building so crucial for their enforcement. With fluctuating degrees of commitment, the States embarked on reshaping their intellectual property protection regimes. At one end of the spectrum, Oman, which possessed few intellectual property laws in the pre-TRIPS phase, introduced in 2000, in a single swoop, a full suite of laws which addressed the TRIPS areas of intellectual property rights, plus protection for new plant varieties. At the other end, Jordan continues to retain its trademark law of 1952, preferring to enact a series of amending statutes to update it on an ongoing basis. The most recent updates occurred in 2010. Bahrain and Kuwait, meanwhile, both of which had been the early pace-setters in regional intellectual property protection, still relied on copyright, trademark and patent laws which were either pre-TRIPS or were derived from earlier pre-TRIPS laws. Yemen, still to achieve either WTO or GCC membership, had in place an omnibus intellectual property law of 1994 that relied on even earlier statutes until it introduced a new suite of post-TRIPS laws between 2010 and 2012.

The two decades since the creation of the WTO and the emergence of TRIPs experience a round of legislative activity by the States as they strive to meet their statutory obligations to introduce new laws for areas of intellectual property not previously existent or recognised, or to make their current laws TRIPS-compliant and their enforcement effective. Hard on the heels of the transformation required to their respective intellectual property protection regimes as necessitated by the TRIPS and post-TRIPS phase comes a new round of emerging changes as the States enter a TRIPS-plus phase. The dominant driving factor shaping the character of their laws during the first decade is the bilateral strategy pursued by the United States as part of its aim to create a Middle East Free Trade Area under US sponsorship (and, thereby, direction). This new round commences with a series of bilateral trade and investment agreements to which Arabian Peninsula States individually accede during the late 1990s; subsequently, the United States concludes FTAs with Jordan (2000), Bahrain (2004) and Oman (2005), all three agreements incorporating extensive provisions on intellectual property.

The intellectual property provisions of these FTAs constitute much higher standards of protection than those set by TRIPS, and further restrict or remove the limited degree of manouvrability that TRIPS permits developing and least-developed countries to enjoy by reducing or eliminating the Agreement's exception or discretionary provisions. The bilateral agreements are reinforced by demands that the signatory States not only adopt the higher standards enshrined in the FTAs themselves but also adopt and adhere to a range of multilateral treaties which constitute TRIPS-plus standards. The multilateral treaties also reduce and restrict the discretion that TRIPS grants to signatories to craft their laws so that they may include some allowances sympathetic to their respective national needs and objectives. As a consequence, Jordan, Bahrain and Oman have subsequently again upgraded their intellectual property laws with enhanced protection standards and committed themselves to a further number of multilateral intellectual property conventions to meet their FTA obligations.

However, the second decade of this TRIPS-plus phase is accompanied by an emerging diametric shift in the regional geopolitical dynamics, with a consequent change in the nature and pace of the development of national intellectual property protection regimes. The nature of this shift is characterised by a global financial crisis, by changes in the United States administration accompanied by a directional shift in foreign policy, by Europe and members of the European Union (EU) being diverted by becoming embroiled in a series of home financial crises and bailouts, and by increasing interest and involvement in the region being displayed by other emerging players, notably Russia and China. The global financial crisis and the crash in oil and energy prices also cause the States and the GCC to focus more on inward retrospection and regional issues rather than promoting further international trade agreements.

The second decade is also marked by the GCC itself taking a more prominent role in regional intellectual property leadership. The GCC had previously floated regional patents and trademark registration schemes from the late 1990s with little if no effective uptake by individual members. That situation changes during this second decade with both regional patents and trademarks schemes gaining increasing acceptance. The Unified Trademarks Law, for example, has already been formally adopted by four of the GCC member States, and there is speculation that the others may follow in the foreseeable future.

10.2 A climate of domestic change

The efforts of the Arabian Peninsula States to protect mainstream intellectual property rights in a remarkably short period of time are impressive. However, the picture is still one of active change. Attention has largely focused on the major areas of activity and concern, namely copyright, patents and trademarks; the intellectual property rights which have received a lesser degree of attention, such as industrial designs, integrated circuits, new plant varieties, and trade secrets, have not attracted the same imperative for preservation of interests and investment. Hence, they have received only fairly brief attention by most States, or have gained some degree of protection by association with other laws, or have been largely passed over. They will attract attention as the major areas become settled and established.

The rapid rate of progress has meant that enactment of a law is not necessarily followed in reasonably rapid succession by the necessary implementing regulations, with the consequence of generating confusion and uncertainty as to the current law in force and thus the law to be enforced. For example, Bahrain does not appear to have yet issued the implementing for Legislative Decree No. 22 of 2006 concerning Copyright and Neighbouring Rights, which was gazetted in June 2006. Similarly, Qatar does not appear to have yet issued the implementing regulations for Law No. 3 of 2006, the Patents Law, which was issued on 6 August 2006, or Law No. 7 of 2002 on Copyright. On occasion, laws and enforcement initiatives can become superseded almost before they have had time to come into practical effect. Delays amounting to years on the passage of a necessary implementing regulation or enforcement strategy for a particular law have meant that the regulation gets overtaken by amending or repealing legislation. But the administrative processes to rectify this conundrum and remove the invalidated regulation are themselves not always in place or operationally effective.

Domestically, some current intellectual property laws still require further refinement to remove the idiosyncratic remnants of former laws, to bring them up to at least TRIPS standards or even current TRIPS-plus, and to introduce sanctions that are generally seen to be effective deterrents. Furthermore, some will also need to re-examine and upgrade their laws and enforcement strategies to now take account of the TRIPS-plus obligations to which they have agreed under their respective bilateral agreements, and the TRIPS-plus treaties to which they have recently acceded.

Kuwait in particular still has on its statute books intellectual property laws which not only fall well short of the current so-called 'highest international standard' but are also perceived to be TRIPS-deficient. Kuwait remains on the USTR Special 301 Priority Watch Listing for 2016, in part because of its perceived failure to make progress on amending its outdated intellectual property laws, particularly copyright, and because of alleged ineffective enforcement against copyright and trademark infringement.[1] The implication here is that, among other measures, the United States will continue to apply pressure for compliance through its Annual Special 301 Report process. However, Kuwait's issuance of a new copyright law in late 2016 (Law No. 22 of 2016) with considerably strengthened sanctions may well see it removed from the Special 301 Report in 2017.

Saudi Arabia, as the largest and most strategically important economy in the Middle East region may also continue to face criticism from US quarters that its copyright law still lacks some basic standards that are required by TRIPs and the current international standards. Saudi Arabia has also been criticised for its failure to ensure transparency in the Saudi enforcement system generally, particularly in respect of timely information on policing and judicial action to aggrieved right holders, and to apply sanctions that serve as harsh and effective deterrents to potential infringers. Being removed from the Special 301 List does not ensure that a State cannot return in the future.

In any case, the benchmark for the quality of an intellectual property rights protection regime cannot be measured solely by the number of laws on the statute books or the number of international bodies joined or conventions adopted. 'Any nation, industrialized or not, can choose virtually overnight to introduce any amount of intellectual property law it chooses but that would not necessarily change its backwardness.'[2] 'Shorn of the economic and cultural roots that it is, or supposed to be, based on and evolve around, intellectual property is a set of indeterminate value except to those that the rules happen to serve because they codify the latter's national needs.'[3]

The most challenging element of the TRIPS and TRIPS-plus phases, as perceived by both the States themselves and the industrialised nations, is the regional enforcement of their intellectual property protection obligations consistent with the standards enshrined in TRIPS, the TRIPS-plus treaties and the bilateral

1 USTR, *2016 Special 301 Report*, p. 46.

2 Assafa Endeshaw (2001), 'The Paradox of Intellectual Property Lawmaking in the New Millennium: Universal Templates as Terms of Surrender for Non-industrial Nations; Piracy as an Offshoot', p. 24, available at https://papers.ssrn.com/sol3/papers.cfm?abstract_id=291692, last accessed 26 May 2017.

3 Ibid.

agreements to which the States have made commitment. Notwithstanding the presence of comprehensive sets of laws and treaty commitments, there has nevertheless existed something of a disjunct between the principle of enforcement as enshrined in the various legislative regimes and the practice as exemplified by the degree of effective policing and judicial action.

The principal barriers to successfully dealing with intellectual property infringements do not subsist so much in the substantive law as in the practical application of the available remedies and sanctions. In a number of States, the negative impact of the barriers is exacerbated by the presence of sanctions which are deemed both inadequate and incomplete in scope and scale. But, irrespective of inadequacies in a few older laws, the sanctions available to the authorities across the broad spectrum of the region's intellectual property laws are not being fully exploited. The reasons do not rest solely with the enforcement authorities or the judiciary; entrenched local societal, cultural and commercial attitudes also contribute to the development of this enforcement challenge.

The establishment of the national and regional intellectual property infrastructures, and the skills development of the human resources to give effect to these national needs and aspirations, will continue to be significant but surmountable challenges. The States readily acknowledge that their infrastructures and human resource expertise are such that they face considerable challenges in the medium to long term to enforce their intellectual property laws to the standards they would seek and the standard expected of them by the developed countries and intellectual property right holders.

There will be other factors remaining in play as the systemic and structural challenges are resolved. It has been suggested that counterfeiting and piracy are not necessarily simply manifestations of the lack of intellectual property protection or enforcement, but rather characterisation of the incongruity of the laws to the degree of industrial development in the State.[4] It may also be a manifestation of the denial of the sovereign right of a State to engage in lawmaking as it sees fit that pushes it to adopt a position of indifference at best, or active resentment at worst, as regards the enforcement of foreign intellectual property rights.[5] The perceived lack of legitimacy and fairness in forcing developing countries to subscribe to laws that significantly ignore their plight, and in particular to set up legal forms that are not congruent with the state of their economy and technology, will make the enforcement of foreign intellectual property in these countries an uphill struggle.[6]

Societies in developing countries will continue to resist changes to their intellectual property laws, and when they do make changes, they will be slow to enforce them in favour of foreign corporations at the expense of local merchants. To the extent that TRIPS-plus rules may adversely affect the economic interests of

4 Endeshaw, op. cit., p. 31.
5 Ibid.
6 Ibid., p. 34.

developing countries, passive resistance may be the most likely counter mechanism. The enforcement disjunct shall remain for the time being, even though some of the States will continue to achieve major successes against the virtually uncontrolled counterfeiting and piracy that existed in the past. But as the imperative for change becomes more internally driven, the successes against piracy will accelerate.

The next major phase unfolding in this ongoing and fascinating story is undoubtedly the development of human resources and infrastructural development in the administration of the intellectual property regimes. Another major phase will then be the introduction of strategies and initiatives more attuned to national interests and needs, such as a stronger protective regime for traditional knowledge and cultural heritage. Associated with this initiative will be a fine-tuning of the more conventional intellectual property laws to also better reflect national interests. However, in this latter case, the opportunities for such refinements will be confined by, and will need to take place in the context of, the multilateral conventions and bilateral agreements into which the States have already entered.

10.3 Current status of intellectual property protection in the Arabian Peninsula States

The aforementioned shift in the regional geopolitical focus during the second decade of the TRIPS-plus phase seems to have been followed by something of a relaxation in the pace of legislative activity in respect of domestic statutory intellectual property protection frameworks. This domestic relaxation – a legislative drawing of breath – could be explained in part by a perception among the GCC member States that their laws now represent, or are close enough to, prevailing international standards. It could also be explained by the focus of attention moving away from standards enshrined in upgraded *sui generis* domestic intellectual property laws in favour of bilateral and regional trade agreements with enhanced trade (and therefore intellectual property protection standards) access and exploitation opportunities.

Nevertheless, there has been ongoing activity to reinforce or add to the mainstream intellectual property protection regime. For example, in March 2017, Jordan ratified the Patent Cooperation Treaty; during 2016, Bahrain and Saudi Arabia separately issued their implementing regulations to bring their adoption of the GCC Unified Trademark Law into effect; Kuwait issued a long-awaited new copyright and neighbouring rights law; the UAE issued regulations to establish a specialised federal intellectual property court; and in March 2015, Qatar ratified the Budapest Treaty.

By the end of 2016 and the twenty-first anniversary of the WTO and TRIPS, all States have established comprehensive legislative regimes for the protection of intellectual property. Most, but by no means all, of their intellectual property laws generally reveal a willingness to comply with the international standards as enshrined in both TRIPS and the TRIPS-plus conventions, even if at times some still fall a little short in respect of the detail and practice. The comprehensive fabric of intellectual property protection that has now been constructed through a network of domestic laws and international conventions stands in stark contrast to the status 21 years ago when TRIPS first came into force. The States' current laws post-date and together encompass the major areas of intellectual property addressed in the Agreement.

The status in respect of membership of the international bodies and adherence to the major international conventions and treaties encompassing intellectual property protection has also advanced apace, with most States now having acceded to the key treaties. All States are now members of both WIPO and the WTO, and all have acceded to the Berne and Paris Conventions. A majority of States have also acceded to the WIPO internet treaties – the WCT and WPPT – and to the Patent Cooperation Treaty (PCT). Most States refer to or use the Madrid Protocol on the international registration of trademarks. Although few States have formally acceded to the Nice Agreement for the classification of marks for goods and services, all utilise a recent edition of the Agreement, primarily being the tenth edition (in force from 1 January 2012), for their domestic trademark registration purposes. A few have even acted proactively and acceded to recently introduced treaties such as the Beijing Treaty on Audiovisual Performances (2012) and the Marrakesh Treaty to Facilitate Access to Published Works for Persons Who Are Blind, Visually Impaired or Otherwise Print Disabled (2013).

Table 10.1 summarises the current situation in respect of domestic laws and international commitments in intellectual property in the Arabian Peninsula States. The years listed in respect of national laws represent the year of introduction of the current law rather than the most recent amendment, and the year in which an international convention came into force domestically.

Outside the conventional intellectual property paradigm, the GCC member States have also been active in attempting to identify, preserve and protect elements of their own cultures and societies – areas in which there has been much debate in the international forums but little effective progress in establishing global standards of protection, notably traditional knowledge and cultural heritage, genetic resources, biodiversity, traditional medicines and indigenous plant species. The States themselves have for some years held a particular interest in these areas and have taken the initiative in introducing some protection standards. They have introduced laws to protect both their tangible and intangible cultural heritage; the exposure to the international norms of intellectual property rights have engendered an appreciation that these subjects are also forms of intellectual property entitled to protection within a domestic and international context. A number of States have constructed national databases to register a range of forms of cultural heritage that encompass song and dance, traditional arts and crafts, and traditional medicines. Some have also made great strides in projects for the registration of native plant species and their applications in traditional and folk medicines.

As the paradigm in international intellectual property protection moves from the traditional and well-established trade-related forms of protection – centring on trademarks, copyright and neighbouring rights and patents – to encompass the

TABLE 10.1 Current intellectual property laws and international conventions in the Arabian Peninsula States (as at March 2017)

	Bahrain	*Jordan*	*Kuwait*	*Oman*	*Qatar*	*Saudi Arabia*	*UAE*	*Yemen*
Copyright	2014	2014	2016	2008	2002	2003	2006	2012
GCC trademarks	2014	–	2015	–	2014	2014	–	–
Trademarks	–	1952	–		2002	–	2002	2010
Patents	2006	1999	2013		2006	2004	2002	2011
Industrial Designs	2006	2000	2001	2008	2002			2010
Geographical indications	2006	2000	–		2002	2002	2002	2010
Integrated Circuits	2006	2000	2001		2005	2004	2002	2011
Trade Secrets	2006	2000	–		2005	2005	2002	2011
New Plant Varieties	2005	2000	–	2009	–	2004	–	–
GCC Patent Reg'n	2004	–	2013	2000	2003	2001	2000	–
Arab Agreement on Author's rights (1981)	–	–	1986	–	1986	1985	–	–
Arab Treaty on Cybercrime	–	2013	–	2015	2012	–	2011	–
GCC	1981	–	1981	1981	1981	1981	1981	–
Arab League	1971	1945	1961	1971	1971	1945	1971	1945
WTO (and TRIPS)	1995	2000	1995	2000	1996	2005	1996	2014
WIPO	1995	1972	1998	1997	1976	1982	1974	1990
IP protection treaties								
Beijing, audiovisual performances	–	2012	–	–	2015	–	2014	–
Berne, literary works	1997	1999	2014	1999	2000	2004	2004	2008
Brussels, satellite signals	2007	–	–	2007	–	–	–	–
Geneva, phonograms	–	–	–	–	–	–	–	–
Madrid, False Indications	–	–	–	–	–	–	–	–

Marrakesh, visually impaired print	–	2013	–	–	–	–	2014	–
Nairobi, Olympic Symbol	–	–	–	1986	1983	–	–	–
Paris, Industrial Property	1997	1972	2014	1999	2000	2004	1996	2007
PLT	2005	–	–	2007	–	2013	–	–
Rome, performers, etc	2006	–	–	–	–	–	2005	–
Singapore trademarks	–	–	–	–	–	–	–	–
TLT	2007	–	–	2007	–	–	–	–
Washington, layout designs	–	–	–	–	–	–	–	–
WCT	2005	2004	–	2005	2005	–	2004	–
WPPT	2005	2004	–	2005	2005	–	2005	–
Classification treaties								
Locarno, designs	–	–	–	–	–	–	–	–
Nice, marks	2005 10th ed.	2008 10th ed.	10th ed.	10th ed.	7th ed	10th ed	10th ed.	8th ed.
Strasbourg, patents	–	–	–	–	–	–	–	–
Vienna, marks elements	–	2008	–	–	–	–	–	–
Global protection treaties								
Budapest, microorganism	2012	2008	–	2007	2014	–	–	–
Hague, Industrial designs	–	–	–	2009	–	–	–	–
Lisbon, appellations	–	–	–	–	–	–	–	–
Madrid Protocol, marks	2005	–	–	2007	–	–	–	–
PCT	2007	2017	2016	2001	2011	2013	1999	–
UPOV, plant varieties	2005	2004	–	2007	–	–	–	–
UCC, copyright (1971)	–	–	–	–	–	1994	–	–

Source: compiled by the authors

Note: All states utilise the Nice classifications, although not all have formally acceded to the Agreement.

new emerging areas of traditional knowledge and cultural heritage, biodiversity, global geographical indications (as distinct from a European context) and public health policy, so there will be a shift in the balance of power in the major international forums of WTO and WIPO. The GCC member States, which to date have largely taken a backseat in the international forums, may possibly assume a more vocal role globally as they develop domestically a sophisticated understanding of intellectual property rights in the international context and an expertise and appreciation of the benefits of effective enforcement.

10.4 Emergence of the GCC in regional IP leadership

Membership of the GCC

As discussed in an earlier chapter, the creation of the GCC was essentially in response to a perceived threat from an Islamic fundamentalist Iran, a Ba'athist Iraq, the state of civil war in Yemen and the 1979 Soviet intervention in Afghanistan – all of which threatened to destabilise the ruling dynasties in the Arabian Peninsula and to involve their states in wider conflicts.[7] The GCC is now seeking to expand its membership with countries that share its political and cultural values, as well as similar economic conditions and security issues, in a bid to create a new centre of gravity, influence and control within the region, and more broadly among the other Middle East and MENA countries.[8] By joining the GCC, Jordan will support the other GCC member States with its extensive military, police and intelligence capability, and in return the GCC will help Jordan to boost its economy by trade and investment.[9] Jordan has expressed interest in joining the GCC since 1996, but until the present has been largely ignored.

Due to the political conflict in Yemen that has arisen in 2011 and the civil war that followed in late 2014 which required the Saudi–Emirati intervention to end the war, the GCC is reconsidering including Yemen as a member.[10] The fact that Yemen has become a WTO member will help ease its integration with the other States as their laws are now more consistent and similar with each other. But political and security stability aligned with Saudi Arabia will need to be established before further moves towards integration or membership can be seriously progressed.

7 See R K Ramanazi (1988), *The Gulf Cooperation Council: Record and Analysis.*

8 Saud Al Tamamy (2015), 'GCC Membership Expansion: Possibilities and Obstacles', *Aljazeera Centre for Studies*, 31 March 2015, available at http://studies.aljazeera.net/en/dossiers/2015/03/201533171547520486.html, last accessed 26 May 2017.

9 Curtis Ryan (2014), 'Jordan, Morocco and an Expanded GCC', *Middle East Research and Information Project*, available at www.merip.org/jordan-morocco-expanded-gcc, last accessed 26 May 2017.

10 Farea Al Muslimi (2016), 'A History of Missed Opportunities: Yemen and the GCC', *Carnegie Middle East Center*, 5 January, available at http://carnegie-mec.org/diwan/62405, last accessed 26 May 2017.

The GCC and intellectual property initiatives

The earlier-mentioned period of relative domestic quietude in respect of intellectual property legislative activity, in the last decade or so, has been overtaken by a resurgence of activity on the part of the GCC. Although the GCC as a regional body has been involved in a coordination role in intellectual property activity since the creation of the WTO and TRIPS coming into force, or even earlier, it has taken a more prominent role regionally in recent times. The GCC's initiatives in the field of intellectual property constitute an endeavour to bring a degree of regional harmonisation and unity (and, it must be said, an associated degree of control) to intellectual property rights. Four actions warrant attention, by way of exemplars – namely:

- the GCC Unified Patent Regulation;
- the GCC Unified Trademark Law;
- the GCC Cyber Law; and
- the creation of the GCC Intellectual Property Training Centre.

GCC Unified Patent Regulation

The GCC Unified Patent Regulation first came before the GCC Supreme Council in 1987, but it was not until December 1992 that it was approved. At the same time, the Supreme Council approved the establishment of the GCC Patent Office in Riyadh, Saudi Arabia. The Regulation was subsequently amended in late 1999 and reissued in April 2000. The main benefit of the Regulation is that it allows a member State to obtain protection across all GCC member States by the lodgment of a single patent application with the GCC Patent Office. It should be noted, however, that the Regulation is essentially a registration statute, and includes very little by way of enforcement provisions, notably in respect of infringements, precautionary measures and sanctions. The GCC Regulation defers these matters to each State to establish within their own domestic laws. Similarly, the Patent Office is primarily a unifying filing office. Although it 'granted' its first patent in 2002, formal examination and approval is still undertaken by agreement with other national patent offices with the necessary experience and expertise.[11]

Nevertheless the Regulation filled a crucial gap in regional patent protection, since some GCC member States, notably Kuwait and Qatar, initially deferred to the Regulation for domestic patent protection instead of introducing their own patent laws. Currently, all GCC member States have adopted the GCC Unified Patent Regulation, but each also has retained its own domestic patent law.[12]

11 For example, the GCC Office has recently signed an agreement with the Chinese Patent Office to undertake patent examinations and approvals on its behalf.

12 See Rawan Al-Louzi and Mohamed Salem Abou El Farag (2017), 'The GCC Unified Patent System: An Analytical Study', in David Price and Alhanoof AlDebasi (eds), *Intellectual Property Rights: Development and Enforcement in the Arab States of the Gulf*, pp. 154–72.

GCC Unified Trademark Law

In December 2006, the GCC Supreme Council adopted the long-awaited GCC Unified Trademark Regulation, a statute that was more than 20 years in the making. It was subsequently revised in 2014 and reissued as the Unified Trademark Law. The primary objective of the Law is to largely replace many of the provisions in the trademark laws of each of the GCC member States, thereby introducing a degree of consistency in regional trademark protection. The Law includes provisions which were missing from most of the domestic trademark laws, including:

- extension of the definition of a trademark to include sound and smell marks and collective marks;
- claims of priority based on prior foreign applications;
- protection for marks well known in the GCC, even if not registered;
- civil and criminal action by right holders against infringing parties;
- strengthened sanctions, including terms of imprisonment of up to five years, and fines of up to one million Saudi riyals (US$270,000) or equivalent local currency.

However, the Law does not offer a unified filing system as is the case with the GCC Unified Patent Regulation, and trademark applications will need to continue to be filed separately in each State for protection. The above sanctions are consistent with those prevailing in the Saudi trademark law, but are significantly different from those stipulated in the trademark laws of some of the other States.

The Law will only be fully effective when, or if, it is ratified by all the individual member States and the related implementing regulations are issued. What is also uncertain is whether the GCC Unified Law or domestic trademark laws will take precedence where the two are inconsistent – which is certainly the case for most States in respect of sanctions. What is already clear is that the official fees will not be unified and will vary depending on the individual overhead costs of the respective trademark offices involved. Bahrain, Kuwait, Saudi Arabia and the UAE have considerably increased their official fees during the latter half of 2015.[13] So far, Bahrain, Kuwait, Saudi Arabia and Qatar have announced and enacted their approval of the GCC Unified Trademark Regulation. Oman and the UAE remain uncommitted.

GCC Cyber Law

The GCC is reportedly undertaking to promote GCC regional cooperation among its member States to enhance cyber systems security and to prevent the misuse of information and criminal fraud activity among GCC member States.

13 See '2015: Year in Review' (2015), *SABA Intellectual Property Monthly Bulletin*, 14 December, available at www.sabaip.com/documents/fe_bulletin/Saba-IP-Bulletin--December-2015.pdf, last accessed 26 May 2017.

While the cyber security project will encompass a broad range of online commercial activity, intellectual property-related activity will form a major part.

The project may well lead to the issuance of a GCC-sponsored cyber law to supplement similar laws already in place in a few of the States. It may also offset some of the perceived shortcomings in the Arab League Cyber Crimes Agreement of 2012.[14] To date, only Oman and Saudi Arabia have ratified the Agreement; both States and the UAE have also enacted their own cyber crimes laws.

Establishment of the GCC Intellectual Property Training Centre

In February 2011, the GCC Secretary General issued Resolution No. 6/79 establishing the GCC Intellectual Property Training Centre (IPTC), as a regional training centre in intellectual property for the GCC member States.[15] The GCC declares that the goals of the centre include:

- promoting an awareness of the importance of intellectual property issues;
- highlighting the role and issues of intellectual property in economic development, technology transfer, business and international trade, and national sovereignty matters;
- providing training for experts and specialists in various intellectual property areas across the GCC.[16]

The Centre is also a practical acknowledgement by the GCC of the global interest in intellectual property, as well as its own interest in this key and crucial aspect of the WTO Agreements, and other conventions, treaties and agreements to which the GCC and its member States have made commitment. The GCC sees the Centre as a specialised technical body that will contribute to the development of GCC human resources in intellectual property, as well as to economic, social, political and intellectual development in the GCC States.[17]

The intellectual property laws of the States can still be enhanced by a process of review leading towards a greater degree of regional harmonisation. Such review should focus upon the elimination of some of those idiosyncrasies and the mutual

14 See the Cooperation Council of the Arab States of the Gulf website/laws, available at http://gccegov.org/en/web/guest/laws, last accessed 1 June 2017. See also Riyadh al-Balushi, 'Arab Treaty on Combating Cybercrime', *www.riyadh.om*, 18 March 2015, available at www.riyadh.om/2015/arab-treaty-on-combating-cybercrime, last accessed 26 May 2017.

15 See GCC Intellectual Property Centre (2017), at www.gccpo.org/gccip (in Arabic), last accessed 13 June 2017. The GCC Ministerial Council at its 122nd Session in March 2012 resolved to accept a Kuwaiti offer to host the Centre.

16 Ibid.

17 'Opening the GCCIP in the State of Kuwait' (2014) *GCCIP Media Centre*, 15 May 2014, www.gcc-sg.org/ar-sa/MediaCenter/NewsCooperation/NewsArchive/Pages/2014/مايو/New3324.aspx (in Arabic); see also 'Commerce Ministers' Council for GCC Opens GCC IP Office in Kuwait, *Alwatan Newspaper*, May 2014, available at http://alwatan.kuwait.tt/articledetails.aspx?id=358211 (in Arabic); both accessed 13 June 2017.

adoption of the positive and comprehensive elements of the more recent and robust laws. The existence of intellectual property laws that enjoy a greater degree of regionally common substantive provisions would make a useful contribution to state initiatives towards effective implementation. Given the importance of effective border controls as a crucial element in any enforcement strategy, common provisions relating to movement and control of goods across state borders would make a significant contribution to the campaign to combat the increasing problem of regional intellectual property piracy and counterfeiting. Harmonised laws would also complement other GCC and regional trade initiatives – such as those directed towards regional free trade areas, common customs union, regional power grids, financial structures and the proposed common currency. The States as a regional group have already embraced a regional patents protection law to complement their national patents laws and similarly a regional trademark law – again, to complement national laws.

However, harmonisation at the legislative level alone is inadequate and ineffective. What also needs to take place is a substantive degree of common practice and collaboration in and between the respective States at the operational levels in respect of such requirements as registrations (where required), oppositions, general administration and notably enforcement.[18]

This harmonisation will be particularly important for those States that are relying or utilising a regional protection system such as the GCC Trademark Law or Unified Patent Regulation, if the system is going work effectively.

As a leading legal professional emphasises, there is considerable variation in capacity, expertise and practices between the various intellectual property offices in the region.[19] Designs offices are not functioning in some countries, such as Qatar, while basic services such as trademark searches are not available in others, such as Kuwait. Saudi Arabia and the UAE have both implemented online only trademark registrations, but are apparently using very different software systems and platforms. Kuwait recently announced that it would not be accepting any patent applications following its adoption of the GCC Patent Regulation, notwithstanding the fact that the Regulation (and the PCT to which Kuwait recently acceded) still has a formal role for a national office. Some States rely on the provision of technical and patent examination services and expertise from certain foreign patents offices, while other local patent offices simply act as a mailbox or lodgment repository.

It has been further suggested that the common area of cooperation and harmonisation seems to be in respect of increasing official costs for certain intellectual property registration, with some of the States having the highest official fees in the

18 For an incisive analysis of IP harmonisation in the region, see Omar Obeidat (2015), 'IP Cooperation and Harmonisation in the Gulf: A myth or reality?', *Al Tamimi & Co. Law Update*, April 2015, available at www.tamimi.com/en/magazine/law-update/section-11/october-5/ip-cooperation-and-harmonisation-in-the-gulf-a-myth-or-reality.html, last accessed 26 May 2017.

19 Ibid.

world for registration and prosecution.[20] Soon after their adoption of the GCC Unified Trademark Law, Kuwait reportedly increased official registration fees by approximately 1,200 per cent, and Bahrain increased fees by approximately 400 per cent.[21] Saudi Arabia also increased its fees by a much smaller margin but also introduced a new raft of fees. Issuance of orders increasing fees seems to be a common and fairly quick practice after the enactment of a new intellectual property law or amending legislation.

While harmonisation is a desirable aspirational goal for effective and strong intellectual property laws, it is also essential at the operational levels to advance intellectual property protection, to overcome many of the existing challenges with enforcement, and to promote the growth of commercial practice and growth, and investment.

However, the recent quarrels between GCC member States that has led to Bahrain, Saudi Arabia and the UAE (along with Egypt) severing diplomatic relations with Qatar in early June 2017, and to impose a boycott upon it, over Qatar's alleged support of terrorism, sponsoring of certain radical Islamic groups and cordial relations with Iran. The quarrels demonstrate the fragility of the state of harmony and unity between the individual GCC member States. While relations between Members have been strained in the past, notably in respect of Bahrain's and Oman's unilateral conclusion of FTAs with the United States in apparent contravention of the GCC Charter, this latest quarrel could threaten the unity of the GCC as a whole and its potential as an influential regional and international bloc. It could therefore undermine the objectiveness, effectiveness and operation of the GCC intellectual property statutes and related initiatives. At the time of this writing, Bahrain, Saudi Arabia and the UAE have issued a number of demands with which Qatar refuses to comply. Kuwait and Oman (as well as Jordan) have both continued to maintain diplomatic, social and trade relations with Qatar.

10.5 The Arabian Peninsula States and beyond the WTO

In some respects, TRIPs has become somewhat superseded by the emergence of the new round of intellectual property lawmaking in the post-TRIPS world. The WTO has stumbled at a number of ministerial meetings on efforts to liberalise global trade, and also to inject a greater degree of equity and access into TRIPS. Failure to conclude the Doha Rounds, after 15 years of rounds of largely fruitless negotiations, calls into question in some quarters WTO's continuing status as the lead forum for the global trade agenda. At the same time, the new 'international standard' of intellectual property protection in practical terms has already become

20 Ibid.

21 'GCC Trade Mark Law – Are increased official fees inevitable?', Newsletter, *Clyde & Co. LLP*, 20 August 2016, available at www.clydeco.com/insight/article/gcc-trade-mark-law-are-increased-official-fees-inevitable, last accessed 26 May 2017.

that which is defined by the terms enshrined in the latest bilateral or regional agreement that the United States and the EU in particular may have concluded. The 'highest international standards' have become very much a dynamic formula in a bilateral context rather than the multilateral forums.

While negotiations in the WTO on injecting a greater degree of balance and equity into intellectual property rights falter, developed countries have turned to bilateral dealings to advance their industries' economic interests and obtain higher levels of commitment from developing countries. A number of countries are keen to establish regional and/or bilateral trade and investment agreements with the GCC as a bloc or with individual States. The GCC has been working as a group to negotiate FTAs with other countries including Australia, China, Japan, Jordan, South Korea, Turkey, New Zealand, India, Iran, and with the Mercosur and ASEAN trading blocs.[22] Some of these negotiations represent a recommencement of stalled negotiations of long standing following the GCC's strategic withdrawal from negotiations or lessening of interest in partnerships in the post-2008 period following the global financial crisis and the degeneration in global oil prices. Others constitute new and fresh initiatives, such as those with South Korea and New Zealand. The United Kingdom, following its recent decision to leave the EU (universally known as 'Brexit'), is actively seeking new trade alliances, including an alliance with the GCC. Both the United Kingdom and the EU will be preoccupied with Brexit, with the likely outcome that the Arabian Peninsula State's dealings with Europe are more likely to be on a bilateral basis with individual countries rather than multilateral.

Some negotiations and eventual agreements, such as those with South Korea and Japan, will no doubt include comprehensive intellectual property rights protection provisions, ratcheting up even further TRIPS' minimum standards from what now seems to be so long ago. Others, such as those with China and India, will probably pay much less attention to intellectual property rights. The 'highest international standard' of intellectual property rights continues to be very much a moving target.

10.6 The Arabian Peninsula States and the international arenas – new agendas?

Developing countries have been described as 'observers' in the intellectual property protection process, the implication being that they are unable to match the developed countries in terms of expertise and capacity.[23] And in some sense the

22 Mercosur comprises the South American countries Argentina, Brazil, Paraguay and Uruguay (as full members), Bolivia, Chile, Peru, Colombia, Ecuador and Suriname (as associate members), and Mexico and New Zealand (as observers). ASEAN (Association of South East Asian Nations) comprises Brunei, Cambodia, Indonesia, Laos, Malaysia, Myanmar, the Philippines, Singapore, Thailand and Vietnam.

23 Ahmed Abdel Latif, 'Current Developments and Trends in the Field of Intellectual Property: Implications for Arab Countries', *Bilaterals.Org*, 28 June 2005, p. 6, available at

States appear to have been willing to play such a role because it suits them at this point in time. They are only too aware of their limitations – in terms of legislation, infrastructure, judicial capacity and expertise in strategic intellectual property policy development and implementation. However, in this approach there is an altruistic pragmatism at play that can be too easily overlooked. Since adoption of TRIPS required laws encompassing particular and complex requirements, it made eminent sense to turn to the administrators of this multilateral benchmark, namely WIPO, to obtain such laws.

By the same token, enforcement needs to be a visible action, which may be addressed by raids that are well publicised but ultimately resolved with quietude. Yet, just as there exists a cynicism on the part of some of the major global exporters of intellectual property (the United States being the leader in this regard) in respect of these attitudes, being perceived as a lack of commitment to intellectual property protection, there is also a cynicism about the publicly orated objectives for the region. The States are not taken in by what some see as double standards on the part of the major developed countries. They see the global trade community, of which the United States and the EU have been the driving forces, establishing a particular set of standards, albeit minimum ones, and they are then confronted by governments acting as agents for multinational corporations striving to drive up those standards through bilateral agreements.

The Arab States have been exhorted to play a more active role in the international arena by joining forces with like-minded countries.[24] However, they may be disinclined to do so by their own volition, unless there arises a particular need to develop a regional agenda that pays attention and care to their development needs and priorities. Nevertheless, the States already have in existence a regional structure that could serve as the logical springboard for launching a greater presence in international forums, namely the GCC itself. Yet the GCC Council has its own internal issues on occasion that can militate against acting as a springboard for the creation of a regional voice on behalf of the Middle East, the greater Arab world or another consortium of developing and least-developed nations. The GCC member States, either collectively as a regional bloc or individually, have not attempted to make their presence felt in the affairs of the WTO or WIPO councils and committees. The lack of active participation to date reinforces the view expressed earlier that membership of these two bodies, although necessary, was not always positively viewed and embraced with active participation by the States.

There could emerge a regional bloc which, if it joins forces with other League of Arab States members and with other regional blocs such as ARIPO,[25] and the

www.bilaterals.org/?current-developments-and-trends-in&lang=en, last accessed 26 May 2017.

24 Mohammed El-Said, 'From TRIPS-minus to TRIPS to TRIPS-plus: Implications of IPRs for the Arab World' (2005), 8, *Journal of World Intellectual Property*, p. 60.

25 ARIPO – African Regional Industrial Property Organisation. Member states are: Botswana, Gambia, Ghana, Kenya, Lesotho, Malawi, Mozambique, Sierra Leone, Somalia, Sudan, Swaziland, Uganda, United Republic of Tanzania, Zambia and Zimbabwe.

'Group of the Friends of Development' bloc,[26] may make a significant contribution to a shift in the balance between the developed and developing/least-developed countries in the major intellectual property and development forums. There also arises the opportunity for these eight States to form their own regional influence within a greater Middle East or even wider Arab forum. This, in turn, could possibly make a change to the negotiating dynamics in the WTO.

In some respects, TRIPS has been somewhat superseded by the emergence of the new round of intellectual property lawmaking in the post-TRIPS world through the complex web of bilateral trade agreements. At the same time, the WTO has stumbled in efforts to liberalise global trade generally and also to inject a greater degree of equity and access into TRIPS. The 'new international standard' of intellectual property protection in practical terms is fast becoming that which is defined by the terms enshrined in the latest round of bilateral agreements together with the prescriptions of the TRIPS-plus treaties, such as the WIPO Internet Treaties and TRIPS-plus conventions. The 'highest international standard' has become very much a moving target.

10.7 Concluding remarks

The establishment of the national and regional intellectual property infrastructures, and the skills development of the human resources to give effect to these national needs and aspirations, will continue to be significant but surmountable challenges. The Arabian Peninsula States readily acknowledge that their infrastructures and human resource expertise are such that they face challenges in the medium to long term to enforce their intellectual property laws to the standards they would seek and the standard expected of them by the developed countries and intellectual property right holders.

But there will be other factors remaining in play as the systemic and structural challenges are resolved. It is suggested that piracy is not necessarily simply a manifestation of the lack of intellectual property protection or enforcement, but rather characterisation of the incongruity between the laws and the degree of industrial development in the State. It may also be a manifestation of the denial of the sovereign right of a State to engage in lawmaking as it sees fit, which pushes it to adopt a position of indifference at best, or active resentment at worst, as regards the enforcement of foreign intellectual property rights. The perceived lack of legitimacy and fairness in forcing developing countries to subscribe to laws that significantly ignore their plight, and in particular to set up legal forms that are not congruent with the state of their economy and technology, will make the enforcement of foreign intellectual property laws in these countries an uphill struggle. Societies

26 The 'Group of the Friends of Development' comprises Argentina, Brazil, Bolivia, Cuba, Dominican Republic, Ecuador, Egypt, Iran, Kenya, Peru, Sierra Leone, South Africa, United Republic of Tanzania and Venezuela.

in developing countries will continue to resist changes to their intellectual property laws, and when they do make changes, they will be slow to enforce them in favour of foreign corporations at the expense of local merchants. To the extent that TRIPS-plus rules may adversely affect the economic interests of developing countries, passive resistance may be the most likely counter mechanism. The enforcement dichotomy shall remain for the time being, even though some of the States will continue to achieve major successes against the virtually uncontrolled counterfeiting and piracy that existed in the past. But as the imperative for change becomes more internally driven, the successes against piracy will accelerate.

The States may well accept without great demurral some of the demands of the western industrialised nations for the regional installation of the international frameworks of global intellectual property protection, and the manner in which they are demanded. Arabic cultural mores and a fine appreciation of the relative bargaining strengths of the protagonists dictate that they do so. However, such acceptance does not necessarily mean that the matter is closed and its conditions no longer negotiable. Adoption of an agreement may well constitute the conclusion of a matter and the fixation of its conditions in some minds, but it may also just be a confirmation of the status quo at a particular point of time in other minds. And, as has already been demonstrated, installation of the legislative framework does not guarantee successful implementation of the strategy.

In the intellectual property context, the States will continue to operate within the western-industrial dominated paradigm for the time being. They will work towards developing those elements that suit their needs and advance their public policy objectives, and accept for the time being those elements which they are presently unable to resist or change. However, most matters are always changeable, and nothing is ever really concluded – even a formal agreement. Conditions agreed to in one context or point in time, may no longer be appropriate or tenable as circumstances change or time progresses. In any case, the hypocrisy of some industrialised nations in advocating the minimum (and maximum) mandatory protection standards of TRIPs, while virtually at the same time actively endeavouring to extend those standards in respect of, say, copyright, trademarks, patent and geographical indications, and seeking to prevent new or equitable standards of protection in respect of traditional knowledge and cultural heritage, and sharing of genetic resources, would not be lost on the States.

It would be a mistake to assume that the *Qur'an* and the *Shariah* are no longer relevant in the intellectual property context, and thus will not have any influence in the future dynamics of the States' intellectual property regimes. Public order, morality and the dictates of the *Shariah* currently set protection parameters in the laws of the States in respect of copyright patent and trademark protection, and will continue to do so, and the possibility of their influence growing in the future should not be discounted. In the final analysis, the nature of the intellectual property protection regimes of the States will be subject to further change and development, and that change is likely to involve a greater degree of internal influence and direction than has been seen in the past.

BIBLIOGRAPHY

Books and book chapters

Al-Baharna, H (1998), *British Extra-Territorial Jurisdiction in the Gulf 1913–1971*, Archive Editions, Slough, UK.

Al Balushi, R, Al Lawati, N and Mohsin, M (2017), 'The Term of Protection of Economic Rights under the Copyright Laws of the GCC', in Price, D and AlDebasi, A (eds) *Intellectual Property Rights: Development and Enforcement in the Arab States of the Gulf*, Gerlach Press, Berlin.

Al-Louzi, R and El Farag, M S A (2017), 'The GCC Unified Patent System: An Analytical Study', in Price, D and AlDebasi, A (eds), *Intellectual Property Rights: Development and Enforcement in the Arab States of the Gulf*, Gerlach Press, Berlin.

Al-Tamimi, E (2003), *Practical Guide to Litigation and Arbitration in the United Arab Emirates*, Kluwer Law International.

Amin, S H (1991), *The Legal System of Kuwait*, Royston Publishers, Glasgow.

Amin, S H (1993), *Law of Intellectual and Industrial Property in Developing Countries: Muslim World*, Scottish Institute of International and Comparative Law, Edinburgh.

Ballantyne, W M (1980), *Legal Development in Arabia*, Graham & Trotman, London.

Ballantyne, W M (1986), *Commercial Law in the Arab Middle East: The Gulf States*, Lloyd's of London, London.

Ballantyne, W M (2011), *Essays and Addresses on Arab Laws*, Routledge Cavendish, London.

Braithwaite, J and Drahos, P (2002), *Information Feudalism: Who Owns the Knowledge Economy?* Earthscan, Abingdon, UK.

Correa, C (1998), 'Layout Designs of Integrated Circuits', in Correa, C M and Yusuf, A A (eds), *Intellectual Property and International Trade: The TRIPS Agreement*, Kluwer Law International, London.

Correa, C (1998), 'Patent Rights', in Correa, C M and Yusuf, A A (eds), *Intellectual Property and International Trade: The TRIPS Agreement*, Kluwer Law International, London.

Correa, C (2000), *Intellectual Property Rights, the WTO and Developing Countries: The TRIPS Agreement and Policy Options*, Third World Network, Penang.

Drahos, P and Braithwaite, J (2002), *Information Feudalism: Who Owns the Global Economy?* Cambridge University Press, Cambridge.

El Farag, M S A (2017), 'The Protection of Trade Secrets in Qatar', in Price, D and AlDebasi, A (eds) *Intellectual Property Rights: Development and Enforcement in the Arab States of the Gulf*, Gerlach Press, Berlin.

Kariodimedjo, D W (2017), 'Traditional Knowledge and Cultural Heritage Protection in the Arabian Gulf and Indonesia: A Comparative Study' in Price, D and AlDebasi, A (eds) *Intellectual Property Rights: Development and Enforcement in the Arab States of the Gulf*, Gerlach Press, Berlin.

Naim, N (2017), 'Intellectual Property Regimes in the GCC: Recommendations to Develop an Integrated Approach to Intellectual Property Rights', in Price, D and AlDebasi, A (eds), *Intellectual Property Rights: Development and Enforcement in the Arab States of the Gulf*, Gerlach Press, Berlin.

Phillips, J (1998), 'Protecting Values in Industrial Designs', in Correa, C M and Yusuf, A A (eds) (1998), *Intellectual Property and International Trade: The TRIPS Agreement*, Kluwer Law International, London.

Ramanazi, R K (1988), *The Gulf Cooperation Council: Record and Analysis*, University Press of Virginia, Charlottesville.

Rayner, S (1991), *The Theory of Contracts in Islamic Law*, Graham & Trotman, London.

Reports, monographs and theses

Al-Kamali, M, 'Development of Intellectual Property Law in the UAE', unpublished PhD thesis, University of Exeter, UK, 1994.

Al Muslimi, F (2016), 'A History of Missed Opportunities: Yemen and the GCC', *Carnegie Middle East Center*, 5 January, available at http://carnegie-mec.org/diwan/62405.

Al Tamamy, S (2015), 'GCC Membership Expansion: Possibilities and Obstacles', *Aljazeera Centre for Studies*, 31 March, available at http://studies.aljazeera.net/en/dossiers/2015/03/201533171547520486.html.

Business Software Alliance (2003), *Eighth Annual Global Piracy Study*, June 2003, available at www.bsa.org/country/Research%20and%20Statistics/~/media/Files/Research%20Papers/GlobalStudy/2003/IPR_GlobalStudy2003.ashx.

Business Software Alliance (2004), *First Annual BSA and IDC Global Software Piracy Study*, July 2004, available at www.bsa.org/~/media/Files/Research%20Papers/GlobalStudy/2004/IDC_GlobalPiracyStudy_2004.pdf.

Business Software Alliance (2006), *Third Annual BSA and IDC Global Software Piracy Study 2006*, May 2006, available at www.bsa.org/~/media/Files/Research%20Papers/GlobalStudy/2005/IDC_Global_Software_Piracy_Study_2005.pdf.

Business Software Alliance (2008), *Sixth Annual BSA Global Software Piracy Study 2008*, available at http://globalstudy.bsa.org/2008/studies/globalpiracy2008.pdf.

Business Software Alliance (2016), *Global Software Survey*, May 2016, available at http://globalstudy.bsa.org/2016/downloads/studies/BSA_GSS_US.pdf.

Business Software Alliance (2017), 'About BSA and Members', available at www.bsa.org/about-bsa/bsa-members

Gulf Research Centre (2016), 'Nationals and non-nationals in GCC countries population', available at http://gulfmigration.eu/total-population-and-percentage-of-nationals-and-non-nationals-in-gcc-countries-latest-national-statistics-2010-2015.

Katzman, K (2005), 'The Persian Gulf States: Post-War Issues for US Policy', *CRS Report for Congress*, No. RL31533, US Library of Congress, 21 December 2005, Executive Summary, available at www.dtic.mil/get-tr-doc/pdf?AD=ADA476192, last accessed 31 May 2017.

Leesti, M and Pengelly, T (2002), 'Institutional Issues for Developing Countries in Intellectual Property Policymaking, Administration and Enforcement', *Report of the Commission on Intellectual Property Rights*, Study Paper 9, UK Department for International Development, DfID, London.

Malkawi, B (2005), 'Jordan and the World Trading System: A Case Study for Arab Countries', SJD dissertation, American University Washington College of Law, Washington DC.

Musungu, S and Dutfield, G (2003), 'Multilateral Agreements and a TRIPS-plus World: The World Intellectual Property Organisation', TRIPS Issues Papers No. 3, *Quaker United Nations Office*, Geneva, available at www.iprsonline.org/ictsd/docs/WIPO_Musungu_Dutfield.pdf.

Third World Network (2005), 'Report of the Asian Regional Workshop on Bilateral Free Trade Agreements', August, Kuala Lumpur, available at www.twn.my/title2/twninfo253.htm.

Ryan C (2014), 'Jordan, Morocco and an Expanded GCC', *Middle East Research and Information Project*, 15 April, available at www.merip.org/jordan-morocco-expanded-gcc.

UK Department for International Development (DfID) (2002), 'Integrating Intellectual Property Rights and Development Policy', *Report of the Commission on Intellectual Property Rights*, DfID, London.

United Nations Development Programme in the Arab States (2016), *Arab Human Development Report 2016*, available at www.arabstates.undp.org/content/rbas/en/home/library/huma_development/arab-human-development-report-2016--youth-and-the-prospects-for-/.

Vivas-Egui, D (2003), 'Regional and Bilateral Agreements and a TRIPS-plus World: The Free Trade Area of the Americas', TRIPS Issues Papers No. 1, *Quaker United Nations Office*, Geneva, available at www.wto.org/english/tratop_e/region_e/sem_nov03_e/vivas_eugui_paper_e.pdf.

Journal articles

Ali, R and Haddad, L (1996), 'WTO Membership and Compliance in the Middle East Countries', 16(2), *Middle East Executive Reports*, p. 15.

Al-Tarawneh, B and Al-Zubi, A (2006), 'The Impact of Joining Jordan to the International Agreement for the Protection of New Varieties of Plants (UPOV)', 6(9), *International Journal of Humanities and Social Science*, p. 143.

Angell, N (2006), 'An Overview of Legal Structures in the GCC Countries', World Service Group (December), available at www.worldservicesgroup.com/publications.asp?action=article&artid=1649.

Azmi, I A G (1996), 'Basis for the Recognition of Intellectual Property in the Light of the *Shariah*', 27, *International Review of Intellectual Property and Competition Law*, p. 650.

Bigger, S (1981), 'Notes from Other Nations', 71, *Trademark Reporter*, pp. 657–9.
Bigger, S (1986), 'Notes from Other Nations', 76, *Trademark Reporter*, pp. 354–5.
Carroll, J (2000/2001), 'Intellectual Property Rights in the Middle East: A Cultural Perspective', 11, *Fordham Intellectual Property Media and Entertainment Law Journal*, p. 555.
Choudry, A (2003), 'Bilateral Trade and Investment Deals a Serious Challenge to Global Justice Movements', *GRAIN*, December, p. 1, available at www.grain.org/article/entries/3620-bilateral-trade-and-investment-deals-a-serious-challenge-to-global-justice-movements.
Choudry, A (2004), 'Bombarded by Bilateral Trade and Investment Agreements', *Bilaterals.org*, March, p. 3, available at www.bilaterals.org/IMG/pdf/Bombarded_by_Bilatera_92909-2.pdf.
Correa, C (1998), 'Implementing the TRIPS Agreement in the Patent Field: Options for Developing Countries', 1, *Journal of World Intellectual Property*, p. 75.
Correa, C (2004), 'Bilateral Investment Agreements: Agents of New Global Standards for the Protection of Intellectual Property Rights?', *GRAIN*, August, available at www.grain.org/article/entries/125-bilateral-investment-agreements-agents-of-new-global-standards-for-the-protection-of-intellectual-property-rights.
Drahos, P (2001), 'BITs and BIPs – Bilateralism in Intellectual Property', 4(6), *Journal of World Intellectual Property*, pp. 798.
Drahos, P (2002), 'Developing Countries and International Intellectual Property Standard-Setting', 5, *Journal of World Intellectual Property*, p. 765.
El-Said, M (2005), 'From TRIPS-minus to TRIPS to TRIPS-plus: Implications of IPRs for the Arab World' (2005), 8, *Journal of World Intellectual Property*, p. 53.
El-Said, M (2012), 'The Morning After: TRIPS-Plus, FTAs and Wikileaks – Fresh Insights on the Implementation and Enforcement of IP Protection in Developing Countries', PIJIP Research Paper No. 2012-03. American University Washington College of Law, Washington, DC.
Endeshaw, A (2001), 'The Paradox of Intellectual Property Lawmaking in the New Millennium: Universal Templates as Terms of Surrender for Non-industrial Nations; Piracy as an Offshoot', 27 November, available at https://papers.ssrn.com/sol3/papers.cfm?abstract_id=291692.
Hansen, M (1993), 'Taking a Realistic Approach to Trade Mark Protection in the Gulf Countries', 16, *Middle East Executive Reports*, p. 12.
Hirst, A (1994), 'Developing IPR in the Gulf: Current Coverage, Problems, Post-Uruguay Round Trends', 17(2), *Middle East Executive Reports*, p. 9.
Hirst, A (2002), 'A Comprehensive Reform of the UAE Copyright Law', 1, *Middle East Executive Reports*, p. 17.
Jamar, S (1992), 'The Protection of Intellectual Property under Islamic Law' (1992), 21, *Capital University Law Review*, p. 1082.
Khoury, A (2000), 'The Development of Modern Trademark Legislation and Protection in Arab Countries in the Middle East' (2000), 16, *Transnational Lawyer*, p. 249.
Khoury, A (2003), 'Ancient and Islamic Sources of Intellectual Property Protection in the Middle East' (2003), 43, *IDEA*, p. 151.
Latif, A A (2005), 'Current Developments and Trends in the Field of Intellectual Property: Implications for Arab Countries', *Bilaterals.Org*, 28 June, available at www.bilaterals.org/?current-developments-and-trends-in&lang=en.
Malkawi, B (2013), 'Intellectual Property Protection from a Shariah Perspective', 16, *Southern Cross University Law Review*, p. 92.

Meyer-Reumann, R (2001), 'The Endeavours of Gulf Countries to Meet WTO Requirements', 16(1), *Arab Law Quarterly*, pp. 49–54.

Mo, C (2011), 'Exploring Economic Relations between China and the GCC States', 5(4), *Journal of Middle Eastern and Islamic Studies (in Asia)*, pp. 88–105.

'Regional Update' (1989), 3 *World Intellectual Property Report*, p. 12, BNA (Bureau of National Affairs) International, Arlington, Virginia.

'Results of 1998 "Special 301" Provisions of 1974 Trade Act Regarding Intellectual Property Protection', 12, *World Intellectual Property Report*, p. 201.

'Results of 1999 "Special 301" Provisions of 1974 Trade Act Regarding Intellectual Property Protection' (1999), 13, *World Intellectual Property Report*, p. 216.

Rosenthal, D (1998), 'A Comment on the Special 301 Annual Review', 1, *Journal of World Intellectual Property*, p. 743.

Rutledge, E and Janardhan (2004), 'Bahrain–US FTA Exposes GCC Chinks', *Bilaterals.org*, 28 December, available at www.bilaterals.org/?us-bahrain-trade-deal-exposes-gcc&lang=fr.

Stovall, H (2000), 'Arab Commercial Laws – Into the Future', 34, *The International Lawyer*, p. 842.

Saif, A (2004), 'Constitutionalism in the Arab Gulf States', *GCC Research Program – GCC Constitutions*, Gulf Research Centre.

Shashikant, S (2004), 'The Politics of United States Free Trade Agreements', 167–168, *Third World Network*, available at www.ghwatch.org/sites/www.ghwatch.org/files/freetrade.pdf.

Sohail, M S (2012), 'Consumer Influences on Pirated Software Purchases: Perspectives from an Emerging Gulf Nation', 5(1), *International Journal of Trade and Global Markets*.

Sultani, S and Deans, R (2014), 'Regional Trade Mark Law for the GCC States', *Managing Intellectual Property*, 6 June, available at www.managingip.com/Article/3347490/Regional-Trade-Mark-Law-for-the-GCC-states.html.

Sunna, R M (2003), 'Bridging the Gulf: Harmonisation of Trade Mark Laws in the Gulf Cooperation Council Countries', 1, *Trademark World*, Supplement.

Usmani, M T (undated), 'Copyright according to Islam', *Mufti Taqi Usmani Official page*, available at *Al-Balagh Webzine*, http://muftitaqiusmani.com/en/?p=11064.

'USTR's Annual Report: GCC Trade and Investment Barriers' (1995), 18(5), *Middle East Executive Report*, pp. 13–17.

Varisco, D M (1989), 'The Arab Gulf States Folklore Centre: A Resource for the Study of Folklore and Traditional Culture', 23(2), *Cambridge Journal of Review of Middle East Studies*, pp. 157–67.

Verma, S (2004), 'Protecting Intellectual Property: Is a *Sui Generis* System an Answer?', 7, *Journal of World Intellectual Property*, p. 770.

Zahr, H and Khawand, H (2015), 'Roundtable Discussion: Arab Trade Marks', 249, *Managing Intellectual Property*, pp. 99–103.

Zahraa, M (2000), 'Characteristic Features of Islamic Law: Perceptions and Misconceptions', 15(2), *Arab Law Quarterly*, p. 168.

Media reports

'72 Riyadh stores closed for copyright violations' (2014), *Arab News*, 12 April, available at www.arabnews.com/news/554456.

'123m fake goods seized in 2015' (2016), *Arab News*, 19 March, available at www.arabnews.com/saudi-arabia/news/897461.

Abdullateef, L. (2012), 'تعزيم الشيخ عائض القرني ٣٣٠الف ريال في قضية الكاتبة سلوى العضيدان'. (Translated by Alhanoof AlDebasi), *Almadina* newspaper, available at www.al-madina.com/node/353477.

'Abu Dhabi will set up the Plant Genetic Resources Centre' (2014), *Gulf News*, 24 November, available at http://gulfnews.com/news/uae/environment/abu-dhabi-to-set-up-plant-genetic-resources-centre-1.1417330.

'A Window into the World of Anti-Piracy' (2005), *Arab News*, 11 October.

Bain, B and Alden, E (2005), 'Washington Seals Trade Agreement with Oman', *Financial Times* (London), 4 October 2005.

'Bahrain: 87 Thousand Pirated Work Were Confiscated in 6 Months' (2014), *AlMenara Newspaper*, 8 September, available at www.menara.ma/ar/2014/08/09/1302077--ألف-87-مصادرة-البحرين-أشهر-ستة-خلال-لقانون-مخالف-بصري-سمعي-منتوج.html.

Bailey, R (2013), 'Is China set to become the GCC's most important economic partner by 2020? And what does this mean for the region?', *Gulf Business*, 16 April, available at http://gulfbusiness.com/china-and-gcc-growing-ties/#.ViEQUi6gyoM.

'US–Qatari negotiations on free trade agreement frozen' (2006), *Kuwait News Agency*, 29 April 2006, available at www.kuna.net.kw/ArticlePrintPage.aspx?id=1656345&language=en.

'Consumer protection: more than 6 tons of pills enters the country', (2014), *Yemen Association for Consumer Protection Newsletter*, 30 November, available at www.consumer-yemen.org/index.php?option=com_content&view=article&id=455:2014-12-01-14-31-13&catid=1&Itemid=3.

'Counterfeit software public market' (2008), *Arab News*, 25 June, available at www.arabnews.com/node/313231.

'Court verdict sets new precedent in anti-piracy fight' (2012), *Arab News*, 1 March, available at www.arabnews.com/node/407587.

'Crackdown on pirates' (2005), *Times of Oman*, 5 October, p. 1 (hard copy with the authors).

'Decline in smuggled counterfeits, Dubai Customs says' (2016), *Gulf News*, 19 January, available at http://gulfnews.com/news/uae/society/decline-in-smuggled-counterfeits-dubai-customs-says-1.1656085.

'DED closes down 8,894 social network accounts for peddling counterfeits' (2017), *Arab News Gazette*, 11 March, available at http://arabnewsnetwork.ae/ded-closes-down-8894-social-network-accounts-for-peddling-counterfeits.

'Dh6.7m in counterfeit goods seized by Dubai Customs in 2014 Q1' (2014), *Gulf News*, 27 April, available at http://gulfnews.com/news/uae/government/dh6-7m-in-counterfeit-goods-seized-by-dubai-customs-in-2014-q1-1.1324982.

'Dubai confiscate counterfeit products in amount of 51.7 million dirham' (2016), *Emarat Alyoum Newspaper*, 16 February, available at www.emaratalyoum.com/business/local/2016-02-16-1.870124.

'Dubai customs seizes fake goods worth Dh38.4m' (2016), *Gulf News*, 3 August, available at http://gulfnews.com/news/uae/society/dubai-customs-seizes-fake-goods-worth-dh38-4m-1.1873048.

'Exporters of fake Chinese goods to be blacklisted' (2014), *Arab News*, 16 March, available at www.arabnews.com/news/541006.

'Fake products boom in Saudi Arabia's markets' (2015), *Al-arabiya*, 11 December, available at https://english.alarabiya.net/en/variety/2015/12/11/Fake-products-boom-in-Saudi-Arabia-s-markets.html.

Holder, S (2016), 'GCC countries – review of patent developments', *Rouse, The Magazine*, 28 June, available at www.rouse.com/magazine/news/gcc-countries-review-of-patent-developments.

Husain, S (2007), 'Informal US-UAE Trade Talks to Go On', *Gulf News*, 12 March, available at www.uaeinteract.com/docs/Informal_US-UAE_trade_talks_to_go_on/24368.htm.

'Joining the club' (2014), *Yemen Times*, 23 January, available at www.yementimes.com/en/1749/business/3384/Joining-the-club.htm.

'Low fines do not act as deterrent' (2008), *Gulf News*, 24 January (hard copy with the authors).

'Merchants of death' (2013), Editorial, *Arab News*, 15 February, available at www.arabnews.com/editorial-merchants-death.

Mu, X (2014), 'China, Gulf states outline 2014–2017 cooperation', *Xinhua*, 17 January, available at http://news.xinhuanet.com/english/china/2014-01/17/c_126023632.htm.

'Oman cautious on US trade talks' (2004), *Arab News*, 30 November, available at www.arabnews.com/search/site/Oman%20Cautious%20on%20US%20Trade%20Talks%E2%80%99%2C.

'Opening the GCCIP in the State of Kuwait' (2014), *GCCIP Media Centre*, 15 May, available at www.gcc-sg.org/ar-sa/MediaCenter/NewsCooperation/NewsArchive/Pages/2014/مايو/New3324.aspx (in Arabic); see also 'Commerce Ministers' Council for GCC Opens GCC IP Office in Kuwait, *Alwatan Newspaper*, May 2014, available at http://alwatan.kuwait.tt/articledetails.aspx?id=358211 (in Arabic).

'Over 57 tons of expired, counterfeit goods destroyed' (2013), *Yemen Times*, 8 July, available at www.yementimes.com/en/1692/report/2602/Over-57-tons-of-expired-counterfeit-goods-destroyed.htm.

'Patent and Utility Model Applications Now Accepted in Bahrain' (2006), *Abu Ghazaleh Intellectual Property Newsletter*, 14 June, available at www.agip.com/News.aspx?id=1008.

'Piracy blues' (2010), *Gulf News*, 19 September, available at http://gulfnews.com/business/technology/piracy-blues-1.683896.

Rahman, S (2006), 'GCC–China free trade deal by 2007', *Gulf News*, 8 September, available at http://gulfnews.com/business/economy/gcc-china-free-trade-deal-by-2007-1.254236.

'Raising the stakes' (2008), *Business.com*, 16 December, available at www.arabianbusiness.com/raising-stakes-42023.html.

'Saudi Trade Ministry closes 75 social media accounts for promoting fake goods' (2017), *Arab News*, 12 March, available at www.arabnews.com/node/1067061/saudi-arabia.

'Shadowy Traders, Shady Deals . . . the Piracy Business Continues' (2003), *Bahrain Tribune*, 16 October (hard copy with the authors).

Statement of Why the United States–Oman Free Trade Agreement is in the Interest of U.S. Commerce', *Oman American Business Center*, March 2005, p. 2, available at www.oabcoman.org/outlining-benefits-of-fta.pdf.

'Super Dupers! Fake items in Oman's markets' (2014), *Times of Oman*, 5 June, available at http://timesofoman.com/article/35427/HI/Super-Dupers!-Fake-items-in-Oman's-markets.

'The GCC in 2020: Outlook for the Gulf and the Global Economy' (2009), *The Economist* Intelligence Unit, March, available at www.graphics.eiu.com/marketing/pdf/Gulf2020.pdf.

'The Jordan Customs Department (JCD) Foiled an Attempt to Smuggle Cigarettes in a Large Amount' (2017), *Jordan Customs News*, 17 January, available at www.customs.gov.jo/ar/CMS_content_View.aspx?Key=10462.

'Thousands of pirated films seized in raids' (2005), *Times of Oman*, 5 December, p. 4 (hard copy with the authors).

'TV piracy is not a "victimless crime", says OSN CEO' (2016), *Khaleej Times*, 26 April, available at www.khaleejtimes.com/nation/general/tv-piracy-is-not-a-victimless-crime-says-osn-ceo.

'UAE legal experts welcome court changes' (2013), *The National, UAE*, 16 September, available at www.thenational.ae/uae/uae-legal-experts-welcome-court-changes.

'US pulls out of Saudi Arabia' (2003), *BBC News*, 29 April, available at http://news.bbc.co.uk/1/hi/world/middle_east/2984547.stm, last accessed 26 May 2017.

'Washington Seals Trade Agreement with Oman' (2005), *Financial Times* (London), 4 October.

'Why the fight against fake goods is important to economic growth' (2016), *Times of Oman, Opinion*, 29 October, available at http://timesofoman.com/article/95326/Opinion/Columnist/Why-the-fight-against-fake-goods-is-important-to-economic-growth.

Legal profession reports and news services

'2015: Year in Review' (2015), *SABA Intellectual Property Monthly Bulletin*, 14 December, available at www.sabaip.com/documents/fe_bulletin/Saba-IP-Bulletin--December-2015.pdf.

'Filing of Patent Applications Ceased in Bahrain' (2004), *Abu Ghazaleh Intellectual Property Newsletter*, May, 1 May, available at www.agip.com/News.aspx?id=126&group_key=news&keywords=Filing+of+Patent+Applications+Ceased+in+Bahrain.

Al Azzeh, B (2016), 'Copyright Violation can Lead to Deportation from the UAE', *Al Tamimi Law Update*, May, available at www.tamimi.com/en/magazine/law-update/section-14/may-9/copyright-violation-can-lead-to-deportation-from-the-uae.html.

Al-Tamimi & Co, Legal Advocates (UAE), *Law Update*, Issue No. 120, March 2001.

Al-Tamimi & Co, Legal Advocates (UAE), *Law Update*, Issue No. 133, April 2002.

Al-Tamimi & Co, Legal Advocates (UAE), *Law Update*, Issue No. 162, September 2004.

Al-Tamimi & Co, Legal Advocates (UAE), Law Update, Issue No. 194, May 2007.

Deans, R and Dunne, J (2016), 'GCC Trade Mark Law – Are increased official fees inevitable?', *Newsletter, Clyde & Co. LLP*, 20 August, available at www.clydeco.com/insight/article/gcc-trade-mark-law-are-increased-official-fees-inevitable.

Deans, R and Human, A (2010), 'United Arab Emirates: Major Changes to UAE IP Laws Announced', *Mondaq*, available at www.mondaq.com/x/95168/Patent/Major+Changes+To+UAE+IP+Laws+Announced.

Hansen, P (2016), 'UAE Federal Supreme Court says Chinese and English trademarks are the same but different', *Hogan Lovells Lime Green IP News*, 12 April, available at www.limegreenipnews.com/2016/04/uae-federal-supreme-court-says-chinese-and-english-trademarks-are-the-same-but-different.

'Jordan: Upcoming PCT Accession' (2016), *Saba Bulletin*, 20 December, available at www.sabaip.com/en/documents/fe_bulletin/Saba-IP-Bulletin--January-2017.pdf.

'Jordan: TMO Sets Precedent for the Protection of Geographic Indicators' (2014), *SABA Intellectual Property Bulletin*, 1 December, available at www.sabaip.com/en/documents/fe_bulletin/Saba--Co.-IP-Bulletin--December-2014.pdf.

'Kuwait: Adopting the Tenth Edition of the Nice Classification' (2016), *SABA Intellectual Property Bulletin*, 13 October, available at www.sabaip.com/en/documents/fe_bulletin/Saba-IP-Bulletin--November-2016.pdf.

'Kuwait: Final GCC Country with PCT Membership' (2016), *SABA Intellectual Property Bulletin*, 30 May, available at www.sabaip.com/en/documents/fe_bulletin/Saba-IP-Bulletin--July-2016.pdf.

'Largest seizure of counterfeit cigarettes ever in UAE' (2002), *Al-Tamimi Law Update*, Issue No. 131, February, p. 1.

'NICE Classification 11th Edition' (2017), *SABA Intellectual Property Bulletin*, 14 February, available at www.sabaip.com/en/documents/fe_bulletin/Saba-IP-Bulletin--February-2017.pdf.

Obeidat, O (2015), 'IP Cooperation and Harmonisation in the Gulf: A myth or reality?', *Al Tamimi & Co. Law Update*, April, available at www.tamimi.com/en/magazine/law-update/section-11/october-5/ip-cooperation-and-harmonisation-in-the-gulf-a-myth-or-reality.html.

Obeidat, O and Nakhaei, S (2016), 'GCC Unified Trademark Law: Key Provisions and Challenges', *Al-Tamimi Law Update*, February, available at www.tamimi.com/en/magazine/law-update/section-14/february-8/gcc-unified-trademark-law-key-provisions-and-challenges.html.

'Oman: Patent Official Fees Due (2016)', *SABA Intellectual Property Bulletin*, 10 October, available at www.sabaip.com/en/documents/fe_bulletin/Saba-IP-Bulletin--November-2016.pdf.

Said, M B (2008), 'Protection of IP rights for Mobile Apps', *Al-Tamimi Law Update*, May, available at www.tamimi.com/en/magazine/law-update/section-11/may-8/protection-of-ip-rights-for-mobile-apps.html?utm_source=Mondaq&utm_medium=syndication&utm_campaign=View-Original.

'Special IP Court Circuit Launched in the UAE under Federal Courts' (2016), *Abu Ghazaleh Intellectual Property (AGIP) Bulletin*, 24 March, available at www.agip.com/News.aspx?id=6367.

World Intellectual Property Organisation (WIPO) documents, reports and publications

Blakeney, M (2004), 'Enforcement of Intellectual Property Rights: Challenges, Remedies and Public Awareness', *WIPO National Seminar on Intellectual Property for Faculty Members and Students of Ajman University*, May, WIPO Document WIPO/IP/UNI/DUB/04/7.

Hirst, A (1999), 'The Role of the Government Authorities in the Enforcement of Intellectual Property Rights', *WIPO Workshop on the Enforcement of Intellectual Property Rights for Judges*, Beirut, December, WIPO Document WIPO/IPR/JU/BEY/99/5B.

WIPO (2001), 'Intellectual Property Needs and Expectations of Traditional Knowledge Holders', *WIPO Report on Fact-Finding Missions on Intellectual Property and Traditional Knowledge (1998–9)*, WIPO Publication No. 768(E), April 2001.

WIPO (1978), *Situation of Industrial Property in the Arab States*, WIPO, Geneva.

WIPO (2002), International Bureau, 'Intellectual Property and Traditional Knowledge: Our Identity, Our Future', *WIPO International Forum on Matters Concerning Intellectual Property and Genetic Resources, Traditional Knowledge and Folklore*, Oman, 21–22 January 2002, WIPO Document IPTK/MCT/02/INF.11, November 2002.

WIPO (2002), 'Synthesis of Issues Concerning Difficulties and Practices in the Field of Enforcement', *WIPO Consultation Meeting on Enforcement, Geneva, 11–13 September*, WIPO Document WIPO/CME/3, 26 July 2002.

WIPO (2003), 'Legislative Assistance Provided by the World Intellectual Property Organization (WIPO) in Relation to the Implementation of the Agreement on Trade-Related Aspects of Intellectual Property Rights (the TRIPS Agreement) and the Doha Declaration', 8 July 2003, available at www.wipo.int/ip-development/en/legislative_assistance.

WIPO (2016), *Developing a National Strategy on Intellectual Property, Traditional Knowledge and Traditional Cultural Expressions*, WIPO Publication No. 3, available at www.wipo.int/edocs/pubdocs/en/wipo_pub_tk_3.pdf.

WIPO (2015), *Intellectual Property and Genetic Resources, Traditional Knowledge and Cultural Expressions*, WIPO Publication No. 933, available at www.wipo.int/edocs/pubdocs/en/tk/933/wipo_pub_933.pdf.

WIPO, 'Draft Act on the Protection of Layout Designs (Topographies) of Integrated Circuits', available at www.wipo.int/treaties/en/text.jsp?file_id=295136.

WIPO, *General Information*, 1 (Publication No. 400(E)).

WIPO, 'Statistical Country Profiles' (2016), available at www.wipo.int/ipstats/en/statistics/country_profile/#B.

World Trade Organisation (WTO) documents

WTO Working Party on the Accession of the Kingdom of Saudi Arabia (1996), *Additional Questions and Replies*, Document WT/ACC/SAU/6/Add.3 (96-4561), 30 October 1996.

WTO Working Party on the Accession of the Sultanate of Oman (1998), *Accession of the Sultanate of Oman: Additional Questions and Replies*, document WT/ACC/OMN/9 (98-3054), 3 August 1998.

WTO Working Party on the Accession of the Sultanate of Oman (1998), *Accession of the Sultanate of Oman: Communication from the Sultanate of Oman*, Document WT/ACC/SPEC/OMN/5 (98-0272), 26 January 1998.

WTO, Working Party on the Accession of the Sultanate of Oman (2000), *Accession of the Sultanate of Oman: Additional Questions and Replies*, Document WT/ACC/OMN/22 (01-0140), 13 January 2000.

WTO Council for Trade-Related Aspects of Intellectual Property Rights (2001), *Minutes of Meeting*, 27–28 November 2001, Document IP/C/M/34 (01-6407), 20 December 2001.

WTO Council for Trade-Related Aspects of Intellectual Property Rights (2001), *Review of Legislation: Bahrain*, 6 December, WTO Document IP/Q4/BHR/1 (01-6218), 6 December 2001.

WTO Council for Trade-Related Aspects of Intellectual Property Rights (2001), *Review of Legislation: Kuwait*, Document IP/Q4/KWT/1 (01-6332), 13 December 2001.

WTO Council for Trade-Related Aspects of Intellectual Property Rights (2001), *Review of Legislation: the United Arab Emirates*, Document IP/C/W/291 (01-3419), 10 July 2001.

WTO Council for Trade-Related Aspects of Intellectual Property Rights (2002), *Checklist of Issues on Enforcement: Responses from Qatar*, Document IP/C/W/291/ Add. 3 (02-3461), 24 June 2002.

WTO Council for Trade-Related Aspects of Intellectual Property Rights (2002), *Review of Legislation: Responses from Qatar to the questions posed by Australia, Canada, the European Communities and their member states, Switzerland and the United States*, IP/C/W/346 (02-3101), 5 June 2002.

WTO Council for Trade-Related Aspects of Intellectual Property Rights (2002), *Review of Legislation: Responses from the United Arab Emirates to the Questions Posed by Canada, the European Communities and their member States, Switzerland the United States – Addendum*, 5 March, WTO Document IP/C/W/291/Add.2 (02-1093).

WTO Council for Trade-Related Aspects of Intellectual Property Rights (2003), *Review of Legislation: Oman*, WTO Document IP/Q/OMN/1 (03-1675), 24 March 2003.

WTO Dispute Settlement: *Dispute DS199: Brazil – Measure Affecting Patent Protection* and WTO Dispute Settlement: *Dispute DS224: United States – US Patent Code*, Documents WT/DS199/1 and 3 (01-0093 and 01-3506).

Office of the United States Trade Representative (USTR)

USTR (2001), *2001 National Trade Estimates, Gulf Cooperation Council Chapter*, available at https://ustr.gov/archive/assets/Document_Library/Reports_Publications/2001/2001_NTE_Report/asset_upload_file262_6571.pdf.

USTR (2001), *2001 National Trade Estimate Report on Foreign Trade Barriers*, available at https://ustr.gov/archive/Document_Library/Reports_Publications/2001/2001_NTE_Report/Section_Index.html.

USTR (2001), *2001 Special 301 Report*, April, available at https://ustr.gov/sites/default/files/2001%20Special%20301%20Report.pdf.

USTR (2003), *2003 Special 301 Report*, April, available at https://ustr.gov/sites/default/files/2003%20Special%20301%20Report.pdf.

USTR (2005), *2005 Special 301 Report*, available at https://ustr.gov/sites/default/files/2005%20Special%20301%20Report.pdf.

USTR (2009), *2009 Special 301 Report*, 30 April, available at https://ustr.gov/sites/default/files/Full%20Version%20of%20the%202009%20SPECIAL%20301%20REPORT.pdf.

USTR (2010), *2010 Special 301 Report*, 30 April, available at https://ustr.gov/issue-areas/intellectual-property/special-301/2010-special-301-review.

USTR (2016), *2016 Special 301 Report*, 16 April, available at https://ustr.gov/sites/default/files/USTR-2016-Special-301-Report.pdf.

USTR Fact Sheet (2004), 'Middle East Free Trade Initiative', 23 June, available at https://ustr.gov/archive/Document_Library/Fact_Sheets/2004/Middle_East_Free_Trade_Initiative_US_Regional_Plan_to_Spur_Economic_Growth.html.

USTR Press Release (2004), 'US and Bahrain Conclude Free Trade Agreement', 27 May, available at https://ustr.gov/about-us/policy-offices/press-office/press-releases/archives/2004/may/us-and-bahrain-conclude-free-trade-agreement.

USTR Trade Facts (2004), 'Middle East Free Trade Initiative: US Regional Plan to Spur Economic Growth', 2 March, available at https://ustr.gov/about-us/policy-offices/press-office/fact-sheets/archives/2004/march/middle-east-free-trade-initiative-us-regional-.

USTR Press Release (2005), 'United States to Begin Free Trade Negotiations This Week with the United Arab Emirates and Oman', 8 March, available at https://ustr.gov/archive/Document_Library/Press_Releases/2005/March/United_States_to_Begin_Free_Trade_Negotiations_This_Week_with_the_United_Arab_Emirates_Oman.html.

USTR 'Mission of the USTR', available at https://ustr.gov/about-us/about-ustr.

IIPA (2004), 'Submission on Saudi Arabia to the USTR for the 2004 Special 301 Report', available at www.iipawebsite.com/rbc/2004/2004SPEC301SAUDIARABIA.pdf.

IPA (2005), '2005 Special 301 Report on Global Copyright Protection and Enforcement', available at www.iipawebsite.com/special301_TOCs/2005_SPEC301_TOC.html.

IIPA (2005), Testimony before the 'Public Hearing Concerning Proposed United States – Oman Free Trade Agreement, Friday January 14, 2005, Before the Trade Policy Staff Committee', Washington DC, available at www.iipawebsite.com/rbi/2005_Jan5_Oman.pdf.

IIPA (2006), 'Submission to the USTR, Saudi Arabia: Special 301 Out-of-Cycle Review', August, Appendix C, available at www.iipawebsite.com/pressreleases/IIPA%20Saudi%20Arabia%20301%20OCR%20submission%20FINAL%20%20100206.pdf.

IIPA (2007), 'Submission for the 2007 Special 301 Report', available at www.iipawebsite.com/rbc/2007/2007SPEC301SAUDIARABIA.pdf.

IIPA (2016), 'Special 301 Report on Global Copyright Protection and Enforcement', UAE Appendix, available at www.iipawebsite.com/rbc/2016/2016SPEC301UAE.PDF.

ITAC-15 (2004), 'Report on the Bahrain FTA', July 14, available at https://ustr.gov/archive/assets/Trade_Agreements/Bilateral/Bahrain_FTA/Reports/asset_upload_file822_5528.pdf.

ITAC-15 (2005), 'The U.S.–Oman Free Trade Agreement (FTA) The Intellectual Property Provisions', November 15 2005, available at https://ustr.gov/archive/assets/Trade_Agreements/Bilateral/Oman_FTA/Reports/asset_upload_file124_8402.pdf.

PhRMA (2000), 'Pharma Group Again Putting Pressure on UAE for IP Violations' (2000), *PhRMA Newsletter*, 117, December 2000.

PhRMA (2004), 'Submission on the USTR 2004 Special 301 Report', 13 February, available at www.phrma.org/international/resources/13.02.2004.600.cfm.

Other sources

'2012 Investment Climate Statement' (2012), Bureau of Economic and Business Affairs, *U.S. Department of State*, June, available at www.state.gov/e/eb/rls/othr/ics/2012/191265.htm.

'About the Emirates Plant Genetic Resources Knowledge Network' (2015), *Emirates Plant Genetic Resources Knowledge Network*, available at http://emirates.plantgenetic.com/Pages/About.aspx?lang=EN&DId=0&I=0&CId=0&CMSId=5002852#sthash.zZ0Ksavy.dpuf.

'About the GCC: Charter Concept and Foundations' (undated), *Gulf Cooperation Council*, available at http://gcc-sg.org/en-us/AboutGCC/Pages/StartingPointsAndGoals.aspx.

'About the GCCIP Centre' (2017), *GCC Intellectual Property Centre*, available at www.gccpo.org/gccip (in Arabic).

Al-Balushi, R (2015), 'Arab Treaty on Combating Cybercrime', *www.riyadh.om*, 18 March, available at www.riyadh.om/2015/arab-treaty-on-combating-cybercrime.

Australian Government Department of Foreign Affairs and Trade (2017), 'Australia–Gulf Cooperation Council (GCC) FTA', available at http://dfat.gov.au/trade/agreements/agccfta/Pages/australia-gulf-cooperation-council-gcc-fta.aspx#about.

Convention on Biological Diversity 1992 (CBD), available at www.cbd.int/convention/text/default.shtml.

Convention on Biological Diversity 1992, 'Parties to the Nagoya Protocol', available at www.cbd.int/abs/nagoya-protocol/signatories/default.shtml.

'Free Trade Agreement Between the EFTA States and the Member States of the Co-Operation Council for the Arab States of the Gulf' (2009), 22 June, available at www.efta.int/media/documents/legal-texts/free-trade-relations/gulf-cooperation-council-GCC/EFTA-GCC%20Free%20Trade%20Agreement.pdf.

'GCC FTA, General' (2014), *European Free Trade Association*, 1 July, available at www.efta.int/free-trade/free-trade-agreements/gcc.

'International Treaty on Plant Genetic Resources for Food and Agriculture' (undated), *Food and Agriculture of the United Nations*, available at www.fao.org/plant-treaty/overview/en.

'Internet World Stats Middle East' (2016), *Internet World Stats*, 12 September, available at www.internetworldstats.com/middle.htm.

New Zealand Government Foreign Affairs and Trade (2017), 'NZ Inc Gulf Cooperation Council (GCC) strategy', available at www.mfat.govt.nz/assets/_securedfiles/NZ-Inc-stategy/NZ-Inc-GCC/NZInc-Strategy-GCC-09-2013.pdf.

'Outcomes of Current U.S. Trade Agreements' (2017), Bureau of Economic and Business Affairs, *U.S. Department of State*, undated, available at www.state.gov/e/eb/tpp/bta/fta/c26474.htm.

'QHIC: Goals and objectives of the Center' (undated), *Qatar Heritage and Identity Center*, available at www.networkqatar.com/clients/_/qhic/mission_vision.php.

Singapore Government (2017), 'Overview of the Gulf Cooperation Council (GSFTA)', undated, available at www.iesingapore.gov.sg/-/media/IE-Singapore/Files/Publications/Brochures-Free-Trade-Agreements/FTAs_GCCGSFTA_FA.ashx.

'The Arab Network of Plant Genetic Resources' (undated), *Arab Organization for Agricultural Development*, available at www.aoad.org/gb/AboutSystem.aspx.

UAE Ministry of Culture and Knowledge Development, cultural heritage website, (2015), available at www.mcycd.gov.ae/sites/MCYCDVar/en-us/pages/HeritageArtServices.aspx.

'Unified Economic Agreement Between the Countries of the Gulf Cooperation Council' (undated), *Gulf Cooperation Council*, available at www.gcc-sg.org/ar-sa/CognitiveSources/DigitalLibrary/Lists/DigitalLibrary/1111318748548/الاقتصاد.pdf.

United Nations Conference on Trade and Development UNCTAD (2006), 'Investment Provisions in Economic Integration Agreements', 114–6, Document UNCTAD/ITE/IIT/2005/10.

United Nations Conference on Trade and Development UNCTAD (2016), 'UN System Task Team on the Post-2015 UN Development Agenda', available at www.un.org/en/development/desa/policy/untaskteam_undf/thinkpieces/22_thinkpiece_trade.pdf.

United States Patent and Trademark Office (USPTO) (2002), *Patent Counts by Country/State and Year, January 1 1997–December 31 2001*, February, available at www.uspto.gov/web/offices/ac/ido/oeip/taf/reports_stco.htm.

All websites were accessed May/June 2017.

APPENDIX

Dedicated intellectual property laws, regulations and orders in the Arab Gulf states

Bahrain

Main current dedicated intellectual property laws, regulations and orders

1 Ministerial Decree No. 65 of 2016, the Implementing Regulation for Law No. 6 of 2014 (issued 23 May 2016 and published in Official Gazette No. 3263 of 26 May 2016).
2 Law No. 6 of 2014 approving the Trade Marks Law of the Gulf Cooperation Council States (issued 17 February 2014 and published in Official Gazette No. 3145 of 27 February 2014).
3 Legislative Decree No. 5 of 2014 amending provisions of Law No. 22 of 2006 (Copyright and Neighbouring Rights).
4 Law No. 4 of 2012 approving Bahrain's accession to the Budapest Treaty on the International Recognition of the Deposit of Microorganisms for the Purposes of Patent Procedure (published in Official Gazette No. 3038 of 9 February 2012).
5 Ministerial Decree No. 1 of 2010, the Executive Regulations for Law No. 6 of 2006 (Industrial Designs and Models) (issued 17 February 2010 and published in Official Gazette No. 2936 of 25 February 2010).
6 Law No. 29 of 2009 approving Bahrain's adoption of the Protocol Amending the TRIPS Agreement (published in Official Gazette No. 2902 of 2 July 2009).
7 Legislative Decree No. 12 of 2008, amending Article 13 of Law No. 22 of 2006 (published in Official Gazette No. 2841 of 1 May 2008).
8 Ministerial Decree No. 2 of 2007, regarding the registration of the economic rights of copyrights and neighboring rights (published in Official Gazette No. 2778 of 15 February 2007).
9 Ministerial Decree No. 6 of 2007, authorising some employees of the printing and publishing department to act as law enforcement officers (issued 11 March 2007 and published in Official Gazette No. 2782 of 15 March 2007).
10 Law No. 83 of 2006 approving Brussels Convention Relating to the Distribution of Programme-Carrying Signals Transmitted by Satellite (published in Official Gazette No. 2769 of 14 December 2006) (Instrument of Accession lodged 1 February 2007 and entered into force 1 May 2007).
11 Ministerial Decree No. 31 of 2006, publishing judgments, decisions and information regarding enforcement of intellectual property (published in Official Gazette No. 2644 of 21 June 2006).

12 Legislative Decree No. 22 of 2006 concerning Copyright and Neighbouring Rights (issued 25 June 2006 and published in Official Gazette No. 2754 of 28 June 2006).
13 Legislative Decree No. 18 of 2006 ratifying Bahrain's accession to the Trademark Law Treaty (issued 25 June 2006 and published in Official Gazette No. 2745 of 28 June 2006) (Instrument of Accession lodged 18 December 2006 and entered into force 18 March 2007).
14 Legislative Decree No. 16 of 2006 amending Law No. 16 of 2004 concerning Geographical Indications (issued 28 May 2006 and published in Official Gazette No. 2741 of 31 May 2006).
15 Legislative Decree No. 14 of 2006 amending Law No. 1 of 2004 concerning Patents and Utility Models (issued 28 May 2006 and published in Official Gazette No. 2741 of 31 May 2006).
16 Legislative Decree No. 12 of 2006 amending Law No. 7 of 2003 concerning Trade Secrets (issued 28 May 2006 and published in Official Gazette No. 2741 of 31 May 2006).
17 Ministerial Decree No. 54 of 2006, the Implementing Regulations for Law No. 1 of 2004 in respect of Patents and Utility Models (issued 8 May 2006 and published in Official Gazette No. 2738 of 10 May 2006).
18 Legislative Decree No. 6 of 2006 concerning Industrial Designs (issued 29 April 2006 and published in Official Gazette No. 2737 of 3 May 2006).
19 Legislative Decree No. 5 of 2006 concerning Layout Designs of Integrated Circuits (issued 29 April 2006 and published in Official Gazette No. 2737 of 3 May 2006).
20 Legislative Decree No. 44 of 2005 ratifying Bahrain's accession to the Patent Cooperation Treaty (published in Official Gazette No. 2722 of 18 January 2006) (Instrument of Accession lodged 18 December 2006 and entered into force in Bahrain on 18 March 2007).
21 Law No. 35 of 2005 amending Law No. 7 of 2003 concerning Trade Secrets (issued 14 November 2005 and published in Official Gazette No. 2713 of 16 November 2005).
22 Legislative Decree No. 23 of 2005 ratifying the Free Trade Agreement between Bahrain and the United States (issued 20 July 2005 and published in Official Gazette No. 2697 of 27 July 2005).
23 Legislative Decree No. 19 of 2005 ratifying Bahrain's accession to the WIPO Patent Law Treaty (PLT) (issued 10 July 2005 and published in Official Gazette No. 2695 of 13 July 2005) (Instrument of Accession lodged 15 September 2005 and entered into force in Bahrain on 15 December 2005).
24 Legislative Decree No. 18 of 2005 ratifying Bahrain's accession to the Protocol Relating to the Madrid Agreement Concerning the International Registration of Marks (1989) (issued 10 July 2005 and promulgated in Official Gazette No. 2695 of 13 July 2005) (Instrument of Accession lodged 15 September 2005 and entered into force in Bahrain on 15 December 2005).
25 Legislative Decree No. 17 of 2005 acceding to the Nice Agreement Concerning the International Classification of Goods and Services for the Purpose of the Registration of Marks (8th edition) (issued February 2005) (Instrument of Accession lodged 15 September 2005 and entered into force in Bahrain on 15 December 2005).
26 Legislative Decree No. 12 of 2005 ratifying Bahrain's accession to the International Convention for the Protection of New Plant Varieties (UPOV) (issued 4 June 2005 and promulgated in Official Gazette No. 2690 of 8 June 2005) (Instrument of Accession lodged 15 September 2005 and Convention entered into force in Bahrain on 15 December 2005).
27 Legislative Decree No. 1 of 2005 approving Rome Convention for the Protection of Performers, Producers of Phonograms and Broadcasting Organisations (Instrument of Accession lodged 18 October 2005 and entered into force in Bahrain on 18 January 2006).

28 Legislative Decree No. 16 of 2004 in respect of Geographical Indications (issued 14 August 2004 and published in Official Gazette No. 2648 of 18 August 2004).
29 Legislative Decree No. 15 of 2004 approving the accession of Bahrain to the WIPO Performances and Phonograms Treaty (Instrument of Accession lodged 15 September 2005 and treaty entered into force in Bahrain on 15 December 2005).
30 Legislative Decree No. 14 of 2004 approving the accession of Bahrain to the WIPO Copyright Treaty (Instrument of Accession lodged 15 September 2005 and treaty entered into force in Bahrain on 15 December 2005).
31 Legislative Decree No. 13 of 2004 acceding to the Nice Agreement Concerning the International Classification of Goods and Services for the Purpose of the Registration of Marks (issued 22 June 2004 and published in Official Gazette No. 2640 of 23 June 2004).
32 Legislative Decree No. 12 of 2004 adopting the GCC Unified Patent Regulation in Bahrain (issued 22 June 2004 and published in Official Gazette No. 2640 of 2004).
33 Legislative Decree No. 1 of 2004 in respect of Patents and Utility Models (issued 24 January 2004 and published in Official Gazette No. 2619 of 28 January 2004).
34 Legislative Decree No. 7 of 2003 in respect of Trade Secrets (issued 13 June 2003 and published in Official Gazette No. 2587 of 18 June 2003).
35 Legislative Decree No. 47 of 2002 in respect of the Organisation of the Press, Printing and Publication (published in Official Gazette No. 2554 of 30 October 2002).
36 Legislative Decree No. 31 of 1996 ratifying Bahrain's accession to the Paris Convention for the Protection of Industrial Property (issued 29 October 1996 and published in Official Gazette No. 2240 of 1996) (Instrument of Accession lodged 2 December 1996 and Convention entered into force in Bahrain on 2 March 1997).
37 Legislative Decree No. 30 of 1996 ratifying Bahrain's accession to the Berne Convention for the Protection of Literary and Artistic Works (issued 29 October 1996 and published in Official Gazette No. 2240 of 1996) (Instrument of Accession lodged 2 December 1996 and Convention entered into force in Bahrain on 2 March 1997).
38 Legislative Decree No. 1 of 1995 ratifying Bahrain's accession to the Convention Establishing the World Intellectual Property Organisation (issued 11 February 1995 and published in Official Gazette No. 2151 of 1995) (Instrument of Accession lodged 22 March 1995 and Convention entered into force in Bahrain on 22 June 1995).
39 Legislative Decree No. 7 of 1994 ratifying Bahrain's accession to the Protocol Establishing the World Trade Organisation (issued 12 June 1994 and published in Official Gazette No. 2120 of 1994) (Protocol entered into force in Bahrain on 1 January 1995).

Subordinate, associated and superseded legislation

40 Law No. 3 of 2011 in respect of Trademarks (issued in 13 April 2011 and published in Official Gazette No. 2995 of 14 April 2011).
41 Legislative Decree No. 11 of 2006 concerning Trademarks (issued 28 May 2006 and published in Official Gazette No. 2741 of 31 May 2006).
42 Ministerial Order No. 1 of 1994 on the System of Deposit at the Copyright Protection Office (issued 15 May 1994 and published in Official Gazette No. 2112 of 1994).
43 Ministerial Order No. 12 of 1993, the Implementing Regulations for Amiri Decree No. 10 of 1991 concerning Trade Marks (issued 17 May 1993 and published in Official Gazette No. 2060 of 19 May 1993).
44 Legislative Decree No. 10 of 1993 with respect to the Protection of Copyright (issued 7 June 1993 and published in Official Gazette No. 2063 of 9 June 1993).

45 Ministerial Order No. 4 of 1993 with respect to the establishment of the Copyright Protection Office in the Ministry of Information (issued 14 November 1993 and published in Official Gazette No. 2086 of 1993).
46 Amiri Decree No. 10 of 1991 concerning Trade Marks (issued 25 June 1991 and published in Official Gazette No. 1961 of 26 June 1991).
47 Amiri Decree No. 7 of 1987, the Law of Commerce (published in Official Gazette No. 1739 of 1987).
48 Amiri Decree No. 5 of 1986 establishing the National Council for Culture, Arts and Literature (published in Official Gazette No. 1720 of 1986).
49 Ministerial Order No. 10 of 1981 amending the Implementing Regulations for Decree No. 22 of 1977 concerning Trade Marks (published in Official Gazette No. 1436 of 1981).
50 Amiri Decree No. 14 of 1979, the Law on Printed Matter and Publishing (published in Official Gazette No. 1344 of 1979).
51 Ministerial Order No. 13 of 1978 amending Ministerial Order No. 2 of 1978, the Implementing Regulations for Amiri Decree No. 22 of 1977 (issued 18 June 1978 and published in Official Gazette No. 1285 of 1978).
52 Ministerial Order No. 2 of 1978, the Implementing Regulations for the Patents, Design and Trade Marks Regulation of 1955 as amended by Amiri Decree No. 22 of 1977 (issued 1 February 1978 and published in Official Gazette No. 1266 of 9 February 1978).
53 Amiri Decree No. 22 of 1977 amending certain provisions of the Patents, Designs and Trade Marks Regulation of 1955 (issued 9 November 1977 and published in Official Gazette No. 1253 of 10 November 1977).
54 Amiri Decree No. 20 of 1975 with respect to the Legal Deposit of Intellectual Works (published in Official Gazette No. 114 of 1975).
55 Amiri Decree No. 12 of 1971, the Civil and Commercial Procedures Code (published in Official Gazette No. 926 of 1971).
56 Patents, Designs and Trade Marks Regulation, No. 1 of 1955 (promulgated 15 June 1955).

Jordan

Main current dedicated intellectual property laws, regulations and orders

1 Law No. 16 of 2016 and Law No. 17 of 2017, amending the Patent Law (both published in Official Gazette No. 5760 and entered into force 16 June 2017).
2 Law of 2017 ratifying Jordan's accession to the Patent Cooperation Treaty (Instrument of Accession lodged 9 March 2017, and entered into force 17 June 2017).
3 Law No. 23 of 2014 amending Copyright Protection Law No. 22 of 1992 (published in Official Gazette No. 5289 of 1 June 2014).
4 Law No. 32 of 2012 on Press and Publications amending Law No. 8 of 1998 on Press and Publications.
5 Regulation No. 22 of 2010 amending the Trademarks Law (issued 13 April 2010 and published in Official Gazette No. 5030 of 16 May 2010).
6 Regulation No. 128 of 2009 amending the Trademarks Law (issued 20 October 2009 and published in Official Gazette No. 4998 of 1 December 2009).
7 Law of 2008 ratifying Jordan's accession to the Budapest Treaty on the International Recognition of the Deposit of Microorganisms for the Purposes of Patent Procedure, Law of 2008 Nice Agreement Concerning the International Classification of Goods and Services for the Purposes of the Registration of Marks,

and Vienna Agreement Establishing an International Classification of the Figurative Elements of Marks (Instruments of Accession lodged 14 August 2008, and entered into force 14 November 2008).

8 Law No. 15 of 2008 amending the Trademarks Law (published in Official Gazette No. 4900 16 April 2008).

9 Regulation No. 65 of 2007 amending the Regulation on Trade Names (issued 29 May 2007 and published in Official Gazette No. 4835 of 1 July 2007).

10 Law No. 29 of 2007 amending Trademark Law No. 33 of 1952 (issued 31 March 2007 and published in Official Gazette No. 4823 of 1 May 2007).

11 Law No. 28 of 2007 amending the Patents Law No. 32 of 1999 (issued 31 March 2007 and published in Official Gazette No. 4823 of 1 May 2007).

12 Law No. 8 of 2005 amending Copyright Law No. 22 of 1992 (issued 19 March 2005, and entered into force 16 April 2005).

13 WIPO Performances and Phonograms Treaty (Instrument of Accession lodged 24 February 2004, and entered into force 24 May 2004).

14 WIPO Copyright Treaty (Instrument of Accession lodged 27 January 2004, and entered into force 27 April 2004).

15 International Convention for the Protection of New Varieties of Plants (UPOV) (Instrument of Accession lodged 24 September 2004, and entered into force 24 October 2004).

16 Law No. 88 of 2003 amending Copyright Law No. 22 of 1992.

17 Regulation No. 93 of 2002 on the Protection of Layout Designs of Integrated Circuits Law No. 10 of 2000 (issued 10 September 2002, entered into force 31 October 2002).

18 Regulation No. 76 of 2002 on Protection of New Plant Varieties Law No. 24 of 2000 (issued 18 July 2002 and published in Official Gazette No. 4561 of 28 August 2002).

19 Regulation No. 52 of 2002 on Industrial Designs and Models Law No. 14 of 2000 (issued 16 April 2002 and published in Official Gazette No. 4547 of 16 May 2002).

20 Free Trade Agreement between the United States and Jordan (signed 24 October 2000, implemented 17 December 2000).

21 Regulation No. 97 of 2001 on Patents Law No. 32 of 1999 (issued 6 November 2001, entered into force 13 December 2001).

22 Temporary Law No. 71 of 2001 on Patents (issued 9 October 2001 and published in Official Gazette No. 4520 of 2 December 2001).

23 Regulation No. 37 of 2000 on Trademark Law No. 33 of 1952 (issued 18 July 2000 and published in Official Gazette No. 4453 of 31 August 2000).

24 Law No. 24 of 2000 on the Protection of New Varieties of Plants (issued 11 June 2000 and published in Official Gazette No. 4443 of 22 July 2000).

25 Law No. 15 of 2000 on Unfair Competition and Trade Secrets (issued 24 February 2000 and published in Official Gazette No. 4423 of 2 April 2000).

26 Law No. 14 of 2000 on Industrial Designs and Models (issued 24 February 2000 and published in Official Gazette No. 4423 of 2 April 2000).

27 Law No. 10 of 2000 on the Protection of Layout-Designs of Integrated Circuits (issued 24 February 2000 and published in Official Gazette No. 4423 of 2 April 2000).

28 Law No. 8 of 2000 on Geographical Indications (issued 14 February 2000 and published in Official Gazette No. 4423 of 2 April 2000).

29 Regulation No. 7 of 2000 on Border Measures for the Protection of Intellectual Property Rights.

30 Law No. 4 of 2000 ratifying the Agreement Establishing the World Trade Organisation (entered into force 11 April 2000).

31 Agreement on Trade-Related Aspects of Intellectual Property Rights (entered into force 11 April 2000).

32 Berne Convention for the Protection of Literary and Artistic Works (Instrument of Accession lodged 28 April 1999, and entered into force 28 July 1999).

33 Law No. 32 of 1999 on Patents (issued 20 September 1999 and published in Official Gazette No. 4256 of 1 November 1999).
34 Law No. 22 of 1992, the Copyright Law (issued 19 March 1992 and published in Official Gazette No. 3821 of 16 April 1992).
35 Paris Convention for the Protection of Industrial Property (Instrument of Accession lodged 12 April 1972, and entered into force 17 July 1972).
36 Convention Establishing the World Intellectual Property Organization (Instrument of Accession lodged 12 April 1972, and entered into force 12 July 1972).
37 Law No. 33 of 1952 on Trademarks (issued 20 May 1952, entered into force 1 July 1952).
38 Trademarks Rules No. 1 of 1952 (issued 25 November 1952).

Subordinate, associated and superseded legislation

39 By-Law No. 4 for 1994 on the Deposit of Compilations (1994).
40 Trademarks Rules No. 1 of 1952 (1952).
41 International Plant Protection Convention (2 October 2005).
42 International Treaty on Plant Genetic Resources for Food and Agriculture (29 June 2004).

Kuwait

Main current dedicated intellectual property laws, regulations and orders

1 Law No. 22 of 2016 on Copyright and Neighbouring Rights (issued 7 June 2016 and published in Official Gazette No. 1293 of 17 June 2017).
2 Law No. 11 of 2016 ratifying Kuwait's accession to the Patent Cooperation Treaty (approved 27 March 2016, Instrument of Accession deposited 9 June 2016 and entered into force in Kuwait 9 September 2016).
3 Ministerial Regulation No. 115 of 2016, the Implementing Regulations for Law No. 71 of 2013 ratifying the GCC Patent Regulation as the Patent Law of Kuwait (published 3 April 2016 and entered into force 4 April 2016).
4 Ministerial Regulation No. 500 of 2015, issuing the Implementing Regulations for Law No. 13 of 2015 (published in Official Gazette No. 1268 of 27 December 2015 and entered into force 28 December 2015).
5 Law No. 13 of 2015 ratifying the GCC Trademark Law as the Trademark Law of Kuwait (published in Official Gazette No. 1228 of 22 March 2015).
6 Law No. 36 of 2014 ratifying Kuwait's accession to the Paris Convention for the Protection of Industrial Property (published in Official Gazette No. 1183 of 11 May 2014). (Instrument of Accession lodged 2 September 2014 and entered into force in Kuwait 2 December 2014).
7 Law No. 35 of 2014 ratifying Kuwait's accession to the Berne Convention for the Protection of Literary and Artistic Works (published in Official Gazette No. 1183 of 11 May 2014). (Instrument of Accession lodged 2 September 2014 and entered into force in Kuwait 2 December 2014).
8 Law No. 71 of 2013 adopting the GCC Patent Regulation as the patent law of Kuwait (issued 14 February 2013 and published in Official Gazette No. 1137 of 25 June 2013).
9 Law No. 3 of 2001 amending certain provisions of Law No. 4 of 1962 concerning Patents, Designs and Industrial Models.
10 Law No. 1 of 2001 amending certain provisions relating to Trademarks and Trade Indications of Law No. 68 of 1980, the Commercial Code.

11 Law No. 4 of 1999, amending certain provisions of Law No. 4 of 1962 concerning Patents, Designs and Industrial Models (issued 25 May 1999 and published in Official Gazette No. 414 of 1999).
12 Law No. 3 of 1999, amending certain provisions of Law No. 68 of 1980, the Commercial Code (issued 25 May 1999).
13 Law No. 2 of 1998 ratifying Kuwait's accession to the Convention Establishing the World Intellectual Property Organisation (Instrument of Accession lodged 14 April 1998 and Convention entered into force in Kuwait 14 July 1998).
14 Law No. 16 of 1986, ratifying the Arab Agreement for the Protection of Authors' Rights (published in Official Gazette No. 1657 of 1986).

Subordinate, associated and superseded legislation

15 Ministerial Order No. 127 of 2000 establishing the Directorate of Intellectual Property in the Ministry of Information.
16 Ministerial Order No. 106 of 2000 granting judicial authority to designated Ministry of Information Officials.
17 Law No. 64 of 1999 governing Copyright and Neighbouring Rights.
18 Ministerial Order No. 8 of 1995 establishing the Trade Mark Register (issued 8 January 1995 and published in Official Gazette No. 190 of 15 January 1995).
19 Law No. 68 of 1980, the Commercial Code (published in Official Gazette No. 1338 of 1980).
20 Law No. 67 of 1980, the Civil Code (promulgated in Official Gazette No. 1335 of 1981).
21 Ministerial Order No. 15 of 1965, the Implementing Regulations for Law No. 4 of 1962 governing Patents, Designs and Industrial Models (published in Official Gazette No. 555 of 5 December 1965).
22 Law No. 4 of 1962 governing Patents, Designs and Industrial Models (issued 9 April 1962 and published in Official Gazette No. 373 of 15 April 1962).
23 Law No. 3 of 1961, the Printed Matter and Publications Law (published in Official Gazette No. 312 of 1961).
24 Implementing Regulations for Law No. 2 of 1961, for the Control and Register of Trade Marks (published in Official Gazette No. 317 of 5 March 1961).
25 Law No. 2 of 1961, the Commercial Law (published in Official Gazette No. 311 of 1961).

Oman

Main current dedicated intellectual property laws, regulations and orders

1 Ministerial Decree No. 103/2015, the Implementing Regulations for Royal Decree No. 49/2009 (issued 16 April 2015 and published in Official Gazette No. 1098 of 26 April 2015).
2 Royal Decree No. 5/2015 ratifying the Arab Cybercrime Agreement (issued 8 March 2015 and published in Official Gazette No. 1088 of 26 March 2015).
3 Ministerial Decree No. 51/2010 on service fees for industrial property (issued 28 April 2010 and published in Official Gazette No. 911 of 15 May 2010).
4 Royal Decree No. 49/2009 promulgating the Law on the Protection of Breeders' Rights in New Varieties of Plants (issued 29 August 2009 and published in Official Gazette No. 894 of 1 September 2009).
5 Accession to the Hague Agreement Concerning the International Registration of Industrial Designs (4 March 2009).

6 Royal Decree No. 132/2008 amending Royal Decree No. 65/2008, the Copyright Law (issued 30 November 2008 and published in Official Gazette No. 876 of 1 December 2008).
7 Royal Decree No. 131/2008, amending Royal Decree No. 67/2008, the Law on Industrial Property Rights (issued 30 November 2008 and published in Official Gazette No. 876 of 1 December 2008).
8 Royal Decree No. 86/2008 acceding to the Hague Agreement Concerning the International Registration of Industrial Designs (published in Official Gazette No. 867 of 1 July 2008) (Instrument of Accession lodged 4 December 2008 and entered into force 4 March 2009).
9 Ministerial Regulation No. 105/2008 issuing the executive regulations of Royal Decree 67/2008, the Law on Industrial Property Rights (issued 2 December 2008 and published in Official Gazette No. 877 of 17 December 2008).
10 Ministerial Resolution No. 103/2008 issuing the executive regulations of Royal Decree No. 65/2008, the Law on Copyright and Neighbouring Rights (issued 2 December 2008 and published in Official Gazette. No. 877).
11 Royal Decree No. 132/2008, amending Royal Decree No. 67/2008.
12 Royal Decree No. 67/2008, the Law on Industrial Property Rights (issued 12 May 2008 and published in the Official Gazette of 15 May 2008).
13 Royal Decree No. 65/2008, the Law on Copyright and Related Rights (issued 4 May 2008 and published in the Official Gazette No. 863 of 15 May 2008).
14 Royal Decree No. 37/2007 ratifying the Sultanate's accession to the Convention Relating to the Distribution of Programme-Carrying Signals Transmitted by Satellite (Brussels Convention), the Budapest Treaty on the International Recognition of the Deposit of Microorganism for the Purposes of Patent Procedure, the Protocol Relating to the Madrid Agreement Concerning the International Registration of Marks (Madrid Protocol), International Convention for the Protection of New Varieties of Plants (UPOV Convention), the Patent Law Treaty, and the Trademark Law Treaty (issued 23 April 2007 and published in Official Gazette No. 838 of 1 May 2007) (Instrument of Accession lodged 16 July 2007 and Treaties entered into force in Oman on 16 October 2007).
15 Ministerial Decision No. 73/2005, the Implementing Regulations for Royal Decree No. 82/2000, the Patents Law (issued 10 September 2005 and published in Official Gazette No. 799 of 17 September 2005).
16 Royal Decree No. 53/2006 ratifying the Sultanate's accession to the WIPO Copyright Treaty (WCT) and the WIPO Performances and Phonograms Treaty (WPPT) (Instrument of Accession lodged 20 June 2005 and Treaties entered into force in Oman on 20 September 2005).
17 Ministerial Decision No. 62/2005, the Implementing Regulations for Royal Decree No. 38/2000 on the Protection of Trademarks (issued 25 June 2005 and published in Official Gazette No. 795 of 16 July 2005).
18 Royal Decree No. 56/2005 endorsing the Agreement on the Preservation of non-materialist Cultural Heritage (Paris 2003) (issued 22 June 2005 and published in Official Gazette No. 794 of 2 July 2005).
19 Royal Decree No. 24/2005 establishing the Functions of the Ministry of Heritage and Culture and its organisational structure (issued 26 February 2005 and published in Official Gazette No. 786 of 1 March 2005).
20 Ministerial Decision No. 35/2004, the Implementing Regulations for Royal Decree 92/2000 on the Protection of New Plant Varieties (issued 10 May 2004 and published in Official Gazette No. 768 of 2004).
21 Royal Decree No. 37/2001 ratifying the Sultanate's accession to the WIPO Patent Cooperation Treaty (PCT) (issued 24 April 2001 and published in Official Gazette No. 694 of 1 May 2001) (Instrument of Accession lodged 27 July 2001 and Convention entered into force in Oman on 27 October 2001).
22 Royal Decree No. 112/2000 ratifying the Sultanate's accession to the Protocol Establishing the World Trade Organisation (issued 15 November 2000 and

published in Official Gazette No. 683 of 15 November 2000) (Protocol entered into force in Oman on 20 November 2000).

23 Ministerial Decision No. 14/2000 recognising the GCC Unified Patent Regulation as amended (1999) as the Patent Law of Oman (issued 23 February 2000 and published in Official Gazette No. 667 of 20 March 2000).

24 Royal Decree No. 63/1998 ratifying the Sultanate's accession to the Paris Convention for the Protection of Industrial Property and the Berne Convention for the Protection of Literary and Artistic Works (issued 28 July 1998 and published in Official Gazette No. 632 of 3 October 1998) (Instrument of Accession lodged 14 April 1999 and Conventions entered into force in Oman on 14 July 1999).

25 Royal Decree No. 74/1996 ratifying the Sultanate's accession to the Convention establishing the World Intellectual Property Organization (issued 25 September 1996 and published in Official Gazette No. 584 of 1 October 1996) (Instrument of Accession lodged 19 February 1997 and Convention entered into force in Oman on 14 April 1997).

Subordinate, associated and superseded legislation

26 Royal Decree No. 92/2000, the Law on the Protection of New Plant Varieties (issued 8 October 2000 and published in Official Gazette No. 681 of 15 October 2000).

27 Royal Decree No. 82/2000, the Patents Law (issued 23 September 2000 and published in Official Gazette No. 680 of 10 October 2000).

28 Royal Decree No. 41/2000, the Law on the Topographies Rights of Integrated Circuits (issued 21 May 2000 and published in Official Gazette No. 672 of 3 June 2000).

29 Royal Decree No. 40/2000, the Law on the Protection of Geographical Indications (issued 21 May 2000 and published in Official Gazette No. 672 of 3 June 2000).

30 Royal Decree No. 39/2000, the Law on the Protection of Industrial Designs (issued 21 May 2000 and published in Official Gazette No. 672 of 3 June 2000).

31 Royal Decree No. 38/2000, the Law on Trade Marks, Indications and Secrets and Protection from Unfair Competition (issued 21 May 2000 and published in Official Gazette No. 672 of 3 June 2000).

32 Royal Decree No. 37/2000, the Law on the Protection of Copyrights and Neighbouring Right, and cancelling Royal Decree 47/96 (issued 21 May 2000 and published in Official Gazette No. 672 of 3 June 2000).

33 Ministerial Regulations No. 43/1998 and No. 170/1998, implementing Royal Decree No. 47/1996 concerning copyright (issued 22 April 1998 and published in Official Gazette No. 622 of 2 May 1998).

34 Royal Decree No. 65/1997, the Artistic Works Control Law (issued 5 October 1997 and published in Official Gazette No. 62 of 15 October 1997).

35 Royal Decree No. 47/1996 promulgating the Law on Copyright (issued 8 June 1996 and published on 15 June 1996).

36 Ministerial Resolution No. 219/1993, adopting the GCC Unified Patent Regulations as the Patents Law of Oman (issued September 1993 and published in Official Gazette No. 514 of 1993).

37 Royal Decree No. 33/1991 amending Royal Decree No. 68/1987, the Trade Mark Law (issued 6 April 1991 and published in Official Gazette No. 453 of 1991).

38 Ministerial Decision No. 103/1988, the Implementing Regulations for Royal Decree No. 68/1987 (issued 24 November 1988 and published in Official Gazette No. of 1988).

39 Royal Decree No. 68/1987, the Law of Trade Marks and Commercial Data (issued 5 October 1987 and published in Official Gazette No. 369 of 15 October 1987).

40 Royal Decree No. 7/1986 ratifying Oman's accession to the Nairobi Treaty on the Protection of the Olympic Symbol (published in Official Gazette No. 328 of 1986) (Instrument of Accession lodged 26 February 1986 and Treaty entered into force in Oman on 26 March 1986).
41 Royal Decree No. 49/1984, the Law on Printed Matter and Publications (issued 26 May 1984 and published in Official Gazette No. 289 of 1984).
42 Royal Decree No. 6/1980, the National Heritage Protection Law (issued 10 February 1980 and published in Official Gazette No. 188 of 1980).
43 Royal Decree No. 70/1977, the Law on the Protection of Manuscripts (published in Official Gazette No. 137 of 1977).
44 Royal Decree No. 3/1975, the Law on Printed Matter (published in Official Gazette No. 83 of 1975).
45 Royal Decree No. 7/74, the Oman Penal Code (published in Official Gazette No. 52 of 1974).

Qatar

Main current dedicated intellectual property laws, regulations and orders

1 Decree No. 21 of 2015 acceding to the Budapest Treaty on the International Recognition of the Deposit of Microorganisms for the Purposes of Patent Procedure (issued 22 March 2015 and published in Official Gazette No. 9 of 3 May 2015) (Instrument of Accession deposited 6 December 2013 and entered into force 22 March 2015).
2 Decree No. 20 of 2015 in respect of Qatar's Accession to the Arab League Agreement for the Protection of Authors' Rights and Neighboring rights (amended version) (issued 22 March 2015 and published in Official Gazette No. 9 of 3 May 2015).
3 Law No. 7 of 2014 adopting the GCC Trade Mark Law (issued 8 June 2014 and published in Official Gazette No. 11 of 30 June 2014).
4 Accession to the Budapest Treaty on the International Recognition of the Deposit of Microorganisms for the Purposes of Patent Procedure (Instrument of Accession deposited 6 December 2013 and entered into force 6 March 2014).
5 Ministerial Decision No. 410 of 2014, on copyright service fees (issued 2 December 2014 and published in Official Gazette No. 19 of 20 December 2014).
6 Law No. 17 of 2011 on Border measures for the Protection of Intellectual Property Rights (issued 17 November 2011 and published in Official Gazette No. 12 of 22 December 2011).
7 Decree No. 36 of 2011 acceding to Patent Cooperation Treaty (issued 15 July and published in Official Gazette No. 10 of 27 September 2011) (instrument of accession deposited 3 May 2011 and entered into force 3 August 2011).
8 Patent Cooperation Treaty (3 August 2011).
9 Emirati Decree No. 53 of 2009 on the Establishment of the Centre of the Protection of Intellectual Property.
10 Law No. 18 of 2007 adopting the GCC Unified Trade Marks Regulation in Qatar (issued 6 August 2007 and published in Official Gazette No. 9 of 30 September 2007).
11 Law No. 30 of 2006 issuing the Patents Law (issued 6 August 2006 and published in Official Gazette No.11 of 12 December 2006).
12 Law of 2005 approving Qatar's accession to the WIPO Copyright Treaty (WCT) (Instrument of Accession lodged 28 July 2005 and Treaty entered into force in Qatar on 28 October 2005).

13 Law of 2005 ratifying Qatar's accession to the WIPO Performances and Phonograms Treaty (WPPT) (Instrument of Accession lodged 28 July 2005 and Convention entered into force in Qatar on 28 October 2005).
14 Law No. 6 of 2005 on the Protection of Layout Designs of Integrated Circuits (issued 2 March 2005 and published in Official Gazette No. 5 of 24 May 2005).
15 Law No. 5 of 2005 concerning Trade Secrets (issued 2 March 2005 and published in Official Gazette No. 5 of 24 May 2005).
16 Law No. 12 of 2003 adopting the GCC Unified Patent Regulation as the Patent Law of Qatar (issued 19 February 2003 and published in Official Gazette No. 6 of 20 July 2003).
17 Law No. 9 of 2002, the Law of Trade Marks, Business Names and Data, Industrial Designs and Geographical Indications (issued 15 June 2002 and published in Official Gazette No. 8 of 26 August 2002).
18 Law No. 7 of 2002, the Law of Copyrights and Neighbouring Rights (issued 8 June 2002 and published in the Official Gazette No. 7 of 3 August 2002).
19 Decree No. 33 of 2001 ratifying Qatar's Accession to the Berne Convention for the Protection of Literary and Artistic Works (issued 4 July 2001 and published in the Official Gazette No. 12 of 24 October 2001) (Instrument of Accession lodged 5 April 2000 and Convention entered into force in Qatar on 5 July 2000).
20 Decree No. 31 of 2001 ratifying Qatar's Accession to the Paris Convention for the Protection of Industrial Property (issued 4 July 2001 and published in the Official Gazette No. 11 of 20 October 2001) (Instrument of Accession lodged 5 April 2000 and Convention entered into force in Qatar on 5 July 2000).
21 Decree No. 46 of 1996 ratifying the GCC Patent Law (issued 22 July 1996 and published in Official Gazette No. 9 of 18 September 1996).
22 Decree No. 24 of 1995 in respect of Qatar's Accession to the Protocol establishing the World Trade Organisation (issued 12 March 1995 and published in Official Gazette No. 2 of 1995).
23 Decree No. 50 of 1986 in respect of Qatar's Accession to the Arab League Agreement for the Protection of Authors' Rights (issued 23 September 1986 and published in Official Gazette No. 11 of 1 January 1986).

Subordinate, associated and superseded legislation

24 Law No. 18 of 2007 adopting the GCC Unified Trade Marks Regulation in Qatar (issued 6 August 2007 and published in Official Gazette No. 9 of 30 September 2009).
25 Law No. 25 of 1995 in respect of the Protection of Intellectual Works and Copyrights (issued 22 July 1995 and published in Official Gazette No. 14 of 12 August 1995).
26 Ministerial Order No. 8 of 1995, Executive Regulations for the Trademark Register (published in Official Gazette No. 190 of 15 January 1995).
27 Law No. 16 of 1993 in respect of Public Relations, Artistic Production and Artistic Works (published in Official Gazette No. 13 of 1993).
28 Law No. 37 of 1988 amending Law No. 2 of 1978, the Trade Marks and Descriptions Law (published in Official Gazette No. 11 of 1988).
29 Accession to the Nairobi Treaty on the Protection of the Olympic Symbol (Instrument of Accession lodged on 23 June 1983 and Treaty entered into force in Qatar on 23 July 1983).
30 Law No. 5 of 1983, the Law on Combatting Fraud in Commercial Transactions (published in Official Register No. 2 of 1983).
31 Law No. 14 of 1982 in respect of the Deposit of Works with the Qatar National Library (published in Official Gazette No. 8 of 1982).

32 Ministerial Decision No. 30 of 1980, the Implementing Regulations for Law No. 3 of 1978, the Trade Marks and Commercial Indications Law (issued 11 June 1980 and published in Official Gazette No. 7 of 1 January 1980).
33 Amiri Law No. 8 of 1979 in respect of Printed Materials and Publication (issued 7 October 1979 and published in Official Gazette No. 7 of 1979).
34 Amiri Law No. 3 of 1978, the Trade Marks and Commercial Indications Law (issued 18 April 1978 and published in Official Gazette No. 3 of 20 May 1978).
35 Amiri Law No. 16 of 1971, the Law of Civil and Commercial Matters (issued 25 August 1971 and published in Official Gazette No. 7 of 1 January 1971).
36 Amiri Law No. 11 of 1966, the Law on the Control of Printed Matter (published in Official Gazette No. 4 of 1966).

Saudi Arabia

Main current dedicated intellectual property laws, regulations and orders

1 Ministerial Decree No. 306 of 2014 approving the Implementing Regulations for the GCC Trademark Law (published in the Official Gazette 30 June 2016 and entered into force 27 September 2016).
2 Royal Decree No. M/51 approving the adoption of the GCC Trademark Law (issued 26 April 2014 and published in the Official Gazette of 2 July 2016).
3 Royal Decree No. M/94 notifying Cabinet approval of the GCC Trademark Law (issued 23 May 2014).
4 Royal Decree No. M/27 of 1434 AH (2013) amending Royal decree No. M/63 of 1430 AH in regard to accession to the Patent Cooperation Treaty and the Patent Law Treaty (published in Official Gazette No. 4460 of 4 May 2013) (instrument of accession lodged 3 May 2013 and entered into force 3 August 2013)
5 Ministerial Decision No. 1147 of 2012 amending Royal Decree No. M/21 of 2002 (the Trademark Law) (issued 16 October 2012).
6 Royal Decree No. M/17 8 Rabi 1 1428 (issued 26 March 2007), the Anti-Cyber Crime Law.
7 Ministerial Decision No. 50 of 1426 AH (2005), the Regulations for the Protection of Confidential Commercial Data (issued 4 April 2005), as amended by Ministerial Decision No. 3218 and Ministerial Decision No. 431 of 1426 AH (2005).
8 Ministerial Decision No. 118828/M/10 of 1425 AH (2005) issuing the Implementing Regulations for Royal Decree No. M/27 of 1425 AH (2004) (issued 26 December 2004).
9 Royal Decree No. M/27 of 1425 AH (2004), the Law of Patents, Layout Designs of Integrated Circuits, Plant Varieties and Industrial Models (issued 17 July 2004 and published in Official Gazette No. 4004 of 6 August 2004).
10 Ministerial Decision No. 1277 of 1425 AH (2004), Regulations for Border Procedures for the Protection of Intellectual Property Rights of Trademarks and Copyrights (issued 3 July 2004).
11 Ministerial Decision No. 1688/1 of 1425 AH (2004) issuing the Implementing Regulations for Royal Decree No. M/41 of 2003, the Law of Copyright (issued 29 May 2004 and published in Official Gazette No. 3995 of 4 June 2004).
12 Royal Decree No. M/48 of 1424 AH (2003), ratifying the Kingdom's accession to the Paris Convention for the Protection of Industrial Property and the Berne Convention for the Protection of Literary and Artistic Works (issued 9 September 2003) (Instrument of Accession lodged 11 December 2003 and Conventions entered into force in the Kingdom 11 March 2004).

13 Royal Decree No. M/41 of 1424 AH (2003), the Law of Copyright (issued 30 August 2003 and published in Official Gazette No. 3959 of 19 September 2003).
14 Ministerial Decision No. 1723 issuing the Implementing Regulations for Royal Decree No. M/21 of 1423 AH (2002) (published in the Official Gazette of 18 October 2002).
15 Royal Decree No. M/21 of 1423 AH (2002), the Law of Trademarks (issued 7 August 2002 and published in Official Gazette No. 3907 of 6 September 2002).
16 Royal Decree No. M/15 of 1423 AH (2002), the Law of Commercial Data (issued 25 June 2002).
17 Ministerial Decision No. 159 of 1422 AH (2001), Implementing Regulations for Royal Decree No. M/28 of 1422 AH (2011) for GCC Unified Patent Regulation.
18 Royal Decree No. M/28 of 1422 AH (2011) for GCC Unified Patent Regulation.
19 Ministerial Decision No. 1641 of 1422 AH (2001) amending the Implementing Regulations of the Trade Mark Law in respect of the International Classification of Goods and Services (issued 9 July 2001).
20 Implementing Regulations for Royal Decree No. M/15 of 1420 AH (1999), the Law of Trade Names (date uncertain).
21 Royal Decree No. M/15 of 1420 AH (1999), the Law of Trade Names (issued 20 November 1999).
22 Ministerial Order No. 1339 of 1416 AH (1994) establishing the Permanent Committee for IP rights in the Ministry of Trade and Commerce.
23 Royal Decree No. M/12 of 1414 AH (1994) ratifying the Kingdom's assent to the Universal Copyright Convention (issued 29 December 1993 and published in Official Gazette No. 3489 of 21 January 1994) (Instrument of assent lodged with UNESCO on 13 April 1994 and Convention came into effect in Saudi Arabia on 13 July 1994).
24 Royal Decree No. M/6 of 1406 AH (1985) ratifying the Arab Agreement for the Protection of Authors' Rights (issued 22 December 1985 and published in Official Gazette No. 3096 of January 1986).
25 Accession to the Convention Establishing the World Intellectual Property Organisation (Instrument of Accession lodged with WIPO on 22 February 1982 and Convention came into effect in Saudi Arabia on 22 May 1982).

Subordinate, associated and superseded legislation

26 Royal Decree No. M/63 of 1430 AH (2009) concerning accession to the Patent Cooperation Treat and the Patent Law Treaty.
27 Ministerial Order M/O/158 of 1412 AH (1992) amending the Implementing Regulations for Royal Decree No. M/11 of 1410 AH (issued 9 September 1992).
28 Royal Decree No. M/26 of 1412 AH (1992), the Regulations for the Deposit of Literary Manuscripts (published in Official Gazette No. 3401 of April 1992).
29 Ministerial Resolution No. 35187/M/10, the Implementing Regulations for Royal Decree No. M/38 of 1409 AH, the Patent Regulations (issued 18 June 1990).
30 Ministerial Resolution No. 699 of 1410 AH (1990), the Implementing Regulations for Royal Decree No. M/61 of 1409 AH) (published in Official Gazette No. 3299 of March 1990).
31 Royal Decree No. M/11 of 1410 AH (1989), the Regulation for the Protection of Copyrights (issued 17 December 1989 and published in Official Gazette No. 3291 of 12 January 1990).
32 Royal Decree No. M/61 of 1409 AH (1989), the Commercial Books Regulation (published in Official Gazette No. 3269 of August 1989).
33 Ministerial Resolution No. 473/DS of 1409 AH (1989), the Implementing Regulations for Royal Decree M/17 of 1402 AH (issued 6 June 1989 and published in Official Gazette No. 3266 of July 1989).

34 Royal Decree No. M/38 of 1409 AH (1989), in respect of Patents (issued 17 January 1989 and published in Official Gazette No. 3248 of 17 February 1989).
35 Royal Decree No. M/5 of 1406 AH (1985) ratifying the Kingdom's accession to the Nairobi Treaty on the Protection of the Olympic Symbol (published in Official Gazette No. 3091 of December 1985).[1]
36 Ministerial Resolution No. 94 of 1404 AH (1984), the Implementing Regulations for Royal Decree No. M/5 concerning Trade Marks (issued 6 May 1984 and published in Official Gazette No. 3016 of 25 May 1984).
37 Royal Decree No. M/5 of 1404 AH (1984) concerning Trade Marks (issued 5 February 1984 and published in Official Gazette No. 3004 of 2 March 1984).
38 Royal Decree No. 28 of 1382 AH (1982), the Boycott of Israel Law (issued July 1982).
39 Royal Decree No. M/17 of 1402 AH (1982) concerning the Control of Publications and Publishing (issued 7 February 1982 and published in Official Gazette No. 2904 of 12 February 1982).
40 Royal Decree No. 8762 of 1358 AH (1938) ratifying Rules for the Registration of Trade Marks (also referred to as Royal Decree No. 33/1/4) (issued 10 August 1938).

United Arab Emirates

Main current dedicated intellectual property laws, regulations and orders

1 Ministerial Resolution No. 137 of 2016, establishing federal specialised intellectual property courts (issued 3 February 2016).
2 Ministerial Decision No. 9 of 2015 on fees (issued 29 May 2015).
3 Federal Decree Law No. 5 of 2012 on Combatting Cybercrimes, issued 25 Ramadan 1433 AH (issued 13 August 2012).
4 UAE adoption of the 10th Edition of the Nice Classification of Goods and Services has come into effect on 1 January 2012.
5 Federal Law No. 17 of 2009 on the Protection of New Plant Varieties.
6 Federal Decree No. 52 of 2007, adopting the GCC Unified Trade Mark Regulation in the UAE (issued 25 July 2007 and published in Official Gazette No. 466 of 28 June 2007).
7 Federal Law No. 32 of 2006 amending Law No. 7 of 2002 on Copyright and Neighbouring Rights (issued 1 October 2006 and published in Official Gazette No. 7 of 1 January 2006).
8 Federal Law No.31 of 2006 amending Law No. 17 of 2002 on Patents.
9 Federal Decree No. 10 of 2005, ratifying the UAE's accession to the WIPO Performances and Phonograms Treaty (WPPT) (published in Official Gazette No. 425 of 28 February 2005) (Instrument of Accession lodged on 9 March 2005 and Treaty came into effect in the UAE on 9 June 2005).
10 Federal Decree of 2005 ratifying the UAE's accession to the International Convention for the Protection of Performers, Producers of Phonograms and Broadcasting Organizations (Rome Convention) (Instrument of Accession lodged on 14 October 2004 and Convention came into effect in the UAE on 14 January 2005).
11 Ministerial Decision No. 121 of 2004 concerning the Issuance of Five Patents (issued 19 September 2004 and published in Official Gazette No. 420 of 13 October 2004).

1 WIPO does not record Saudi Arabia as having lodged Instruments of Accession to the Treaty.

12 Federal Law of 2004 ratifying the UAE's accession to the WIPO Copyright Treaty (WCT) (Instrument of Accession lodged on 14 April 2004 and Treaty entered into force in the UAE on 14 July 2004).
13 Federal Decree No. 10 of 2004, acceding to the Berne Convention for the Protection of Literary and Artistic works (issued and published in Official Gazette No. 408 of February 2004) (Instrument of accession lodged with WIPO on 14 April 2004 and Convention entered into force in the UAE on 14 July 2004).
14 Ministerial Decision No. 134 of 2004 on the Mandatory Licencing for Copying or Translating Copyright Works (issued 22 March 2004).
15 Ministerial Decision No. 133 of 2004 on the Collective Management of Copyrights and Neighbouring Rights (issued 22 March 2004).
16 Ministerial Decision No. 132 of 2004 on the Registration of Importers and Distributors of Published Works (issued 22 March 2004).
17 Ministerial Decision No. 131 of 2004 on the Registration of Published Works (issued 22 March 2004).
18 Federal Law No. 17 of 2002 for the Industrial Regulation and Protection of Patents, Industrial Drawings, and Designs, (issued 19 November 2002 and published in Official Gazette No. 390 of 30 November 2002).
19 Federal Law No. 8 of 2002 amending Law No. 37 of 1992 concerning Trademarks (issued 24 July and published in Official Gazette No. 384 of 31 July 2002).
20 Federal Law No. 7 of 2002 concerning Copyright and Neighbouring Rights (issued 1 July 2002 and published in Official Gazette No. 383 of 14 July 2002).
21 Ministerial Decision No. 165 of 2001 adopting the Nice Agreement Concerning the International Classification of Goods and Services for the Purpose of the Registration of Marks (issued 24 November 2001).[2]
22 Ministerial Decision No. 61/16 of 2000, adopting the GCC Unified Patent Regulations as amended (1999) in the UAE (issued April 2000).
23 Ministerial Decree No. 404 of 2000 Regarding Pharmaceutical Patents (issued 28 April 2000).
24 Federal Decree No. 84 of 1998 ratifying the accession of the UAE to the Patent Cooperation Treaty (PCT) (issued 18 August 1998) (Instrument of Accession lodged with WIPO on 10 December 1998 and Treaty entered into force in the UAE on 10 March 1999).
25 Federal Decree No. 21 of 1997, ratifying the accession of the UAE to the Protocol establishing the World Trade Organization (issued 10 April 1996) (Protocol entered into force in the UAE on 10 April 1996).
26 Federal Decree No. 20 of 1996, ratifying the accession of the UAE to the Paris Convention for the Protection of Industrial Property (issued 18 March 1996 and published in Official Gazette No. 291 of 11 March 1996) (Instrument of Accession lodged with WIPO on 19 September 1996 and Convention entered into force in the UAE on 19 December 1996).
27 Federal Law No. 37 of 1992 Governing Trade Marks (issued 28 September 1992 and published in Official Gazette No. 243 of 12 October 1992).
28 Federal Law No. 21 of 1975, ratifying the UAE's accession to the Convention establishing the World Intellectual Property Organisation (published in Official Gazette No. 27 of 1975) (Instrument of accession lodged with WIPO on 24 June 1974 and Convention entered into force in the UAE on 24 September 1974).

Subordinate, associated and superseded legislation

29 Ministerial Decree No. 165 of 2001 concerning the reclassification of services in accordance with WIPO classifications.

2 WIPO does not record the UAE as having lodged Instruments of Accession to the Agreement.

30 Ministerial Decree No. 68 of 2001 amending some of the Provisions of Ministerial Decree No. (6) of 1993 concerning the Implementing Regulations of the Trademark Law (issued on 2 May 2001).
31 Federal Law No. 19 for 2000 amending Some Provisions of Federal Law No. 37 for 1992 with regard to Trademarks (issued 16 September 2000).
32 Ministerial Decision No. 412 of 1993 concerning Regulations for the Deposit of Protected Works (issued 1 September 1993 and published in Official Gazette No. 256 of 1993).
33 Ministerial Decision No. 411 of 1993 concerning the Deposit of Protected Intellectual Works (issued 1 September 1993 and published in Official Gazette No. 256 of 1993).
34 Federal Law No. 18 of 1993, the Commercial Transactions Code (published in Official Gazette No. 255 of 1993).
35 Ministerial Decision No. 11 of 1993, the Implementing Regulations for Federal Law No. 44 of 1992 (issued 12 May 1993 and published in Official Gazette No. 251 of 1993).
36 Ministerial Decision No. 6 of 1993, the Executive Regulations for Federal Law No. 37 of 1992 (issued 2 February 1993).
37 Federal Law No. 44 of 1992 concerning the Organization and Protection of Patents, Industrial Drawings and Industrial Models (issued 12 October 1992 and published in Official Gazette No. 243 of 12 October 1992).
38 Federal Law No. 40 of 1992 concerning the Protection of Intellectual Compilations and Author's Rights (issued 28 September 1992 and published in Official Gazette No. 243 of 12 October 1992).
39 Federal Law No. 11 of 1992, the Civil Procedures Code (published in Official Gazette No. 235 of 1992).
40 Federal Law No. 3 of 1987, the Penal Code (published in Official Gazette No. 182 of 1987).
41 Federal Law No. 5 of 1985, the Civil Transactions Code (published in Official Gazette No. 158 of December 1985).
42 Federal Law No. 28 of 1984 ratifying the Arab Agreement for the Protection of Authors' Rights (published in Official Gazette No. 139 of 1984).
43 Federal Law No. 18 of 1981, the Commercial Agencies Law (published in Official Gazette No. 94 of 1981).
44 Federal Law No. 15 of 1980, the Control of Press and Publications (issued 16 November 1980 and published in Official Gazette No. 85 of 1980).
45 Federal Law No. 4 of 1979 on the Suppression of Fraud and Deceit in Commercial Transactions (published in Official Gazette No. 67 of 1979).
46 Federal Law No. 5 of 1973, the Law on Printed Matter and Publishing (published in Official Gazette No. 12 of August 1993).

Yemen

Main current dedicated intellectual property laws, regulations and orders

1 Prime Ministerial Decree No. 19 of 2014 approving membership of the World Trade Organisation (issued 11 May 2014 and entered into force 26 June 2014).
2 Law No. 15 of 2012 on the Protection of Copyright and Related Rights (issued 22 June 2012).
3 Prime Ministerial Decree No. 213 of 2011, the Executive Regulations for Law No. 23 of 2010, the Trademarks and Geographical Indications Law (issued 3 October 2011).

4 Prime Ministerial Decree No. 212 of 2011, the Executive Regulations for Law No. 28 of 2010, the Industrial Designs Law (issued 3 October 2011).
5 Law No. 2 of 2011 relating to Patents, Utility Models, Integrated Circuit Layouts and Undisclosed Information (issued 12 January 2011).
6 Law No. 28 of 2010 relating to Industrial Designs (issued 26 December 2010).
7 Law No. 23 of 2010 relating to Trademarks and Geographical Indications (issued 21 November 2010).
8 Ministerial Decree No. 217 of 2010 in regard to patent registrations (issued 31 October 2010)
9 Law No. 14 of 2007, approving accession to the Berne Convention (issued 13 July 2007) (instrument of accession lodged 14 April 2008 and entered into force on 14 July 2008).
10 Law No. 27 of 2006, approving accession to the Paris Convention (issued 7 August 2006) (instrument of accession lodged 15 November 2006 and Agreement entered into force in Yemen on 15 February 2007).
11 Law No. 25 of 1990 on Press and Publications (issued 23 December 1990).
12 Accession to the WIPO Convention (December 1990).

Subordinate, associated and superseded legislation

13 Implementing Regulations for Law No. 19 of 1994 (entered into force on 2 July 2007).
14 Law No. 19 of 1994 concerning Copyright and Industrial Property (issued 29 October 1994 and published in Official Gazette No. 20 of 31 October 1994).
15 Trademarks Law No. 45 of 1976 (Yemen Arab Republic, entered into force 1982).

Gulf Cooperation Council

1 GCC Unified Trade Mark Law (issued by the 33rd GCC Supreme Council on 25 December 2012).
2 GCC Unified Customs Law (issued by the 23rd GCC Supreme Council on 31 December 2001).
3 Implementing By-laws for the GCC Patent Regulations of 2000 (issued by the GCC Ministerial Council at its 74th session on 8–9 April 2000).
4 GCC Unified Patent Regulations, amending the 1992 Regulations (issued by the GCC Supreme Council on 29 November 1999 and published in the GCC Patents Gazette No. 1 of 15 May 2000).
5 Unified Economic Agreement Between The Countries Of The Gulf Cooperation Council (second) (issued by GCC Supreme Council at its 22nd session 31 December 2001).
6 Arab Agreement for the Protection of Author's Rights, adopted at the meeting of member states of the Arab Organization for Education, Culture, and Science, Baghdad, 5 November 1981.

Subordinate, associated and superseded legislation

1 GCC Unified Trade Mark Regulation (issued by the 27th GCC Supreme Council on 10 December 2006).
2 Implementing By-Laws for the GCC Unified Patent Regulations (issued by the GCC Ministerial Council in October 1996).
3 GCC Unified Patent Regulations (issued by the GCC Supreme Council 22 September 1992).
4 Unified Economic Agreement Between The Countries Of The Gulf Cooperation Council (first) (issued in 11 November 1981).

INDEX